Contemporary
Moral
Problems

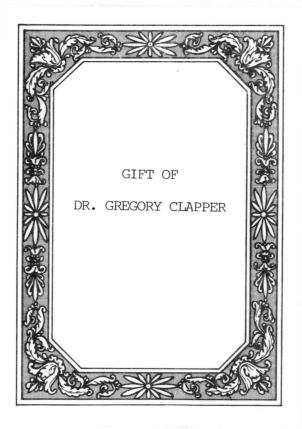

Second Edition

Contemporary Moral Problems

James White
St. Cloud State University

90-290

West Publishing Company
St. Paul   New York   Los Angeles   San Francisco

Copyeditor: *Kimberly Bornhoft*
Interior and Cover Design: *David J. Farr,*
 Imagesmythe, Inc.

Library of Congress Cataloging-in-Publication
Data

Contemporary Moral Problems.
  Includes bibliographies and index.
  1. Ethical problems. 2. Civilization,
Modern—1950–   I. White, James E.
BJ1031.C6   1988   170   87–19045
ISBN 0–314–62485–6

Contents

Chapter 1
Abortion 1

Chapter 2
Euthanasia 49

Chapter 3
Capital Punishment 85

Chapter 4
Hunger and Welfare 131

Preface

The choice of topics for this text was mostly dictated by student interest. Students were surveyed to see what moral issues they wished to discuss, and at the top of the list were issues about killing—abortion, euthanasia, the death penalty, and nuclear war. All of these are included in the text. Next on the list of popular topics was sexual morality. There is one chapter on this topic.

But students these days are not just interested in killing and sex; many of them are planning a career in business, and most hope to get jobs. So it seemed appropriate to add two new chapters, one on corporate responsibility, and the other on discrimination and affirmative action.

Student interest was not the only consideration however. Two topics were added because of their logical connection to the other topics. It makes sense to follow chapters on abortion and euthanasia with a later chapter on hunger and welfare because it involves further questions about the right to life and the right to welfare. Writers on abortion often insist that unborn human beings have a right to life. If so, then why don't starving people in distant countries and poor people also have this right? And why doesn't this right include a welfare right to have basic needs satisfied? Furthermore, if one agrees that there is no moral difference between killing and letting die, as some writers on euthanasia contend, then it seems to follow that letting people die of starvation, even distant

people or poor people, is in the same moral category as killing people.

The chapter on animals and the environment was added because it raises more questions about discrimination, and it prevents the book from having an overemphasis on killing and letting die. If it is unfair to discriminate against women and minorities because of their sex or race, then why isn't it also unjust to discriminate against animals because of their species? In other words, if sexism and racism are wrong, then why isn't *speciesism* (discriminating against other species) wrong too? The argument of Peter Singer and others who defend animal rights is that speciesism is analogous to sexism and racism, and if one rejects these types of discrimination as unjust, then one should also reject speciesism.

But why should our moral concern end with animals? Isn't it morally arbitrary to draw the line at sentience, and have moral concern only for conscious or sentient beings? This is still another form of discrimination, called *sentientism,* the discrimination against nonsentient things such as forests and lakes. The view of Aldo Leopold and his follower William Godfrey-Smith is that the natural environment should be an object of moral concern too.

The chapter on nuclear war and deterrence was placed at the end of the book. It seems best to end with a topic that is one of the most important and pressing issues of our time. Furthermore, it is both an issue about killing and letting die on a massive scale, and an environmental issue about large-scale pollution of the environment.

The choice of particular readings on each topic was influenced by a variety of considerations. First there was an attempt to find readings of high quality. As a result, many of the articles included are semiclassics such as

Mary Anne Warren's "On the Moral and Legal Status of Abortion," and none are previously unpublished. Some of the readings were chosen for their historical importance, e.g., the Supreme Court decisions on abortion and the death penalty. Also, there was an attempt to balance the reading, to have different points of view expressed. On most of these issues it is possible to discern what might be called, loosely speaking, a conservative view and a more liberal view that opposes it. For example, in the first chapter on abortion, John T. Noonan defends the conservative view that abortion is killing an innocent human being, and as such it is almost always wrong; while Mary Anne Warren expounds the liberal view that abortion is not the killing of a person with a right to life, and that women have a right to get an abortion when they want to. Whenever possible, a moderate view, relatively speaking, has been included as well. For example, in the chapter on abortion, Daniel Callahan expresses a conservative-moderate view that allows abortions in a few extreme cases, and Jane English presents a liberal-moderate view that allows abortions justified by the appeal to self-defense.

Last, and certainly not the least important consideration, was suitability for students. The book is intended to be an introductory level textbook that can be read and understood by most college students. Many of the readings were assigned in class, and students were tested for comprehension. It must be admitted that some students had difficulties. To alleviate this problem, several student aids have been provided:

1. Chapter Introductions. Each chapter begins with a general introduction that explains the issue and gives background information. When it is necessary, there is a brief survey of the main philosophical issues, arguments, and theories relevant to the moral issue.

2. Reading Introductions. Each reading is preceded by an author biography and a short summary of the author's main conclusions and arguments.

3. Study Questions. After each reading there are study questions of two kinds. First, there are rather detailed and pedestrian review questions that test the student's grasp of the main points in the reading. They are directed towards the student who has had trouble following the text. Second, there are more difficult discussion questions that probe deeper into the reading. They are aimed at the person who has understood the reading and is ready to discuss it.

4. Problem Cases. At the end of each chapter, there are problem cases that require the student to apply the concepts, principles, arguments, and theories discussed in the chapter to a hard case, either actual or hypothetical. This case-study method (as they call it in law schools and business schools) produces lively discussion, and it is a good way to get the students to think about the moral issues from a moral point of view. Also, the problem cases can be assigned as short paper topics or used on essay tests.

5. Suggested Readings. Specific suggestions are made for further reading. These suggestions are numbered and annotated to make them more useful. Some of them are discussed in the chapter introduction so that the student will see how they are relevant to the topic of the chapter. When this is done, the number of the reading is given after the name of the author, e.g., "See Michael Tooley (13)." Obviously these suggested readings are not intended to take the place of a comprehensive bibliography. Rather, they discuss items that might have been included in the chapter.

6. Glossary. There is a glossary of noncontroversial terms at the end of each chapter.

In revising the book for the second edition, I have benefited from the help and advice of many people. In particular, I want to thank my colleagues John Dienhart, Myron Anderson, and Philip Devine. Andrew Blauvelt made suggestions on nuclear deterrence. I am grateful to Donald Levy of Brooklyn College, the City University of New York, for his advice. The following people were also of help with their reviews of this book: Fred J. Blomgren, Monroe Community College; John P. Clark, Loyola University at New Orleans; Patricia Greenspan, University of Maryland; Ronald J. Koshoshek, University of Wisconsin, Eau Claire; Peter C. List, Oregon State University; Darryl Mehring, Metropolitan State College; Joan Price, Mesa Community College; Leslie C. Read, Sacramento City College; Stephen N. Schwarz, University of Rhode Island; James J. Valone, Bellarmine College; Willard F. Williamson, William Rainey Harper College. I received helpful recommendations and encouragement from Nancy E. Crochiere and Clark Baxter, my editors at West Publishing Company. Finally, I am grateful to many anonymous reviewers for their detailed criticisms and suggestions for improving the text.

Contemporary
Moral
Problems

Chapter 1

Abortion

Introduction

Abortion is the termination of pregnancy involving the death of the fetus. Strictly speaking, the term *fetus* refers to the prenatal organism from about the eighth week of pregnancy until birth. Before the eighth week, the prenatal organism is technically an **embryo,** and when it is a fertilized egg or ovum, it is called a **zygote.** But it is convenient to follow the common practice of using the term *fetus* as a general term covering the prenatal organism from conception to birth.

Since the landmark abortion decision of the United States Supreme Court in *Roe* v. *Wade* (1973) abortion in most cases has been legal. In this case, the Court ruled that restrictive abortion laws, except in certain narrowly defined conditions, are unconstitutional. This decision made abortion legally available to women who could afford it. Thus far the Court has not changed this decision and it seems unlikely to do so. Opponents of the decision have proposed to amend the Constitution with the Human Life Bill, which affirms that human life begins at conception and that every human life has intrinsic worth and equal value under the Constitution. This bill has not been passed.

The Moral Issue   We shall not be concerned with the legal aspects of the abortion controversy; instead we will concentrate on the moral issue. The basic moral issue, of course, is whether or not abortion is morally wrong.

Roughly three positions have been taken on this issue. The conservative view is that abortion is morally wrong except in rare cases where it is necessary to save the mother's life. Conservatives do not agree, however, about when exactly to make this exception. James M. Humber (9—*see* the Suggested Readings at the end of the chapter) holds that abortion to save the mother's life is justifiable only when it is impossible to save the life of the fetus. An example of such a case is tubal or **ectopic pregnancy.** The zygote does not descend to the uterus, but remains lodged in the fallopian tube: The mother will die if an abortion is not performed in this situation, and there is no hope for the survival of the zygote. Almost everyone agrees that abortion is therefore justified in this case.

But what about a case where the fetus can be saved by sacrificing the life of the mother, as, for example, in the case of a pregnant woman who has a cardiac condition such that she will die if she carries the baby to term? Some conservatives might allow an abortion in that case, but Humber (9) and John T. Noonan, following the traditional Roman Catholic position, would not. According to this position, a direct abortion, where the fetus is deliberately and intentionally killed, is never morally permissible. However, the fetus may be allowed to die as a consequence of an action intended to save the life of the mother, for example, the removal of a cancerous uterus. Noonan gives an additional reason for the mother to sacrifice her life for the sake of her child—such a self-sacrifice is meaningful in the Christian tradition because it is an expression of unselfishness and Christlike love.

The second view, the liberal view, is that abortion is morally permissible whenever the mother chooses it. But other than to save her life, why would a pregnant woman want an abortion? There are various answers to this question. If a woman is pregnant due to rape, she may feel justified in getting an abortion. Incest is often cited as a good reason for getting an abortion. Another common reason is to avoid giving birth to a defective child. Or a woman may

want to get an abortion because it is inconvenient for her to be pregnant; for example, the pregnancy might interfere with her career. The liberal insists that abortion is permissible in all of these cases.

Liberals do not agree, however, about the infanticide issue. Mary Anne Warren has a liberal view about abortion, but she claims that it does not follow from her position that infanticide is morally permissible in our society. Warren recognizes that in our society many people value the lives of infants, and she believes that adoption is a better alternative. Michael Tooley (13), on the other hand, sees little difference between abortion and killing newborn babies. He argues that in both cases we are killing something that does not have a right to continued existence because it does not have a concept of a continuing self.

The third view is the moderate view whose supporters hold that abortion is justified in some cases, but not in others. In which cases is it justified and in which not justified? Moderates do not agree on the answer to this question. The Supreme Court decision allows abortions merely for the sake of convenience. Not all moderates agree that abortion for convenience is justified. Judith Jarvis Thomson (12), for example, does not think that abortion is justified merely for the sake of convenience, say to avoid postponing a trip to Europe. Jane English, another moderate, agrees with Thomson (12) that a woman who is seven months pregnant should not get an abortion merely to avoid postponing a trip to Europe, but she says that in the early months of pregnancy, "abortion is permissible whenever it is in the interests of the pregnant woman or her family." Thus it appears that English's position is slightly more liberal than that of Thomson (12). However, English's view is slightly more conservative than that of Justice Blackmun in his opinion in *Roe* v. *Wade* because she thinks that we do have a serious obligation to not kill or harm the fetus in the later stages of development when it is more like a baby. In a reading in this chapter, Daniel Callahan presents a moderate position that is more conservative than the positions of Thomson (12), English, or Justice Blackmun. Callahan thinks that a fetus is an important and valuable human life, not just worthless tissue. He believes that respect for the sanctity of human life should incline every woman to have a strong moral bias against abortion. However, he allows that there might be circumstances in which a woman might justifiably have an abortion because of her responsibilities to herself, her family, and her society. Furthermore, he holds that in a free, pluralistic society a woman should be allowed to make her own choice about abortion.

Philosophical Issues How can we resolve the moral issue about the wrongness of abortion? Most writers agree that settling this issue requires solving some difficult philosophical puzzles. Debate has most often centered on the nature and status of the fetus. Is it a person or not, and how do we tell if something is a person or not? Does the fetus have the full moral status of a person, a partial moral status, or none at all? One common approach to these problems is *line drawing*, that is, making an attempt to find a morally significant point or dividing line in the development of the fetus that divides the period in which it is not a person with rights from the period in which it is a person with rights. Justice Blackmun and Alan Zaitchik (14) both agree that **viability** is such a point. Viability occurs when the fetus is capable of surviving outside the womb; this is said to occur around the twenty-eighth week of pregnancy, given the present state of medical technology. Other writers have chosen different points. Baruch Brody (2) argues that the presence of brain waves, beginning at about the eighth week, is a significant dividing line because their presence marks the beginning of consciousness or the ability to feel pain. In European

common law, abortion is considered killing a person only after **quickening,** the time when a pregnant woman first feels the fetus move on its own.

Opponents of line drawing between conception and birth, such as Noonan, argue that these lines are always arbitrary and inadequate. Viability is a shifting point. The development of artificial incubation may make the fetus viable at any time, even shortly after conception. Furthermore, the time at which the fetus is viable varies according to circumstances such as its weight, age, and race. Opponents of line drawing often use **slippery slope arguments** to argue that a line cannot be securely drawn at any point in the development of the fetus because such a line inevitably slides down the slope of development to conception; they insist that the only place to draw the line is at conception. These arguments are discussed by Thomson (12).

Noonan and other conservatives adopt a different approach to the problem of establishing the moral status of the fetus: Instead of trying to draw a line in the development of the fetus, they try to prove that the fetus is a human being with a right to life from the moment of conception. One argument depends upon the religious doctrine of **ensoulment.** This doctrine states that the soul enters the fetus at the moment of conception; anything with a soul is a person with a right to life; hence the fetus is a person with a right to life from the moment of conception. Noonan avoids appealing to the ensoulment doctrine. Instead he updates the traditional view by discussing genetic coding of the zygote. At conception, the zygote receives the full genetic code, twenty-three pairs of chromosomes. Anything with full human genetic coding is a human being with a right to life; hence the zygote is a human being with a right to life from the moment of conception.

Liberals find it very hard to believe that

a zygote, a single cell, is a human being with a right to life, that is, a person. For one thing, any human cell has the full genetic coding of a human being but any old human cell is hardly a person. Saying that the zygote is a potential person is no help because the rights of an actual person, the mother, would always outweigh the rights of merely a potential person, assuming that potential persons have rights in the first place. Warren thinks that conservatives like Noonan confuse two different senses of the word *human.* There is a genetic sense in which a being is human if it is a member of the biological species *Homo sapiens,* and a moral sense in which a being is human if it is a member of the moral community. Just because the zygote is genetically human does not mean that it is morally human or a member of the moral community. In order to be a person, a being must be capable of consciousness, communication, reasoning, self-motivated activity, and self-concept formation. Obviously the fetus does not have all of these capabilities, therefore, it is not a person.

Conservative critics point out that Warren's position implies that infants are not people either, and thus it can be used to justify infanticide. Because the conservative thinks that babies are undeniably persons with rights, and that infanticide is morally wrong, they find Warren's position to be unacceptable.

An alternative approach to line drawing is to hold, as English does, that the concept of person has *fuzzy borders,* that is, there are borderline cases in which we cannot say whether an entity is a person or not. The fetus constitutes just such a case. Another alternative is to hold that the fetus is neither a full-fledged person nor merely an organism with no moral status at all; rather it has some sort of partial moral status. Callahan seems to suggest such a position when he insists that the fetus is an important and valuable form of human life

even though it does not qualify as a person.

If we cannot conclusively determine the nature and moral status of the fetus, then how can we answer the moral question about abortion? The tactic of Thomson (12) is to shift the focus of debate from the status of the fetus to the rights of the mother. She argues that even if the fetus is a person with a right to life, it still does not follow that abortions are never justified. The rights of the mother can justify an abortion. English adopts a similar tactic and uses it to attack both the conservative and the liberal views. Even if we assume that the fetus is a person, the mother's right of self-defense is sufficient to justify abortion in a number of cases including rape, serious harm, or great inconvenience. On the other hand, even if we assume that the fetus is not a person, it still has some rights because it is at least personlike. Therefore, we have an obligation to not kill it or harm it without a good reason.

The methods of Thomson (12) and English are open to criticism, however. Both of them rely on puzzling imaginary cases, e.g., Thomson's case of the famous violinist who is plugged into another person, and English's case of the mad scientist who hypnotizes people to attack innocent passers-by with knives. They ask us what we would say or think about these cases; that is, they appeal to our moral intuitions. Such an appeal does not always produce agreement, particularly when we are talking about abortion. The conservative Humber (9), for example, does not have the same intuitions about these cases as Thomson (12) does. Another problem with appealing to intuitions, as R.M. Hare (8) points out in his criticism of Thomson (12), is that these intuitions may merely reflect our different backgrounds. If so, they are not an infallible guide to moral conduct.

In trying to decide if abortion is wrong or not, Hare (8) adopts a novel approach. He appeals to the Golden Rule that we should do to others as we wish them to do to us. He finds that this rule does allow abortions in a small minority of cases, e.g., where a person wishes she had been aborted. In using a general moral rule, Hare is following a respectable tradition in ethics of formulating a general moral principle or theory and then applying it to a particular problem. Unfortunately, there is no agreement about which principles or theories are correct, or about how they are properly applied to particular problems.

The Supreme Court

Excerpts from *Roe* v. *Wade* (1973)

Harry A. Blackmun is an associate justice of the United States Supreme Court. He is a graduate of Harvard Law School, and he was appointed to the Court in 1970.

Byron R. White is also an associate justice of the United States Supreme Court. He was appointed in 1962, and he is a graduate of Yale Law School.

In the case of Roe v. Wade, a pregnant single woman challenged a Texas abortion law making abortion (except to save the mother's life) a crime punishable by a prison sentence of two to five years. The Court invalidated this law.

The reading includes excerpts from the majority opinion written by Justice Blackmun (concurred in by six other justices), and from the dissenting opinion written by Justice White (concurred in by Justice William H. Rehnquist).

Justice Blackmun argues that the abortion decision is included in the right of personal privacy. But this right is not absolute. It must yield at some point to the state's legitimate interest in protecting potential life, and this interest becomes compelling at the point of viability.

Justice White in his dissenting opinion holds that the Court has no constitutional basis for its decision, and that it values the convenience of the mother more than the existence and development of human life.

MAJORITY OPINION

A recent review of the common law prece-dents argues ... that even post-quickening abortion was never established as a common law crime. This is of some importance because while most American courts ruled, in holding or dictum, that abortion of an un-quickened fetus was not criminal under their received common law, others followed Coke in stating that abortion of a quick fetus was a "misprison," a term they translated to mean "misdemeanor." That their reliance on Coke on this aspect of the law was uncritical and, apparently in all the reported cases, dictum (due probably to the paucity of common law prosecutions for post-quickening abortion), makes it now appear doubtful that abortion was ever firmly established as a common law crime even with respect to the destruction of a quick fetus....

It is thus apparent that at common law, at the time of the adoption of our Constitution, and throughout the major portion of the 19th century, abortion was viewed with less disfa-vor than under most American statutes cur-rently in effect. Phrasing it another way, a woman enjoyed a substantially broader right to terminate a pregnancy than she does in most States today. At least with respect to the early stage of pregnancy, and very possibly without such a limitation, the opportunity to make this choice was present in this country well into the 19th century. Even later, the law continued for some time to treat less puni-tively an abortion procured in early pregnan-cy....

Three reasons have been advanced to ex-plain historically the enactment of criminal abortion laws in the 19th century and to justify their continued existence.

It has been argued occasionally that these laws were the product of a Victorian social concern to discourage illicit sexual conduct. Texas, however, does not advance this justification in the present case, and it appears that no court or commentator has taken the argument seriously. . . .

A second reason is concerned with abortion as a medical procedure. When most criminal abortion laws were first enacted, the procedure was a hazardous one for the woman. This was particularly true prior to the development of antisepsis. Antiseptic techniques, of course, were based on discoveries by Lister, Pasteur, and others first announced in 1867, but were not generally accepted and employed until about the turn of the century. Abortion mortality was high. Even after 1900, and perhaps until as late as the development of antibiotics in the 1940s, standard modern techniques such as dilation and curettage were not nearly so safe as they are today. Thus it has been argued that a State's real concern in enacting a criminal abortion law was to protect the pregnant woman, that is, to restrain her from submitting to a procedure that placed her life in serious jeopardy.

Modern medical techniques have altered this situation. Appellants and various *amici* refer to medical data indicating that abortion in early pregnancy, that is, prior to the end of first trimester, although not without its risk, is now relatively safe. Mortality rates for women undergoing early abortions, where the procedure is legal, appear to be as low as or lower than the rates for normal childbirth. Consequently, any interest of the State in protecting the woman from an inherently hazardous procedure, except when it would be equally dangerous for her to forgo it, has largely disappeared. Of course, important state interests in the area of health and medical standards do remain. The State has a legitimate interest in seeing to it that abortion, like any other medical procedure, is performed under circumstances that insure maximum safety for the patient. This interest obviously extends at least to the performing physician and his staff, to the facilities involved, to the availability of aftercare, and to adequate provision for any complication or emergency that might arise. The prevalence of high mortality rates at illegal "abortion mills" strengthens, rather than weakens, the State's interest in regulating the conditions under which abortions are performed. Moreover, the risk to the woman increases as her pregnancy continues. Thus the State retains a definite interest in protecting the woman's own health and safety when an abortion is performed at a late stage of pregnancy.

The third reason is the State's interest— some phrase it in terms of duty—in protecting prenatal life. Some of the argument for this justification rests on the theory that a new human life is present from the moment of conception. . . .

Parties challenging state abortion laws have sharply disputed in some courts the contention that a purpose of these laws, when enacted, was to protect prenatal life. Pointing to the absence of legislative history to support the contention, they claim that most state laws were designed solely to protect the woman. Because medical advances have lessened this concern, at least with respect to abortion in early pregnancy, they argue that with respect to such abortions the laws can no longer be justified by any state interest. There is some scholarly support for this view of original purpose. The few state courts called upon to interpret their laws in the late 19th and early 20th centuries did focus on the State's interest in protecting the woman's health rather than in preserving embryo and fetus. . . .

The Constitution does not explicitly mention any right of privacy. In a line of decisions, however, going back perhaps as far as *Union Pacific R. Co.* v. *Botsford,* 141 U.S. 250, 251 (1891), the Court has recognized that a right of personal privacy, or a guarantee of certain areas or zones of privacy, does exist under the Constitution. In varying contexts the Court or individual Justices have indeed found at least the roots of that right in the First Amendment, . . . in the Fourth and Fifth Amendments . . . in the penumbras of the Bill of Rights . . . in the Ninth Amendment . . . or in the concept of liberty guaranteed by the first section of the Fourteenth Amendment. . . . These decisions make it clear that only personal rights that can be deemed "fundamental" or "implicit in the concept of ordered liberty," . . . are included in this guarantee of personal privacy. They also make it clear that the right has some extension to activities relating to marriage, . . . procreation, . . . contraception, . . . family relationships, . . . and child rearing and education. . . .

This right of privacy, whether it be founded in the Fourteenth Amendment's concept of personal liberty and restrictions upon state action, as we feel it is or, as the District Court determined, in the Ninth Amendment's reservation of rights to the people, is broad enough to encompass a woman's decision whether or not to terminate her pregnancy. . . .

. . . Appellants and some *amici* argue that the woman's right is absolute and that she is entitled to terminate her pregnancy at whatever time, in whatever way, and for whatever reason she alone chooses. With this we do not agree. Appellants' arguments that Texas either has no valid interest at all in regulating the abortion decision, or no interest strong enough to support any limitation upon the woman's sole determination, is unpersuasive. The Court's decisions recognizing a right of privacy also acknowledge that some state regulation in areas protected by that right is appropriate. As noted above, a state may properly assert important interests in safeguarding health, in maintaining medical standards, and in protecting potential life. At some point in pregnancy, these respective interests become sufficiently compelling to sustain regulation of the factors that govern the abortion decision. The privacy right involved, therefore, cannot be said to be absolute. . . .

We therefore conclude that the right of personal privacy includes the abortion decision, but that this right is not unqualified and must be considered against important state interests in regulation.

We note that those federal and state courts that have recently considered abortion law challenges have reached the same conclusion. . . .

Although the results are divided, most of these courts have agreed that the right of privacy, however based, is broad enough to cover the abortion decision; that the right, nonetheless, is not absolute and is subject to some limitations; and that at some point the state interests as to protection of health, medical standards, and prenatal life, become dominant. We agree with this approach.

The appellee and certain *amici* argue that the fetus is a "person" within the language and meaning of the Fourteenth Amendment. In support of this they outline at length and in detail the well-known facts of fetal development. If this suggestion of personhood is established, the appellant's case, of course, collapses, for the fetus' right to life is then guaranteed specifically by the Amendment. The appellant conceded as much on reargument. On the other hand, the appellee conceded on reargument that no case could be cited that holds that a fetus is a person within the meaning of the Fourteenth Amendment.

All this, together with our observation, *supra*, that throughout the major portion of the 19th century prevailing legal abortion practices were far freer than they are today, persuades us that the word "person," as used in the Fourteenth Amendment, does not include the unborn. . . . Indeed, our decision in *United States* v. *Vuitch,* 402 U.S. 62 (1971), inferentially is to the same effect, for we there would not have indulged in statutory interpretation favorable to abortion in specified circumstances if the necessary consequence was the termination of life entitled to Fourteenth Amendment protection.

. . . As we have intimated above, it is reasonable and appropriate for a State to decide that at some point in time another interest, that of health of the mother or that of potential human life, becomes significantly involved. The woman's privacy is no longer sole and any right of privacy she possesses must be measured accordingly.

... We need not resolve the difficult question of when life begins. When those trained in the respective disciplines of medicine, philosophy, and theology are unable to arrive at any consensus, the judiciary, at this point in the development of man's knowledge, is not in a position to speculate as to the answer.

It should be sufficient to note briefly the wide divergence of thinking on this most sensitive and difficult question. There has always been strong support for the view that life does not begin until live birth. This was the belief of the **Stoics.** It appears to be the predominant, though not the unanimous, attitude of the Jewish faith. It may be taken to represent also the position of a large segment of the Protestant community, insofar as that can be ascertained; organized groups that have taken a formal position on the abortion issue have generally regarded abortion as a matter for the conscience of the individual and her family. As we have noted, the common law found greater significance in quickening. Physicians and their scientific colleagues have regarded that event with less interest and have tended to focus either upon conception or upon live birth or upon the interim point at which the fetus becomes "viable," that is, potentially able to live outside the mother's womb, albeit with artificial aid. Viability is usually placed at about seven months (28 weeks) but may occur earlier, even at 24 weeks....

In areas other than criminal abortion the law has been reluctant to endorse any theory that life, as we recognize it, begins before live birth or to accord legal rights to the unborn except in narrowly defined situations and except when the rights are contingent upon live birth.... In short, the unborn have never been recognized in the law as persons in the whole sense.

In view of all this, we do not agree that, by adopting one theory of life, Texas may override the rights of the pregnant woman that are at stake. We repeat, however, that the State does have an important and legitimate interest in preserving and protecting the health of the pregnant woman, whether she be a resident of the State or a nonresident who seeks medical consultation and treatment there, and that it has still *another* important and legitimate interest in protecting the potentiality of human life. These interests are separate and distinct. Each grows in substantiality as the woman approaches term and, at a point during pregnancy, each becomes "compelling."

With respect to the State's important and legitimate interest in the health of the mother, the "compelling" point, in the light of present medical knowledge, is at approximately the end of the first trimester. This is so because of the now established medical fact ... that until the end of the first trimester mortality in abortion is less than mortality in normal childbirth. It follows that, from and after this point, a State may regulate the abortion procedure to the extent that the regulation reasonably relates to the preservation and protection of maternal health. Examples of permissible state regulation in this area are requirements as to the qualifications of the person who is to perform the abortion; as to the licensure of that person; as to the facility in which the procedure is to be performed, that is, whether it must be a hospital or may be a clinic or some other place of less-than-hospital status; as to the licensing of the facility; and the like.

This means, on the other hand, that, for the period of pregnancy prior to this "compelling" point, the attending physician, in consultation with his patient, is free to determine, without regulation by the State, that in his medical judgment the patient's pregnancy should be terminated. If that decision is reached, the judgment may be effectuated by an abortion free of interference by the State.

With respect to the State's important and

legitimate interest in potential life, the "compelling" point is at viability.... State regulation protective of fetal life after viability thus has both logical and biological justifications. If the State is interested in protecting fetal life after viability, it may go so far as to proscribe abortion during that period except when it is necessary to preserve the life or health of the mother....

To summarize and repeat:

1. A state criminal abortion statute of the current Texas type, that excepts from criminality only a *life-saving* procedure on behalf of the mother, without regard to pregnancy stage and without recognition of the other interests involved, is violative of the Due Process Clause of the Fourteenth Amendment.

(a) For the stage prior to approximately the end of the first **trimester,** the abortion decision and its effectuation must be left to the medical judgment of the pregnant woman's attending physician.

(b) For the stage subsequent to approximately the end of the first trimester, the State, in promoting its interest in the health of the mother, may, if it chooses, regulate the abortion procedure in ways that are reasonably related to maternal health.

(c) For the stage subsequent to viability the State, in promoting its interest in the potentiality of human life, may, if it chooses, regulate, and even proscribe, abortion except where it is necessary, in appropriate medical judgment, for the preservation of the life or health of the mother.

2. The State may define the term "physician," as it has been employed in the preceding numbered paragraphs of this Part XI of this opinion, to mean only a physician currently licensed by the State, and may proscribe any abortion by a person who is not a physician as so defined.

... The decision leaves the State free to place increasing restrictions on abortion as the period of pregnancy lengthens, so long as those restrictions are tailored to the recognized state interests. The decision vindicates the right of the physician to administer medical treatment according to his professional judgment up to the points where important state interests provide compelling justifications for intervention. Up to those points the abortion decision in all its aspects is inherently, and primarily, a medical decision, and basic responsibility for it must rest with the physician. If an individual practitioner abuses the privilege of exercising proper medical judgment, the usual remedies, judicial and intraprofessional, are available....

DISSENT

At the heart of the controversy in these cases are those recurring pregnancies that pose no danger whatsoever to the life or health of the mother but are nevertheless unwanted for any one or more of a variety of reasons— convenience, family planning, economics, dislike of children, the embarrassment of illegitimacy, etc. The common claim before us is that for any one of such reasons, or for no reason at all, and without asserting or claiming any threat to life or health, any woman is entitled to an abortion at her request if she is able to find a medical advisor willing to undertake the procedure.

The Court for the most part sustains this position: During the period prior to the time the fetus becomes viable, the Constitution of the United States values the convenience, whim or caprice of the putative mother more than the life or potential life of the fetus; the Constitution, therefore, guarantees the right to an abortion as against any state law or policy seeking to protect the fetus from an abortion not prompted by more compelling reasons of the mother.

With all due respect, I dissent. I find nothing in the language or history of the Constitution to support the Court's judgment.... As an exercise of raw judicial power, the

Court perhaps has authority to do what it does today; but in my view its judgment is an improvident and extravagant exercise of the power of judicial review which the Constitution extends to this Court.

The Court apparently values the convenience of the pregnant mother more than the continued existence and development of the life or potential life which she carries....

It is my view, therefore, that the Texas statute is not constitutionally infirm because it denies abortions to those who seek to serve only their convenience rather than to protect their life or health....

Review Questions

1. Justice Blackmun discusses three reasons for the enactment of criminal abortion laws. Why doesn't he accept these reasons?

2. Where does the Constitution guarantee a right of privacy according to Justice Blackmun?

3. Is the fetus a person in the legal sense according to Justice Blackmun?

4. According to Justice Blackmun, when is the *compelling* point in the state's interest in the health of the mother?

5. When, according to Justice Blackmun, is the *compelling* point in the state's interest in potential life?

6. Explain Justice Blackmun's conclusions.

7. What are Justice White's objections?

Discussion Questions

1. What is the right of privacy? Try to define it.

2. What do you think is properly included in the right of privacy, and what is properly excluded?

3. Do you think that the fetus has any legal rights or any moral rights? Defend your view.

4. Justice White complains that Justice Blackmun's opinion allows a woman to get an abortion "without asserting or claiming any threat to life or health" provided she is able to find a doctor willing to undertake the procedure. Do you think that women should be allowed to get such abortions? Explain your answer. Do you believe that doctors have any obligation to perform such abortions? Why or why not?

∞

John T. Noonan, Jr.

An Almost Absolute Value in History

John T. Noonan, Jr., is professor of law at the University of California, Berkeley. His books include Contraception: A History of Its Treatment by the Catholic Theologians and Canonists *(1965), (1970), and* Persons and Masks of the Law *(1976).*

Noonan begins with the question, How do you determine the humanity of a being? The answer he defends is what he says is the view of traditional Christian theology, namely that you are human if you are conceived by human parents. This view is compared to other alleged criteria of humanity such as viability, experience, feelings of adults, sensations of adults, and social visibility. Each of these is rejected as inadequate and arbitrary. In his defense of the traditional view, Noonan does not appeal to the medieval theory of ensoulment, that is, the theory that the soul enters the body at conception. Instead, he rests his case on the fact that at conception the fetus (or strictly speaking, the zygote) receives the full genetic code of a human being. He assumes that anything with human genetic coding is a human being with rights equal to those of other humans. It follows that the fetus is a human being with rights

Reprinted by permission of the publishers from *The Morality of Abortion: Legal and Historical Perspectives,* ed. by John T. Noonan, Jr., Cambridge, Massachusetts: Harvard University Press, Copyright © 1970 by the President and Fellows of Harvard College.

from the moment of conception. Once this has been granted, we can see that abortion is morally wrong except in rare cases where it is necessary to save the mother's life.

The most fundamental question involved in the long history of thought on abortion is: How do you determine the humanity of a being? To phrase the question that way is to put in comprehensive humanistic terms what the theologians either dealt with as an explicitly theological question under the heading of "ensoulment" or dealt with implicitly in their treatment of abortion. The Christian position as it originated did not depend on a narrow theological or philosophical concept. It had no relation to theories of infant baptism.[1] It appealed to no special theory of instantaneous ensoulment. It took the world's view on ensoulment as that view changed from Aristotle to Zacchia. There was, indeed, theological influence affecting the theory of ensoulment finally adopted, and, of course, ensoulment itself was a theological concept, so that the position was always explained in theological terms. But the theological notion of ensoulment could easily be translated into humanistic language by substituting "human" for "rational soul"; the problem of knowing when a man is a man is common to theology and humanism.

If one steps outside the specific categories used by the theologians, the answer they gave can be analyzed as a refusal to discriminate among human beings on the basis of their varying potentialities. Once conceived, the being was recognized as man because he had man's potential. The **criterion for humanity,** thus, was simple and all-embracing: if you are conceived by human parents, you are human.

The strength of this position may be tested by a review of some of the other distinctions offered in the contemporary controversy over legalizing abortion. Perhaps the most popular distinction is in terms of viability. Before an age of so many months, the fetus is not viable, that is, it cannot be removed from the mother's womb and live apart from her. To that extent, the life of the fetus is absolutely dependent on the life of the mother. This dependence is made the basis of denying recognition to its humanity.

There are difficulties with this distinction. One is that the perfection of artificial incubation may make the fetus viable at any time: it may be removed and artificially sustained. Experiments with animals already show that such a procedure is possible. This hypothetical extreme case relates to an actual difficulty: there is considerable elasticity to the idea of viability. Mere length of life is not an exact measure. The viability of the fetus depends on the extent of its anatomical and functional development. The weight and length of the fetus are better guides to the state of its development than age, but weight and length vary. Moreover, different racial groups have different ages at which their fetuses are viable. Some evidence, for example, suggests that Negro fetuses mature more quickly than white fetuses. If viability is the norm, the standard would vary with race and with many individual circumstances.

The most important objection to this approach is that dependence is not ended by viability. The fetus is still absolutely dependent on someone's care in order to continue existence; indeed a child of one or three or even five years of age is absolutely dependent on another's care for existence; uncared for, the older fetus or the younger child will die as surely as the early fetus detached from the mother. The unsubstantial lessening in dependence at viability does not seem to signify any special acquisition of humanity.

A second distinction has been attempted in terms of experience. A being who has had experience, has lived and suffered, who possesses memories, is more human than one who has not. Humanity depends on formation by experience. The fetus is thus "unformed" in the most basic human sense.

This distinction is not serviceable for the embryo which is already experiencing and reacting. The embryo is responsive to touch after eight weeks and at least at that point is experiencing. At an earlier stage the zygote is certainly alive and responding to its environment. The distinction may also be challenged by the rare case where **aphasia** has erased adult memory: has it erased humanity? More fundamentally, this distinction leaves even the older fetus or the younger child to be treated as an unformed inhuman thing. Finally, it is not clear why experience as such confers humanity. It could be argued that certain central experiences such as loving or learning are necessary to make a man human. But then human beings who have failed to love or to learn might be excluded from the class called man.

A third distinction is made by appeal to the sentiments of adults. If a fetus dies, the grief of the parents is not the grief they would have for a living child. The fetus is an unnamed "it" till birth, and is not perceived as personality until at least the fourth month of existence when movements in the womb manifest a vigorous presence demanding joyful recognition by the parents.

Yet feeling is notoriously an unsure guide to the humanity of others. Many groups of humans have had difficulty in feeling that persons of another tongue, color, religion, sex, are as human as they. Apart from reactions to alien groups, we mourn the loss of a ten-year-old boy more than the loss of his one-day-old brother or his 90–year-old grandfather. The difference felt and the grief expressed vary with the potentialities extinguished, or the experience wiped out; they do not seem to point to any substantial difference in the humanity of baby, boy, or grandfather.

Distinctions are also made in terms of sensation by the parents. The embryo is felt within the womb only after about the fourth month. The embryo is seen only at birth. What can be neither seen nor felt is different from what is tangible. If the fetus cannot be seen or touched at all, it cannot be perceived as man.

Yet experience shows that sight is even more untrustworthy than feeling in determin-ing humanity. By sight, color became an appropriate index for saying who was a man, and the evil of racial discrimination was given foundation. Nor can touch provide the test; a being confined by sickness, "out of touch" with others, does not thereby seem to lose his humanity. To the extent that touch still has appeal as a criterion, it appears to be a survival of the old English idea of "quickening"—a possible mistranslation of the Latin *animatus* used in the canon law. To that extent touch as a criterion seems to be dependent on the Aristotelian notion of ensoulment, and to fall when this notion is discarded.

Finally, a distinction is sought in social visibility. The fetus is not socially perceived as human. It cannot communicate with others. Thus, both subjectively and objectively, it is not a member of society. As moral rules are rules for the behavior of members of society to each other, they cannot be made for behavior toward what is not yet a member. Excluded from the society of men, the fetus is excluded from the humanity of men.[2]

By force of the argument from the consequences, this distinction is to be rejected. It is more subtle than that founded on an appeal to physical sensation, but it is equally dangerous in its implications. If humanity depends on social recognition, individuals or whole groups may be dehumanized by being denied any status in their society. Such a fate is fictionally portrayed in *1984* and has actually been the lot of many men in many societies. In the Roman empire, for example, condemnation to slavery meant the practical denial of most human rights; in the Chinese Communist world, landlords have been classified as enemies of the people and so treated as nonpersons by the state. Humanity does not depend on social recognition, though often the failure of society to recognize the prisoner, the alien, the heterodox as human has led to the destruction of human beings. Anyone conceived by a man and a woman is human. Recognition of this condition by society follows a real event in the objective order, however imperfect and halting the recognition.

Any attempt to limit humanity to exclude some group runs the risk of furnishing authority and precedent for excluding other groups in the name of the consciousness or perception of the controlling group in the society.

A philosopher may reject the appeal to the humanity of the fetus because he views "humanity" as a secular view of the soul and because he doubts the existence of anything real and objective which can be identified as humanity. One answer to such a philosopher is to ask how he reasons about moral questions without supposing that there is a sense in which he and the others of whom he speaks are human. Whatever group is taken as the society which determines who may be killed is thereby taken as human. A second answer is to ask if he does not believe that there is a right and wrong way of deciding moral questions. If there is such a difference, experience may be appealed to: to decide who is human on the basis of the sentiment of a given society has led to consequences which rational men would characterize as monstrous.

The rejection of the attempted distinctions based on viability and visibility, experience and feeling, may be buttressed by the following considerations: Moral judgments often rest on distinctions, but if the distinctions are not to appear arbitrary *fiat,* they should relate to some real difference in probabilities. There is a kind of continuity in all life, but the earlier stages of the elements of human life possess tiny probabilities of development. Consider, for example, the spermatozoa in any normal ejaculate: There are about 200,000,000 in any single ejaculate, of which one has a chance of developing into a zygote. Consider the oocytes which may become ova: there are 100,000 to 1,000,000 oocytes in a female infant, of which a maximum of 390 are ovulated. But once spermatozoon and ovum meet and the conceptus is formed, such studies as have been made show that roughly in only 20 percent of the cases will spontaneous abortion occur. In other words,

the chances are about 4 out of 5 that this new being will develop. At this stage in the life of the being there is a sharp shift in probabilities, an immense jump in potentialities. To make a distinction between the rights of spermatozoa and the rights of the fertilized ovum is to respond to an enormous shift in possibilities. For about twenty days after conception the egg may split to form twins or combine with another egg to form a **chimera,** but the probability of either event happening is very small.

It may be asked, What does a change in biological probabilities have to do with establishing humanity? The argument from probabilities is not aimed at establishing humanity but at establishing an objective discontinuity which may be taken into account in moral discourse. As life itself is a matter of probabilities, as most moral reasoning is an estimate of probabilities, so it seems in accord with the structure of reality and the nature of moral thought to found a moral judgment on the change in probabilities at conception. The appeal to probabilities is the most commonsensical of arguments; to a greater or smaller degree all of us base our actions on probabilities, and in morals, as in law, prudence and negligence are often measured by the account one has taken of the probabilities. If the chance is 200,000,000 to 1 that the movement in the bushes into which you shoot is a man's, I doubt if many persons would hold you careless in shooting; but if the chances are 4 out of 5 that the movement is a human being's, few would acquit you of blame. Would the argument be different if only one out of ten children conceived came to term? Of course this argument would be different. This argument is an appeal to probabilities that actually exist, not to any and all states of affairs which may be imagined.

The probabilities as they do exist do not show the humanity of the embryo in the sense of a demonstration in logic any more than the probabilities of the movement in the bush being a man demonstrate beyond all doubt that the being is a man. The appeal is a "buttressing" consideration, showing the plausibility of the standard adopted. The argument focuses on the decisional factor in any moral judgment and assumes that part of the business of a moralist is drawing lines. One evidence of the nonarbitrary character of the line drawn is the difference of probabilities on either side of it. If a spermatozoon is destroyed, one destroys a being which had a chance of far less than 1 in 200 million of developing into a reasoning being, possessed of the genetic code, a heart and other organs, and capable of pain. If a fetus is destroyed, one destroys a being already possessed of the genetic code, organs, and sensitivity to pain, and one which had an 80 percent chance of developing further into a baby outside the womb who, in time, would reason.

The positive argument for conception as the decisive moment of humanization is that at conception the new being receives the genetic code. It is this genetic information which determines his characteristics, which is the biological carrier of the possibility of human wisdom, which makes him a self-evolving being. A being with a human genetic code is man.

This review of current controversy over the humanity of the fetus emphasizes what a fundamental question the theologians resolved in asserting the inviolability of the fetus. To regard the fetus as possessed of equal rights with other humans was not, however, to decide every case where abortion might be employed. It did decide the case where the argument was that the fetus should be aborted for its own good. To say a being was human was to say it had a destiny to decide for itself which could not be taken from it by another man's decision. But human beings with equal rights often come in conflict with each other, and some decision must be made as to whose claims are to prevail. Cases of conflict involving the fetus are different only in two respects: the total inability of the fetus to speak for itself and the fact that the right of the fetus regularly at stake is the right to life itself.

The approach taken by the theologians to these conflicts was articulated in terms of "direct" and "indirect." Again, to look at what they were doing from outside their categories, they may be said to have been drawing lines or "balancing values." "Direct" and "indirect" are spatial metaphors; "line-drawing" is another. "To weigh" or "to balance" values is a metaphor of a more complicated mathematical sort hinting at the process which goes on in moral judgments. All the metaphors suggest that, in the moral judgments made, comparisons were necessary, that no value completely controlled. The principle of double effect was no doctrine fallen from heaven, but a method of analysis appropriate where two relative values were being compared. In Catholic moral theology, as it developed, life even of the innocent was not taken as an absolute. Judgments on acts affecting life issued from a process of weighing. In the weighing, the fetus was always given a value greater than zero, always a value separate and independent from its parents. This valuation was crucial and fundamental in all Christian thought on the subject and marked it off from any approach which considered that only the parents' interests needed to be considered.

Even with the fetus weighed as human, one interest could be weighed as equal or superior: that of the mother in her own life. The **casuists** between 1450 and 1895 were willing to weigh this interest as superior. Since 1895, that interest was given decisive weight only in the two special cases of the cancerous uterus and the ectopic pregnancy. In both of these cases the fetus itself had little chance of survival even if the abortion were not performed. As the balance was once struck in favor of the mother whenever her life was endangered, it could be so struck again. The balance reached between 1895 and 1930 attempted prudentially and pastorally to forestall a multitude of exceptions for interests less than life.

The perception of the humanity of the fetus and the weighing of fetal rights against other human rights constituted the work of the moral analysts. But what spirit animated their abstract judgments? For the Christian community it was the injunction of Scripture to love your neighbor as yourself. The fetus as human was a neighbor; his life had parity with one's own. The commandment gave life to what otherwise would have been only rational calculation.

The commandment could be put in humanistic as well as theological terms: Do not injure your fellow man without reason. In these terms, once the humanity of the fetus is perceived, abortion is never right except in self-defense. When life must be taken to save life, reason alone cannot say that a mother must prefer a child's life to her own. With this exception, now of great rarity, abortion violates the rational humanist tenet of the equality of human lives.

For Christians the commandment to love had received a special imprint in that the exemplar proposed of love was the love of the Lord for his disciples. In the light given by this example, self-sacrifice carried to the point of death seemed in the extreme situations not without meaning. In the less extreme cases, preference for one's own interests to the life of another seemed to express cruelty or selfishness irreconcilable with the demands of love.

Footnotes

1. According to Glanville Williams (*The Sanctity of Human Life supra* n. 169, at 193), "The historical reason for the Catholic objection to abortion is the same as for the Christian Church's historical opposition to infanticide: the horror of bringing about the death of an unbaptized child." This statement is made without any citation of evidence. As has been seen, desire to administer baptism could, in the Middle Ages, even be urged as a reason for procuring an abortion. It is highly regrettable that the American Law Institute was apparently misled by Williams' account and repeated after him the same baseless statement. See American Law Institute, *Model Penal Code: Tentative Draft No. 9* (1959), p. 148, n. 12.

2. ... Thomas Aquinas gave an analogous reason against baptizing a fetus in the womb: "As long as it exists in the womb of the mother, it cannot be subject to the operation of the ministers of the Church as it is not known to men" (*In sententias Petri Lombardi* 4.6 1.1.2).

Review Questions

1. According to Noonan, what is the simple Christian criterion for humanity?

2. Noonan discusses five different distinctions (starting with viability) used by defenders of abortion. Explain Noonan's critique of these distinctions.

3. State and explain Noonan's argument from probabilities.

4. What is Noonan's positive argument for saying that conception is "the decisive moment of humanization?"

5. In Noonan's view, why does the fetus have rights equal to those of other human beings?

6. According to Noonan, how do Christian theologians resolve conflicts of rights such as that between the mother's right to life and the fetus' right to life?

7. According to the traditional view defended by Noonan, in which cases do the fetus' right to life outweigh the mother's right to life?

Discussion Questions

1. Consider the following objection to Noonan's claim that "a being with a human genetic code is a man." A human cell also is a being with a human genetic code, but obviously it is not a man in the sense of being a human being; therefore, Noonan's claim is false. How could Noonan respond to this objection?

2. Is it possible for a nonhuman being, for example an angel or an intelligent alien being, to have rights equal to those of human beings? Defend your answer.

3. Noonan admits that abortion can be justified by appealing to the right of self-defense. Does this right justify an abortion in a case of rape? Why or why not?

Mary Anne Warren

On the Moral and Legal Status of Abortion

Mary Anne Warren teaches at San Francisco State University. She is the author of several articles including "Do Potential People Have Moral Rights?" and "Secondary Sexism and Quota Hiring."

The first part of Warren's article in this text is a response to Thomson (12). She argues that even though Thomson's argument from analogy is probably conclusive in showing that abortion is justified in the case of pregnancy due to rape, it does not show that abortion is permissible in numerous other cases where pregnancy is not due to rape and is not life threatening. Warren feels that more argument is needed to show the permissibility of abortion in those cases.

In the second part of the article, Warren presents her case for the liberal view that abortion can be justified in any case. Her argument depends on a distinction between two senses of the word human. *The first sense is a* genetic *sense where something is human if it is a member of the biological species* Homo sapiens; *the second is a* moral *sense where something is human if it is a member of the moral community. She claims that conservatives like Noonan confuse these two senses of human. They fallaciously argue from the fact that fetuses are genetically human to the conclusion that they are morally human, that is, persons with a right to life. But an analysis of the concept of person shows that fetuses are unlike persons in too many areas to have a significant right to life. There are five features central to personhood—consciousness, reasoning, self-motivated activity, the capacity to communicate, and self-awareness. The fetus lacks all of these features in the early stages of development and continues to lack most of them in the later stages. Furthermore, the fetus' potential for becoming a person does not pro-*

vide us with a good reason for ascribing to it a significant right to life. The rights of merely a potential person, even assuming it has rights, would always be outweighed by the rights of an actual person, in this case, the mother. The mother's right to have an abortion, then, is absolute; it can never be outweighed by the rights of the fetus.

In the postscript, Warren replies to the objection that her view would justify infanticide. She admits that infants do not have a significant right to life in her view, but she claims that it does not follow that infanticide is permissible for two reasons. First, there may be people willing to adopt the unwanted child and in that case it would be wrong to kill it. Second, many people in our country value infants and would prefer that they be preserved, even if foster parents are not available.

We will be concerned with both the moral status of abortion, which for our purposes we may define as the act which a woman performs in voluntarily terminating, or allowing another person to terminate, her pregnancy, and the legal status which is appropriate for this act. I will argue that, while it is not possible to produce a satisfactory defense of a woman's right to obtain an abortion without showing that a fetus is not a human being, in the morally relevant sense of that term, we ought not to conclude that the difficulties involved in determining whether or not a fetus is human make it impossible to produce any satisfactory solution to the problem of the moral status of abortion. For it is possible to show that, on the basis of intuitions which we may expect even the opponents of abortion to share, a fetus is not a person, and hence not the sort of entity to which it is proper to ascribe full moral rights.

Of course, while some philosophers would deny the possibility of any such proof,[1] others will deny that there is any need for it, since the moral permissibility of abortion appears to them to be too obvious to require proof. But the inadequacy of this attitude should be evident from the fact that both the friends and the foes of abortion consider their position to be morally self-evident. Be-

From "On the Moral and Legal Status of Abortion," *The Monist*, vol. 57, no. 1 (January 1973), pp. 43–61. Reprinted with permission from *The Monist* and Dr. Mary Anne Warren, San Francisco State University.

cause pro-abortionists have never adequately come to grips with the conceptual issues surrounding abortion, most if not all, of the arguments which they advance in opposition to laws restricting access to abortion fail to refute or even weaken the traditional antiabortion argument, i.e., that a fetus is a human being, and therefore abortion is murder.

These arguments are typically one of two sorts. Either they point to the terrible side effects of the restrictive laws, e.g., the deaths due to illegal abortions, and the fact that it is poor women who suffer the most as a result of these laws, or else they state that to deny a woman access to abortion is to deprive her of her right to control her own body. Unfortunately, however, the fact that restricting access to abortion has tragic side effects does not, in itself, show that the restrictions are unjustified, since murder is wrong regardless of the consequences of prohibiting it; and the appeal to the right to control one's body, which is generally construed as a property right, is at best a rather feeble argument for the permissibility of abortion. Mere ownership does not give me the right to kill innocent people whom I find on my property, and indeed I am apt to be held responsible if such people injure themselves while on my property. It is equally unclear that I have any moral right to expel an innocent person from my property when I know that doing so will result in his death.

Furthermore, it is probably inappropriate to describe a woman's body as her property, since it seems natural to hold that a person is something distinct from her property, but not from her body. Even those who would object to the identification of a person with his body, or with the conjunction of his body and his mind, must admit that it would be very odd to describe, say, breaking a leg, as damaging one's property, and much more appropriate to describe it as injuring one*self*. Thus it is probably a mistake to argue that the right to obtain an abortion is in any way derived from the right to own and regulate property.

But however we wish to construe the right to abortion, we cannot hope to convince those who consider abortion a form of murder of the existence of any such right unless we are able to produce a clear and convincing refutation of the traditional antiabortion argument, and this has not, to my knowledge, been done. With respect to the two most vital issues which that argument involves, i.e., the humanity of the fetus and its implication for the moral status of abortion, confusion has prevailed on both sides of the dispute.

Thus, both pro-abortionists and antiabortionists have tended to abstract the question of whether abortion is wrong to that of whether it is wrong to destroy a fetus, just as though the rights of another person were not necessarily involved. This mistaken abstraction has led to the almost universal assumption that if a fetus is a human being, with a right to life, then it follows immediately that abortion is wrong (except perhaps when necessary to save the woman's life), and that it ought to be prohibited. It has also been generally assumed that unless the question about the status of the fetus is answered, the moral status of abortion cannot possibly be determined.

Two recent papers, one by B.A. Brody,[2] and one by Judith Thomson,[3] have attempted to settle the question of whether abortion ought to be prohibited apart from the question of whether or not the fetus is human. Brody examines the possibility that the following two statements are compatible: (1) that abortion is the taking of innocent human life, and therefore wrong; and (2) that nevertheless it ought not to be prohibited by law, at least under the present circumstances.[4] Not surprisingly, Brody finds it impossible to reconcile these two statements, since, as he rightly argues, none of the unfortunate side effects of the prohibition of abortion is bad enough to justify legalizing the *wrongful* taking of human life. He is mistaken, however, in concluding that the incompatibility of (1) and (2), in itself, shows that "the legal problem about abortion cannot be resolved independently of the status of the fetus problem" . . . .

What Brody fails to realize is that (1) embodies the questionable assumption that if a fetus is a human being, then of course abortion is morally wrong, and that an attack on *this* assumption is more promising, as a way of reconciling the humanity of the fetus with the claim that laws prohibiting abortion are unjustified, than is an attack on the assumption that if abortion is the wrongful killing of innocent human beings then it ought to be prohibited. He thus overlooks the possibility that a fetus may have a right to life and abortion still be morally permissible, in that the right of a woman to terminate an unwanted pregnancy might override the right of the fetus to be kept alive. The immorality of abortion is no more demonstrated by the humanity of the fetus, in itself, than the immorality of killing in self-defense is demonstrated by the fact that the assailant is a human being. Neither is it demonstrated by the *innocence* of the fetus, since there may be situations in which the killing of innocent human beings is justified.

It is perhaps not surprising that Brody fails to spot this assumption, since it has been accepted with little or no argument by nearly everyone who has written on the morality of abortion. John Noonan is correct in saying that "the fundamental question in the long history of abortion is, How do you determine the humanity of a being?"[5] He summarizes his own antiabortion argument, which is a version of the official position of the Catholic Church, as follows:

> . . . *it is wrong to kill humans, however poor, weak, defenseless, and lacking in opportunity to develop their potential they may be. It is therefore morally wrong to kill Biafrans. Similarly, it is morally wrong to kill embryos.*[6]

Noonan bases his claim that fetuses are human upon what he calls the theologians' criterion of humanity: that whoever is conceived of human beings is human. But although he argues at length for the appropriateness of this criterion, he never questions the assumption that if a fetus is human then abortion is wrong for exactly the same reason that murder is wrong.

Judith Thomson is, in fact, the only writer I am aware of who has seriously questioned this assumption; she has argued that, even if we grant the antiabortionist his claim that a fetus is a human being, with the same right to life as any other human being, we can still demonstrate that, in at least some and perhaps most cases, a woman is under no moral obligation to complete an unwanted pregnancy.[7] Her argument is worth examining, since if it holds up it may enable us to establish the moral permissibility of abortion without becoming involved in problems about what entitles an entity to be considered human, and accorded full moral rights. To be able to do this would be a great gain in the power and simplicity of the pro-abortion position, since, although I will argue that these problems can be solved at least as decisively as can any other moral problem, we should certainly be pleased to be able to avoid having to solve them as part of the justification of abortion.

On the other hand, even if Thomson's argument does not hold up, her insight, i.e., that it requires *argument* to show that if fetuses are human then abortion is properly classified as murder, is an extremely valuable one. The assumption she attacks is particularly invidious, for it amounts to the decision that it is appropriate, in deciding the moral status of abortion, to leave the rights of the pregnant woman out of consideration entirely, except possibly when her life is threatened. Obviously, this will not do; determining what moral rights, if any, a fetus possesses is only the first step in determining the moral status of abortion. Step two, which is at least equally essential, is finding a just solution to the conflict between whatever rights the fetus may have, and the rights of the woman who is unwillingly pregnant. While the historical error has been to pay far too little attention to the second step, Ms. Thomson's suggestion is that if we look at the second step first we may find that a woman has a right to obtain an abortion *regardless* of what rights the fetus has.

Our own inquiry will also have two stages. In Section I, we will consider whether or not it is possible to establish that abortion is morally permissible even on the assumption that a fetus is an entity with a full-fledged right to life. I will argue that in fact this cannot be established, at least not with the conclusiveness which is essential to our hopes of convincing those who are skeptical about the morality of abortion, and that we therefore cannot avoid dealing with the question of whether or not a fetus really does have the same right to life as a (more fully developed) human being.

In Section II, I will propose an answer to this question, namely, that a fetus cannot be considered a member of the moral community, the set of beings with full and equal moral rights, for the simple reason that it is not a person, and that it is personhood, and not genetic humanity, i.e., humanity as defined by Noonan, which is the basis for membership in this community. I will argue that a fetus, whatever its stage of development, satisfies none of the basic criteria of personhood, and is not even enough *like* a person to be accorded even some of the same rights on the basis of this resemblance. Nor, as we will see, is a fetus's *potential* personhood a threat to the morality of abortion, since, whatever the rights of potential people may be, they are invariably overridden in any conflict with the moral rights of actual people.

I

We turn now to Professor Thomson's case for the claim that even if a fetus has full moral rights, abortion is still morally permissible, at least sometimes, and for some reasons other than to save the woman's life. Her argument is based upon a clever, but I think faulty, analogy. She asks us to picture ourselves waking up one day, in bed with a famous violinist. Imagine that you have been kidnapped, and your bloodstream hooked up to that of the violinist, who happens to have an ailment which will certainly kill him unless he is per-

mitted to share your kidneys for a period of nine months. No one else can save him, since you alone have the right type of blood. He will be unconscious all that time, and you will have to stay in bed with him, but after the nine months are over he may be unplugged, completely cured, that is provided that you have cooperated.

Now then, she continues, what are your obligations in this situation? The antiabortionist, if he is consistent, will have to say that you are obligated to stay in bed with the violinist: for all people have a right to life, and violinists are people, and therefore it would be murder for you to disconnect yourself from him and let him die .... But this is outrageous, and so there must be something wrong with the same argument when it is applied to abortion. It would certainly be commendable of you to agree to save the violinist, but it is absurd to suggest that your refusal to do so would be murder. His right to life does not obligate you to do whatever is required to keep him alive; nor does it justify anyone else in forcing you to do so. A law which required you to say in bed with the violinist would clearly be an unjust law, since it is no proper function of the law to force unwilling people to make huge sacrifices for the sake of other people toward whom they have no such prior obligation.

Thomson concludes that, if this analogy is an apt one, then we can grant the antiabortionist his claim that a fetus is a human being, and still hold that it is at least sometimes the case that a pregnant woman has the right to refuse to be a Good Samaritan towards the fetus, i.e., to obtain an abortion. For there is a great gap between the claim that *x* has a right to life, and the claim that *y* is obligated to do whatever is necessary to keep *x* alive, let alone that he ought to be forced to do so. It is *y*'s duty to keep *x* alive only if he has somehow contracted a *special* obligation to do so; and a woman who is unwillingly pregnant, e.g., who was raped, has done nothing which obligates her to make the enormous sacrifice which is necessary to preserve the conceptus.

This argument is initially quite plausible, and in the extreme case of pregnancy due to rape it is probably conclusive. Difficulties arise, however, when we try to specify more exactly the range of cases in which abortion is clearly justifiable even on the assumption that the fetus is human. Professor Thomson considers it a virtue of her argument that it does not enable us to conclude that abortion is *always* permissible. It would, she says, be "indecent" for a woman in her seventh month to obtain an abortion just to avoid having to postpone a trip to Europe. On the other hand, her argument enables us to see that "a sick and desperately frightened schoolgirl pregnant due to rape may *of course* choose abortion, and that any law which rules this out is an insane law" . . . . So far, so good; but what are we to say about the woman who becomes pregnant not through rape but as a result of her own carelessness, or because of contraceptive failure, or who gets pregnant intentionally and then changes her mind about wanting a child? With respect to such cases, the violinist analogy is of much less use to the defender of the woman's right to obtain an abortion.

Indeed, the choice of a pregnancy due to rape, as an example of a case in which abortion is permissible even if a fetus is considered a human being, is extremely significant; for it is only in the case of pregnancy due to rape that the woman's situation is adequately analogous to the violinist case for our intuitions about the latter to transfer convincingly. The crucial difference between a pregnancy due to rape and the *normal* case of an unwanted pregnancy is that in the normal case we cannot claim that the woman is in no way responsible for her predicament; she could have remained chaste, or taken her pills more faithfully, or abstained on dangerous days, and so on. If, on the other hand, you are kidnapped by strangers, and hooked up to a strange violinist, then you are free of any shred of responsibility for the situation, on the basis of which it could be argued that you are obligated to keep the violinist alive.

Only when her pregnancy is due to rape is a woman clearly just as nonresponsible.[8]

Consequently, there is room for the antiabortionist to argue that in the normal case of unwanted pregnancy a woman has, by her own actions, assumed responsibility for the fetus. For if x behaves in a way which he could have avoided, and which he knows involves, let us say, a 1 percent chance of bringing into existence a human being, with a right to life, and does so knowing that if this should happen then that human being will perish unless x does certain things to keep him alive, then it is by no means clear that when it does happen x is free of any obligation to what he knew in advance would be required to keep that human being alive.

The plausibility of such an argument is enough to show that the Thomson analogy can provide a clear and persuasive defense of a woman's right to obtain an abortion only with respect to those cases in which the woman is in no way responsible for her pregnancy, e.g., where it is due to rape. In all other cases, we would almost certainly conclude that it was necessary to look carefully at the particular circumstances in order to determine the extent of the woman's responsibility, and hence the extent of her obligation. This is an extremely unsatisfactory outcome, from the viewpoint of the opponents of restrictive abortion laws, most of whom are convinced that a woman has a right to obtain an abortion regardless of how and why she got pregnant.

Of course a supporter of the violinist analogy might point out that it is absurd to suggest that forgetting her pill one day might be sufficient to obligate a woman to complete an unwanted pregnancy. And indeed it *is* absurd to suggest this. As we will see, the moral right to obtain an abortion is not in the least dependent upon the extent to which the woman is responsible for her pregnancy. But unfortunately, once we allow the assumption that a fetus has full moral rights, we cannot avoid taking this absurd suggestion seriously. Perhaps we can make this point more clear by altering the violinist story just enough to make it more analogous to a normal unwanted pregnancy and less to a pregnancy due to rape, and then seeing whether it is still obvious that you are not obligated to stay in bed with the fellow.

Suppose, then, that violinists are peculiarly prone to the sort of illness the only cure for which is the use of someone else's bloodstream for nine months, and that because of this there has been formed a society of music lovers who agree that whenever a violinist is stricken they will draw lots and the loser will, by some means, be made the one and only person capable of saving him. Now then, would you be obligated to cooperate in curing the violinist if you had voluntarily joined this society, knowing the possible consequences, and then your name had been drawn and you had been kidnapped? Admittedly, you did not promise ahead of time that you would, but you did deliberately place yourself in a position in which it might happen that a human life would be lost if you did not. Surely this is at least a prima facie reason for supposing that you have an obligation to stay in bed with the violinist. Suppose that you had gotten your name drawn deliberately; surely *that* would be quite a strong reason for thinking that you had such an obligation.

It might be suggested that there is one important disanalogy between the modified violinist case and the case of an unwanted pregnancy, which makes the woman's responsibility significantly less, namely, the fact that the fetus *comes into existence* as the result of the woman's actions. This fact might give her a right to refuse to keep it alive, whereas she would not have had this right had it existed previously, independently, and then as a result of her actions become dependent upon her for its survival.

My own intuition, however, is that *x* has no more right to bring into existence, either deliberately or as a foreseeable result of actions he could have avoided, a being with full moral rights *(y)*, and then refuse to do what he knew beforehand would be required to keep that being alive, than he has to enter into an agreement with an existing person, whereby he may be called upon to save that person's life, and then refuse to do so when so called upon. Thus, *x*'s responsibility for *y*'s existence does not seem to lessen his obligation to keep *y* alive, if he is also responsible for *y*'s being in a situation in which only he can save him.

Whether or not this intuition is entirely correct, it brings us back once again to the conclusion that once we allow the assumption that a fetus has full moral rights it becomes an extremely complex and difficult question whether and when abortion is justifiable. Thus the Thomson analogy cannot help us produce a clear and persuasive proof of the moral permissibility of abortion. Nor will the opponents of the restrictive laws thank us for anything less; for their conviction (for the most part) is that abortion is obviously *not* a morally serious and extremely unfortunate, even though sometimes justified act, comparable to killing in self-defense or to letting the violinist die, but rather is closer to being a morally neutral act, like cutting one's hair.

The basis of this conviction, I believe, is the realization that a fetus is not a person, and thus does not have a full-fledged right to life. Perhaps the reason why this claim has been so inadequately defended is that it seems self-evident to those who accept it. And so it is, insofar as it follows from what I take to be perfectly obvious claims about the nature of personhood, and about the proper grounds for ascribing moral rights, claims which ought, indeed, to be obvious to both the friends and foes of abortion. Nevertheless, it is worth examining these claims, and showing how they demonstrate the moral innocuousness of abortion, since this apparently has not been adequately done before.

II

The question which we must answer in order to produce a satisfactory solution to the problem of the moral status of abortion is this: How are we to define the moral community, the set of beings with full and equal moral rights, such that we can decide whether a human fetus is a member of this community or not? What sort of entity, exactly, has the inalienable rights to life, liberty, and the pursuit of happiness? Jefferson attributed these rights to all *men*, and it may or may not be fair to suggest that he intended to attribute them *only* to men. Perhaps he ought to have attributed them to all human beings. If so, then we arrive, first, at Noonan's problem of defining what makes a being human, and, second, at the equally vital question which Noonan does not consider, namely, What reason is there for identifying the moral community with the set of all human beings, in whatever way we have chosen to define that term?

On the Definition of "Human"

One reason why this vital second question is so frequently overlooked in the debate over the moral status of abortion is that the term "human" has two distinct, but not often distinguished, senses. This fact results in a slide of meaning, which serves to conceal the fallaciousness of the traditional argument that since (1) it is wrong to kill innocent human beings, and (2) fetuses are innocent human beings, then (3) it is wrong to kill fetuses. For if "human" is used in the same sense in both (1) and (2) then, whichever of the two senses is meant, one of these premises is question-begging. And if it is used in two different senses then of course the conclusion doesn't follow.

Thus, (1) is a self-evident moral truth,[9] and avoids begging the question about abortion, only if "human being" is used to mean something like "a full-fledged member of the moral community." (It may or may not also be meant to refer exclusively to members of the species *Homo sapiens.*) We may call this the *moral* sense of "human." It is not to be confused with what we will call the *genetic* sense, i.e., the sense in which *any* member of the species is a human being, and no member of any other species could be. If (1) is acceptable only if the moral sense is intended, (2) is

non-question-begging only if what is intended is the genetic sense.

In "Deciding Who Is Human," Noonan argues for the classification of fetuses with human beings by pointing to the presence of the full genetic code, and the potential capacity for rational thought .... It is clear that what he needs to show, for his version of the traditional argument to be valid, is that fetuses are human in the moral sense, the sense in which it is analytically true that all human beings have full moral rights. But, in the absence of any argument showing that whatever is genetically human is also morally human, and he gives none, nothing more than genetic humanity can be demonstrated by the presence of the human genetic code. And, as we will see, the *potential* capacity for rational thought can at most show that an entity has the potential for *becoming* human in the moral sense.

Defining the Moral Community

Can it be established that genetic humanity is sufficient for moral humanity? I think that there are very good reasons for not defining the moral community in this way. I would like to suggest an alternative way of defining the moral community, which I will argue for only to the extent of explaining why it is, or should be, self-evident. The suggestion is simply that the moral community consists of all and only *people*, rather than all and only human beings;[10] and probably the best way of demonstrating its self-evidence is by considering the concept of personhood, to see what sorts of entity are and are not persons, and what the decision that a being is or is not a person implies about its moral rights.

What characteristics entitle an entity to be considered a person? This is obviously not the place to attempt a complete analysis of the concept of personhood, but we do not need such a fully adequate analysis just to determine whether and why a fetus is or isn't a person. All we need is a rough and approximate list of the most basic criteria of personhood, and some idea of which, or how many, of these an entity must satisfy in order to properly be considered a person.

In searching for such criteria, it is useful to look beyond the set of people with whom we are acquainted, and ask how we would decide whether a totally alien being was a person or not. (For we have no right to assume that genetic humanity is necessary for personhood.) Imagine a space traveler who lands on an unknown planet and encounters a race of beings utterly unlike any he has ever seen or heard of. If he wants to be sure of behaving morally toward these beings, he has to somehow decide whether they are people, and hence have full moral rights, or whether they are the sort of thing which he need not feel guilty about treating as, for example, a source of food.

How should he go about making this decision? If he has some anthropological background, he might look for such things as religion, art, and the manufacturing of tools, weapons, or shelters, since these factors have been used to distinguish our human from our prehuman ancestors, in what seems to be closer to the moral than the genetic sense of "human." And no doubt he would be right to consider the presence of such factors as good evidence that the alien beings were people, and morally human. It would, however, be overly anthropocentric of him to take the absence of these things as adequate evidence that they were not, since we can imagine people who have progressed beyond, or evolved without ever developing, these cultural characteristics.

I suggest that the traits which are most central to the concept of personhood, or humanity in the moral sense, are, very roughly, the following:

1. consciousness (of objects and events external and/or internal to the being), and in particular the capacity to feel pain;
2. reasoning (the *developed* capacity to solve new and relatively complex problems);
3. self-motivated activity (activity which is relatively independent of either genetic or direct external control);
4. the capacity to communicate, by whatever means, messages of an indefinite variety of types, that is, not just with an indefinite number of possible contents, but on indefinitely many possible topics;
5. the presence of self-concepts, and self-awareness, either individual or racial, or both.

Admittedly, there are apt to be a great many problems involved in formulating precise definitions of these criteria, let alone in developing universally valid behavioral criteria for deciding when they apply. But I will assume that both we and our explorer know approximately what (1)–(5) mean, and that he is also able to determine whether or not they apply. How, then, should he use his findings to decide whether or not the alien beings are people? We needn't suppose that an entity must have *all* of these attributes to be properly considered a person; (1) and (2) alone may well be sufficient for personhood, and quite probably (1)–(3) are sufficient. Neither do we need to insist that any one of these criteria is *necessary* for personhood, although once again (1) and (2) look like fairly good candidates for necessary conditions, as does (3), if "activity" is construed so as to include the activity of reasoning.

All we need to claim, to demonstrate that a fetus is not a person, is that any being which satisfies *none* of (1)–(5) is certainly not a person. I consider this claim to be so obvious that I think anyone who denied it, and claimed that a being which satisfied none of (1)–(5) was a person all the same, would thereby demonstrate that he had no notion at all of what a person is—perhaps because he had confused the concept of a person with that of genetic humanity. If the opponents of abortion were to deny the appropriateness of these five criteria, I do not know what further arguments would convince them. We would probably have to admit that our conceptual schemes were indeed irreconcilably different, and that our dispute could not be settled objectively.

I do not expect this to happen, however, since I think that the concept of a person is one which is very nearly universal (to people), and that it is common to both proabortionists and antiabortionists, even though neither group has fully realized the relevance of this concept to the resolution of their dispute. Furthermore, I think that on reflection even the antiabortionists ought to agree not only that (1)–(5) are central to the concept of personhood, but also that it is a part of this concept that all and only people have full moral rights. The concept of a person is in part a moral concept; once we have admitted that *x* is a person we have recognized, even if we have not agreed to respect, *x* 's right to be treated as a member of the moral community. It is true that the claim that *x* is a *human being* is more commonly voiced as part of an appeal to treat *x* decently than is the claim that *x* is a person, but this is either because "human being" is here used in the sense which implies personhood, or because the genetic and moral senses of "human" have been confused.

Now if (1)–(5) are indeed the primary criteria of personhood, then it is clear that genetic humanity is neither necessary nor sufficient for establishing that an entity is a person. Some human beings are not people, and there may well be people who are not human beings. A man or woman whose consciousness has been permanently obliterated but who remains alive is a human being which is no longer a person; defective human beings, with no appreciable mental capacity, are not and presumably never will be people; and a fetus is a human being which is not yet a person, and which therefore cannot coherently be said to have full moral rights. Citizens of the next century should be prepared to recognize highly advanced, self-aware robots or computers, should such be developed, and intelligent inhabitants of other worlds, should such be found, as people in the fullest sense, and to respect their moral rights. But to ascribe full moral rights to an entity which is not a person is as absurd as to ascribe moral obligations and responsibilities to such an entity.

Fetal Development and the Right to Life

Two problems arise in the application of these suggestions for the definition of the moral community to the determination of the precise moral status of a human fetus. Given that the paradigm example of a person is a normal adult human being, then (1) How like this paradigm, in particular how far advanced since conception, does a human being need to be before it begins to have a right to life by virtue, not of being fully a person as of yet, but of being *like* a person? and (2) To what extent, if any, does the fact that a fetus has the *potential* for becoming a person endow it with some of the same rights? Each of these questions requires some comment.

In answering the first question, we need not attempt a detailed consideration of the moral rights of organisms which are not developed enough, aware enough, intelligent enough, etc., to be considered people, but which resemble people in some respects. It does seem reasonable to suggest that the more like a person, in the relevant respects, a being is, the stronger is the case for regarding it as having a right to life, and indeed the stronger its right to life is. Thus we ought to take seriously the suggestion that, insofar as "the human individual develops biologically in a continuous fashion ... the rights of a human person might develop in the same way." [11] But we must keep in mind that the attributes which are relevant in determining whether or not an entity is enough like a person to be regarded as having some of the same moral rights are no different from those which are relevant to determining whether or not it is fully a person—i.e., are no different from (1)–(5)—and that being genetically human, or having recognizably human facial and other physical features, or detectable brain activity, or the capacity to survive outside the uterus, are simply not among these relevant attributes.

Thus it is clear that even though a seven-or

eight-month fetus has features which make it apt to arouse in us almost the same powerful protective instinct as is commonly aroused by a small infant, nevertheless it is not significantly more personlike than is a very small embryo. It is *somewhat* more personlike; it can apparently feel and respond to pain, and it may even have a rudimentary form of consciousness, insofar as its brain is quite active. Nevertheless, it seems safe to say that it is not fully conscious, in the way that an infant of a few months is, and that it cannot reason, or communicate messages of indefinitely many sorts, does not engage in self-motivated activity, and has no self-awareness. Thus, in the *relevant* respects, a fetus, even a fully developed one, is considerably less personlike than is the average mature mammal, indeed the average fish. And I think that a rational person must conclude that if the right to life of a fetus is to be based upon its resemblance to a person, then it cannot be said to have any more right to life than, let us say, a newborn guppy (which also seems to be capable of feeling pain), and that a right of that magnitude could never override a woman's right to obtain an abortion, at any stage of her pregnancy.

There may, of course, be other arguments in favor of placing legal limits upon the stage of pregnancy in which an abortion may be performed. Given the relative safety of the new techniques of artificially inducing labor during the third trimester, the danger to the woman's life or health is no longer such an argument. Neither is the fact that people tend to respond to the thought of abortion in the later stages of pregnancy with emotional repulsion, since mere emotional responses cannot take the place of moral reasoning in determining what ought to be permitted. Nor, finally, is the frequently heard argument that legalizing abortion, especially late in the pregnancy, may erode the level of respect for human life, leading, perhaps, to an increase in unjustified euthanasia and other crimes. For this threat, if it is a threat, can be better met by educating people to the kinds of moral distinctions which we are making here than

by limiting access to abortion (which limitation may, in its disregard for the rights of women, be just as damaging to the level of respect for human rights).

Thus, since the fact that even a fully developed fetus is not person-like enough to have any significant right to life on the basis of its person-likeness shows that no legal restrictions upon the stage of pregnancy in which an abortion may be performed can be justified on the grounds that we should protect the rights of the older fetus; and since there is no other apparent justification for such restrictions, we may conclude that they are entirely unjustified. Whether or not it would be *indecent* (whatever that means) for a woman in her seventh month to obtain an abortion just to avoid having to postpone a trip to Europe, it would not, in itself, be *immoral*, and therefore it ought to be permitted.

Potential Personhood and the Right to Life

We have seen that a fetus does not resemble a person in any way which can support the claim that it has even some of the same rights. But what about its *potential*, the fact that if nurtured and allowed to develop naturally it will very probably become a person? Doesn't that alone give it at least some right to life? It is hard to deny that the fact that an entity is a potential person is a strong prima facie reason for not destroying it; but we need not conclude from this that a potential person has a right to life, by virtue of that potential. It may be that our feeling that it is better, other things being equal, not to destroy a potential person is better explained by the fact that potential people are still (felt to be) an invaluable resource, not to be lightly squandered. Surely, if every speck of dust were a potential person, we would be much less apt to conclude that every potential person has a right to become actual.

Still, we do not need to insist that a potential person has no right to life whatever. There may well be something immoral, and not just imprudent, about wantonly destroying potential people, when doing so isn't necessary to protect anyone's rights. But even if a potential person does have some **prima facie right** to life, such a right could not possibly outweigh the right of a woman to obtain an abortion, since the rights of any actual person invariably outweigh those of any potential person, whenever the two conflict. Since this may not be immediately obvious in the case of a human fetus, let us look at another case.

Suppose that our space explorer falls into the hands of an alien culture, whose scientists decide to create a few hundred thousand or more human beings, by breaking his body into its component cells, and using these to create fully developed human beings, with, of course, his genetic code. We may imagine that each of these newly created men will have all of the original man's abilities, skills, knowledge, and so on, and also have an individual self-concept, in short that each of them will be a bona fide (though hardly unique) person. Imagine that the whole project will take only seconds, and that its chances of success are extremely high, and that our explorer knows all of this, and also knows that these people will be treated fairly. I maintain that in such a situation he would have every right to escape if he could, and thus to deprive all of these potential people of their potential lives; for his right to life outweighs all of theirs together, in spite of the fact that they are all genetically human, all innocent, and all have a very high probability of becoming people very soon, if only he refrains from acting.

Indeed, I think he would have a right to escape even if it were not his life which the alien scientists planned to take, but only a year of his freedom, or, indeed, only a day. Nor would he be obligated to stay if he had gotten captured (thus bringing all these people-potentials into existence) because of his own carelessness, or even if he had done so deliberately, knowing the consequences. Regardless of how he got captured, he is not morally obligated to remain in captivity for *any* period of time for the sake of permitting any number of potential people to come into actuality, so great is the margin by which one actual person's right to liberty outweighs whatever right to life even a hundred thousand potential people have. And it seems reasonable to conclude that the rights of a woman will outweigh by a similar margin whatever right to life a fetus may have by virtue of its potential personhood.

Thus, neither a fetus's resemblance to a person, nor its potential for becoming a person provides any basis whatever for the claim that it has any significant right to life. Consequently, a woman's right to protect her health, happiness, freedom, and even her life,[12] by terminating an unwanted pregnancy, will always override whatever right to life it may be appropriate to ascribe to a fetus, even a fully developed one. And thus, in the absence of any overwhelming social need for every possible child, the laws which restrict the right to obtain an abortion, or limit the period of pregnancy during which an abortion may be performed, are a wholly unjustified violation of a woman's most basic moral and constitutional rights.[13]

POSTSCRIPT ON INFANTICIDE

Since the publication of this article, many people have written to point out that my argument appears to justify not only abortion, but infanticide as well. For a new-born infant is not significantly more person-like than an advanced fetus, and consequently it would seem that if the destruction of the latter is permissible so too must be that of the former. Inasmuch as most people, regardless of how they feel about the morality of abortion, consider infanticide a form of murder, this might appear to represent a serious flaw in my argument.

Now, if I am right in holding that it is only people who have a full-fledged right to life, and who can be murdered, and if the criteria of personhood are as I have described them, then it obviously follows that killing a new-born infant isn't murder. It does *not* follow, however, that infanticide is permissible, for two reasons. In the first place, it would be wrong, at least in this country and in this period of history, and other things being equal, to kill a new-born infant, because even if its parents do not want it and would not suffer from its destruction, there are other people who would like to have it, and would, in all probability, be deprived of a great deal of pleasure by its destruction. Thus, infanticide is wrong for reasons analogous to those which make it wrong to wantonly destroy natural resources, or great works of art.

Secondly, most people, at least in this country, value infants, and would much prefer that they be preserved, even if foster parents are not immediately available. Most of us would rather be taxed to support orphanages than allow unwanted infants to be destroyed. So long as there are people who want an infant preserved, and who are willing and able to provide the means of caring for it, under reasonably humane conditions, it is, *ceteris parabis,* wrong to destroy it.

But, it might be replied, if this argument shows that infanticide is wrong, at least at this time and in this country, doesn't it also show that abortion is wrong? After all, many people value fetuses, are disturbed by their destruction, and would much prefer that they be preserved, even at some cost to themselves. Furthermore, as a potential source of pleasure to some foster family, a fetus is just as valuable as an infant. There is, however, a crucial difference between the two cases: so long as the fetus is unborn, its preservation, contrary to the wishes of the pregnant woman, violates her rights to freedom, happiness, and self-determination. Her rights override the rights of those who would like the fetus preserved, just as if someone's life or limb is threatened by a wild animal, his right to protect himself by destroying the animal overrides the rights of those who would prefer that the animal not be harmed.

The minute the infant is born, however, its preservation no longer violates any of its mother's rights, even if she wants it de-stroyed, because she is free to put it up for adoption. Consequently, while the moment of birth does not mark any sharp discontinuity in the degree to which an infant possesses the right to life, it does mark the end of its mother's right to determine its fate. Indeed, if abortion could be performed without killing the fetus, she would never possess the right to have the fetus destroyed, for the same reasons that she has no right to have an infant destroyed.

On the other hand, it follows from my argument that when an unwanted or defective infant is born into a society which cannot afford and/or is not willing to care for it, then its destruction is permissible. This conclusion will, no doubt, strike many people as heartless and immoral; but remember that the very existence of people who feel this way, and who are willing and able to provide care for unwanted infants, is reason enough to conclude that they should be preserved.

Footnotes

1. For example, Roger Wertheimer, who in "Understanding the Abortion Argument" (*Philosophy and Public Affairs,* 1, No. 1 [Fall 1971], 67–95), argues that the problem of the moral status of abortion is insoluble, in that the dispute over the status of the fetus is not a question of fact at all, but only a question of how one responds to the facts.

2. B.A. Brody, "Abortion and the Law," *The Journal of Philosophy,* 68, No. 12 (June 17, 1971), 357–69.

3. Judith Thomson, "A Defense of Abortion," *Philosophy and Public Affairs,* 1, No. 1 (Fall 1971), 47–66.

4. I have abbreviated these statements somewhat, but not in a way which affects the argument.

5. John Noonan, "Abortion and the Catholic Church: A Summary History," *Natural Law Forum,* 12 (1967), 125.

6. John Noonan, "Deciding Who Is Human," *Natural Law Forum,* 13 (1968), 134.

7. "A Defense of Abortion."

8. We may safely ignore the fact that she might have avoided getting raped, e.g., by carrying a gun, since by similar means you might likewise have avoided getting kidnapped, and in neither case does the victim's failure to take all possible precautions against a highly unlikely event (as opposed to reasonable precautions against a rather likely event) mean that he is morally responsible for what happens.

9. Of course, the principle that it is (always) wrong to kill innocent human beings is in need of many modifications, e.g., that it may be permissible to do so to save a greater number of other innocent human beings, but we may safely ignore these complications here.

10. From here on, we will use "human" to mean genetically human, since the moral sense seems closely connected to, and perhaps derived from, the assumption that genetic humanity is sufficient for membership in the moral community.

11. Thomas L. Hayes, "A Biological View," *Commonweal*, 85 (March 17, 1967), 677–78; quoted by Daniel Callahan, in *Abortion, Law, Choice, and Morality* (London: Macmillan & Co., 1970).

12. That is, insofar as the death rate, for the woman, is higher for childbirth than for early abortion.

13. My thanks to the following people, who were kind enough to read and criticize an earlier version of this paper: Herbert Gold, Gene Glass, Anne Lauterbach, Judith Thomson, Mary Mothersill, and Timothy Binkley.

Review Questions

1. What is the traditional antiabortion argument according to Warren?

2. According to Warren, why are the two typical pro-abortion arguments inadequate?

3. What difficulties does Warren raise in Thomson's argument?

4. Warren claims that the word *human* has two different senses, a *genetic sense* and a *moral sense.* Explain the distinction between the two.

5. Why does Warren think that it is obvious that a fetus is not a person, and why does she expect antiabortionists to agree with her?

6. Warren admits that she has two problems when it comes to applying her account of personhood to human fetuses. What are these two problems, and how does Warren solve them?

7. How does Warren reply to the objection that her position justifies infanticide as well as abortion?

Discussion Questions

1. Warren asserts that neither defective humans with little mental capacity nor permanently comatose humans are persons with moral rights. Do you agree? Why or why not?

2. Warren also claims that there can be nonhuman persons, for example, self-aware robots and alien beings from other planets. Is this possible? Explain your answer.

3. Warren says that an infant of a few months is less personlike than the average fish. Is this true?

4. Warren says, in opposition to Thomson (12), that a woman in her seventh month of pregnancy ought to be permitted to have an abortion just to avoid postponing a trip to Europe. Do you agree with this judgment? Defend your answer.

Daniel Callahan

Abortion Decisions and Personal Morality

Daniel Callahan is the director of the Hastings Center. He is the author of Ethics and Population Limitation *(1971) and the coeditor of* Science, Ethics and Medicine *(1976).*

Callahan begins by affirming his view that in a pluralistic society such as ours a woman should be free to make her own moral choice about abortion. This implies that there should be no laws prohibiting abortion. However, the moral dilemma concerning abortion remains: Even if it is legal, is it ever morally right to get an abortion? Callahan rejects the so-called tissue theory, *which holds that the fetus is merely worthless human tissue, because it ignores the biological evidence about fetal development. But on the other hand, he admits that the fetus does not qualify as a full-fledged person. His own view is somewhere in between these two extremes; the fetus is an important and valuable form of human life, and respect for the sanctity of human life should incline women toward a general and strong moral bias against abortion. Nevertheless, he allows that there may be extreme or unusual circumstances in which there are good reasons for having an abortion; these are circumstances in which the woman's duties to herself, her family, or her society outweigh the duty not to take an innocent human life. One example that he cites is a case of extreme overpopulation where the woman is responsible for the survival of a whole species.*

The strength of pluralistic societies lies in the personal freedom they afford individuals. One is free to choose among religious, philosophical, ideological and political creeds; or one can create one's own highly personal, idiosyncratic moral code and view of the universe. Increasingly, the individual is free to ignore the morals, manners and mores of society. The only limitations are upon those actions which seem to present clear and present dangers to the common good, and even there the range of prohibited actions is diminishing as more and more choices are left to personal and private decisions. I have contended that, apart from some regulatory laws, abortion decisions should be left, finally, up to the women themselves. Whatever one may think of the morality of abortion, it cannot be established that it poses a clear and present danger to the common good. Thus society does not have the right decisively to interpose itself between a woman and the abortion she wants. It can only intervene where it can be shown that some of its own interests are at stake *qua* society. Regulatory laws of a minimal kind therefore seem in order, since in a variety of ways already mentioned society will be affected by the number, kind and quality of legal abortions. In short, with a few important stipulations, what I have been urging is tantamount to saying that abortion decisions should be private decisions. It is to accept, in principle, the contention of those who believe that, in a free, pluralistic society, the woman should be allowed to make her own moral choice on abortion and be allowed to implement that choice.

But pluralistic societies also lay a few traps for the unwary. It is not a large psychological step from saying that individuals should be left free to make up their own minds on some crucial moral issues (of which abortion is one) to an adoption of the view that one personal decision is as good as another, that any decision is a good one as long as it is honest or sincere, that a free decision equals a correct decision. However short the psychological step, the logical gap is very large. An absence of cant, hypocrisy and coercion may prepare the way for good personal decisions. But that is only to clean the room, and something must then be put in it. The hazard is that, once cleaned, it will be filled with capriciousness, sentimentality, a thinly disguised conformity to the reigning moral taste, or strongly felt but inadequately analyzed moral opinions. This is a particular danger in affluent pluralistic societies, heavily dominated by popular tastes, communication media and the absence of shared values. Philosophically, the view that all values are equally good and all private moral choices on a par is all but dead; but it still has a strong life at the popular level, where there is a tendency to act as if, once personal freedom is legally and socially achieved, moral questions cease to exist.

A considerable quantity of literature exists in the field of ethics concerned with such problems as subjective and objective values, the meaning and use of ethical principles and moral rules, the role of intentionality. That literature need not be reviewed here. But it is directly to the point to observe that a particular failing of the abortion-on-request literature is that it persistently scants the moral problem of how a woman, if granted the desired legal freedom to make her own decision about abortion, should go about making that decision. Up to a point, this deficiency is understandable. The immediate tactical problem has been to get the laws changed or repealed; that has been the burden of the public struggle, which has concentrated on statutes and legislators rather than on the moral contents and problems of personal decision-making. It is reasonable and legitimate to say that a woman should be left free to make the decision in the light of her own personal values; that is, I believe, the best legal solution. But it leaves totally untouched the question of how, once freedom is achieved, she ought to go about the personal business of forming a coherent, rational, sensitive moral perspective and opinion on abortion. After freedom, what then? Society may have no right to demand that a woman give it good reasons why she should have an abortion before permitting it. But this does not entail that the woman should not, as a morally responsible person, have good reasons to justify her desires or acts in her own eyes.

This is only to say that a solution of the legal problem is not the same as a solution to the moral problem. That the moral struggle is transferred from the public to the private sphere should not be taken to mean that the moral problem has been solved; only its public aspect, under a permissive law or a repeal of all laws, has been dealt with. The personal problem will remain.

Some women will be part of a religious group or ethical tradition which they freely choose and which can offer them something, possibly very much, in the way of helpful moral insight consistent with that tradition. The obvious course in that instance is for them to turn to their tradition to see what it has to offer them on the particular problem of abortion. But what of those who have no tradition to repair to or those who find their tradition wanting on this problem? One way or another, they will have to find some way of developing a set of ethical principles and moral rules to help them act responsibly, to justify their own conduct in their own eyes. To press the problem to a finer point, what ought they to think about as they try to work out their own views on abortion?

Only a few suggestions will be made here, taking the form of arguing for an ethic of personal responsibility which tries, in the process of decision-making, to make itself aware of a number of things. The biological evidence should be considered, just as the problem of methodology must be considered; the philosophical assumptions implicit in different uses of the word "human" need to be considered; a philosophical theory of biological analysis is required; the social consequences of different kinds of analyses and different meanings of the word "human" should be thought through; consistency of meaning and use should be sought to avoid *ad hoc* **and arbitrary solutions.**

It is my own conviction that the "developmental school" offers the most helpful and illuminating approach to the problem of the beginning of human life, avoiding, on the one hand, a too narrow genetic criterion of human life and, on the other, a too broad and socially dangerous social definition of the "human." Yet the kinds of problems which appear in any attempt to decide upon the beginning of life suggest that no one position can be either proved or disproved from biological evidence alone. It becomes a question of trying to do justice to the evidence while, at the same time, realizing that how the evidence is approached and used will be a function of one's way of looking at reality, one's moral policy, the values and rights one believes need balancing, and the type of questions one thinks need to be asked. At the very least, however, the genetic evidence for the uniqueness of zygotes and embryos (a uniqueness of a different kind than that of the uniqueness of sperm and ova), their potentiality for development into a human person, their early development of human characteristics, their genetic and organic distinctness from the organism of the mother, appear to rule out a treatment even of zygotes, much less the more developed stages of the conceptus, as mere pieces of "tissue," of no human significance or value. The "tissue" theory of the significance of the conceptus can only be made plausible by a systematic disregard of the biological evidence. Moreover, though one may conclude that a conceptus is only potential human life, in the process of continually actualizing its potential through growth and development, a respect for the sanctity of life, with its bias in favor even of undeveloped life, is enough to make the taking of such life a moral problem. There is a choice to be made and it is a moral choice. In the near future, it is likely that some kind of simple, safe abortifacient drug will be developed, which either prevents implantation or destroys the conceptus before it can develop. It will be tempting then to think that the moral dilemma has vanished, but I do not believe it will have.

It is possible to imagine a huge number of situations where a woman could, in good and sensitive conscience, choose abortion as a moral solution to her personal or social difficulties. But, at the very least, the bounds of morality are overstepped when either through a systematic intellectual negligence or a willful choosing of that moral solution most personally convenient, personal choice is deliberately made easy and problem-free. Yet it seems to me that a pressure in that direction is a growing part of the ethos of technological societies; it is easily possible to find people to reassure us that we need have no scruples about the way we act, whether the issue is war, the suppression of rebellion and revolution, discrimination against minorities or the use of technological advances. Pluralism makes possible the achieving of free, more subtle moral thinking; but it is a possibility constantly endangered by cultural pressures which would simplify or dissolve moral doubts and anguish.

The question of abortion "indications" returns at the level of personal choice. I have contended that the advent of permissive laws should not mean a cessation of efforts to explore the problem of "indications." When a woman asks herself, as she ought, whether her reasons for wanting an abortion are sound reasons—which presumes abortion is a serious enough moral issue to warrant the need to provide oneself with good reasons for choosing it—she will be asking herself about justifiable indications. Thus, transposed from the legal to the personal level,

the kinds of concerns adumbrated in the earlier chapters on indications remain fully pertinent. It was argued in those chapters that, with the possible exception of exceedingly rare instances of a direct threat to the physical life of the mother, one cannot speak of general categories of abortion indications as *necessitating* an abortion. In a number of circumstances, abortion may be a wise and justifiable solution to a distressed pregnancy. But when the language of necessity is used, the implication is that no other conceivable alternative is available. It may be granted, willingly enough, that some set of practical circumstances in some (possibly very many) concrete cases may indicate that abortion is the only feasible option open. But these cases cannot readily be determined in advance, and, for that reason, it is necessary to say that no formal indication as such (e.g., a psychiatric indication) entails a necessary, predetermined choice in favor of abortion.

The word "indication" remains the best word, suggesting that a number of given circumstances will bring the possibility or desirability of abortion to the fore. But to escalate the concept of an indication into that of a required procedure is to go too far. Abortion is *one* way to solve the problem of an unwanted or hazardous pregnancy (physically, psychologically, economically or socially), but it is rarely the only way, at least in affluent societies (I would be considerably less certain about making the same statement about poor societies). Even in the most extreme cases—rape, incest, psychosis, for instance—alternatives will usually be available and different choices open. It is not necessarily the end of every woman's chance for a happy, meaningful life to bear an illegitimate child. It is not necessarily the automatic destruction of a family to have a seriously defective child born into it. It is not necessarily the ruination of every family living in overcrowded housing to have still another child. It is not inevitable that every immature woman would become even more so if she bore a child or another child. It is not inevitable that a gravely handicapped child can hope for nothing from life. It is not inevitable that every unwanted child is doomed to misery. It is not written in the essence of things, as a fixed law of human nature, that a woman cannot come to accept, love and be a good mother to a child who was initially unwanted. Nor is it a fixed law that she could not come to cherish a grossly deformed child. Naturally, these are only generalizations. The point is only that human beings are as a rule flexible, capable of doing more than they sometimes think they can, able to surmount serious dangers and challenges, able to grow and mature, able to transform inauspicious beginnings into satisfactory conclusions. Everything in life, even in procreative and family life, is not fixed in advance; the future is never wholly unalterable.

Yet the problem of personal question-asking must be pushed a step farther. The way the questions are answered will be very much determined by a woman's way of looking at herself and at life. A woman who has decided, as a personal moral policy, that nothing should be allowed to stand in the way of her own happiness, goals and self-interest will have no trouble solving the moral problem. For her, an unwanted pregnancy will, by definition, be a pregnancy to be terminated. But only by a **Pickwickian use of words** could this form of reasoning be called moral. It would preclude any need to consult the opinion of others, any need to examine the validity of one's own viewpoint, any need to, for instance, ask when human life begins, any need to interrogate oneself in any way, intellectually or morally; will and desire would be king.

Assuming, however, that most women would seek a broader ethical horizon than that of their exclusively personal self-interest, what might they think about when faced with an abortion decision? A respect for the sanctity of human life should, I believe, incline them toward a general and strong bias against abortion. Abortion is an act of killing, the violent, direct destruction of potential human life, already in the process of development. That fact should not be disguised, or glossed over by euphemism and circumlocution. It is not the destruction of a human person—for at no stage of its development does the conceptus fulfill the definition of a person, which implies a developed capacity for reasoning, willing, desiring and relating to others—but it is the destruction of an important and valuable form of human life. Its value and its potentiality are not dependent upon the attitude of the woman toward it; it grows by its own biological dynamism and has a genetic and morphological potential distinct from that of the woman. It has its own distinctive and individual future. If contraception and abortion are both seen as forms of birth limitation, they are distinctly different acts; the former precludes the possibility of a conceptus being formed, while the latter stops a conceptus already in existence from developing. The bias implied by the principle of the sanctity of human life is toward the protection of all forms of human life, especially, in ordinary circumstances, the protection of the right to life. That right should be accorded even to doubtful life; its existence should not be wholly dependent upon the personal self-interest of the woman.

Yet she has her own rights as well, and her own set of responsibilities to those around her; that is why she may have to choose abortion. In extreme situations of overpopulation, she may also have a responsibility for the survival of the species or of a people. In many circumstances, then, a decision in favor of abortion—one which overrides the right to life of that potential human being she carries within—can be a responsible moral decision, worthy neither of the condemnation of others nor of self-condemnation. But the bias of the principle of the sanctity of life is against a routine, unthinking employment of abortion; it bends over backwards not to take life and gives the benefit of the doubt to life. It does not seek to diminish the range of responsibility toward life—potential or actual—but to extend it. It does not seek the narrowest definition of life, but the widest and the richest. It is mindful of individual possibility, on the one hand, and of a destructive human tendency, on the other hand, to exclude from the category of "the human" or deny rights to those beings whose existence is or could prove burdensome to others.

The language used to describe abortion will have an important bearing on the sensitivities and imagination of those women who must make abortion decisions. Abortion can be talked about in the language of medical technology and technique—as, say, "a therapeutic procedure involving the emptying of the uterine contents." That language is neutral, clinical, unemotional. Or abortion can be talked about in the emotive language of relieving woman from suffering, or meeting the need for freedom among women, or saving a nation from a devastating overpopulation. Both kinds of language have their place, for abortion has more than one result and meaning and abortion can legitimately be talked about in more than one way. What is objectionable is a conscious manipulation of language to incite an irrational emotional response, to allay doubts or to mislead the imagination. Particularly misleading is one commonly employed mixture of rhetorical modes by advocates of abortion on request. That is the use of a detached, clinical language to describe the actual operation itself combined with an emotive rhetoric to evoke the personal and social goods which an abortion can bring about. Thus, when every effort is made to suggest that emotion and feeling are perfectly appropriate to describe the social and personal goals of abortion, but that a clinical language only is appropriate when the actual technique and medical objective of an abortion is described, then the moral imagination is being misled.

Any human act can be described in impersonal, technological language, just as any act can be described in emotive language. What is wanted is an equity in the language. It is fair enough and to the point to say that in

many circumstances abortion will save a woman's health or her family. It only becomes misleading when the act itself, as distinguished from its therapeutic goal, is talked about in an entirely different way. For, abortion is not just an "emptying of the uterine contents." It is also an act of killing; there will be no abortion unless the conceptus is killed (or its further existence made impossible, which amounts to the same thing). If it is appropriate to evoke the imagination and elicit sympathy for those women in a distressed pregnancy who could be helped by abortion, it is no less appropriate to evoke the imagination about what actually occurs in an abortion "procedure."

Imagination should also come into play at another point. It is often argued by proponents of abortion that there is no need for a woman ever to take any chances in a distressed pregnancy, particularly in the instance of an otherwise healthy woman who, if she has an abortion on one occasion, could simply get pregnant again on another, more auspicious occasion. This might be termed the "replacement theory" of abortion indications: since fetus "x" can be replaced by fetus "y," then there is no reason why a woman should have any scruples about such a replacement. This way of conceiving the choices effectively dissolves them; it becomes important only to know whether a woman can get pregnant again when she wants to. But this strategy can be employed only at the price of convincing oneself that there is no difference whatever among embryos or fetuses, that they all have exactly the same potentiality. But even the sketchiest knowledge of the genetic uniqueness of each conceptus (save in the instance of **monozygotic twins**), and thus the different genetic potentialities of each, should raise doubts on that point. Yet, having said that, I would not want to deny that the possibility of a further pregnancy could have an important bearing on the moral reasoning of a woman whose present pregnancy was threatening. If, out of a sense of responsibility toward her present children or her present life situation, a woman decided that an abortion was the wisest, most moral course, then the possibility that she could become pregnant later, when these responsibilities would be less pressing, would be a pertinent consideration.

The goal of these remarks is to keep alive in the consciences of women who have an abortion choice a moral tension; and it is to hope that they will be willing to bear the pain and the uncertainty of having to make a moral choice. It is the automatic, unthinking and unimaginative personal solution of abortion questions which women themselves should be extremely wary of, either for or against an abortion. A woman can, with little trouble, find both people and books to reassure her that there is no problem about abortion at all; or people and books to convince her that she would be a moral monster if she chose abortion. A woman can choose in advance the views she will listen to and thus have her predispositions confirmed. Yet a willingness to keep alive a moral tension, and to be wary of precipitous solutions, presupposes two things. First, that the woman herself wants to do what is right, realizing that what is right may not always be that which is most convenient, most easy or most immediately apt to solve a pressing problem. It is simply not the case that what one wants to do, or would like to do, or is predisposed to do is necessarily the right thing to do. A willingness seriously to entertain that moral perception—which, of course, does not in itself imply a decision for or against an abortion—is one sign of moral seriousness.

Second, moral seriousness presupposes one is concerned with the protection and furthering of life. This means that, out of respect for human life, one bends over backwards not to eliminate human life, not to desensitize oneself to the meaning and value of potential life, not to seek definitions of the "human" which serve one's self-interest only. A desire to respect human life in all of its forms means, therefore, that one voluntarily imposes upon oneself a pressure against the taking of life; that one demands of oneself serious reasons for doing so, even in the case of a very early embryo; that one use not only the mind but also the imagination when a decision is being made; that one seeks not to evade the moral issues but to face them; that one searches out the alternatives and conscientiously entertains them before turning to abortion. A bias in favor of the sanctity of human life in all of its forms would include a bias against abortion on the part of women; it would be the last rather than the first choice when unwanted pregnancies occurred. It would be an act to be avoided if at all possible.

A bias of this kind, voluntarily imposed by a woman upon herself, would not trap her; for it is also part of a respect for the dignity of life to leave the way open for an abortion when other reasonable choices are not available. For she also has duties toward herself, her family and her society. There can be good reasons for taking the life even of a very late fetus; once that also is seen and seen as a counterpoise in particular cases to the general bias against the taking of potential life, the way is open to choose abortion. The bias of the moral policy implies the need for moral rules which seek to preserve life. But, as a policy which leaves room for choice—rather than entailing a fixed set of rules—it is open to flexible interpretation when the circumstances point to the wisdom of taking exception to the normal ordering of the rules in particular cases. Yet, in that case, one is not genuinely taking exception to the rules. More accurately, one would be deciding that, for the preservation or furtherance of other values or rights—species-rights, person-rights— a choice in favor of abortion would be serving the sanctity of life. That there would be, in that case, conflict between rights, with one set of rights set aside (reluctantly) to serve another set, goes without saying. A subversion of the principle occurs when it is made out that there is no conflict and thus nothing to decide.

Review Questions

1. Why does Callahan hold that abortion decisions should be left to women alone?
2. What is the *tissue theory* and why does Callahan reject it?
3. Why does Callahan believe that women should have a strong bias against abortion?
4. What is the *replacement theory of abortion?*
5. State and explain Callahan's conclusions about the morality of abortion.

Discussion Questions

1. In what circumstances, if any, would a woman's "duties toward herself, her family and her society" require her to get an abortion? Be specific.
2. Do you think that Callahan has effectively defeated the conservative view of Noonan, and the liberal view of Warren? Explain your answer.

Jane English

Abortion and the Concept of a Person

Jane English (1947–1978) taught at the University of North Carolina, Chapel Hill, and published several articles in ethics. She was the editor of Sex Equality *(1977).*

> *English argues that one of the central issues in the abortion debate, whether the fetus is a person or not, cannot be conclusively settled because of the nature of the concept of a person. This concept is said to be a cluster concept because it cannot be defined in terms of necessary and sufficient conditions. Given this lack of defining features, we cannot say whether a fetus is a person or not; it remains in a conceptually fuzzy borderline area.*
>
> *English argues that regardless of whether or not the fetus is a person we must accept the moderate view that abortion is justified in some cases and not in others. Even if the fetus is a person, as the conservatives hold, it does not follow that abortion is never morally permissible. For the self-defense model not only justifies abortion to save the mother's life, but also justifies abortion to avoid serious harm or*

Reprinted with the permission of the editors from *Canadian Journal of Philosophy*, vol. V, no. 2, October 1975, pp. 233–243.

> *injury. On the other hand, the liberal view that the fetus is not a person does not warrant abortion on demand because we still have a duty to not harm or kill nonpersons that are sufficiently personlike. This duty makes late abortions for the sake of convenience (such as the woman who does not want to postpone a trip to Europe) morally wrong.*

The abortion debate rages on. Yet the two most popular positions seem to be clearly mistaken. Conservatives maintain that a human life begins at conception and that therefore abortion must be wrong because it is murder. But not all killings of humans are murders. Most notably, self defense may justify even the killing of an innocent person.

Liberals, on the other hand, are just as mistaken in their argument that since a fetus does not become a person until birth, a woman may do whatever she pleases in and to her own body. First, you cannot do as you please with your own body if it affects other people adversely.[1] Second, if a fetus is not a person, that does not imply that you can do to it anything you wish. Animals, for example, are not persons, yet to kill or torture them for no reason at all is wrong.

At the center of the storm has been the issue of just when it is between ovulation and adulthood that a person appears on the scene. Conservatives draw the line at conception, liberals at birth. In this paper I first examine our concept of a person and conclude that no single criterion can capture the concept of a person and no sharp line can be drawn. Next I argue that if a fetus is a person, abortion is still justifiable in many cases; and if a fetus is not a person, killing it is still wrong in many cases. To a large extent, these two solutions are in agreement. I conclude that our concept of a person cannot and need not bear the weight that the abortion controversy has thrust upon it.

I

The several factions in the abortion argument have drawn battle lines around various proposed criteria for determining what is and what is not a person. For example, Mary Anne Warren[2] lists five features (capacities for reasoning, self-awareness, complex communication, etc.) as her criteria for personhood and argues for the permissibility of abortion because a fetus falls outside this concept. Baruch Brody[3] uses brain waves. Michael Tooley[4] picks having-a-concept-of-self as his criterion and concludes that infanticide and abortion are justifiable, while the killing of adult animals is not. On the other side, Paul Ramsey[5] claims a certain gene structure is the defining characteristic. John Noonan[6] prefers conceived-of-humans and presents counterexamples to various other candidate criteria. For instance, he argues against viability as the criterion because the newborn and infirm would then be nonpersons, since they cannot live without the aid of others. He rejects any criterion that calls upon the sorts of sentiments a being can evoke in adults on the grounds that this would allow us to exclude other races as nonpersons if we could just view them sufficiently unsentimentally.

These approaches are typical: foes of abortion propose sufficient conditions for personhood which fetuses satisfy, while friends of abortion counter with necessary conditions for personhood which fetuses lack. But these both presuppose that the concept of a person can be captured in a strait jacket of necessary and/or sufficient conditions.[7] Rather, 'person' is a cluster of features, of which rationality, having a self concept and being conceived of humans are only part.

What is typical of persons? Within our concept of a person we include, first, certain biological factors: descended from humans, having a certain genetic makeup, having a head, hands, arms, eyes, capable of locomotion, breathing, eating, sleeping. There are psychological factors: sentience, perception, having a concept of self and of one's own interests and desires, the ability to use tools, the ability to use language or symbol systems, the ability to joke, to be angry, to doubt. There are rationality factors: the ability to reason and draw conclusions, the ability to generalize and to learn from past experience, the ability to sacrifice present interests for greater gains in the future. There are social factors: the ability to work in groups and respond to peer pressures, the ability to recognize and consider as valuable the interests of others, seeing oneself as one among "other minds," the ability to sympathize, encourage, love, the ability to evoke from others the responses of sympathy, encouragement, love, the ability to work with others for mutual advantage. Then there are legal factors: being subject to the law and protected by it, having the ability to sue and enter contracts, being counted in the census, having a name and citizenship, the ability to own property, inherit, and so forth.

Now the point is not that this list is incomplete, or that you can find counterinstances to each of its points. People typically exhibit rationality, for instance, but someone who was irrational would not thereby fail to qualify as a person. On the other hand, something could exhibit the majority of these features and still fail to be a person, as an advanced robot might. There is no single core of necessary and sufficient features which we can draw upon with the assurance that they constitute what really makes a person; there are only features that are more or less typical.

This is not to say that no necessary or sufficient conditions can be given. Being alive is a necessary condition for being a person, and being a U.S. Senator is sufficient. But rather than falling inside a sufficient condition or outside a necessary one, a fetus lies in the penumbra region where our concept of a person is not so simple. For this reason I think a conclusive answer to the question whether a fetus is a person is unattainable.

Here we might note a family of simple fallacies that proceed by stating a necessary condition for personhood and showing that a fetus has that characteristic. This is a form of the **fallacy of affirming the consequent.** For example, some have mistakenly reasoned from the premise that a fetus is human (after all, it is a human fetus rather than, say, a canine fetus), to the conclusion that it is a human. Adding an **equivocation** on 'being', we get the fallacious argument that since a fetus is something both living and human, it is a human being.

Nonetheless, it does seem clear that a fetus has very few of the above family of characteristics, whereas a newborn baby exhibits a much larger proportion of them—and a two-year-old has even more. Note that one traditional anti-abortion argument has centered on pointing out the many ways in which a fetus resembles a baby. They emphasize its development ("It already has ten fingers . . .") without mentioning its dissimilarities to adults (it still has gills and a tail). They also try to evoke the sort of sympathy on our part that we only feel toward other persons ("Never to laugh . . . or feel the sunshine?"). This all seems to be a relevant way to argue, since its purpose is to persuade us that a fetus satisfies so many of the important features on the list that it ought to be treated as a person. Also note that a fetus near the time of birth satisfies many more of these factors than a fetus in the early months of development. This could provide reason for making distinctions among the different stages of pregnancy, as the U.S. Supreme Court has done.[8]

Historically, the time at which a person has been said to come into existence has varied widely. Muslims date personhood from fourteen days after conception. Some medievals followed Aristotle in placing ensoulment at forty days after conception for a male fetus and eighty days for a female fetus.[9] In European common law since the Seventeenth Century, abortion was considered the killing of a person only after quickening, the time when a pregnant woman first feels the fetus move on its own. Nor is this variety of opinions surprising. Biologically, a human being develops gradually. We shouldn't expect there to be any specific time or sharp dividing point when a person appears on the scene.

For these reasons I believe our concept of a person is not sharp or decisive enough to bear the weight of a solution to the abortion controversy. To use it to solve that problem is to clarify *obscurum per obscurius.*

II

Next let us consider what follows if a fetus is a person after all. Judith Jarvis Thomson's landmark article, "A Defense of Abortion,"[10] correctly points out that some additional argumentation is needed at this point in the conservative argument to bridge the gap between the premise that a fetus is an innocent person and the conclusion that killing it is always wrong. To arrive at this conclusion, we would need the additional premise that killing an innocent person is always wrong. But killing an innocent person is sometimes permissible, most notably in self-defense. Some examples may help draw out our intuitions or ordinary judgments about self-defense.

Suppose a mad scientist, for instance, hypnotized innocent people to jump out of the bushes and attack innocent passers-by with knives. If you are so attacked, we agree you have a right to kill the attacker in self-defense, if killing him is the only way to protect your life or to save yourself from serious injury. It does not seem to matter here that the attacker is not malicious but himself an innocent pawn, for your killing of him is not done in a spirit of retribution but only in self-defense.

How severe an injury may you inflict in self-defense? In part this depends upon the severity of the injury to be avoided: you may not shoot someone merely to avoid having your clothes torn. This might lead one to the mistaken conclusion that the defense may only equal the threatened injury in severity; that to avoid death you may kill, but to avoid a black eye you may only inflict a black eye or the equivalent. Rather, our laws and customs seem to say that you may create an injury somewhat, but not enormously, greater than the injury to be avoided. To fend off an attack whose outcome would be as serious as rape, a severe beating or the loss of a finger, you may shoot; to avoid having your clothes torn, you may blacken an eye.

Aside from this, the injury you may inflict should only be the minimum necessary to deter or incapacitate the attacker. Even if you know he intends to kill you, you are not justified in shooting him if you could equally well save yourself by the simple expedient of running away. Self-defense is for the purpose of avoiding harms rather than equalizing harms.

Some cases of pregnancy present a parallel situation. Though the fetus is itself innocent, it may pose a threat to the pregnant woman's well-being, life prospects or health, mental or physical. If the pregnancy presents a slight threat to her interests, it seems self-defense cannot justify abortion. But if the threat is on a par with a serious beating or the loss of a finger, she may kill the fetus that poses such a threat, even if it is an innocent person. If a lesser harm to the fetus could have the same defensive effect, killing it would not be justified. It is unfortunate that the only way to free the woman from the pregnancy entails the death of the fetus (except in very late stages of pregnancy). Thus a self-defense model supports Thomson's point that the woman has a right only to be freed from the fetus, not a right to demand its death.[11]

The self-defense model is most helpful when we take the pregnant woman's point of view. In the pre-Thomson literature, abortion is often framed as a question for a third party: do you, a doctor, have a right to choose between the life of the woman and that of the fetus? Some have claimed that if you were a passer-by who witnessed a struggle between the innocent hypnotized attacker and his equally innocent victim, you would have no reason to kill either in defense of the other. They have concluded that the self defense model implies that a woman may attempt to abort herself, but that a doctor should not assist her. I think the position of the third party is somewhat more complex. We do feel some inclination to intervene on behalf of the victim rather than the attacker, other things equal. But if both parties are innocent, other factors come into consideration. You would rush to the aid of your husband whether he was attacker or attackee. If a hypnotized famous violinist were attacking a skid row bum, we would try to save the individual who is of more value to society. These considerations would tend to support abortion in some cases.

But suppose you are a frail senior citizen who wishes to avoid being knifed by one of these innocent hypnotics, so you have hired a bodyguard to accompany you. If you are attacked, it is clear we believe that the bodyguard, acting as your agent, has a right to kill the attacker to save you from a serious beating. Your rights of self defense are transferred to your agent. I suggest that we should similarly view the doctor as the pregnant woman's agent in carrying out a defense she is physically incapable of accomplishing herself.

Thanks to modern technology, the cases are rare in which a pregnancy poses as clear a threat to a woman's bodily health as an attacker brandishing a switchblade. How does self defense fare when more subtle, complex and long-range harms are involved?

To consider a somewhat fanciful example, suppose you are a highly trained surgeon when you are kidnapped by the hypnotic attacker. He says he does not intend to harm you but to take you back to the mad scientist who, it turns out, plans to hypnotize you to have a permanent mental block against all your knowledge of medicine. This would automatically destroy your career which would in turn have a serious adverse impact on your family, your personal relationships and your happiness. It seems to me that if the only way you can avoid this outcome is to shoot the innocent attacker, you are justified in so doing. You are defending yourself from a drastic injury to your life prospects. I think it is no exaggeration to claim that unwanted pregnancies (most obviously among teenagers) often have such adverse life-long consequences as the surgeon's loss of livelihood.

Several parallels arise between various views on abortion and the self defense model. Let's suppose further that these hypnotized attackers only operate at night, so that it is well known that they can be avoided completely by the considerable inconvenience of never leaving your house after dark. One view is that since you could stay home at night, therefore if you go out and are selected by one of these hypnotized people, you have no right to defend yourself. This parallels the view that abstinence is the only acceptable way to avoid pregnancy. Others might hold that you ought to take along some defense such as mace which will deter the hypnotized person without killing him, but that if this defense fails, you are obliged to submit to the resulting injury, no matter how severe it is. This parallels the view that contraception is all right but abortion is always wrong, even in cases of contraceptive failure.

A third view is that you may kill the hypnotized person only if he will actually kill you, but not if he will only injure you. This is like the position that abortion is permissible only if it is required to save a woman's life. Finally we have the view that it is all right to kill the attacker, even if only to avoid a very slight inconvenience to yourself and even if you knowingly walked down the very street where all these incidents have been taking place without taking along any mace or protective escort. If we assume that a fetus is a person, this is the analogue of the view that abortion is always justifiable, "on demand."

The self-defense model allows us to see an important difference that exists between abortion and infanticide, even if a fetus is a person from conception. Many have argued that the only way to justify abortion without justifying infanticide would be to find some characteristic of personhood that is acquired at birth. Michael Tooley, for one, claims infanticide is justifiable because the really significant characteristics of person are acquired some time after birth. But all such approaches look to characteristics of the developing human and ignore the relation between the fetus and the woman. What if, after birth, the presence of an infant or the need to support it posed a grave threat to the woman's sanity or life prospects? She could escape this threat by the simple expedient of running away. So a solution that does not entail the death of the infant is available. Before birth, such solutions are not available because of the biological dependence of the fetus on the woman. Birth is the crucial point not because of any characteristics the fetus gains, but because after birth the woman can defend herself by a means less drastic than killing the infant. Hence self defense can be used to justify abortion without necessarily thereby justifying infanticide.

III

On the other hand, supposing a fetus is not after all a person, would abortion always be morally permissible? Some opponents of abortion seem worried that if a fetus is not a full-fledged person, then we are justified in treating it in any way at all. However, this does not follow. Nonpersons do get some consideration in our moral code, though of course they do not have the same rights as persons have (and in general they do not have moral responsibilities), and though their interests may be overridden by the interests of persons. Still, we cannot just treat them in any way at all.

Treatment of animals is a case in point. It is wrong to torture dogs for fun or to kill wild birds for no reason at all. It is wrong Period, even though dogs and birds do not have the same rights persons do. However, few people think it is wrong to use dogs as experimental animals, causing them considerable suffering in some cases, provided that the resulting research will probably bring discoveries of great benefit to people. And most of us think it all right to kill birds for food or to protect our crops. People's rights are different from the consideration we give to animals, then, for it is wrong to experiment on people, even if others might later benefit a great deal as a result of their suffering. You might volunteer to be a subject, but this would be supererogatory; you certainly have a right to refuse to be a medical guinea pig.

But how do we decide what you may or may not do to nonpersons? This is a difficult problem, one for which I believe no adequate account exists. You do not want to say, for instance, that torturing dogs is all right whenever the sum of its effects on people is good—when it doesn't warp the sensibilities of the torturer so much that he mistreats people. If that were the case, it would be all right to torture dogs if you did it in private, or if the torturer lived on a desert island or died soon afterward, so that his actions had no effect on people. This is an inadequate account, because whatever moral consideration animals get, it has to be indefeasible, too. It will have to be a general proscription of certain actions, not merely a weighing of the impact on people on a case-by-case basis.

Rather, we need to distinguish two levels on which consequences of actions can be taken into account in moral reasoning. The traditional objections to **Utilitarianism** focus on the fact that it operates solely on the first level, taking all the consequences into account in particular cases only. Thus Utilitarianism is open to "desert island" and "life-boat" counterexamples because these cases are rigged to make the consequences of ac-

tions severely limited.

Rawls' theory could be described as a teleological sort of theory, but with teleology operating on a higher level.[12] In choosing the principles to regulate society from the original position, his hypothetical choosers make their decision on the basis of the total consequences of various systems. Furthermore, they are constrained to choose a general set of rules which people can readily learn and apply. An ethical theory must operate by generating a set of sympathies and attitudes toward others which reinforces the functioning of that set of moral principles. Our prohibition against killing people operates by means of certain moral sentiments including sympathy, compassion and guilt. But if these attitudes are to form a coherent set, they carry us further: we tend to perform **supererogatory actions,** and we tend to feel similar compassion toward person-like nonpersons.

It is crucial that psychological facts play a role here. Our psychological constitution makes it the case that for our ethical theory to work, it must prohibit certain treatment of nonpersons which are significantly person-like. If our moral rules allowed people to treat some person-like nonpersons in ways we do not want people to be treated, this would undermine the system of sympathies and attitudes that makes the ethical system work. For this reason, we would choose in the original position to make mistreatment of some sorts of animals wrong in general (not just wrong in the cases with public impact), even though animals are not themselves parties in the original position. Thus it makes sense that it is those animals whose appearance and behavior are most like those of people that get the most consideration in our moral scheme.

It is because of "coherence of attitudes," I think, that the similarity of a fetus to a baby is very significant. A fetus one week before birth is so much like a newborn baby in our psychological space that we cannot allow any cavalier treatment of the former while expecting full sympathy and nurturative support for the latter. Thus, I think that anti-abortion forces are indeed giving their strongest arguments when they point to the similarities between a fetus and a baby, and when they try to evoke our emotional attachment to and sympathy for the fetus. An early horror story from New York about nurses who were expected to alternate between caring for six-week premature infants and disposing of viable 24–week aborted fetuses is just that—a horror story. These beings are so much alike that no one can be asked to draw a distinction and treat them so very differently.

Remember, however, that in the early weeks after conception, a fetus is very much unlike a person. It is hard to develop these feelings for a set of genes which doesn't yet have a head, hands, beating heart, response to touch or the ability to move by itself. Thus it seems to me that the alleged "slippery slope" between conception and birth is not so very slippery. In the early stages of pregnancy, abortion can hardly be compared to murder for psychological reasons, but in the latest stages it is psychologically akin to murder.

Another source of similarity is the bodily continuity between fetus and adult. Bodies play a surprisingly central role in our attitudes toward persons. One has only to think of the philosophical literature on how far physical identity suffices for personal identity or Wittgenstein's remark that the best picture of the human soul is the human body. Even after death, when all agree the body is no longer a person, we still observe elaborate customs of respect for the human body; like people who torture dogs, necrophiliacs are not to be trusted with people.[13] So it is appropriate that we show respect to a fetus as the body continuous with the body of a person. This is a degree of resemblance to persons that animals cannot rival.

Michael Tooley also utilizes a parallel with animals. He claims that it is always permissible to drown newborn kittens and draws conclusions about infanticide.[14] But it is only permissible to drown kittens when their survival would cause some hardship. Perhaps it would be a burden to feed and house six more cats or to find other homes for them. The alternative of letting them starve produces even more suffering than the drowning. Since the kittens get their rights second-hand, so to speak, *via* the need for coherence in our attitudes, their interests are often overridden by the interests of full-fledged persons. But if their survival would be no inconvenience to people at all, then it is wrong to drown them, *contra* Tooley.

Tooley's conclusions about abortion are wrong for the same reason. Even if a fetus is not a person, abortion is not always permissible, because of the resemblance of a fetus to a person. I agree with Thomson that it would be wrong for a woman who is seven months pregnant to have an abortion just to avoid having to postpone a trip to Europe. In the early months of pregnancy when the fetus hardly resembles a baby at all, then, abortion is permissible whenever it is in the interests of the pregnant woman or her family. The reasons would only need to outweigh the pain and inconvenience of the abortion itself. In the middle months, when the fetus comes to resemble a person, abortion would be justifiable only when the continuation of the pregnancy or the birth of the child would cause harms—physical, psychological, economic or social—to the woman. In the late months of pregnancy, even on our current assumption that a fetus is not a person, abortion seems to be wrong except to save a woman from significant injury or death.

The Supreme Court has recognized similar gradations in the alleged slippery slope stretching between conception and birth. To this point, the present paper has been a discussion of the moral status of abortion only, not its legal status. In view of the great physical, financial and sometimes psychological costs of abortion, perhaps the legal arrangement most compatible with the proposed moral solution would be the absence of restrictions, that is, so-called abortion "on demand."

So I conclude, first, that application of our concept of a person will not suffice to settle the abortion issue. After all, the biological development of a human being is gradual. Second, whether a fetus is a person or not, abortion is justifiable early in pregnancy to avoid modest harms and seldom justifiable late in pregnancy except to avoid significant injury or death.[15]

Footnotes

1. We also have paternalistic laws which keep us from harming our own bodies even when no one else is affected. Ironically, anti-abortion laws were originally designed to protect pregnant women from a dangerous but tempting procedure.

2. Mary Anne Warren, "On the Moral and Legal Status of Abortion," *Monist* 57 (1973), [*supra*, pp. 102–119].

3. Baruch Brody, "Fetal Humanity and the Theory of Essentialism," in Robert Baker and Frederick Elliston (eds.), *Philosophy and Sex* (Buffalo, N.Y., 1975).

4. Michael Tooley, "Abortion and Infanticide," *Philosophy and Public Affairs* 2 (1971). [Revised version *supra*, pp. 120–134.]

5. Paul Ramsey, "The Morality of Abortion," in James Rachels, ed., *Moral Problems* (New York, 1971).

6. John Noonan, "Abortion and the Catholic Church: A Summary History," *Natural Law Forum* 12 (1967), pp. 125–131.

7. Wittgenstein has argued against the possibility of so capturing the concept of a game, *Philosophical Investigations* (New York, 1958), § 66–71.

8. Not because the fetus is partly a person and so has some of the rights of persons, but rather because of the rights of person-like non-persons. This I discuss in part III below.

9. Aristotle himself was concerned, however, with the different question of when the soul takes form. For historical data, see Jimmye Kimmey, "How the Abortion Laws Happened," *Ms.* 1 (April, 1973), pp. 48ff, and John Noonan, *loc. cit.*

10. J.J. Thomson, "A Defense of Abortion," *Philosophy and Public Affairs* 1 (1971). [*Infra*, pp. 173–187.]

11. *Ibid.* [p. 187].

12. John Rawls, *A Theory of Justice* (Cambridge, Mass., 1971), § 3–4.

13. On the other hand, if they can be trusted with people, then our moral customs are mistaken. It all depends on the facts of psychology.

14. *Op. cit.,* pp. 40, 60–61.

15. I am deeply indebted to Larry Crocker and Arthur Kuflik for their constructive comments.

Review Questions

1. What is wrong with the conservative view according to English?

2. What two objections does she make to the liberal argument?

3. According to English, why do the various attempts to find the necessary and/or sufficient conditions for personhood all fail?

4. Explain English's own account of the concept of person including the biological, psychological, rationality, social, and legal factors.

5. According to English, in what cases does the self-defense model justify abortion, as distinguished from merely extracting the fetus and keeping it alive?

6. English discusses four different views of abortion and self-defense. Distinguish between these four different views.

7. According to English, why isn't abortion always morally permissible even if the fetus is not a person?

Discussion Questions

1. Is English's analysis of the concept of person correct? To find out, try to state necessary and sufficient conditions for being a person.

2. English never commits herself to one of the four views on abortion and self-defense. Which of these do you think is the most plausible? Why?

3. English asserts that it is wrong—period—to kill wild birds for no reason at all. Do you agree? Why or why not?

Problem Cases

1. Mrs. Sherri Finkbine and Thalidomide In 1962 Mrs. Sherri Finkbine, the mother of four normal children, became pregnant. During the pregnancy, Mrs. Finkbine had trouble sleeping so, without consulting her physician, she took some tranquilizers containing the drug thalidomide which her husband had brought back from a trip to Europe. In Europe, the sedative was widely used.

Later Mrs. Finkbine read that a number of severely deformed children had been born in Europe. These children's limbs failed to develop, or developed in malformed ways; some were born blind and deaf, and others had seriously defective internal organs. The birth defects were traced to the use during pregnancy of a popular tranquilizer whose active ingredient was thalidomide. This was the same tranquilizer that Mrs. Finkbine had taken.

Mrs. Finkbine went to her physician who confirmed her fears. The tranquilizer did contain thalidomide, and she had a very good chance of delivering a seriously deformed baby. Consequently, the physician recommended an abortion. Mrs. Finkbine then presented her case to the three-member medical board of Phoenix. They granted approval for the abortion.

In her concern for other women who might have taken thalidomide, Mrs. Finkbine told her story to a local newspaper, and it was printed on the front page. Before long however, reporters discovered that Mrs. Finkbine was the subject of the article and then revealed her identity to the public. She became the object of an intense antiabortion campaign and was condemned as a murderer in the Vatican newspaper.

In view of the controversy, the members of medical board decided that their approval of the Finkbine abortion would not survive a court test because the Arizona statute at that time allowed abortion only when necessary to save the mother's life. Therefore they withdrew their approval.

Eventually Mrs. Finkbine found it necessary to get an abortion in Sweden. After the abortion, Mrs. Finkbine asked if the fetus was a boy or a girl. The doctor could not say because the fetus was too badly deformed.

Do you think that Mrs. Finkbine acted wrongly in having an abortion? Explain your answer.

Do you think that the government has a right to prohibit abortions in such cases? Why or why not?

2. (*This is another actual case, but the name has been changed.*) Mrs. Jones was a devout Catholic. She was a wonderful wife and mother of eight children. Because she did not use any artificial method of birth control, she became pregnant with her ninth child. Tragically, her doctor discovered that she had cancer of the uterus. Rather than getting an abortion to save her life, she decided to have the child and risk dying of cancer. She delivered the child successfully and died a short time later, leaving her husband with nine children.

Do you think that Mrs. Jones made the morally correct decision? Explain your answer.

3. A Rape Case Suppose that a sixteen-year-old girl who is an honor student, is living with her mother in New York city. One day while walking home from school she is caught by a gang of thugs from a different neighborhood. The gang rapes and beats her in an alley one block from her apartment; nobody comes to her aid despite her screams and cries for help. She is left unconscious in the alley until she is discovered by the police and taken to the hospital. The girl has a concussion and a punctured lung, and she must stay in the hospital for three weeks. At the end of this time, just when she is about to be released, she finds out that she is pregnant. Her doctor advises her to have an abortion. She is not sure what to do and feels very angry, hurt, and depressed.

What would you advise this girl to do? Should she get an abortion or should she have the child?

4. Replacing a Defective Fetus Imagine that Jane is a forty-four-year-old divorced mother with one child. The child has Down's syndrome and is severely retarded. Nevertheless, Jane has chosen the difficult task of caring for the child. Because she wants very much to have a normal child, she becomes pregnant by artificial insemination. However, she is concerned about the possibility of another defective child. Her doctor has warned her that the risk of having a Down's syndrome child increases sharply with the age of the mother. He has advised her to undergo amniocentesis, a test of the embryonic fluid that can detect Down's syndrome. She undergoes the test and the results are positive. The fetus has Down's syndrome. After careful consideration, she decides to get an abortion. She also firmly intends to get pregnant again so that she can replace the defective fetus with a normal one. Is abortion morally right or wrong in this case? Defend your answer.

5. *The Punker* Jane is a twenty-three-year-old lead singer in a punk rock band, and she loves it. With the other male members of the band, she takes drugs, and, when she feels like it, she has sex. Sometimes she uses contraceptives and sometimes she doesn't, particularly when she uses drugs. Despite her destructive lifestyle, she is very successful—after two gold records she has three new cars, two houses, and a couple of million dollars in the bank. During the week of the recording sessions for her third record, she discovers that she is pregnant. The father is unknown. This is not a good time to be pregnant because after the release of the record she has a nation-wide tour. If she cancels the tour, she will take a big loss of profit and also hurt the band. Besides, she thinks that motherhood is a drag to say the least. So without giving it much thought, she has a quick abortion and then gets back to business.

Does Jane have a right to get an abortion? Explain your answer.

Suggested Readings

(1) Bok, Sissela. "Ethical Problems of Abortion." *Hastings Center Studies* 2 (January 1974): 33–52. Bok rejects attempts to define humanity and suggests that various reasons for not getting an abortion become stronger as the fetus develops.

(2) Brody, Baruch. "On the Humanity of the Foetus." In *Abortion: Pro and Con.* edited by Robert L. Perkins, 69–90, Cambridge, Mass: Schenkman, 1974. After critically examining various proposals for *drawing the line* on the humanity of the fetus, Brody suggests that the most defensible view is to draw the line at the point when fetal brain waves can be detected.

(3) Callahan, Daniel. *Abortion: Law, Choice and Morality.* New York: Macmillan, 1970. Callahan provides factual material relevant to medical, social, and legal questions about abortion. He defends the moderate view that the fetus has what he calls a "partial moral status."

(4) Cohen, Marshall, Nagel, Thomas and Scanlon, Thomas eds. *The Rights and Wrongs of Abortion.* Princeton, NJ: Princeton University Press, 1974. This short anthology has five articles including two by Judith Jarvis Thomson; all originally appeared in the journal *Philosophy and Public Affairs.*

(5) Engelhardt, H. Tristram, Jr. "The Ontology of Abortion." *Ethics* 84 (April 1974): 217–234. Engelhardt deals with the question of whether or not the fetus is a person. He decides that it is not, strictly speaking, a person until the later stages of infancy. However, after viability, the fetus can be treated as if it were a person.

(6) Feinberg, Joel, ed. *The Problem of Abortion.* Belmont, CA: Wadsworth, 1984. This is the best anthology available on the subject. It contains a wide range of good articles representing different points of view.

(7) Grisez, Germain. *Abortion: The Myths, the Realities, and the Arguments.* New York: Corpus Books, 1970. This is a long and difficult book; Grisez defends the conservative view on abortion in Chapter 6.

(8) Hare, R.M. "Abortion and the Golden Rule." *Philosophy and Public Affairs* 4 (Spring 1975): 201–222. Hare attacks those who appeal to intuition, such as Thomson, and relies on the Golden Rule as a basic ethical principle to support a roughly moderate view of abortion.

(9) Humber, James M. "Abortion: The Avoidable Moral Dilemma," *Journal of Value Inquiry* 9 (Winter 1975): 282–302. Humber asserts that abortion is immoral because it violates the fetus' right to life. He attacks the defenses of abortion as merely "after-the-fact rationalizations" resulting from sympathy for the mother rather than for the fetus.

(10) Nicholson, Susan. *Abortion and the Roman Catholic Church.* Knoxville, Tenn.: Religious Ethics, 1974. Nicholson explains the position of the Church.

(11) Perkins, Robert L., ed. *Abortion: Pro and Con.* Cambridge, MA: Schenkman, 1974. This anthology contains a variety of articles representing different positions on abortion.

(12) Thomson, Judith Jarvis. "A Defense of Abortion." *Philosophy and Public Affairs* I (Fall 1971): 47–66. In this famous article, Thomson attacks the conservative view that abortion is morally wrong except to save the mother's life. She denies that a zygote is a person with a right to life. But instead of trying to draw a line dividing the stage of development where the fetus is a person from the stage where it is not, she decides to grant, for the sake of argument, that the fetus is a person from conception. Even assuming this, it still does not follow, she argues, that the fetus' right to life always outweighs the mother's rights. In some cases, e.g., rape, the mother's rights outweigh those of the fetus.

(13) Tooley, Michael. "Abortion and Infanticide." *Philosophy and Public Affairs* 1 (Fall 1971): 47–66. Tooley presents a classic defense of the extreme liberal view that neither a fetus nor a newborn infant have a serious right to continued existence, and that both abortion and infanticide are morally acceptable.

(14) Zaitchik, Alan. "Viability and the Morality of Abortion." *Philosophy & Public Affairs* 10:1 (1981): 18–24. Zaitchik defends the view that viability is a morally significant dividing line against criticisms made by conservatives.

Glossary

Ad hoc Solution   a solution made up specifically for a particular problem.

Amici   a Latin term literally meaning "friends of the court;" Lawyers who file briefs or present arguments to a court on behalf of another person.

Aphasia   the loss or impairment of the power to use words as symbols of ideas resulting from a brain lesion.

Casuists   persons skilled in the practice of casuistry; the resolution of questions about moral right or wrong through the application of religious or secular rules and principles.

Chimera   an organism consisting of tissues of diverse genetic constitution.

Criterion (pl. criteria)   something that provides a conclusive way of knowing whether something exists, or whether a word is used correctly. In the abortion controversy, writers have tried to find criteria for the fetus being a person, that is, features that provide logically conclusive evidence that fetuses are persons. Sometimes criteria are formulated in terms of necessary and sufficient conditions. *See* necessary and sufficient conditions.

Ectopic pregnancy   gestation elsewhere than in the uterus (as in the fallopian tube).

Embryo   a medical term used to refer to the unborn human entity from the time of implantation in the uterine wall, about the second week of pregnancy, until about the eighth week, or roughly the point at which brain waves can be detected. It is in this embryonic period that organ systems and other human characteristics begin to appear. Before this time the unborn entity is formally designated a *zygote,* and after this time it is formally designated a *fetus*

Ensoulment   the infusion of the soul into the body. The *special theory of instantaneous ensoulment* is that God puts the soul into the zygote at the moment of conception. This is a common Roman Catholic belief that is sometimes used to defend the conservative view of abortion.

Equivocation   using a word in two different senses. The fallacy of equivocation is committed by an argument that gives one word different meanings. The example given by Jane English is this: A fetus is a being that is living and human, so a fetus is a human being (the word *being* is used equivocally).

Fallacy of affirming the consequence   a fallacy committed by arguments having the logical form *P implies Q; Q; therefore P,* where P and Q are statements that are true or false. In the conditional statement P implies Q, Q is called the *consequence* and P the *antecedent.* For example, consider this argument: If the fetus is a person, then the fetus is conscious. The fetus is conscious after the eighth week. So the fetus is a person after the eighth week. Here is an argument with the same logical form, only it is about Fido the dog: If Fido is a person, then Fido is conscious. Fido is conscious when barking. So Fido is a person when barking.

Monozygotic twins   twins produced by a single zygote. This possibility raises a serious difficulty for the claim that a zygote is a single and unique individual.

Necessary and sufficient conditions   a necessary condition for something is one without which the thing would not exist or occur. The presence of oxygen is a necessary condition for human life. Being alive is a necessary condition for being a person. A sufficient condition for something is one given the occurrence or presence of which the thing does exist or occur. Prolonged absence of oxygen is a sufficient condition for human death. Being a United States Senator is a sufficient condition for being a person. Something can be a necessary condition and not a sufficient condition and vice versa.

Pickwickian Use of Words   using words in an unusual or nonstandard way.

Prima facie duty (or obligation)   a moral duty which everyone has unless it is overridden by some other duty. *Prima facie* means literally on the face of it. The key idea is that one prima facie duty (say the mother's right of self-defense) can override another prima facie duty (say the fetus' right to life). By contrast, an *absolute duty* is one that cannot be overridden by any other duties.

Prima facie right   a moral right that can be overridden by another right. To be contrasted with *absolute right,* which is a right that cannot be overridden by any other right.

Quickening   when the mother begins to feel the movements of the fetus, somewhere between the twelfth and sixteenth week of pregnancy.

Rawls' theory   the theory of Harvard philosopher John Rawls as presented in his book, *A Theory of Justice* (1971). Rawls offers his theory as a modern alternative to utilitarianism that gives a better account of justice as equality. On this theory, the principles that regulate society are to be chosen by people in an "original position" involving a "veil of ignorance" about their circumstances so that they choose fairly. The two main principles thus arrived at, according to Rawls, are the principles of equal liberty and difference. The equal liberty principle is that each person has an equal right to liberty comparable with like liberty for all. The difference principle is that social and economic inequalities are to be arranged so that they are the greatest benefit to the least advantaged.

Slippery slope argument   the argument that if an infant is a person, and the development of the infant from the zygote is a *slippery slope,* that is, a smooth continuous curve of development without any sharp breaks or discontinuities so that no lines can be drawn, then the zygote is a person too. This argument is attacked by Thomson as no better than saying that an acorn is an oak tree because the oak tree grew from the acorn.

Stoics   followers of Zeno of Citium (c 336—c 264 B.C.). The Stoic movement was named after the porch (*stoa*) where Zeno taught.

Supererogatory actions   actions above and beyond the call of duty.

Supra   above.

Trimester   period of three months.

Utilitarianism   a standard theory of moral conduct which uses the principle of utility to determine the moral rightness or wrongness of actions. This principle can be formulated in different ways, but a standard version is this: Everyone ought to act so as to bring about the greatest possible balance of good over evil. Utilitarians do not agree about what is good or bad. Some of them, called *hedonists,* think that only pleasure is intrinsically good (that is, good in itself), and that only pain is intrinsically bad. For example, the classical utilitarians Jeremy Bentham (1748–1832) and John Stuart Mill (1806–1873), were *hedonistic utilitarians.* Other utilitarians believe that satisfaction of one's desires is what is good and not having them satisfied is bad. They are called *preference utilitarians*

Critics of utilitarianism try to give counterexamples, examples of morally wrong actions that are supposed to be right based on the theory. The two examples mentioned by English involve lifeboats and desert islands. A lifeboat example is this: Seven people are on a lifeboat which only holds six; so they throw one person overboard. This seems wrong, but not in utilitarianism. A desert island example is this: On a desert island Joe promises Jane that he will take care of her garden after she dies even though he hates the garden. After she dies, he takes great pleasure in tearing up the garden. Again, this seems wrong, but it would be right according to utilitarianism.

Viability the point in the development of the fetus at which the fetus is able to survive outside the mother's womb, usually said to occur at about the twenty-eighth week of pregnancy.

Zygote fertilized egg formed by the combination of the male germ cell (the spermatazoon) with the female germ cell (the ovum) that embodies the full genetic code of twenty-three pairs of chromosomes.

Chapter 2

Euthanasia

Introduction

The term *euthanasia* is usually defined as mercy killing, or the killing of those who are incurably ill or experiencing great pain in order to spare them from further suffering.

It is customary to distinguish between different types of euthanasia. *Voluntary euthanasia* is mercy killing with the consent of the terminally ill person. For example, a patient suffering from a very painful and terminal form of cancer may ask to be killed with a fatal injection of morphine. *Nonvoluntary euthanasia,* by contrast, is mercy killing without the consent of the person who is ill (although the consent of others such as parents or relatives can be obtained). Authors who discuss nonvoluntary euthanasia usually have in mind the killing of those who are unable to give consent, for example, a comatose person such as Karen Ann Quinlan or a defective infant. There is another possibility, however, and that is the mercy killing of a person who is able to give consent but is not asked. If the person killed does not wish to die, it might be more accurate to call this involuntary euthanasia.

A further distinction is often made between active and passive euthanasia, or between killing and letting die for the sake of mercy. Just how this distinction should be drawn is a matter of some debate. As James Rachels (7) defines it in the reading, active euthanasia means "taking some positive action designed to kill the patient," for example, giving the patient a lethal injection of **potassium chloride.** Rachels defines passive euthanasia as "simply refraining from doing anything to keep the patient alive," for example, not performing

49

life-saving surgery on a defective infant.

Rachels maintains that the 1973 policy statement of the AMA (the American Medical Association) rests on the mistaken assumption that there is an important moral difference between active and passive euthanasia. He argues that there is no difference. Both active and passive euthanasia can be intentional and can precede from the same motives, and in such cases the same moral evaluation is used to make the decision.

Steinbock defends the AMA statement against Rachels' attack. She argues that the AMA statement does not make the distinction that Rachels criticises. Instead, she says it allows the cessation of extraordinary means of treatment, which is not the same as passive euthanasia, despite Rachels' contentions to the contrary. Steinbock does not object to the basic distinction between active and passive euthanasia, however, and she agrees with Rachels that in some cases active euthanasia is preferable to passive euthanasia.

Some authors object to the basic distinction between active and passive euthanasia. Gay-Williams claims that the phrase *passive euthanasia* is misleading and mistaken. In his view, what is called passive euthanasia is not really euthanasia at all because it is not intentional killing. Either the killing is an unintended consequence, a side effect of the real intention—elimination of the suffering—or the cause of death is the person's injuries or disease, not the failure to receive treatment.

The traditional position that Gay-Williams adopts rests on a distinction between the intended consequence of an act and the foreseen but unintended consequence. Although Gay-Williams does not discuss it, it is worth noting that this distinction is part of a traditional doctrine called the **doctrine of double effect.** According to this doctrine, as long as the intended consequence of an act is good, a bad foreseen consequence (such as death)

can be morally allowed provided it is not intended and that it prevents a greater evil (such as great suffering). To use Gay-Williams' example, suppose that a doctor gives a terminal cancer patient an overdose of morphine sufficient to kill the patient. If the doctor intends only to reduce or eliminate the patient's pain, but not to kill him, and if the death of the patient is not as bad as the patient's suffering, then, according to the doctrine of double effect, the doctor's action is not wrong, even though the doctor of course foresees that the patient will die from the overdose.

John Ladd (6) takes a different position than either Gay-Williams or Rachels. Ladd rejects the doctrine of double effect as nothing more than a "verbal trick" that does not give us any clear criterion for determining what is and is not part of the intention of an act. He also denies that any absolute distinction between active and passive euthanasia, or between killing and letting die, can be made. Instead, Ladd presents an alternative view that he calls *contextualism.* In this view, the distinction between killing and letting die is always relative to the context, to the moral acts that come before and after the act in question. Some acts of letting die could be virtuous and others could be vicious, depending on the context. The same can be said for acts of killing.

Philippa Foot (2), in sharp contrast to both Ladd and Rachels, and in disagreement with Gay-Williams, thinks that an absolute and morally relevant distinction between active and passive euthanasia can be drawn in terms of the right to life. This right creates a duty of noninterference which conflicts with actively killing a person, but not with letting a person die. There are, however, different sorts of interference. Fatally shooting a person is obviously an interference with his or her life, but turning off a **respirator** is merely interference with treatment, and as such it should be classified as passive rather than active euthanasia.

Having made a distinction between active and passive euthanasia, and also between voluntary and nonvoluntary euthanasia, Foot distinguishes between four different types of euthanasia: (1) active voluntary euthanasia, (2) passive voluntary euthanasia, (3) active nonvoluntary euthanasia, and (4) passive nonvoluntary euthanasia.

The Moral Issue   The moral issue is whether euthanasia is wrong or not. It is complicated by the fact that all parties do not agree about the meaning of the term *euthanasia*. It seems safe to say that the traditional conservative view is that active euthanasia is always wrong. This is the view of Gay-Williams and the AMA. However, conservatives on euthanasia do grant that patients may be morally right to allow someone to die or even to be *indirectly killed* in some cases. As we have said, Gay-Williams allows indirect killing when death is not intended but is merely a side effect. For example, a patient is given an injection of a drug necessary to treat the disease; however, rather than treating the disease, the drug kills the patient. Gay-Williams also argues that allowing a patient with no chance of recovery to die by failing to treat his or her injuries or disease results in the cause of death being the injuries or disease, not the failure to provide treatment—so it is not regarded as passive euthanasia. (This claim is examined and rejected by Rachels in the reading in his discussion of the "first counter-argument.") The AMA position is somewhat different. It allows the cessation of extraordinary means of treatment, and in some cases this seems to be passive euthanasia, even though the AMA statement does not make any distinction between active and passive euthanasia.

The liberal view of euthanasia, as distinguished from what we are calling the traditional, conservative view, is that active euthanasia can be morally right in some

cases, and it is even preferable to passive euthanasia when by a quick and painless death the patient avoids suffering. This view is defended by Rachels and Brandt and is accepted by Steinbock. Various moderate positions exist between these extreme positions. For example, Foot finds that nonvoluntary active euthanasia is wrong, and this makes her more conservative than Rachels and Brandt. Yet, she allows that voluntary active euthanasia and passive euthanasia (whether voluntary or nonvoluntary), can be morally right. This position is more liberal than either Gay-Williams' position or the AMA policy statement.

Philosophical Issues   As far as voluntary euthanasia is concerned, one basic issue is whether or not terminally ill persons who are rational and fully informed should be free to decide to die, and then to bring about that decision by themselves or with another person's help. Philosophers such as Jonathan Glover (4) and H. Tristram Engelhardt, Jr. (1), assume that adults who satisfy the appropriate criteria should be free to make such a decision, but other writers disagree. Gay-Williams argues that a person who chooses to die, whether by suicide or by active euthanasia, is acting contrary to nature and to self-interest.

When discussing nonvoluntary euthanasia, one of the issues, as we have seen, is whether or not there is a morally significant difference between the act of killing and of letting die. A related issue is whether or not the doctrine of double effect is acceptable. Critics such as John Ladd (6) and Philippa Foot (3) complain that no clear distinction can be made between the two effects, the intended one and the unintended but foreseen one. Furthermore, assuming that a distinction between the two effects can be made, then it seems to follow that the doctrine can be used to defend any evil act provided it is merely foreseen and not intended. All that is required is an appropriate manipulation of intentions. Defenders of the doctrine insist that a clear distinction between the two effects in question can be made, and that the doctrine actually prevents an evil act from occurring.

Another matter of controversy is the distinction between ordinary and extraordinary means of prolonging life. This distinction is defended as important and relevant by both Thomas D. Sullivan (10) and Bonnie Steinbock. In his reply to Sullivan, Rachels (8) claims that the distinction begs the question and is irrelevant. It begs the question because the definitions of ordinary and extraordinary cited by Sullivan employ terms like *excessive cost* which already assume that the life in question is not worth saving. It is irrelevant because there are cases in which even ordinary means of prolonging life should not be used. Giving insulin to a diabetic is an ordinary means of preserving life. However, suppose a diabetic has terminal cancer and does not want his or her insulin shots; in that case, Rachels (8) claims, failing to give the shots would not be wrong, even if they are an ordinary means of prolonging life.

Rachels thinks that the cessation of extraordinary means of treatment amounts to passive euthanasia because it is the intentional termination of life. Steinbock does not agree. She argues that the reason for stopping extraordinary treatment is to avoid treatment that causes more discomfort than the disease; the reason is not to terminate life. As she explains it, extraordinary treatment is treatment that causes excessive discomfort to the patient, thus what is extraordinary in one situation might be ordinary in another. According to Steinbock, the use of a respirator to sustain a patient through a respiratory disease is considered ordinary treatment, but its use to keep alive a person in an irreversible coma is considered extraordinary. Ordinary treatment, then, is the care a doctor would normally be expected to provide, and if a doctor does not provide it, he or she is guilty of neglect. So giving insulin to a diabetic would be ordinary treatment, as Rachels says.

Another important issue is how to make life-or-death decisions. One standard answer, given by Rachels, Brandt, and Glover, is to appeal to the quality of a person's life. If a person will have a bad life, then her life should be ended; but if a person will have a good life, then his life should be continued. How do we distinguish between good and bad lives? That is a classical problem in ethics that resists an easy solution. Glover's answer is that we should ask ourselves if we would want to live the life in question. But it seems unlikely that everyone will agree about which lives are or are not worth living. Taking surveys may not be the answer. Brandt's suggestion is that we use a "happiness criterion." A life is good or worth living if over the whole lifetime there are more moments of happiness (moments of experience that are liked) than moments of unhappiness (moments of experience that are disliked). But is happiness the only thing to be considered? What about other things like knowledge and achievement? Perhaps an unhappy life could still be good because of achievements or knowledge.

J. Gay-Williams

The Wrongfulness of Euthanasia

J. Gay-Williams has requested that no biographical information be provided.

Gay-Williams defines "euthanasia" as intentionally taking the life of a presumably hopeless person. Suicide can count as euthanasia, but not "passive euthanasia" because the latter does not involve intentional killing. Three main arguments are presented to show that euthanasia is wrong: the argument from nature, the argument from self-interest, and the argument from practical effects.

My impression is that euthanasia—the idea, if not the practice—is slowly gaining acceptance within our society. Cynics might attribute this to an increasing tendency to devalue human life, but I do not believe this is the major factor. The acceptance is much more likely to be the result of unthinking sympathy and benevolence. Well-publicized, tragic stories like that of Karen Quinlan elicit from us deep feelings of compassion. We think to ourselves, "She and her family would be better off if she were dead." It is an easy step from this very human response to the view that if someone (and others) would be better off dead, then it must be all right to kill that person.[1] Although I respect the compassion that leads to this conclusion, I believe the conclusion is wrong. I want to show that euthanasia is wrong. It is inherently wrong, but it is also wrong judged from the standpoints of self-interest and of practical effects.

Before presenting my arguments to support this claim, it would be well to define "euthanasia." An essential aspect of euthanasia is that it involves taking a human life, ei-

ther one's own or that of another. Also, the person whose life is taken must be someone who is believed to be suffering from some disease or injury from which recovery cannot reasonably be expected. Finally, the action must be deliberate and intentional. Thus, euthanasia is intentionally taking the life of a presumably hopeless person. Whether the life is one's own or that of another, the taking of it is still euthanasia.

It is important to be clear about the deliberate and intentional aspect of the killing. If a hopeless person is given an injection of the wrong drug by mistake and this causes his death, this is wrongful killing but not euthanasia. The killing cannot be the result of accident. Furthermore, if the person is given an injection of a drug that is believed to be necessary to treat his disease or better his condition and the person dies as a result, then this is neither wrongful killing nor euthanasia. The intention was to make the patient well, not kill him. Similarly, when a patient's condition is such that it is not reasonable to hope that any medical procedures or treatments will save his life, a failure to implement the procedures or treatments is not euthanasia. If the person dies, this will be as a result of his injuries or disease and not because of his failure to receive treatment.

The failure to continue treatment after it has been realized that the patient has little chance of benefiting from it has been characterized by some as "passive euthanasia." This phrase is misleading and mistaken.[2] In such cases, the person involved is not killed (the first essential aspect of euthanasia), nor is the death of the person intended by the withholding of additional treatment (the third essential aspect of euthanasia). The aim may be to spare the person additional and unjustifiable pain, to save him from the indignities of hopeless manipulations, and to avoid increasing the financial and emotional burden on his family. When I buy a pencil it is so that I can use it to write, not to contribute to an increase in the gross national product. This may be the unintended consequence of my action, but it is not the aim of my action. So it is with failing to continue the treatment of a dying person. I intend his death no more than I intend to reduce the GNP by not using medical supplies. His is an unintended dying, and so-called "passive euthanasia" is not euthanasia at all.

THE ARGUMENT FROM NATURE

Every human being has a natural inclination to continue living. Our reflexes and responses fit us to fight attackers, flee wild animals, and dodge out of the way of trucks. In our daily lives we exercise the caution and care necessary to protect ourselves. Our bodies are similarly structured for survival right down to the molecular level. When we are cut, our **capillaries** seal shut, our blood clots, and fibrogen is produced to start the process of healing the wound. When we are invaded by bacteria, antibodies are produced to fight against the alien organisms, and their remains are swept out of the body by special cells designed for clean-up work.

Euthanasia does violence to this natural goal of survival. It is literally acting against nature because all the processes of nature are bent towards the end of bodily survival. Euthanasia defeats these subtle mechanisms in a way that, in a particular case, disease and injury might not.

It is possible, but not necessary, to make an appeal to revealed religion in this connection.[3] Man as trustee of his body acts against God, its rightful possessor, when he takes his own life. He also violates the commandment to hold life sacred and never to take it without just and compelling cause. But since this appeal will persuade only those who are prepared to accept that religion has access to revealed truths, I shall not employ this line of argument.

It is enough, I believe, to recognize that the organization of the human body and our patterns of behavioral responses make the continuation of life a natural goal. By reason alone, then, we can recognize that euthanasia sets us against our own nature.[4] Further-

more, in doing so, euthanasia does violence to our dignity. Our dignity comes from seeking our ends. When one of our goals is survival, and actions are taken that eliminate that goal, then our natural dignity suffers. Unlike animals, we are conscious through reason of our nature and our ends. Euthanasia involves acting as if this dual nature—inclination towards survival and awareness of this as an end—did not exist. Thus, euthanasia denies our basic human character and requires that we regard ourselves or others as something less than fully human.

THE ARGUMENT FROM SELF–INTEREST

The above arguments are, I believe, sufficient to show that euthanasia is inherently wrong. But there are reasons for considering it wrong when judged by standards other than reason. Because death is final and irreversible, euthanasia contains within it the possibility that we will work against our own interest if we practice it or allow it to be practiced on us.

Contemporary medicine has high standards of excellence and a proven record of accomplishment, but it does not possess perfect and complete knowledge. A mistaken diagnosis is possible, and so is a mistaken prognosis. Consequently, we may believe that we are dying of a disease when, as a matter of fact, we may not be. We may think that we have no hope of recovery when, as a matter of fact, our chances are quite good. In such circumstances, if euthanasia were permitted, we would die needlessly. Death is final and the chance of error too great to approve the practice of euthanasia.

Also, there is always the possibility that an experimental procedure or a hitherto untried technique will pull us through. We should at least keep this option open, but euthanasia closes it off. Furthermore, spontaneous remission does occur in many cases. For no apparent reason, a patient simply recovers when those all around him, including his physicians, expected him to die. Euthanasia would just guarantee their expectations and leave no room for the "miraculous" recoveries that frequently occur.

Finally, knowing that we can take our life at any time (or ask another to take it) might well incline us to give up too easily. The will to live is strong in all of us, but it can be weakened by pain and suffering and feelings of hopelessness. If during a bad time we allow ourselves to be killed, we never have a chance to reconsider. Recovery from a serious illness requires that we fight for it, and anything that weakens our determination by suggesting that there is an easy way out is ultimately against our own interest. Also, we may be inclined towards euthanasia because of our concern for others. If we see our sickness and suffering as an emotional and financial burden on our family, we may feel that to leave our life is to make their lives easier.[5] The very presence of the possibility of euthanasia may keep us from surviving when we might.

THE ARGUMENT FROM PRACTICAL EFFECTS

Doctors and nurses are, for the most part, totally committed to saving lives. A life lost is, for them, almost a personal failure, an insult to their skills and knowledge. Euthanasia as a practice might well alter this. It could have a corrupting influence so that in any case that is severe doctors and nurses might not try hard enough to save the patient. They might decide that the patient would simply be "better off dead" and take the steps necessary to make that come about. This attitude could then carry over to their dealings with patients less seriously ill. The result would be an overall decline in the quality of medical care.

Finally, euthanasia as a policy is a slippery slope. A person apparently hopelessly ill may be allowed to take his own life. Then he may be permitted to deputize others to do it for him should he no longer be able to act. The judgment of others then becomes the ruling factor. Already at this point euthanasia is not personal and voluntary, for others are acting "on behalf of" the patient as they see fit. This may well incline them to act on behalf of others patients who have not authorized them to exercise their judgment. It is only a short step, then, from voluntary euthanasia (self-inflicted or authorized), to directed euthanasia administered to a patient who has given no authorization, to involuntary euthanasia conducted as part of a social policy.[6] Recently many psychiatrists and sociologists have argued that we define as "mental illness" those forms of behavior that we disapprove of.[7] This gives us license then to lock up those who display the behavior. The category of the "hopelessly ill" provides the possibility of even worse abuse. Embedded in a social policy, it would give society or its representatives the authority to eliminate all those who might be considered too "ill" to function normally any longer. The dangers of euthanasia are too great to all to run the risk of approving it in any form. The first slippery step may well lead to a serious and harmful fall.

I hope that I have succeeded in showing why the benevolence that inclines us to give approval of euthanasia is misplaced. Euthanasia is inherently wrong because it violates the nature and dignity of human beings. But even those who are not convinced by this must be persuaded that the potential personal and social dangers inherent in euthanasia are sufficient to forbid our approving it either as a personal practice or as a public policy.

Suffering is surely a terrible thing, and we have a clear duty to comfort those in need and to ease their suffering when we can. But suffering is also a natural part of life with values for the individual and for others that we should not overlook. We may legitimately seek for others and for ourselves an easeful death, as Arthur Dyck has pointed out.[8] Euthanasia, however, is not just an easeful death. It is a wrongful death. Euthanasia is not just dying. It is killing.

Footnotes

1. For a sophisticated defense of this position see Philippa Foot, "Euthanasia," *Philosophy and Public Affairs* 6

(1977): 85–112. Foot does not endorse the radical conclusion that euthanasia, voluntary and involuntary, is
always right.

2. James Rachels rejects the distinction between active
and passive euthanasia as morally irrelevant in his "Active and Passive Euthanasia," *New England Journal of
Medicine,* 292: 78–80. But see the criticism by Foot, pp.
100–103.

3. For a defense of this view see J.V. Sullivan, "The
Immorality of Euthanasia," in *Beneficent Euthanasia,* ed.
Marvin Kohl (Buffalo, NY: Prometheus Books, 1975),
pp. 34–44.

4. This point is made by Ray V. McIntyre in "Voluntary Euthanasia: The Ultimate Perversion," *Medical Coun-
terpoint* 2: 26–29.

5. See McIntyre, p. 28.

6. See Sullivan, "Immorality of Euthanasia," pp. 34–
44, for a fuller argument in support of this view.

7. See, for example, Thomas S. Szasz, *The Myth of
Mental Illness,* rev. ed. (New York: Harper & Row,
1974).

8. Arthur Dyck, "Beneficent Euthanasia and
Benemoriasia," Kohl, op. cit., pp. 117–129.

Review Questions

1. How does Gay-Williams define euthanasia?

2. Why does he object to the phrase passive euthanasia?

3. Explain the three arguments he uses to show
that euthanasia is wrong.

Discussion Questions

1. Is Gay-Williams' definition of euthanasia acceptable? Defend your view.

2. Are his arguments sound or not?

James Rachels

Euthanasia, Killing, and Letting Die

*James Rachels is professor of philosophy at the Uni-
versity of Alabama in Birmingham. He is the author
of several articles in ethics; he is the editor of* Moral
Problems: A Collection of Philosophical Essays *(1st ed., 1971, 3rd ed., 1979); and the author of* The Elements of Moral Philosophy
(1986).

*Rachels attacks the 1973 policy statement of the
AMA. He thinks that it rests on the unjustified assumption that there is an important moral difference
between killing and letting die, and that in practice
this assumption produces terrible consequences for
patients. Rachels rejects this assumption; he argues
that there is no significant moral difference between
killing and letting die. Both can be intentional and
deliberate and can proceed from the same motives.
Furthermore, when killing and letting die are similar
in these respects, our moral evaluation of these acts is
similar. Rachels concludes with a consideration of
two counter-arguments to his view. The first focuses
on an irrelevant distinction between causing and not
causing a person's death, while the second claims
that the duty to not harm is stronger than the duty to
help. In his reply to the second argument, Rachels
makes the important claim, further developed in his
article "Killing and Starving to Death" (found in
Chapter 4), that our duty to help people is just as
strong as our duty to not harm them.*

"Euthanasia, Killing, and Letting Die" by James
Rachels in John Ladd, ed., *Ethical Issues Relating to Life
and Death.* Copyright © 1979 by Oxford University
Press, Inc. Reprinted by permission. A shortened
version of this paper (about one-third the length), with
the title "Active and Passive Euthanasia," appeared in
The New England Journal of Medicine, 292, no. 2 (9 January 1975), pp. 78–80.

Dr. F.J. Ingelfinger, former editor of the *The
New England Journal of Medicine,* observes that

*This is the heyday of the ethicist in medicine. He
delineates the rights of patients, of experimental subjects,
of fetuses, of mothers, of animals, and even of doctors.
(And what a far cry it is from the days when medical
"ethics" consisted of condemning economic improprieties
such as fee splitting and advertising!) With impeccable*

logic—once certain basic assumptions are granted—and with graceful prose, the ethicist develops his arguments.... Yet his precepts are essentially the products of armchair exercise and remain abstract and idealistic until they have been tested in the laboratory of experience.[1]

One problem with such armchair exercises, he complains, is that in spite of the impeccable logic and the graceful prose, the result is often an absolutist ethic which is unsatisfactory when applied to particular cases, and which is therefore of little use to the practicing physician. Unlike some absolutist philosophers, "the practitioner appears to prefer the principles of individualism. As there are few atheists in fox holes, there tend to be few absolutists at the bedside."[2]

I must concede at the outset that this chapter is another exercise in "armchair ethics" in the sense that I am not a physician but a philospher. Yet I am no absolutist; and my purpose is to examine a doctrine that *is* held in an absolute form by many doctors. The doctrine is that there is an important moral difference between active and passive euthanasia, such that even though the latter is sometimes permissible, the former is always forbidden. This is an absolute which doctors hold "at the bedside" as well as in the seminar room, and the "principles of individualism" make little headway against it. But I will argue that this is an irrational dogma, and that there is no sound moral basis for it.

I will not argue, simply, that active euthanasia is all right. Rather, I will be concerned with the *relation* between active euthanasia and passive euthanasia: I will argue that there is no moral difference between them. By this I mean that there is no reason to prefer one over the other as a matter of principle—the fact that one case of euthanasia is active, while another is passive, is not *itself* a reason to think one morally better than the other. If you already think that passive euthanasia is all right, and you are convinced by my arguments, then you may conclude that active euthanasia must be all right, too. On the other hand, if you believe that active euthanasia is

immoral, you may want to conclude that passive euthanasia must be immoral, too. Although I prefer the former alternative, I will not argue for it here. I will only argue that the two forms of euthanasia are morally equivalent—either both are acceptable or both are unacceptable.

I am aware that this will at first seem incredible to many readers, but I hope that this impression will be dispelled as the discussion proceeds. The discussion will be guided by two methodological considerations, both of which are touched on in the editorial quoted above. The first has to do with my "basic assumptions." My arguments are intended to appeal to all reasonable people, and not merely to those who already share my philosophical preconceptions. Therefore, I will try not to rely on any assumptions that cannot be accepted by any reasonable person. None of my arguments will depend on morally eccentric premises. Second, Dr. Ingelfinger is surely correct when he says that we must be as concerned with the realities of medical practice as with the more abstract issues of moral theory. As he notes, the philosopher's precepts "remain abstract and idealistic until they are tested in the laboratory of experience." Part of my argument will be precisely that, when "tested in the laboratory of experience," the doctrine in question has terrible results. I believe that if this doctrine were to be recognized as irrational, and rejected by the medical profession, the benefit to both doctors and patients would be enormous. In this sense, my paper is not intended as an "armchair exercise" at all.

THE AMERICAN MEDICAL ASSOCIATION POLICY STATEMENT

"Active euthanasia," as the term is used, means taking some positive action designed to kill the patient; for example, giving him a lethal injection of **potassium chloride.** "Passive euthanasia," on the other hand, means simply refraining from doing anything to keep the patient alive. In passive euthanasia we withhold medication or other life-sustaining therapy, or we refuse to perform surgery, etc., and let the patient die "naturally" of whatever ills already afflict him.

Many doctors and theologians prefer to use the term "euthanasia" only in connection with active euthanasia, and they use other words to refer to what I am calling "passive euthanasia"—for example, instead of "passive euthanasia" they may speak of "the right to death with dignity." One reason for this choice of terms is the emotional impact of the words: it *sounds* so much better to defend "death with dignity" than to advocate "euthanasia" of any sort. And of course if one believes that there is a great moral difference between active and passive euthanasia—as most doctors and religious writers do—then one may prefer a terminology which puts as much psychological distance as possible between them. However, I do not want to become involved in a pointless dispute about terminology, because nothing of substance depends on which label is used. I will stay with the terms "active euthanasia" and "passive euthanasia" because they are the most convenient; but if the reader prefers a different terminology he may substitute his own throughout, and my arguments will be unaffected.

The belief that there is an important moral difference between active and passive euthanasia obviously has important consequences for medical practice. It makes a difference to what doctors are willing to do. Consider, for example, the following familiar situation. A patient who is dying from incurable cancer of the throat is in terrible pain that we can no longer satisfactorily alleviate. He is certain to die within a few days, but he decides that he does not want to go on living for those days since the pain is unbearable. So he asks the doctor to end his life now; and his family joins in the request. One way that the doctor might comply with this request is simply by killing the patient with a lethal injection. Most doctors would not do that, not only because of the possible legal conse-

quences, but because they think such a course would be immoral. And this is understandable: the idea of killing someone goes against very deep moral feelings; and besides, as we are often reminded, it is the special business of doctors to save and protect life, not to destroy it. Yet, even so, the physician may sympathize with the dying patient's request and feel that it is entirely reasonable for him to prefer death now rather than after a few more days of agony. The doctrine that we are considering tells the doctor what to do: it says that although he may not administer the lethal injection—that would be "active euthanasia," which is forbidden—he *may* withhold treatment and let the patient die sooner than he otherwise would.

It is no wonder that this simple idea is so widely accepted, for it seems to give the doctor a way out of his dilemma without having to kill the patient, and without having to prolong the patient's agony. The idea is not a new one. What *is* new is that the idea is now being incorporated into official statements of medical ethics. What was once unofficially done is now becoming official policy. The idea is expressed, for example, in a 1973 policy statement of the American Medical Association, which says (in its entirety):

The intentional termination of the life of one human being by another—mercy killing—is contrary to that for which the medical profession stands and is contrary to the policy of the American Medical Association.
The cessation of the employment of extraordinary means to prolong the life of the body when there is irrefutable evidence that biological death is imminent is the decision of the patient and/or his immediate family. The advice and judgment of the physician should be freely available to the patient and/or his immediate family.[3]

This is a cautiously worded statement, and it is not clear *exactly* what is being affirmed. I take it, however, that at least these three propositions are intended:

1. Killing patients is absolutely forbidden; however, it is sometimes permissible to allow patients to die.

2. It is permissible to allow a patient to die if

    a. there is irrefutable evidence that he will die soon anyway;

    b. "extraordinary" measures would be required to keep him alive; and

    c. the patient and/or his immediate family requests it.

3. Doctors should make their own advice and judgments available to the patient and/or his immediate family when the latter are deciding whether to request that the patient be allowed to die.

The first proposition expresses the doctrine which is the main subject of this paper. As for the third, it seems obvious enough, provided that 1 and 2 are accepted, so I shall say nothing further about it.

I do want to say a few things about 2. Physicians often allow patients to die; however, they do *not* always keep to the guidelines set out in 2. For example, a doctor may leave instructions that if a hopeless, comatose patient suffers cardiac arrest, nothing be done to start his heart beating again. "No-coding" is the name given to this practice, and the consent of the patient and/or his immediate family is not commonly sought. This is thought to be a medical decision (in reality, of course, it is a moral one) which is the doctor's affair. To take a different sort of example, when a Down's infant (a **mongoloid**) is born with an intestinal blockage, the doctor and parents may agree that there will be no operation to remove the blockage, so that the baby will die.[4] (If the same infant were born without the obstruction, it certainly would not be killed. This is a clear application of the idea that "letting die" is all right even though killing is forbidden.) But in such cases it is clear that the baby is *not* going to die soon anyway. If the surgery were performed, the baby would proceed to a "normal" infancy—normal, that is, for a mongoloid. Moreover, the treatment required to save the baby—abdominal surgery—can hardly be called "extraordinary" by today's medical standards.

Therefore, all three conditions which the AMA statement places on the decision to let die are commonly violated. It is beyond the scope of this paper to determine whether doctors are right to violate those conditions. But I firmly believe that the second requirement—2b—is not acceptable. Only a little reflection is needed to show that the distinction between ordinary and extraordinary means is not important. Even a very conservative, religiously-oriented writer such as Paul Ramsey stresses this. Ramsey gives these examples:

Suppose that a diabetic patient long accustomed to self-administration of insulin falls victim to terminal cancer, or suppose that a terminal cancer patient suddenly develops diabetes. Is he in the first case obliged to continue, and in the second case obliged to begin, insulin treatment and die painfully of cancer, or in either or both cases may the patient choose rather to pass into diabetic coma and an earlier death? ... Or an old man slowly deteriorating who from simply being inactive and recumbent gets pneumonia: are we to use antibiotics in a likely successful attack upon this disease which from time immemorial has been called "the old man's friend"? [5]

I agree with Ramsey, and with many other writers, that in such cases treatment may be withheld even though it is not "extraordinary" by any reasonable standard. Contrary to what is implied by the AMA statement, the distinction between heroic and nonheroic means of treatment can *not* be used to determine when treatment is or is not mandatory.

KILLING AND LETTING DIE

I return now to the distinction between active and passive euthanasia. Of course, not every doctor believes that this distinction is morally important. Over twenty years ago Dr. D.C.S. Cameron of the American Cancer Society said that "Actually the difference between euthanasia [i.e., killing] and letting the patient die by omitting life-sustaining treatment is a moral quibble." [6] I argue that Cameron was right.

The initial thought can be expressed quite simply. In any case in which euthanasia seems desirable, it is because we think that the patient would literally be better off dead—or at least, no worse off dead—than continuing the kind of life available to him. (Without this assumption, even *passive* euthanasia would be unthinkable.) But, as far as the main question of ending the patient's life is concerned, it does not matter whether the euthanasia is active or passive: *in either case,* he ends up dead sooner than he otherwise would. And if the results are the same, why should it matter so much which method is used?

Moreover, we need to remember that, in cases such as that of the terminal cancer-patient, the justification for allowing him to die, rather than prolonging his life for a few more hopeless days, is that he is in horrible pain. But if we simply withhold treatment, it may take him *longer* to die, and so he will suffer *more* than he would if we were to administer the lethal injection. This fact provides strong reason for thinking that, once we have made the initial decision not to prolong his agony, active euthanasia is actually preferable to passive euthanasia rather than the reverse. It also shows a kind of incoherence in the conventional view: to say that passive euthanasia is preferable is to endorse the option which leads to more suffering rather than less, and is contrary to the humanitarian impulse which prompts the decision not to prolong his life in the first place.

But many people are convinced that there is an important moral difference between active and passive euthanasia because they think that, in passive euthanasia, the doctor does not really *do* anything. No action whatever is taken; the doctor simply does nothing, and the patient dies of whatever ills already afflict him. In active euthanasia, however, we *do something* to bring about the patient's death. We kill him. Thus, the difference between active and passive euthanasia is thought to be the difference between doing something to bring about someone's death, and not doing anything to bring about anyone's death. And of course if we conceive the matter in *this* way, passive euthanasia seems preferable. Ramsey, who denounces the view

I am defending as "extremist" and who regards the active/passive distinction as one of the "flexibly wise categories of traditional medical ethics," takes just this view of the matter. He says that the choice between active and passive euthanasia "is not a choice between directly and indirectly willing and doing something. *It is rather the important choice between doing something and doing nothing,* or (better said) ceasing to do something that was begun in order to do something that is better because now more fitting." [7]

This is a very misleading way of thinking, for it ignores the fact that in passive euthanasia the doctor *does* do one thing which is very important: namely, he lets the patient die. We may overlook this obvious fact—or at least, we may put it out of our minds—if we concentrate only on a very restricted way of describing what happens: "The doctor does not administer medication or any other therapy; he does not instruct the nurses to administer any such medication; he does not perform any surgery"; and so on. And of course this description of what happens is correct, as far as it goes—these are all things that the doctor does not do. But the point is that the doctor *does* let the patient die when he could save him, and this must be included in the description, too.

There is another reason why we might fall into this error. We might confuse *not saving* someone with *letting him die.* Suppose a patient is dying, and Dr. X could prolong his life. But he decides not do so and the patient dies. Now it is true of everyone on earth that he did not save the patient. Dr. X did not save him, and neither did you, and neither did I. So we might be tempted to think that all of us are in the same moral position, reasoning that since neither you nor I are responsible for the patient's death, neither is Dr. X. None of us did anything. This, however, is a mistake, for even though it is true that none of us saved the patient, it is *not* true that we all let him die. In order to let someone die, one must be *in a position* to save him. You and I were not in a position to save the patient, so we did not let him die. Dr. X, on the other hand, was in a position to save him, and did let him die. Thus the doctor is in a special moral position which not just everyone is in.

Here we must remember some elementary points, which are so obvious that they would not be worth mentioning except for the fact that overlooking them is a source of so much confusion in this area. The act of letting someone die may be intentional and deliberate, just as the act of killing someone may be intentional and deliberate. Moreover, the doctor is *responsible* for his decision to let the patient die, just as he would be responsible for giving the patient a lethal injection. The decision to let a patient die is subject to moral appraisal in the same way that a decision to kill is subject to moral appraisal: it may be assessed as wise or unwise, compassionate or sadistic, right or wrong. If a doctor deliberately let a patient die who was suffering from a routinely curable illness, then he would be to blame for what he did, just as he would be to blame if he had needlessly killed the patient. It would be no defense at all for him to insist that, *really*, he didn't "do anything" but just stand there. We would all know that he did do something very serious indeed, for he let the patient die.

These considerations show how misleading it is to characterize the difference between active and passive euthanasia as a difference between doing something (killing), for which the doctor may be morally culpable; and doing nothing (just standing there while the patient dies), for which the doctor is not culpable. The real difference between them is, rather, the difference between *killing* and letting die, both of which are actions for which a doctor, or anyone else, will be morally responsible.

Now we can formulate our problem more precisely. If there is an important moral difference between active and passive euthanasia, it must be because *killing someone is morally worse than letting someone die.* But is it? Is killing, in itself, worse than letting die? In order to investigate this issue, we may consider two cases which are exactly alike except that one involves killing where the other involves letting someone die. Then we can ask whether this difference makes any difference to our moral assessments. It is important that the cases be *exactly* alike except for this one difference, since otherwise we cannot be confident that it is *this* difference which accounts for any variation in our assessments.

1. Smith stands to gain a large inheritance if anything should happen to his six-year-old cousin. One evening while the child is taking his bath, Smith sneaks into the bathroom and drowns the child, and then arranges things so that it will look like an accident.

2. Jones also stands to gain if anything should happen to his six-year-old cousin. Like Smith, Jones sneaks in planning to drown the child in his bath. However, just as he enters the bathroom Jones sees the child slip, hit his head, and fall face down in the water. Jones is delighted; he stands by, ready to push the child's head back under if it is necessary, but it is not necessary. With only a little thrashing about, the child drowns all by himself, "accidentally," as Jones watches and does nothing.

Now Smith killed the child, while Jones "merely" let the child die. That is the only difference between them. Did either man behave better, from a moral point of view? Is there a moral difference between them? *If the difference between killing and letting die were itself a morally important matter, then we should say that Jones's behavior was less reprehensible than Smith's.* But do we actually want to say that? I think not, for several reasons. In the first place, both men acted from the same motive, personal gain, and both had exactly the same end in view when they acted. We may infer from Smith's conduct that he is a bad man, although we may withdraw or modify that judgment if we learn certain further facts about him; for example, that he is mentally deranged. But would we not also infer the very same thing about Jones from his conduct? And would not the same further considerations also be relevant to any modification of that judgment? Moreover, suppose Jones pleaded in his defense, "After all, I didn't kill the child. I only stood there and let him die." Again, if letting die were in itself less bad than killing, this defense should have some weight. But—morally, at least—it does not. Such a "defense" can only be regarded as a grotesque perversion of moral reasoning.

Thus, it seems that when we are careful not to smuggle in any further differences which prejudice the issue, the mere difference between killing and letting die does not itself make any difference to the morality of actions concerning life and death.[8]

Now it may be pointed out, quite properly, that the cases of euthanasia with which doctors are concerned are not like this at all. They do not involve personal gain or the destruction of normal, healthy children. Doctors are concerned only with cases in which the patient's life is of no further use to him, or in which the patient's life has become or soon will become a positive burden. However, the point is the same in those cases: the difference between killing and letting die does not, *in itself*, make a difference, from the point of view of morality. If a doctor lets a patient die, for humane reasons, he is in the same moral position as if he had given the patient a lethal injection for humane reasons. If his decision was wrong—if, for example, the patient's illness was in fact curable—then the decision would be equally regrettable no matter which method was used to carry it out. And if the doctor's decision was the right one, then the method he used is not itself important.

The AMA statement isolates the crucial issue very well: "the intentional termination of the life of one human being by another." But then the statement goes on to deny that the cessation of treatment *is* the intentional termination of a life. This is where the mistake comes in, for what is the cessation of treatment, in those circumstances, if it is not "the intentional termination of the life of one human being by another"? Of course it is exactly that; if it were not, there would be no point to it.

COUNTER–ARGUMENTS

Our argument has now brought us to this point: we cannot draw any moral distinction between active and passive euthanasia on the grounds that one involves killing while the other only involves letting someone die, because that is a difference that does not make a difference, from a moral point of view. Some people will find this hard to accept. One reason, I think, is that they fail to distinguish the question of whether killing is, in itself, worse than letting die, from the very different question of whether most actual cases of killing are more reprehensible than most actual cases of letting die. Most actual cases of killing are clearly terrible—think of the murders reported in the newspapers—and we hear of such cases almost every day. On the other hand, we hardly ever hear of a case of letting die, except for the actions of doctors who are motivated by humanitarian reasons. So we learn to think of killing in a much worse light than letting die; and we conclude, invalidly, that there must be something about killing which makes it *in itself* worse than letting die. But this does not follow for it is not the bare difference between killing and letting die that makes the difference in these cases. Rather, it is the other factors—the murderer's motive of personal gain, for example, contrasted with the doctor's humanitarian motivation, or the fact that the murderer kills a healthy person while the doctor lets die a terminal patient racked with disease—that account for our different reactions to the different cases.

There are, however, some substantial arguments that may be advanced to oppose my conclusion. Here are two of them:

The first counter-argument focuses specifically on the concept of *being the cause of someone's death*. If we kill someone, then we are the cause of his death. But if we merely let someone die, we are not the cause; rather, he dies of whatever condition he already has. The doctor who gives the cancer patient a lethal injection will have caused his patient's death, and will have this on his conscience; whereas if he merely ceases treatment, the cancer and not the doctor is the cause of death. This is supposed to make a moral difference. This argument has been advanced many times. Ramsey, for example, urges us to remember that "In omission no human agent causes the patient's death, directly or indirectly." [9] And, writing in the *Villanova Law Review* for 1968, Dr. J. Russell Elkinton said that what makes the active/passive distinction important is that in passive euthanasia, "the patient does not die from the act [e.g. the act of turning off the respirator] but from the underlying disease or injury." [10]

This argument will not do, for two reasons. First, just as there is a distinction to be drawn between being and not being the cause of someone's death, there is also a distinction to be drawn between letting someone die and not letting anyone die. It is certainly desirable, in general, not to be the cause of anyone's death; but it is also desirable, in general, not to let anyone die when we can save them. (Doctors act on this precept every day.) Therefore, we cannot draw any special conclusion about the relative desirability of passive euthanasia just on these grounds. Second, the reason why we think it is bad to be the cause of someone's death is that we think that death is a great evil—and so it is. However, if we have decided that euthanasia, even passive euthanasia, is desirable in a given case, then we have decided that in *this* instance death is no greater an evil than the patient's continued existence. And if this is true, then the usual reason for not wanting to be the cause of someone's death simply does not apply. To put the point just a bit differently: There is nothing wrong with being the cause of someone's death if his death is, all things considered, a good thing. And if his death is *not* a good thing, then *no* form of euthanasia, active or passive, is justified. So

once again we see that the two kinds of euthanasia stand or fall together.

The second counter-argument appeals to a favorite idea of philosophers, namely that our duty not to harm people is generally more stringent than our duty to help them. The law affirms this when it forbids us to kill people, or steal their goods, but does not require us in general to save people's lives or give them charity. And this is said to be not merely a point about the law, but about morality as well. We do not have a strict moral duty to help some poor man in Ethiopa—although it might be kind and generous of us if we did—but we *do* have a strict moral duty to refrain from doing anything to harm him. Killing someone is a violation of our duty not to harm, whereas letting someone die is merely a failure to give help. Therefore, the former is a more serious breach of morality than the latter; and so, contrary to what was said above, there is a morally significant difference between killing and letting die.

This argument has a certain superficial plausibility, but it cannot be used to show that there is a morally important difference between active and passive euthanasia. For one thing, it only seems that our duty to help people is less stringent than our duty not to harm them when we concentrate on certain sorts of cases: cases in which the people we could help are very far away, and are strangers to us; or cases in which it would be very difficult for us to help them, or in which helping would require a substantial sacrifice on our part. Many people feel that, in *these* types of cases, it may be kind and generous of us to give help, but we are not morally required to do so. Thus it is felt that when we give money for famine relief we are being especially big-hearted, and we deserve special praise—even if it would be immodest of us to seek such praise—because we are doing more than, strictly speaking, we are required to do.[11]

However, if we think of cases in which it would be very easy for us to help someone who is close at hand and in which no great personal sacrifice is required, things look very different. Think again of the child drowning in the bathtub: *of course* a man standing next to the tub would have a strict moral duty to help the child. Here the alleged asymmetry between the duty to help and the duty not to do harm vanishes. Since most of the cases of euthanasia with which we are concerned are of this latter type—the patient is close at hand, it is well within the professional skills of the physician to keep him alive—the alleged asymmetry has little relevance.

It should also be remembered, in considering this argument, that the duty of doctors toward their patients *is* precisely to help them; that is what doctors are supposed to do. Therefore, even if there were a general asymmetry between the duty to help and the duty not to harm—which I deny—it would not apply in the special case of the relation between doctors and their patients. Finally, it is not clear that killing such a patient *is* harming him, even though in other cases it certainly is a great harm to someone to kill him, for as I said before, we are going under the assumption that the patient would be no worse off dead than he is now; if this is so, then killing him is not harming him. For the same reason we should not classify letting such a patient die as failing to help him. Therefore, even if we grant that our duty to help people is less stringent than our duty not to harm them, nothing follows about our duties with respect to killing and letting die in the special case of euthanasia.

PRACTICAL CONSEQUENCES

This is enough, I think, to show that the doctrine underlying the AMA statement is false. There is no general moral difference between active and passive euthanasia; if one is permissible, so is the other. Now if this were merely an intellectual mistake, having no significant consequences for medical practice, the whole matter would not be very important. But the opposite is true: the doctrine has terrible consequences for, as I have already mentioned—and as doctors know very well—the process of being "allowed to die" can be relatively slow and painful, while being given a lethal injection is relatively quick and painless. Dr. Anthony Shaw describes what happens when the decision has been made not to perform the surgery necessary to "save" a mongoloid infant:

When surgery is denied [the doctor] must try to keep the infant from suffering while natural forces sap the baby's life away. As a surgeon whose natural inclination is to use the scalpel to fight off death, standing by and watching a salvageable baby die is the most emotionally exhausting experience I know. It is easy at a conference, in a theoretical discussion, to decide that such infants should be allowed to die. It is altogether different to stand by in the nursery and watch as dehydration and infection wither a tiny being over hours and days. This is a terrible ordeal for me and the hospital staff—much more so than for the parents who never set foot in the nursery.[12]

Why must the hospital staff "stand by in the nursery and watch as dehydration and infection wither a tiny being over hours and days"? Why must they merely "try" to reduce the infant's suffering? The doctrine which says that the baby may be allowed to dehydrate and wither, but not be given an injection which would end its life without suffering, is not only irrational but cruel.

The same goes for the case of the man with cancer of the throat. Here there are three options: with continued treatment, he will have a few more days of pain, and then die; if treatment is stopped, but nothing else is done, it will be a few more hours; and with a lethal injection, he will die at once. Those who oppose euthanasia in all its forms say that we must take the first option, and keep the patient alive for as long as possible. This view is so patently inhumane that few defend it; nevertheless, it does have a certain kind of integrity. It is at least consistent. The third option is the one I think best. But the *middle* position—that, although the patient need not suffer for days before dying, he must nevertheless suffer for a few more hours—is a "moderate" view which incorporates the worst, and not the best, features of both extremes.

Let me mention one other practice that we would be well rid of if we stopped thinking that the distinction between active and passive euthanasia is important. About one in six hundred babies born in the United States is mongoloid. Most of these babies are otherwise healthy—that is, with only the usual pediatric care, they will proceed to a "normal" infancy. Some, however, are born with other congenital defects such as intestinal obstructions which require surgery if the baby is to live. As I have already mentioned, sometimes the surgery is withheld and the baby dies. But when there is no defect requiring surgery, the baby lives on.[13] Now surgery to remove an intestinal obstruction is not difficult; the reason why it is not performed in such cases is, clearly, that the child is mongoloid and the parents and doctor judge that because of *this* it is better for the child to die.

But notice that this situation is absurd, no matter what view one takes of the lives and potentials of such babies. If you think that the life of such an infant is worth preserving, then what does it matter if it needs a simple operation? Or, if you think it better that such a baby not live on, then what difference does it make if its intestinal tract is *not* blocked? In either case, the matter of life or death is being decided on irrelevant grounds. It is the mongolism, and not the intestine, that is the issue. The matter should be decided, if at all, on *that* basis, and not be allowed to depend on the essentially irrelevant question of whether the intestinal tract is blocked.

What makes this situation possible, of course, is the idea that when there is an intestinal obstruction we can "let the baby die," but when there is no such defect there is nothing we can do, for we must not "kill" it. The fact that this idea leads to such results as deciding life or death on irrelevant grounds is another good reason why it should be rejected.

Doctors may think that all of this is only of academic interest, the sort of thing which philosophers may worry about but which has no practical bearing on their own work. After all, doctors must be concerned about the legal consequences of what they do, and active euthanasia is clearly forbidden by the law. They are right to be concerned about this. There have not been many prosecutions of doctors in the United States for active euthanasia, but there have been some. Prosecutions for passive euthanasia, on the other hand, are virtually nonexistent, even though there are laws under which charges could be brought, and even though this practice is much more wide-spread. Passive euthanasia, unlike active euthanasia, is by and large tolerated by the law. The law may sometimes compel a doctor to take action which he might not otherwise take to keep a patient alive,[14] but of course this is very different from bringing criminal charges against him after the patient is dead.

Even so, doctors should be concerned with the fact that the law and public opinion are forcing upon them an indefensible moral position, which has a considerable effect on their practices. Of course, most doctors are not now in the position of being coerced in this matter, for they do not regard themselves as merely going along with what the law requires. Rather, in statements such as the AMA statement that I quoted, they are endorsing the doctrine as a central point of medical ethics. In that statement, active euthanasia is condemned not merely as illegal but as "contrary to that for which the medical profession stands," while passive euthanasia is approved. However, if my arguments have been sound, there really is no intrinsic moral difference between them (although there may be morally important differences in their consequences, varying from case to case); so while doctors may have to discriminate between them to satisfy the law, they should not do any *more* than that. In particular, they should not give the distinction any added authority and weight by writing it into official statements of medical ethics.

Footnotes

1. F.J. Ingelfinger, "Bedside Ethics for the Hopeless Case," *The New England Journal of Medicine* 289 (25 October 1973), p. 914.

2. Ibid.

3. This statement was approved by the House of Delegates of the AMA on December 4, 1973. It is worth noting that some state medical societies have advised *patients* to take a similar attitude toward the termination of their lives. In 1973 the Connecticut State Medical Society approved a "background statement" to be signed by terminal patients which includes this sentence: "I value life and the dignity of life, so that I am not asking that my life be directly taken, but that my life not be unreasonably prolonged or the dignity of life be destroyed." Other state medical societies have followed suit.

4. A discussion of this type of case can be found in Anthony Shaw, " 'Doctor, Do We Have a Choice?' " *The New York Times Magazine,* 30 January 1972, pp. 44–54. Also see Shaw's "Dilemmas of 'Informed Consent' in Children," *The New England Journal of Medicine* 289 (25 October 1973), pp. 885–90.

5. Paul Ramsey, *The Patient as Person* (New Haven, Conn.: Yale University Press, 1970), pp. 115–16.

6. D.C.S. Cameron, *The Truth About Cancer* (Englewood Cliffs, N.J.: Prentice-Hall, 1956), p. 116.

7. Ramsey, *The Patient as Person*, p. 151.

8. Judith Jarvis Thomson has argued that this line of reasoning is unsound. Consider, she says, this argument which is parallel to the one involving Smith and Jones:

> Alfrieda knows that if she cuts off Alfred's head he will die, and wanting him to die, cuts if off; Bertha knows that if she punches Bert in the nose he will die—Bert is in peculiar physical condition—and, wanting him to die, punches him in the nose. But what Bertha does is surely every bit as bad as what Alfrieda does. So cutting off a man's head isn't worse than punching a man in the nose. ["Killing, Letting Die, and the Trolley Problem," *The Monist* 59 (1976), p. 204.]

She concludes that, since this absurd argument doesn't prove anything, the Smith/Jones argument doesn't prove anything either.

However, I think that the Alfrieda/Bertha argument is not absurd, as strange as it is. A little analysis shows that it is a sound argument and that its conclusion is true. We need to notice first that the reason why it is wrong to chop someone's head off is, obviously, that this causes death. The act is objectionable because of its consequences. Thus, a different act with the same consequences may be equally objectionable. In Thomson's example, punching Bert in the nose has the same consequences as chopping off Alfred's head; and, indeed, the two actions are equally bad.

Now the Alfrieda/Bertha argument presupposes a distinction between the act of chopping off someone's head, and the results of this act, the victim's death. (It is stipulated that, except for the fact that Alfrieda chops off someone's head, while Bertha punches some-one in the nose, the two acts are "in all other respects alike." The "*other* respects" include the act's consequence, the victim's death.) This is not a distinction we would normally think to make, since we cannot in fact cut off someone's head without killing him. Yet in thought the distinction can be drawn. The question raised in the argument, then, is whether, *considered apart from their consequences,* head-chopping is worse than nose-punching. And the answer to *this* strange question is No, just as the argument says it should be.

The conclusion of the argument should be construed like this: The bare fact that one act is an act of head-chopping, while another act is an act of nose-punching, is not a reason for judging the former to be worse than the latter. At the same time—and this is perfectly compatible with the argument—the fact that one act causes death, while another does not, *is* a reason for judging the former to be worse. The parallel construal of my conclusion is: The bare fact that one act is an act of killing, while another act is an act of letting die, is not a reason for judging the former to be worse than the latter. At the same time—and this is perfectly compatible with my argument—the fact that an act (of killing, for example) prevents suffering, while another act (of letting die, for example) does not, *is* a reason for preferring one over the other. So once we see exactly how the Alfrieda/Bertha argument *is* parallel to the Smith/Jones argument, we find that Thomson's argument is, surprisingly, quite all right.

9. Ramsey, *The Patient as Person*, p. 151.

10. J. Russell Elkinton, "The Dying Patient, the Doctor, and the Law," *Villanova Law Review* 13 (Summer 1968), p. 743.

11. For the purposes of this essay we do not need to consider whether this way of thinking about "charity" is justified. There are, however, strong arguments that it is morally indefensible: see Peter Singer, "Famine, Affluence, and Morality," *Philosophy and Public Affairs* 1 (Spring 1972), pp. 229–43. Also see James Rachels, "Killing and Letting People Die of Starvation," forthcoming in *Philosophy,* for a discussion of the killing/letting die distinction in the context of world hunger, as well as further arguments that the distinction is morally unimportant.

12. Shaw, " 'Doctor, Do We Have a Choice?' " p. 54.

13. See the articles by Shaw cited in note 4.

14. For example, in February 1974 a Superior Court judge in Maine ordered a doctor to proceed with an operation to repair a hole in the esophagus of a baby with multiple deformities. Otherwise the operation would not have been performed. The baby died anyway a few days later. "Deformed Baby Dies Amid Controversy," *The Miami Herald,* 25 February 1974, p. 4–B.

Review Questions

1. According to Rachels, what absolute doctrine is held by many doctors?

2. Explain the position that Rachels defends, including the distinction between active and passive euthanasia.

3. How does Rachels attack the 1973 policy statement of the AMA?

4. What is Ramsey's view of the active/passive distinction, and why does Rachels reject it?

5. Explain Rachels' argument (using the example about Smith and Jones) for saying that there is no important moral difference between killing and letting die.

6. What are the two counter-arguments, and how does Rachels reply to them?

7. According to Rachels, on what basis should life and death decisions about defective infants be made?

Discussion Questions

1. Do you agree with Rachels that in some cases active euthanasia is better than passive euthanasia? Why or why not?

2. Is Rachels' argument that there is no significant moral difference between killing and letting die acceptable to you? Explain your answer.

3. Rachels denies that there is a general asymmetry between the duty to help and the duty to not harm. Do you agree that, in general, these two duties have equal moral force? Why or why not?

4. Should the law be changed to allow active euthanasia or not? Defend your view.

Bonnie Steinbock

The Intentional Termination of Life

Bonnie Steinbock teaches philosophy at the State University of New York at Albany.

Steinbock defends the AMA statement on euthanasia from the attack made by Rachels. She argues that the AMA statement does not make the distinction between active and passive euthanasia that Rachels attacks. According to Steinbock, the AMA statement instead rejects both active and passive euthanasia, but does permit the cessation of extraordinary means of treatment. This is not the same as passive euthanasia. Cessation of extraordinary means can be done to respect the patient's right to refuse treatment, or because continued treatment is painful; neither reason is the same as letting the patient die. She grants, however, that in some cases the cessation of extraordinary means does amount to letting the patient die, and that in some cases a quick

and painless death may be preferable to letting a patient die slowly.

According to James Rachels [1] a common mistake in medical ethics is the belief that there is a moral difference between active and passive euthanasia. This is a mistake, [he] argues, because the rationale underlying the distinction between active and passive euthanasia is the idea that there is a significant moral difference between intentionally killing and letting die.... Whether the belief that there is a significant moral difference (between intentionally killing and intentionally letting die) is mistaken is not my concern here. For it is far from clear that this distinction *is* the basis of the doctrine of the American Medical Association which Rachels attacks. And if the killing/letting die distinction is not the basis of the AMA doctrine, then arguments showing that the distinction has no moral force do not, in themselves, reveal in the doctrine's adherents either "confused thinking" or "a moral point of view unrelated to the interests of individuals". Indeed, as we examine the AMA doctrine, I think it will become clear that it appeals to and makes use of a number of overlapping distinctions, which may have moral significance in particular

From Bonnie Steinbock, "The International Termination of Life," in *Ethics in Science and Medicine* (Pergamon Press, Ltd., 1979), pp. 59–64. Reprinted with permission.

cases, such as the distinction between intending and foreseeing, or between ordinary and extraordinary care. Let us then turn to the statement, from the House of Delegates of the American Medical Association, which Rachels cites:

The intentional termination of the life of one human being by another—mercy-killing—is contrary to that for which the medical profession stands and is contrary to the policy of the American Medical Association.
The cessation of the employment of extraordinary means to prolong the life of the body when there is irrefutable evidence that biological death is imminent is the decision of the patient and/or his immediate family. The advice and judgment of the physician should be freely available to the patient and/or his immediate family.[2]

Rachels attacks this statement because he believes that it contains a moral distinction between active and passive euthanasia....

I intend to show that the AMA statement does not imply support of the active/passive euthanasia distinction. In forbidding the intentional termination of life, the statement rejects both active and passive euthanasia. It does allow for "... the cessation of the employment of extraordinary means ..." to prolong life. The mistake Rachels makes is in identifying the cessation of life-prolonging treatment with passive euthanasia, or intentionally letting die. If it were right to equate the two, then the AMA statement would be self-contradictory, for it would begin by condemning, and end by allowing, the intentional termination of life. But if the cessation of life-prolonging treatment is not always or necessarily passive euthanasia, then there is no confusion and no contradiction.

Why does Rachels think that the cessation of life-prolonging treatment is the intentional termination of life? He says:

The AMA policy statement isolates the crucial issue very well: the crucial issue is "the intentional termination of the life of one human being by another". But after identifying this issue, and forbidding "mercy-killing", the statement goes on to deny that the cessation of treatment is the intentional termination of a life. This is where the mistake comes in, for what is the cessation of treatment, in these circumstances, if it is not "the intentional termination of the life of one human being by another"? Of course it is exactly that, and if it were not, there would be no point to it.[3]

However, there *can* be a point (to the cessation of life-prolonging treatment) other than an endeavor to bring about the patient's death, and so the blanket identification of cessation of treatment with the intentional termination of a life is inaccurate. There are at least two situations in which the termination of life-prolonging treatment cannot be identified with the intentional termination of the life of one human being by another.

The first situation concerns the patient's right to refuse treatment. Rachels gives the example of a patient dying of an incurable disease, accompanied by unrelievable pain, who wants to end the treatment which cannot cure him but can only prolong his miserable existence. Why, they ask, may a doctor accede to the patient's request to stop treatment, but not provide a patient in a similar situation with a lethal dose? The answer lies in the patient's right to refuse treatment. In general, a competent adult has the right to refuse treatment, even where such treatment is necessary to prolong life. Indeed, the right to refuse treatment has been upheld even when the patient's reason for refusing treatment is generally agreed to be inadequate.[4] This right can be overridden (if, for example, the patient has dependent children) but, in general, no one may legally compel you to undergo treatment to which you have not consented. "Historically, surgical intrusion has always been considered a technical battery upon the person and one to be excused or justified by consent of the patient or justified by necessity created by the circumstances of the moment...."[5]

At this point, it might be objected that if one has the right to refuse life-prolonging treatment, then consistency demands that one have the right to decide to end his life, and to obtain help in doing so. The idea is that the right to refuse treatment somehow implies a right to voluntary euthanasia, and we need to see why someone might think this. The right to refuse treatment has been considered by legal writers as an example of the right to privacy or, better, the right to bodily self-determination. You have the right to decide what happens to your own body, and the right to refuse treatment is an instance of that more general right. But if you have the right to determine what happens to your body, then should you not have the right to choose to end your life, and even a right to get help in doing so?

However, it is important to see that the right to refuse treatment is not the same as, nor does it entail, a right to voluntary euthanasia, even if both can be derived from the right to bodily self-determination. The right to refuse treatment is not itself a "right to die"; that one may choose to exercise this right even at the risk of death, or even *in order to die,* is irrelevant. The purpose of the right to refuse medical treatment is not to give persons a right to decide whether to live or die, but to protect them from the unwanted interferences of others. Perhaps we ought to interpret the right to bodily self-determination more broadly so as to include a right to die: but this would be a substantial extension of our present understanding of the right to bodily self-determination, and not a consequence of it. Should we recognize a right to voluntary euthanasia, we would have to agree that people have the right not merely to be left alone, but also the right to be killed. I leave to one side that substantive moral issue. My claim is simply that there can be a reason for terminating life-prolonging treatment other than "to bring about the patient's death".

The second case in which termination of treatment cannot be identified with intentional termination of life is where continued treatment has little chance of improving the patient's condition and brings greater discomfort than relief.

The question here is what treatment is appropriate to the particular case. A cancer specialist describes it in this way:

*My general rule is to administer therapy as long as a patient responds well and has the potential for a reasonably good quality of life. But when all feasible therapies have been administered and a patient shows signs of rapid deterioration, the continuation of therapy can cause more discomfort than the cancer. From that time I recommend surgery, **radiotherapy,** or **chemotherapy** only as a means of relieving pain. But if a patient's condition should once again stabilize after the withdrawal of active therapy and if it should appear that he could still gain some good time, I would immediately reinstitute active therapy. The decision to cease anticancer treatment is never irrevocable, and often the desire to live will push a patient to try for another remission, or even a few more days of life.*[6]

The decision here to cease anticancer treatment cannot be construed as a decision that the patient die, or as the intentional termination of life. It is a decision to provide the most appropriate treatment for that patient at that time. Rachels suggests that the point of the cessation of treatment is the intentional termination of life. But here the point of discontinuing treatment is not to bring about the patient's death, but to avoid treatment that will cause more discomfort than the cancer and has little hope of benefiting the patient. Treatment that meets this description is often called "extraordinary".[7] The concept is flexible, and what might be considered "extraordinary" in one situation might be ordinary in another. The use of a respirator to sustain a patient through a severe bout with a respiratory disease would be considered ordinary; its use to sustain the life of a severely brain damaged person in an irreversible coma would be considered extraordinary.

Contrasted with extraordinary treatment is ordinary treatment, the care a doctor would normally be expected to provide. Failure to provide ordinary care constitutes neglect, and can even be construed as the intentional infliction of harm, where there is a legal obligation to provide care. The importance of the ordinary/extraordinary care distinction lies partly in its connection to the doctor's intention. The withholding of extraordinary care should be seen as a decision not to inflict painful treatment on a patient without reasonable hope of success. The withholding of ordinary care, by contrast, must be seen as neglect. Thus, one doctor says, "We have to draw a distinction between ordinary and extraordinary means. We never withdraw what's needed to make a baby comfortable, we would never withdraw the care a parent would provide. We never kill a baby. . . . But we may decide certain heroic intervention is not worthwhile."[8]

We should keep in mind the ordinary/ extraordinary care distinction when considering an example given by Rachels to show the irrationality of the active/passive distinction with regard to infanticide. The example is this: a child is born with **Down's syndrome** and also has an intestinal obstruction which requires corrective surgery. If the surgery is not performed, the infant will starve to death, since it cannot take food orally. This may take days or even weeks, as dehydration and infection set in. Commenting on this situation, Rachels says:

I can understand why some people are opposed to all euthanasia, and insist that such infants must be allowed to live. I think I can also understand why other people favor destroying these babies quickly and painlessly. But why should anyone favor letting "dehydration and infection wither a tiny being over hours and days"? The doctrine that says that a baby may be allowed to dehydrate and wither, but may not be given an injection that would end its life without suffering, seems so patently cruel as to require no further refutation.[9]

Such a doctrine perhaps does not need further refutation; but this is not the AMA doctrine. For the AMA statement criticized by Rachels allows only for the cessation of extraordinary means to prolong life when death is imminent. Neither of these conditions is satisfied in this example. Death is not imminent in this situation, any more than it would be if a normal child had an attack of appendicitis. Neither the corrective surgery to remove the intestinal obstruction, nor the intravenous feeding required to keep the infant alive until such surgery is performed, can be regarded as extraordinary means, for neither is particularly expensive, nor does either place an overwhelming burden on the patient or others. (The continued existence of the child might be thought to place an overwhelming burden on its parents, but that has nothing to do with the characterization of the means to prolong its life as extraordinary. If it had, then *feeding* a severely defective child who required a great deal of care could be regarded as extraordinary.) The chances of success if the operation is undertaken are quite good, though there is always a risk in operating on infants. Though the Down's syndrome will not be alleviated, the child will proceed to an otherwise normal infancy.

It cannot be argued that the treatment is withheld for the infant's sake, unless one is prepared to argue that all mentally retarded babies are better off dead. This is particularly implausible in the case of Down's syndrome babies who generally do not suffer and are capable of giving and receiving love, of learning and playing, to varying degrees.

In a film on this subject entitled, "Who Should Survive?", a doctor defended a decision not to operate, saying that since the parents did not consent to the operation, the doctors' hands were tied. As we have seen, surgical intrusion requires consent, and in the case of infants, consent would normally come from the parents. But, as their legal guardians, parents are required to provide medical care for their children, and failure to do so can constitute criminal neglect or even homicide. In general, courts have been understandably reluctant to recognize a parental right to terminate life-prolonging treatment.[10] Although prosecution is unlikely, physicians who comply with invalid instructions from the parents and permit the infant's death could be liable for aiding and abetting, failure to report child neglect, or even homicide. So it is not true that, in this situation, doctors are legally bound to do as the parents wish.

To sum up, I think that Rachels is right to regard the decision not to operate in the Down's syndrome example as the intentional termination of life. But there is no reason to believe that either the law or the AMA would regard it otherwise. Certainly the decision to withhold treatment is not justified by the AMA statement. That such infants have been allowed to die cannot be denied; but this, I think, is the result of doctors misunderstanding the law and the AMA position.

Withholding treatment in this case is the intentional termination of life because the infant is deliberately allowed to die; that is the point of not operating. But there are other cases in which that is not the point. If the point is to avoid inflicting painful treatment on a patient with little or no reasonable hope of success, this is not the intentional termination of life. The permissibility of such withholding of treatment, then, would have no implications for the permissibility of euthanasia, active or passive.

The decision whether or not to operate, or to institute vigorous treatment, is particularly agonizing in the case of children born with **spina bifida,** an opening in the base of the spine usually accompanied by **hydrocephalus** and mental retardation. If left unoperated, these children usually die of **meningitis** or kidney failure within the first few years of life. Even if they survive, all affected children face a lifetime of illness, operations and varying degrees of disability. The policy used to be to save as many as possible, but the trend now is toward selective treatment, based on the physician's estimate of the chances of success. If operating is not likely to improve significantly the child's condition, parents and doctors may agree not to operate. This is not the intentional termination of life, for again the purpose is not the termination of the child's life but the avoidance of painful and pointless treatment. Thus, the fact that withholding treatment is justified does not imply that killing the child would be equally justified.

Throughout the discussion, I have claimed that intentionally ceasing life-prolonging treatment is not the intentional termination of life unless the doctor has, as his or her purpose in stopping treatment, the patient's death.

It may be objected that I have incorrectly characterized the conditions for the intentional termination of life. Perhaps it is enough that the doctor intentionally ceases treatment, foreseeing that the patient will die; perhaps the reason for ceasing treatment is irrelevant to its characterization as the intentional termination of life. I find this suggestion implausible, but am willing to consider arguments for it. Rachels has provided no such arguments: indeed, he apparently shares my view about the intentional termination of life. For when he claims that the cessation of life-prolonging treatment is the intentional termination of life, his reason for making the claim is that "if it were not, there would be no point to it". Rachels believes that the point of ceasing treatment, "in these cases", is to bring about the patient's death. If that were not the point, he suggests, why would the doctor cease treatment? I have shown, however, that there can be a point to ceasing treatment which is not the death of the patient. In showing this, I have refuted Rachels' reason for identifying the cessation of life-prolonging treatment with the intentional termination of life, and thus his argument against the AMA doctrine.

Here someone might say: Even if the withholding of treatment is not the intentional termination of life, does that make a difference, morally speaking? If life-prolonging treatment may be withheld, for the sake of the child, may not an easy death be provided, for the sake of the child, as well? The unoperated child with spina bifida may take months or even years to die. Distressed by the spectacle of children "lying around waiting to die", one doctor has written, "It is time that society and medicine stopped perpetuating the fiction that withholding treatment is ethically different from terminating a life. It is time that society began to discuss mechanisms by which we can alleviate the pain and suffering for those individuals whom we cannot help."[11]

I do not deny that there may be cases in which death is in the best interests of the patient. In such cases, a quick and painless death may be the best thing. However, I do not think that, once active or vigorous treatment is stopped, a quick death is always preferable to a lingering one. We must be cautious about attributing to defective children *our* distress at seeing them linger. Waiting for them to die may be tough on parents, doctors and nurses—it isn't necessarily tough on the child. The decision not to operate need not mean a decision to neglect, and it may be possible to make the remaining months of the child's life comfortable, pleasant and filled with love. If this alternative is possible, surely it is more decent and humane than killing the child. In such a situation, withholding treatment, foreseeing the child's death, is not ethically equivalent to killing the child, and we cannot move from the permissibility of the former to that of the latter. I am worried that there will be a tendency to do precisely that if active euthanasia is regarded as morally equivalent to the withholding of life-prolonging treatment.

CONCLUSION

The AMA statement does not make the distinction Rachels wishes to attack, i.e. that between active and passive euthanasia. Instead, the statement draws a distinction between the intentional termination of life, on the one hand, and the cessation of the employment of extraordinary means to prolong life, on the other. Nothing said by Rachels shows that this distinction is confused. It may be that doctors have misinterpreted the AMA statement, and that this had led, for example, to decisions to allow defective infants slowly to starve to death. I quite agree with Rachels that the decisions to which they allude were cruel and made on irrelevant grounds. Certainly it is worth pointing out that allowing someone to die can be the intentional termination of life, and that it can be just as bad as, or worse than, killing someone. However, the withholding of life-prolonging treatment is not necessarily the intentional termination of life, so that if it is permissible to withhold life-prolonging treatment, it does not follow that, other things being equal, it is permissible to kill. Furthermore, most of the time, other things are not equal. In many of the cases in which it would be right to cease treatment, I do not think that it would also be right to kill.

Footnotes

1. James Rachels. Active and passive euthanasia. *New Engl.J.Med.,* 292, 78–80, 1975.

2. Rachels, p. 78.

3. Rachels, pp. 79–80.

4. For example, *In re Yetter,* 62 Pa. D. & C. 2d 619, C.P., Northampton County Ct., 1974.

5. David W. Meyers, Legal aspects of voluntary euthanasia, *Dilemmas of Euthanasia,* (Edited by John Behnke and Sissela Bok), p. 56. Anchor Books, New York, 1975.

6. Ernest H. Rosenbaum, Md., *Living with Cancer,* p. 27. Praeger, New York, 1975.

7. Cf. H. Tristram Engelhardt, Jr., Ethical issues in aiding the death of young children, *Beneficent Euthanasia* (Edited by Marvin Kohl), Prometheus Books, Buffalo, N.Y. 1975.

8. B.D. Colen, *Karen Ann Quinlan: Living and Dying in the Age of Eternal Life,* p. 115. Nash, 1976.

9. Rachels, p. 79.

10. Cf. Norman L. Cantor, Law and the termination of an incompetent patient's life-preserving care. *Dilemmas of Euthanasia. op. cit.,* pp. 69–105.

11. John Freeman, Is there a right to die—quickly?, *J. Pediat.* 80. p. 905.

Review Questions

1. According to Steinbock, what mistake does Rachels make in his interpretation of the AMA statement?

2. How does Steinbock understand the right to refuse treatment?

3. How does Steinbock distinguish between extraordinary and ordinary treatment?

4. What is Steinbock's view of the case of the child with Down's syndrome, and how does her view differ from that of Rachels?

5. What is Steinbock's view of the treatment of children with spina bifida?

6. Why does Steinbock think that she has refuted Rachels' attack against the AMA statement?

7. Explain Steinbock's conclusion.

1. In your opinion, in what cases can the right to refuse medical treatment be overriden and why?

2. Steinbock grants that in some cases "a quick

and painless death may be the best thing." Can you think of any such cases? Why are they the best thing?

Richard B. Brandt

Defective Newborns and the Morality of Termination

Richard B. Brandt is Professor of Philosophy at the University of Michigan. His most recent book on ethics is A Theory of the Good and the Right *(1979).*

Brandt argues that it is morally right to actively or passively terminate the life of a defective newborn if its life is bad according to a "happiness criterion". Consent is irrelevant; the infant cannot give consent, and it will be indifferent to continued life. But the cost of caring for the infant is relevant to the decision to terminate in addition to the quality of the prospective life.

The *legal* rights of a fetus are very different from those of a newborn. The fetus may be aborted, legally, for any reason or no reason up to twenty-four or twenty-eight weeks (U.S. Supreme Court, *Roe* v. *Wade*). But, at least in theory, immediately after birth an infant has all the legal rights of the adult, including the right to life.

The topic of this paper, however, is to identify the moral rights of the newborn, specifically whether *defective* newborns have a right to life. But it is simpler to talk, not about "rights to life," but about when or

From *Infanticide and the Value of Life,* ed. by Marvin Kohl (Prometheus Books, 1978). Reprinted with permission.

whether it is *morally right* either actively or passively (by withdrawal of life-supportive measures) to terminate defective newborns. It is also better because the conception of a right involves the notion of a sphere of autonomy—something is to be done or omitted, but only if the subject of the rights wants or consents—and this fact is apt to be confusing or oversimplifying. Surely what we want to know is whether termination is morally right or wrong, and nothing can turn on the **semantics** of the concept of a "right."[1]

What does one have to do in order to support some answers to these questions? One thing we can do is ask—and I think myself that the answer to this question is definitive for our purposes—whether rational or fully informed persons would, in view of the total consequences, support a moral code for a society in which they expected to live, with one or another, provision on this matter. (I believe a fully rational person will at least normally have some degree of benevolence, or positive interest in the welfare or happiness of others; I shall not attempt to specify how much.) Since, however, I do not expect that everyone else will agree that answering this question would show what is morally right, I shall, for their benefit, also argue that certain moral principles on this matter are coherent with strong moral convictions of reflective people; or, to use Rawls's terminology, that a certain principle on the matter would belong to a system of moral principles in "reflective equilibrium."

Historically, many writers, including Pope Pius XI in *Casti Connubii* (1930), have affirmed an absolute prohibition against killing anyone who is neither guilty of a capital crime nor an unjust assailant threatening one's life (self-defense), except in case of "extreme necessity." Presumably the prohibition is intended to include withholding of food or liquid from a newborn, although strictly speaking this is only *failing* to do something, not actually *doing* something to bring about a death. (Would writers in this tradition demand, on moral grounds, that complicated and expensive surgery be undertaken to save a life? Such surgery is going beyond normal care, and in some cases beyond what earlier writers even conceived.) However the intentions of these writers may be, we should observe that historically their moral condemnation of all killing (except for the cases mentioned) derives from the Biblical injunction, "Thou shalt not kill," which, as it stands and without interpretation, may be taken to forbid suicide, killing of animals, perhaps even plants, and hence cannot be taken seriously.

Presumably a moral code that is coherent with our intuitions and that rational persons would support for their society would include some prohibition of killing, but it is another matter to identify the exact class to which such a prohibition is to apply. For one thing, I would doubt that killing one's self would be included—although one might be forbidden to kill one's self if that would work severe hardship on others, or conflict with the discharge of one's other moral obligations. And, possibly, defective newborns would *not* be included in the class. Further, a decision has to be made whether the prohibition of killing is *absolute* or only *prima facie*, meaning by "prima facie" that the duty not to kill might be outweighed by some other duty (or right) stronger in the circumstances, which could be fulfilled only by killing. In case this distinction is made, we would have to decide whether defective newborns fall within the scope of even a prima facie moral prohibition against killing. I shall, however, not attempt to make this fine distinction here, and shall simply inquire whether, everything considered, defective newborns—or some identifiable group of

them—are excluded from the moral prohibition against killing.

THE PROSPECTIVE QUALITY OF LIFE OF DEFECTIVE NEWBORNS

Suppose that killing a defective newborn, or allowing it to die, would not be an *injury*, but would rather be doing the infant a favor. In that case we should feel intuitively less opposed to termination of newborns, and presumably rational persons would be less inclined to support a moral code with a prohibition against such action. In that case we would feel rather as we do about a person's preventing a suicide attempt from being successful, in order that the person be elaborately tortured to death at a later stage. It is no favor to the prospective suicide to save his life; similarly, if the prospective life of defective newborns is bad we are doing them a favor to let them die.

It may be said that we have no way of knowing what the conscious experiences of defective children are like, and that we have no competence in any case to decide when or what kind of life is bad or not worth living. Further, it may be said that predictions about a defective newborn's prospects for the future are precarious, in view of possible further advances of medicine. It does seem, however, that here, as everywhere, the rational person will follow the evidence about the present or future facts. But there is a question how to decide whether a life is bad or not worth living.

In the case of *some* defective newborns, it seems clear that their prospective life is bad. Suppose, as sometimes happens, a child is hydrocephalic with an extremely low I.Q., is blind and deaf, has no control over its body, can only lie on its back all day and have all its needs taken care of by others, and even cries out with pain when it is touched or lifted. Infants born with spina bifida—and these number over two per one thousand births—are normally not quite so badly off, but are often nearly so.

But what criterion are we using if we say

that such a life is bad? One criterion might be called a "happiness" criterion. If a person *likes* a moment of experience while he is having it, his life is so far good; if a person *dislikes* a moment of experience while he is having it, his life is so far bad. Based on such reactions, we might construct a "happiness curve" for a person, going up above the indifference axis when a moment of experience is liked—and how far above depending on how strongly it is liked—and dipping down below the line when a moment is disliked. Then this criterion would say that a life is worth living if there is a net balance of positive area under the curve over a lifetime, and that it is bad if there is a net balance of negative area. One might adopt some different criterion: for instance, one might say that a life is worth living if a person would *want* to live it over again given that, at the end, he could remember the whole of it with perfect vividness in some kind of grand intuitive awareness. Such a response to this hypothetical holistic intuition, however, would likely be affected by the state of the person's drives or moods at the time, and the conception strikes me as unconvincing, compared with the moment-by-moment reaction to what is going on. Let us, for the sake of the argument, adopt the happiness criterion.[2]

Is the prospective life of the seriously defective newborn, like the one described above, bad or good according to this criterion? One thing seems clear: that it is *less* good than is the prospective life of a normal infant. But is it bad?

We have to do some extrapolating from what we know. For instance, such a child will presumably suffer from severe sensory deprivation; he is simply not getting interesting stimuli. On the basis of laboratory data, it is plausible to think the child's experience is at best boring or uncomfortable. If the child's experience is painful, of course, its moments are, so far, on the negative side. One must suppose that such a child hardly suffers from disappointment, since it will not learn to expect anything exciting, beyond being fed and

fondled, and these events will be regularly forthcoming. One might expect such a child to suffer from isolation and loneliness, but insofar as this is true, the object of dislike probably should be classified as just sensory deprivation; dislike of loneliness seems to depend on the deprivation of past pleasures of human company. There are also some positive enjoyments: of eating, drinking, elimination, seeing the nurse coming with food, and so on. But the brief enjoyments can hardly balance the long stretches of boredom, discomfort, or even pain. On the whole, the lives of such children are bad according to the happiness criterion.

Naturally we cannot generalize about the cases of all "defective" newborns; there are all sorts of defects, and the cases I have described are about the worst. A child with spina bifida may, if he survives the numerous operations, I suppose, adjust to the frustrations of immobility; he may become accustomed to the embarrassments of no bladder or bowel control; he may have some intellectual enjoyments like playing chess; he will suffer from observing what others have but he cannot, such as sexual satisfactions, in addition to the pain of repeated surgery. How does it all balance out? Surely not as very good, but perhaps above the indifference level.

It may fairly be said, I think, that the lives of some defective newborns are destined to be bad on the whole, and it would be a favor to them if their lives were terminated. Contrariwise, the prospective lives of many defective newborns are modestly pleasant, and it would be some injury to them to be terminated, albeit the lives they will live are ones some of us would prefer not to live at all.

CONSENT

Let us now make a second suggestion, not this time that termination of a defective newborn would be doing him a favor, but this time that he *consents* to termination, in the sense of expressing a rational deliberated preference for this. In that case I suggest that intuitively we would be *more* favorably inclined to judge that it is right to let the defective die, and I suggest also that for that case rational persons would be more ready to support a moral code permitting termination. Notice that we think that if an ill person has signified what we think a rational and deliberated desire to die, we are morally better justified in withdrawing life-supporting measures than we otherwise would be.

The newborn, however, is incapable of expressing his preference (giving consent) at all, much less expressing a rational deliberated preference. There could in theory be court-appointed guardians or proxies, presumably disinterested parties, authorized to give such consent on his behalf, but even so this would not be *his* consent.

Nevertheless, there is a fact about the mental life of the newborn (defective or not) such that, if he could understand the fact, it seems he would not object—even rationally or after deliberation, if that were possible—to his life being terminated, or to his parents substituting another child in his place. This suggestion may seem absurd, but let us see. The explanation runs along the lines of an argument I once used to support the morality of abortion. I quote the paragraph in which this argument was introduced.[3]

Suppose I were seriously ill, and were told that, for a sizeable fee, an operation to save "my life" could be performed, of the following sort: my brain would be removed to another body which could provide a normal life, but the unfortunate result of the operation would be that my memory and learned abilities would be wholly erased, and that the forming of memory brain traces must begin again from scratch, as in a newborn baby. Now, how large a fee would I be willing to pay for this operation, when the alternative is my peaceful demise? My own answer would be: None at all. I would take no interest in the continued existence of "myself" in that sense, and I would rather add the sizeable fee to the inheritance of my children.... I cannot see the point of forfeiting my children's inheritance in order to start off a person who is brand new except that he happens to enjoy the benefit of having my present brain, without the memory traces. It appears that some continuity of memory is a necessary condition for personal identity in an important sense.

My argument was that the position of a fetus, at the end of the first trimester, is essentially the same as that of the person contemplating this operation: he will consider that the baby born after six months will not be *he* in any *important* and *motivating* sense (there will be no continuity of memory, and, indeed, maybe nothing to have been remembered), and the later existence of this baby, in a sense bodily continuous with his present body, would be a matter of indifference to him. So, I argued, nothing is being done to the fetus that he would object to having done if he understood the situation.

What do I think is necessary in order for the continuation of my body with its conscious experiences to be worthwhile? One thing is that it is able to remember the events I can now remember; another is that it takes some interest in the projects I am now planning and remembers them as my projects; another is that it recognizes my friends and has warm feelings for them, and so on. Reflection on these states of a future continuation of my body with its experiences is what makes the idea motivating. But such motivating reflection for a newborn is impossible: he has no memories that he wants recalled later; he has no plans to execute; he has no warm feelings for other persons. He has simply not had the length of life necessary for these to come about. Not only that: the conception of these things cannot be motivating because the concept of some state of affairs being motivating requires roughly a past experience in which similar states of affairs were satisfying, and he has not lived long enough for the requisite conditioning to have taken place. (The most one could say is that the image of warm milk in his mouth is attractive; he might answer affirmatively if it could be put to him whether he would be aversive to the idea of no more warm milk.) So we can say not merely that the newborn does not want the continuation of himself as a subject of experiences (he has not the conceptual framework for this), he does not want *anything* that his own survival would promote. It is like the case of the operation: there is nothing I want that the survival of my brain with no memory would promote. Give the newborn as much *conceptual* framework as you like; the *wants* are not there, which could give significance to the continuance of his life.

The newborn, then, is bound to be *indifferent* to the idea of a continuation of the stream of his experiences, even if he clearly has the idea of that. It seems we can know this about him.

The truth of all this is still not for it to be the case that the newborn, defective or not, gives *consent* to, or expresses a preference for, the termination of his life. *Consent* is a performance, normally linguistic, but always requiring some conventional *sign.* A newborn, who has not yet learned how to signalize consent, cannot give consent. And it may be thought that this difference makes all the difference.

In order to see what difference it does make in this case, we should ask what makes adult consent morally important. Why is it that we think euthanasia can be practiced on an adult only if he gives his consent, at least his implied consent (e.g., by previous statements)? There seem to be two reasons. The first is that a person is more likely to be concerned with his own welfare, and to take steps to secure it, than are others, even his good friends. Giving an individual control over his own life, and not permitting others to take control except when he consents, is normally to promote his welfare. An individual may, of course, behave stupidly or shortsightedly, but we think that on the whole a person's welfare is best secured if decisions about it are in his hands; and it is best for society in the normal case (not for criminals, etc.) if persons' own lives are well-served. The second reason is the feeling of security a person can have if he knows the major decisions about himself are in his own hands. When they are not, a person can easily, and in some cases very reasonably, suppose that other persons may well be able to do something to him that he would

very much like them not to do. He does not have to worry about that if he knows they cannot do it without his consent.

Are things different with the newborn? At least he, like the fetus, is not yet able to suffer from insecurity; he cannot worry about what others may do to him. So the second reason for requiring consent cannot have any importance in his case. His situation is thus very unlike that of the senile adult, for an adult can worry about what others may do to him if they judge him senile. And this worry can well cast a shadow over a lot of life. But how about the first reason? Here matters are more complex. In the case of children, we think their own lives are better cared for if certain decisions are in the hands of others; the child may not want to visit the dentist, but the parents know that his best interests are served by going, and they make him go. The same for compulsory school attendance. And the same for the newborn. But there is another point: that society has an interest, at certain crucial points, that may not be served by doing just exactly what is for the lifelong interest of the newborn. There are huge costs that are relevant, in the case of the defective newborn. I shall go into that problem in a moment. It seems, then, that in the case of the newborn, *consent* cannot have the moral importance that it has in the case of adults.

On the other hand, then, the newborn will not *care* whether his life is terminated, even if he understands his situation perfectly; and, on the other hand, consent does not have the moral importance in his case that it has for adults. So, while it seems true that we would feel better about permitting termination of defective newborns if only they could give rational and deliberated consent and gave it, nevertheless when we bear the foregoing two points in mind, the absence of consent does not seem morally crucial in their case. We can understand why rational persons deciding which moral code to support for their society would not make the giving of consent a necessary condition for feeling free to terminate an infant's life when such action was morally indicated by the other features of the situation.

REPLACEMENT IN ORDER TO GET A BETTER LIFE

Let us now think of an example owing to Derek Parfit. Suppose a woman wants a child, but is told that if she conceives a child now it will be defective, whereas if she waits three months she will produce a normal child. Obviously we think it would be wrong for the mother not to delay. (If she delays, the child she will have is not the *same* child as the one she would have had if she had not delayed, but it will have a better life.) This is the sole reason why we think she should delay and have the later-born child.

Suppose, however, a woman conceives but discovers only three months later that the fetus will become a defective child, but that she can have a normal child if she has an abortion and tries again. Now this time there is still the same reason for having the abortion that there formerly was for the delay: that she will produce a child with a better life. Ought she not then to have the abortion? If the child's life is bad, he could well complain that he had been injured by deliberately being brought to term. Would he complain if he were aborted, in favor of the later normal child? Not if the argument of the preceding section is correct.

But now suppose the woman does not discover until after she gives birth, that the child is severely defective, but that she could conceive again and have a normal child. Are things really different, in the first few days? One might think that a benevolent person would want, in each of these cases, the substitution of a normal child for the defective one, of the better life for the worse one.

THE COST AND ITS RELEVANCE

It is agreed that the burden of care for a defective infant, say one born with spina bifida, is huge. The cost of surgery alone for an infant with spina bifida has been estimated to be around $275,000.[4] In many places this cost must be met by the family of the child, and there is the additional cost of care in an institution, if the child's condition does not permit care at home—and a very modest estimate of the monthly cost at present is $1,100. To meet even the surgical costs, not to mention monthly payments for continuing care, the lives of members of the family must be at a most spartan level for many years. The psychological effects of this, and equally, if not more so, of care provided at home, are far-reaching; they are apt to destroy the marriage and to cause psychological problems for the siblings. There is the on-going anxiety, the regular visits, the continuing presence of a caretaker if the child is in the home. In one way or another the continued existence of the child is apt to reduce dramatically the quality of life of the family as a whole.

It can be and has been argued that such costs, while real, are irrelevant to the moral problem of what should be done.[5] It is obvious, however, that rational persons, when deciding which moral code to support, would take these human costs into account. As indeed they should: the parents and siblings are also human beings with lives to live, and any sacrifices a given law or moral system might call on them to make must be taken into account in deciding between laws and moral codes. Everyone will feel sympathy for a helpless newborn; but everyone should also think, equally vividly, of all the others who will suffer and just how they will suffer—and, of course, as indicated above, of just what kind of life the defective newborn will have in any case. There is a choice here between allowing a newborn to die (possibly a favor to it, and in any case not a serious loss), and imposing a very heavy burden on the family for many years to come.

Philosophers who think the cost to others is irrelevant to what should be done should reflect that we do not accept the general principle that lives should be saved at no matter what cost. For instance, ships are deliberately built with only a certain margin of safety; that could be built so that they would hardly sink in any storm, but to do so would be economically unfeasible. We do not think we should require a standard of safety for automobiles that goes beyond a certain point of expense and inconvenience; we are prepared to risk a few extra deaths. And how about the lives we are willing to lose in war, in order to assure a certain kind of economic order or democracy or free speech? Surely there is a point at which the loss of a life (or the abbreviation of a life) and the cost to others become comparable. Is it obvious that the continuation of a marginal kind of life for a child takes moral precedence over providing a college education for one or more of his siblings? Some comparisons will be hard to make, but continuing even a marginally pleasant life hardly has absolute priority.

DRAWING LINES

There are two questions that must be answered in any complete account of what is the morally right thing to do about defective newborns.

The first is: If a decision to terminate is made, how soon must it be made? Obviously it could not be postponed to the age of five, or of three, or even a year and a half. At those ages, all the reasons for insisting on consent are already cogent. And at those ages, the child will already care what happens to him. But ten days is tolerable. Doubtless advances in medicine will permit detection of serious prospective defects early in pregnancy, and this issue of how many days will not arise.

Second, the argument from the quality of the prospective life of the defective newborn requires that we decide which defects are so serious that the kind of life the defective child can have gives it no serious claim as compared with the social costs. This issue must be thought through, and some guidelines established, but I shall not attempt this here.

One might argue that, if the newborn cannot rationally care whether its life ends or not, the parents are free to dispose of a child irrespective of whether he is defective, if they simply do not want it. To this there are two replies. First, in practice there are others who want a child if the parents do not, and they can put it up for adoption. But second, the parents are *injuring* a child if they prevent it from having the good life it could have had. We do not in general accept the argument that a person is free to injure another, for no reason, even if he has that person's consent. In view of these facts, we may expect that rational, benevolent persons deciding which moral code to support would select one that required respect for the life of a normal child, but would permit the termination of the life of a seriously defective child.

ACTIVE AND PASSIVE PROCEDURES

There is a final question: that of a choice between withdrawal of life-supporting measures (such as feeding), and the active, painless taking of life. It seems obvious, however, that once the basic decision is made that an infant is not to receive the treatment necessary to sustain life beyond a few days, it is mere stupid cruelty to allow it to waste away gradually in a hospital bed—for the child to suffer, and for everyone involved also to suffer in watching the child suffer. If death is the outcome decided upon, it is far kinder for it to come quickly and painlessly.

Footnotes

1. Here I disagree with Michael Tooley, "Abortion and Infanticide," *Philosophy and Public Affairs* 2 (1972): 37–65, especially pp. 44–49.

2. Professor P. Foot has made interesting remarks on when a life is worth living. See her "Euthanasia," *Philosophy and Public Affairs,* 6 (1977): 85–112, especially pp. 95–96. She suggests that a good life must "contain a minimum of basic goods," although not necessarily a favorable balance of good over evil elements. When does she think this minimum fails? For one thing, in extreme senility or severe brain damage. She also cites as examples of conditions for minimal goods that "a man is not driven to work far beyond his capacity; that he has the support of a family or community; that he can more or less satisfy his hunger; that he has hopes for the future; that he can lie down to rest at night." Overwhelming pain or nausea, or crippling depression, she says, also can make life not worth living. All of these, of course, except for cases of senility and brain damage, are factors fixing whether stretches of living are highly unpleasant.

If a person thinks that life is not good unless it realizes certain human potentialities, he will think life can be bad even if liked—and so far sets a higher standard than the happiness criterion. But Foot and such writers may say that even when life is not pleasant on balance, it can still be good if human potentialities are being realized or these basic minimal conditions are met; and in that sense they set a lower standard.

3. Richard B. Brandt, "The Morality of Abortion," in an earlier form in *The Monist* 56 (1972): 504–526, and in revised form in R.L. Perkins, ed., *Abortion: Pro and Con* (Cambridge, MA: Schenkman Publishing Co., 1974).

4. See A.M. Shaw and I.A. Shaw, in S. Gorovitz, et al., *Moral Problems in Medicine* (Englewood Cliffs, NJ: Prentice-Hall, Inc., 1976), pp. 335–341.

5. See, for instance, Philippa Foot, "Euthanasia," especially pp. 109–111. She writes: "So it is not for their sake but to avoid trouble to others that they are allowed to die. When brought out into the open this seems unacceptable; at least we do not easily accept the principle that adults who need special care should be counted too burdensome to be kept alive." I would think that "to avoid trouble to others" is hardly the terminology to describe the havoc that is apt to be produced. I agree that adults should not be allowed to die, or actively killed, without their consent, possibly except when they cannot give consent but are in great pain; but the reasons that justify different behavior in the two situations have appeared in the section, "Consent."

Review Questions

1. According to Brandt, how should one answer questions about moral rightness?

2. According to Brandt, why can't the Biblical injunction "Thou shalt not kill" be taken seriously?

3. Explain Brandt's "happiness criterion."

4. In Brandt's view, in what cases would the life of a defective infant be bad?

5. Why would a newborn be indifferent to continued life according to Brandt?

6. In Brandt's view, why is it better to replace a defective child with a normal one?

7. According to Brandt, why is active euthanasia better than passive euthanasia in some cases?

Discussion Questions

1. Is Brandt's "happiness criterion" acceptable? Defend your view.

2. Is the cost of caring for a defective infant morally relevant? Defend your position.

3. Do you agree that in some cases active euthanasia is better than passive euthanasia? Why or why not?

Problem Cases

1. The Case of Karen Quinlan On the night of April 15, 1975, for reasons still unclear, Karen Quinlan ceased breathing. She was at a birthday party, and after a few drinks, she passed out. Her friends thought she was drunk and put her to bed. Later they discovered that she had stopped breathing. Her friends gave her mouth-to-mouth resuscitation and took her to the nearest hospital. There she had a temperature of 100 degrees, her pupils did not react to stimulus, and she did not respond to even deep pain.

Blood and urine tests showed that Karen had not consumed a dangerous amount of alcohol. A small amount of aspirin and the tranquilizer Valium was present, but not enough to be toxic or lethal. Why Karen had stopped breathing was a mystery. It was clear that part of her brain had died from oxygen deprivation.

After a week of unconsciousness, she was moved to St. Clare's Hospital in nearby Denville where she was examined by Dr. Robert J. Morse, a neurologist. Dr. Morse found that she was in a "chronic persistent vegetative state," but not brain dead by the ordinary medical standard. It was judged that no form of treatment could restore her to cognitive life.

Nevertheless, she was kept breathing by means of a respirator that pumped air through a tube in her throat, and fed by means of a nasal-gastro tube. Her condition began to deteriorate. Her weight dropped to seventy pounds, and her five-foot-two-inch frame bent into a rigid fetal position about three feet in length. After a few months, her father, Joseph Quinlan, asked to be appointed her legal guardian with the expressed purpose of requesting that the use of the respirator be discontinued. Experts testified that there was a strong likelihood that death would follow the removal of the respirator. The lower court refused his request that the respirator be discontinued; it said that "to do so would be homicide and an act of euthanasia." But in a famous decision (Supreme Court of New Jersey 355 A.2d 647), the Supreme Court of New Jersey granted the request on the condition that (1) attending physicians of Joseph Quinlan's choice conclude that there was no reasonable possibility of Karen being restored to cognitive life, and (2) the ethics committee of the institution where Karen was hospitalized concurred in the physician's judgment.

Do you agree with the Supreme Court of New Jersey decision? Why or why not?

2. The Case of Karen Quinlan Continued Six weeks after the court decision the respirator still had not been turned off because the attending physicians, Dr. Robert Morse, the neurologist, and Dr. Javed, a pulmonary internist, were reluctant to do so. After Mr. Quinlan demanded that they remove her from the respirator, they agree to wean her slowly from the machine. Soon she was breathing without mechanical assistance, and she was moved to a chronic-care hospital.

At this point, would it have been morally right, in your opinion, to give Karen a fatal injection of morphine? Explain your answer.

3. Karen Quinlan as Irreversibly Comatose For about ten years Karen was kept alive in the Morris View Nursing Home with high-nutrient feedings and regular doses of antibiotics to prevent infections. During this time she never regained consciousness, but sometimes she made reflexive responses to touch and sound. After about ten years of comatose existence, Karen Quinlan died.

Would it have been morally right, during this long comatose period, to withhold the antibiotics so that she would die from infections? Defend your view.

Was it a good idea to keep her alive for the ten years? Why or why not?

Was her death a good thing? How would you evaluate it?

4. The Case of George Zygmaniak (Taken from Peter Singer, *Practical Ethics* [Cambridge: Cambridge University Press, 1979], 128). In 1973 George Zygmaniak was injured in a motorcycle accident near his home in New Jersey. He was taken to a hospital, where he was found to be totally

paralysed from the neck down. He was also in considerable pain. He told his doctor and his brother, Lester, that he did not want to live in this condition. He begged them both to kill him. Lester questioned the doctor and the hospital staff about George's prospects of recovery; he was told that they were nil. Then he smuggled a gun into the hospital, and said to his brother, "I am here to end your pain, George. Is it all right with you?" George, who was now unable to speak because of an operation to assist his breathing, nodded his assent. Lester shot him through the temple and killed him.

It is undeniable that Lester's action was illegal; the law in New Jersey, as in most states, regards active euthanasia as murder. But was it morally wrong? Explain your position on this.

Suppose you were in the jury at Lester's trial for murder. Would you find him guilty or not? If guilty, then what should his sentence be? If not guilty, then what is the justification for this decision?

5. The Case of Baby Jane Doe In October 1983, Baby Jane Doe (as the infant was called by the court to protect her anonymity) was born with spina bifida and a host of other congenital defects. According to the doctors consulted by the parents, the child would be severely mentally retarded, bedridden, and suffer considerable pain. After consultations with doctors and religious counselors, Mr. and Mrs. A (as the parents were called in the court documents) decided not to consent to life-saving surgery.

Did the parents make the right decision? Explain and defend your position.

6. The Baby Doe Case Continued A right-to-life activist lawyer tried to legally force life-saving surgery in the Baby Doe case, but two New York appeals courts and a state children's agency decided not to override the parent's right to make a decision in the case. At this point, the United States Justice Department intervened in the case. It sued to obtain records from the University Hospital in Stony Brook, New York to determine if the hospital had violated a federal law that forbids discrimination against the handicapped. Dr. C. Everett Koop, the United States Surgeon General, appeared on television to express the view that the government has the moral obligation to intercede on behalf of such infants in order to protect their right to life.

Two weeks later, Federal District Judge Leonard Wexler threw out the Justice Department's unusual suit. Wexler found no discrimination. The hospital had been willing to do the surgery, but had failed to do so because the parents refused to consent to the surgery. Wexler found the parent's decision to be a reasonable one in view of the circumstances.

The day after the ruling, the Justice Department appealed. On January 9, 1984, federal regulations were issued preventing federally funded hospitals from withholding treatment in such cases.

Do parents have a right to make life and death decisions for their defective children? Why or why not?

Do you agree with Dr. Koop that the government has a moral obligation to save the lives of such infants, even when their parents do not wish it? Explain your position.

If the government forces us to save the lives of defective infants like Baby Doe, then should it assume the responsibility for the cost of surgery, intensive care, and so on? If so, then how much money should be spent on this program? If not, then who is going to pay the bills?

Suggested Readings

(1) Engelhardt, H. Tristram, Jr. "Ethical Issues in Aiding the Death of Young Children." In *Beneficent Euthanasia.* edited by Marvin Kohl, 180–192. Buffalo, NY: Prometheus Books, 1975. Engelhardt distinguishes between adult euthanasia and euthanasia of children. He assumes that adult euthanasia can be justified by the appeal to freedom. Adults have a right to choose to die. But, Engelhardt claims, children do not have this right because they are not persons in a strict sense; they are persons only in a social sense. He argues that child euthanasia is justified when parents decide that the child has little chance of a full human life and a great chance of suffering, and the cost of prolonging life is great.

(2) Foot, Philippa. "Euthanasia." *Philosophy and Public Affairs* 6 (Winter 1977): 85–112. Foot defines euthanasia as producing a death (by act or omission) that is good for the one who dies. She distinguishes between voluntary and nonvoluntary euthanasia, and between active and passive euthanasia. The latter distinction is based on the right to life and the correlative duty of noninterference. This duty is usually violated by active euthanasia but not by passive euthanasia. She finds that nonvoluntary active euthanasia is never justified; however, she allows that the other types can be justified in some cases.

(3) _____. "The Problem of Abortion and the Doctrine of the Double Effect." Oxford Review no. 5: 5–15. Foot gives a classic discussion of the doctrine of double effect. As Foot defines it, this is the doctrine that it is permissible to bring about by oblique intention (that is, to foresee as a consequence of action, but to not directly intend) what is wrong to directly intend. Appealing to this doctrine, conservatives hold that it is permissible to perform an abortion to save the mother's life since the direct intention is to save the mother's life and the death of the fetus is only indirectly or obliquely intended (to use Foot's example).

(4) Glover, Jonathan. *Causing Death and Saving Lives,* 182–189. Harmondsworth, Middlesex, England: Penguin Books, Ltd., 1977. Glover applies utilitarianism to the problem of euthanasia and to other problems of killing such as abortion and capital punishment.

(5) Kohl, Marvin, ed. *Beneficent Euthanasia.* Buffalo, NY: Prometheus Books, 1975. This anthology has a number of excellent articles on euthanasia.

_____. ed. *Infanticide and the Value of Life.* Buffalo, NY: Prometheus Books, 1978. This anthology concentrates on the morality of euthanasia for severely defective newborns.

(6) Ladd, John. "Positive and Negative Euthanasia." In *Ethical Issues Relating to Life & Death,* edited by John Ladd, 164–186. Oxford: Oxford University Press, 1979. Ladd prefers to talk about positive euthanasia instead of active euthanasia, and negative euthanasia instead of passive euthanasia. He rejects two positions, the absolutist position that a clear-cut and absolute distinction can be made between killing and letting die, and the consequentialist position that the consequences of killing and letting die are the same. Therefore, the consequentialist sees no significant moral difference between the two. His own position is called a contextual position; it is the view that the distinction always depends on the context.

(7) Rachels, James. "Active and Passive Euthanasia." *The New England Journal of Medicine* 292 (Jan. 9, 1975): 78–80. This paper is attacked by Thomas D. Sullivan; it is a shorter version of Rachels' "Euthanasia, Killing and Letting Die."

(8) ———. "More Impertinent Distinctions." In *Biomedical Ethics* edited by T.A. Mappes and J.S. Zembaty, 355–359. New York: McGraw-Hill, Inc., 1981. This article is a response to Sullivan's view.

(9) Robertson, John A. "Involuntary Euthanasia of Defective Newborns." *Stanford Law Review* vol. 27 (Jan. 1975): 213–261. In opposition to Engelhardt, Brandt, and others, Robertson argues that the utilitarian or consequentialist defense of euthanasia for defective newborns does not succeed in showing that euthanasia is justified.

(10) Sullivan, Thomas D. "Active and Passive Euthanasia: An Impertinent Distinction?" *Human Life Review* III (Summer 1977): 40–46. Sullivan defends the AMA statement against Rachels' attack in "Active and Passive Euthanasia." He argues that Rachels' distinction between active and passive euthanasia is impertinent and irrelevant.

(11) Young, Robert. "Voluntary and Nonvoluntary Euthanasia." *The Monist* 59 (April 1976): 2264–82. Young reviews a number of arguments used to show that voluntary active euthanasia is not justified, and he concludes that none of them are successful.

Glossary

Chemotherapy   the treatment of a disease with chemical substances.

Capillaries   minute, thin-walled blood vessels of the body.

Down's syndrome   a congenital idiocy in which the child is born with slanting eyes, a broad, short skull, and broad hands with short fingers. Also called *mongolism.*

Hydrocephalus   an abnormal increase in the amount of cerebrospinal fluid within the cranial cavity which causes an enlargement of the skull.

Meningitis   a disease in which inflamation of the meninges (the membranes enveloping the brain and spinal cord) occurs.

Mongoloid   a child suffering from mongolism or Down's syndrome. See *Down's syndrome*

Potassium chloride   a crystalline salt used chiefly as a fertilizer; this substance is a poison.

Principle of double effect (or doctrine of double effect)   a traditional doctrine that makes a distinction between two effects of an action, an unintended but foreseen consequence, and an intended consequence. According to this doctrine, a foreseen evil consequence of an action is allowable provided it is unintended, and provided that the intended consequence is good. *See* Foot (3) in the Suggested Readings.

Radiotheraphy   treatment of a disease by means of X rays or radioactive substances such as radium.

Respirator   a mechanical device that maintains breathing artificially.

Semantics   the study of linguistic meanings.

Spina bifida   a congenital cleft of the vertebral column with protrusion of the meninges, the membranes enveloping the brain and the spinal cord.

Chapter 3

Capital Punishment

Introduction

The Eighth Amendment to the Constitution of the United States prohibits "cruel and unusual" punishment. Is the death penalty an example of cruel and unusual punishment, and thus unconstitutional? This is a matter of debate. In the case of *Furman* v. *Georgia* (1972), the Supreme Court ruled (by a five-to-four majority) that the death penalty was unconstitutional because it was being administered in an arbitrary and capricious manner. Juries were allowed to inflict the death sentence without any explicit guidelines or standards, and the result was that blacks were much more likely to receive the sentence than whites.

After the *Furman* decision, states wishing to retain the death sentence reacted in two ways. One way was to meet the objection about standardless discretion of juries by making the death penalty mandatory for certain crimes. But in *Woodson* v. *North Carolina* (1976), the Court ruled (again by a mere five-to-four majority) that mandatory death sentences are unconstitutional.

The second approach to the objection raised in *Furman* was to provide standards for juries. Georgia specified in its law ten statutory aggravating circumstances, one of which had to be found by the jury to exist beyond reasonable doubt before a death sentence could be imposed. This second approach proved to be successful. For in *Gregg* v. *Georgia* (1976), the majority ruled, with only Justice Marshall and Justice Brennan dissenting, that the death penalty is not unconstitutional for the crime of murder, provided there are safeguards against any arbitrary or capricious imposition by juries.

But why isn't the death penalty cruel and unusual? In their majority opinion, Justices

Stewart, Powell, and Stevens answered this important question. First, they gave an explanation of *cruel and unusual*. In their view, a punishment is cruel and unusual if it either fails to accord with "evolving standards of decency" or fails to accord with the "dignity of man" that is the "basic concept underlying the Eighth Amendment." This second stipulation rules out "excessive" punishment that involves unnecessary pain or is disproportionate to the crime. Second, they argued that the death penalty does not satisfy either of these stipulations. It is acceptable to the majority of the people, since thirty-five states have statutes providing for the death penalty, and it is not excessive because it achieves two important social purposes, retribution and deterrence.

Retribution   To fully understand the appeal to retribution, it is necessary to examine the theory on which it is based, namely retributivism. The classical formulation of this theory was given by the eighteenth-century German philosopher Immanuel Kant (8). According to Kant, the only justification for punishing a person is guilt. If a person is guilty of a crime, then he or she must be punished; and if a person is not guilty, then no punishment is justified. In other words, guilt is both a necessary and a sufficient condition for punishment. Furthermore, in Kant's view the punishment must fit the crime, or be proportionate to the crime, according to the traditional principle of retaliation (**lex talionis**) that says, "life for life, eye for eye, tooth for tooth." Now what punishment fits the crime of murder in this principle? Kant insists that death, and only death, is the proper punishment for murder; no other punishment will satisfy the requirements of legal justice.

But why must a criminal be punished? Why is it necessary for a criminal to pay for his or her crime? After all, punishing the criminal causes suffering, and suffering is bad. Walter Berns tries to explain why

criminals must be paid back for their crimes, and in particular why murderers must pay with their lives. In Bern's view, this punishment is an expression of anger, but this anger is morally right because it serves justice, and it acknowledges the humanity of the criminal by holding the criminal responsible for his or her actions.

Various objections have been made to the retributive view. Glover thinks that it leads to what he considers to be pointless suffering. With pointless suffering there are no real benefits to either the person punished or other people. But the retributivist can reply that punishment does provide an important benefit, namely that justice is served by giving the criminal the punishment he or she deserves. If punishment is not given, then people will not be held accountable for their actions, nor will they realize the consequences of their deeds.

Anthony G. Amsterdam rejects the principle of strict retaliation according to which there must be "an eye for an eye, a life for a life." He claims that appealing to this principle does not justify capital punishment because of the simple fact that most murderers are not executed but just sent to prison. Obviously we think that many crimes of murder do not deserve the death penalty; for example, we do not have the death sentence for homicides that are unpremeditated or accidental. Another objection to the strict principle of retaliation made by Hugo Adam Bedau (1) is that we do have the death sentence for nonhomicidal crimes such as treason. This shows that the death sentence can be justified for crimes other than murder.

The principle of strict retaliation can be revised to say that the punishment should fit the crime, so that serious crimes are severely punished. But as Amsterdam points out, this does not tell us how severely we ought to punish any particular crime. Should we punish vicious murderers by burning them at the stake or boiling them in oil? Now it seems that retributivism can be used to justify punishment that is indeed cruel.

But retributivism can be defended against the charge that it justifies cruel and unusual punishment. Perhaps it does not even justify the death sentence after all. According to Robert S. Gerstein, retributivism requires us to punish a member of the community who has acted unjustly, but there are limits to the severity of the punishment. We must treat the criminal with the respect due to a member of the community, and because of this requirement, it may be that we cannot deliberately kill a person because such a punishment might show a lack of respect for the moral worth and dignity of the person.

Deterrence   The appeal to deterrence is an appeal to the social benefits of punishment. The particular social benefits claimed for the death penalty by its defenders are deterrence and prevention: It deters other potential criminals from killing, and it prevents the criminal who is executed from committing further crimes. But does the death penalty actually have these consequences? This is a factual question that is much debated.

Amsterdam reviews some of the evidence for the death penalty being a deterrent and he finds it to be inconclusive—it does not show that the death penalty is a better deterrent than life imprisonment for murder. Amsterdam also discusses and rejects the appeal to intuition, namely, that the fear of death would intuitively seem to deter potential murderers.

Glover argues that capital punishment has not been shown to be a substantial deterrent, and that there is a strong presumption against it because of its special evils and bad side effects.

Bedau claims that the verdict of scientists who have studied the issue is that the deterrence achieved by the death penalty is not measurably greater than the deterrence achieved by life imprisonment. As for preventing convicted murderers from killing again, Bedau asserts that there is little evidence that the death sentence does this. In fact, less than one convicted murderer in a hundred commits another murder.

Hook (7) does not agree that the death penalty should never be applied. He thinks that there are two cases in which the death sentence is justified. One is the case in which a defendant convicted of murder chooses the death sentence rather than life imprisonment. Hook is assuming, of course, that the satisfaction of the criminal's desire is good, and that we ought to do what is good. The second case is one in which a criminal who has been sentenced to prison for premeditated murder commits another murder. Such a second offender ought to get the death sentence because it is likely that this criminal will kill again and again, and this should be prevented.

The Supreme Court
Gregg v. Georgia (1976)

Potter Stewart, Lewis F. Powell, Jr., and John Paul

Stevens are associate justices of the United States Supreme Court. (Justice Powell has recently announced his retirement.) Justice Stewart, a graduate of Yale Law School, was appointed to the Court in 1958. Justice Powell, LL.M (Harvard), was appointed in 1971. Justice Stevens graduated from Northwestern University School of Law, and was appointed to the Court in 1975. Thurgood Marshall, associate justice of the United States Supreme Court, was appointed in 1967; he was the first black person ever to be appointed.

The main issue before the Court in the case of Gregg *v.* Georgia *(1976) was whether or not the death penalty violates the Eighth Amendment prohibition of cruel and unusual punishment. The majority of the Court, with Justice Marshall and Justice Brennan dissenting, held that the death penalty does not violate the Eighth Amendment because it is in accord with contemporary standards of decency. It serves both a deterrent and retributive purpose, and in the case of the Georgia law being reviewed, it is no longer arbitrarily applied.*

In his dissenting opinion, Justice Marshall objects that the death sentence is excessive because a less severe penalty—life imprisonment—would accomplish the legitimate purposes of punishment. In reply to the claim that the death sentence is necessary for deterrence, Marshall asserts that the available evidence shows that this is not the case. As for the appeal to retribution, Marshall argues that the purely retributive justification for the death penalty is not consistent with human dignity.

The issue in this case is whether the imposition of the sentence of death for the crime of murder under the law of Georgia violates the Eighth and Fourteenth Amendments.

I

The petitioner, Troy Gregg, was charged with committing armed robbery and murder. In accordance with Georgia procedure in capital cases, the trial was in two stages, a guilt stage and a sentencing stage. . . .

. . . The jury found the petitioner guilty of two counts of armed robbery and two counts of murder.

At the penalty stage, which took place before the same jury, . . . the trial judge instructed the jury that it could recommend either a death sentence or a life prison sentence on each count. . . . The jury returned verdicts of death on each count.

The Supreme Court of Georgia affirmed the convictions and the imposition of the

death sentences for murder. . . . The death sentences imposed for armed robbery, however, were vacated on the grounds that the death penalty had rarely been imposed in Georgia for that offense. . . .

II

. . . The Georgia statute, as amended after our decision in *Furman* v. *Georgia* (1972), retains the death penalty for six categories of crime: murder, kidnaping for ransom or where the victim is harmed, armed robbery, rape, treason, and aircraft hijacking. . . .

III

We address initially the basic contention that the punishment of death for the crime of murder is, under all circumstances, "cruel and unusual" in violation of the Eighth and Fourteenth Amendments of the Constitution. In Part IV of this opinion, we will consider the sentence of death imposed under the Georgia statutes at issue in this case.

The Court on a number of occasions has both assumed and asserted the constitutionality of capital punishment. In several cases that assumption provided a necessary foundation for the decision, as the Court was asked to decide whether a particular method of carrying out a capital sentence would be allowed to stand under the Eighth Amendment. But until *Furman* v. *Georgia* (1972), the Court never confronted squarely the fundamental claim that the punishment of death always, regardless of the enormity of the offense or the procedure followed in imposing the sentence, is cruel and unusual punishment in violation of the Constitution. Although this issue was presented and addressed in *Furman*, it was not resolved by the Court. Four Justices would have held that capital punishment is not unconstitutional *per se*; two Justices would have reached the opposite conclusion; and three Justices, while agreeing that the statutes then before the Court were invalid as applied, left open the question whether such punishment may ever be imposed. We now hold that the punishment of death does not invariably violate the Constitution.

A

The history of the prohibition of "cruel and unusual" punishment already has been reviewed at length. The phrase first appeared in the English Bill of Rights of 1689, which was drafted by Parliament at the accession of William and Mary. The English version appears to have been directed against punishments unauthorized by statute and beyond the jurisdiction of the sentencing court, as well as those disproportionate to the offense involved. The American draftsmen, who adopted the English phrasing in drafting the Eighth Amendment, were primarily concerned, however, with proscribing "tortures" and other "barbarous" methods of punishment.

In the earliest cases raising Eighth Amendment claims, the Court focused on particular methods of execution to determine whether they were too cruel to pass constitutional muster. The constitutionality of the sentence of death itself was not at issue, and the criterion used to evaluate the mode of execution was its similarity to "torture" and other "barbarous" methods. . . .

But the Court has not confined the prohibition embodied in the Eighth Amendment to "barbarous" methods that were generally outlawed in the 18th century. Instead, the Amendment has been interpreted in a flexible and dynamic manner. The Court early recognized that "a principle to be vital must be capable of wider application than the mischief which gave it birth." Thus the clause forbidding "cruel and unusual" punishments "is not fastened to the obsolete but may acquire meaning as public opinion becomes enlightened by a humane justice." . . .

It is clear from the foregoing precedents that the Eighth Amendment has not been regarded as a static concept. As Mr. Chief Justice Warren said, in an oftquoted phrase, "[t]he Amendment must draw its meaning from the evolving standards of decency that mark the progress of a maturing society." Thus, an assessment of contemporary values concerning the infliction of a challenged sanction is relevant to the application of the Eighth Amendment. As we develop below more fully, this assessment does not call for a subjective judgment. It requires, rather, that we look to objective indicia that reflect the public attitude toward a given sanction.

But our cases also make clear that public perceptions of standards of decency with respect to criminal sanctions are not conclusive. A penalty also must accord with "the dignity of man," which is the "basic concept underlying the Eighth Amendment." This means, at least, that the punishment not be "excessive." When a form of punishment in the abstract (in this case, whether capital punishment may ever be imposed as a sanction for murder) rather than in the particular (the propriety of death as a penalty to be applied to a specific defendant for a specific crime) is under consideration, the inquiry into "excessiveness" has two aspects. First, the punishment must not involve the unnecessary and wanton infliction of pain. Second, the punishment must not be grossly out of proportion to the severity of the crime.

B

Of course, the requirements of the Eighth Amendment must be applied with an awareness of the limited role to be played by the courts. This does not mean that judges have no role to play, for the Eighth Amendment is a restraint upon the exercise of legislative power. . . .

But, while we have an obligation to ensure that constitutional bounds are not overreached, we may not act as judges as we might as legislators. . . .

Therefore, in assessing a punishment selected by a democratically elected legislature against the constitutional measure, we presume its validity. We may not require the legislature to select the least severe penalty possible so long as the penalty selected is not cruelly inhumane or disproportionate to the crime involved. And a heavy burden rests on those who would attack the judgment of the representatives of the people.

This is true in part because the constitutional test is intertwined with an assessment of contemporary standards and the legislative judgment weighs heavily in ascertaining such standards. "[I]n a democratic society legislatures, not courts, are constituted to respond to the will and consequently the moral values of the people."

The deference we owe to the decisions of the state legislatures under our federal system is enhanced where the specification of punishments is concerned, for "these are peculiarly questions of legislative policy." Caution is necessary lest this Court become, "under the aegis of the Cruel and Unusual Punishment Clause, the ultimate arbiter of the standards of criminal responsibility ... throughout the country." A decision that a given punishment is impermissible under the Eighth Amendment cannot be reversed short of a constitutional amendment. The ability of the people to express their preference through the normal democratic processes, as well as through ballot referenda, is shut off. Revisions cannot be made in the light of further experience.

C

In the discussion to this point we have sought to identify the principles and considerations that guide a court in addressing an Eighth Amendment claim. We now consider specifically whether the sentence of death for the crime of murder is a *per se* violation of the Eighth and Fourteenth Amendments to the Constitution. We note first that history and precedent strongly support a negative answer to this question.

The imposition of the death penalty for the crime of murder has a long history of acceptance both in the United States and in England. . . .

It is apparent from the text of the Constitution itself that the existence of capital punishment was accepted by the Framers. At the time the Eighth Amendment was ratified, capital punishment was a common sanction in every State. Indeed, the First Congress of the United States enacted legislation providing death as the penalty for specified crimes. . . .

For nearly two centuries, this Court, repeatedly and often expressly, has recognized that capital punishment is not invalid *per se*. . . .

Four years ago, the petitioners in *Furman* and its companion cases predicated their argument primarily upon the asserted proposition that standards of decency had evolved to the point where capital punishment no longer could be tolerated. The petitioners in those cases said, in effect, that the evolutionary process had come to an end, and that standards of decency required that the Eighth Amendment be construed finally as prohibiting capital punishment for any crime regardless of its depravity and impact on society. This view was accepted by two Justices. Three other Justices were unwilling to go so far; focusing on the procedures by which convicted defendants were selected for the death penalty rather than on the actual punishment inflicted, they joined in the conclusion that the statutes before the Court were constitutionally invalid.

The petitioners in the capital cases before the Court today renew the "standards of decency" argument, but developments during the four years since *Furman* have undercut substantially the assumptions upon which their argument rested. Despite the continuing debate, dating back to the nineteenth century, over the morality and utility of capital punishment, it is now evident that a large proportion of American society continues to regard it as an appropriate and necessary criminal sanction.

The most marked indication of society's endorsement of the death penalty for murder is the legislative response to *Furman*. The legislatures of at least thirty-five States have enacted new statutes that provide for the death penalty for at least some crimes that result in the death of another person. And the Congress of the United States, in 1974, enacted a statute providing the death penalty for aircraft piracy that results in death. These recently adopted statutes have attempted to address the concerns expressed by the Court in *Furman* primarily (i) by specifying the factors to be weighed and the procedures to be followed in deciding when to impose a capital sentence, or (ii) by making the death penalty mandatory for specified crimes. But all of the post-*Furman* statutes make clear that capital punishment itself has not been rejected by the elected representatives of the people. . . .

The jury also is a significant and reliable objective index of contemporary values because it is so directly involved. The Court has said that "one of the most important functions any jury can perform in making . . . a selection [between life imprisonment and death for a defendant convicted in a capital case] is to maintain a link between contemporary community values and the penal system." It may be true that evolving standards have influenced juries in recent decades to be more discriminating in imposing the sentence of death. But the relative infrequency of jury verdicts imposing the death sentence does not indicate rejection of capital punishment *per se*. Rather, the reluctance of juries in many cases to impose the sentence may well reflect the humane feeling that this most irrevocable of sanctions should be reserved for a small number of extreme cases. Indeed, the actions of juries in many states since *Furman* are fully compatible with the legislative judgments, reflected in the new statutes, as to the continued utility and necessity of capital punishment in appropriate cases. At the close of 1974 at least 254 persons had been sentenced to death since *Furman*, and by the end of March 1976, more than 460 persons were subject to death sentences.

As we have seen, however, the Eighth Amendment demands more than that a challenged punishment be acceptable to contemporary society. The Court also must ask whether it comports with the basic concept of human dignity at the core of the amendment. Although we cannot "invalidate a category of penalties because we deem less severe penalties adequate to serve the ends of **penology**," the sanction imposed cannot be so totally without penological justification that it results in the gratuitous infliction of suffering.

The death penalty is said to serve two principal social purposes: retribution and deterrence of capital crimes by prospective offenders.[1]

In part, capital punishment is an expression of society's moral outrage at particularly offensive conduct. This function may be unappealing to many, but it is essential in an ordered society that asks its citizens to rely on legal processes rather than self-help to vindicate their wrongs.

The instinct for retribution is part of the nature of man, and channeling that instinct in the administration of criminal justice serves an important purpose in promoting the stability of a society governed by law. When people begin to believe that organized society is unwilling or unable to impose upon criminal offenders the punishment they "deserve," then there are sown the seeds of anarchy—if self-help, vigilante justice, and lynch law. Furman v. Georgia (Stewart, J., concurring).

"Retribution is no longer the dominant objective of the criminal law," but neither is it a forbidden objective nor one inconsistent with our respect for the dignity of men. Indeed, the decision that capital punishment may be the appropriate sanction in extreme cases is an expression of the community's belief that certain crimes are themselves so grievous an affront to humanity that the only adequate response may be the penalty of death.

Statistical attempts to evaluate the worth of the death penalty as a deterrent to crimes by potential offenders have occasioned a great deal of debate. The results simply have been inconclusive. . . .

Although some of the studies suggest that the death penalty may not function as a significantly greater deterrent than lesser penalties, there is no convincing empirical evidence either supporting or refuting this view.

We may nevertheless assume safely that there are murderers, such as those who act in passion, for whom the threat of death has little or no deterrent effect. But for many others, the death penalty undoubtedly is a significant deterrent. There are carefully contemplated murders, such as murder for hire, where the possible penalty of death may well enter into the cold calculus that precedes the decision to act. And there are some categories of murder, such as murder by a life prisoner, where other sanctions may not be adequate.

The value of capital punishment as a deterrent of crime is a complex factual issue the resolution of which properly rests with the legislatures, which can evaluate the results of statistical studies in terms of their own local conditions and with a flexibility of approach that is not available to the courts. Indeed, many of the post-*Furman* statutes reflect just such a responsible effort to define those crimes and those criminals for which capital punishment is most probably an effective deterrent.

In sum, we cannot say that the judgment of the Georgia Legislature that capital punishment may be necessary in some cases is clearly wrong. Considerations of **federalism,** as well as respect for the ability of a legislature to evaluate, in terms of its particular State, the moral consensus concerning the death penalty and its social utility as a sanction, require us to conclude, in the absence of more convincing evidence, that the infliction of death as a punishment for murder is not without justification and thus is not unconstitutionally severe.

Finally, we must consider whether the punishment of death is disproportionate in relation to the crime for which it is imposed. There is no question that death as a punishment is unique in its severity and irrevocability. When a defendant's life is at stake, the Court has been particularly sensitive to insure that every safeguard is observed. But we are concerned here only with the imposition of capital punishment for the crime of murder, and when a life has been taken deliber-

ately by the offender,[2] we cannot say that the punishment is invariably disproportionate to the crime. It is an extreme sanction, suitable to the most extreme of crimes.

We hold that the death penalty is not a form of punishment that may never be imposed, regardless of the circumstances of the offense, regardless of the character of the offender, and regardless of the procedure followed in reaching the decision to impose it.

IV

We now consider whether Georgia may impose the death penalty on the petitioner in this case.

A

While *Furman* did not hold that the infliction of the death penalty *per se* violates the Constitution's ban on cruel and unusual punishments, it did recognize that the penalty of death is different in kind from any other punishment imposed under our system of criminal justice. Because of the uniqueness of the death penalty, *Furman* held that it could not be imposed under sentencing procedures that created a substantial risk that it would be inflicted in an arbitrary and capricious manner. . . .

Furman mandates that where discretion is afforded a sentencing body on a matter so grave as the determination of whether a human life should be taken or spared, that discretion must be suitably directed and limited so as to minimize the risk of wholly arbitrary and capricious action.

It is certainly not a novel proposition that discretion in the area of sentencing be exercised in an informed manner. We have long recognized that "[f]or the determination of sentences, justice generally requires . . . that there be taken into account the circumstances of the offense together with the character and propensities of the offender." . . .

Jury sentencing has been considered desirable in capital cases in order "to maintain a link between contemporary community values and the penal system—a link without which the determination of punishment could hardly reflect 'the evolving standards of decency that mark the progress of a maturing society.' " But it creates special problems. Much of the information that is relevant to the sentencing decision may have no relevance to the question of guilt, or may even be extremely prejudicial to a fair determination of that question. This problem, however, is scarcely insurmountable. Those who have studied the question suggest that a **bifurcated** procedure—one in which the question of sentence is not considered until the determination of guilt has been made—is the best answer. ... When a human life is at stake and when the jury must have information prejudicial to the question of guilt but relevant to the question of penalty in order to impose a rational sentence, a bifurcated system is more likely to ensure elimination of the constitutional deficiencies identified in *Furman.*

But the provision of relevant information under fair procedural rules is not alone sufficient to guarantee that the information will be properly used in the imposition of punishment, especially if sentencing is performed by a jury. Since the members of a jury will have had little, if any, previous experience in sentencing, they are unlikely to be skilled in dealing with the information they are given. To the extent that this problem is inherent in jury sentencing, it may not be totally correctable. It seems clear, however, that the problem will be alleviated if the jury is given guidance regarding the factors about the crime and the defendant that the State, representing organized society, deems particularly relevant to the sentencing decision. ...

While some have suggested that standards to guide a capital jury's sentencing deliberations are impossible to formulate, the fact is that such standards have been developed. When the drafters of the Model Penal Code faced this problem, they concluded "that it is within the realm of possibility to point to the main circumstances of aggravation and of **mitigation** that should be weighed *and weighed against each other* when

they are presented in a concrete case." [3] While such standards are by necessity somewhat general, they do provide guidance to the sentencing authority and thereby reduce the likelihood that it will impose a sentence that fairly can be called capricious or arbitrary. Where the sentencing authority is required to specify the factors it relied upon in reaching its decision, the further safeguard of meaningful **appellate** review is available to ensure that death sentences are not imposed capriciously or in a freakish manner.

In summary, the concerns expressed in *Furman* that the penalty of death not be imposed in an arbitrary or capricious manner can be met by a carefully drafted statute that ensures that the sentencing authority is given adequate information and guidance. As a general proposition these concerns are best met by a system that provides for a bifurcated proceeding at which the sentencing authority is apprised of the information relevant to the imposition of sentence and provided with standards to guide its use of the information.

We do not intend to suggest that only the above-described procedures would be permissible under *Furman* or that any sentencing system constructed along these general lines would inevitably satisfy the concerns of *Furman,* for each distinct system must be examined on an individual basis. Rather, we have embarked upon this general exposition to make clear that it is possible to construct capital-sentencing systems capable of meeting *Furman* 's constitutional concerns.

B

We now turn to consideration of the constitutionality of Georgia's capital-sentencing procedures. In the wake of *Furman,* Georgia amended its capital punishment statute, but chose not to narrow the scope of its murder provisions. Thus, now as before *Furman,* in Georgia "[a] person commits murder when he unlawfully and with malice aforethought, either express or implied, causes the death of another human being." All persons convicted of murder "shall be punished by death or by imprisonment for life."

Georgia did act, however, to narrow the class of murderers subject to capital punishment by specifying ten statutory aggravating circumstances, one of which must be found by the jury to exist beyond a reasonable doubt before a death sentence can ever be imposed. In addition, the jury is authorized to consider any other appropriate aggravating or mitigating circumstances. The jury is not required to find any mitigating circumstance in order to make a recommendation of mercy that is binding on the trial court, but it must find a *statutory* aggravating circumstance before recommending a sentence of death.

These procedures require the jury to consider the circumstances of the crime and the criminal before it recommends sentence. No longer can a Georgia jury do as Furman's jury did: reach a finding of the defendant's guilt and then, without guidance or direction, decide whether he should live or die. Instead, the jury's attention is directed to the specific circumstances of the crime: Was it committed in the course of another capital felony? Was it committed for money? Was it committed upon a peace officer or judicial officer? Was it committed in a particularly **heinous** way or in a manner that endangered the lives of many persons? In addition, the jury's attention is focused on the characteristics of the person who committed the crime: Does he have a record of prior convictions for capital offenses? Are there any special facts about this defendant that mitigate against imposing capital punishment (*e.g.*, his youth, the extent of his cooperation with the police, his emotional state at the time of the crime)? As a result, while some jury discretion still exists, "the discretion to be exercised is controlled by clear and objective standards so as to produce nondiscriminatory application."

As an important additional safeguard against arbitrariness and caprice, the Georgia statutory scheme provides for automatic appeal of all death sentences to the State's Supreme Court. That court is required by statute to review each sentence of death and determine whether it was imposed under the influence of passion or prejudice, whether the evidence supports the jury's finding of a statutory aggravating circumstance, and whether the sentence is disproportionate compared to those sentences imposed in similar cases.

In short, Georgia's new sentencing procedures require as a prerequisite to the imposition of the death penalty, specific jury findings as to the circumstances of the crime or the character of the defendant. Moreover, to guard further against a situation comparable to that presented in *Furman*, the Supreme Court of Georgia compares each death sentence with the sentences imposed on similarly situated defendants to ensure that the sentence of death in a particular case is not disproportionate. On their face these procedures seem to satisfy the concerns of *Furman*. No longer should there be "no meaningful basis for distinguishing the few cases in which [the death penalty] is imposed from the many cases in which it is not." ...

V

The basic concern of *Furman* centered on those defendants who were being condemned to death capriciously and arbitrarily. Under the procedures before the Court in that case, sentencing authorities were not directed to give attention to the nature or circumstances of the crime committed or to the character or record of the defendant. Left unguided, juries imposed the death sentence in a way that could only be called freakish. The new Georgia sentencing procedures, by contrast, focus the jury's attention on the particularized nature of the crime and the particularized characteristics of the individual defendant. While the jury is permitted to consider any aggravating or mitigating circumstances, it must find and identify at least one statutory aggravating factor before it may impose a penalty of death. In this way the jury's discretion is channeled. No longer can a jury wantonly and freakishly impose the death sentence; it is always circumscribed by the legislative guidelines. In addition, the review function of the Supreme Court of Georgia affords additional assurance that the concerns that prompted our decision in *Furman* are not present to any significant degree in the Georgia procedure applied here.

For the reasons expressed in this opinion, we hold that the statutory system under which Gregg was sentenced to death does not violate the Constitution. Accordingly, the judgment of the Georgia Supreme Court is affirmed.

DISSENTING OPINION

In *Furman* v. *Georgia* (1972) (concurring opinion), I set forth at some length my views on the basic issue presented to the Court in [this case]. The death penalty, I concluded, is a cruel and unusual punishment prohibited by the Eighth and Fourteenth Amendments. That continues to be my view.

I have no intention of retracing the "long and tedious journey" that led to my conclusion in *Furman*. My sole purposes here are to consider the suggestion that my conclusion in *Furman* has been undercut by developments since then, and briefly to evaluate the basis for my Brethren's holding that the extinction of life is a permissible form of punishment under the Cruel and Unusual Punishments Clause.

In *Furman* I concluded that the death penalty is constitutionally invalid for two reasons. First, the death penalty is excessive. And second, the American people, fully informed as to the purposes of the death penalty and its liabilities, would in my view reject it as morally unacceptable.

Since the decision in *Furman,* the legislatures of thirty-five States have enacted new statutes authorizing the impositin of the death sentence for certain crimes, and Congress has enacted a law providing the death penalty for air piracy resulting in death. I would be less than candid if I did not acknowledge that these developments have a significant bearing on a realistic assessment of the moral acceptability of the death penal-ty to the American people. But if the constitutionality of the death penalty turns, as I have urged, on the opinion of an *informed* citizenry, then even the enactment of new death statutes cannot be viewed as conclusive. In *Furman,* I observed that the American people are largely unaware of the information critical to a judgment on the morality of the death penalty, and concluded that if they were better informed they would consider it shocking, unjust, and unacceptable. A recent study, conducted after the enactment of the post-*Furman* statutes, has confirmed that the American people know little about the death penalty, and that the opinions of an informed public would differ significantly from those of a public unaware of the consequences and effects of the death penalty.

Even assuming, however, that the post-*Furman* enactment of statutes authorizing the death penalty renders the prediction of the views of an informed citizenry an uncertain basis for a constitutional decision, the enactment of those statutes has no bearing whatsoever on the conclusion that the death penalty is unconstitutional because it is excessive. An excessive penalty is invalid under the Cruel and Unusual Punishments Clause "even though popular sentiment may favor" it. The inquiry here, then, is simply whether the death penalty is necessary to accomplish the legitimate legislative purposes in punishment, or whether a less severe penalty—life imprisonment—would do as well.

The two purposes that sustain the death penalty as nonexcessive in the Court's view are general deterrence and retribution. In *Furman,* I canvassed the relevant data on the deterrent effect of capital punishment. The state of knowledge at that point, after literally centuries of debate, was summarized as follows by a United Nations Committee:

It is generally agreed between the retentionists and **abolitionists,** *whatever their opinions about the validity of comparative studies of deterrence, that the data which now exist show no correlation between the existence of capital punishment and lower rates of capital crime.*

The available evidence, I concluded in *Furman,* was convincing that "capital punishment is not necessary as a deterrent to crime in our society." ...

The evidence I reviewed in *Furman* remains convincing, in my view, that "capital punishment is not necessary as a deterrent to crime in our society." The justification for the death penalty must be found elsewhere.

The other principal purpose said to be served by the death penalty is retribution. The notion that retribution can serve as a moral justification for the sanction of death finds credence in the opinion of my Brothers Stewart, Powell, and Stevens. ... It is this notion that I find to be the most disturbing aspect of today's unfortunate [decision].

The concept of retribution is a multifaceted one, and any discussion of its role in the criminal law must be undertaken with caution. On one level, it can be said that the notion of retribution or **reprobation** is the basis of our insistence that only those who have broken the law be punished, and in this sense the notion is quite obviously central to a just system of criminal sanctions. But our recognition that retribution plays a crucial role in determining who may be punished by no means requires approval of retribution as a general justification for punishment. It is the question whether retribution can provide a moral justification for punishment—in particular, capital punishment—that we must consider.

My Brothers Stewart, Powell, and Stevens offer the following explanation of the retributive justification for capital punishment:

The instinct for retribution is part of the nature of man, and channeling that instinct in the administration of criminal justice serves an important purpose in promoting the stability of a society governed by law. When people begin to believe that organized society is unwilling or unable to impose upon criminal offenders the punishment they "deserve," then there are sown the seeds of anarchy—of self-help, vigilante justice, and lynch law.

This statement is wholly inadequate to justify the death penalty. As my Brother Brennan stated in *Furman,* "[t]here is no evidence whatever that utilization of imprisonment rather than death encourages private blood feuds and other disorders." It simply defies belief to suggest that the death penalty is necessary to prevent the American people from taking the law into their own hands.

In a related vein, it may be suggested that the expression of moral outrage through the imposition of the death penalty serves to reinforce basic moral values—that it marks some crimes as particularly offensive and therefore to be avoided. The argument is akin to a deterrence argument, but differs in that it contemplates the individual's shrinking from antisocial conduct, not because he fears punishment, but because he has been told in the strongest possible way that the conduct is wrong. This contention, like the previous one, provides no support for the death penalty. It is inconceivable that any individual concerned about conforming his conduct to what society says is "right" would fail to realize that murder is "wrong" if the penalty were simply life imprisonment.

The foregoing contentions—that society's expression of moral outrage through the imposition of the death penalty preempts the citizenry from taking the law into its own hands and reinforces moral values—are not retributive in the purest sense. They are essentially utilitarian in that they portray the death penalty as valuable because of its beneficial results. These justifications for the death penalty are inadequate because the penalty is, quite clearly I think, not necessary to the accomplishment of those results.

There remains for consideration, however, what might be termed the purely retributive justification for the death penalty—that the death penalty is appropriate, not because of its beneficial effect on society, but because the taking of the murderer's life is itself morally good. Some of the language of the opinion of my Brothers Stewart, Powell, and Stevens ... appears positively to embrace this notion of retribution for its own sake as a justification for capital punishment. They state:

[T]he decision that capital punishment may be the appropriate sanction in extreme cases is an expression of the community's belief that certain crimes are themselves so grievous an affront to humanity that the only adequate response may be the penalty of death.

They then quote with approval from Lord Justice Denning's remarks before the British Royal Commission on Capital Punishment:

The truth is that some crimes are so outrageous that society insists on adequate punishment, because the wrong-doer deserves it, irrespective of whether it is a deterrent or not.

Of course, it may be that these statements are intended as no more than observations as to the popular demands that it is thought must be responded to in order to prevent anarchy. But the implication of the statements appears to me to be quite different—namely, that society's judgment that the murderer "deserves" death must be respected not simply because the preservation of order requires it, but because it is appropriate that society make the judgment and carry it out. It is this latter notion, in particular, that I consider to be fundamentally at odds with the Eighth Amendment. The mere fact that the community demands the murderer's life in return for the evil he has done cannot sustain the death penalty, for as Justices Stewart, Powell, and Stevens remind us, "the Eighth Amendment demands more than that a challenged punishment be acceptable to contemporary society." To be sustained under the Eighth Amendment, the death penalty must "compor[t] with the basic concept of human dignity at the core of the Amendment;" the objective in imposing it must be "[consistent] with our respect for the dignity of [other] men." Under these standards, the taking of life "because the wrongdoer deserves it" surely must fail, for such a punishment has as its very basis the total denial of the wrongdoer's dignity and worth.

The death penalty, unnecessary to promote the goal of deterrence or to further any legitimate notion of retribution, is an excessive penalty forbidden by the Eighth and Fourteenth Amendments. I respectfully dissent from the Court's judgment upholding the [sentence] of death imposed upon the [petitioner in this case].

Footnotes

1. Another purpose that has been discussed is the incapacitation of dangerous criminals and the consequent prevention of crimes that they may otherwise commit in the future.

2. We do not address here the question whether the taking of the criminal's life is a proportionate sanction where no victim has been deprived of life—for example, when capital punishment is imposed for rape, kidnapping, or armed robbery that does not result in the death of any human being.

3. The Model Penal Code proposes the following standards:

"(3) Aggravating Circumstances.

"(a) The murder was committed by a convict under sentence of imprisonment.

"(b) The defendant was previously convicted of another murder or of a felony involving the use or threat of violence to the person.

"(c) At the time the murder was committed the defendant also committed another murder.

"(d) The defendant knowingly created a great risk of death to many persons.

"(e) The murder was committed while the defendant was engaged or was an accomplice in the commission of, or an attempt to commit, or flight after committing or attempting to commit robbery, rape or deviate sexual intercourse by force or threat of force, arson, burglary or kidnapping.

"(f) The murder was committed for the purpose of avoiding or preventing a lawful arrest or effecting an escape from lawful custody.

"(g) The murder was committed for pecuniary gain.

"(h) The murder was especially heinous, atrocious or cruel, manifesting exceptional depravity.

"(4) Mitigating Circumstances.

"(a) The defendant has no significant history of prior criminal activity.

"(b) The murder was committed while the defendant was under the influence of extreme mental or emotional disturbance.

"(c) The victim was a participant in the defendant's homicidal conduct or consented to the homicidal act.

"(d) The murder was committed under circumstances which the defendant believed to provide a moral justification or extenuation for his conduct.

"(e) The defendant was an accomplice in a murder committed by another person and his participation in the homicidal act was relatively minor.

"(f) The defendant acted under duress or under

the domination of another person.

"(g) At the time of the murder, the capacity of the defendant to appreciate the criminality [wrongfulness] of his conduct or to conform his conduct to the requirements of law was impaired as a result of mental disease or defect or intoxication.

"(h) The youth of the defendant at the time of the crime." ALI Model Penal Code § 210.6 (Proposed Official Draft 1962).

Review Questions

1. How did the justices rule in *Furman* v. *Georgia* (1972), and by contrast, how do they rule in this case?

2. According to the justices, what is the "basic concept underlying the Eighth Amendment?"

3. According to the justices, in what two ways may a punishment be excessive?

4. According to the justices, why doesn't the death penalty violate contemporary standards of decency?

5. The justices say that the death penalty serves "two principal social purposes." What are they,

and how are they supposed to work?

6. What safeguards against the arbitrary and capricious application of the death sentence are suggested by the justices?

7. Explain Justice Marshall's objections and his criticisms of the majority opinion.

Discussion Questions

1. The Georgia statute retains the death penalty for six crimes, including rape, armed robbery, and treason. Do you agree that persons guilty of these crimes should receive the death sentence? Explain your view.

2. Try to give a precise definition of the phrase "cruel and unusual." Can you do it?

3. How could it be conclusively proven that the death penalty deters potential criminals better than life imprisonment?

4. Should the "instinct for retribution" be satisfied? Defend your answer.

Walter Berns

For Capital Punishment

Walter Berns teaches political science at Georgetown University. He is the author of For Capital Punishment *(New York: Basic Books, 1979).*

Berns wants to explain the retributive view that requires us to pay criminals back for their crimes, and that requires us to make murderers pay for their crimes with their lives. Berns thinks that punishing criminals, including murderers, is an expression of anger. But this anger is morally right, he believes, because it acknowledges the humanity of the criminals, it holds them responsible for their actions,

and it serves justice. A criminal who has violated the trust of a moral community has thereby injured it, therefore, the criminal must be punished for the sake of justice. Berns concludes with an interesting discussion of the views of capital punishment that he finds in Camus The Stranger *and Shakespeare's* Macbeth; *he asserts that Shakespeare gives us a truer account of murder than Camus.*

INTRODUCTION

Until recently, my business did not require me to think about the punishment of criminals in general or the legitimacy and efficacy of capital punishment in particular. In a vague way, I was aware of the disagreement among professionals concerning the purpose of punishment—whether it was intended to deter others, to rehabilitate the criminal, or to pay him back—but like most laymen I had no particular reason to decide which purpose was right or to what extent they may all have been right. I did know that retribution was held in ill repute among criminologists and jurists—to them, retribution was a fancy name for revenge, and revenge was barbaric—and, of course, I knew that capital punishment had the support only of policemen, prison guards, and some local politicians, the sort of people Arthur Koestler calls "hanghards" (Philadelphia's Mayor Rizzo comes to mind). The intellectual community denounced it as both unnecessary and immoral. It was the phenomenon of Simon Wiesenthal that allowed me to understand why the intellectuals were wrong and why the police, the politicians, and the majority of the voters were right: we punish criminals principally in order to pay them back, and we execute the worst of them out of moral necessity. Anyone who respects Wiesenthal's mission will be driven to the same conclusion.

Of course, not everyone will respect that mission. It will strike the busy man—I mean the sort of man who sees things only in the light cast by a concern for his own interests—as somewhat bizarre. Why should anyone devote his life—more than thirty years of it!—exclusively to the task of hunting down the Nazi war criminals who survived World War II and escaped punishment? Wiesenthal says his conscience forces him, "to bring the guilty ones to trial." But why punish them? What do we hope to accomplish now by punishing SS Obersturmbannführer Adolf Eichmann or SS Obersturmführer Franz Stangl or someday—who knows?—Reichsleiter Martin Bormann? We surely don't expect to rehabilitate them, and it would be foolish to think that by punishing them we might thereby deter others. The answer, I think, is clear: We want to punish them in order *to pay them back.* We think they must be made to pay for their crimes with their lives, and we think that we, the survivors of the world they violated, may legitimately exact that payment because we, too, are their victims. By punishing them, we demonstrate that there are laws that bind men across generations as well as across (and within) nations, that we are not simply isolated individuals, each pursuing his selfish inter-

ests and connected with others by a mere contract to live and let live. To state it simply, Wiesenthal allows us to see that it is right, morally right, to be angry with criminals and to express that anger publicly, officially, and in an appropriate manner, which may require the worst of them to be executed.

Modern civil-libertarian opponents of capital punishment do not understand this. They say that to execute a criminal is to deny his human dignity; they also say that the death penalty is not useful, that nothing useful is accomplished by executing anyone. Being utilitarians, they are essentially selfish men, distrustful of passion, who do not understand the connection between anger and justice, and between anger and human dignity.

ANGER AS RESPONSE DUE

ANGER IS EXPRESSED or manifested on those occasions when someone has acted in a manner that is thought to be unjust, and one of its origins is the opinion that men are responsible, and should be held responsible, for what they do. Thus, as Aristotle teaches us, anger is accompanied not only by the pain caused by the one who is the object of anger, but by the pleasure arising from the expectation of inflicting revenge on someone who is thought to deserve it. We can become angry with an inanimate object (the door we run into and then kick in return) only by foolishly attributing responsibility to it, and we cannot do that for long, which is why we do not think of returning later to revenge ourselves on the door. For the same reason, we cannot be more than momentarily angry with any one creature other than man; only a fool or worse would dream of taking revenge on a dog. And, finally, we tend to pity rather than to be angry with men who—because they are insane, for example—are not responsible for their acts. Anger, then, is a very human passion not only because only a human being can be angry, but also because anger acknowledges the humanity of its objects: it holds them accountable for what they do.

And in holding particular men responsible, it pays them the respect that is due them as men. Anger recognizes that only men have the capacity to be moral beings and, in so doing, acknowledges the dignity of human beings. Anger is somehow connected with *justice,* and it is this that modern penology has not understood; it tends, on the whole, to regard anger as a selfish indulgence.

Anger can, of course, be that; and if someone does not become angry with an insult or an injury suffered unjustly, we tend to think he does not think much of himself. But it need not be selfish, not in the sense of being provoked only by an injury suffered by oneself. There were many angry men in America when President Kennedy was killed; one of them—Jack Ruby—took it upon himself to exact the punishment that, if indeed deserved, ought to have been exacted by the law. There were perhaps even angrier men when Martin Luther King, Jr., was killed, for King, more than anyone else at the time, embodied a people's quest for justice; the anger—more, the "black rage"—expressed on that occasion was simply a manifestation of the great change that had occurred among black men in America, a change wrought in large part by King and his associates in the civil-rights movement: the servility and fear of the past had been replaced by pride and anger, and the treatment that had formerly been accepted as a matter of course or as if it were deserved was now seen for what it was, unjust and unacceptable. King preached love, but the movement he led depended on anger as well as love, and that anger was not despicable, being neither selfish nor unjustified. On the contrary, it was a reflection of what was called solidarity and may more accurately be called a profound caring for others, black for other blacks, white for blacks, and, in the world King was trying to build, American for other Americans. If men are not saddened when someone else suffers, or angry when someone else suffers unjustly, the implication is that they do not care for anyone other than themselves or that they lack some quality that befits a man. When we criticize them for this, we acknowledge that they ought to care for others. If men are not angry when a neighbor suffers at the hands of a criminal, the implication is that their moral faculties have been corrupted, that they are not good citizens.

Criminals are properly the objects of anger, and the perpetrators of terrible crimes— for example, Lee Harvey Oswald and James Earl Ray—are properly the objects of great anger. They have done more than inflict an injury on an isolated individual; they have violated the foundations of trust and friendship, the necessary elements of a moral community, the only community worth living in. A moral community, unlike a hive of bees or a hill of ants, is one whose members are expected freely to obey the laws and, unlike those in a tyranny, are trusted to obey the laws. The criminal has violated that trust, and in so doing has injured not merely his immediate victim but the community as such. He has called into question the very possibility of that community by suggesting that men cannot be trusted to respect freely the property, the person, and the dignity of those with whom they are associated. If, then, men are not angry when someone else is robbed, raped, or murdered, the implication is that no moral community exists, because those men do not care for anyone other than themselves. Anger is an expression of that caring, and society needs men who care for one another, who share their pleasures and their pains, and do so for the sake of the others. It is the passion that can cause us to act for reasons having nothing to do with selfish or mean calculation; indeed, when educated, it can become a generous passion, the passion that protects the community or country by demanding punishment for its enemies. It is the stuff from which heroes are made.

CAMUS VS. SHAKESPEARE

A MORAL COMMUNITY is not possible without anger and the moral indignation that accompanies it. Thus the most powerful attack on capital punishment was written by a man, Albert Camus, who denied the legitimacy of anger and moral indignation by denying the very possibility of a moral community in our time. The anger expressed in our world, he said, is nothing but hypocrisy. His novel *L'Etranger* (variously translated as *The Stranger* or *The Outsider*) is a brilliant portrayal of what Camus insisted is our world, a world deprived of God, as he put it. It is a world we would not choose to live in and one that Camus, the hero of the French Resistance, disdained. Nevertheless, the novel is a modern masterpiece, and Meursault, its antihero (for a world without anger can have no heroes), is a murderer.

He is a murderer whose crime is excused, even as his lack of hypocrisy is praised, because the universe, we are told, is "benignly indifferent" to how we live or what we do. Of course, the law is not indifferent; the law punished Meursault and it threatens to punish us if we do as he did. But Camus the novelist teaches us that the law is simply a collection of arbitrary conceits. The people around Meursault apparently were not indifferent; they expressed dismay at his lack of attachment to his mother and disapprobation of his crime. But Camus the novelist teaches us that other people are hypocrites. They pretend not to know what Camus the opponent of capital punishment tells us: namely, that "our civilization has lost the only values that, in a certain way, can justify that penalty ... [the existence of] a truth or a principle that is superior to man." There is no basis for friendship and no moral law; therefore, no one, not even a murderer, can violate the terms of friendship or break that law; and there is no basis for the anger that we express when someone breaks that law. The only thing we share as men, the only thing that connects us one to another, is a "solidarity against death," and a judgment of capital punishment "upsets" that solidarity. The purpose of human life is to stay alive.

Like Meursault, Macbeth was a murderer, and like *L'Etranger,* Shakespeare's *Macbeth* is the story of a murder; but there the similarity ends. As Lincoln said, "Nothing equals *Macbeth.* " He was comparing it with the other Shakespearean plays he knew, the plays he had "gone over perhaps as frequently as any unprofessional reader ...*Lear, Richard Third, Henry Eighth, Hamlet* "; but I think he meant to say more than that none of these equals *Macbeth.* I think he meant that no other literary work equals it. "It is wonderful," he said. Macbeth is wonderful because, to say nothing more here, it teaches us the awesomeness of the commandment "Thou shalt not kill."

What can a dramatic poet tell us about murder? More, probably, than anyone else, if he is a poet worthy of consideration, and yet nothing that does not inhere in the act itself. In *Macbeth,* Shakespeare shows us murders committed in a political world by a man so driven by ambition to rule that world that he becomes a tyrant. He shows us also the consequences, which were terrible, worse even than Macbeth feared. The cosmos rebelled, turned into chaos by his deeds. He shows a world that was not "benignly indifferent" to what we call crimes and especially to murder, a world constituted by laws divine as well as human, and Macbeth violated the most awful of those laws. Because the world was so constituted, Macbeth suffered the torments of the great and the damned, torments far beyond the "practice" of any physician. He had known glory and had deserved the respect and affection of king, countrymen, army, friends, and wife; and he lost it all. At the end he was reduced to saying that life "is a tale told by an idiot, full of sound and fury, signifying nothing"; yet, in spite of the horrors provoked in us by his acts, he excites no anger in us. We pity him; even so, we understand the anger of his countrymen and the dramatic necessity of his death. *Macbeth* is a play about ambition, murder, tyranny; about horror, anger, vengeance, and, perhaps more than any other of Shakespeare's plays, justice. Because of justice, Macbeth has to die, not by his own hand—he will not "play the Roman fool, and die on [his] own sword"—but at the hand of the avenging Macduff. The dramatic necessity of his death would appear to rest on its *moral* necessity. Is that right? Does this play conform to our sense of what a murder means? Lincoln thought it was "wonderful."

Surely Shakespeare's is a truer account of murder than the one provided by Camus, and by truer I mean truer to our moral sense of what a murder is and what the consequences that attend it must be. Shakespeare shows us vengeful men because there is something in the souls of men—then and now—that requires such crimes to be revenged. Can we imagine a world that does not take its revenge on the man who kills Macduff's wife and children? (Can we imagine the play in which Macbeth does not die?) Can we imagine a people that does not hate murderers? (Can we imagine a world where Meursault is an outsider only because he does not *pretend* to be outraged by murder?) Shakespeare's poetry could not have been written out of the moral sense that the death penalty's opponents insist we ought to have. Indeed, the issue of capital punishment can be said to turn on whether Shakespeare's or Camus' is

the more telling account of murder.

Review Questions

1. According to Berns, what is the principle reason for punishing criminals?

2. Explain Bern's account of anger, including the connection between anger, justice, and humanity.

3. Why are criminals properly the objects of anger according to Berns?

4. What views of capital punishment does Berns find in Camus' *The Stranger?*

5. What view does he find in Shakespeare's *Macbeth?*

Discussion Questions

1. Do you agree that Shakespeare has given a better account of murder than Camus? Why or why not?

2. Are there any other reasons for punishing criminals besides "paying them back?" What are they?

3. Are there any criminals who do *not* deserve to be punished? Who are they?

Anthony G. Amsterdam
Capital Punishment

Anthony G. Amsterdam is a lawyer who has represented many clients who have received the death sentence.

Amsterdam begins by asserting that capital punishment is a great evil simply because it is intentionally killing a person. Furthermore, it is wrong because it results in killing people in error, and these errors cannot be corrected. Moreover, it is unfairly

applied. The death sentence is disproportionately imposed on the poor and blacks.

Amsterdam concludes with a discussion of retribution and deterrence. He argues that neither the appeal to retribution nor the appeal to deterrence justifies capital punishment.

My discussion of capital punishment will proceed in three stages.

First, I would like to set forth certain basic factual realities about capital punishment, like the fact that capital punishment is a fancy phrase for legally killing people. Please forgive me for beginning with such obvious and ugly facts. Much of our political and philosophical debate about the death penalty is carried on in language calculated to conceal these realities and their implications. The im-

From the *Stanford Magazine,* Fall/Winter 1977. Copyright © Stanford Alumni Association. Reprinted with permission.

plications, I will suggest, are that capital punishment is a great evil—surely the greatest evil except for war that our society can intentionally choose to commit.

This does not mean that we should do away with capital punishment. Some evils, like war, are occasionally necessary, and perhaps capital punishment is one of them. But the fact that it is a great evil means that we should not choose to do it without some very good and solid reason of which we are satisfactorily convinced upon sufficient evidence. The conclusion of my first point simply is that the burden of proof upon the question of capital punishment rightly rests on those who are asking us to use our laws to kill people with, and that this is a very heavy burden.

Second, I want to review the justifications that have been advanced to support capital punishment. I want to explore with you concepts such as retribution and deterrence, and some of the assumptions and evidence about them. The conclusion of my second point will be that none of these reasons which we like to give ourselves for executing criminals can begin to sustain the burden of proof that rightfully rests upon them.

Third, I would like to say a word about history—about the slow but absolutely certain progress of maturing civilization that will bring an inevitable end to punishment by death. That history does not give us the choice between perpetuating and abolishing capital punishment, because we could not perpetuate it if we wanted to. A generation or two within a single nation can retard but not reverse a long-term, worldwide evolution of this magnitude. Our choice is narrower although it is not unimportant: whether we shall be numbered among the last generations to put legal killing aside. I will end by asking you to cast your choice for life instead of death. But, first, let me begin with some basic facts about the death penalty.

1. The most basic fact, of course, is that capital punishment means taking, living, breathing men and women, stuffing them into a chair, strapping them down, pulling a lever, and exterminating them. We have almost forgotten this fact because there have been no executions in this country for more than ten years, except for Gary Gilmore whose combined suicide and circus were so wildly extravagant as to seem unreal. For many people, capital punishment has become a sanitized and symbolic issue: Do you or do you not support you local police? Do you or do you not care enough about crime to get tough with criminals? These abstractions were never what capital punishment was about, although it was possible to think so during the ten-year moratorium on executions caused by constitutional challenges to the death penalty in the courts. That is no longer possible. The courts have now said that we can start up executions again, if we want to. Today, a vote for capital punishment is a vote to kill real, live people.

What this means is, first, that we bring men or women into court and put them through a trial for their lives. They are expected to sit back quietly and observe decent courtroom decorum throughout a proceeding whose purpose is systematically and deliberately to decide whether they should be killed. The jury hears evidence and votes; and you can always tell when a jury has voted for death because they come back into court and they will not look the defendant or defense counsel in the eyes. The judge pronounces sentence and the defendant is taken away to be held in a cell for two to six years, hoping that his appeals will succeed, not really knowing what they are all about, but knowing that if they fail, he will be taken out and cinched down and put to death. Most of the people in prison are reasonably nice to him, and even a little apologetic; but he realizes every day for that 700 or 2,100 days that they are holding him there helpless for the approaching slaughter; and that, once the final order is given, they will truss him up and kill him, and that nobody in that vast surrounding machinery of public officials and servants of the law will raise a finger to save him. This is why Camus once wrote that an execution

is not simply death. It is just as different . . . from the privation of life as a concentration camp is from prison. . . . It adds to death a rule, a public premeditation known to the future victim, an organization . . . which is itself a source of moral sufferings more terrible than death . . . [Capital punishment] is . . . the most premeditated of murders, to which no criminal's deed, however calculated . . . can be compared. . . . For there to be an equivalency, the death penalty would have to punish a criminal who had warned his victim of the date at which he would inflict a horrible death on him and who, from that moment onward, had confined him at his mercy for months. Such a monster is not encountered in private life.

I will spare you descriptions of the execution itself. Apologists for capital punishment commonly excite their readers with descriptions of extremely gruesome, gory murders. All murders are horrible things, and executions are usually a lot cleaner physically—although, like Camus, I have never heard of a murderer who held his victim captive for two or more years waiting as the minutes and hours ticked away toward his preannounced death. The clinical details of an execution are as unimaginable to me as they are to most of you. We have not permitted public executions in this country for over 40 years. The law in every state forbids more than a few people to watch the deed done behind prison walls. In January of 1977, a federal judge in Texas ruled that executions could be photographed for television, but the attorneys general of 25 states asked the federal Court of Appeals to set aside that ruling, and it did. I can only leave to your imagination what they are trying so very hard to hide from us. Oh, of course, executions are too hideous to put on television; we all know that. But let us not forget that it is the same hideous thing, done in secret, which we are discussing under abstract labels like "capital punishment" that permit us to talk about the subject in after-dinner conversation instead of spitting up.

In any event, the advocates of capital punishment can and do accentuate their arguments with descriptions of the awful physical details of such hideous murders as that of poor Sharon Tate. All of us naturally and rightly respond to these atrocities with shock and horror. You can read descriptions of executions that would also horrify you (for example, in Byron Eshelman's 1962 book, *Death Row Chaplain*, particularly pages 160–61), but I prefer not to insult your intelligence by playing "can you top this" with issues of life and death. I ask you only to remember two things, if and when you are exposed to descriptions of terrifying murders.

First, the murders being described are not murders that are being done by us, or in our name, or with our approval; and our power to stop them is exceedingly limited even under the most exaggerated suppositions of deterrence, which I shall shortly return to question. Every execution, on the other hand, is done by our paid servants, in our collective name, and we can stop them all. Please do not be bamboozled into thinking that people who are against executions are in favor of murders. If we had the individual or the collective power to stop murders, we would stop them all—and for the same basic reason that we want to stop executions. Murders and executions are both ugly, vicious things, because they destroy the same sacred and mysterious gift of life which we do not understand and can never restore.

Second, please remember therefore that descriptions of murders are relevant to the subject of capital punishment only on the theory that two wrongs make a right, or that killing murderers can assuage their victims' sufferings or bring them back to life, or that capital punishment is the best deterrent to murder. The first two propositions are absurd, and the third is debatable—although, as I shall later show, the evidence is overwhelmingly against it. My present point is only that deterrence *is* debatable, whereas we *know* that persons whom we execute are dead beyond recall, no matter how the debate about deterrence comes out. That is a sufficient reason, I believe, why the burden of proof on the issue of deterrence should be placed squarely upon the executioners.

There are other reasons too. Let me try to state them briefly.

Capital punishment not merely kills people, it also kills some of them in error, and these are errors which we can never correct. When I speak about legal error, I do not mean only the question whether "they got the right man" or killed somebody who "didn't do it." Errors of that sort do occur: Timothy Evans, for example, an innocent man whose execution was among the reasons for the abolition of the death penalty in Great Britain. If you read Anthony Scaduto's recent book, *Scapegoat*, you will come away with unanswerable doubts whether Bruno Richard Hauptmann was really guilty of the kidnaping of the Lindbergh infant for which he was executed, or whether we killed Hauptmann, too, for a crime he did not commit.

In 1975, the Florida Cabinet pardoned two black men, Freddie Lee Pitts and Wilbert Lee, who were twice tried and sentenced to death and spent 12 years apiece on death row for a murder committed by somebody else. This one, I am usually glibly told, "does not count," because Pitts and Lee were never actually put to death. Take comfort if you will but I cannot, for I know that only the general constitutional attack which we were then mounting upon the death penalty in Florida kept Pitts and Lee alive long enough to permit discovery of the evidence of their innocence. Our constitutional attack is now dead, and so would Pitts and Lee be if they were tried tomorrow. Sure, we catch some errors. But we often catch them by extremely lucky breaks that could as easily not have happened. I represented a young man in North Carolina who came within a hair's breadth of being the Gary Gilmore of his day. Like Gilmore, he became so depressed under a death sentence that he tried to dismiss his appeal. He was barely talked out of it, his conviction was reversed, and on retrial a jury acquitted

him in 11 minutes.

We do not know how many "wrong men" have been executed. We think and pray that they are rare—although we can't be sure because, after a man is dead, people seldom continue to investigate the possibility that he was innocent. But that is not the biggest source of error anyway.

What about *legal* error? In 1968, the Supreme Court of the United States held that it was unconstitutional to exclude citizens from capital trial juries simply because they had general conscientious or religious objections to the death penalty. That decision was held retroactive; and I represented 60 or 70 men whose death sentences were subsequently set aside for constitutional errors in jury selection. While researching their cases, I found the cases of at least as many more men who had already been executed on the basis of trials infected with identical errors. On June 29, 1977, we finally won a decision from the Supreme Court of the United States that the death penalty is excessively harsh and therefore unconstitutional for the crime of rape. Fine, but it comes too late for the 455 men executed for rape in this country since 1930—405 of them black.

In 1975, the Supreme Court held that the constitutional presumption of innocence forbids a trial judge to tell the jury that the burden of proof is on a homicide defendant to show provocation which reduces murder to manslaughter. On June 17, 1977, the Court held that this decision was also retroactive. Jury charges of precisely that kind were standard forms for more than a century in many American states that punished murder with death. Can we even begin to guess how many people were unconstitutionally executed under this so-called retroactive decision?

Now what about errors of fact that go to the degree of culpability of a crime? In almost every state, the difference between first- and second-degree murder—or between capital and noncapital murder—depends on whether the defendant acted with something called "premeditation" as distinguished from intent to kill. Premeditation means intent formed beforehand, but no particular amount of time is required. Courts tell juries that premeditation "may be as instantaneous as successive thoughts in the mind." Mr. Justice Cardozo wrote that *he* did not understand the concept of premeditation after several decades of studying and trying to apply it as a judge. Yet this is the kind of question to which a jury's answer spells out life or death in a capital trial—this, and the questions whether the defendant had "malice aforethought," or "provocation and passion," or "insanity," or the "reasonableness" necessary for killing in self-defense.

I think of another black client, Johnny Coleman, whose conviction and death sentence for killing a white truck driver named "Screwdriver" Johnson we twice got reversed by the Supreme Court of the United States. On retrial a jury acquitted him on the grounds of self-defense upon exactly the same evidence that an earlier jury had had when it sentenced him to die. When ungraspable legal standards are thus applied to intangible mental states, there is not merely the possibility but the actuarial certainty that juries deciding substantial volumes of cases are going to be wrong in an absolutely large number of them. If you accept capital punishment, you must accept the reality—not the risk, but the reality—that we shall kill people whom the law says that it is not proper to kill. No other outcome is possible when we presume to administer an infallible punishment through a fallible system.

You will notice that I have taken examples of black defendants as some of my cases of legal error. There is every reason to believe that discrimination on grounds of race and poverty fatally infect the administration of capital justice in this country. Since 1930, an almost equal number of white and black defendants has been executed for the crime of murder, although blacks constituted only about a tenth of the nation's population during this period. No sufficiently careful studies have been done of these cases, controlling variables other than race, so as to determine exactly what part race played in the outcome. But when that kind of systematic study *was* done in rape cases, it showed beyond the statistical possibility of a doubt that black men who raped white women were disproportionately sentenced to die on the basis of race alone. Are you prepared to believe that juries which succumbed to conscious or unconscious racial prejudices in rape cases were or are able to put those prejudices wholly aside where the crime charged is murder? Is it not much more plausible to believe that even the most conscientious juror—or judge, or prosecuting attorney—will be slower to want to inflict the death penalty on a defendant with whom he can identify as a human being; and that the process of identification in our society is going to be very seriously affected by racial identity?

I should mention that there have been a couple of studies—one by the *Stanford Law Review* and the other by the Texas Judicial Council—which found no racial discrimination in capital sentencing in certain murder cases. But both of these studies had methodological problems and limitations; and both of them also found death-sentencing discrimination against the economically poor, who come disproportionately from racial minorities. The sum of the evidence still stands where the National Crime Commission found it ten years ago, when it described the following discriminatory patterns. "The death sentence," said the Commission, "is disproportionately imposed and carried out on the poor, the Negro, and members of unpopular groups."

Apart from discrimination, there is a haphazard, crazy-quilt character about the administration of capital punishment that every knowledgeable lawyer or observer can describe but none can rationally explain. Some juries are hanging juries, some counties are hanging counties, some years are hanging years; and men live or die depending on these flukes.

However atrocious the crime may have

been for which a particular defendant is sentenced to die, "[e]xperienced wardens know many prisoners serving life or less whose crimes were equally, or more atrocious." That is a quotation, by the way, from former Attorney General Ramsey Clark's statement to a congressional subcommittee; and wardens Lewis Lawes, Clinton Duffy, and others have said the same thing.

With it I come to the end of my first point. I submit that the deliberate judicial extinction of human life is intrinsically so final and so terrible an act as to cast the burden of proof for its justification upon those who want us to do it. But certainly when the act is executed through a fallible system which assures that we kill some people wrongly, others because they are black or poor or personally unattractive or socially unacceptable, and all of them quite freakishly in the sense that whether a man lives or dies for any particular crime is a matter of luck and happenstance, *then,* at the least, the burden of justifying capital punishment lies fully and heavily on its proponents.

II. Let us consider those justifications. The first and the oldest is the concept of *retribution:* an eye for an eye, a life for a life. You may or may not believe in this kind of retribution, but I will not waste your time debating it because it cannot honestly be used to justify the only form of capital punishment that this country has accepted for the past half-century. Even before the judicial moratorium, executions in the United States had dwindled to an average of about 30 a year. Only a rare, sparse handful of convicted murderers was being sentenced to die or executed for the selfsame crimes for which many, many times as many murderers were sent away to prison. Obviously, as Professor Herbert Wechsler said a generation ago, the issue of capital punishment is no longer "whether it is fair or just that one who takes another person's life should lose his own. . . . [W]e do not and cannot act upon . . . [that proposition] generally in the administration of the penal

law. The problem rather is whether a small and highly random sample of people who commit murder. . . . ought to be despatched, while most of those convicted of . . . [identical] crimes are dealt with by imprisonment."

Sometimes the concept of retribution is modernized a little with a notion called *moral reinforcement*—the ideal that we should punish very serious crimes very severely in order to demonstrate how much we abhor them. The trouble with *this* justification for capital punishment, of course, is that it completely begs the question, which is *how severely* we ought to punish any particular crime to show appropriate abhorrence for it. The answer can hardly be found in a literal application of the eye-for-an-eye formula. We do not burn down arsonists' houses or cheat back at bunco artists. But if we ought not punish all crimes exactly according to their kind, then what is the fit moral reinforcement for murder? You might as well say burning at the stake or boiling in oil as simple gassing or electrocution.

Or is it not more plausible—if what we really want to say is that the killing of a human being is wrong and ought to be condemned as clearly as we can—that we should choose the punishment of prison as the fitting means to make this point? So far as moral reinforcement goes, the difference between life imprisonment and capital punishment is precisely that imprisonment continues to respect the value of human life. The plain message of capital punishment, on the other hand, is that life ceases to be sacred whenever someone with the power to take it away decides that there is a sufficiently compelling pragmatic reason to do so.

But there is still another theory of a retributive sort which is often advanced to support the death penalty, particularly in recent years. This is the argument that *we*—that is, the person making the argument—we no longer believe in the outworn concept of retribution, but the *public*—they believe in retribution, and so we must let them have their prey or they will lose respect for law. Watch for this argument because it is the surest sign of demogagic depravity. It is disgusting in its patronizing attribution to "the public" of a primitive, uneducable bloodthirstiness which the speaker is unprepared to defend but is prepared to exploit as a means of sidestepping the rational and moral limitations of a *just* theory of retribution. It out-judases Judas in its abnegation of governmental responsibility to respond to popular misinformation with enlightenment, instead of seizing on it as a pretext for atrocity. This argument asserts that the proper way to deal with a lynch mob is to string its victim up before the mob does.

I don't think "the public" is a lynch mob or should be treated as one. People today are troubled and frightened by crime, and legitimately so. Much of the apparent increase of violent crime in our times is the product of intensified statistics keeping, massive and instantaneous and graphic news reporting, and manipulation of figures by law enforcement agencies which must compete with other sectors of the public economy for budget allocations. But part of the increase is also real, and very disturbing. Murders ought to disturb us all, whether or not they are increasing. Each and every murder is a terrible human tragedy. Nevertheless, it is irresponsible for public officials—particularly law enforcement officials whom the public views as experts—first to exacerbate and channel legitimate public concern about crime into public support for capital punishment by advertising unsupportable claims that capital punishment is an answer to the crime problem, and then to turn around and cite public support for capital punishment as justification when all other justifications are shown to be unsupportable. Politicians do this all the time, for excellent political reasons. It is much easier to advocate simplistic and illusory solutions to the crime problem than to find real and effective solutions. Most politicians are understandably afraid to admit that our society knows

frighteningly little about the causes or cure of crime, and will have to spend large amounts of taxpayers' money even to begin to find out. The facile politics of crime do much to explain our national acceptance of capital punishment, but nothing to justify it.

Another supposed justification for capital punishment that deserves equally brief treatment is the notion of *isolation* or *specific deterrence*—the idea that we must kill a murderer to prevent him from murdering ever again. The usual forms that this argument takes are that a life sentence does not mean a life sentence—it means parole after 7, or 12, or 25 years; and that, within prisons themselves, guards and other prisoners are in constant jeopardy of death at the hands of convicted but unexecuted murderers.

It amazes me that these arguments can be made or taken seriously. Are we really going to kill a human being because we do not trust other people—the people whom we have chosen to serve on our own parole boards—to make a proper judgment in his case at some future time? We trust this same parole board to make far more numerous, difficult, and dangerous decisions: hardly a week passes when they do not consider the cases of armed robbers, for example, although armed robbers are much, much more likely statistically to commit future murders than any murderer is to repeat his crime. But if we really do distrust the public agencies of law—if we fear that they may make mistakes—then surely that is a powerful argument *against* capital punishment. Courts which hand out death sentences because they predict that a man will still be criminally dangerous 7 or 25 years in the future cannot conceivably make fewer mistakes than parole boards who release a prisoner after 7 or 25 years of close observation in prison have convinced them that he is reformed and no longer dangerous.

But pass this point. If we refuse to trust the parole system, then let us provide by law that the murderers whose release we fear shall be given sentences of life imprisonment without parole which *do* mean life imprisonment without parole. I myself would be against that, but it is far more humane than capital punishment, and equally safe.

As for killings inside prisons, if you examine them you will find that they are very rarely done by convicted murderers, but are almost always done by people imprisoned for crimes that no one would think of making punishable by death. Warden Lawes of Sing Sing and Governor Wallace of Alabama, among others, regularly employed murder convicts as house servants because they were among the very safest of prisoners. There are exceptions, of course; but these can be handled by adequate prison security. You cannot tell me or believe that a society which is capable of putting a man on the moon is incapable of putting a man in prison, keeping him there, and keeping him from killing while he is there. And if anyone says that this is costly, and that we should kill people in order to reduce government expenditures, I can only reply that the cost of housing a man for life in the most physically secure conditions imaginable is considerably less than the cost of putting the same man through all of the extraordinary legal proceedings necessary to kill him.

That brings me to the last supposed justification for the death penalty: *deterrence*. This is the subject that you most frequently hear debated, and many people who talk about capital punishment talk about nothing else. I have done otherwise here, partly for completeness, partly because it is vital to approach the subject of deterrence knowing precisely what question you want to ask and have answered. I have suggested that the proper question is *whether there is sufficiently convincing evidence that the death penalty deters murder better than does life imprisonment so that you are willing to accept responsibility for doing the known evil act of killing human beings—with all of the attending ugliness that I have described—on the faith of your conviction in the superior deterrent efficacy of capital punishment.*

If this is the question, then I submit that there is only one fair and reasonable answer.

When the Supreme Court of the United States reviewed the evidence in 1976, it described that evidence as "inconclusive." Do not let anybody tell you—as death-penalty advocates are fond of doing—that the Supreme Court held the death penalty justifiable as a deterrent. What the Court's plurality opinion said, exactly, was that "there is no convincing evidence *either supporting or refuting* . . . [the] view" that "the death penalty may not function as a significantly greater deterrent than lesser penalties." *Because* the evidence was inconclusive, the Court held that the Constitution did not forbid judgment either way. But if the evidence is inconclusive, is it *your* judgment that we should conclusively kill people on a factual theory that the evidence does not conclusively sustain?

I hope not. But let us examine the evidence more carefully because—even though it is not conclusive—it is very, very substantial; and the overwhelming weight of it refutes the claims of those who say that capital punishment is a better deterrent than life imprisonment for murder.

For more than 40 years, criminologists have studied this question by a variety of means. They have compared homicide rates in countries and states that did and did not have capital punishment, or that actually executed people more and less frequently. Some of these studies compared large aggregates of abolitionist and retentionist states; others compared geographically adjacent pairs or triads of states, or states that were chosen because they were comparable in other socioeconomic factors that might affect homicide. Other studies compared homicide rates in the same country or state before and after the abolition or reinstatement of capital punishment, or they compared homicide rates for the same geographic area during periods preceding and following well publicized executions. Special comparative studies were done relating to police killings and prison killings. All in all, there were dozens of studies. Without a single exception, *none* of them found that the death penalty had any statistically significant effect upon the rate of homicide or murder. Often I have heard advocates of capital punishment explain away its failures by likening it to a great lighthouse: "We count the ships that crash," they say, "but we never know how many saw the light and were saved." What these studies show, however, is that coastlines of the same shape and depth and tidal structure, with and without lighthouses, invariably have the same number of shipwrecks per year. On that evidence, would you invest your money in a lighthouse, or would you buy a sonar if you really wanted to save lives?

In 1975, the first purportedly scientific study ever to find that capital punishment *did* deter homicides was published. This was done by Isaac Ehrlich of Chicago, who is not a criminologist but an economist. Using regression analysis involving an elaborate mathematical model, Ehrlich reported that every execution deterred something like eight murders. Naturally, supporters of capital punishment hurriedly clambered on the Ehrlich bandwagon.

Unhappily, for them, the wagon was a factory reject. Several distinguished econometricians—including a team headed by Lawrence Klein, president of the American Economic Association—reviewed Ehrlich's work and found it fatally flawed with numerous methodological errors. Some of these were technical: it appeared, for example, that Ehrlich had produced his results by the unjustified and unexplained use of a logarithmic form of regression equation instead of the more conventional linear form—which made his findings of deterrence vanish. Equally important, it was shown that Ehrlich's findings depended entirely on data from the post-1962 period, when executions declined and the homicide rate rose *as a part of a general rise, in the overall crime rate that Ehrlich incredibly failed to consider.*

Incidentally, the nonscientific proponents of capital punishment are also fond of suggesting that the rise in homicide rates in the 1960s and the 1970s, when executions were halted, proves that executions used to deter homicides. This is ridiculous when you consider that crime as a whole has increased during this period; that homicide rates have increased about *half* as much as the rates for all other FBI Index crimes; and that whatever factors are affecting the rise of most noncapital crimes (which *cannot* include cessation of executions) almost certainly affect the homicide-rate rise also.

In any event, Ehrlich's study was discredited and a second, methodologically inferior study by a fellow named Yunker is not even worth criticizing here. These are the only two scientific studies in 40 years, I repeat, which have ever purported to find deterrence. On the other hand, several recent studies have been completed by researchers who adopted Ehrlich's basic regression-analysis approach but corrected its defects. Peter Passell did such a study finding no deterrence. Kenneth Avio did such a study finding no deterrence. Brian Forst did such a study finding no deterrence. If you want to review all of these studies yourselves, you may find them discussed and cited in an excellent article in the 1976 *Supreme Court Review* by Hans Zeisel, at page 317. The conclusion you will have to draw is that—during 40 years and today—the scientific community has looked and looked and looked for any reliable evidence that capital punishment deters homicide better than does life imprisonment, and it has found no such evidence at all.

Proponents of capital punishment frequently cite a different kind of study, one that was done by the Los Angeles Police Department. Police officers asked arrested robbers who did not carry guns, or did not use them, *why* they did not; and the answers, supposedly, were frequently that the robber "did not want to get the death penalty." It is noteworthy that the Los Angeles Police Department has consistently refused to furnish copies of this study and its underlying data to professional scholars, apparently for fear of criticism. I finally obtained a copy of the study from a legislative source, and I can tell you that it shows two things. First, an arrested person will tell a police officer anything that he thinks the officer wants to hear. Second, police officers, like all other human beings, hear what they want to hear. When a robber tries to say that he did not carry or use a gun because he did not wish to risk the penalties for homicide, he will describe those penalties in terms of whatever the law happens to be at the time and place. In Minnesota, which has no death penalty, he will say, "I didn't want to get life imprisonment." In Los Angeles, he will say, "I didn't want to get the death penalty." Both responses mean the same thing; neither tells you that death is a superior deterrent to life imprisonment.

The real mainstay of deterrence thesis, however, is not evidence but intuition. You and I ask ourselves: Are we not afraid to die? Of course! Would the threat of death, then, not intimidate us to forbear from a criminal act? Certainly! *Therefore,* capital punishment must be a deterrent. The trouble with this intuition is that the people who are doing the reasoning and the people who are doing the murdering are not the same people. You and I do not commit murder for a lot of reasons other than the death penalty. The death penalty might perhaps also deter us from murdering—but altogether needlessly, since we would not murder with it or without it. Those who are sufficiently dissocialized to murder and are not responding to the world in the way that we are, and we simply cannot "intuit" their thinking processes from ours.

Consider, for example, the well-documented cases of persons who kill *because* there is a death penalty. One of these was Pamela Watkins, a babysitter in San Jose who had made several unsuccessful suicide attempts and was frightened to try again. She finally strangled two children so that the state of California would execute her. In various bizarre forms, this "suicide-murder" syndrome is reported by psychiatrists again and again. (Parenthetically, Gary Gilmore was probably such a case.) If you intuit that somewhere, sometime, the death penalty *does* deter some potential murders, are you also prepared to intuit that their numbers mathematically exceed the numbers of these wretched people who are actually induced to murder by the existence of capital punishment?

Here, I suggest, our intuition does—or should—fail, just as the evidence certainly does fail, to establish a deterrent justification for the death penalty. There is simply no credible evidence, and there is no rational way of reasoning about the real facts once you know them, which can sustain this or any other justification with the degree of confidence that should be demanded before a civilized society deliberately extinguishes human life.

III. I have only a little space for my final point, but it is sufficient because the point is perfectly plain. Capital punishment is a dying institution in this last quarter of the twentieth century. It has already been abandoned in law or in fact throughout most of the civilized world. England, Canada, the Scandinavian countries, virtually all of Western Europe except for France and Spain have abolished the death penalty. The vast majority of countries in the Western Hemisphere have abolished it. Its last strongholds in the world—apart from the United States—are in Asia and Africa, particularly South Africa. Even the countries which maintain capital punishment on the books have almost totally ceased to use it in fact. In the United States, considering only the last half century, executions have plummeted from 199 in 1935 to approximately 29 a year during the decade before 1967, when the ten-year judicial moratorium began.

Do you doubt that this development will continue? Do you doubt that it will continue because it is the path of civilization—the path up out of fear and terror and the barbarism that terror breeds, into self-confidence and decency in the administration of justice? The road, like any other built by men, has its detours, but over many generations it has run true, and will run true. And there will therefore come a time—perhaps in 20 years, perhaps in 50 or 100, but very surely and very shortly as the lifetime of nations is measured—when our children will look back at us in horror and unbelief because of what we did in their names and for their supposed safety, just as we look back in horror and unbelief at the thousands of crucifixions and beheadings and live disembowelments that our ancestors practiced for the supposed purpose of making our world safe from murderers and robbers, thieves, shoplifters, and pickpockets.

All of these kinds of criminals are still with us, and will be with our children—although we can certainly decrease their numbers and their damage, and protect ourselves from them a lot better, if we insist that our politicians stop pounding on the whipping boy of capital punishment and start coming up with some real solutions to the real problems of crime. Our children will cease to execute murderers for the same reason that we have ceased to string up pickpockets and shoplifters at the public crossroads, although there are still plenty of them around. Our children will cease to execute murderers because executions are a self-deluding, self-defeating, self-degrading, futile, and entirely stupid means of dealing with the crime of murder, and because our children will prefer to be something better than murderers themselves. Should we not—can we not—make the same choice now?

Review Questions

1. Why does Amsterdam think that capital punishment is a great evil?

2. What additional reasons does Amsterdam give for saying that capital punishment is wrong?

3. Why does Amsterdam reject the oldest concept of retribution, an eye for an eye, a life for a life?

4. What is the notion of moral reinforcement, and why doesn't Amsterdam accept it?

5. How does Amsterdam reply to the argument that the public's desire for retribution must be satisfied?

6. What is wrong with the notion of specific deterrence according to Amsterdam?

7. How does Amsterdam deal with the appeal to deterrence?

Discussion Questions

1. Do you agree with Amsterdam that capital punishment is a great evil? Why or why not?

2. Has Amsterdam successfully defeated the appeal to retribution?

3. Are you convinced that capital punishment is not a better deterrent than life imprisonment? Explain your answer.

Robert S. Gerstein

Capital Punishment—"Cruel and Unusual?": A Retributivist Response

Robert S. Gerstein is a professor of political science at the University of California at Los Angeles and is an adjunct professor of law at Loyola Law School in Los Angeles.

Gerstein argues that retributivism should not be equated with vengeance. Rather it is the view that punishment restores the balance of advantages to a just community. The punishment must be proportionate to the offense, but also it must treat the offender with the respect due a member of a community founded on principles of justice. Insofar as it does not do this, but rather negates the moral worth of a person, the death penalty is not justified by retributivism.

Thomas Long, in his article "Capital Punishment—'Cruel and Unusual'?" [1] canvasses the various arguments made for the view that capital punishment is cruel and unusual punishment and comes to the conclusion that the only argument with substantial merit is that which holds that capital punishment is unconstitutional because the pain and suffering it involves cannot be shown to be justified by its effectiveness as a deterrent. It must therefore be regarded as an irrational imposition of pain and suffering until such time as it can be shown that it is a more effective deterrent than less severe punishments would be. He then goes on to admit that this argument has its "sinister" aspects: it is probably true that no punishment could meet the burden of proof required by this standard of rationality. The force of the argument then is to under-

mine the justification for punishment generally.

I would suggest that Long arrives at this surprising result largely because he has chosen to restrict his consideration of the legitimacy of capital punishment to utilitarian considerations. The key to understanding this restriction is to be found, I believe in his decision to disregard the retributivist view because "nonretributive views are today predominant among theoreticians of crime and punishment." [2] Having rejected retributivism, and any consideration of whether people "deserve" certain sorts of punishments or not, he is left with a classic utilitarian calculus in which the pain caused to the criminal is to be balanced against the benefits society would gain from the example his punishment sets to others. The dilemma in which he finds himself at the end of his indecisive calculations serves to underline Kant's warning to the penologist who stops being concerned with giving people what they deserve and instead "rummages around in the winding paths of a theory of happiness" [3] for guidance.

It is true that many judges and scholars simply reject retributivism out of hand. [4] It is also true, however, that there has in recent years been a revival of interest in retributive theory. [5] I would like to suggest that the rejection of retributivism is largely a product of misunderstanding and that, properly understood, the retributive view offers a more plausible basis for the solution of the problems surrounding cruel and unusual punishment generally, and capital punishment in particular, than do utilitarian views such as Long's.

The most common way of misunderstanding retributivism is to take it to be a fancy word for revenge. Those who assume that it is simply a rationalization for the venting of our passion for vengeance [6] quite rightly conclude that retributivism can offer us little help in deciding what is cruel and unusual punishment. Obviously this passion is not subject to any inherent limits on cruelty: it

From Robert S. Gerstein, "Capital Punishment—'Cruel and Unusual'?: A Retributivist Response" Ethics, vol. 85, no. 1, pp. 75–79. Published by the University of Chicago Press. Reprinted with permission.

has been known to lead people to kill not only wrongdoers, but their whole families as well; it has led to boilings in oil and burnings at the stake. Others who connect retributivism with revenge construe it as a kind of utilitarian argument. In this view the retributivist is not one who justifies the urge to vengeance, but one who thinks that punishment is useful because it allows people to vent this emotion in a (relatively) harmless and orderly way.[7] People who see retributivism in this way also quite rightly come to the conclusion that it offers us no help in deciding what kinds of punishments should be ruled out as cruel and unusual.

These misunderstandings have at their heart the equation of vengeance with retribution. The equation is made understandable by the fact that there are connections, historical and conceptual, between these two ideas. It is mistaken because it misses the enormous and crucial differences between them.

Vengefulness is an emotional response to injuries done to us by others: we feel a desire to injure those who have injured us. Retributivism is not the idea that it is good to have and satisfy this emotion. It is rather the view that there are good arguments for including that kernel of rationality to be found in the passion for vengeance as a part of any just system of laws. Assuming the existence of a generally just legal system, the argument for making retributive punishment a part of it has been succinctly stated in this way:

In order to enjoy the benefits that a legal system makes possible, each man must be prepared to make an important sacrifice—namely, the sacrifice of obeying the law even when he does not desire to do so. Each man calls on others to do this, and it is only just or fair that he bear a comparable burden when his turn comes. Now if the system is to remain just, it is important to guarantee that those who disobey will not thereby gain an unfair advantage over those who obey voluntarily. Criminal punishment thus attempts to maintain the proper balance between benefit and obedience by insuring that there is no profit in criminal wrongdoing.[8]

It has been seen that some critics of retributivism regard it as a theory that would lead us to use criminals as objects upon which to vent our emotions, as scapegoats to be dealt with without regard to their value as people. In fact, nothing could be further from the truth. It is a major tenet of the standard form of retributivism that "a human being can never be manipulated merely as a means to the purposes of someone else."[9] Punishment is not, in this view, a matter of injuring people because it is useful to us but of dealing with them in the way they deserve to be dealt with. The question for the retributivist is not: what will be the most advantageous way of disposing of this criminal? Rather it is: what is the just way to treat one of our fellow citizens who has willfully taken unjust advantage of the rest of us?

It is especially surprising that critics suggest that retributivism leads to the destruction of all limits on the severity of punishment. Retributivism in its classic form has within it a standard that measures out the severity of the punishment with great care: *lex talionis.*[10] Indeed, if the purpose of punishment is to restore the balance of advantages necessary to a just community, then punishment must be proportioned to the offense; any unduly severe punishment would unbalance things in the other direction.

In fact, one of the great advantages of retributivism over other views is that it serves not only as a justification for punishment but also as a guide to the appropriate kind of punishment and a limit on the severity of punishment. Most other views require us to balance various utilitarian considerations against each other to come to our conclusions. So, for example, a very harsh punishment might be warranted for a particular crime from the point of view of the needs of deterrence, but we might decide to mitigate it because it would simply be too painful to those that would undergo it. Understood from this perspective, the problem of deciding whether some particular punishment was cruel and unusual would, of course, be a matter of weighing the social advantages to be derived from it against the pain it would cause the criminal. A variety of policies, including deterrence, security, and rehabilitation, must all be taken into account.

In retributivism, on the other hand, we have a single coherent perspective from which to make a principled judgment as to the punishment appropriate for this offense and this person. Because punishment is justified as the deserved response of the community to a member who has acted unjustly, it is essential that the punishment meted out to him be consistent with his position as a member of the community. He is not to be treated as an object or even as an enemy. Our duty to treat him justly is no less stringent than that which we have toward any other member of the community. The purpose of punishment is to restore the balance of justice within the community, not further to derange it.

What then would retributivism regard as cruel and unusual punishment? Clearly, any punishment the severity of which was out of proportion with the offense. But further, any punishment that would be inconsistent with the criminal's status as a member of the community whose capacity for a sense of justice (a capacity of which he did not make use when he committed his crime)[11] is worthy of our respect. This is not to say that we may not cause him pain, and even very great pain. To say that punishment is justified is to say that a man with the capacity for a sense of justice ought to feel guilty and recognize that he should suffer for what he has done. The line is not to be drawn in terms of degree, but in terms of the kind of suffering that is inflicted. As Plato pointed out, it can never be the business of a just man to make another man less just than he was.[12] An affliction that undermines a man's self-respect rather than awakening his conscience, that impairs his capacity for justice rather than stimulating it, could not serve as just punishment.

In fact, one of the most widely accepted views of the meaning of "cruel and unusual punishment," that developed by Justice Brennan,[13] fits very well into the retributivist perspective. Brennan argues that cruel and unusual punishments are those that "treat members of the human race as nonhumans, as objects to be toyed with and discarded."[14] He sums up his view in terms of the "primary principle ... that a punishment must not in its severity be degrading to human dignity."[15] Brennan's position gains both force and clarity when it is seen in the context of retributivism. In this context the distinction between punishments that destroy human dignity and those that do not becomes more plausible because the theory shows us how we can justify the imposition of some afflictive punishments on a person while giving full respect to his human dignity. The idea of human dignity is also given content when it is explicated in terms of the capacity for a sense of justice. Just as we justify punishment as a response to those who abuse this capacity, so we shape and limit punishment out of the desire to preserve and stimulate it.

How does capital punishment fit into this scheme? The retributivist view, to the extent it is dealt with at all, is dealt with only as providing arguments in favor of capital punishment.[16] This is, first, because it does offer a justification for punishment in general, and, second, because the *lex talionis* can be seen as a justification for capital punishment in particular: "life for life, eye for eye, tooth for tooth." Of course, this should make it clear that retributivism would almost certainly rule out as cruel and unusual the use of capital punishment for rape, or for any other crime but murder. But is the retributivist committed to the support of capital punishment for murder? Kant argued that because there is "no sameness of kind between death and remaining alive even under the most miserable conditions" only capital punishment can restore the balance of justice where murder has been committed.[17]

The retributive theory contains the foundation of a very different sort of argument, however.[18] It can lead us to ask how it is possible for us to continue to respect the moral capacity of another while we prepare for and carry out his execution. The answer to this question might depend on attitudes that do change over time. Perhaps the people involved in the ceremony surrounding the public beheading of a nobleman in the eighteenth century could continue to have profound respect for him as a moral being.[19] But ceremonial public executions would not be tolerated among us today. Given our surreptitious and mechanical approach to execution, it is hard to see that the condemned are treated as anything more than "objects to be . . . discarded." The condemned man's physical suffering may be minimized, but that is no more than we would do for a domestic animal to be disposed of. It is not the degree of suffering that might lead the retributivist to regard capital punishment as cruel and unusual, but its dehumanizing character, its total negation of the moral worth of the person to be executed.

I have not attempted here to give a justification of retributivism but only to establish that it would be a serious mistake not to include it among the alternative positions to be considered in gaining a full understanding of the issues involved in declaring the death penalty unconstitutional. Retributivism does offer a coherent and intuitively sound approach to understanding what the phrase "cruel and unusual punishment" can be taken to mean. It is not subject to the difficulties that beset positions like that developed by Long. And if it does not give us an easy answer to the question whether the death penalty is cruel and unusual, it does present the question to us in a form that presses us to make a principled judgment of the most serious sort: when, if ever, can we say that a person whom we continue to respect as a fellow member of a community founded on the principles of justice is deserving of death at our hands?

Footnotes

1. *Ethics* 83 (April 1973): 214–23.
2. Ibid., p. 220, n. 21.
3. Kant, *The Metaphysical Elements of Justice,* trans. John Ladd (Indianapolis: Bobbs-Merrill Co., 1965), p. 100.
4. See Furman v. Georgia, 92 S.Ct. 2726, 2779–80 (Marshall, J., concurring 1972), and the authorities cited at 2780, no. 86.
5. See Moberly, *The Ethics of Punishment* (London: Faber & Faber, 1968); Herbert Morris, "Persons and Punishment," *Monist* 52 (October 1968): 475; Jeffrey Murphy, "Three Mistakes about Retributivism," *Analysis* 31 (April 1971): 166.
6. See Furman v. Georgia, 92 S.Ct. 2726, 2779 (Marshall, J. concurring 1972).
7. Ibid., at 2761 (Stewart, J., concurring), 2836 (Powell, J., dissenting); Goldberg and Dershowitz, "Declaring the Death Penalty Unconstitutional," *Harvard Law Review* 83 (June 1970); 1773, 1796.
8. Murphy, p. 166.
9. Kant, p. 100.
10. Ibid., p. 101.
11. The concept of the capacity for a sense of justice is developed in Rawls, "The Sense of Justice," *Philosophical Review* 72 (1963): 281.
12. *Republic,* trans. Cornford (Oxford: Oxford University Press, 1941), p. 13.
13. Concurring in Trop v. Dulles, 356 U.S. 86, 102 (1958), and Furman v. Georgia, 92 S.Ct. 2726, 2742–48 (1972).
14. Furman v. Georgia, at 2743.
15. Ibid., at 2748.
16. See ibid., 92 S.Ct. 2726, 2779 (Marshall, J., concurring), 2761 (Stewart, J., concurring), 2836 (Powell, J., dissenting).
17. Kant, p. 102.
18. Moberly, on whose view I have drawn extensively here, is one leading retributivist who opposes capital punishment (see *The Ethics of Punishment,* pp. 296–99).
19. See Kant, p. 103, where such an execution is used as an example.

Review Questions

1. Explain Long's argument for saying that capital punishment is cruel and unusual.

2. According to Gerstein, what is the "classic utilitarian calculus" as it is applied to punishment?

3. What is Kant's warning?

4. According to Gerstein, why isn't retributivism "a fancy word for revenge?"

5. According to Gerstein, what would retributivism regard as a cruel and unusual punishment?

6. How does Gerstein characterize the law of retribution (*lex talionis*)?

7. Does retributivism support the death penalty or not? What is Gerstein's view on this?

ber of the community? Explain your answer.

2. In your opinion, is the principle of *lex talionis* acceptable or not? Why or why not?

❧

Jonathan Glover

Execution and Assassination

Jonathan Glover is a Fellow and tutor in philosophy at New College, Oxford, and has written Responsibility (1970).

Glover begins with a discussion of Kant's retributive view and the absolutist rejection of capital punishment. He finds both of these to be unacceptable from a utilitarian point of view. The utilitarian approach is that the death penalty is justified if the number of lives saved exceeds the number of executions. But due to the bad side effects of execution on the person executed and on others, as well as other undesirable features, the death penalty is not justified unless it has a substantial deterrent effect. After considering arguments for this deterrent effect, Glover concludes that the case for capital punishment as a substantial deterrent fails.

The Penal Law is a Categorical Imperative; and woe to him who creeps through the serpent-windings of Utilitarianism to discover some advantage that may discharge him from the Justice of Punishment, or even from the due measure of it ... For if Justice and Righteousness perish, human life would no longer have any value in the world ... Whoever has committed murder must die.

Immanuel Kant, The Philosophy of Law

It is curious, but till that moment I had never realized

what it means to destroy a healthy, conscious man. When I saw the prisoner step aside to avoid the puddle I saw the mystery, the unspeakable wrongness, of cutting a life short when it is in full tide. This man was not dying, he was alive just as we are alive. All the organs of his body were working—bowels digesting food, skin renewing itself, nails growing, tissues forming—all toiling away in solemn foolery. His nails would still be growing when he stood on the drop, when he was falling through the air with a tenth of a second to live. His eyes saw the yellow gravel and the grey walls, and his brain still remembered, foresaw, reasoned, even about puddles. He and we were a party of men walking together, seeing, hearing, feeling, understanding the same world; and in two minutes, with a sudden snap, one of us would be gone—one mind less, one world less.

George Orwell, "A Hanging," Adelphi, 1931

The debate about capital punishment for murder is, emotionally at least, dominated by two absolutist views. On the retributive view, the murderer must be given the punishment he deserves, which is death. On the other view, analogous to pacifism about war, there is in principle no possibility of justifying capital punishment; in execution there is only "the unspeakable wrongness of cutting a life short when it is in full tide." Supporters of these two approaches agree only in rejecting the serpent-windings of utilitarianism.

Let us look first at the retributive view. According to retributivism in its purest form, the aim of punishment is quite independent of any beneficial social consequences it may have. To quote Kant again:

Even if a Civil Society resolved to dissolve itself with the consent of all its members—as might be supposed in the case of a people inhabiting an island resolving to separate and scatter themselves throughout the whole world—the last Murderer lying in the prison ought to be executed before the resolution was carried out. This ought to be done in order that everyone may realize the desert of his deeds, and that blood-guiltiness may not remain upon the people; for otherwise they might all be regarded as participators in the murder as a public violation of justice.

This view of punishment, according to which it has a value independent of its contribution to reducing the crime rate, is open to the objection that acting on it leads to what many consider to be pointless suffering. To impose suffering or deprivation on someone, or to take his life, is something that those of us who are not retributivists think needs very strong justification in terms of benefits, either to the person concerned or to other people. The retributivist has to say either that the claims of justice can make it right to harm someone where no one benefits, or else to cite the curiously **metaphysical** "benefits" of justice being done, such as Kant's concern that we should have "blood-guiltiness" removed. I have no way of refuting these positions, as they seem to involve no clear intellectual mistake. I do not expect to win the agreement of those who hold them, and I am simply presupposing the other view, that there is already enough misery in the world, and that adding to it requires a justification in terms of nonmetaphysical benefits to people.

This is not to rule out retributive moral principles perhaps playing a limiting role in a general theory of punishment. There is a lot to be said for the retributive restrictions that *only* those who deserve punishment should receive it and that they should never get more punishment than they deserve. (The case for this, which at least partly rests on utilitarian considerations, has been powerfully argued by H.L.A. Hart.[1]) But the approach to be adopted here rules out using retributive considerations to justify any punishment not already justifiable in terms of social benefits. In particular it rules out the argument that capital punishment can be justified, whether or not it reduces the crime rate, because the criminal deserves it.

This approach also has the effect of casting doubt on another way of defending capi-

tal punishment, which was forthrightly expressed by Lord Denning: "The ultimate justification of any punishment is not that it is a deterrent, but that it is the emphatic denunciation by the community of a crime: and from this point of view, there are some murders which, in the present state of public opinion, demand the most emphatic denunciation of all, namely the death penalty."[2] The question here is whether the point of the denunciation is to reduce the murder rate, in which case this turns out after all to be a utilitarian justification, or whether denunciation is an end in itself. If it is an end in itself, it starts to look like the retributive view in disguise, and should be rejected for the same reasons.

If we reject retribution for its own sake as a justification for capital punishment we are left with two alternative general approaches to the question. One is an absolute rejection in principle of any possibility of capital punishment being justified, in the spirit of Orwell's remarks. The other is the rather more messy approach, broadly utilitarian in character, of weighing up likely social costs and benefits.

THE ABSOLUTIST REJECTION OF CAPITAL PUNISHMENT

To some people, it is impossible to justify the act of killing a fellow human being. They are absolute pacifists about war and are likely to think of capital punishment as "judicial murder." They will sympathize with Beccaria's question: "Is it not absurd that the laws which detest and punish homicide, in order to prevent murder, publicly commit murder themselves?"

The test of whether an opponent of capital punishment adopts this absolutist position is whether he would still oppose it if it could be shown to save many more lives than it cost, if, say, every execution deterred a dozen potential murderers. The absolutist, unlike the utilitarian opponent of the death penalty, would be unmoved by any such evidence. This question brings out the links between the absolutist position and the **acts and omissions doctrine.** For those of us who reject the acts and omissions doctrine, the deaths we fail to prevent have to be given weight, as well as the deaths we cause by execution. So those of us who do not accept the acts and omissions doctrine cannot be absolutist opponents of capital punishment.

There is a variant on the absolutist position that at first sight seems not to presuppose the acts and omissions doctrine. On this view, while saving a potential murder victim is in itself as important as not killing a murderer, there is something so cruel about the kind of death involved in capital punishment that this rules out the possibility of its being justified. Those of us who reject the acts and omissions doctrine have to allow that sometimes there can be side effects associated with an act of killing, but not with failure to save a life, which can be sufficiently bad to make a substantial moral difference between the two. When this view is taken of the cruelty of the death penalty, it is not usually the actual method of execution that is objected to, though this can seem important, as in the case where international pressure on General Franco led him to substitute shooting for the garrote. What seems pecularily cruel and horrible about capital punishment is that the condemned man has the period of waiting, knowing how and when he is to be killed. Many of us would rather die suddenly than linger for weeks or months knowing we were fatally ill, and the condemned man's position is several degrees worse than that of the person given a few months to live by doctors. He has the additional horror of knowing exactly when he will die, and of knowing that his death will be in a ritualized killing by other people, symbolizing his ultimate rejection by the members of his community. The whole of his life may seem to have a different and horrible meaning when he sees it leading up to this end.

For reasons of this kind, capital punishment can plausibly be claimed to fall under the United States Constitution's ban on "cruel and unusual punishments," so long as the word unusual is not interpreted too strictly. The same reasons make the death penalty a plausible candidate for falling under a rather similar ethical ban, which has been expressed by H.L.A. Hart: "There are many different ways in which we think it morally incumbent on us to *qualify* or *limit* the pursuit of the utilitarian goal by methods of punishment. Some punishments are ruled out as too barbarous to use *whatever their social utility* " [3] (final italics mine). Because of the extreme cruelty of capital punishment, many of us would, if forced to make a choice between two horrors, prefer to be suddenly murdered than be sentenced to death and executed. This is what makes it seem reasonable to say that the absolutist rejection of the death penalty need not rest on the acts and omissions doctrine.

But this appearance is illusory. The special awfulness of capital punishment may make an execution even more undesirable than a murder (though many would disagree on the grounds that this is outweighed by the desirability that the guilty rather than the innocent should die). Even if we accept that an execution is worse than an average murder, it does not follow from this that capital punishment is too barbarous to use *whatever its social utility.* For supposing a single execution deterred many murders? Or suppose that some of the murders deterred would themselves have been as cruel as an execution? When we think of the suffering imposed in a famous kidnapping case, where the mother received her son's ear through the post, we may feel uncertain even that capital punishment is more cruel than some "lesser" crimes than murder. The view that some kinds of suffering are too great to impose, whatever their social utility, rules out the possibility of justifying them, however much more suffering they would prevent. And this does presuppose the acts and omissions doctrine, and so excludes some of us even from this version of absolutism.

A UTILITARIAN APPROACH

It is often supposed that the utilitarian alternative to absolutism is simply one of adopting an unqualified maximizing policy. On such a view, the death penalty would be justified if, and only if, it was reasonable to think the number of lives saved exceeded the number of executions. (The question of what to do where the numbers exactly balance presupposes a fineness of measurement that is unattainable in these matters.) On any utilitarian view, numbers of lives saved must be a very important consideration. But there are various special features that justify the substantial qualification of a maximizing policy.

The special horror of the period of waiting for execution may not justify the absolutist rejection of the death penalty, but it is a powerful reason for thinking that an execution may normally cause more misery than a murder, and so for thinking that, if capital punishment is to be justified, it must do better than break even when lives saved through deterrence are compared with lives taken by the executioner.

This view is reinforced when we think of some of the other side effects of the death penalty. It must be appalling to be told that your husband, wife, or child has been murdered, but this is surely less bad than the experience of waiting a month or two for your husband, wife, or child to be executed. And those who think that the suffering of the murderer himself matters less than that of an innocent victim will perhaps not be prepared to extend this view to the suffering of the murderer's parents, wife, and children.

There is also the possibility of mistakenly executing an innocent man, something which it is very probable happened in the case of Timothy Evans. The German Federal Ministry of Justice is quoted in the Council of Europe's report on *The Death Penalty in European Countries* as saying that in the hundred years to 1953, there were twenty-seven death sentences "now established or presumed" to be miscarriages of justice. This point is often used as an argument against capital punishment, but what is often not noticed is that its force must depend on the special horrors of execution as compared with other forms of death, including being murdered. For the victim of murder is innocent too, and he also has no form of redress. It is only the (surely correct) assumption that an innocent man faces something much worse in execution than in murder that gives this argument its claim to prominence in this debate. For, otherwise, the rare cases of innocent men being executed would be completely overshadowed by the numbers of innocent men being murdered. (Unless, of course, the acts and omissions doctrine is again at work here, for execution is something that we, as a community, *do* while a higher murder rate is something, we at most *allow*.)

The death penalty also has harmful effects on people other than the condemned man and his family. For most normal people, to be professionally involved with executions, whether as judge, prison warden, chaplain, or executioner, must be highly disturbing. Arthur Koestler quotes the case of the executioner Ellis, who attempted suicide a few weeks after he executed a sick woman "whose insides fell out before she vanished through the trap." [4] (Though the chances must be very small of the experience of Mr. Pierrepoint, who describes in his autobiography how he had to execute a friend with whom he often sang duets in a pub.[5]) And there are wider effects on society at large. When there is capital punishment, we are all involved in the horrible business of a long-premeditated killing, and most of us will to some degree share in the emotional response George Orwell had so strongly when he had to be present. It cannot be good for children at school to know that there is an execution at the prison down the road. And there is another bad effect, drily stated in the *Report of the Royal Commission on Capital Punishment:* "No doubt the ambition that prompts an average of five applications a week for the post of hangman, and the craving that draws a crowd to the prison where a notorious murderer is being executed, reveal psychological qualities that no state would wish to foster in its citizens.''

Capital punishment is also likely to operate erratically. Some murderers are likely to *go* free because the death penalty makes juries less likely to convict. (Charles Dickens, in a newspaper article quoted in the 1868 Commons debate, gave the example of a forgery case, where a jury found a £ 10 note to be worth thirty-nine shillings, in order to save the forger's life.) There are also great problems in operating a reprieve system without arbitrariness, say, in deciding whether being pregnant or having a young baby should qualify a woman for a reprieve.

Finally, there is the drawback that the retention or reintroduction of capital punishment contributes to a tradition of cruel and horrible punishment that we might hope would wither away. Nowadays we never think of disemboweling people or chopping off their hands as a punishment. Even if these punishments would be especially effective in deterring some very serious crimes, they are not regarded as a real possibility. To many of us, it seems that the utilitarian benefits from this situation outweigh the loss of any deterrent power they might have if reintroduced for some repulsive crime like kidnapping. And the longer we leave capital punishment in abeyance, the more its use will seem as out of the question as the no more cruel punishment of mutilation. (At this point, I come near to Hart's view that some punishments are too barbarous to use whatever their social utility. The difference is that I think that arguments for and against a punishment should be based on social utility, but that a widespread view that some things are unthinkable is itself of great social utility.)

For these reasons, a properly thought-out utilitarianism does not enjoin an unqualified policy of seeking the minimum loss of life, as the no trade-off view does. Capital punishment has its own special cruelties and horrors, which change the whole position. In order to be justified, it must be shown, with good evidence, that it has a deterrent effect not obtainable by less awful means, and one that is quite substantial rather than marginal.

DETERRENCE AND MURDER

The arguments over whether capital punishment deters murder more effectively than less drastic methods are of two kinds: statistical and intuitive. The statistical arguments are based on various kinds of comparisons of murder rates. Rates are compared before and after abolition in a country, and, where possible, further comparisons are made with rates after reintroduction of capital punishment. Rates are compared in neighboring countries, or neighboring states of the U.S.C.A., with and without the death penalty. I am not a statistician and have no special competence to discuss the issue, but will merely purvey the received opinion of those who have looked into the matter. Those who have studied the figures are agreed that there is no striking correlation between the absence of capital punishment and any alteration in the curve of the murder rate. Having agreed on this point, they then fall into two schools. On one view, we can conclude that capital punishment is not a greater deterrent to murder than the prison sentences that are substituted for it. On the other, more cautious, view, we can only conclude that we do not know that capital punishment is a deterrent. I shall not attempt to choose between these interpretations. For, given that capital punishment is justified only where there is good evidence that it is a substantial deterrent, either interpretation fails to support the case for it.

If the statistical evidence were conclusive that capital punishment did not deter more than milder punishments, this would leave no room for any further discussion. But, since the statistical evidence may be inconclusive, many people feel there is room left for intuitive arguments. Some of these deserve examination. The intuitive case was forcefully stated in 1864 by Sir James Fitzjames Stephen: [6]

No other punishment deters men so effectually from

committing crimes as the punishment of death. This is one of those propositions which it is difficult to prove, simply because they are in themselves more obvious than any proof can make them. It is possible to display ingenuity in arguing against it, but that is all. The whole experience of mankind is in the other direction. The threat of instant death is the one to which resort has always been made when there was an absolute necessity for producing some result. . . . No one goes to certain inevitable death except by compulsion. Put the matter the other way. Was there ever yet a criminal who, when sentenced to death and brought out to die, would refuse the offer of a commutation of his sentence for the severest secondary punishment? Surely not. Why is this? It can only be because "All that a man has will he give for his life." In any secondary punishment, however terrible, there is hope; but death is death; its terrors cannot be described more forcibly.

These claims turn out when scrutinized to be much more speculative and doubtful than they at first sight appear.

The first doubt arises when Stephen talks of "certain inevitable death." The Royal Commission, in their *Report,* after quoting the passage from Stephen above, quote figures to show that, in the fifty years from 1900 to 1949, there was in England and Wales one execution for every twelve murders known to the police. In Scotland in the same period there was less than one execution for every twenty-five murders known to the police. Supporters of Stephen's view could supplement their case by advocating more death sentences and fewer reprieves, or by optimistic speculations about better police detection or greater willingness of juries to convict. But the reality of capital punishment as it was in these countries, unmodified by such recommendations and speculations, was not one where the potential murderer faced certain, inevitable death. This may incline us to modify Stephen's estimate of its deterrent effect, unless we buttress his view with the further speculation that a fair number of potential murderers falsely believed that what they would face was certain, inevitable death.

The second doubt concerns Stephen's talk of "the threat of instant death." The reality again does not quite fit this. By the time

the police conclude their investigation, the case is brought to trial, and verdict and sentence are followed by appeal, petition for reprieve, and then execution, many months have probably elapsed, and when this time factor is added to the low probability of the murderers being executed, the picture looks very different. For we often have a time bias, being less affected by threats of future catastrophes than by threats of instant ones. The certainty of immediate death is one thing; it is another thing merely to increase one's chances of death in the future. Unless this were so, no one would smoke or take on such high-risk jobs as diving in the North Sea.

There is another doubt when Stephen very plausibly says that virtually all criminals would prefer life imprisonment to execution. The difficulty is over whether this entitles us to conclude that it is therefore a more effective deterrent. For there is the possibility that, compared with the long term of imprisonment that is the alternative, capital punishment is what may appropriately be called an "overkill." It may be that, for those who will be deterred by threat of punishment, a long prison sentence is sufficient deterrent. I am not suggesting that this is so, but simply that it is an open question whether a worse alternative here generates any additional deterrent effect. The answer is *not* intuitively obvious.

Stephen's case rests on the speculative psychological assumptions that capital punishment is not an overkill compared with a prison sentence, and that its additional deterrent effect is not obliterated by time bias, nor by the low probability of execution, nor by a combination of these factors. Or else it must be assumed that, where the additional deterrent effect would be obliterated by the low probability of death, either on its own or in combination with time bias, the potential murderer thinks the probability is higher than it is. Some of these assumptions may be true, but, when they are brought out into the open, it is by no means obvious that the required combination of them can be relied upon.

Supporters of the death penalty also sometimes use what David A. Conway, in his valuable discussion of this issue, calls "the best-bet argument." [7] On this view, since there is no certainty whether or not capital punishment reduces the number of murders, either decision about it involves gambling with lives. It is suggested that it is better to gamble with the lives of murderers than with the lives of their innocent potential victims. This presupposes the attitude, rejected here, that a murder is a greater evil than the execution of a murderer. But, since this attitude probably has overwhelmingly widespread support, it is worth noting that, even if it is accepted, the best-bet argument is unconvincing. This is because, as Conway has pointed out, it overlooks the fact that we are not choosing between the chance of a murderer dying and the chance of a victim dying. In leaving the death penalty, we are opting for the certainty of the murderer dying that we hope will give us a chance of a potential victim being saved. This would look like a good bet only if we thought an execution substantially preferable to a murder and either the statistical evidence or the intuitive arguments made the effectiveness of the death penalty as a deterrent look reasonably likely.

Since the statistical studies do not give any clear indication that capital punishment makes any difference to the number of murders committed, the only chance of its supporters discharging the heavy burden of justification would be if the intuitive arguments were extremely powerful. We might then feel justified in supposing that other factors distorted the murder rate, masking the substantial deterrent effect of capital punishment. The intuitive arguments, presented as the merest platitudes, turn out to be speculative and unobvious. I conclude that the case for capital punishment as a substantial deterrent fails.

DETERRENCE AND POLITICAL CRIMES BY OPPOSITION GROUPS

It is sometimes suggested that the death penalty may be an effective deterrent in the case of a special class of "political" crimes. The "ordinary" murder (killing one's wife in a moment of rage, shooting a policeman in panic after a robbery, killing someone in a brawl) may not be particularly sensitive to different degrees of punishment. But some killings for political purposes have a degree of preparation and thought that may allow the severity of the penalty to affect the calculation. Two different kinds of killing come to mind here. There are killings as part of a political campaign, ranging from assassination through terrorist activities up to full-scale guerrilla war. And then there are policies carried out by repressive governments, varying from "liquidation" of individual opponents with or without "trial" to policies of wholesale extermination, sometimes, but not always, in wartime.

Let us look first at killings by groups opposed to governments. Would the various sectarian terrorist groups in Ireland stop their killings if those involved were executed? Would independence movements in countries like Algeria or Kenya have confined themselves to nonviolent means if more executions had taken place? Could the Nazis have deterred the French resistance by more executions? Could the Americans have deterred guerrillas war in Vietnam by more executions?

To ask these questions is to realize both the variety of different political situations in which the question of deterrent killing arises, and also to be reminded, if it is necessary, that moral right is not always on the side of the authorities trying to do the deterring. But let us, for the sake of argument, assume a decent government is trying to deal with terrorists or guerrillas whose cause has nothing to be said for it. People have always gone to war knowing they risk their lives, and those prepared to fight in a guerrilla war seem scarcely likely to change their mind because of the marginal extra risk of capital punishment if they are arrested. If the case is to be made, it must apply to lower levels of violence than full-scale guerrilla war.

Given the death penalty's drawbacks, is there any reason to think it would be sufficiently effective in deterring a campaign of terrorist violence to be justified? The evidence is again inconclusive. In many countries there have been terrorist campaigns where the authorities have responded with executions without stopping the campaign. It is always open to someone to say that the level of terrorist activity might have been even higher but for the executions, but it is hard to see why this should be likely. Those who do the shooting or the planting of bombs are not usually the leaders and can be easily replaced by others willing to risk their lives. Danger to life does not deter people from fighting in wars, and a terrorist gunman may be just as committed to his cause as a soldier. And executions create martyrs, which helps the terrorist cause. They may even raise the level of violence by leading to reprisals.

But it may be that a sufficiently ruthless policy of executions would be effective enough to overcome these drawbacks. It has been claimed that the policy of the Irish government in 1922–3 is an instance of this. David R. Bates describes it as follows: [8]

In the turbulent period following the establishment of the Irish Free State, military courts with power to inflict the death penalty were set up to enable the Irregulars (opposing the Treaty) to be crushed. These powers were first used on 17 November 1922, when four young men were arrested in Dublin and, on being found to be armed, were executed. Shortly afterwards the Englishman, Erskine Childers, captured while carrying a revolver, was also executed. On 7 December two Deputies were shot (one fatally) by the Irregulars. The Minister for Defense, with the agreement of the Cabinet, selected four Irregular leaders who had been in prison since the fall of the Four Courts on 29 June. They were wakened, told to prepare themselves, and were executed by firing squad at dawn. During a six-month period, almost twice as many Irregular prisoners were executed as had been executed by the British from 1916 to 1921. At the end of April 1923, the Irregulars sought a cease fire to discuss terms. The Free State Government refused. In May 1924, the Irregulars conceded military defeat.

This is an impressive case, and it may be that this degree of ruthlessness by the government involved fewer deaths than would have taken place during a prolonged terrorist campaign. But against this must be set some doubts. What would have happened if the terrorists had been as ruthless in reprisal as the government, perhaps announcing that for every man executed there would be two murders? Is it clear that after a period of such counter-retaliation it would have been the Irregulars rather than the government who climbed down? Does not any net saving of lives by the government's ruthless policy depend on the terrorists refraining from counter-retaliation, and can this be relied on in other cases? And is there not something dangerous in the precedent set when a government has prisoners executed without their having been convicted and sentenced for a capital offence? And, in this case, is it even clear that the defeat of the Irregulars ended once and for all the violence associated with the issues they were campaigning about? I raise these questions, not to claim that the government policy was clearly wrong, but to show how even a case like this is ambiguous in the weight it lends to the argument for using the death penalty against terrorism.

I do not think that the chance of a net saving of lives will in general outweigh the combination of the general drawbacks of capital punishment combined with the danger of its merely leading to a higher level of violence in a terrorist situation. But this is a matter of judgment rather than proof, and I admit that it *may* be that the opposite view had better results than mine would have had in 1922.

DETERRENCE AND POLITICAL CRIMES BY THE AUTHORITIES

The other category of political crimes that sometimes seems so special as to justify the death penalty is atrocities committed by governments or their agents. The executions of leading Nazis after the Nuremberg trials and the execution of Eichmann after his trial in Jerusalem come to mind. The justification usually advanced for these executions is retributive, and it is hard to imagine any more deserving candidates for the death penalty. But, for those of us who do not consider retribution an acceptable aim of punishment, the question must be whether executing them made their kind of activity less likely to happen again in the future. For, if not, we have no answer to the question asked by Victor Gollancz at the time of the Eichmann trial: why should we think we improve the world by turning six million deaths into six million and one?

The chances of people who design or carry out governmental policies of murder being tried and sentenced must often be very small. Sometimes this happens as the result of revolution or defeat in war, but those in power stand a fairly good chance of being killed under these circumstances anyway, and the additional hazard of capital punishment may not have much deterrent effect. As with "ordinary" murderers, the hope of not being caught reduces the punishment's terrors. Some of those who murdered for Hitler were executed; their opposite numbers under Stalin paid no penalty. The torturers who worked for the Greek colonels were brought to trial, but those now at work in Chile, Brazil, and South Africa have every expectation of not being punished.

When considering isolated cases of governmental murder (perhaps the assassination of a troublesome foreign leader by a country's intelligence agency, or the single killing of a political opponent) there seems no reason to think capital punishment more of a deterrent than it is of "ordinary" nonpolitical murder. If anything, it is likely to be less of a deterrent because of the reduced chance of a murder charge ever being brought. So there seems no case for treating these crimes as other than ordinary murders. But when considering large-scale atrocities, on the scale of those of Hitler or Stalin, or even on the scale of Lyndon Johnson in Vietnam or General Gowon in Nigeria, a version of the best-bet argument comes into play. There are two possible advantages to the death penalty here. One is simply that of totally eliminating the chance of the same mass murderer occupying a position of leadership again. Suppose Hitler had been captured at the end of the Second World War and the question of executing him had arisen. If he had not been executed, it is overwhelmingly probable that he would have spent the rest of his life in Spandau prison, writing his memoirs and giving increasingly senile lectures on world history to visiting journalists. But there would always be the very slight risk of an escape and return to power in the style of Napoleon. This slight risk is removed by execution. The other advantage of the death penalty is the chance, which we have seen to be probably very slight, of deterring repetition of such policies by other leaders.

The best-bet argument in these cases can be used by someone who accepts that the dangers of a defeated leader returning to power are very small and that the chances of execution deterring future leaders from similar policies are also very small. The argument is simply that, where the prevention of such enormous atrocities is in question, even an extremely small probability of prevention is valuable. Consider a case in which numbers and probabilities are parallel, but in which act and omission are reversed. Suppose someone in the hospital can have his life saved only by the making of some organism that has previously been banned. The reason for the ban is that there is a danger, but only a very faint one, of the organism getting out of control. If it does this, the death rate will run into millions. Let us suppose that our intuitive estimate of the unquantifiable risk here is the same as our intuitive estimate of the unquantifiable reduction of risk caused by executing the murdering leader. Those who would rather let the hospital patient die than breach the ban on the dangerous organism must either rely on the acts and omissions doctrine, or else rely on some difference of side effects, if they are not prepared to support executing the murdering politician or official.

Part of the difficulty in interpreting comparisons of this sort arises from the fact that we are dealing with probabilities that cannot be measured. And, even if they could be measured, most of us are unclear what sacrifices are worth making for the reduction of some risk that is already very small. But if we make the highly artificial assumption that the alterations in probability of risk are the same in the medical case as in the execution case, the dilemma remains. Let us suppose that the risk is one that we would not take in the medical case to save a single life. Those of us who do not accept the acts and omissions doctrine must then either find some difference of side effects or else support the execution.

Side effects do go some way towards separating the two cases. For, to breach the ban on producing the organism, even if it does no harm itself, contributes by example to a less strict observance of that ban (and possibly others) in cases in which the risk may be much greater. In the case of the Nazi leaders, such bad side effects as exist follow from execution rather than from saving their lives. These side effects include the contribution made to a climate of opinion where the death penalty seems more acceptable in other contexts, and the precedent that may encourage politicians to have their overthrown rivals, at home or abroad, executed. This last effect could be mitigated by more effort than was made at Nuremberg to remove the impression of the defeated being tried by the victors. It would be possible to set up a court of a genuinely international kind, independent of governmental pressure, to which prosecutions for a large-scale murder could be brought. But the general effect on the public consciousness of having capital punishment as a serious possibility would remain. I am uncertain how to weigh this against the small chance of helping to avert a great evil. For this reason my own views on this question are undecided.

Footnotes

1. H.L.A. Hart, "Prolegomenon to the Principles of Punishment," *Proceedings of the Aristotelian Society*, 1959–60.

2. Quoted in the *Report of the Royal Commission on Capital Punishment*, 1953.

3. H.L.A. Hart, "Murder and the Principles of Punishment," *Northwestern Law Review*, 1958.

4. Arthur Koestler, *Reflections on Hanging*, London, 1956.

5. Albert Pierrepoint, *Executioner: Pierrepoint*, London, 1974.

6. James Fitzjames Stephen, "Capital Punishments," *Fraser's Magazine*, 1864.

7. David A. Conway, "Capital Punishment and Deterrence," *Philosophy and Public Affairs*, 1974.

8. Professor David R. Bates, Letter to *The Times*, 14 October 1975.

Review Questions

1. Why doesn't Glover accept Kant's view of capital punishment?

2. What is the "other view" that Glover is presupposing?

3. Why doesn't Glover accept the absolutist rejection of capital punishment?

4. Why does Glover think that capital punishment can plausibly be claimed to be a "cruel and unusual punishment?"

5. According to Glover, in what cases can capital punishment be justified even if it is cruel?

6. State the maximizing policy, and the considerations that Glover introduces to qualify it.

7. According to Glover, how can capital punishment be justified?

8. Glover discusses three arguments (beginning with the statistical argument) that are used to defend capital punishment. What are these arguments, and why doesn't Glover accept them?

9. What is Glover's position on capital punishment for political crimes?

Discussion Questions

1. "Whoever has committed murder must *die*." Do you agree with this statement? Explain your view.

2. Is the death penalty a cruel and unusual pun-

ishment? Explain your answer.

3. Glover concludes that the case for capital punishment as a substantial deterrent fails. Do you agree? Defend your position.

4. Can you think of any cases in which capital punishment would be justified? What are they?

Problem Cases

1. The Case of Troy Gregg (*Gregg* v. *Georgia,* 428 U.S. 153, 1976) Troy Gregg and Floyd Allen were hitchhiking when they were picked up by Fred Simmons and Bob Moore. Simmons and Moore left the car at a rest stop. According to the testimony of Allen, Gregg said that they were going to rob Simmons and Moore. He fired at them when they came back to the car, then shot each of them in the head, robbed them, and finally drove away with Allen. Gregg first admitted that Allen's account was accurate, but later denied it. Gregg's story was that Simmons had attacked him, and that he had killed the two men in self-defense. The jury found Gregg guilty of two counts of murder, and determined that the murders were committed for the purpose of robbery.

Should Gregg be given the death sentence or not? Defend your answer?

2. The Case of Paul Crump (*See* Ronald Bailey, "Facing Death: A New Life Perhaps Too Late," *Life,* [July 27, 1962]: 28–29.) In the early 1950's, Paul Crump was convicted of a vicious murder, sentenced to death, and put in an Illinois prison. At his trial he was said to be full of hatred, "animalistic and belligerent," and a danger to society. Yet under the influence of Warden Jack Johnson and his prison reforms, Crump became rehabilitated. Even though he had only a ninth-grade education, he took courses in reading and writing. Soon he was reading poetry, fiction, and philosophy, and writing stories, articles and poems which were published in small magazines. He wrote an autobiographical novel, *Burn, Killer, Burn.* Also he began to help his fellow prisoners. He was put in charge of caring for the sick and disabled in the convalescent section of the jail hospital. All this did not happen overnight, but took a period of seven years. At the end of this time, Warden Johnson claimed that Crump was "completely rehabilitated," and on August 1, 1962, Illinois Governor Otto Kerner commuted Crump's death sentence to 199 years with the possibility of parole.

Do you think that Governor Kerner made the right decision? Explain your answer.

Would it have been morally right to free Crump? Why or why not?

Would it have been morally justifiable to execute Crump despite his rehabilitation? What do you think?

3. The Sacco-Vanzetti Case On April 15, 1920, a paymaster for a shoe company in South Braintree, MA, and his guard were shot and killed by two men who escaped with over $15,000. Witnesses thought the two men were Italians, and Nicola Sacco and Bartolomeo Vanzetti were arrested. Both men were anarchists and had evaded the army draft. Upon their arrest they made false statements, and both carried firearms; but neither had a criminal record, nor was there any evidence that they had the money. In July, 1921, they were found guilty and sentenced to death. The conduct of the trial by Judge Webster Thayer was criticised, and indeed much of the evidence against them was later discredited. The appeal for a new trial was denied, and Governor Alvan T. Fuller, after postponing the execution, allowed them to be executed on August 22, 1927. They were widely regarded as being innocent, and there were worldwide sympathy demonstrations. The case has been the subject of many books, most of which agree that Vanzetti was innocent, but that Sacco may have been guilty. The gun found on Sacco was tested with modern ballistics equipment in 1961. These tests seemed to show that the gun had been used to kill the guard.

Was it morally right to execute these two men? Why or why not?

4. The "Angel of Death" Case In New York City there is a series of unsolved murders. In each case an elderly man or woman is found dead from arsenic poisoning. Fingerprints are found at the scene of one of the crimes, and they are identified as belonging to George Smith, a twenty-year-old man with a record of drug offenses. He is picked up and he admits he is the killer. It also turns out that he is a heavy user of drugs, especially LSD. At the trial he testifies that he was an "angel of death" commanded by God to help old people die and go to heaven. Three psychiatrists testify that Smith is legally sane, but that while on drugs he suffers from psychotic episodes in which he hears voices that he believes are from God. The jury determines that Smith is legally sane, and that he is guilty of five counts of murder.

Should Smith be given the death sentence? If not, then what sentence would be appropriate?

Suggested Readings

(1) Bedau, Hugo Adam. "Capital Punishment." In *Matters of Life and Death,* edited by Tom Regan, 148–182 New York: Random House, 1980. Bedau is an abolitionist who argues that neither the appeal to retribution nor deterrence justifies the death penalty as opposed to the lesser penalty of life imprisonment.

(2) Bedau, Hugo Adam, ed. *The Death Penalty in America,* 3d ed. New York: Oxford, 1982. This excellent anthology provides a number of useful articles on factual data relevant to the death penalty, as well as articles both for and against it.

(3) Ezorsky, Gertrude, ed. *Philosophical Perspectives on Punishment.* Albany: State University of New York Press, 1972. This is an anthology on general philosophical questions about punishment. It includes a section on capital punishment.

(4) Goldberg, Steven. "On Capital Punishment." *Ethics* 85 (October 1974): 67–74. Goldberg examines the factual issue of whether or not the death penalty is a uniquely effective deterrent. A revised version entitled "Does Capital Punishment Deter?" appears in Richard A. Wasserstrom, ed., *Today's Moral Problems,* 2d ed. (New York: Macmillan, 1979, pp. 538–551).

(5) van den Haag, Ernest. "In Defense of the Death Penalty: A Practical and Moral Analysis." In *The Death Penalty in America,* 3d ed., edited by Hugo Adam Bedau, 323–333 New York: Oxford, 1982. Van den Haag offers a retentionist argument based on our uncertainty concerning the deterrent effect of the death penalty: Faced with this uncertainty, it is better to risk the lives of the convicted murderers than to risk the lives of innocent people. This "best-bet" argument is rejected by Glover and Bedau.

(6) van den Haag, Ernest, and John P. Conrad. *The Death Penalty: A Debate.* New York: Plenum, 1983. Conrad is against the death penalty and van den Haag is for it; each presents his case and critically responds to the other's arguments.

(7) Hook, Sidney. "The Death Sentence." In Hugo *The Death Penalty in America,* rev. ed., edited by Hugo Adam Bedau. Garden City, NY: Doubleday, 1967. Hook supports the retention of the death penalty in two cases: (1) defendants convicted of murder who choose the death sentence rather than life imprisonment, and (2) those who have been sentenced to prison for premeditated murder, and then murder again. Since the publication of the original essay, Professor Hook advises that he is now prepared to extend the scope of discretionary death sentences in cases of multiple and aggravated capital crimes.

(8) Kant, Immanuel. *The Metaphysical Elements of Justice,* trans. John Ladd. Indianapolis, Indiana: Bobbs-Merrill, 1965. Kant's views on capital punishment are found on pages 96–106.

(9) Long, Thomas. "Capital Punishment—'Cruel and Unusual'?" *Ethics* 83 (April 1973): 214–223. Long discusses various arguments for the view that capital punishment is cruel and unusual.

(10) Murphy, Jeffrie G. ed. *Punishment and Rehabilitation,* 2d ed. Belmont, CA: Wadsworth, 1985. This anthology covers various philosophical aspects of punishment including capital punishment.

Glossary

Appellate relating to appeals; an appellate court has the power to affirm, reverse, or modify the decision of a lower court.

Abolitionists in this context, those who want to abolish the death penalty. As opposed to retentionists, who want to retain the death penalty.

Acts and omissions doctrine the doctrine that there is an important moral difference between acts and omissions (failures to act) such that an act can be wrong but an omission with the same effect not wrong. As it is applied to killing and letting die, the doctrine says that killing an innocent person is wrong, but letting her die may not be wrong, or is less wrong. The application of the doctrine to euthanasia is attacked by Rachels in "Euthanasia, Killing, and Letting Die" (Chapter 2); he attacks its application to the problem of hunger in "Killing and Starving to Death" (Chapter 4). Glover discusses and rejects the doctrine and its application to euthanasia in Chapter 7 of *Causing Death and Saving Lives.* A limited defense of the doctrine as it is applied to killing and letting die can be found in Foot's "Euthanasia" and Ladd's "Positive and Negative Euthanasia" (*see* the Suggested Readings for Chapter 2).

Bifurcated combining or made up of two aspects, factors, or parts.

Federalism the principle of federal control of an organization or group.

Heinous hateful or shockingly evil.

Lex talionis the principle of retributive justice based on the Mosaic law of "eye for eye, tooth for tooth" in Exodus 21: 23–25, and usually expressed as "a life for a life."

Metaphysical relating to metaphysics; in Glover's article, it means something transcendental or beyond the sensible world.

Mitigation the diminution or lessening of something painful or harsh such as punishment.

Penology the study of punishment for crime.

Reprobation the act of raising legal exceptions or objections.

Chapter 4

Hunger and Welfare

Introduction

The World Health Organization conservatively estimates that in the world there are ten million children under five who are chronically malnourished. If these children survive at all, they will suffer lasting effects—stunted growth and brain damage from lack of protein. In addition, if we calculate the ratio of children to adults in the world, we get a total of about seventy million chronically malnourished people in the world. Some of these people are in rich countries such as the United States. According to the latest reports (1987), the United States has thirty million people living below the poverty level, including two million homeless people. What to do about these poor people is part of the welfare problem. Most of these malnourished people, however, are in other countries— countries on the subcontinent (India, Pakistan, and Bangladesh) and in poor nations of the Caribbean, Latin America, Southeast Asia, and Africa. What to do about starving people in other countries is the world hunger problem.

Before turning to these two related problems, we should briefly discuss two factual issues: 1) Are all countries able to provide welfare for their needy citizens, and 2) is it possible to feed all the hungry people in the world?

The first question is easily answered. No doubt some poor countries cannot provide welfare for their citizens; that is one reason why world hunger is a problem. However, rich countries such as the United States can and do provide welfare for some of their poor citizens, and they could easily provide welfare for all their needy citizens if it was considered important, as important, say, as national defense. The main issue about welfare is not whether it is actually possible in rich countries—obviously it is, rather the moral question is whether or not citizens in rich countries have a right to welfare, and whether or not the governments have a corresponding duty to provide it.

The second factual question is not so easy to answer. Is it even possible to feed all the hungry people in the world? To determine the amount of aid actually required to do this, we need to know how many people need food, what their nutritional requirements are, how distribution can be made, what population growth will be, and other facts relevant to the problem. According to Nick Eberstadt (2), there are no accurate figures in these areas. If there are more than a billion people to be fed, as the Overseas Development Council claims, then perhaps the task is hopeless. But if there are only seventy million people to feed (this is Eberstadt's estimate), which is less than two percent of the world's population, then food relief and development projects are a manageable undertaking, with international cooperation. According to Eberstadt, enough food is produced each year to feed everyone comfortably. If 1.3 billion tons of grain are produced each year, and one person needs 500 pounds, then 5.2 billion people could be fed, and this is more than the highest estimate for the world's population.

But if enough food is produced to feed everyone, then why do people starve to death? In Eberstadt's view, the answer is that the rich nations consume more than their fair share of the food; statistically, the rich nations (e.g., the United States, Russia, European countries, Japan) consume seventy percent more protein than the rest of the world. They do this by consuming grain indirectly via feedstocks converted into animal protein, rather than directly in the form of bread, noodles, rice, and so on. In other words, the problem is the result of unequal food distribution rather than inadequate food production.

The World Hunger Problem   Let us assume with Eberstadt that it is at least theoretically possible to feed all of the world's hungry people. Is there any moral obligation to do this? Do rich nations have any moral obligation to help people in poor countries from starving to death?

One standard view on the problem, expressed by Foot (see her article "Euthanasia," cited in the Suggested Readings for Chapter 2) and others who distinguish between killing and letting die, is that we have a negative duty to not kill people, but we do not have a **positive duty** to prevent people from dying of starvation. To be sure, it is a good thing to give to charity to prevent this, but this is an optional duty, it is not required by morality.

As we have seen in the last chapter, however, the claim that there is a significant moral difference between killing and letting die is problematic. In Chapter 2, Rachels denies that this distinction has any moral relevance to euthanasia, and he takes the same line on starvation in this chapter. His view is that letting people die from starvation is just as bad as killing them. He tries to convince us of this with a simple example. Suppose there is a starving child in the room right now, and you have a sandwich you don't need. Wouldn't you be a "moral monster" if you allowed her to die? But is there really any morally relevant difference between this case and the case of the millions of people who are starving right now? Rachels discusses such possible differences as spatial location, the number of people, "dischargeability," the action/inaction distinction, and "optionality." He finds that none of these differences have any moral significance. He concludes that we do not have a good reason for not giving money to support famine relief efforts.

At this point, the conservative will object that starving people do not have any right to be fed—they do not have any claim against us such that we must help them. At best, our duty to help them is merely optional; helping others is an act of charity that is morally praiseworthy, but not morally required.

Against this, Henry Shue (8) and others contend that the malnourished children and adults in the world who cannot provide for themselves have a right to subsistence. This right includes not just a right to adequate food, but also to air, water, clothing, shelter, and minimum health care. This right, along with the right to security, is basic in that it must be fulfilled before any other rights can be enjoyed. Shue thinks that rich nations should transfer food or money to the poor nations; they could do this, he claims, without impoverishing themselves or even causing a decline in their growth rate.

Garrett Hardin raises objections to such welfare-style transfers from rich nations to poor ones. In his view, nations are lifeboats with limited carrying capacity; they cannot afford to feed poor nations. Besides, aid to poor nations just makes matters worse—the result is a vicious cycle of more overpopulation, more starvation, more aid, and so on until there is ecological disaster. The implication is that we should let people in poor nations die.

The Welfare Problem   Even if we agree that rich nations should not help people in poor nations, there remains the question of what to do about the poor people within the rich nations themselves. As I said, it seems un-deniable that welfare for these people is theoretically possible in rich countries such as the United States, particularly if welfare programs were considered as important as other matters, such as national defense. But does a rich nation like the United States have a moral obligation to provide for the basic needs (food, clothing, shelter, and medical care) of its poor citizens?

Trudy Govier examines three different positions on the welfare problem: the individualist position which holds that no one has a right to welfare, the permissive view that everyone in a rich country has a right to welfare, and the more moderate puritan view that the right to welfare in an affluent society is conditional on one's willingness to work. She formulates these positions in terms of rights rather than obligations, but she agrees that rights imply obligations. If a person in a rich country has a legal or moral right to welfare, then the country has a moral obligation to provide welfare benefits. Which position does Govier accept? After a careful evaluation of the three positions with respect to social justice and the social consequences, Govier concludes that the permissive view is the most acceptable.

In vivid contrast, Hospers strongly believes that only individualism, or libertarianism (as he calls it), is acceptable. As Hospers explains it, libertarianism posits two positive principles: 1) a principle of liberty which says that individuals have a right to act as they choose unless their action interferes with the similar right of others to act as they choose, and 2) a principle of government which says that the only function of the government is to protect people from interference. In other words, the second principle says that the government should only recognize the rights of noninterference (sometimes called negative rights) and not positive rights such as the right to welfare benefits.

James Rachels
Killing and Starving to Death

James Rachels is Professor of Philosophy at the University of Alabama in Birmingham. He is the author of several articles on ethics, and he is the editor of Moral Problems: A Collection of Philosophical Essays *(1971, 3rd ed., 1979).*

Rachels argues that our duty not to let people die of starvation is as strong as our duty not to kill them. He defends this Equivalence Thesis against various attempts to show that there is a moral difference between killing and letting die.

Although we do not know exactly how many people die each year of malnutrition or related health problems, the number is very high, in the millions.[1] By giving money to support famine relief efforts, each of us could save at least some of them. By not giving, we let them die.

Some philosophers have argued that letting people die is not as bad as killing them, because in general our "positive duty" to give aid is weaker than our "negative duty" not to do harm.[2] I maintain the opposite: letting die is just as bad as killing.[3] At first this may seem wildly implausible. When reminded that people are dying of starvation while we spend money on trivial things, we may feel a bit guilty, but certainly we do not feel like murderers. Philippa Foot writes:

Most of us allow people to die of starvation in India and Africa, and there is surely something wrong with us that we do; it would be nonsense, however, to pretend that it is only in law that we make a distinction between allowing people in the underdeveloped countries to die of starvation and sending them poisoned food. There is

From James Rachels, "Killing and Starving to Death," *Philosophy* 54, no. 208 (April 1979): 159–171.
Reprinted with the permission of Cambridge University Press.

worked into our moral system a distinction between what we owe people in the form of aid and what we owe them in the way of noninterference.[4]

No doubt this would be correct if it were intended only as a description of what most people believe. Whether this feature of "our moral system" is rationally defensible is, however, another matter. I shall argue that we are wrong to take comfort in the fact that we *only* let these people die, because our duty not to let them die is equally as strong as our duty not to kill them, which, of course, is very strong indeed.

Obviously, this Equivalence Thesis is not morally neutral, as philosophical claims about ethics often are. It is a radical idea that, if true, would mean that some of our "intuitions" (our prereflective beliefs about what is right and wrong in particular cases) are mistaken and must be rejected. Neither is the view I oppose morally neutral. The idea that killing is worse than letting die is a relatively conservative thesis that would allow those same intuitions to be preserved. However, the Equivalence Thesis should not be dismissed merely because it does not conform to all our prereflective intuitions. Rather than being perceptions of the truth, our "intuitions" might sometimes signify nothing more than our prejudices or selfishness or cultural conditioning. Philosophers often admit that, in theory at least, some intuitions might be unreliable—but usually this possibility is not taken seriously, and conformity to prereflective intuition is used uncritically as a test of the acceptability of moral theory. In what follows I shall argue that many of our intuitions concerning killing and letting die *are* mistaken, and should not be trusted.

I

We think that killing is worse than letting die, not because we overestimate how bad it is to kill, but because we underestimate how bad it is to let die. The following chain of reasoning is intended to show that letting people in foreign countries die of starvation is very much worse than we commonly assume.

Suppose there were a starving child in the room where you are now—hollow-eyed, belly bloated, and so on—and you have a sandwich at your elbow that you don't need. Of course you would be horrified; you would stop reading and give her the sandwich or, better, take her to a hospital. And you would not think this an act of supererogation; you would not expect any special praise for it, and you would expect criticism if you did not do it. Imagine what you would think of someone who simply ignored the child and continued reading, allowing her to die of starvation. Let us call the person who would do this Jack Palance, after the very nice man who plays such vile characters in the movies. Jack Palance indifferently watches the starving child die; he cannot be bothered even to hand her the sandwich. There is ample reason for judging him very harshly; without putting too fine a point on it, he shows himself to be a moral monster.

When we allow people in faraway countries to die of starvation, we may think, as Mrs. Foot puts it, that "there is surely something wrong with us". But we most emphatically do not consider ourselves moral monsters. We think this, in spite of the striking similarity between Jack Palance's behavior and our own. He could easily save the child; he does not, and the child dies. We could easily save some of those starving people; we do not, and they die. If we are not monsters, there must be some important difference between him and us. But what is it?

One obvious difference between Jack Palance's position and ours is that the person he lets die is in the same room with him, while the people we let die are mostly far away. Yet the spatial location of the dying people hardly seems a relevant consideration.[5] It is absurd to suppose that being located at a certain map coordinate entitles one to treatment that one would not merit if situated at a different longitude or latitude. Of course, if a dying person's location meant that we *could not* help, that would excuse us. But, since there are efficient famine relief agencies

willing to carry our aid to the faraway countries, this excuse is not available. It would be almost as easy for us to send these agencies the price of the sandwich as for Palance to hand the sandwich to the child.

The location of the starving people does make a difference, psychologically, in how we feel. If there were a starving child in the same room with us, we could not avoid realizing, in a vivid and disturbing way, how it is suffering and that it is about to die. Faced with this realization our consciences probably would not allow us to ignore the child. But if the dying are far away, it is easy to think of them only abstractly, or to put them out of our thoughts altogether. This might explain why our conduct would be different if we were in Jack Palance's position, even though, from a moral point of view, the location of the dying is not relevant.

There are other differences between Jack Palance and us, which may seem important, having to do with the sheer numbers of people, both affluent and starving, that surround us. In our fictitious example Jack Palance is one person, confronted by the need of one other person. This makes his position relatively simple. In the real world our position is more complicated, in two ways: first, in that there are millions of people who need feeding, and none of us has the resources to care for all of them; and second, in that for any starving person we *could* help there are millions of other affluent people who could help as easily as we.

On the first point, not much needs to be said. We may feel, in a vague sort of way, that we are not monsters because no one of us could possibly save *all* the starving people—there are just too many of them, and none of us has the resources. This is fair enough, but all that follows is that, individually, none of us is responsible for saving everyone. We may still be responsible for saving someone, or as many as we can. This is so obvious that it hardly bears mentioning, yet it is easy to lose sight of, and philosophers have actually lost sight of it. In his article "Saving Life and

Taking Life,"[6] Richard Trammell says that one morally important difference between killing and letting die is "dischargeability." By this he means that, while each of us can discharge completely a duty not to kill anyone, no one among us can discharge completely a duty to save everyone who needs it. Again, fair enough; but all that follows is that since we are only bound to save those we can, the class of people we have an obligation to save is much smaller than the class of people we have an obligation not to kill. It does *not* follow that our duty with respect to those we can save is any less stringent. Suppose Jack Palance were to say: "I needn't give this starving child the sandwich because, after all, I can't save everyone in the world who needs it." If this excuse will not work for him, neither will it work for us with respect to the children we could save in India or Africa.

The second point about numbers was that, for any starving person we *could* help, there are millions of other affluent people who could help as easily as we. Some are in an even better position to help since they are richer. But by and large these people are doing nothing. This also helps explain why we do not feel especially guilty for letting people starve. How guilty we feel about something depends, to some extent, on how we compare with those around us. If we were surrounded by people who regularly sacrificed to feed the starving and we did not, we would probably feel ashamed. But because our neighbors do not do any better than we, we are not so ashamed.

But again, this does not imply that we should not feel more guilty or ashamed than we do. A psychological explanation of our feelings is not a moral justification of our conduct. Suppose Jack Palance were only one of twenty people who watched the child die; would that decrease his guilt? Curiously, I think many people assume it would. Many people seem to feel that if twenty people do nothing to prevent a tragedy, each of them is only one-twentieth as guilty as he would have been if he had watched the tragedy alone. It

is as though there is only a fixed amount of guilt, which divides. I suggest, rather, that guilt multiplies, so that each passive viewer is fully guilty, if he could have prevented the tragedy but did not. Jack Palance watching the girl die alone would be a moral monster; but if he calls in a group of his friends to watch with him, he does not diminish his guilt by dividing it among them. Instead, they are all moral monsters. Once the point is made explicit, it seems obvious.

The fact that most other affluent people do nothing to relieve hunger may very well have implications for one's own obligations. But the implication may be that one's own obligations *increase* rather than decrease. Suppose Palance and a friend were faced with two starving children, so that, if each did his "fair share," Palance would only have to feed one of them. But the friend will do nothing. Because he is well-off, Palance could feed both of them. Should he not? What if he fed one and then watched the other die, announcing that he has done *his* duty and that the one who died was his friend's responsibility? This shows the fallacy of supposing that one's duty is only to do one's fair share, where this is determined by what would be sufficient *if* everyone else did likewise.

To summarize: Jack Palance, who refuses to hand a sandwich to a starving child, is a moral monster. But we feel intuitively that we are not so monstrous, even though we also let starving children die when we could feed them almost as easily. If this intuition is correct, there must be some important difference between him and us. But when we examine the most obvious differences between his conduct and ours—the location of the dying, the differences in numbers—we find no real basis for judging ourselves less harshly than we judge him. Perhaps there are some other grounds on which we might distinguish our moral position, with respect to actual starving people, from Jack Palance's position with respect to the child in my story. But I cannot think of what they might be. Therefore, I conclude that if he is a monster, then so are we—or at least, so are we after our **rationalizations** and thoughtlessness have been exposed.

This last qualification is important. We judge people, at least in part, according to whether they can be expected to realize how well or how badly they behave. We judge Palance harshly because the consequences of his indifference are so immediately apparent. By contrast, it requires an unusual effort for us to realize the consequences of our indifference. It is normal behavior for people in the affluent countries not to give to famine relief, or if they do give, to give very little. Decent people may go along with this normal behavior pattern unthinkingly, without realizing, or without comprehending in a clear way just what this means for the starving. Thus, even though those decent people may act monstrously, we do not judge them monsters. There is a curious sense, then, in which moral reflection can transform decent people into indecent ones; for if a person thinks things through, and realizes that he is, morally speaking, in Jack Palance's position, his continued indifference is more blameworthy than before.

The preceding is not intended to prove that letting people die of starvation is as bad as killing them. But it does provide strong evidence that letting die is much worse than we normally assume, and so that letting die is much *closer* to killing than we normally assume. These reflections also go some way towards showing just how fragile and unreliable our intuitions are in this area. They suggest that, if we want to discover the truth, we are better off looking at arguments that do not rely on unexamined intuitions.

II

Before arguing that the Equivalence Thesis is true, let me explain more precisely what I mean by it. I take it to be a claim about what does, or does not, count as a morally good reason in support of a value judgment: the bare fact that one act is an act of killing, while another act is an act of *merely* letting someone

die, is not a morally good reason in support of the judgment that the former is worse than the latter. Of course there may be *other* differences between such acts that are morally significant. For example, the family of an irreversibly comatose hospital patient may want their loved one to be allowed to die, but not killed. Perhaps the reason for their preference is religious. So we have at least one reason to let the patient die rather than to kill him—the reason is that the family prefers it that way. This does not mean, however, that the distinction between killing and letting die *itself* is important. What is important is respecting the family's wishes. (It is often right to respect people's wishes even if we think those wishes are based on false beliefs.) In another sort of case, a patient with a painful terminal illness may want to be killed rather than allowed to die because a slow, lingering death would be agonizing. Here we have a reason to kill and not let die, but once again the reason is not that one course is intrinsically preferable to the other. The reason is, rather, that the latter course would lead to no more suffering.

It should be clear then, that I will *not* be arguing that every act of letting die is equally as bad as every act of killing. There are lots of reasons why a particular act of killing may be morally worse than a particular act of letting die, or vice versa. If a healthy person is murdered, from a malicious motive, while a person in irreversible coma is allowed to die upon a calm judgment that maintaining him alive is pointless, certainly this killing is very much worse than this letting die. Similarly, if an ill person who could be saved is maliciously allowed to die, while a terminal patient is killed, upon his request, as an act of kindness, we have good reason to judge the letting die worse than the killing. All that I want to argue is that, whatever reasons there may be for judging one act worse than another, the simple fact that one is killing, whereas the other is only letting die, is not among them.

The first stage of the argument is concerned with some formal relations between moral judgments and the reasons that support them. I take it to be a point of logic that moral judgments are true only if good reasons support them; for example, if there is no good reason why you ought to do some action, it cannot be true that you ought to do it. Moreover, when there is a choice to be made from among several possible actions, the preferable alternative is the one that is backed by the strongest reasons.

But when are the reasons for or against one act stronger than those for or against another act? A complete answer would have to include some normative theory explaining why some reasons are intrinsically weightier than others. Suppose you are in a situation in which you can save someone's life only by lying: the normative theory would explain why "Doing A would save someone's life" is a stronger reason in favor of doing A than "Doing B would be telling the truth" is in favor of doing B.

However, there are also some purely formal principles that operate here. The simplest and least controversial such principle is this:

(i) If there are the *same* reasons for or against A as for or against B, then the reasons in favor of A are neither stronger nor weaker than the reasons in favor of B; and so A and B are morally equivalent—neither is preferable to the other.

Now, suppose we ask why killing is morally objectionable. When someone is killed, there may of course be harmful effects for people other than the victim himself. Those who loved him may grieve, and those who were depending on him in one way or another may be caused hardship because, being dead, he will be unable to perform as expected. However, we cannot explain the wrongness of killing purely, or even mainly, in terms of the bad effects for the survivors. The primary reason why killing is wrong is that something very bad is done to the victim himself: he ends up dead; he no longer has a

good—his life—that he possessed before. But notice that exactly the same can be said about letting someone die. The primary reason why it is morally objectionable to let someone die, when we could save him, is that he ends up dead; he no longer has a good—his life—that he possessed before. Secondary reasons again have to do with harmful effects on those who survive. Thus, the explanation of why killing is bad mentions features of killing that are also features of letting die, and vice versa. Since there are no comparably general reasons in favor of either, this suggests that:

(ii) There are the same reasons for and against letting die as for and against killing.

And if this is true, we get the conclusion:

(iii) Therefore, killing and letting die are morally equivalent—neither is preferable to the other.

The central idea of this argument is that there is no morally relevant difference between killing and letting die, that is, no difference that may be cited to show that one is worse than the other. The argument therefore contains a premise—(ii)—that is supported only inductively. The fact that the explanation of why killing is wrong applies equally well to letting die, and vice versa, provides strong evidence that the **inductive generalization** is true. Nevertheless, no matter how carefully we analyze the matter, it will always be possible that there is some subtle, morally relevant difference between the two that we have overlooked. In fact, philosophers who believe that killing is worse than letting die have sometimes tried to identify such differences. I believe that these attempts have failed; here are three examples.

1. The first is one that I have already mentioned. Trammell urges that there is an important difference in the "dischargeability" of duties not to kill and not to let die. We can completely discharge a duty not to kill anyone; but we cannot completely discharge a duty to save everyone who needs aid. This is obviously correct, but it does not show that the Equivalence Thesis is false, for two reasons. In the first place, the difference in dischargeability only shows that the class of people we have a duty to save is smaller than the class of people we have a duty not to kill. It does not show that our duty with respect to those we *can* save is any less stringent. In the second place, if we *cannot* save someone, and that person dies, then we do not let him die. It is not right to say that I let Josef Stalin die, for example, since there is no way I could have saved him. So if I cannot save everyone, then neither can I let everyone die.

2. It has also been urged that, in killing someone, we are *doing* something—namely, killing him—whereas, in letting someone die, we are not doing anything. In letting people die of starvation, for example, we only *fail* to do certain things, such as sending food. The difference is between action and inaction; somehow this is supposed to make a moral difference.[7]

There are also two difficulties with this suggestion. First, it is misleading to say, without further ado, that in letting someone die we do nothing. For there is one very important thing that we do: we let someone die. "Letting someone die" is different, in some ways, from other sorts of actions, mainly in that it is an action we perform *by way of* not performing other actions. We may let someone die by way of not feeding him, just as we may insult someone by way of not shaking his hand. (If it is said, "I didn't do anything; I simply refrained from taking his hand when he offered it," it may be replied "You did do one thing—you insulted him.") The distinction between action and inaction is relative to a specification of *what* actions are or are not done. In insulting someone, we may *not* smile, speak, shake hands, and so on—but we *do* insult or snub the person. And in letting

someone die, the following may be among the things that are not done: we do not feed the person, we do not give medication, and so on. But the following is among the things that are done: we let him die.

Second, even if letting die were only a case of inaction, why should any moral conclusion follow from *that* fact? It may seem that a significant conclusion follows if we assume that we are not responsible for inactions. However, there is no general correlation between the action-inaction distinction and any sort of moral assessment. We ought to do some things, and we ought not do others, and we can certainly be morally blameworthy for not doing things as well as for doing them—Jack Palance was blameworthy for not feeding the child. (In many circumstances we are even legally liable for not doing things: tax fraud may involve only "inaction"—failing to report certain things to the Department of Internal Revenue—but what of it?) Moreover, failing to act can be subject to all the other kinds of moral assessment. Not doing something may, depending on the circumstances, be right, wrong, obligatory, wise, foolish, compassionate, sadistic, and so on. Since there is no general correlation between the action-inaction distinction and *any* of these matters, it is hard to see how anything could be made out of this distinction in the present context.

3. My final example is from Trammell again. He argues that "optionality" is a morally relevant difference between killing and letting die. The point here is that if we fail to save someone, we leave open the option for someone else to save him; whereas if we kill, the victim is dead and that is that. This point, I think, has little significance. For one thing, while "optionality" may mark a difference between killing and *failing to save,* it does not mark a comparable difference between killing and *letting die.* If X fails to save Y, it does not follow that Y dies; someone else may come along and save him. But if X lets

Y die, it does follow that Y dies; Y is dead and that is that.[8] When Palance watches the child die, he does not merely fail to save the child; he lets her die. And when we fail to send food to the starving, and they die, we let them die—we do not merely fail to save them.

The importance of "optionality" in any particular case depends on the actual chances of someone else's saving the person we do not save. Perhaps it is not so bad not to save someone if we know that someone else *will* save him. (Although even here, we do not behave as we ought; for we ought not simply to leave what needs doing to others.) And perhaps it even gets us off the hook a little if there is the *strong chance* that someone else will step in. But in the case of the world's starving, we know very well that no person or group of persons is going to come along tomorrow and save all of them. We know that there are at least some people who will *not* be saved, if we do not save them. So, as an excuse for not giving aid to the starving, the "optionality" argument is clearly in bad faith. To say to those people, after they are dead, that someone else *might* have saved them, in the very weak sense in which that will be true, does not excuse us at all. The others who might have saved them, but did not, are as guilty as we, but that does not diminish our guilt—as I have already remarked, guilt in these cases multiplies, not divides.

III

I need now to say a few more things about the counter-intuitive nature of the Equivalence Thesis.

The fact that this view has radical implications for conduct has been cited as a reason for rejecting it. Trammell complains that "Denial of the distinction between negative and positive duties leads straight to an ethic so strenuous that it might give pause even to a philosophical John the Baptist." [9] Suppose John is about to buy a phonograph record, purely for his enjoyment, when he is remind-

ed that with this five dollars a starving person could be fed. On the view I am defending, he ought to give the money to feed the hungry person. This may not seem exceptional until we notice that the reasoning is reiterable. Having given the first five dollars, John is not free to use another five to buy the record. For the poor are always with him; there is always *another* starving person to be fed, and then another, and then another. "The problem," Trammell says, "is that, even though fulfillment of one particular act of aid involves only minimal effort, it sets a precedent for millions of such efforts." [10] So we reach the bizarre conclusion that it is almost always immoral to buy phonograph records! And the same goes for fancy clothes, cars, toys, and so on.

This sort of *reductio argument* is of course familiar in philosophy. Such arguments may be divided into three categories. The strongest sort shows that a theory entails a contradiction, and, since contradictions cannot be tolerated, the theory must be modified or rejected. Such arguments, when valid, are of course devastating. Second, an argument may show that a theory has a consequence that, while not inconsistent, is nevertheless demonstrably false—that is, an independent proof can be given that the offensive consequence is unacceptable. Arguments of this second type, while not quite so impressive as the first, can still be irresistible. The third type of *reductio* is markedly weaker than the others. Here, it is merely urged that some consequence of a theory is counter-intuitive. The supposedly embarrassing consequence is perfectly consistent, and there is no proof that it is false; the complaint is only that it goes against our unreflective, pretheoretical beliefs. Now sometimes even this weak sort of argument can be effective, especially when we have not much confidence in the theory, or when our confidence in the pretheoretical belief is unaffected by the reasoning that supports the theory. However, it may happen that *the same reasoning that leads one to accept a theory also persuades one that the pretheoretical beliefs were wrong.* (If this did not happen, philosophy would always be in the service of what we already think; it could never challenge and change our beliefs, and would be, in an important sense, useless.) The present case, it seems to me, is an instance of this type. The same reasoning that leads to the view that we are as wicked as Jack Palance, and that killing is no worse than letting die, also persuades (me, at least) that the prereflective belief in the rightness of our affluent lifestyle is mistaken.[11]

So, I want to say about all this what H.P. Grice once said at a conference when someone objected that his theory of meaning had an unacceptable implication. Referring to the supposedly embarrassing consequence, Grice said, "See here, that's not an *objection* to my theory—*that's* my theory!"[12] Grice not only accepted the implication, he claimed it as an integral part of what he wanted to say. Similarly, the realization that we are morally wrong to spend money on inessentials, when that money could go to feed the starving, is an integral part of the view I am defending. It is not an embarrassing consequence of the view; it is (part of) the view itself.

There is another way in which the counter-intuitive nature of the Equivalence Thesis may be brought out. It follows from that thesis that if the *only* difference between a pair of acts is that one is killing, while the other is letting die, those actions are equally good or bad—neither is preferable to the other. Defenders of the distinction between positive and negative duties have pointed out that in such cases our intuitions often tell us just the opposite: killing seems obviously worse. Here is an example produced by Daniel Dinello:

Jones and Smith are in a hospital. Jones cannot live longer than two hours unless he gets a heart transplant. Smith, who has had one kidney removed, is dying of an infection in the other kidney. If he does not get a kidney transplant, he will die in about four hours. When Jones dies, his one good kidney can be transplanted to Smith, or Smith could be killed and his heart transplanted to Jones ... it seems clear that it would, in fact, be wrong to kill Smith and save Jones, rather than letting Jones

die and saving Smith.[13]

And another from Trammell:

If someone threatened to steal $1000 from a person if he did not take a gun and shoot a stranger between the eyes, it would be very wrong for him to kill the stranger to save his $1000. But if someone asked from that person $1000 to save a stranger, it would seem that his obligation to grant this request would not be as great as his obligation to refuse the first demand—even if he has good reason for believing that without his $1000 the stranger would certainly die. ... In this particular example, it seems plausible to say that a person has a greater obligation to refrain from killing someone, even though the effort required of him ($1000) and his motivation toward the stranger be assumed identical in both cases.[14]

The conclusion we are invited to draw from these examples is that, contrary to what I have been arguing, the bare difference between killing and letting die *must be* morally significant.

Now Dinello's example is badly flawed, since the choice before the doctor is not a choice between killing and letting die at all. If the doctor kills Smith in order to transplant his heart to Jones, he will have killed Smith. But if he waits until Jones dies, and then transfers the kidney to Smith, he will *not* have "let Jones die." The reason is connected with the fact that not every case of not saving someone is a case of letting him die. (Josef Stalin died, and I did not save him, but I did not let Stalin die.) Dinello himself points out that, in order for it to be true that X lets Y die, X must be "in a position" to save Y, but not do so.[15] (I was never in a position to save Stalin.) Now the doctor is in a position to save Jones only if there is a heart available for transplantation. But no such heart is available—Smith's heart, for example, is not available since Smith is still using it. Therefore, since the doctor is not in a position to save Jones, he does not let Jones die.[16]

Trammell's example is not quite so easy to dismiss. Initially, I share the intuition that it would be worse to kill someone to prevent $1000 from being stolen than to refuse to pay

$1000 to save someone. Yet on reflection I have not much confidence in this feeling. What is at stake in the situation described is the person's $1000 and the stranger's life. But we end up with the *same* combination of lives and money, no matter which option the person chooses: if he shoots the stranger, the stranger dies and he keeps his $1000; and if he refuses to pay to save the stranger, the stranger dies and he keeps his $1000. It makes no difference, either to the person's interests or to the stranger's interests, which option is chosen; why, then, do we have the curious intuition that there is a big difference here?

I conceded at the outset that most of us believe that in letting people die we are not behaving as badly as if we were to kill them. I think I have given good reasons for concluding that this belief is false. Yet giving reasons is often not enough, even in philosophy. For if an intuition is strong enough, we may continue to rely on it and assume that *something* is wrong with the arguments opposing it, even though we are not sure exactly what is wrong. It is a familiar remark: "X is more certain than any argument that might be given against it." So in addition to the arguments, we need some account of why people have the allegedly mistaken intuition and why it is so persistent. Why do people believe so firmly that killing is so much worse than letting die, both in fictitious cases such as Trammell's, and in the famine relief cases in the real world? In some ways the explanation of this is best left to the psychologists; the distinctly philosophical job is accomplished when the intuition is shown to be false. However, I shall hazard a hypothesis, since it shows how our intuitions can be explained without assuming that they are perceptions of the truth.

Human beings are to some degree **altruistic,** but they are also to a great degree selfish, and their attitudes on matters of conduct are largely determined by what is in their own interests, and what is in the interests of the few other people they especially care about.

In terms of both the costs and the benefits, it is to their own advantage for people in the affluent countries to regard killing as worse than letting die. First, the *costs* of never killing anyone are not great; we can live very well without ever killing. But the cost of not allowing people to die, when we could save them, would be very great. For any one of us to take seriously a duty to save the starving would require that we give up our affluent lifestyles; money could no longer be spent on luxuries while others starve. On the other side, we have much more to *gain* from a strict prohibition on killing than from a like prohibition on letting die. Since we are not in danger of starving, we will not suffer if people do not regard feeding the hungry as so important; but we would be threatened if people did not regard killing as very, very bad. So, both the costs and the benefits encourage us, selfishly, to view killing as worse than letting die. It is to our own advantage to believe this, and so we do.

Footnotes

1. For an account of the difficulties of getting reliable information in this area, see Nick Eberstadt, "Myths of the Food Crisis," *New York Review of Books* (19 February 1976); 32–37.

2. Richard L. Trammell, "Saving Life and Taking Life," *Journal of Philosophy* 72 (1975): 131–137, is the best defense of this view of which I am aware.

3. This article is a companion to an earlier one, "Active and Passive Euthanasia," *New England Journal of Medicine* 292 (9 January 1975): 78–80, in which I discuss the (mis)use of the killing/letting die distinction in medical contexts. But nothing in this article depends on the earlier one.

4. Philippa Foot, "The Problem of Abortion and the Doctrine of the Double Effect," *Oxford Review* No. 5 (1967); reprinted in J. Rachels (ed.), *Moral Problems,* 2nd ed. (New York: Harper and Row, 1975), p. 66.

5. On this point, and more generally on the whole subject of our duty to contribute for famine relief, see Peter Singer, "Famine, Affluence, and Morality," *Philosophy and Public Affairs* 1 (Spring 1972): 232.

6. Trammell, p. 133.

7. This argument is suggested by Paul Ramsey in *The Patient as Person* (New Haven, CN: Yale University Press, 1970), p. 151.

8. This difference between failing to save and letting die was pointed out by David Sanford in a very helpful paper, "On Killing and Letting Die," read at the Western Division meeting of the American Philosophical Association, New Orleans, 30 April 1976.

9. Trammell, p. 133.

10. Trammell, p. 134.

11. There is also some independent evidence that this prereflective belief is mistaken; see Singer, "Famine, Affluence, and Morality."

12. Grice made this remark several years ago at Oberlin. I do not remember the surrounding details of the discussion, but the remark seems to me an important one that applies to lots of "objections" to various theories. The most famous objections to act-utilitarianism, for example, are little more than descriptions of the theory, with the question-begging addendum, "Because it says *that*, it can't be right."

13. Daniel Dinello, "On Killing and Letting Die," *Analysis* 31 (January 1971): 85–86.

14. Trammell, p. 131.

15. Dinello, p. 85.

16. There is another way to meet Dinello's counter-example. A surprisingly strong case can be made that it would *not* be any worse to kill Smith than to "let Jones die." I have in mind adapting John Harris's argument in "The Survival Lottery," *Philosophy* 50 (1975): 81–87.

Review Questions

1. What is the Equivalence Thesis?

2. According to Rachels, why isn't spatial location a morally relevant consideration?

3. What is "dischargeability?" Why isn't it relevant according to Rachels?

4. According to Rachels, why isn't there a difference between action and inaction?

5. What is "optionality?" Why isn't it morally relevant according to Rachels?

6. Rachels distinguishes between three sorts of *reductio* arguments. What are they?

7. Why doesn't Rachels accept the objection that the Equivalence Thesis is counter-intuitive?

Discussion Questions

1. Does Rachels refute Foot's view of the duty to give aid? Defend your answer.

2. Rachels says that many of our moral intuitions are mistaken. Is this true? If you agree, give some examples.

3. Does Rachels himself appeal to intuition in his examples? Why, or why not?

Garrett Hardin

Living on a Lifeboat

Garrett Hardin is Professor of Biology at the University of California at Santa Barbara. He is the author of many books, including The Limits of Altruism: An Ecologist's View of Survival *(1977).*

Hardin uses the metaphor of a lifeboat to argue that rich nations such as the United States do not have a moral obligation to help poor nations. In fact, he claims, aid in the form of food makes matters worse; it results in more population growth, and eventually the ruin of natural resources such as oceans.

Susanne Langer (1942) has shown that it is probably impossible to approach an unsolved problem save through the door of metaphor. Later, attempting to meet the demands of rigor, we may achieve some success in cleansing theory of metaphor, though our success is limited if we are unable to avoid using common language, which is shot through and through with fossil metaphors. (I count no less than five in the preceding two sentences.)

Since metaphorical thinking is inescapable it is pointless merely to weep about our human limitations. We must learn to live with them, to understand them, and to control them. "All of us," said George Eliot in *Middlemarch*, "get our thoughts entangled in metaphors, and act fatally on the strength of them." To avoid unconscious suicide we are well advised to pit one metaphor against another. From the interplay of competitive metaphors, thoroughly developed, we may come closer to metaphor-free solutions to our problems.

No generation has viewed the problem of the survival of the human species as seriously as we have. Inevitably, we have entered this world of concern through the door of metaphor. Environmentalists have emphasized the image of the earth as a spaceship—Spaceship Earth. Kenneth Boulding (1966) is the principal architect of this metaphor. It is time, he says, that we replace the wasteful "cowboy economy" of the past with the frugal "spaceship economy" required for continued survival in the limited world we now see ours to be. The metaphor is notably useful in justifying pollution-control measures.

Unfortunately, the image of a spaceship is also used to promote measures that are suicidal. One of these is a generous immigration policy, which is only a particular instance of a class of policies that are in error because they lead to the tragedy of the commons (Hardin 1968). These suicidal policies are attractive because they mesh with what we unthinkingly take to be the ideals of "the best people." What is missing in the idealistic view is an insistence that rights and responsibilities must go together. The "generous" attitude of all too many people results in asserting inalienable rights while ignoring or denying matching responsibilities.

For the metaphor of a spaceship to be correct the aggregate of people on board would have to be under unitary sovereign control (Ophuls 1974). A true ship always has a captain. It is conceivable that a ship could be run by a committee. But it could not possibly survive if its course were determined by bickering tribes that claimed rights without responsibilities.

What about Spaceship Earth? It certainly has no captain, and no executive committee. The United Nations is a toothless tiger, because the signatories of its charter wanted it that way. The spaceship metaphor is used only to justify spaceship demands on common resources without acknowledging corresponding spaceship responsibilities.

An understandable fear of decisive action leads people to embrace "incrementalism"—moving toward reform by tiny stages. As we shall see, this strategy is counterproductive in the area discussed here if it means accepting rights before responsibilities. Where human survival is at stake, the acceptance of responsibilities is a precondition to the acceptance of rights, if the two cannot be introduced simultaneously.

LIFEBOAT ETHICS

Before taking up certain substantive issues let us look at an alternative metaphor, that of a lifeboat. In developing some relevant examples the following numerical values are assumed. Approximately two-thirds of the world is desperately poor, and only one-third is comparatively rich. The people in poor countries have an average per capita GNP (Gross National Product) of about $200 per year; the rich, of about $3,000. (For the United States it is nearly $5,000 per year.) Metaphorically, each rich nation amounts to a lifeboat full of comparatively rich people. The poor of the world are in other, much more crowded lifeboats. Continuously, so to speak, the poor fall out of their lifeboats and swim for a while in the water outside, hoping to be admitted to a rich lifeboat, or in some other way to benefit from the "goodies" on board. What should the passengers on a rich lifeboat do? This is the central problem of "the ethics of a lifeboat."

First we must acknowledge that each lifeboat is effectively limited in capacity. The land of every nation has a limited carrying capacity. The exact limit is a matter for argument, but the energy crunch is convincing more people every day that we have already exceeded the carrying capacity of the land. We have been living on "capital"—stored petroleum and coal—and soon we must live on income alone.

Let us look at only one lifeboat—ours. The ethical problem is the same for all, and is as follows. Here we sit, say fifty people in a lifeboat. To be generous, let us assume our boat has a capacity of ten more, making sixty. (This, however, is to violate the engineering principle of the "safety factor." A new plant disease or a bad change in the weather may decimate our population if we don't preserve some excess capacity as a safety factor.)

The fifty of us in the lifeboat see 100 others swimming in the water outside, asking for admission to the boat, or for handouts. How shall we respond to their calls? There are several possibilities.

One. We may be tempted to try to live by the Christian ideal of being "our brother's keeper," or by the Marxian ideal (Marx 1875) of "from each according to his abilities, to each according to his needs." Since the needs of all are the same, we take all the needy into our boat, making a total of 150 in a boat with a capacity of sixty. The boat is swamped, and everyone drowns. Complete justice, complete catastrophe.

Two. Since the boat has an unused excess capacity of ten, we admit just ten more to it. This has the disadvantage of getting rid of the safety factor, for which action we will sooner or later pay dearly. Moreover, *which* ten do we let in? "First come, first served?" The best ten? The neediest ten? How do we *discriminate?* And what do we say to the ninety who are excluded?

Three. Admit no more to the boat and preserve the small safety factor. Survival of the people in the lifeboat is then possible (though we shall have to be on our guard against boarding parties).

The last solution is abhorrent to many people. It is unjust, they say. Let us grant that it is.

"I feel guilty about my good luck," say some. The reply to this is simple: *Get out and yield your place to others.* Such a selfless action might satisfy the conscience of those who are addicted to guilt but it would not change the ethics of the lifeboat. The needy person to whom a guilt-addict yields his place will not himself feel guilty about his sudden good

luck. (If he did he would not climb aboard.) The net result of conscience-stricken people relinquishing their unjustly held positions is the elimination of their kind of conscience from the lifeboat. The lifeboat, as it were, purifies itself of guilt. The ethics of the lifeboat persist, unchanged by such momentary aberrations.

This then is the basic metaphor within which we must work out our solutions. Let us enrich the image step by step with substantive additions from the real world.

REPRODUCTION

The harsh characteristics of lifeboat ethics are heightened by reproduction, particularly by reproductive differences. The people inside the lifeboats of the wealthy nations are doubling in numbers every eighty-seven years; those outside are doubling every thirty-five years, on the average. And the relative difference in prosperity is becoming greater.

Let us, for a while, think primarily of the U.S. lifeboat. As of 1973 the United States had a population of 210 million people, who were increasing by 0.8% per year, that is, doubling in number every eighty-seven years.

Although the citizens of rich nations are outnumbered two to one by the poor, let us imagine an equal number of poor people outside our lifeboat—a mere 210 million poor people reproducing at a quite different rate. If we imagine these to be the combined populations of Columbia, Venezuela, Ecuador, Morocco, Thailand, Pakistan, and the Philippines, the average rate of increase of the people "outside" is 3.3% per year. The doubling time of this population is twenty-one years.

Suppose that all these countries, and the United States, agreed to live by the Marxian ideal, "to each according to his needs," the ideal of most Christians as well. Needs, of course, are determined by population size, which is affected by reproduction. Every nation regards its rate of reproduction as a sovereign right. If our lifeboat were big enough in the beginning it might be possible to live *for a while* by Christian-Marxian ideals. *Might.*

Initially, in the model given, the ratio of non-Americans to Americans would be one to one. But consider what the ratio would be eighty-seven years later. By this time Americans would have doubled to a population of 420 million. The other group (doubling every twenty-one years) would now have swollen to 3,540 million. Each American would have more than eight people to share with. How could the lifeboat possibly keep afloat?

All this involves extrapolation of current trends into the future, and is consequently suspect. Trends may change. Granted: but the change will not necessarily be favorable. If—as seems likely—the rate of population increase falls faster in the ethnic group presently inside the lifeboat than it does among those now outside, the future will turn out to be even worse than mathematics predicts, and sharing will be even more suicidal.

RUIN IN THE COMMONS

The fundamental error of the sharing ethics is that it leads to the tragedy of the commons. Under a system of private property the man (or group of men) who own property recognize their responsibility to care for it, for if they don't they will eventually suffer. A farmer, for instance, if he is intelligent, will allow no more cattle in a pasture than its carrying capacity justifies. If he overloads the pasture, weeds take over, erosion sets in, and the owner loses in the long run.

But if a pasture is run as a commons open to all, the right of each to use it is not matched by an operational responsibility to take care of it. It is no use asking independent herdsmen in a commons to act responsibly, for they dare not. The considerate herdsman who refrains from overloading the commons suffers more than a selfish one who says his needs are greater. (As Leo Durocher says, "Nice guys finish last.") Christian-Marxian idealism is counterproductive. That it *sounds* nice is no excuse. With distribution systems, as with individual morality, good intentions are no substitute for good performance.

A social system is stable only if it is insensitive to errors. To the Christian-Marxian idealist a selfish person is a sort of "error." Prosperity in the system of the commons cannot survive errors. If *everyone* would only restrain himself, all would be well; but it takes *only one less than everyone* to ruin a system of voluntary restraint. In a crowded world of less than perfect human beings—and we will never know any other—mutual ruin is inevitable in the commons. This is the core of the tragedy of the commons.

One of the major tasks of education today is to create such an awareness of the dangers of the commons that people will be able to recognize its many varieties, however disguised. There is pollution of the air and water because these media are treated as commons. Further growth of population and growth in the per capita conversion of natural resources into pollutants require that the system of the commons be modified or abandoned in the disposal of "externalities."

The fish populations of the oceans are exploited as commons, and ruin lies ahead. No technological invention can prevent this fate; in fact, all improvements in the art of fishing merely hasten the day of complete ruin. Only the replacement of the system of the commons with a responsible system can save oceanic fisheries.

The management of western range lands, though nominally rational, is in fact (under the steady pressure of cattle ranchers) often merely a government-sanctioned system of the commons, drifting toward ultimate ruin for both the rangelands and the residual enterprisers.

WORLD FOOD BANKS

In the international arena we have recently heard a proposal to create a new commons, namely an international depository of food reserves to which nations will contribute according to their abilities, and from which nations may draw according to their needs. Nobel laureate Norman Borlaug has lent the prestige of his name to this proposal.

A world food bank appeals powerfully to our humanitarian impulses. We remember John Donne's celebrated line, "Any man's death diminishes me." But before we rush out to see for whom the bell tolls let us recognize where the greatest political push for international granaries comes from, lest we be disillusioned later. Our experience with Public Law 480 clearly reveals the answer. This was the law that moved billions of dollars worth of U.S. grain to food-short, population-long countries during the past two decades. When P.L. 480 first came into being, a headline in the business magazine *Forbes* (Paddock and Paddock 1970) revealed the power behind it: "Feeding the World's Hungry Millions: How it will mean billions for U.S. business."

And indeed it did. In the years 1960 to 1970 a total of $7.9 billion was spent on the "Food for Peace" program, as P.L. 480 was called. During the years 1948 to 1970 an additional $49.9 billion were extracted from American taxpayers to pay for other economic aid programs, some of which went for food and food-producing machinery. (This figure does *not* include military aid.) That P.L. 480 was a giveaway program was concealed. Recipient countries went through the motions of paying for P.L. 480 food—with IOUs. In December 1973 the charade was brought to an end as far as India was concerned when the United States "forgave" India's $3.2 billion debt (Anonymous 1974). Public announcement of the cancellation of the debt was delayed for two months; one wonders why.

"Famine—1974!" (Paddock and Paddock 1970) is one of the few publications that points out the commercial roots of this humanitarian attempt. Though all U.S. taxpayers lost by P.L. 480, special interest groups gained handsomely. Farmers benefited because they were not asked to contribute the grain—it was bought from them by the taxpayers. Besides the direct benefit there was the indirect effect of increasing demand and thus raising prices of farm products general-ly. The manufacturers of farm machinery, fertilizers, and pesticides benefited by the farmers' extra efforts to grow more food. Grain elevators profited from storing the grain for varying lengths of time. Railroads made money hauling it to port, and shipping lines by carrying it overseas. Moreover, once the machinery for P.L. 480 was established an immense bureaucracy had a vested interest in its continuance regardless of its merits.

Very little was ever heard of these selfish interests when P.L. 480 was defended in public. The emphasis was always on its humanitarian effects. The combination of multiple and relatively silent selfish interests with highly vocal humanitarian apologists constitutes a powerful lobby for extracting money from taxpayers. Foreign aid has become a habit that can apparently survive in the absence of any known justification. A news commentator in a weekly magazine (Lansner 1974), after exhaustively going over all the conventional arguments for foreign aid—self-interest, social justice, political advantage, and charity—and concluding that none of the known arguments really held water, concluded: "So the search continues for some logically compelling reasons for giving aid...." In other words, *Act now, justify later*—if ever. (Apparently a quarter of a century is too short a time to find the justification for expending several billion dollars yearly).

The search for a rational justification can be short-circuited by interjecting the word "emergency." Borlaug uses this word. We need to look sharply at it. What is an "emergency?" It is surely something like an accident, which is correctly defined as *an event that is certain to happen, though with a low frequency* (Hardin 1972a). A well-run organization prepares for everything that is certain, including accidents and emergencies. It budgets for them. It saves for them. It expects them—and mature decision-makers do not waste time complaining about accidents when they occur.

What happens if some organizations budget for emergencies and others do not? If each organization is solely responsible for its own well-being, poorly managed ones will suffer. But they should be able to learn from experience. They have a chance to mend their ways and learn to budget for infrequent but certain emergencies. The weather, for instance, always varies and periodic crop failures are certain. A wise and competent government saves out of the production of the good years in anticipation of bad years that are sure to come. This is not a new idea. The Bible tells us that Joseph taught this policy to Pharaoh in Egypt more than 2,000 years ago. Yet it is literally true that the vast majority of the governments of the world today have no such policy. They lack either the wisdom or the competence, or both. Far more difficult than the transfer of wealth from one country to another is the transfer of wisdom between sovereign powers or between generations.

"But it isn't their fault! How can we blame the poor people who are caught in an emergency? Why must we punish them?" The concepts of blame and punishment are irrelevant. The question is, what are the operational consequences of establishing a world food bank? If it is open to every country every time a need develops, slovenly rulers will not be motivated to take Joseph's advice. Why should they? Others will bail them out whenever they are in trouble.

Some countries will make deposits in the world food bank and others will withdraw from it; there will be almost no overlap. Calling such a depository-transfer unit a "bank" is stretching the metaphor of *bank* beyond its elastic limits. The proposers, of course, never call attention to the metaphorical nature of the word they use.

THE RATCHET EFFECT

An "international food bank" is really, then, not a true bank but a disguised one-way transfer device for moving wealth from rich countries to poor. In the absence of such a bank, in a world inhabited by individually responsible sovereign nations, the population of each nation would repeatedly go through a cycle of the sort shown in Exhibit A. P_2 is greater than P_1, either in absolute numbers or because a deterioration of the food supply has removed the safety factor and produced a dangerously low ratio of resources to population. P_2 may be said to represent a state of overpopulation, which becomes obvious upon the appearance of an "accident," e.g., a crop failure. If the "emergency" is not met by outside help, the population drops back to the "normal" level—the "carrying capacity" of the environment—or even below. In the absence of population control by a sovereign, sooner or later the population grows to P_2 again and the cycle repeats. The long-term population curve (Hardin 1966) is an irregularly fluctuating one, equilibrating more or less about the carrying capacity.

A demographic cycle of this sort obviously involves great suffering in the restrictive phase, but such a cycle is normal to any independent country with inadequate population control. The third century theologian Tertullian (Hardin 1969a) expressed what must have been the recognition of many wise men when he wrote: "The scourges of pestilence, famine, wars, and earthquakes have come to be regarded as a blessing to overcrowded nations, since they serve to prune away the lux-

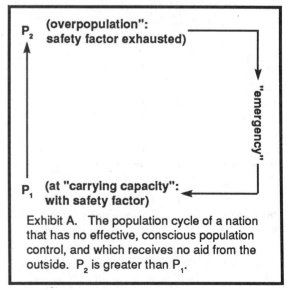

Exhibit A. The population cycle of a nation that has no effective, conscious population control, and which receives no aid from the outside. P_2 is greater than P_1.

uriant growth of the human race."

Only under a strong and farsighted sovereign—which theoretically could be the people themselves, democratically organized—can a population equilibrate at some set point below the carrying capacity, thus avoiding the pains normally caused by periodic and unavoidable disasters. For this happy state to be achieved it is necessary that those in power be able to contemplate with equanimity the "waste" of surplus food in times of bountiful harvests. It is essential that those in power resist the temptation to convert extra food into extra babies. On the public relations level it is necessary that the phrase "surplus food" be replaced by "safety factor."

But wise sovereigns seem not to exist in the poor world today. The most anguishing problems are created by poor countries that are governed by rulers insufficiently wise and powerful. If such countries can draw on a world food bank in times of "emergency," the population *cycle* of Exhibit A will be re-placed by the population *escalator* of Exhibit B. The input of food from a food bank acts as the pawl of a ratchet, preventing the population from retracting its steps to a lower level. Reproduction pushes the population upward, inputs from the world bank prevent its moving downward. Population size escalates, as does the absolute magnitude of "accidents" and "emergencies." The process is brought to an end only by the total collapse of the whole system, producing a catastrophe of scarcely imaginable proportions.

Such are the implications of the well-meant sharing of food in a world of irresponsible reproduction.

I think we need a new word for systems like this. The adjective "melioristic" is applied to systems that produce continual improvement; the English word is derived from the Latin *meliorare,* to become or make better. Parallel with this it would be useful to bring in the word *pejoristic* (from the Latin *pejorare,* to become or make worse). This word can be

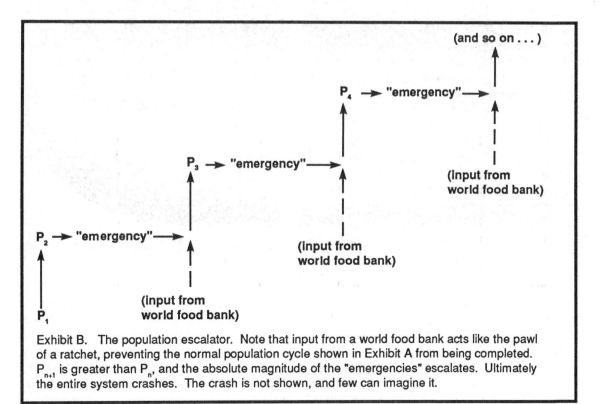

Exhibit B. The population escalator. Note that input from a world food bank acts like the pawl of a ratchet, preventing the normal population cycle shown in Exhibit A from being completed. P_{n+1} is greater than P_n, and the absolute magnitude of the "emergencies" escalates. Ultimately the entire system crashes. The crash is not shown, and few can imagine it.

applied to those systems that by their very nature, can be relied upon to make matters worse. A world food bank coupled with sovereign state irresponsibility in reproduction is an example of a pejoristic system.

This pejoristic system creates an unacknowledged commons. People have more motivation to draw from than to add to the common store. The license to make such withdrawals diminishes whatever motivation poor countries might otherwise have to control their populations. Under the guidance of this ratchet, wealth can be steadily moved in one direction only, from the slowly-breeding rich to the rapidly-breeding poor, the process finally coming to a halt only when all countries are equally and miserably poor.

All this is terribly obvious once we are acutely aware of the pervasiveness and danger of the commons. But many people still lack this awareness and the euphoria of the "benign demographic transition" (Hardin 1973) interferes with the realistic appraisal of pejoristic mechanisms. As concerns public policy, the deductions drawn from the benign demographic transition are these:

1. If the per capita GNP rises the birth rate will fall; hence, the rate of population increase will fall, ultimately producing ZPG (Zero Population Growth).
2. The long-term trend all over the world (including the poor countries) is of a rising per capita GNP (for which no limit is seen).
3. Therefore, all political interference in population matters is unnecessary; all we need to do is foster economic "development"—*note the metaphor*—and population problems will solve themselves.

Those who believe in the benign demographic transition dismiss the pejoristic mechanism of Exhibit B in the belief that each input of food from the world outside fosters development within a poor country thus resulting in a drop in the rate of population increase. Foreign aid has proceeded on this assumption for more than two decades.

Unfortunately it has produced no indubitable instance of the asserted effect. It has, however, produced a library of excuses. The air is filled with plaintive calls for more massive foreign aid appropriations so that the hypothetical melioristic process can get started.

The **doctrine of demographic laissez-faire** implicit in the hypothesis of the benign demographic transition is immensely attractive. Unfortunately there is more evidence against the melioristic system than there is for it (Davis 1963). On the historical side there are many counter-examples. The rise in per capita GNP in France and Ireland during the past century has been accompanied by a rise in population growth. In the twenty years following the Second World War the same positive correlation was noted almost everywhere in the world. Never in world history before 1950 did the worldwide population growth reach one percent per annum. Now the average population growth is over two percent and shows no signs of slackening.

On the theoretical side, the denial of the pejoristic scheme of Exhibit B probably springs from the hidden acceptance of the "cowboy economy" that Boulding castigated. Those who recognize the limitations of a spaceship, if they are unable to achieve population control at a safe and comfortable level, accept the necessity of the corrective feedback of the population cycle shown in Exhibit A. No one who knew in his bones that he was living on a true spaceship would countenance political support of the population escalator shown in Exhibit B.

ECO–DESTRUCTION VIA THE GREEN REVOLUTION

The demoralizing effect of charity on the recipient has long been known. "Give a man a fish and he will eat for a day; teach him how to fish and he will eat for the rest of his days." So runs an ancient Chinese proverb. Acting on this advice the Rockefeller and Ford Foundations have financed a multipronged program for improving agriculture in the hungry nations. The result, known as the

"Green Revolution," has been quite remarkable. "Miracle wheat" and "miracle rice" are splendid technological achievements in the realm of plant genetics.

Whether or not the Green Revolution can increase food production is doubtful (Harris 1972, Paddock 1970, Wilkes 1972), but in any event not particularly important. What is missing in this great and well-meaning humanitarian effort is a firm grasp of fundamentals. Considering the importance of the Rockefeller Foundation in this effort it is ironic that the late Alan Gregg, a much-respected vice-president of the Foundation, strongly expressed his doubts of the wisdom of all attempts to increase food production some two decades ago. (This was before Borlaug's work—supported by Rockefeller—had resulted in the development of "miracle wheat.") Gregg (1955) likened the growth and spreading of humanity over the surface of the earth to the metastasis of cancer in the human body, wryly remarking that "Cancerous growths demand food; but, as far as I know, they have never been cured by getting it."

"Man does not live by bread alone"—the scriptural statement has a rich meaning even in the material realm. Every human being born constitutes a draft on all aspects of the environment—food, air, water, unspoiled scenery, occasional and optional solitude, beaches, contact with wild animals, fishing, hunting—the list is long and incompletely known. Food can, perhaps, be significantly increased, but what about clean beaches, unspoiled forests, and solitude? If we satisfy the need for food in a growing population we necessarily decrease the supply of other goods, and thereby increase the difficulty of equitably allocating scarce goods (Hardin 1969b, 1972b).

The present population of India is 600 million, and it is increasing by fifteen million per year. The environmental load of this population is already great. The forests of India are only a small fraction of what they were three centuries ago. Soil erosion, floods, and the psychological costs of crowding are serious. Every one of the net fifteen million lives added each year stresses the Indian environment more severely. *Every life saved this year in a poor country diminishes the quality of life for subsequent generations.*

Observant critics have shown how much harm we wealthy nations have already done to poor nations through our well-intentioned but misguided attempts to help them (Paddock and Paddock 1973). Particularly reprehensible is our failure to carry out post-audits of these attempts (Farvar and Milton 1972). Thus have we shielded our tender consciences from knowledge of the harm we have done. Must we Americans continue to fail to monitor the consequences of our external "do-gooding?" If, for instance, we thoughtlessly make it possible for the present 600 million Indians to swell to 1,200 million by the year 2001—as their present growth rate promises—will posterity in India thank *us* for facilitating an even greater destruction of *their* environment? Are good intentions ever a sufficient excuse for bad consequences?

IMMIGRATION CREATES A COMMONS

I come now to the final example of a commons in action, one for which the public is least prepared for rational discussion. The topic is at present enveloped by a great silence that reminds me of a comment made by Sherlock Holmes in A. Conan Doyle's story, "Silver Blaze." Inspector Gregory had asked, "Is there any point to which you wish to draw my attention?" To this Holmes responded:

"To the curious incident of the dog in the night-time."
"The dog did nothing in the night-time," said the Inspector.
"That was the curious incident," remarked Sherlock Holmes.

By asking himself what would repress the normal barking instinct of a watch dog Holmes realized that it must be the dog's recognition of his master as the criminal trespasser. In a similar way we should ask ourselves what repression keeps us from discussing something as important as immigration?

It cannot be that immigration is numerically of no consequence. Our government acknowledges a *net* inflow of 400,000 a year. Hard data are understandably lacking on the extent of illegal entries, but a not implausible figure is 600,000 per year. (Buchanan 1973). The natural increase of the resident population is now about 1.7 million per year. This means that the yearly gain from immigration is at least nineteen percent and may be thirty-seven percent, of the total increase. It is quite conceivable that educational campaigns like that of Zero Population Growth, Inc., coupled with adverse social and economic factors—inflation, housing shortage, depression, and loss of confidence in national leaders—may lower the fertility of American women to a point at which all of the yearly increase in population would be accounted for by immigration. Should we not at least ask if that is what we want? How curious it is that we so seldom discuss immigration these days!

Curious, but understandable—as one finds out the moment he publicly questions the wisdom of the status quo in immigration. He who does so is promptly charged with *isolationism, bigotry, prejudice, **ethnocentrism,** chauvinism,* and *selfishness.* These are hard accusations to bear. It is pleasanter to talk about other matters, leaving immigration policy to wallow in the crosscurrents of special interests that take no account of the good of the whole—*or of the interests of posterity.*

We Americans have a bad conscience because of things we said in the past about immigrants. Two generations ago the popular press was rife with references to *Dagos, Wops, Pollacks, Japs, Chinks,* and *Krauts*—all pejorative terms that failed to acknowledge our indebtedness to Goya, Leonardo, Copernicus, Hiroshige, Confucius, and Bach. Because the implied inferiority of foreigners was *then* the justification for keeping them out, it is *now* thoughtlessly assumed that restrictive policies can only be based on the assumption of immigrant inferiority. *This is not so.*

Existing immigration laws exclude idiots and known criminals; future laws will almost certainly continue this policy. But should we also consider the quality of the average immigrant, as compared with the quality of the average resident? Perhaps we should, perhaps we shouldn't. (What is "quality" anyway?) But the quality issue is not our concern here.

From this point on, *it will be assumed that immigrants and native-born citizens are of exactly equal quality,* however quality may be defined. The focus is only on quantity. The conclusions reached depend on nothing else, so all charges of ethnocentrism are irrelevant.

World food banks move food to the people, thus facilitating the exhaustion of the environment of the poor. By contrast, unrestricted immigration moves people to the food, thus speeding up the destruction of the environment in rich countries. Why poor people should want to make this transfer is no mystery, but why should rich hosts encourage it? This transfer, like the reverse one, is supported by both selfish interests and humanitarian impulses.

The principal selfish interest in unimpeded immigration is easy to identify: it is the interest of the employers of cheap labor, particularly that needed for degrading jobs. We have been deceived about the forces of history by the lines of Emma Lazarus inscribed on the Statue of Liberty:

Give me your tired, your poor,
Your huddled masses yearning to breathe free,
The wretched refuse of your teeming shore,
Send these, the homeless, tempest-tossed to me:
I lift my lamp beside the golden door.

The image is one of an infinitely generous earth-mother, passively opening her arms to hordes of immigrants who come here on their own initiative. Such an image may have been adequate for the early days of colonization, but by the time these lines were written (1886) the force for immigration was largely manufactured inside our own borders by factory and mine owners who sought cheap labor not to be found among laborers already here. One group of foreigners after another was thus enticed into the United States to work at wretched jobs for wretched wages.

At present, it is largely the Mexicans who are being so exploited. It is particularly to the advantage of certain employers that there be many illegal immigrants. Illegal immigrant workers dare not complain about their working conditions for fear of being **repatriated.** Their presence reduces the bargaining power of all Mexican-Amercian laborers. Cesar Chavez has repeatedly pleaded with congressional committees to close the doors to more Mexicans so that those here can negotiate effectively for higher wages and decent working conditions. Chavez understands the ethics of a lifeboat.

The interests of the employers of cheap labor are well served by the silence of the **intelligentsia** of the country. WASPS—White Anglo-Saxon Protestants—are particularly reluctant to call for a closing of the doors to immigration for fear of being called ethnocentric bigots. It was, therefore, an occasion of pure delight for this particular WASP to be present at a meeting when the points he would like to have made were made better by a non-WASP speaking to other non-WASPS. It was in Hawaii, and most of the people in the room were second-level Hawaiian officials of Japanese ancestry. All Hawaiians are keenly aware of the limits of their environment, and the speaker had asked how it might be practically and constitutionally possible to close the doors to more immigrants to the islands. (To Hawaiians, immigrants from the other forty-nine states are as much of a threat as those from other nations. There is only so much room in the islands, and the islanders know it. Sophistical arguments that imply otherwise do not impress them.)

Yet the Japanese-Americans of Hawaii have active ties with the land of their origin. This point was raised by a Japanese-American member of the audience who asked the Japanese-American speaker: "But how can we shut the doors now? We have many friends and relations in Japan that we'd like to bring to Hawaii some day so that they can enjoy this beautiful land."

The speaker smiled sympathetically and responded slowly, "Yes, but we have children now and someday we'll have grandchildren. We can bring more people here from Japan only by giving away some of the land that we hope to pass on to our grandchildren some day. What right do we have to do that?"

To be generous with one's own possessions is one thing; to be generous with posterity's is quite another. This, I think, is the point that must be gotten across to those who would, from a commendable love of **distributive justice,** institute a ruinous system of the commons, either in the form of a world food bank or that of unrestricted immigration. Since every speaker is a member of some ethnic group it is always possible to charge him with ethnocentrism. But even after purging an argument of ethnocentrism the rejection of the commons is still valid and necessary if we are to save at least some parts of the world from environmental ruin. Is it not desirable that at least some of the grandchildren of people now living should have a decent place in which to live?

THE ASYMMETRY OF DOOR–SHUTTING

We must now answer this telling point: "How can you justify slamming the door once you're inside? You say that immigrants should be kept out. But aren't we all immigrants, or the descendants of immigrants? Since we refuse to leave, must we not, as a matter of justice and symmetry, admit all others?"

It is literally true that we Americans of non-Indian ancestry are the descendants of thieves. Should we not, then, "give back" the land to the Indians, that is, give it to the now-living Americans of Indian ancestry? As an exercise in pure logic I see no way to reject this proposal. Yet I am unwilling to live by it, and I know no one who is. Our reluctance to embrace pure justice may spring from pure selfishness. On the other hand, it may arise from an unspoken recognition of consequences that have not yet been clearly spelled out.

Suppose, becoming intoxicated with pure justice, we "Anglos" should decide to turn our land over to the Indians. Since all our other wealth has also been derived from the land, we would have to give that to the Indians, too. Then what would we non-Indians do? Where would we go? There is no open land in the world on which men without capital can make their living (and not much unoccupied land on which men with capital can either). Where would 209 million putatively justice-loving, non-Indian Americans go? Most of them—in the persons of their ancestors—came from Europe, but they wouldn't be welcomed back there. Anyway, Europeans have no better title to their land than we to ours. They also would have to give up their homes. (But to whom? And where would *they* go?)

Clearly, the concept of pure justice produces an **infinite regress.** The law long ago invented statutes of limitations to justify the rejection of pure justice, in the interest of preventing massive disorder. The law zealously defends property rights—but only *recent* property rights. It is as though the physical principle of exponential decay applies to property rights. Drawing a line in time may be unjust, but any other action is practically worse.

We are all the descendants of thieves, and the world's resources are inequitably distributed, but we must begin the journey to tomorrow from the point where we are today. We cannot remake the past. We cannot, without violent disorder and suffering, give land and resources back to the "original" owners—who are dead anyway.

We cannot safely divide the wealth equitably among all present peoples, so long as people reproduce at different rates, because to do so would guarantee that our grandchildren—everyone's grandchildren—would have only a ruined world to inhabit.

MUST EXCLUSION BE ABSOLUTE?

To show the logical structure of the immigration problem I have ignored many factors that would enter into real decisions made in a real world. No matter how convincing the logic may be, it is probable that we would want, from time to time, to admit a few people from the outside to our lifeboat. Political refugees in particular are likely to cause us to make exceptions: We remember the Jewish refugees from Germany after 1933, and the Hungarian refugees after 1956. Moreover, the interests of national defense, broadly conceived, could justify admitting many men and women of unusual talents, whether refugees or not. (This raises the quality issue, which is not the subject of this essay.)

Such exceptions threaten to create runaway population growth inside the lifeboat, i.e., the receiving country. However, the threat can be neutralized by a population policy that includes immigration. An effective policy is one of flexible control.

Suppose, for example, that the nation has achieved a stable condition of ZPG, which (say) permits 1.5 million births yearly. We must suppose that an acceptable system of allocating birth-rights to potential parents is in effect. Now suppose that an inhumane regime in some other part of the world creates a horde of refugees, and that there is a widespread desire to admit some to our country. At the same time, we do not want to sabotage our population control system. Clearly, the rational path to pursue is the following. If we decide to admit 100,000 refugees this year we should compensate for this by reducing the allocation of birth-rights in the following year by a similar amount, that is, downward to a total of 1.4 million. In that way we could achieve both humanitarian and population control goals. (And the refugees would have to accept the population controls of the society that admits them. It is not inconceivable that they might be given proportionally fewer rights than the native population.)

In a democracy, the admission of immigrants should properly be voted on. But by whom? It is not obvious. The usual rule of a democracy is votes for all. But it can be questioned whether a universal franchise is the most just one in a case of this sort. Whatever benefits there are in the admission of immigrants presumably accrue to everyone. But the costs would be seen as falling most heavily on potential parents, some of whom would have to postpone or forego having their (next) child because of the influx of immigrants. The double question *Who benefits? Who pays?* suggests that a restriction of the usual democratic franchise would be appropriate and just in this case. Would our particular quasi-democratic form of government be flexible enough to institute such a novelty? If not, the majority might, out of humanitarian motives, impose an unacceptable burden (the foregoing of parenthood) on a minority, thus producing political instability.

Plainly many new problems will arise when we consciously face the immigration question and seek rational answers. No workable answers can be found if we ignore population problems. And—if the argument of this essay is correct—so long as there is no true world government to control reporduction everywhere it is impossible to survive in dignity if we are to be guided by spaceship ethics. Without a world government that is sovereign in reproductive matters mankind lives, in fact, on a number of sovereign lifeboats. For the foreseeable future survival demands that we govern our actions by the ethics of a lifeboat. Posterity will be ill served if we do not.

References

Anonymous. 1974. *Wall Street Journal* 19 Feb.

Borlaug, N. 1973. Civilization's future: a call for international granaries. *Bull.At.Sci.* 29: 7–15.

Boulding, K. 1966. The economics of the coming Spaceship Earth. *In* H. Jarrett, ed. Environmental Quality in a Growing Economy. Baltimore: John Hopkins Press.

Buchanan, W. 1973. Immigration statistics. *Equilibrium* 1(3): 16–19.

Davis, K. 1963. Population. *Sci.Amer.* 209(3): 62–71.

Farvar, M.T., and J.P. Milton. 1972. The Careless Technology. Garden City, NY: Natural History Press.

Gregg, A. 1955. A medical aspect of the population problem. *Science* 121:681–682.

Hardin, G. 1966. Chap. 9 *in* Biology: Its Principles and Implications, 2nd ed. San Francisco: Freeman.

———. 1968. The tragedy of the commons. *Science* 162: 1243–1248.

———. 1969a Page 18 *in* Population, Evolution, and Birth Control, 2nd ed. San Francisco: Freeman.

———. 1969b. The economics of wilderness. *Nat.Hist.* 78(6): 20–27.

———. 1972a. Pages 81–82 *in* Exploring New Ethics for Survival: The Voyage of the Spaceship *Beagle*. New York: Viking.

———. 1972b. Preserving quality on Spaceship Earth. *In* J.B. Trefethen, ed. Transactions of the Thirty-Seventh North American Wildlife and Natural Resources Conference. Wildlife Management Institute, Washington, D.C.

———. 1973. Chap. 23 *in* Stalking the Wild Taboo. Los Altos, CA: Kaufmann.

Harris, M. 1972. How green the revolution. *Nat. Hist.* 81(3): 28–30.

Langer, S.K. 1942. Philosophy in a New Key. Cambridge, MA: Harvard University Press.

Lansner, K. 1974. Should foreign aid begin at home? *Newsweek,* 11 Feb., p. 32.

Marx, K. 1875. Critique of the Gotha program. Page 388 *in* R.C. Tucker, ed. The Marx-Engels Reader. New York: Norton, 1972.

Ophuls, W. 1974. The scarcity society. *Harpers* 248(1487): 47–52.

Paddock, W.C. 1970. How green is the green revolution? *BioScience* 20: 897–902.

Paddock, W., and E. Paddock. 1973. We Don't Know How. Ames, IA: Iowa State University Press.

Paddock, W., and P. Paddock. 1967. Famine—1975! Boston: Little, Brown.

Wilkes, H.G. 1972. The green revolution. *Environment* 14(8): 32–39.

Review Questions

1. What is wrong with the spaceship metaphor according to Hardin?

2. Explain Hardin's lifeboat metaphor.

3. According to Hardin, why can't we live by the Christian or the Marxian ideal?

4. Explain what Hardin calls the "tragedy of the commons." How is this supposed to apply to rich and poor nations?

5. Explain the "ratchet effect" and a "pejoristic system."

6. Why isn't a "benign demographic transition" possible according to Hardin?

7. Why doesn't Hardin think that the "Green Revolution" will solve the problem of world hunger?

8. Explain Hardin's opposition to present immigration policies.

1. Are there any respects in which the United States is not a lifeboat?

2. Is there any solution to the problem of over-population in poor countries that does not involve letting people die? What is it?

3. Is there any way to avoid the "tragedy of the commons" that does not involve private ownership? Explain.

4. Is there any way to avoid the "ratchet effect?" Explain.

5. Should we allow more people to immigrate into the United States? Why or why not?

Trudy Govier

The Right to Eat and the Duty to Work

Trudy Govier has taught philosophy at Trent University in Ontario. She has written several articles on moral philosophy.

*Govier discusses three different positions on the welfare question: Do needy people in an affluent society have a legal right to welfare benefits? First, there is the individualist position (called libertarianism by Hospers) that no one has a legal right to welfare benefits, not even in an affluent society. Second, there is the permissive position that in an affluent society, everyone has an unconditional legal right to welfare benefits. Third, there is the puritan position that everyone has a legal right to welfare, but this right ought to be conditional on one's willingness to work. After evaluating these three positions in terms of their social consequences (the "**teleological appraisal**") and social justice, Govier concludes that the permissive position is superior.*

Although the topic of welfare is not one with which philosophers have often concerned themselves, it is a topic which gives rise to many complex and fascinating questions— some in the area of political philosophy, some in the area of ethics, and some of a more practical kind. The variety of issues related to the subject of welfare makes it particularly necessary to be clear just which issue one is examining in a discussion of welfare. In a recent book on the subject, Nicholas Rescher asks:

In what respects and to what extent is society, working through the instrumentality of the state, responsible for the welfare of its members? What demands for the promotion of his welfare can an individual reasonably make upon his society? These are questions to which no answer can be given in terms of some **a priori** *approach with reference to universal ultimates. Whatever answer can appropriately be given will depend, in the final analysis, on what the society decides it should be.*[1]

Rescher raises this question only to avoid it. His response to his own question is that a society has all and only those responsibilities for its members that it thinks it has. Although this claim is trivially true as regards legal responsibilities, it is inadequate from a moral perspective. If one imagines the case of an affluent society which leaves the blind, the disabled, and the needy to die of starvation, the incompleteness of Rescher's account becomes obvious. In this imagined case one is naturally led to raise the question as to whether those in power ought to supply those in need with the necessities of life. Though the needy have no legal right to welfare benefits of any kind, one might very well say that they ought to have such a right. It is this claim which I propose to discuss here.[2]

I shall approach this issue by examining

From Trudy Govier, "The Right to Eat and the Duty to Work," *Philosophy of the Social Sciences*, vol. 5 (1975), pp. 125–143. Reprinted with permission of the author and *Philosophy of the Social Sciences.*

three positions which may be adopted in response to it. These are:

1. *The Individualist Position:* Even in an affluent society, one ought not to have any legal right to state-supplied welfare benefits.
2. *The Permissive Position:* In a society with sufficient resources, one ought to have an unconditional legal right to receive state supplied welfare benefits. (That is, one's right to receive such benefits ought not to depend on one's behaviour; it should be guaranteed).
3. *The Puritan Position:* In a society with sufficient resources one ought to have a legal right to state-supplied welfare benefits; this right ought to be conditional, however, on one's willingness to work.

But before we examine these positions, some preliminary clarification must be attempted....

Welfare systems are state-supported systems which supply benefits, usually in the form of cash income, to those who are in need. Welfare systems thus exist in the sort of social context where there is some private ownership of property. If no one owned anything individually (except possibly his own body), and all goods were considered to be the joint property of everyone, then this type of welfare system could not exist. A state might take on the responsibility for the welfare of its citizens, but it could not meet this responsibility by distributing a level of cash income which such citizens would spend to purchase the goods essential for life. The welfare systems which exist in the western world do exist against the background of extensive private ownership of property. It is in this context that I propose to discuss moral questions about having a right to welfare benefits. By setting out my questions in this way, I do not intend to endorse the institution of private property, but only to discuss questions which many people find real and difficult in the context of the social organization which they actually do experience. The present analysis of welfare is intended to apply to societies which (*a*) have the institution of private property, if not for means of production, at least for some basic good; and (*b*) possess sufficient resources so that it is at least possible for every member of the society to be supplied with the necessities of life.

The Individualist View

It might be maintained that a person in need has no legitimate moral claim on those around him and that the hypothetical inattentive society which left its blind citizens to beg or starve cannot rightly be censured for doing so. This view, which is dramatically at odds with most of contemporary social thinking, lives on in the writings of Ayn Rand and her followers.[3] The Individualist sets a high value on uncoerced personal choice. He sees each person as a responsible agent who is able to make his own decisions and to plan his own life. He insists that with the freedom to make decisions goes responsibility for the consequences of those decisions. A person has every right, for example, to spend ten years of his life studying Sanskrit—but if, as a result of this choice, he is unemployable, he ought not to expect others to labour on his behalf. No one has a proper claim on the labour of another, or on the income ensuing from that labour, unless he can repay the labourer in a way acceptable to that labourer himself. Government welfare schemes provide benefits from funds gained largely by taxing earned income. One cannot "opt out" of such schemes. To the Individualist, this means that a person is forced to work part of his time for others.

Suppose that a man works forty hours and earns two hundred dollars. Under modern-day taxation, it may well be that he can spend only two-thirds of that money as he chooses. The rest is taken by government and goes to support programmes which the working individual may not himself endorse. The beneficiaries of such programmes—those beneficiaries who do not work themselves—are as though they have slaves working for them.

Backed by the force which government authorities can command, they are able to exist on the earnings of others. Those who support them do not do so voluntarily, out of charity; they do so on government command.

Someone across the street is unemployed. Should you be taxed extra to pay for his expenses? Not at all. You have not injured him, you are not responsible for the fact that he is unemployed (unless you are a senator or bureaucrat who agitated for further curtailing of business which legislation passed, with the result that your neighbour was laid off by the curtailed business). You may voluntarily wish to help him out, or better still, try to get him a job to put him on his feet again; but since you have initiated no aggressive act against him, and neither purposefully nor accidentally injured him in any way, you should not be legally penalized for the fact of his unemployment.[4]

The Individualist need not lack concern for those in need. He may give generously to charity; he might give more generously still, if his whole income were his to use, as he would like it to be. He may also believe that, as a matter of empirical fact, existing government programmes do not actually help the poor. They support a cumbersome bureaucracy and they use financial resources which, if untaxed, might be used by those with initiative to pursue job-creating endeavours. The thrust of the Individualist's position is that each person owns his own body and his own labour; thus each person is taken to have a virtually unconditional right to the income which that labour can earn him in a free market place.[5] For anyone to pre-empt part of a worker's earnings without that worker's voluntary consent is tantamount to robbery. And the fact that the government is the intermediary through which this deed is committed does not change its moral status one iota.

On an Individualist's view, those in need should be cared for by charities or through other schemes to which contributions are voluntary. Many people may wish to insure themselves against unforeseen calamities and they should be free to do so. But there is no justification for non-optional government schemes financed by taxpayers' money....

The Permissive View

Directly contrary to the Individualist view of welfare is what I have termed the Permissive view. According to this view, in a society which has sufficient resources so that everyone could be supplied with the necessities of life, every individual ought to be given the legal right to social security, and this right ought not to be conditional in any way upon an individual's behavior. *Ex hypothesi* the society which we are discussing has sufficient goods to provide everyone with food, clothing, shelter and other necessities. Someone who does without these basic goods is scarcely living at all, and a society which takes no steps to change this state of affairs implies by its inaction that the life of such a person is without value. It does not execute him; but it may allow him to die. It does not put him in prison; but it may leave him with a life of lower quality than that of some prison inmates. A society which can rectify these circumstances and does not can justly be accused of imposing upon the needy either death or lifelong deprivation. And those characteristics which make a person needy—whether they be illness, old age, insanity, feeblemindedness, inability to find paid work, or even poor moral character—are insufficient to make him deserve the fate to which an inactive society would in effect condemn him. One would not be executed for inability or failure to find paid work; neither should one be allowed to die for this misfortune or failing.

A person who cannot or does not find his own means of social security does not thereby forfeit his status as a human being. If other human beings, with physical, mental and moral qualities different from his, are regarded as having the right to life and to the means of life, then so too should he be regarded. A society which does not accept the responsibility for supplying such a person with the basic necessities of life is, in effect, endorsing a difference between its members which is without moral justification....

The adoption of a Permissive view of welfare would have significant practical implications. If there were a legal right, unconditional upon behaviour, to a specified level of state-supplied benefits, then state investigation of the prospective welfare recipient could be kept to a minimum. Why he is in need, whether he can work, whether he is willing to work, and what he does while receiving welfare benefits are on this view quite irrelevant to his right to receive those benefits. A welfare recipient is a person who claims from his society that to which he is legally entitled under a morally based welfare scheme. The fact that he makes this claim licenses no special state or societal interference with his behaviour. If the Permissive view of welfare were widely believed, then there would be no social stigma attached to being on welfare. There is such a stigma, and many long-term welfare recipients are considerably demoralized by their dependent status.[6] These facts suggest that the Permissive view of welfare is not widely held in our society.

The Puritan View

This view of welfare rather naturally emerges when we consider that no one can have a right to something without someone else's, or some group of other persons', having responsibilities correlative to this right. In the case in which the right in question is a legal right to social security, the correlative responsibilities may be rather extensive. They have been deemed responsibilities of "the state." The state will require resources and funds to meet these responsibilities, and these do not emerge from the sky miraculously, or zip into existence as a consequence of virtually effortless acts of will. They are taken by the state from its citizens, often in the form of taxation on earned income. The funds given to the welfare recipient and many of the goods which he purchases with these funds are produced by other members of society, many of whom give a considerable portion of their time and their energy to this end. If a state has the moral responsibility to ensure the social security of its citizens then all the citizens of that state have the responsibility to provide state agencies with the means to carry out their duties. This responsibility, in our present contingent circumstances, seems to generate an obligation to *work*.

A person who works helps to produce the goods which all use in daily living and, when paid, contributes through taxation to government endeavours. The person who does not work, even though able to work, does not make his contribution to social efforts towards obtaining the means of life. He is not entitled to a share of the goods produced by others if he chooses not to take part in their labours. Unless he can show that there is a moral justification for his not making the sacrifice of time and energy which others make, he has no legitimate claim to welfare benefits. If he is disabled or unable to obtain work, he cannot work; hence he has no need to justify his failure to work. But if he does choose not to work, he would have to justify his choice by saying "others should sacrifice their time and energy for me; I have no need to sacrifice time and energy for them." This principle, a version of what Rawls refers to as a **free-rider's** principle, simply will not stand up to criticism.[7] To deliberately avoid working and benefit from the labours of others is morally indefensible.

Within a welfare system erected on these principles, the right to welfare is conditional upon one's satisfactorily accounting for his failure to obtain the necessities of life by his own efforts. Someone who is severely disabled mentally or physically, or who for some other reason cannot work, is morally entitled to receive welfare benefits. Someone who chooses not to work is not. The Puritan view of welfare is a kind of compromise between the Individualist view and the Permissive view....

The Puritan view of welfare, based as it is on the inter-relation between welfare and work, provides a rationale for two connected principles which those establishing welfare schemes in Canada and in the United States seem to endorse. First of all, those on welfare should never receive a higher income than the working poor. Secondly, a welfare scheme should, in some way or other, incorporate incentives to work. These principles, which presuppose that it is better to work than not to work, emerge rather naturally from the contingency which is at the basis of the Puritan view: the goods essential for social security are products of the labour of some members of society. If we wish to have a continued supply of such goods, we must encourage those who work to produce them....

APPRAISAL OF POLICIES: SOCIAL CONSEQUENCES AND SOCIAL JUSTICE

In approaching the appraisal of prospective welfare policies under these two aspects I am, of course, making some assumptions about the moral appraisal of suggested social policies. Although these cannot possibly be justified here, it may be helpful to articulate them, at least in a rough way.

Appraisal of social policies is in part teleological. To the extent that a policy, P, increases the total human welfare more than does an alternative policy, P', P is a better social policy then P'. Or, if P leaves the total human welfare as it is, while P' diminishes it, then to that extent, P is a better social policy than P'. Even this skeletal formulation of the teleological aspect of appraisal reveals why appraisal cannot be entirely teleological. We consider total consequences—effects upon the total of "human well-being" in a society. But this total is a summation of consequences on different individuals. It includes no judgements as to how far we allow one individual's well-being to decrease while another's increases, under the same policy. Judgements relating to the latter problems are judge-

ments about social justice.

In appraising social policies we have to weigh up considerations of total well-being against considerations of justice. Just how this is to be done, precisely, I would not pretend to know. However, the absence of precise methods does not mean that we should relinquish attempts at appraisal: some problems are already with us, and thought which is necessarily tentative and imprecise is still preferable to no thought at all.

Consequences of Welfare Schemes

First, let us consider the consequences of the non-scheme advocated by the Individualist. He would have us abolish all non-optional government programmes which have as their goal the improvement of anyone's personal welfare. This rejection extends to health schemes, pension plans and education, as well as to welfare and unemployment insurance. So following the Individualist would lead to very sweeping changes.

The Individualist will claim (as do Hospers and Ayn Rand) that on the whole his non-scheme will bring beneficial consequences. He will admit, as he must, that there are people who would suffer tremendously if welfare and other social security programmes were simply terminated. Some would even die as a result. We cannot assume that spontaneously developing charities would cover every case of dire need. Nevertheless the Individualist wants to point to benefits which would accrue to businessmen and to working people and their families if taxation were drastically cut. It is his claim that consumption would rise, hence production would rise, job opportunities would be extended, and there would be an economic boom, if people could only spend all their earned income as they wished. This boom would benefit both rich and poor.

There are significant omissions which are necessary in order to render the Individualist's optimism plausible. Either workers and businessmen would have insurance of various kinds, or they would be insecure in their prosperity. If they did have insurance to cover health problems, old age and possible job loss, then they would pay for it; hence they would not be spending their whole earned income on consumer goods. Those who run the insurance schemes could, of course, put this money back into the economy—but government schemes already do this. The economic boom under Individualism would not be as loud as originally expected. Furthermore the goal of increased consumption-increased productivity must be questioned from an ecological viewpoint: many necessary materials are available only in limited quantities.

Finally, a word about charity. It is not to be expected that those who are at the mercy of charities will benefit from this state, either materially or psychologically. Those who prosper will be able to choose between giving a great deal to charity and suffering from the very real insecurity and guilt which would accompany the existence of starvation and grim poverty outside their padlocked doors. It is to be hoped that they would opt for the first alternative. But, if they did, this might be every bit as expensive for them as government-supported benefit schemes are now. If they did not give generously to charity, violence might result. However one looks at it, the consequences of Individualism are unlikely to be good.

Welfare schemes operating in Canada today are almost without exception based upon the principles of the Puritan view. To see the consequences of that type of welfare scheme we have only to look at the results of our own welfare programmes. Taxation to support such schemes is high, though not so intolerably so as to have led to widescale resentment among taxpayers. Canadian welfare programmes are attended by complicated and often cumbersome bureaucracy, some of which results from the interlocking of municipal, provincial and federal governments in the administration and financing of welfare programmes. The cost of the programmes is no doubt increased by this bureaucracy; not

all the tax money directed to welfare programmes goes to those in need. Puritan welfare schemes do not result in social catastrophe or in significant business stagnation—this much we know, because we already live with such schemes. Their adverse consequences, if any, are felt primarily not by society generally nor by businessmen and the working segment of the public, but rather by recipients of welfare.

Both the Special Senate Committee Report on Poverty and the Real Poverty Report criticize our present system of welfare for its demoralization of recipients, who often must deal with several levels of government and are vulnerable to arbitrary interference on the part of administering officials. Welfare officials have the power to check on welfare recipients and cut off or limit their benefits under a large number of circumstances. The dangers to welfare recipients in terms of anxiety, threats to privacy and loss of dignity are obvious. According to the Senate Report, the single aspect shared by all Canada's welfare systems is "a record of failure and insufficiency, of bureaucratic rigidities that often result in the degradation, humiliation and alienation of recipients." [8] The writers of this report cite many instances of humiliation, leaving the impression that these are too easily found to be "incidental aberrations." [9] Concern that a welfare recipient either be unable to work or be willing to work (if unemployed) can easily turn into concern about how he spends the income supplied him, what his plans for the future are, where he lives, how many children he has. And the rationale underlying the Puritan scheme makes the degradation of welfare recipients a natural consequence of welfare institutions. Work is valued and only he who works is thought to contribute to society. Welfare recipients are regarded as parasites and spongers—so when they are treated as such, this is only what we should have expected. Being on welfare in a society which thinks and acts in this fashion can be psychologically debilitating. Welfare recipients who are demoralized by their downgraded status and relative lack of personal freedom can be expected to be made less capable of self-sufficiency. To the extent that this is so, welfare systems erected on Puritan principles may defeat their own purposes.

In fairness, it must be noted here that bureaucratic checks and controls are not a feature only of Puritan welfare systems. To a limited extent, Permissive systems would have to incorporate them too. Within those systems, welfare benefits would be given only to those whose income was inadequate to meet basic needs. However, there would be no checks on "willingness to work," and there would be no need for welfare workers to evaluate the merits of the daily activities of recipients. If a Permissive guaranteed income system were administered through income tax returns, everyone receiving the basic income and those not needing it paying it back in taxes, then the special status of welfare recipients would fade. They would no longer be singled out as a special group within the population. It is to be expected that living solely on government-supplied benefits would be psychologically easier in that type of situation.

Thus it can be argued that for the recipients of welfare, a Permissive scheme has more advantages than a Puritan one. This is not a very surprising conclusion. The Puritan scheme is relatively disadvantageous to recipients, and Puritans would acknowledge this point; they will argue that the overall consequences of Permissive schemes are negative in that these schemes benefit some at too great a cost to others. (Remember, we are not yet concerned with the *justice* of welfare policies, but solely with their consequences as regards *total* human well-being within the society in question.) The concern which most people have regarding the Permissive scheme relates to its costs and its dangers to the "work ethic." It is commonly thought that people work only because they have to work to survive in a tolerable style. If a guaranteed income scheme were adopted by the govern-ment, this incentive to work would disappear. No one would be faced with the choice between a nasty and boring job and starvation. Who would do the nasty and boring jobs then? Many of them are not eliminable and they have to be done somehow, by someone. Puritans fear that a great many people—even some with relatively pleasant jobs—might simply cease to work if they could receive non-stigmatized government money to live on. If this were to happen, the permissive society would simply grind to a halt.

In addressing these anxieties about the consequences of Permissive welfare schemes, we must recall that welfare benefits are set to ensure only that those who do not work have a bearable existence, with an income sufficient for basic needs, and that they have this income regardless of why they fail to work. Welfare benefits will not finance luxury living for a family of five! If jobs are adequately paid so that workers receive more than the minimum welfare income in an earned salary, then there will still be a financial incentive to take jobs. What guaranteed income schemes will do is to raise the salary floor. This change will benefit the many non-unionized workers in service and clerical occupations.

Furthermore it is unlikely that people work solely due to (i) the desire for money and the things it can buy and (ii) belief in the Puritan work ethic. There are many other reasons for working, some of which would persist in a society which had adopted a Permissive welfare system. Most people are happier when their time is structured in some way, when they are active outside their own homes, when they feel themselves part of an endeavour whose purposes transcend their particular egoistic ones. Women often choose to work outside the home for these reasons as much as for financial ones. With these and other factors operating I cannot see that the adoption of a Permissive welfare scheme would be followed by a level of slothfulness which would jeopardize human well-being.

Another worry about the Permissive scheme concerns cost. It is difficult to comment on this in a general way, since it would vary so much from case to case. Of Canada at the present it has been said that a guaranteed income scheme administered through income tax would cost less than social security payments administered through the present bureaucracies. It is thought that this saving would result from a drastic cut in administrative costs. The matter of the work ethic is also relevant to the question of costs. Within a Puritan framework it is very important to have a high level of employment and there is a tendency to resist any reorganization which results in there being fewer jobs available. Some of these proposed reorganizations would save money; strictly speaking we should count the cost of keeping jobs which are objectively unnecessary as part of the cost of Puritanism regarding welfare.

In summary, we can appraise Individualism, Puritanism and Permissivism with respect to their anticipated consequences, as follows: Individualism is unacceptable; Puritanism is tolerable, but has some undesirable consequences for welfare recipients; Permissivism appears to be the winner. Worries about bad effects which Permissive welfare schemes might have due to high costs and (alleged) reduced work-incentives appear to be without solid basis.

Social Justice under Proposed Welfare Schemes

We must now try to consider the merits of Individualism, Puritanism and Permissivism with regard to their impact on the distribution of the goods necessary for well-being. [Robert] Nozick has argued against the whole conception of a distributive justice on the grounds that it presupposes that goods are like manna from heaven: we simply get them and then have a problem—to whom to give them. According to Nozick we know where things come from and we do not have the problem of to whom to give them. There is not really a problem of distributive justice, for there is no central distributor giving out manna from heaven! It is necessary to

counter Nozick on this point since his reaction to the (purported) problems of distributive justice would undercut much of what follows.[10]

There is a level at which Nozick's point is obviously valid. If A discovers a cure for cancer, then it is A and not B or C who is responsible for this discovery. On Nozick's view this is taken to imply that A should reap any monetary profits which are forthcoming; other people will benefit from the cure itself. Now although it cannot be doubted that A is a bright and hardworking person, neither can it be denied that A and his circumstances are the product of many co-operative endeavours: schools and laboratories, for instance. Because this is so, I find Nozick's claim that "we know where things come from" unconvincing at a deeper level. Since achievements like A's presuppose extensive social co-operation, it is morally permissible to regard even the monetary profits accruing from them as shareable by the "owner" and society at large.

Laws support existing income levels in many ways. Governments specify taxation so as to further determine net income. Property ownership is a legal matter. In all these ways people's incomes and possibilities for obtaining income are affected by deliberate state action. It is always possible to raise questions about the moral desirability of actual conventional arrangements. Should university professors earn less than lawyers? More than waitresses? Why? Why not? Anyone who gives an account of distributive justice is trying to specify principles which will make it possible to answer questions such as these, and nothing in Nozick's argument suffices to show that the questions are meaningless or unimportant.

Any human distribution of anything is unjust insofar as differences exist for no good reason. If goods did come like manna from heaven and the Central Distributor gave A ten times more than B, we should want to know why. The skewed distribution might be deemed a just one if A's needs were objectively ten times greater than B's, or if B refused to accept more than his small portion of goods. But if no reason at all could be given for it, or if only an irrelevant reason could be given (e.g., A is blue-eyed and B is not), then it is an unjust distribution. All the views we have expounded concerning welfare permit differences in income level. Some philosophers would say that such differences are never just, although they may be necessary, for historical or utilitarian reasons. Whether or not this is so, it is admittedly very difficult to say just what would constitute a good reason for giving A a higher income than B. Level of need, degree of responsibility, amount of training, unpleasantness of work— all these have been proposed and all have some plausibility. We do not need to tackle all this larger problem in order to consider justice under proposed welfare systems. For we can deal here solely with the question of whether everyone should receive a floor level of income; decisions on this matter are independent of decisions on overall equality or principles of variation among incomes above the floor. The Permissivist contends that all should receive at least the floor income; the Individualist and the Puritan deny this. All would claim justice for their side.

The Individualist attempts to justify extreme variations in income, with some people below the level where they can fulfill their basic needs, with reference to the fact of people's actual accomplishments. This approach to the question is open to the same objections as those which have already been raised against Nozick's non-manna-from-heaven argument, and I shall not repeat them here. Let us move on to the Puritan account. It is because goods emerge from human efforts that the Puritan advances his view of welfare. He stresses the unfairness of a system which would permit some people to take advantage of others. A Permissive welfare system would do this, as it makes no attempt to distinguish between those who choose not to work and those who cannot work. No one should be able to take advantage of another under the auspices of a government institution. The Puritan scheme seeks to eliminate this possibility, and for that reason, Puritans would allege, it is a more just scheme than the Permissive one.

Permissivists can best reply to this contention by acknowledging that any instance of free-riding would be an instance where those working were done an injustice, but by showing that any justice which the Puritan preserves by eliminating free-riding is outweighted by *injustice* perpetrated elsewhere. Consider the children of the Puritan's free-riders. They will suffer greatly for the "sins" of their parents. Within the institution of the family, the Puritan cannot suitably hurt the guilty without cruelly depriving the innocent. There is a sense, too, in which Puritanism does injustice to the many people on welfare who are not free-riders. It perpetuates the opinion that they are non-contributors to society and this doctrine, which is over-simplified if not downright false, has a harmful effect upon welfare recipients.

Social justice is not simply a matter of the distribution of goods, or the income with which goods are to be purchased. It is also a matter of the protection of rights. Western societies claim to give their citizens equal rights in political and legal contexts; they also claim to endorse the larger conception of a right to life. Now it is possible to interpret these rights in a limited and formalistic way, so that the duties correlative to them are minimal. On the limited, or negative, interpretation, to say that A has a right to life is simply to say that others have a duty not to interfere with A's attempts to keep himself alive. This interpretation of the right to life is compatible with Individualism as well as with Puritanism. But it is an inadequate interpretation of the right to life and of other rights. A right to vote is meaningless if one is starving and unable to get to the polls; a right to equality before the law is meaningless if one cannot afford to hire a lawyer. And so on.

Even a Permissive welfare scheme will go only a very small way towards protecting people's rights. It will amount to a meaningful acknowledgement of a right to life, by ensuring income adequate to purchase food, clothing and shelter—at the very least. These minimum necessities are presupposed by all other rights a society may endorse in that their possession is a precondition of being able to exercise these other rights. Because it protects the rights of all within a society better than do Puritanism and Individualism, the Permissive view can rightly claim superiority over the others with regard to justice.

Footnotes

1. Nichols Rescher, *Welfare: Social Issues in Philosophical Perspective*, p. 114.

2. One might wish to discuss moral questions concerning welfare in the context of **natural rights** doctrines. Indeed, Article 22 of the United Nations Declaration of Human Rights states, "Everyone, as a member of society, has the right to social security and is entitled, through national effort and international cooperation and in accordance with the organization and resources of each State, to the economic, social and cultural rights indispensable for his dignity and the free development of his personality." I make no attempt to defend the right to welfare as a **natural right.** Granting that rights imply responsibilities or duties and that "ought" implies "can," it would only be intelligible to regard the right to social security as a natural right if all states were able to ensure the minimum well-being of their citizens. This is not the case. And a natural right is one which is by definition supposed to belong to all human beings simply in virtue of their status as human beings. The analysis given here in the permissive view is compatible with the claim that all human beings have a *prima facie* natural right to social security. It is not, however, compatible with the claim that all human beings have a natural right to social security if this right is regarded as one which is so absolute as to be inviolable under any and all conditions.

3. See, for example, Ayn Rand's *Atlas Shrugged, The Virtue of Selfishness,* and *Capitalism: the Unknown Ideal.*

4. John Hospers, *Libertarianism: A Political Philosophy for Tomorrow,* p. 67.

5. I say virtually unconditional, because an Individualist such as John Hospers sees a legitimate moral role for government in preventing the use of force by some citizens against others. Since this is the case, I presume that he would also regard as legitimate such taxation as was necessary to support this function. Presumably that taxation would be seen as consented to by all, on the grounds that all "really want" government protection.

6. Ian Adams, William Cameron, Brian Hill, and Peter Penz, *The Real Poverty Report,* pp. 167–187.

7. See *A Theory of Justice,* pp. 124, 136. Rawls defines the free-rider as one who relies on the principle "everyone is to act justly except for myself, if I choose not to," and says that his position is a version of egoism which is eliminated as a morally acceptable principle by formal constraints. This conclusion regarding the tenability of egoism is one which I accept and which is taken for granted in the present context.

8. *Senate Report on Poverty,* p. 73.

9. The Hamilton Public Welfare Department takes automobile licence plates from recipients, making them available again only to those whose needs meet with the Department's approval. (*Real Poverty Report,* p. 186.) The *Globe and Mail* for 12 January 1974 reported that welfare recipients in the city of Toronto are to be subjected to computerized budgeting. In the summer of 1973, the two young daughters of an Alabama man on welfare were sterilized against their own wishes and without their parents' informed consent. (See *Time,* 23 July 1973.)

10. Robert Nozick, "Distributive Justice," *Philosophy and Public Affairs,* Fall 1973.

Review Questions

1. Distinguish between the individualist view, the permissive view, and the puritan view (as Govier explains them).

2. State the "free-rider principle." Why does Govier reject it?

3. Compare the consequences of the three views as Govier describes them.

4. What is Govier's conclusion with respect to the consequences of the three positions?

5. What is Govier's objection to the individualist's view with respect to justice?

6. How does Govier characterize social justice?

7. Which of the three positions is superior according to Govier and why?

Discussion Questions

1. Does everyone in a rich society such as the United States have a right to welfare? Explain your answer.

2. Does everyone in a society who is able to work have a right to work? Why or why not?

3. Is a person who is able to work, but who chooses not to work entitled to welfare? What is your position on this "free-rider" problem?

4. Some women with dependent children receive more money from welfare than they could make working at low-paying jobs. This gives them an incentive not to work. Is this acceptable? What is your view?

5. Is a guaranteed income administered through the income tax a good idea? What do you think of Govier's suggestion?

John Hospers
What Libertarianism Is

John Hospers is professor of philosophy at the University of Southern California. He is the author of Human Conduct: Problems of Ethics *(1972),* Libertarianism: A Political Philosophy for Tomorrow *(1971), and* Understanding the Arts *(1982). He was the Libertarian party's candidate for the president of the United States in the last presidential election.*

Hospers begins with several different statements of the libertarian thesis which says that every person is the owner of his or her life. This basic thesis entails a right to liberty and a right to act as you choose, unless your action infringes on the equal liberty of others to act as they choose. Hospers also recognizes a right to life and a right to property. These rights are interpreted negatively, that is, they imply only that no one, including the government, has a right to interfere with a person's liberty, life, or property, however, they do not require any positive actions. Since these rights are violated by an initial use of force, the only proper role of government is to prevent this use of force and to retaliate against those who do initiate the use of force. All other possible roles of government, including protecting individuals from themselves, or requiring people to help each other, are emphatically rejected by Hospers.

The political philosophy that is called libertarianism (from the Latin *libertas,* liberty) is the doctrine that every person is the owner of his own life, and that no one is the owner of anyone else's life; and that consequently every human being has the right to act in accordance with his own choices, unless those actions infringe on the equal liberty of other human beings to act in accordance with their choices.

There are several other ways of stating the same libertarian thesis:

1. No one is anyone else's master, and no one is anyone else's slave. Since I am the one to decide how my life is to be conducted just as you decide about yours, I have no right (even if I had the power) to make you my slave and be your master, nor have you the right to become the master by enslaving me. Slavery is *forced* servitude, and since no one owns the life of anyone else, no one has the right to enslave another. Political theories past and present have traditionally been concerned with who should be the master (usually the king, the dictator, or government bureaucracy) and who should be the slaves, and what the extent of the slavery should be. Libertarianism holds that no one has the right to use force to enslave the life of another, or any portion or aspect of that life.

2. Other men's lives are not yours to dispose of. I enjoy seeing operas; but operas are expensive to produce. Opera-lovers often say, "The state (or the city, etc.) should subsidize opera, so that we can all see it. Also it would be for people's betterment, cultural benefit, etc." But what they are advocating is nothing more or less than legalized plunder. They can't pay for the productions themselves, and yet they want to see opera, which involves a large number of

From John Hospers, "What Libertarianism Is," in Tibor R. Machan, ed., *The Libertarian Alternative* (Chicago: Nelson-Hall Co., 1974), pp. 3–20. Reprinted with permission.

people and their labor; so what they are saying in effect is, "Get the money through legalized force. Take a little bit more out of every worker's paycheck every week to pay for the operas we want to see." But I have no right to take by force from the workers' pockets to pay for what I want.

Perhaps it would be better if he *did* go to see opera—then I should try to convince him to go voluntarily. But to take the money from him forcibly, because in my opinion it would be good for *him,* is still seizure of his earnings, which is plunder.

Besides, if I have the right to force him to help pay for my pet projects, hasn't he equally the right to force me to help pay for his? Perhaps he in turn wants the government to subsidize rock-and-roll, or his new car, or a house in the country? If I have the right to milk him, why hasn't he the right to milk me? If I can be a moral cannibal, why can't he too?

We should beware of the inventors of **utopias.** They would remake the world according to their vision—with the lives and fruits of the labor of *other* human beings. Is it someone's utopian vision that others should build pyramids to beautify the landscape? Very well, then other men should provide the labor; and if he is in a position of political power, and he can't get men to do it voluntarily, then he must *compel* them to "cooperate"—i.e. he must enslave them.

A hundred men might gain great pleasure from beating up or killing just one insignificant human being; but other men's lives are not theirs to dispose of. "In order to achieve the worthy goals of the next five-year-plan, we must forcibly collectivize the peasants ..."; but other men's lives are not theirs to dispose of. Do you want to occupy, rent-free, the mansion that another man has worked for twenty years to buy? But other men's lives are not yours to dispose of. Do you want operas so badly that everyone is forced to work harder to pay for their subsidization through taxes? But other

men's lives are not yours to dispose of. Do you want to have free medical care at the expense of other people, whether they wish to provide it or not? But this would require them to work longer for you whether they want to or not, and other men's lives are not yours to dispose of....

3. No human being should be a nonvoluntary mortgage on the life of another. I cannot claim your life, your work, or the products of your effort as mine. The fruit of one man's labor should not be fair game for every freeloader who comes along and demands it as his own. The orchard that has been carefully grown, nurtured, and harvested by its owner should not be ripe for the plucking for any bypasser who has a yen for the ripe fruit. The wealth that some men have produced should not be fair game for looting by government, to be used for whatever purposes its representatives determine, no matter what their motives in so doing may be. The theft of your money by a robber is not justified by the fact that he used it to help his injured mother.

It will already be evident that libertarian doctrine is embedded in a view of the rights of man. Each human being has the right to live his life as he chooses, compatibly with the equal right of all other human beings to live their lives as they choose.

All man's rights are implicit in the above statement. Each man has the right to life: any attempt by others to take it away from him, or even to injure him, violates this right, through the use of coercion against him. Each man has the right to liberty: to conduct his life in accordance with the alternatives open to him without coercive action by others. And every man has the right to property: to work to sustain his life (and the lives of whichever others he chooses to sustain, such as his family) and to retain the fruits of his labor.

People often defend the rights of life and liberty but **denigrate** property rights, and yet the right to property is as basic as the other two: indeed, without property rights no other rights are possible. Depriving you of property is depriving you of the means by which you live. . . .

I have no right to decide how *you* should spend your time or your money. I can make that decision for myself, but not for you, my neighbor. I may deplore your choice of lifestyle, and I may talk with you about it provided you are willing to listen to me. But I have no right to use force to change it. Nor have I the right to decide how you should spend the money you have earned. I may appeal to you to give it to the Red Cross, and you may prefer to go to prize-fights. But that is your decision, and however much I may chafe about it I do not have the right to interfere forcibly with it, for example by robbing you in order to use the money in accordance with *my* choices. (If I have the right to rob you, have you also the right to rob me?)

When I claim a right, I carve out a niche, as it were, in my life, saying in effect, "This activity I must be able to perform without interference from others. For you and everyone else, this is off limits." And so I put up a "no trespassing" sign, which marks off the area of my right. Each individual's right is his "no trespassing" sign in relation to me and others. I may not encroach upon his domain any more than he upon mine, without my consent. Every right entails a duty, true—but the duty is only that of *forbearance* —that is, of *refraining* from violating the other person's right. If you have a right to life, I have no right to take your life; if you have a right to the products of your labor (property), I have no right to take it from you without your consent. The nonviolation of these rights will not guarantee you protection against natural catastrophes such as floods and earthquakes, but it will protect you against the aggressive activities *of other men.* And rights, after all, have to do with one's relations to other human beings, not with one's relations to physical nature.

Nor were these rights created by govern-ment; governments—some governments, obviously not all—*recognize* and *protect* the rights that individuals already have. Governments regularly forbid homicide and theft; and, at a more advanced stage, protect individuals against such things as libel and breach of contract. . . .

The *right to property* is the most misunderstood and unappreciated of human rights, and it is one most constantly violated by governments. "Property" of course does not mean only real estate; it includes anything you can call your own—your clothing, your car, your jewelry, your books and papers.

The right of property is not the right to just *take* it from others, for this would interfere with *their* property rights. It is rather the right to work for it, to obtain non-coercively, the money or services which you can present in voluntary exchange.

The right to property is consistently underplayed by intellectuals today, sometimes even frowned upon, as if we should feel guilty for upholding such a right in view of all the poverty in the world. But the right to property is absolutely basic. It is your hedge against the future. It is your assurance that what you have worked to earn will still be there and be yours, when you wish or need to use it, especially when you are too old to work any longer.

Government has always been the chief enemy of the right to property. The officials of government, wishing to increase their power, and finding an increase of wealth an effective way to bring this about seize some or all of what a person has earned—and since government has a monopoly of physical force within the geographical area of the nation, it has the power (but not the right) to do this. When this happens, of course, every citizen of that country is insecure: he knows that no matter how hard he works the government can swoop down on him at any time and confiscate his earnings and possessions. A person sees his life savings wiped out in a moment when the tax-collectors descend to deprive him of the fruits of his work; or, an industry which has been fifty years in the making and cost millions of dollars and millions of hours of time and planning, is nationalized overnight. Or the government, via inflation, cheapens the currency, so that hard-won dollars aren't worth anything any more. The effect of such actions, of course, is that people lose hope and incentive: if no matter how hard they work the government agents can take it all away, why bother to work at all, for more than today's needs? Depriving people of property is *depriving them of the means by which they live* —the freedom of the individual citizen to do what he wishes with his own life and to plan for the future. Indeed only if property rights are respected is there any point to planning for the future and working to achieve one's goals. *Property rights are what makes long-range planning possible* —the kind of planning which is a distinctively human endeavor, as opposed to the day-by-day activity of the lion who hunts, who depends on the supply of game tomorrow but has no real insurance against starvation in a day or a week. Without the right to property, the right to life itself amounts to little: how can you sustain your life if you cannot plan ahead? and how can you plan ahead if the fruits of your labor can at any moment be confiscated by government? . . .

Indeed, the right to property may well be considered second only to the right to life. Even the freedom of speech is limited by considerations of property. If a person visiting in your home behaves in a way undesired by you, you have every right to evict him; he can scream or agitate elsewhere if he wishes, but not in your home without your consent. Does a person have a right to shout obscenities in a cathedral? No, for the owners of the cathedral (presumably the Church) have not allowed others on their property for that purpose; one may go there to worship or to visit, but not just for any purpose one wishes. Their property right is prior to your or my wish to scream or expectorate or write graffiti on their building. Or, to take the stock example, does a person have a right to shout "Fire!" falsely in a crowded theater? No, for

the theater owner has permitted others to enter and use his property only for a specific purpose, that of seeing a film or watching a stage show. If a person heckles or otherwise disturbs other members of the audience, he can be thrown out. (In fact, he can be removed for any reason the owner chooses, provided his admission money is returned). And if he shouts "Fire!" when there is no fire, he may be endangering other lives by causing a panic or stampede. The right to free speech doesn't give one the right to say anything anywhere; it is circumscribed by property rights.

Again, some people seem to assume that the right to free speech (including written speech) means that they can go to a newspaper publisher and demand that he print in his newspaper some propaganda or policy statement for their political party (or other group). But of course they have no right to the use of his newspaper. Ownership of the newspaper is the product of his labor, and he has a right to put into his newspaper whatever he wants, for whatever reason. If he excludes material which many readers would like to have in, perhaps they can find it in another newspaper or persuade him to print it himself (if there are enough of them, they will usually do just that). Perhaps they can even cause his newspaper to fail. But as long as he owns it, he has the right to put in it what he wishes; what would a property right be if he could not do this? They have no right to place their material in his newspaper without his consent—not for free, nor even for a fee. Perhaps other newspapers will include it, or perhaps they can start their own newspaper (in which case they have a right to put in it what they like). If not, an option open to them would be to mimeograph and distribute some handbills.

In exactly the same way, no one has a right to "free television time" unless the owner of the television station consents to give it; it is his station, he has the property rights over it, and it is for him to decide how to dispose of his time. He may not decide wisely, but it is his right to decide as he wishes. If he makes enough unwise decisions, and courts enough unpopularity with the viewing public or the sponsors, he may have to go out of business; but as he is free to make his own decisions, so is he free to face their consequences. (If the government owns the television station, then government officials will make the decisions, and there is no guarantee of *their* superior wisdom. The difference is that when "the government" owns the station, you are forced to help pay for its upkeep through your taxes, whether the bureaucrat in charge decides to give you television time or not.)

"But why have *individual* property rights? Why not have lands and houses owned by everybody together?" Yes, this involves no violation of individual rights, as long as everybody consents to this arrangement and no one is forced to join it. The parties to it may enjoy the communal living enough (at least for a time) to overcome certain inevitable problems: that some will work and some not, that some will achieve more in an hour than others can do in a day, and still they will all get the same income. The few who do the most will in the end consider themselves "workhorses" who do the work of two or three or twelve, while the others will be "freeloaders" on the efforts of these few. But as long as they can get out of the arrangement if they no longer like it, no violation of rights is involved. They got in voluntarily, and they can get out voluntarily; no one has used force.

"But why not say that everybody owns everything? That we *all* own everything there is?"

To some this may have a pleasant ring—but let us try to analyze what it means. If everybody owns everything, then everyone has an equal right to go everywhere, do what he pleases, take what he likes, destroy if he wishes, grow crops or burn them, trample them under, and so on. Consider what it would be like in practice. Suppose you have saved money to buy a house for yourself and

your family. Now suppose that the principle, "everybody owns everything," becomes adopted. Well then, why shouldn't every itinerant hippie just come in and take over, sleeping in your beds and eating in your kitchen and not bothering to replace the food supply or clean up the mess? After all, it belongs to all of us, doesn't it? So we have just as much right to it as you, the buyer, have. What happens if we *all* want to sleep in the bedroom and there's not room for all of us? Is it the strongest who wins?

What would be the result? Since no one would be responsible for anything, the property would soon be destroyed, the food used up, the facilities nonfunctional. Beginning as a house that *one* family could use, it would end up as a house that *no one* could use. And if the principle continued to be adopted, no one would build houses any more—or anything else. What for? They would only be occupied and used by others, without remuneration.

Suppose two men are cast ashore on an island, and they agree that each will cultivate half of it. The first man is industrious and grows crops and builds a shelter, making the most of the situation with which he is confronted. The second man, perhaps thinking that the warm days will last forever, lies in the sun, picks coconuts while they last, and does a minimum of work to sustain himself. At the time of harvest, the second man has nothing to harvest, nor does he assist the first man in his labors. But later when there is a dearth of food on the island, the second man comes to the first man and demands half of the harvest as his right. But of course he has no right to the product of the first man's labors. The first man may freely choose to give part of his harvest to the second out of charity rather than see him starve; but that is just what it is—charity, not the second man's right.

How can any of man's rights be violated? Ultimately, only by the use of force. I can make suggestions to you, I can reason with you, entreat you (if you are willing to listen), but I cannot *force* you without violating your rights; only by forcing you do I cut the cord between your free decisions and your actions. Voluntary relations between individuals involve no deprivation of rights, but murder, assault, and rape do, because in doing these things I make you the unwilling victim of my actions. A man's beating his wife involves no violation of rights if she *wanted* to be beaten. *Force is behavior that requires the unwilling involvement of other persons.*

Thus the use of force need not involve the use of physical violence. If I trespass on your property or dump garbage on it, I am violating your property rights, as indeed I am when I steal your watch; although this is not force in the sense of violence, it *is* a case of your being an unwilling victim of my action. Similarly, if you shout at me so that I cannot be heard when I try to speak, or blow a siren in my ear, or start a factory next door which pollutes my land, you are again violating my rights (to free speech, to property); I am, again, an unwilling victim of your actions. Similarly, if you steal a manuscript of mine and publish it as your own, you are confiscating a piece of my property and thus violating my right to keep what is the product of my labor. Of course, if I give you the manuscript with permission to sign your name to it and keep the proceeds, no violation of rights is involved—any more than if I give you permission to dump garbage on my yard.

According to libertarianism, the role of government should be limited to the retaliatory use of force against those who have initiated its use. It should not enter into any other areas, such as religion, social organization, and economics.

GOVERNMENT

Government is the most dangerous institution known to man. Throughout history it has violated the rights of men more than any individual or group of individuals could do: it has killed people, enslaved them, sent them to forced labor and concentration camps, and regularly robbed and pillaged them of the fruits of their expended labor. Unlike individual criminals, government has the power to arrest and try; unlike individual criminals, it can surround and encompass a person totally, dominating every aspect of one's life, so that one has no recourse from it but to leave the country (and in totalitarian nations even that is prohibited). Government throughout history has a much sorrier record than any individual, even that of a ruthless mass murderer. The signs we see on bumper stickers are chillingly accurate: "Beware: the Government Is Armed and Dangerous."

The only proper role of government, according to libertarians, is that of the protector of the citizen against aggression by other individuals. The government, of course, should never initiate aggression; its proper role is as the embodiment of the *retaliatory* use of force against anyone who initiates its use.

If each individual had constantly to defend himself against possible aggressors, he would have to spend a considerable portion of his life in target practice, karate exercises, and other means of self-defenses, and even so he would probably be helpless against groups of individuals who might try to kill, maim, or rob him. He would have little time for cultivating those qualities which are essential to civilized life, nor would improvements in science, medicine, and the arts be likely to occur. The function of government is to take this responsibility off his shoulders: the government undertakes to defend him against aggressors and to punish them if they attack him. When the government is effective in doing this, it enables the citizen to go about his business unmolested and without constant fear for his life. To do this, of course, government must have physical power—the police, to protect the citizen from aggression within its borders, and the armed forces, to protect him from aggressors outside. Beyond that, the government should not intrude upon his life, either to run his business, or adjust his daily activities, or prescribe his personal moral code.

Government, then, undertakes to be the individual's protector; but historically governments have gone far beyond this function. Since they already have the physical power, they have not hesitated to use it for purposes far beyond that which was entrusted to them in the first place. Undertaking initially to protect its citizens against aggression, it has often itself become an aggressor—a far greater aggressor, indeed, than the criminals against whom it was supposed to protect its citizens. Governments have done what no private citizen can do: arrest and imprison individuals without a trial and send them to slave labor camps. Government must have power in order to be effective—and yet the very means by which alone it can be effective make it vulnerable to the abuse of power, leading to managing the lives of individuals and even inflicting terror upon them.

What then should be the function of government? In a word, the *protection of human rights.*

1. The right to life: libertarians support all such legislation as will protect human beings against the use of force by others, for example, laws against killing, attempted killing, maiming, beating, and all kinds of physical violence.

2. The right to liberty: there should be no laws compromising in any way freedom of speech, of the press, and of peaceable assembly. There should be no censorship of ideas, books, films, or of anything else by government.

3. The right to property: libertarians support legislation that protects the property rights of individuals against confiscation, nationalization, eminent domain, robbery, trespass, fraud and misrepresentation, patent and copyright, libel and slander.

Someone has violently assaulted you. Should he be legally liable? Of course. He has violated one of your rights. He has knowingly injured you, and since he has initiated aggression against you he should be made to expiate.

Someone has negligently left his bicycle on the sidewalk where you trip over it in the dark and injure yourself. He didn't do it intentionally; he didn't mean you any harm. Should he be legally liable? Of course; he has, however unwittingly, injured you, and since the injury is caused by him and you are the victim, he should pay.

Someone across the street is unemployed. Should you be taxed extra to pay for his expenses? Not at all. You have not injured him, you are not responsible for the fact that he is unemployed (unless you are a senator or bureaucrat who agitated for further curtailing of business, which legislation passed, with the result that your neighbor was laid off by the curtailed business). You may voluntarily wish to help him out, or better still, try to get him a job to put him on his feet again; but since you have initiated no aggressive act against him, and neither purposely nor accidentally injured him in any way, you should not be legally penalized for the fact of his unemployment. (Actually, it is just such penalties that increase unemployment.)

One man, A, works hard for years and finally earns a high salary as a professional man. A second man, B, prefers not to work at all, and to spend wastefully what money he has (through inheritance), so that after a year or two he has nothing left. At the end of this time he has a long siege of illness and lots of medical bills to pay. He demands that the bills be paid by the government—that is, by the taxpayers of the land, including Mr. A.

But of course B has no such right. He chose to lead his life in a certain way—that was his voluntary decision. One consequence of that choice is that he must depend on charity in case of later need. Mr. A chose not to live that way. (And if everyone lived like Mr. B, on whom would he depend in case of later need?) Each has a right to live in the way he pleases, but each must live with the consequences of his own decision (which, as always, fall primarily on himself). He cannot, in time of need, claim A's beneficence as his right....

Laws may be classified into three types:

(1) laws protecting individuals against themselves, such as laws against fornication and other sexual behavior, alcohol, and drugs; (2) laws protecting individuals against aggressions by other individuals, such as laws against murder, robbery, and fraud; (3) laws requiring people to help one another; for example, all laws which rob Peter to pay Paul, such as welfare.

Libertarians reject the first class of laws totally. Behavior which harms no one else is strictly the individual's own affair. Thus, there should be no laws against becoming intoxicated, since whether or not to become intoxicated is the individual's own decision; but there should be laws against driving while intoxicated, since the drunken driver is a threat to every other motorist on the highway (drunken driving falls into type 2). Similarly, there should be no laws against drugs (except the prohibition of sale of drugs to minors) as long as the taking of these drugs poses no threat to anyone else. Drug addiction is a psychological problem to which no present solution exists. Most of the social harm caused by addicts, other than to themselves, is the result of thefts which they perform in order to continue their habit—and then the *legal* crime is the theft, not the addiction. The actual cost of heroin is about ten cents a shot; if it were legalized, the enormous traffic in illegal sale and purchase of it would stop, as well as the accompanying proselytization to get new addicts (to make more money for the pusher) and the thefts performed by addicts who often require eighty dollars a day just to keep up the habit. Addiction would not stop, but the crimes would: it is estimated that 75 percent of the burglaries in New York City today are performed by addicts, and all these crimes could be wiped out at one stroke through the legalization of drugs. (Only when the taking of drugs could be shown to constitute a threat to *others,* should it be prohibited by law. It is only laws protecting people against *themselves* that libertarians oppose.)

Laws should be limited to the second class only: aggression by individuals against other individuals. These are laws whose function is to protect human beings against encroachment by others; and this, as we have seen, is (according to libertarianism) the sole function of government.

Libertarians also reject the third class of laws totally: no one should be forced by law to help others, not even to tell them the time of day if requested, and certainly not to give them a portion of one's weekly paycheck. Governments, in the guise of humanitarianism, have given to some by taking from others (charging a "handling fee" in the process, which, because of the government's waste and inefficiency, sometimes is several hundred percent). And in so doing they have decreased incentive, violated the rights of individuals, and lowered the standard of living of almost everyone.

All such laws constitute what libertarians call *moral cannibalism.* A cannibal in the physical sense is a person who lives off the flesh of other human beings. A *moral* cannibal is one who believes he has a right to live off the "spirit" of other human beings—who believes that he has a moral claim on the productive capacity, time, and effort expended by others.

It has become fashionable to claim virtually everything that one needs or desires as one's *right.* Thus, many people claim that they have a right to a job, the right to free medical care, to free food and clothing, to a decent home, and so on. Now if one asks, apart from any specific context, whether it would be desirable if everyone had these things, one might well say yes. But there is a gimmick attached to each of them: *At whose expense?* Jobs, medical care, education, and so on, don't grow on trees. These are goods and services *produced only by men.* Who, then, is to provide them, and under what conditions?

If you have a right to a job, who is to supply it? Must an employer supply it even if he doesn't want to hire you? What if you are unemployable, or incurably lazy? (If you say "the government must supply it," does that mean that a job must be created for you which no employer needs done, and that you must be kept in it regardless of how much or little you work?) If the employer is forced to supply it at his expense even if he doesn't need you, then isn't *he* being enslaved to that extent? What ever happened to *his* right to conduct his life and his affairs in accordance with his choices?

If you have a right to free medical care, then, since medical care doesn't exist in nature as wild apples do, some people will have to supply it to you for free: that is, they will have to spend their time and money and energy taking care of you whether they want to or not. What ever happened to *their* right to conduct their lives as they see fit? Or do you have a right to violate theirs? Can there be a right to violate rights?

All those who demand this or that as a "free service" are consciously or unconsciously evading the fact that there is in reality no such thing as free services. All manmade goods and services are the result of human expenditure of time and effort. There is no such thing as "something for nothing" in this world. If you demand something free, you are demanding that other men give their time and effort to you without compensation. If they voluntarily choose to do this, there is no problem; but if you demand that they be *forced* to do it, you are interfering with their right not to do it if they so choose. "Swimming in this pool ought to be free!" says the indignant passerby. What he means is that others should build a pool, others should provide the materials, and still others should run it and keep it in functioning order, so that *he* can use it without fee. But what right has he to the expenditure of *their* time and effort? To expect something "for free" is to expect it *to be paid for by others* whether they choose to or not.

Many questions, particularly about economic matters, will be generated by the libertarian account of human rights and the role of government. Should government have no role in assisting the needy, in providing social security, in legislating minimum wages, in fixing prices and putting a ceiling on rents, in curbing monopolies, in erecting tariffs, in guaranteeing jobs, in managing the money supply? To these and all similar questions the libertarian answers with an unequivocal no.

"But then you'd let people go hungry!" comes the rejoinder. This, the libertarian insists, is precisely what would not happen; with the restrictions removed, the economy would flourish as never before. With the controls taken off business, existing enterprises would expand and new ones would spring into existence satisfying more and more consumer needs; millions more people would be gainfully employed instead of subsisting on welfare, and all kinds of research and production, released from the stranglehold of government, would proliferate, fulfilling man's needs and desires as never before. It has always been so whenever government has permitted men to be free traders on a free market. But *why* this is so, and how the free market is the best solution to all problems relating to the material aspect of man's life, is another and far longer story. . . .

Review Questions

1. How does Hospers explain libertarianism?

2. What are the three most basic human rights according to Hospers?

3. According to Hospers, why is the government "the chief enemy of the right to property?"

4. In Hospers' view, what is wrong with holding that "everybody owns everything?"

5. Hospers claims that human rights can be violated in only one way. How?

6. What is the only proper role of government according to libertarians?

7. How does Hospers propose to deal the problem of unemployment?

8. Which type of laws do libertarians accept? Which laws do they reject?

9. Why does Hospers think that people will not be hungry if libertarianism is followed?

Discussion Questions

1. Hospers thinks that the right to property is just as important as the right to life. Do you agree? Why or why not?

2. Compare Hospers' account of the right to life to that given by Rachels. Which account is more acceptable and why?

3. Hospers says, "I may deplore your choice of life-style, . . . but I have no right to use force to change it." Can you think of any exceptions to this? What are they?

4. Hospers claims that human rights can be violated "only by the use of force." Is this true? Explain your answer.

5. "A man's beating his wife involves no violation of rights if she *wanted* to be beaten." What is your view of voluntary wife-beating? Is this an acceptable practice?

6. Hospers says, "Libertarians support all such legislation as will protect human beings against the use of force by others." How would he apply this to abortion, euthanasia, and capital punishment?

7. Hospers rejects all laws which protect individuals from themselves, for example, laws prohibiting prostitution and drugs. Do you agree that all such laws should be abolished? Explain your view of these paternalistic laws.

8. Hospers is totally opposed to any welfare laws. Should all such laws be eliminated? What is your view?

9. Hospers denies that you have a right to a job, medical care, food, or anything free. Do you agree? Do you have any positive rights at all, as distinguished from the negative rights of noninterference?

Problem Cases

1. *Famine in Africa* For several years there has been a drought in central Africa affecting an area about one-half the size of the United States. Thousands of people have already died despite substantial aid given to the country by many countries and volunteers. The area is rapidly turning into a barren desert, and it may not be able to support human life. Even though the people can no longer grow food in the area, they refuse to leave, even if this means death.

Should these people be forced to leave the area? Why or why not?

Assuming that the people stay where they are, should massive aid be provided to save them from death by starvation or disease? Explain your answer.

2. *The Poor in Brazil* The population of Brazil is growing rapidly. If its present rate of growth of 2.8 percent continues, it will soon become the most populous country in the Western hemisphere. Although Brazil is rich in natural resources and has significant economic growth, the majority of benefits has gone to the rich. Forty percent of the population is under fifteen years of age and unemployment is high. Population growth in the cities has made it difficult for the government to provide education, health care, water, sanitation, food, and housing for the poor. What steps, if any, should be taken to provide for the poor and needy people in this country? Explain your proposals.

3. *The "Boarder Baby Scandal"* (As reported by Andrew Stein, president of the New York City Council in the New York Times, Saturday, Jan. 17, 1987.) New York City is the most prosperous city in the world with a 21 billion dollar budget and immense private and community wealth. Yet it has a very serious problem—abandoned and homeless children. At the end of 1986, the city officially counted 11,000 such children and babies living in municipal shelters, decrepit welfare hotels, and hospitals. Some have been living in such conditions for years. Some of the victims are called "boarder babies" because they were abandoned by their parents in hospitals; they will stay there because of the lack of certified foster parents, or qualified parents willing to adopt them. Others have been removed from their homes for their own protection; reports of child abuse and neglect (including a 250 percent increase in cases of drug-addicted babies) have ris-

en so dramatically that welfare offices are overwhelmed with children, often keeping them overnight in the offices or placing them illegally in group foster homes.

What, if anything, should be done about these babies and children? Explain your recommendations carefully.

4. A Case of Unemployment John Smith and his wife Jane have three small children. Until recently, John had a good job in a factory in Dallas, Texas, and a good life: a house, car, T.V., new furniture, and so on. Unfortunately he lost his job when the factory closed, and he cannot find another one. He has sold all his possessions, and his unemployment compensation payments have run out. Married men and women do not qualify for Aid to Families with Dependent Children (AFDC) and, in fact, no welfare at all is available for him in Dallas. Jane has tried working as a waitress, leaving John to care for the children, but she did not make enough money to pay the bills. Now they are living on the street, and getting one free meal a day at the Salvation Army. The children are suffering from exposure and malnutrition, and John and Jane are tired, hun-

gry, dirty, and depressed.

Should such a family receive welfare benefits or not? Explain your answer.

5. Another Case of Unemployment Ralph Jones has a violent temper; he cannot stand people telling him what to do, and if they do, he gets angry and violent, and sometimes assaults them. Because of this character defect, he has been unable to keep a job. For awhile he received unemployment compensation payments, but they have run out. Currently he is living on the street, begging, eating garbage, and sleeping in a cardboard box under a bridge. Occasionally he eats food in grocery stores without paying for it, but he does not consider this stealing. In fact, he is generally a very law-abiding citizen. He is not a danger to himself or others unless, of course, they start bossing him around, then he is likely to assault them, either verbally or physically.

Should Ralph receive welfare payments for food, clothing, shelter, and medical care? Why or why not?

Suppose that Ralph is not a man, but a woman. Would that make any difference in your view?

Suggested Readings

(1)   Brown, Peter G., Conrad Johnson, and Paul Vernier, eds. *Income Support: Conceptual and Policy Issues.* Totowa, NJ: Rowman and Littlefield, 1981. This anthology has articles on the moral and conceptual issues involved in the income support policies in the United States.

(2)   Eberstadt, Nick. "Myths of the Food Crisis." *The New York Review of Books* (February 19, 1976): 32–37. Eberstadt argues that the cause of starvation today is not overpopulation, but inequalities in food distribution. He feels that this inequality cannot be eliminated by welfare-style transfers of income; instead the productivity of the world's poor must be improved.

(3)   Friedman, Milton. *Capitalism and Freedom.* Chicago: University of Chicago Press, 1962. Friedman is an economist who thinks that the principle of distributing income in a free society should be that one gets what one produces or what the instruments one owns produce.

(4)   Harrington, Michael. *Socialism.* New York:

Saturday Review Press, 1970. Harrington presents a version of socialism that is different from both communism and the welfare state.

(5)   Nozick, Robert. *Anarchy, State, and Utopia.* New York: Basic Books, 1974. Nozick defends a libertarian conception of justice. This book has produced a great deal of discussion among philosophers concerned with distributive justice, some of it very hostile.

(6)   O'Neill, Onora. "Lifeboat Earth." *Philosophy & Public Affairs* vol. 4, no. 3 (Spring, 1975). O'Neill assumes that people on the lifeboat Earth have a right not to be killed (except in cases of unavoidable killing and self-defense), and that there is a corollary duty not to kill others. It follows from this, she argues, that we ought to adopt policies that will prevent others from dying from starvation.

(7)   Rawls, John. *A Theory of Justice.* Cambridge, MA: Harvard University Press, 1971. This is a very important book on justice. In Rawls' account of

justice, everyone who is rational will agree to two principles that are in the equal interests of everyone: (1) everyone has the right to equal liberty, and (2) the difference of wealth and privilege can be justified only if everyone has an opportunity to compete for them and everyone benefits from them.

(8) Shue, Henry. *Basic Rights.* Princeton, NJ: Princeton University Press, 1980. Shue defends the view that everyone has a right to subsistence, and that this economic right is as important as political rights such as the right to liberty. An implication of this, Shue thinks, is that rich nations (those with a gross domestic product per capita of United States $400 or more) should make welfare-style transfers of food or money to poor nations. He claims that they could do this without impoverishing themselves or even causing a decline in their growth rate.

(9) Shuman, Charles B. "Food aid and the free market." In *Food Policy*, edited by Peter G. Brown and Henry Shue, 145–163. New York: The Free Press, 1977. In opposition to Shue, Shuman advocates a free-market approach to the problem of hunger and starvation.

(10) Simon, Julian L. *The Ultimate Resource.* Princeton, NJ: Princeton University Press, 1981. Simon argues for a position directly opposed to Hardin.

(11) Singer, Peter. *Practical Ethics.* Cambridge, MA: Cambridge University Press, 1979. Singer argues that rich nations have a moral obligation to help poor ones (See pages 158–181 for specific discussion).

Glossary

Altruistic   concerned with other people, as opposed to being selfish.

A priori   known prior to experience, as distinguished from a posteriori, known after experience. The statement "No statement can be both true and false" is known a priori, while the statement "Some crows are black," is known a posteriori.

Denigrate   to belittle maliciously.

Distributive justice   the problem or theory of how to allocate goods and services in a society.

Doctrine of demographic laissez-faire   the doctrine that people should be free to have as many children as they wish.

Ethnocentrism   the belief that one's own race or ethnic group is superior to other races or ethnic groups.

Ex hypothesi   a Latin phrase meaning "by hypothesis."

Free-rider   one who gets or tries to benefit without paying, for example, a worker who gets the benefits of a union contract without being a member of the union.

Inductive generalization   in the broad sense, an inference from some things of a certain kind to a conclusion about all the remaining things of that kind. For example, all observed crows are black; so all crows (including the unobserved ones) are black.

Infinite regress   a series of events that continues without end; usually there is the implication that this is impossible. A "vicious infinite regress" is one that is impossible, while a "benign or virtuous infinite regress" is not impossible.

Intelligentsia   the class of people engaged in activities requiring the use of the intellect, as distinguished from those who do manual labor.

Natural right   a right that any human being has simply by virtue of being human.

Postitive duty   an obligation to do something, e.g., give food to a starving person. Contrasted with negative duty, an obligation *not* to do something, e.g., not to kill an innocent person.

Rationalization   a term from Freudian psychology referring to reasons given to explain behavior that hide the real, unconscious motivation.

Reductio **argument**   an argument that shows a

statement or thesis to have absurd consequences; it "reduces the statement to an absurdity."

Repatriated returned to one's own country.

Teleological teleological ethics determine the rightness or wrongness of acts or policies in terms of their consequences.

Utopia an imaginary country with ideal laws and social conditions.

Chapter 5

Corporate Responsibility

Introduction

Businesses engage in a variety of practices that seem to be morally questionable: polluting the environment with toxic chemical wastes, producing unsafe or lethal products, discriminating against women and minorities, bribing government officials, lying and deceiving in advertising, and so on. Consider, for example, the waste disposal practices of Hooker Chemical Company, the tenth largest chemical company in the United States, with thirty plants in eleven countries. Critics claim that this company is one of the worst polluters in the country. It has dumped kepone (a known carcinogen) into the James River in Virginia, and allowed mirex (another carcinogen) to run into Lake Ontario from improperly stored barrels. It has released a variety of dangerous gases (chlorine, phosphorous, mercury, and so on) into the air outside the company's Niagara Falls plant. From 1942 to 1953 it dumped over 21,000 tons of toxic chemical wastes into an abandoned canal digging called Love Canal. This site was sold, and an elementary school and a tract of houses were built adjacent to it. The site eventually leaked its toxic chemicals into houses causing a number of health problems: liver damage, miscarriages, birth defects, cancer, epilepsy, suicide, and rectal bleeding, to name a few.

Another disturbing practice of business is the discrimination against women and minorities. In Chapter 6 substantial evidence for sexual and racial discrimination in business will be discussed in greater detail. Multinational corporations also do business with countries that discriminate against blacks such as South Africa.

179

A Philosophical Problem Critics of Hooker Chemical assume that this company has a moral responsibility to avoid immoral actions such as polluting the environment. But do corporations have moral responsibilities over and above the responsibility to make money? Should they adopt a moral point of view in which they are concerned with the welfare of others, or should they act only in their own self-interest by pursuing profits? The latter view is accepted by Milton Friedman. He believes that the only responsibility of business is to increase its profits by open and free competition without deception or fraud. Friedman attacks what he calls the "doctrine of social responsibility." This is the view that business has other social responsibilities besides making money, for example, the duty to reduce pollution or eliminate racial and sexual discrimination. To begin with, Friedman points out only persons have responsibilities, and since business as a whole and corporations are not strictly speaking persons, they cannot be said to have responsibilities. Of course business executives are persons who have responsibilities, but their responsibility is to make money for their stockholders, and not to spend the money of the stockholders without their consent. If business executives do this in the pursuit of some socially responsible goal such as reducing pollution, then they are in effect imposing taxes on the stockholders and the consumers, and this is "taxation without representation." Furthermore, the doctrine of social responsibility has bad consequences: executives who follow it will be fired, and wage restraints justified by it will produce strikes and worker revolts. Finally, Friedman denounces the doctrine of social responsibility as a "fundamentally subversive doctrine" that is incompatible with the ideal of a free society.

Friedman's position has been attacked by several writers. Kenneth E. Goodpaster and John B. Matthews, Jr. (6) attack Friedman's contention that corporations cannot meaningfully be said to be "persons" who have "responsibilities." In their analysis of the concept of moral responsibility, a person is morally responsible if he or she takes a moral point of view in making decisions. This means that in making the decision the person is rational and concerned for the welfare of others. But corporations are legally persons who act and make decisions, and it makes sense to say that these decisions are rational and concerned for the welfare of others. Therefore, it makes sense to say that corporations are morally responsible.

Christopher D. Stone states and criticizes other arguments used by Friedman. The "promissory argument" (as Stone calls it) claims that the management of a corporation has promised the shareholders that it will maximize profits, so if it does not do this, management has broken its promise. Stone objects that management has made no such promise, and that even if it did, the promise is only to existent shareholders, and anyway a promise can always be overridden by more important moral concerns. The "agency argument" is another argument used by Friedman. According to this argument, the management is the agent of the individuals who own the corporation, and as such it has a duty to maximize profits. In reply, Stone points out that management often does not act like such an agent. Management not only ignores the wishes of the shareholders, it also actively opposes them in some cases.

Stone does not try to refute the so-called "polestar argument," the argument that the single-minded pursuit of profits by corporations is a means of charting a straight course for what is best for society. This argument, or a version of it, is attacked by Robert Almeder. As Almeder formulates it, the argument is a utilitarian one: the greatest good for the greatest number can only be achieved if corporations act only in the pursuit of profits and ignore moral concerns. Almeder thinks that this argument makes the doubtful factual assumption that a selfish society in which everyone pursues their own self-interest will turn out to be better than a moral society in which people are regulated by moral concerns.

Another argument used by Friedman is that there is no sure way for corporations to discover what their moral responsibilities are, even assuming that they have them. In reply, Almeder claims that we do agree about some moral responsibilities, for example, the duty to not kill innocent persons for money. Almeder concludes with a positive argument based on the duty to not kill innocent people. Corporations engage in certain practices that amount to killing innocent persons for money. But we all agree, he insists, that killing an innocent person for money is morally wrong. Hence, corporations are guilty of doing something that is morally wrong, and they have a strong moral obligation to stop doing it.

Tom L. Beauchamp & Martha W. Elliott

Hooker Chemical and Love Canal

Tom L. Beauchamp is a member of the philosophy department at Georgetown University. He is the author of Philosophical Ethics, *and coauthor of* Hume and the Problem of Causation, Medical Ethics, *and* Principles of Biomedical Ethics.

Martha W. Elliott was a member of Beauchamp's research staff.

The authors describe the toxic chemical waste dumping by Hooker Chemical at the Love Canal site, and the consequences of the resulting pollution for the residents living near the site. Many other cases of pollution and exposure to dangerous chemicals involving Hooker Chemical are described. The efforts of the EPA to solve the problem of dangerous waste disposal are discussed. Finally, the defense of Hooker Chemical is presented.

Today the Love Canal area of Niagara Falls looks like a war zone. The 235 houses nearest the landfill are boarded up and empty, surrounded by an 8-foot-high cyclone fence that keeps tourists and looters away. Still other houses outside the fenced area are also boarded up and deserted, their owners having fled the unknown. Here and there throughout the neighborhood, newly erected green signs mark the pickup points for emergency evacuation in case there is a sudden release of toxins. An ambulance and a fire truck stand by in the area as workers struggle to seal off the flow of chemicals and render the area once again safe—if not exactly habitable.[1]

What is Love Canal? How did this desolation occur? Who, if anyone, is responsible?

Love Canal is named for William T. Love, a businessman and visionary who in the late nineteenth century attempted to create a model industrial city near Niagara Falls. Love proposed to build a canal that would figure in the generation and transmission of hydroelectric power from the falls to the city's industries. An economic recession that made financing difficult and the development of cheaper methods of transmitting electricity dampened Love's vision, and the partially dug canal in what is now the southeast corner of the city of Niagara Falls is the sole tangible legacy of the project.

However, industry was still drawn to the area, which provided easy access to transportation, cheap electricity, and abundant water for industrial processes. Several chemical companies were among those who took advantage of the natural resources. The Hooker Electrochemical Company, now Hooker Chemical and a major figure in the later events at Love Canal, built its first plant in the area in 1905. Presently a subsidiary of Occidental Petroleum, Hooker manufactures plastics, pesticides, chlorine, caustic soda, fertilizers, and a variety of other chemical products. With over 3,000 employees, Hooker is still one of the largest employers and an economic force in the Niagara Falls area.[2]

In the early 1940s, the abandoned section of Love Canal—for many years a summer swimming hole—became a dump for barrels of waste materials produced by the various chemical companies. Hooker received permission in 1942 to use the site for chemical dumping. It is estimated (though no accurate records were kept) that between the early dumping period and 1953, when this tract of land was sold, approximately 21,800 tons of many different kinds of chemical wastes—some extremely toxic—were put into the old canal. The chemicals were in drums, which were eventually covered with clay-like materials—a reasonable maneuver at the time, since the site was ideal for chemical dumping. It was in an undeveloped and largely unpopulated area and had highly impermeable clay walls that retained liquid chemical materials with virtually no penetration at all. Research indicated that the canal's walls permitted water penetration at the rate of ⅓ of an inch over a 25–year period.

In 1947 Hooker purchased the Love Canal site from Niagara Power and Development Company. In 1953 the dump was closed and covered with an impermeable clay top. The land encompassing and surrounding the dump was acquired by the Niagara Falls School Board. This acquisition was against the advice of Hooker, which had warned of the toxic wastes. However, the Board persist-ed and started condemnation proceedings to acquire land in the area. Subsequently an elementary school and a tract of houses were built adjacent to the site. Thousands of cubic yards of soil were removed from the top of the canal in the process. This series of developments set the stage for the desolate scene described in the opening quotation. Apparently, the construction damaged the integrity of the clay covering. Water from rains and heavy snows then seeped through the covering and entered the chemical-filled, clay-lined basin. Eventually the basin overflowed on the unfortunate residents, who were treated to the noxious smell and unwholesome sight of chemicals seeping into their basements and surfacing to the ground.

In April of 1978 evidence of toxic chemicals was found in the living area of several homes and the state health commissioner ordered an investigation. A number of health hazards came to light. Many of the adults examined showed incipient liver damage; young women in certain areas experienced three times the normal incidence of miscarriages; and the area had 3.5 times the normal incidence of birth defects. Epilepsy, suicide, rectal bleeding, hyperactivity, and a variety of other ills were also reported.

Upon review of these findings, the health commissioner recommended that the elementary school be temporarily closed and that pregnant women and children under the age of two be temporarily evacuated. Shortly thereafter the Governor of New York announced that the state would purchase the 235 houses nearest the canal and would assist in the relocation of dispossessed families. President Carter declared Love Canal a disaster area, qualifying the affected families for federal assistance.[3] However, families in the adjacent ring of houses were not able to move—although they firmly believed that their health was endangered. Early studies tended to confirm this view, but in mid-July, 1982, EPA released a study that concluded there was "no evidence that Love Canal has contributed to environmental contamination" in the outer ring of 400 homes. However, this report was on "health hazards" and did not address symptoms of stress that have been noted: For example, the divorce rate among remaining families increased as wives and children fled, while husbands tried to hold onto their investments: their houses and jobs.[4]

Since the investigation first began more than 100 different chemicals, some of them mutagens, teratogens, or carcinogens, have been identified. A number of unanswered questions are still being probed. One question has to do with the long range effects of chemical exposure. Cancer, for instance, often doesn't develop for 20 to 25 years after exposure to the cancer-producing agent. Chromosomal damage may appear only in subsequent generations. Other unanswered questions involve determining how to clean up the "mess" and who should be held responsible for it.

Hooker Chemical Company figures in both of these questions. In 1977 the city of Niagara Falls employed an engineering consulting firm to study Love Canal and make recommendations. Hooker supplied technical assistance, information, and personnel. The cost of a second study was shared equally by Hooker, the city, and the school board, which had originally purchased the land from Hooker. Hooker also offered to pay one-third of the estimated $850,000 cost of clean-up.[5]

In 1980 Hooker was faced with over $2 billion in lawsuits stemming from its activities at Love Canal and other locations. Thirteen-hundred private suits had been filed against Hooker by mid-1982. The additional complaints and suits stemmed from past and current activities in other states as well as from additional sites in New York. In addition, in 1976 suits of more than $100 million were filed by Virginia employees of Life Sciences who had been exposed to kepone, a highly toxic chemical known to cause trembling and sterility in humans. Hooker was named in the suit as a supplier of some of the raw materials used in the Virginia manufacturing process.

(This suit was ultimately settled out of court.) In 1977 Hooker was ordered to pay $176,000 for discharging HCCPD, a chemical used in the manufacture of Kepone and Mirex, which causes cancer in laboratory animals, into White Lake. In 1979 Michigan officials sued Hooker for a $200 million cleanup due to air, water, and land pollution around its White Lake plant. Hooker in 1978 acknowledged that it had buried an estimated 3,700 tons of trichlorophenol waste—which includes some quantities of the potent chemical dioxin—at various sites around Niagara Falls from 1942–1972.[6]

At the same time that Hooker was defending itself in Virginia and Michigan, the state of California was investigating the company and ultimately brought suit on charges that Hooker's Occidental Chemical Plant at Lathrop, California had for years violated state law by dumping toxic pesticides, thereby polluting nearby ground water. While Hooker officials denied the charges, a series of memos written by Robert Edson, Occidental's environmental engineer at Lathrop, suggests the company knew of the hazard as early as 1975 but chose to ignore it until pressured by the state investigation. In April 1975 Edson wrote, "Our laboratory records indicate that we are slowly contaminating all wells in our area, and two of our own wells are contaminated to the point of being toxic to animals or humans...." A year later he wrote, "To date, we have been discharging waste water ... containing about five tons of pesticide per year to the ground.... I believe we have fooled around long enough and already over-pressed our luck." Another year later, Edson reiterated his charges and added that "if anyone should complain, we could be the party named in an action by the Water Quality Control Board.... Do we correct the situation before we have a problem or do we hold off until action is taken against us?"[7]

Other complaints stemmed from the same general area as Love Canal. In 1976 the New York Department of Environmental Conservation banned consumption of seven species of fish taken from Lake Ontario claiming that they were contaminated with chemicals, including Mirex. It was alleged that Mirex had been discharged from the Hooker Niagara Falls plant. A Hooker-sponsored study of Lake Ontario fish disputed this allegation of Mirex contamination. While this study has not been accepted by the state, the ban has, for the most part, been lifted.

Hooker's Hyde Park chemical waste dump, located in the Niagara Falls area, has also been a source of continuing concern and dispute to residents and government officials. In 1972 the manager of a plant adjacent to the dump complained to Hooker about "an extremely dangerous condition affecting our plant and employees ... our midnight shift workers has [sic] complained of coughing and sore throats from the obnoxious and corrosive permeating fumes from the disposal site." [8] Apparently the "dangerous condition" was not adequately rectified, and in 1979 Hooker's Hyde Park landfill became the subject of a nearly $26 million suit filed by the town of Niagara. New York State filed a suit for more than $200 million for alleged damages at the Hyde Park site. A remedial program agreement, signed by the state, entailed an estimated $16 million in proposed work at this site.

In 1980 Hooker was also faced with four additional suits for $124.5 million in remedial work by the Environmental Protection Agency. Barbara Blum, EPA Deputy Administrator, explains the EPA concern and strategy as follows:

To help protect against toxic by-products, EPA has launched a major regulatory and enforcement drive, including suits using EPA's "imminent hazard" or "emergency" provisions to force the cleanup of the most dangerous hazardous waste problems. I anticipate that 50 such cases will be filed before the end of 1980.

The most widely recognized symbol of the hazardous waste crisis is Love Canal in Niagara Falls, where an entire neighborhood has been abandoned. There are, however, hundreds of other graphic examples scattered across the country.

The issue of how to deal with our legacy of

dangerous waste disposal sites and to prevent the development of new "Love Canals" may be the most difficult environmental challenge of the 1980's. EPA has launched four interrelated efforts to bring this problem under control. [9]

Two of these efforts are relevant to the actions against Hooker: (1) litigation under "imminent hazard" provisions of existing EPA laws and (2) the creation of programs, financed by government and industry, to clean up hazardous waste sites. The "imminent hazard" litigation is described as follows:

Primarily emphasizing injunctive relief, this program seeks to halt dangerous disposal practices and to force privately-funded clean-up. This approach gets results, of course, only where a responsible party can be identified and has adequate financial resources to carry some or all of the clean-up costs. [10]

Blum goes on to describe the specific statutes the EPA is acting under and the EPA's collaboration with the Justice Department in enforcing the statutes:

Sections of the Resource Conservation and Recovery Act, Safe Drinking Water Act, Toxic Substances Control Act, Clean Water Act, and Clean Air Act all authorize EPA to ask the court for injunctive relief in situations which pose threats to public health or the environment. Section 309 of the Clean Water Act levies a penalty of up to $10,000 a day for unpermitted discharges to navigable waters (a leaking dump can be considered a discharge). The 1899 "Refuse Act" provides additional penalties for unauthorized discharges or dumping. Available common law remedies include the common law of nuisance and trespass, restitution, and "strict liability" for damages caused by those who engaged in ultra-hazardous activities. We are aggressively using each of these legal tools to address the hazardous waste disposal problem.

The Agency—working with the Department of Justice—has launched a top-priority effort to pursue imminent hazard cases . . . .

People are frightened by Love Canal and by the emergence of threatening hazardous waste sites in their local communities. They are demanding action—and they are getting it. [11]

The EPA currently estimates that only 10% of all hazardous wastes are disposed of in strict compliance with federal regulations. According to Thomas H. Maugh, II, writing in 1979 in *Science* magazine, "nearly 50 percent is disposed of by lagooning in unlined surface impoundments, 30 percent in non-secure landfills, and about 10 percent by dumping into sewers, spreading on roads, injection into deep wells, and incineration under uncontrolled conditions." [12] Maugh goes on to argue that "legal dumpsites gone awry" are actually a lesser problem than the growing problem of illegally dumped wastes in unsecured dumpsites, often in the middle of cities.[13] In October 1981 the EPA announced that "there are at least 29 toxic waste disposal sites around the country as dangerous or more so than Love Canal. . . ." [14] This is partly because some clean-up has already been done at Love Canal and many of the endangered people have moved away.

Hooker Chemical believes that its role and defense have been misunderstood. While the company neither denies using the canal as a chemical dump nor denies that the dump has created a serious problem, officials of the company contend that (1) the company's efforts to prevent first the public and then the private development of the canal area are generally unrecognized; (2) the company has been an industry leader in safety; (3) Hooker is being unfairly blamed and singled out for waste disposal practices that were then almost universal throughout the chemical industry; and (4) a certain level of risk is an inevitable hazard in an industrial society.

Hooker has marshaled data to support its contentions. In the first place, Hooker believes that its efforts to warn the School Board and City against interfering with the waste disposal area are unappreciated. When the Niagara Falls School Board expressed an interest in selling a portion of the Love Canal tract to a developer, Hooker representatives argued against the plan in a public meeting and later reiterated to the Board its warnings of possible hazards. When the school board

persisted in its plans and began to obtain adjacent parcels of land through condemnation proceedings, Hooker, in the deed to the School Board, again referred to the past use of the property and stipulated that all future risks and liabilities be passed to the School Board. One part of the deed stipulated:

Prior to the delivery of this instrument of conveyance, the grantee herein has been advised by the grantor that the premises above described have been filled, in whole or in part, to the present grade level thereof with waste products resulting from the manufacturing of chemicals by the grantor at its plant in the City of Niagara Falls, New York, and the grantee assumes all risk and liability incident to the use thereof. It is, therefore, understood and agreed that, as a part of the consideration for this conveyance and as a condition thereof, no claim, suit, action or demand of any nature whatsoever shall ever be made by the grantee, its successors or assigns, against the grantor, its successors or assigns, for injury to a person or persons, including death resulting therefrom, or loss of or damage to property caused by, in connection with or by reason of the presence of said industrial wastes.[15]

When the school board later sold part of the land to a private developer who planned to build houses, Hooker officials protested the sale both verbally and in writing. Executives believe that the company is being unjustly blamed for the improvidence of others. Hooker also claims that it has no legal responsibility for the problem at Love Canal and that it has more than met its social and moral obligations in time and money spent on the clean-up effort. Through its experiences at Love Canal, Hooker environmental health and safety specialists have developed knowledge and skills that have enabled the company to take a leadership role in problems of underground pollution.

Hooker officials also argue that their past practices more than met then acceptable industry standards for waste disposal. During the period from 1942 to 1953 when Hooker was filling Love Canal with barrels of chemical wastes, the long-term environmental and personal hazzards of these industrial "leftovers" were not adequately recognized either by the industries involved or by the health and regulatory professions. Putting the chemical wastes into a clay canal was actually an improvement on common methods of disposal in unlined and unsecured landfills.

The company's defense of its behavior in the Love Canal situation parallels in some respects the reaction of certain Love Canal residents. They directed the major thrust of their antagonism not toward Hooker Chemical, but toward the New York State Health Department, which had failed to provide open access to the results of state-conducted health studies and left unexplained delays in admitting that a health problem existed. The Health Department attempted to discourage, and even actively harassed independent researchers whose reports indicated more widespread risks to the health of the community than the Department was willing to admit—or prepared to pay to rectify. Given these considerations, it was the Health Department, not Hooker Chemical, who did not meet its obligations to the community in the eyes of many residents.[16]

Hooker supports the common industry position that society will have to learn to accept a certain level of risk in order to enjoy the products of industrial society. Environmental hazards are just one more form of industrial "trade-offs." They cite such persons as Margery W. Shaw, an independent scientist who reviewed a chromosomal study of Love Canal residents. She points out that the level of acceptable risk is a general societal problem merely instanced in this case.

In our democratic society, perhaps we will decide that 500,000 deaths per year is an acceptable price for toxic chemicals in our environment, just as we have decided that 50,000 traffic deaths per year is an acceptable price for automobile travel. On the other hand, we may say that 5,000 deaths per year is an unacceptable price for toxic chemicals.[17]

Over the years Hooker has been among the most heavily criticized corporations for its environmental policies. Ralph Nader attacked Hooker as a "callous corporation" leaving toxic "cesspools." An ABC News documenta-ry was highly critical of the company, concentrating on the increased incidence of disease at Love Canal. On the other hand, Hooker has picked up a number of defenders in recent years. In a July 27, 1981 editorial in *Fortune* magazine, the corporation was defended for having explicitly conformed to government standards of waste disposal, for resisting the construction at the canal, and for being the victim of exaggerated and irresponsible reports about the incidence of disease in the region.[18] An April 1981 editorial in *Discover* magazine laid the blame on the Niagara Falls board of education for Love Canal, but argued that Hooker did act irresponsibly in waste dumpage at a number of other sites.[19] The 1982 study released by the EPA had the effect of blunting some federal efforts and some law suits.

Footnotes

1. Thomas H. Maugh, II, "Toxic Waste Disposal a Gnawing Problem," *Science* 204 (May 1979), p. 820.

2. John F. Steiner, "Love can be Dangerous to your Health," in George A. Steiner and John F. Steiner, *Casebook for Business, Government and Society*, 2nd ed. (New York: Random House, Business Division, 1980), pp. 108–109.

3. Maugh, "Toxic Waste Disposal."

4. Constance Holden, "Love Canal Residents Under Stress," *Science* 208 (June 13, 1980), pp. 1242–1244. "Some Love Canal Areas Safe, A New EPA Study Concludes." *The Washington Post*, July 15, 1982. Sec. A, pp. 1, 9 (Byline: Sandra Sugawara). See also Beverly Paigen below on the earlier data.

5. Steiner, "Love can be Dangerous," p. 112.

6. Michael H. Brown, "Love Canal, U.S.A.," *New York Times Magazine* (January 21, 1979), p. 23, passim; and Gary Whitney, "Hooker Chemical and Plastics" (HBS Case Services, Harvard Business School, 1979), p. 3.

7. "The Hooker Memos," in Robert J. Baum, ed., *Ethical Problems in Engineering*, 2nd ed. (Troy, N.Y.: Center for the Study of the Human Dimensions of Science and Technology, Rensselaer Polytechnic Institute, 1980), Vol. 2: Cases, p. 38; and "An Occidental Unit Knowingly Polluted California Water, House Panel Charges," *The Wall Street Journal*, June 20, 1979, p. 14.

8. Whitney, "Hooker Chemical and Plastics."

9. Barbara Blum, "Hazardous Waste Action," *EPA Journal* (June 1980), p. 2.

10. *Ibid.*

11. *Ibid.*, p. 8.

12. Maugh, "Toxic Waste Disposal," pp. 819, 821.

13. *Ibid.*, p. 110.

14. Joanne Omong, "EPA Names 115 Toxic Waste Dump Sites for Cleanup," *The Washington Post*, October 24, 1981, p. 4.

15. Steiner, "Love can be Dangerous," p. 110.

16. Beverly Paigen, "Controversy at Love Canal," *Hastings Center Report* 12 (June 1982), pp. 29–37.

17. Margery W. Shaw, "Love Canal Chromosome Study," *Science* 209 (August 15, 1980), p. 752.

18. *Fortune* (July 27, 1981), pp. 30–31.

19. *Discover* 2 (4) (April 1981), p. 8.

Review Questions

1. Describe the use of Love Canal as a site for chemical waste dumping by Hooker Chemical before 1953.

2. Why did the Love Canal site overflow with toxic chemicals? What effect did this have on the residents?

3. What did the government, the residents, and Hooker Chemical do about the pollution?

4. How does Hooker Chemical defend itself against the charge that it acted irresponsibly?

5. Why does Hooker Chemical claim that it has more than met its social and moral obligations?

6. Who do some residents blame?

Discussion Questions

1. Has Hooker Chemical adequately defended itself against the charge of acting irresponsibly? What do you think?

2. Has Hooker Chemical really met all of its social and moral obligations? If so, how have they done this? If not, where have they failed?

3. Is 500,000 deaths per year an acceptable price to pay for toxic chemicals in our environment, just as 50,000 traffic deaths per year is an acceptable price to pay for automobile travel?

Milton Friedman

The Social Responsibility of Business is to Increase Its Profits

Milton Friedman is professor of economics at the University of Chicago, and the author of Capitalism and Freedom.

Friedman defends the conservative view that the only responsibility of business is to increase its profits by open and free competition without deception or fraud. He attacks the view that business has any other social responsibilities, such as eliminating discrimination or reducing pollution. He calls this view the doctrine of social responsibility. Friedman thinks that the business executive who follows such doctrine will end up spending the money of the stockholders or the customers without their consent—in effect imposing taxes and spending tax money independent of the wishes of the public. He believes that this is wrong, it amounts to "taxation without representation." Furthermore, the doctrine of social responsibility has bad consequences: business executives who try to follow it will be fired, and wage restraints justified by it will produce wildcat strikes and revolts by workers. Finally, Friedman condemns the doctrine of social responsibility as a "fundamentally subversive doctrine" that is incompatible with the ideal of a free society because if it is applied to every human activity, the result would be total conformity to general social interests and no freedom at all.

When I hear businessmen speak eloquently about the "social responsibilities of business in a free-enterprise system," I am reminded of the wonderful line about the Frenchman who discovered at the age of 70 that he had been speaking prose all his life. The businessmen believe that they are defending free enterprise when they declaim that business is not concerned "merely" with profit but also with promoting desirable "social" ends; that business has a "social conscience" and takes seriously its responsibilities for providing employment, eliminating discrimination, avoiding pollution and whatever else may be the catchwords of the contemporary crop of reformers. In fact they are—or would be if they or anyone else took them seriously— preaching pure and unadulterated socialism. Businessmen who talk this way are unwitting puppets of the intellectual forces that have been undermining the basis of a free society these past decades.

The discussion of the "social responsibilities of business" are notable for their analytical looseness and lack of rigor. What does it mean to say that "business" has responsibilities? Only people can have responsibilities. A corporation is an artificial person and in this sense may have artificial responsibilities, but "business" as a whole cannot be said to have responsibilities, even in this vague sense. The first step toward clarity to examining the doctrine of the social responsibility of business is to ask precisely what it implies for whom.

Presumably, the individuals who are to be responsible are businessmen, which means individual proprietors or corporate executives. Most of the discussion of social responsibility is directed at corporations, so in what follows I shall mostly neglect the individual proprietors and speak of corporate executives.

In a free-enterprise, private-property system, a corporate executive is an employee of the owners of the business. He has direct responsibility to his employers. That responsibility is to conduct the business in accordance with their desires, which generally will be to make as much money as possible while conforming to the basic rules of the society, both those embodied in law and those embodied in ethical custom. Of course, in some cases his employers may have a different objective. A group of persons might establish a corporation for an **eleemosynary** purpose—for ex-

ample, a hospital or a school. The manager of such a corporation will not have money profit as his objectives but the rendering of certain services.

In either case, the key point is that, in his capacity as a corporate executive, the manager is the agent of the individuals who own the corporation or establish the eleemosynary institution, and his primary responsibility is to them.

Needless to say, this does not mean that it is easy to judge how well he is performing his task. But at least the criterion of performance is straightforward, and the persons among whom a voluntary contractual arrangement exists are clearly defined.

Of course, the corporate executive is also a person in his own right. As a person, he may have many other responsibilities that he recognizes or assumes voluntarily—to his family, his conscience, his feelings of charity, his church, his clubs, his city, his country. He may feel impelled by these responsibilities to devote part of his income to causes he regards as worthy, to refuse to work for particular corporations, even to leave his job, for example, to join his country's armed forces. If we wish, we may refer to some of these responsibilities as "social responsibilities." But in these respects he is acting as a principal, not an agent; he is spending his own money or time or energy, not the money of his employers or the time or energy he has contracted to devote to their purposes. If these are "social responsibilities," they are the social responsibilities of individuals, not of business.

What does it mean to say that the corporate executive has a "social responsibility" in his capacity as businessman? If this statement is not pure rhetoric, it must mean that he is to act in some way that is not in the interest of his employers. For example, that he is to refrain from increasing the price of the product in order to contribute to the social objective of preventing inflation, even though a price increase would be in the best interests of the corporation. Or that he is to make expenditures on reducing pollution beyond the amount that is in the best interests of the corporation or that is required by law in order to contribute to the social objective of improving the environment. Or that, at the expense of corporate profits, he is to hire "hardcore" unemployed instead of better qualified available workmen to contribute to the social objective of reducing proverty.

In each of these cases, the corporate executive would be spending someone else's money for a general social interest. Insofar as his actions in accord with his "social responsibility" reduce returns to stockholders, he is spending their money. Insofar as his actions raise the price to customers, he is spending the customers' money. Insofar as his actions lower the wages of some employees, he is spending their money.

The stockholders or the customers or the employees could separately spend their own money on the particular action if they wished to do so. The executive is exercising a distinct "social responsibility," rather than serving as an agent of the stockholders or the customers or the employees, only if he spends the money in a different way than they would have spent it.

But if he does this, he is in effect imposing taxes, on the one hand, and deciding how the tax proceeds shall be spent, on the other.

This process raises political questions on two levels: principle and consequences. On the level of political principle, the imposition of taxes and the expenditure of tax proceeds are governmental functions. We have established elaborate constitutional, parliamentary and judicial provisions to control these functions, to assure that taxes are imposed so far as possible in accordance with the preferences and desires of the public—after all, "taxation without representation" was one of the battle cries of the American Revolution. We have a system of checks and balances to separate the legislative function of imposing taxes and enacting expenditures from the executive function of collecting taxes and administering expenditure programs and from

the judicial function of mediating disputes and interpreting the law.

Here the businessman—self-selected or appointed directly or indirectly by stockholders—is to be simultaneously legislator, executive and jurist. He is to decide whom to tax by how much and for what purpose, and he is to spend the proceeds—all this guided only by general exhortations from on high to restrain inflation, improve the environment, fight poverty and so on and on.

The whole justification for permitting the corporate executive to be selected by the stockholders is that the executive is an agent serving the interests of his principal. This justification disappears when the corporate executive imposes taxes and spends the proceeds for "social" purposes. He becomes in effect a public employee, a civil servant, even though he remains in name an employee of a private enterprise. On grounds of political principle, it is intolerable that such civil servants—insofar as their actions in the name of social responsibility are real and not just window-dressing—should be selected as they are now. If they are to be civil servants, then they must elected through a political process. If they are to impose taxes and make expenditures to foster "social" objectives, then political machinery must be set up to make the assessment of taxes and to determine through a political process the objectives to be served.

This is the basic reason why the doctrine of "social responsibility" involves the acceptance of the socialist view that political mechanisms, not market mechanisms, are the appropriate way to determine the allocation of scarce resources to alternative uses.

On the grounds of consequences, can the corporate executive in fact discharge his alleged "social responsibilities"? On the one hand, suppose he could get away with spending the stockholders' or customers' or employees' money. How is he to know how to spend it? He is told that he must contribute to fighting inflation. How is he to know what action of his will contribute to that end? He is presumably an expert in running his company—in producing a product or selling it or financing it. But nothing about his selection makes him an expert on inflation. Will his holding down the price of his product reduce inflationary pressure? Or, by leaving more spending power in the hands of his customers, simply divert it elsewhere? Or, by forcing him to produce less because of the lower price, will it simply contribute to shortages? Even if he could answer these questions, how much cost is he justified in imposing on his stockholders, customers, and employees for this social purpose? What is his appropriate share and what is the appropriate share of others?

And, whether he wants to or not, can he get away with spending his stockholders', customers' or employees' money? Will not the stockholders fire him? (Either the present ones or those who take over when his actions in the name of social responsibility have reduced the corporation's profits and the price of its stock.) His customers and his employees can desert him for other producers and employers less scrupulous in exercising their social responsibilities.

This facet of "social responsibility" doctrine is brought into sharp relief when the doctrine is used to justify wage restraint by trade unions. The conflict of interest is naked and clear when union officials are asked to subordinate the interest of their members to some more general purpose. If the union officials try to enforce wage restraint, the consequence is likely to be wildcat strikes, rank-and-file revolts and the emergence of strong competitors for their jobs. We thus have the ironic phenomenon that union leaders—at least in the U.S.—have objected to Government interference with the market far more consistently and courageously than have business leaders.

The difficulty of exercising "social responsibility" illustrates, of course, the great virtue of private competitive enterprise—it forces people to be responsible for their own actions and makes it difficult for them to "ex-ploit" other people for either selfish or unselfish purposes. They can do good—but only at their own expense.

Many a reader who has followed the argument this far may be tempted to remonstrate that it is all well and good to speak of Government's having the responsibility to impose taxes and determine expenditures for such "social" purposes as controlling pollution or training the hard-core unemployed, but that the problems are too urgent to wait on the slow course of political processes, that the exercise of social responsibility by businessmen is a quicker and surer way to solve pressing current problems.

Aside from the question of fact—I share Adam Smith's skepticism about the benefits that can be expected from "those who affected to trade for the public good"—this argument must be rejected on grounds of principle. What it amounts to is an assertion that those who favor the taxes and expenditures in question have failed to persuade a majority of their fellow citizens to be of like mind and that they are seeking to attain by undemocratic procedures what they cannot attain by democratic procedures. In a free society, it is hard for "evil" people to do "evil," especially since one man's good is another's evil.

I have, for simplicity, concentrated on the special case of the corporate executive, except only for the brief digression on trade unions. But precisely the same argument applies to the newer phenomenon of calling upon stockholders to require corporations to exercise social responsibility (the recent G.M. crusade for example). In most of these cases, what is in effect involved is some stockholders trying to get other stockholders (or customers or employees) to contribute against their will to "social" causes favored by the activists. Insofar as they succeed, they are again imposing taxes and spending the proceeds.

The situation of the individual proprietor is somewhat different. If he acts to reduce the returns of his enterprise in order to exercise his "social responsibility," he is spending his own money, not someone else's. If he wishes to spend his money on such purposes, that is his right, and I cannot see that there is any objection to his doing so. In the process, he, too, may impose costs on employees and customers. However, because he is far less likely than a large corporation or union to have monopolistic power, any such side effects will tend to be minor.

Of course, in practice the doctrine of social responsibility is frequently a cloak for actions that are justified on other grounds rather than a reason for those actions.

To illustrate, it may well be in the long-run interest of a corporation that is a major employer in a small community to devote resources to providing amenities to that community or to improving its government. That may make it easier to attract desirable employees, it may reduce the wage bill or lessen losses from pilferage and sabotage or have other worthwhile effects. Or it may be that, given the laws about the deductibility of corporate charitable contributions, the stockholders can contribute more to charities they favor by having the corporation make the gift than by doing it themselves, since they can in that way contribute an amount that would otherwise have been paid as corporate taxes.

In each of these—and many similar—cases, there is a strong temptation to rationalize these actions as an exercise of "social responsibility." In the present climate of opinion, with its widespread aversion to "capitalism," "profits," and "soulless corporation" and so on, this is one way for a corporation to generate goodwill as a by-product of expenditures that are entirely justified in its own self-interest.

It would be inconsistent of me to call on corporate executives to refrain from this hypocritical window-dressing because it harms the foundations of a free society. That would be to call on them to exercise a "social responsibility"! If our institutions, and the attitudes of the public make it in their self-interest to cloak their actions in this way, I cannot summon much indignation to denounce

them. At the same time, I can express admiration for those individual proprietors or owners of closely held corporations or stockholders of more broadly held corporations who disdain such tactics as approaching fraud.

Whether blameworthy or not, the use of the cloak of social responsibility, and the nonsense spoken in its name by influential and prestigious businessmen, does clearly harm the foundations of a free society. I have been impressed time and again by the schizophrenic character of many businessmen. They are capable of being extremely far-sighted and clear-headed in matters that are internal to their businesses. They are incredibly short-sighted and muddle-headed in matters that are outside their businesses but affect the possible survival of business in general. This short-sightedness is strikingly exemplified in the calls from many businessmen for wage and price guidelines or controls or income policies. There is nothing that could do more in a brief period to destroy a market system and replace it by a centrally controlled system than effective governmental control of prices and wages.

The short-sightedness is also exemplified in speeches by businessmen on social responsibility. This may gain them kudos in the short run. But it helps to strengthen the already too prevalent view that the pursuit of profits is wicked and immoral and must be curbed and controlled by external forces. Once this view is adopted, the external forces that curb the market will not be the social consciences, however highly developed, of the pontificating executives; it will be the iron fist of Government bureaucrats. Here, as with price and wage controls, businessmen seem to me to reveal a suicidal impulse.

The political principle that underlies the market mechanism is unanimity. In an ideal free market resting on private property, no individual can coerce any other, all cooperation is voluntary, all parties to such cooperation benefit or they need not participate. There are no values, no "social" responsibilities in any sense other than the shared values and responsibilities of individuals. Society is a collection of individuals and of the various groups they voluntarily form.

The political principle that underlies the political mechanism is conformity. The individual must serve a more general social interest—whether that be determined by a church or a dictator or a majority. The individual may have a vote and say in what is to be done, but if he is overruled, he must conform. It is appropriate for some to require others to contribute to a general social purpose whether they wish to or not.

Unfortunately, unanimity is not always feasible. There are some respects in which conformity appears unavoidable, so I do not see how one can avoid the use of the political mechanism altogether.

But the doctrine of "social responsibility" taken seriously would extend the scope of the political mechanism to every human activity. It does not differ in philosophy from the most explicitly collectivist doctrine. It differs only by professing to believe that collectivist ends can be attained without collectivist means. That is why, in my book *Capitalism and Freedom,* I have called it a "fundamentally subversive doctrine" in a free society, and have said that in such a society, "there is one and only one social responsibility of business—to use its resources and engage in activities designed to increase its profits so long as it stays within the rules of the game, which is to say, engages in open and free competition without deception or fraud."

Review Questions

1. According to Friedman, why doesn't it make sense to say that business itself has responsibilities?

2. In Friedman's view, who in business does have responsibilities, and what are they?

3. Explain Friedman's account of the corporate executive who acts out of social responsibility.

4. Why does Friedman think that a corporate executive should direct his or her actions by other considerations than social responsibility?

5. According to Friedman, why does the doctrine of social responsibility involve socialism?

6. How does Friedman reply to the objection that social activities such as pollution control should be left to the government?

7. Why does Friedman find the doctrine of social responsibility to be a "fundamentally subversive doctrine?"

8. What is the one and only social responsibility of business according to Friedman?

Discussion Questions

1. Can a business have responsibilities? Why or why not?

2. Is it possible for a business executive to follow the doctrine of social responsibility and not end up spending the money of consumers or stockholders? How?

3. If business ignores social problems such as discrimination in hiring and pay, pollution, unemployment, and so on, then how can these problems be solved? What is your view?

Christopher D. Stone

Why Shouldn't Corporations Be Socially Responsible?

Christopher D. Stone is a member of the department of law at the University of Southern California, and the author of Should Trees have Standing?

Stone attacks four arguments used by conservatives such as Milton Friedman to defend the view that corporations have no responsibilities other than maximizing profits. The four arguments are the "promissory argument," the "agency argument," the "role argument," and the "polestar argument." He finds the first three to be defective; they rest on false assumptions and they are inconclusive. Stone says that the fourth argument, the so-called "polestar" argument, makes a number of assumptions, and that the arguments based on these assumptions have a "germ of validity." Their essential failure is in not pursuing the alternatives to controlling corporations by market forces and by law. Such alternatives should be pursued because corporations need additional constraints.

The opposition to corporate social responsibility comprises at least four related though separable positions. I would like to challenge the fundamental assumption that underlies all four of them. Each assumes in its own degree that the managers of the corporation are to be steered almost wholly by profit, rather than by what they think proper for society on the whole. Why should this be so? So far as ordinary morals are concerned, we often expect human beings to act in a fashion that is calculated to benefit others, rather than themselves, and commend them for it. Why should the matter be different with corporations?

THE PROMISSORY ARGUMENT

The most widespread but least persuasive arguments advanced by the "antiresponsibility" forces take the form of a moral claim based upon the corporation's supposed obligations to its shareholders. In its baldest and least tenable form, it is presented as though management's obligation rested upon the keeping of a promise—that the management of the corporation "promised" the shareholders that it would maximize the shareholders' profits. But this simply isn't so.

Consider for contrast the case where a widow left a large fortune goes to a broker, asking him to invest and manage her money so as to maximize her return. The broker, let us suppose, accepts the money and the conditions. In such a case, there would be no disagreement that the broker had made a promise to the widow, and if he invested her money in some venture that struck his fancy for any reason other than that it would increase her fortune, we would be inclined to advance a moral (as well, perhaps, as a legal) claim against him. Generally, at least, we believe in the keeping of promises; the broker, we should say, had violated a promissory obligation to the widow.

But that simple model is hardly the one that obtains between the management of major corporations and their shareholders. Few if any American shareholders ever put their money into a corporation upon the express promise of management that the company would be operated so as to maximize their returns. Indeed, few American shareholders ever put their money directly *into* a corporation at all. Most of the shares outstanding today were issued years ago and found their way to their current shareholders only circuitously. In almost all cases, the current shareholder gave his money to some prior shareholder, who, in turn, had gotten it from B, who, in turn, had gotten it from A, and so on back to the purchaser of the original issue, who, many years before, had bought the shares through an underwriting syndicate. In the course of these transactions, one of the basic elements that exists in the broker case is missing: The manager of the corporation, unlike the broker, was never even offered a chance to refuse the shareholder's "terms" (if they were that) to maximize the shareholder's profits.

There are two other observations to be made about the moral argument based on a supposed promise running from the management to the shareholders. First, even if we do infer from all the circumstances a "promise" running from the management to the shareholders, but not one, or not one of comparable weight running elsewhere (to the company's employees, customers, neighbors, etc.), we ought to keep in mind that as a moral matter (which is what we are discussing here) sometimes it is deemed morally justified to break promises (even to break the law) in the furtherance of other social interests of higher concern. Promises can advance moral arguments, by way of creating presumptions, but few of us believe that promises, per se, can end them. My promise to appear in class on time would not ordinarily justify me from refusing to give aid to a drowning man. In other words, even if management *had* made an express promise to its shareholders to "maximize your profits," (a) I am not persuaded that the ordinary person would interpret it to mean "maximize *in every way you can possibly get away with,* even if that means polluting the environment, ignoring or breaking the law"; and (b) I am not persuaded that, even if it were interpreted as so blanket a promise, most people would not suppose it ought—morally—to be broken in some cases.

Finally, even if, in the face of all these considerations, one still believes that there is an overriding, unbreakable promise of some sort running from management to the shareholders, I do not think that it can be construed to be any stronger than one running to *existent* shareholders, arising from *their* expectations as measured by the price *they* paid. That is to say, there is nothing in the argument from promises that would wed us to a regime in which management was bound to

maximize the income of shareholders. The argument might go so far as to support compensation for existent shareholders if the society chose to announce that henceforth management would have other specified obligations, thereby driving the price of shares to a lower adjustment level. All future shareholders would take with "warning" of, and a price that discounted for, the new "risks" of shareholding (i.e., the "risks" that management might put corporate resources to *pro bonum* ends).

THE AGENCY ARGUMENT

Related to the promissory argument but requiring less stretching of the facts is an argument from agency principles. Rather than trying to infer a promise by management to the shareholders, this argument is based on the idea that the shareholders designated the management their agents. This is the position advanced by Milton Friedman in his *New York Times* article. "The key point," he says, "is that . . . the manager is the agent of the individuals who own the corporation. . . ." [1]

Friedman, unfortunately, is wrong both as to the state of the law (the directors are *not* mere agents of the shareholders) [2] and on his assumption as to the facts of corporate life (surely it is closer to the truth that in major corporations the shareholders are *not,* in any meaningful sense, selecting the directors; management is more often using its control over the proxy machinery to designate who the directors shall be, rather than the other way around).

What Friedman's argument comes down to is that for some reason the directors ought morally to consider themselves more the agents for the shareholders than for the customers, creditors, the state, or the corporation's immediate neighbors. But why? And to what extent? Throwing in terms like "principal" and "agent" begs the fundamental questions.

What is more, the "agency" argument is not only morally inconclusive, it is embarrassingly at odds with the way in which supposed "agents" actually behave. If the managers truly considered themselves the agents of the shareholders, as agents they would be expected to show an interest in determining how their principals wanted them to act—and to act accordingly. In the controversy over Dow's production of napalm, for example, one would expect, on this model, that Dow's management would have been glad to have the napalm question put to the shareholders at a shareholders' meeting. In fact, like most major companies faced with shareholder requests to include "social action" measures on proxy statements, it fought the proposal tooth and claw.[3] It is a peculiar agency where the "agents" will go to such lengths (even spending tens of thousands of dollars of their "principals'" money in legal fees) to resist the determination of what their "principals" want.

THE ROLE ARGUMENT

An argument so closely related to the argument from promises and agency that it does not demand extensive additional remarks is a contention based upon supposed considerations of *role.* Sometimes in moral discourse, as well as in law, we assign obligations to people on the basis of their having assumed some role or status, independent of any specific verbal promise they made. Such obligations are assumed to run from a captain to a seaman (and vice versa), from a doctor to a patient, or from a parent to a child. The antiresponsibility forces are on somewhat stronger grounds resting their position on this basis, because the model more nearly accords with the facts—that is, management never actually promised the shareholders that they would maximize the shareholders' investment, nor did the shareholders designate the directors their agents for this express purpose. The directors and top management are, as lawyers would say, fiduciaries. But what does this leave us? So far as the directors are fiduciaries of the shareholders in a legal sense, of course they are subject to the legal limits on fiduciaries—that is to say, they

cannot engage in self-dealing, "waste" of corporate assets, and the like. But I do not understand any proresponsibility advocate to be demanding such corporate largesse as would expose the officers to legal liability; what we are talking about are expenditures on, for example, pollution control, above the amount the company is required to pay by law, but less than an amount so extravagant as to constitute a violation of these legal **fiduciary** duties. (Surely no court in America today would enjoin a corporation from spending more to reduce pollution than the law requires.) What is there about assuming the role of corporate officer that makes it immoral for a manager to involve a corporation in these expenditures? A father, one would think, would have stronger obligations to his children by virtue of his status than a corporate manager to the corporation's shareholders. Yet few would regard it as a compelling moral argument if a father were to distort facts about his child on a scholarship application form on the grounds that he had obligations to advance his child's career; nor would we consider it a strong moral argument if a father were to leave unsightly refuse piled on his lawn, spilling over into the street, on the plea that he had obligations to give every moment of his attention to his children, and was thus too busy to cart his refuse away.

Like the other supposed moral arguments, the one from role suffers from the problem that the strongest moral obligations one can discover have at most only prima facie force, and it is not apparent why those obligations should predominate over some contrary social obligations that could be advanced.

Then too, when one begins comparing and weighing the various moral obligations, those running back to the shareholder seem fairly weak by comparison to the claims of others. For one thing, there is the consideration of alternatives. If the shareholder is dissatisfied with the direction the corporation is taking, he can sell out, and if he does so quickly enough, his losses may be slight. On the other hand, as Ted Jacobs observes, "those most vitally affected by corporate decisions—people who work in the plants, buy the products, and consume the **effluents**—cannot remove themselves from the structure with a phone call." [4]

THE "POLESTAR" ARGUMENT

It seems to me that the strongest moral argument corporate executives can advance for looking solely to profits is not one that is based on a supposed express, or even implied promise to the shareholder. Rather, it is one that says, if the managers act in such fashion as to maximize profits—if they act *as though* they had promised the shareholders they would do so—then it will be best for all of us. This argument might be called the polestar argument, for its appeal to the interests of the shareholders is not justified on supposed obligations to the shareholders per se, but as a means of charting a straight course toward what is best for the society as a whole.

Underlying the polestar argument are a number of assumptions—some express and some implied. There is, I suspect, an implicit **positivism** among its supporters—a feeling (whether its proponents own up to it or not) that moral judgments are peculiar, arbitrary, or vague—perhaps even "meaningless" in the philosophic sense of not being amenable to rational discussion. To those who take this position, profits (or sales, or price-earnings ratios) at least provide some solid, tangible standard by which participants in the organization can measure their successes and failures, with some efficiency, in the narrow sense, resulting for the entire group. Sometimes the polestar position is based upon a related view—not that the moral issues that underlie social choices are meaningless, but that resolving them calls for special expertise. "I don't know any investment adviser whom I would care to act in my behalf in any matter except turning a profit.... The value of these specialists ... lies in their limitations; they ought not allow themselves to see so

much of the world that they become distracted." [5] A slightly modified point emphasizes not that the executives lack moral or social expertise per se, but that they lack the social authority to make policy choices. Thus, Friedman objects that if a corporate director took "social purposes" into account, he would become "in effect a public employee, a civil servant.... On grounds of political principle, it is intolerable that such civil servants ... should be selected as they are now." [6]

I do not want to get too deeply involved in each of these arguments. That the moral judgments underlying policy choices are vague, I do not doubt—although I am tempted to observe that when you get right down to it, a wide range of actions taken by businessmen every day, supposedly based on solid calculations of "profit," are probably as rooted in hunches and intuition as judgments of ethics. I do not disagree either that, ideally, we prefer those who have control over our lives to be politically accountable; although here, too, if we were to pursue the matter in detail we would want to inspect both the premise of this argument, that corporate managers are not *presently* custodians of discretionary power over us anyway, and also its logical implications: Friedman's point that "if they are to be civil servants, then they must be selected through a political process" [7] is not, as Friedman regards it, a *reductio ad absurdum*—not, at any rate, to Ralph Nader and others who want publicly elected directors.

The reason for not pursuing these counterarguments at length is that, whatever reservations one might have, we can agree that there is a germ of validity to what the "antis" are saying. But their essential failure is in not pursuing the alternatives. Certainly, *to the extent* that the forces of the market and the law can keep the corporation within desirable bounds, it may be better to trust them than to have corporate managers implementing their own vague and various notions of what is best for the rest of us. But are the "antis" blind to the fact that there are circumstances in which the law—and the forces of the market—are simply not competent to keep the corporation under control? The shortcomings of these traditional restraints on corporate conduct are critical to understand, not merely for the defects they point up in the "antis'" position. More important, identifying where the traditional forces are inadequate is the first step in the design of new and alternative measures of corporate control.

Footnotes

1. *New York Times,* September 12, 1962, sect. 6, p. 33, col. 2.
2. See, for example, *Automatic Self-Cleansing Filter Syndicate Co. Ltd. v. Cunninghame* (1906) 2 Ch. 34.
3. "Dow Shalt Not Kill," in S. Prakash Sethi, *Up Against the Corporate Wall,* (Englewood Cliffs, N.J.: Prentice-Hall, 1971), pp. 236–266, and the opinion of Judge Tamm in *Medical Committee for Human Rights v. S.E.C.,* 432 F.2d 659 (D.C.Cir.1970), and the dissent of Mr. Justice Douglas in the same case in the U.S. Supreme Court, 404 U.S. 403, 407–411 (1972).
4. Theodore J. Jacobs, "Pollution, Consumerism, Accountability," *Center Magazine* 5, 1 (January–February 1971): 47.
5. Walter Goodman, "Stocks Without Sin," *Harper's,* August 1971, p. 66.
6. *New York Times,* September 12, 1962, sec. 6, p. 122, col. 3.
7. Ibid., p. 122, cols. 3–4.

Review Questions

1. How does Stone attack the promissory argument?

2. What is wrong with Friedman's agency argument according to Stone?

3. How does Stone reply to the role argument?

4. State and explain the so-called "polestar" argument.

5. What assumptions does Stone find underlying this argument?

6. What is Stone's appraisal of the "polestar" argument and the assumptions underlying it?

Discussion Questions

1. Has Stone given a decisive refutation of Friedman's position? Why or why not?

2. Stone admits that there is a "germ of validity" in what his opposition is saying. What is this "germ of validity?" Can you clarify this?

Robert Almeder

Morality in the Marketplace

Robert Almeder is professor of philosophy at Georgia State University.

In direct opposition to Friedman, Almeder tries to prove that corporations have a moral obligation to be socially responsible in ways that go beyond merely

Reprinted from *Business Ethics,* © 1983 by Milton Snoeyenbos, Robert Almeder, and James Humber, eds., with permission of Prometheus Books, Buffalo, New York.

making money. He begins with a statement and criticism of two main arguments used by defenders of Friedman's position that the only responsibility of business is to make as much money as legally possible. The first is that the greatest good for the greatest number can only be achieved if corporations act only in the pursuit of profit and ignore moral concerns. Almeder claims that this argument rests on the questionable factual assumption that a society in which everyone pursues his or her self-interst will be better than a society in which people are regulated by moral concerns. The second argument is that there is no noncontroversial way for corporations to discover what their moral responsibilities are, assuming that they have them. Almeder replies that we do agree about some moral responsibilities. Finally, Almeder presents a positive argument for his thesis: We all believe that it is wrong to kill an innocent human being for money. But corporations engage in certain practices that amount to doing this. Hence they are guilty of immoral practices, and they have a strong moral obligation to stop them.

I

In order to create a climate more favorable for corporate activity, International Telephone and Telegraph allegedly contributed large sums of money to "destabilize" the duly elected government of Chile. Even though advised by the scientific community that the practice is lethal, major chemical companies reportedly continue to dump large amounts of carcinogens into the water supply of various areas and, at the same time, lobby to prevent legislation against such practices. General Motors Corporation, other automobile manufacturers, and Firestone Tire and Rubber Corporation have frequently defended themselves against the charge that they knowingly and willingly marketed a product that, owing to defective design, had been reliably predicted to kill a certain percentage of its users and, moreover, refused to recall promptly the product even when government agencies documented the large incidence of death as a result of the defective product. Finally, people often say that numerous advertising companies happily accept, and earnestly solicit, accounts to advertise cigarettes knowing full well that as a direct result of their advertising activities a certain number of people will die considerably prematurely and painfully. We need not concern ourselves with whether these and other similar charges are true because our concern here is with what might count as a justification for such corporate conduct were it to occur. There can be no question that such behavior is frequently legal. The question is whether corporate behavior should be constrained by nonlegal or moral considerations. As things presently stand, it seems to be a dogma of contemporary capitalism that the sole responsibility of business is to make as much money as is legally possible. But the question

is whether this view is rationally defensible.

Sometimes, although not very frequently, corporate executives will admit to the sort of behavior depicted above and then proceed proximately to justify such behavior in the name of their responsibility to the shareholders or owners (if the shareholders are not the owners) to make as much profit as is legally possible. Thereafter, less proximately and more generally, they will proceed to urge the more general utilitarian point that the increase in profit engendered by such corporate behavior begets such an unquestionable overall good for society that the behavior in question is morally acceptable if not quite praiseworthy. More specifically, the justification in question can, and usually does, take two forms.

The first and most common form of justification consists in urging that, as long as one's corporate behavior is not illegal, the behavior will be morally acceptable because the sole purpose of being in business is to make a profit; and the rules of the marketplace are somewhat different from those in other places and must be followed if one is to make a profit. Moreover, proponents of this view hasten to add that, as Adam Smith has claimed, the greatest good for society is achieved not by corporations seeking to act morally, or with a sense of social responsibility in their pursuit of profit, but rather by each corporation seeking to maximize its own profit, unregulated in that endeavor except by the laws of supply and demand along with whatever other laws are inherent to the competition process. Smith's view, that there is an invisible hand, as it were, directing an economy governed solely by the profit motive to the greatest good for society,[1] is still the dominant motivation and justification for those who would want an economy unregulated by any moral concern that would, or could, tend to decrease profits for some *alleged* social or moral good.

Milton Friedman, for example, has frequently asserted that the sole moral responsibility of business is to make as much profit as is legally possible; and by that he means to suggest that attempts to regulate or restrain the pursuit of profit in accordance with what some people believe to be socially desirable ends are in fact *subversive* of the common good since the greatest good for the greatest number is achieved by an economy maximally competitive and unregulated by moral rules in its pursuit of profit.[2] So, on Friedman's view, the greatest good for society is achieved by corporations acting legally, but with no further regard for what may be morally desirable; and this view begets the paradox that, *in business,* the greatest good for society can be achieved only by acting without regard for morality. Moreover, adoption of this position constitutes a fairly conscious commitment to the view that while one's personal life may well need governance by moral considerations, when pursuing profit, it is necessary that one's corporate behavior be unregulated by any moral concern other than that of making as much money as is legally possible; curiously enough, it is only in this way that society achieves the greatest good. So viewed, it is not difficult to see how a corporate executive could consistently adopt rigorous standards of morality in his or her personal life and yet feel quite comfortable in abandoning those standards in the pursuit of profit. Albert Carr, for example, likens the conduct of business to that of playing poker.[3] As Carr would have it, moral busybodies who insist on corporations acting morally might do just as well to censure a good bluffer in poker for being deceitful. Society, of course, lacking a perspective such as Friedman's and Carr's, is only too willing to view such behavior as strongly hypocritical and fostered by an unwholesome avarice.

The second way of justifying, or defending, corporate practices that may appear morally questionable consists in urging that even if corporations were to take seriously the idea of limiting profits because of a desire to be moral or more responsible to social needs, then corporations would be involved in the unwholesome business of selecting and implementing moral values that may not be shared by a large number of people. Besides, there is the overwhelming question of whether there can be any nonquestionable moral values or noncontroversial list of social priorities for corporations to adopt. After all, if **ethical relativism** is true, or if **ethical nihilism** is true (and philosophers can be counted upon to argue for both positions), then it would be fairly silly of corporations to limit profits for what may be a quite dubious reason, namely, for being moral, when there are no clear grounds for doing it, and when it is not too clear what would count for doing it. In short, business corporations could argue (as Friedman has done)[4] that corporate actions in behalf of society's interests would require of corporations an ability to clearly determine and rank in noncontroversial ways the major needs of society; and it would not appear that this could be done successfully.

Perhaps another, and somewhat easier, way of formulating this second argument consists in urging that because philosophers generally fail to agree on what are the proper moral rules (if any), as well as on whether we should be moral, it would be imprudent to sacrifice a clear profit for a dubious or controversial moral gain. To authorize such a sacrifice would be to abandon a clear responsibility for one that is unclear or questionable.

If there are any other basic ways of justifying the sort of corporate behavior noted at the outset, I cannot imagine what they might be. So, let us examine these two modes of justification. In doing this, I hope to show that neither argument is sound and, moreover, that corporate behavior of the sort in question is clearly immoral if anything is immoral—and if nothing is immoral, then such corporate behavior is clearly contrary to the long-term interest of a corporation. In the end, we will reflect on ways to prevent such behavior, and on what is philosophically implied by corporate willingness to act in clearly immoral ways.

II

Essentially, the first argument is that the greatest good for the greatest number will be, and can only be, achieved by corporations acting legally but unregulated by any moral concern in the pursuit of profit. As we saw earlier, the evidence for this argument rests on a fairly classical and unquestioning acceptance of Adam Smith's view that society achieves a greater good when each person is allowed to pursue her or his own self-interested ends than when each person's pursuit of self-interested ends is regulated in some way or another by moral rules or concern. But I know of no evidence Smith ever offered for this latter claim, although it seems clear that those who adopt it generally do so out of respect for the perceived good that has emerged for various modern societies as a direct result of the free enterprise system and its ability to raise the overall standard of living of all those under it.

However, there is nothing inevitable about the greatest good occurring in an unregulated economy. Indeed, we have good inductive evidence from the age of the Robber Barons that unless the profit motive is regulated in various ways (by statute or otherwise) untold social evil can (and some say *will*) occur because of the natural tendency of the system to place ever-increasing sums of money in ever-decreasing numbers of hands. If all this is so, then so much the worse for all philosophical attempts to justify what would appear to be morally questionable corporate behavior on the grounds that corporate behavior, unregulated by moral concern, is necessarily or even probably productive of the greatest good for the greatest number. Moreover, a **rule utilitarian** would not be very hard pressed to show the many unsavory implications to society as a whole if society were to take seriously a rule to the effect that, provided only that one acts legally, it is morally permissible to do whatever one wants to do to achieve a profit. Some of those implications we shall discuss below before drawing a conclusion.

The second argument cited above asserts that even if we were to grant, for the sake of argument, that corporations have social responsibilities beyond that of making as much money as is legally possible for the shareholders, there would be no noncontroversial way for corporations to discover just what these responsibilities are in the order of their importance. Owing to the fact that even distinguished moral philosophers predictably disagree on what one's moral responsibilities are, if any, it would seem irresponsible to limit profits to satisfy dubious moral responsibilities.

For one thing, this argument unduly exaggerates our potential for moral disagreement. Admittedly, there might well be important disagreements among corporations (just as there could be among philosophers) as to a priority ranking of major social needs; but that does not mean that most of us could not, or would not, agree that certain things ought not be done in the name of profit even when there is no law prohibiting such acts. There will always be a few who would do anything for a profit; but that is hardly a good argument in favor of their having the moral right to do so rather than a good argument that they refuse to be moral. In sum, it is hard to see how this second argument favoring corporate moral nihilism is any better than the general argument for ethical nihilism based on the variability of ethical judgments or practices; and apart from the fact that it tacitly presupposes that morality is a matter of what we all in fact would, or should, accept, the argument is maximally counterintuitive (as I shall show) by way of suggesting that we cannot generally agree that corporations have certain clear social responsibilities to avoid certain practices. Accordingly, I would now like to argue that if anything is immoral, a certain kind of corporate behavior is quite immoral although it may not be illegal.

III

Without caring to enter into the reasons for the belief, I assume we all believe that it is wrong to kill an innocent human being for no other reason than that doing so would be more financially rewarding for the killer than if he were to earn his livelihood in some other way. Nor, I assume, should our moral feelings on this matter change depending on the amount of money involved. Killing an innocent baby for fifteen million dollars would not seem to be any less objectionable than killing it for twenty cents. It is possible, however, that some self-professing utilitarian might be tempted to argue that the killing of an innocent baby for fifteen million dollars would not be objectionable if the money were to be given to the poor; under these circumstances, greater good would be achieved by the killing of the innocent baby. But, I submit, if anybody were to argue in this fashion, his argument would be quite deficient because he has not established what he needs to establish to make his argument sound. What he needs is a clear, convincing argument that raising the standard of living of an indefinite number of poor persons by the killing of an innocent person is a greater good for all those affected by the act than if the standard of living were not raised by the killing of an innocent person. This is needed because part of what we mean by having a basic right to life is that a person's life cannot be taken from him or her without a good reason. If our utilitarian cannot provide a convincing justification for his claim that a greater good is served by killing an innocent person in order to raise the standard of living for a large number of poor people, then it is hard to see how he can have the good reason he needs to deprive an innocent person of his or her life. Now, it seems clear that there will be anything but unanimity in the moral community on the question of whether there is a greater good achieved in raising the standard of living by killing an innocent baby than in leaving the standard of living alone and not killing an innocent baby. Moreover, even if everybody were to agree that the greater good is achieved by the killing of the innocent baby, how could that be shown to be

true? How does one compare the moral value of a human life with the moral value of raising the standard of living by the taking of that life? Indeed, the more one thinks about it, the more difficult it is to see just what would count as objective evidence for the claim that the greater good is achieved by the killing of the innocent baby. Accordingly, I can see nothing that would justify the utilitarian who might be tempted to argue that if the sum is large enough, and if the sum were to be used for raising the standard of living for an indefinite number of poor people, then it would be morally acceptable to kill an innocent person for money.

These reflections should not be taken to imply, however, that no utilitarian argument could justify the killing of an innocent person for money. After all, if the sum were large enough to save the lives of a large number of people who would surely die if the innocent baby were not killed, then I think one would as a rule be justified in killing the innocent baby for the sum in question. But this situation is obviously quite different from the situation in which one would attempt to justify the killing of an innocent person in order to raise the standard of living for an indefinite number of poor people. It makes sense to kill one innocent person in order to save, say, twenty innocent persons; but it makes no sense at all to kill one innocent person to raise the standard of living of an indefinite number of people. In the latter case, but not in the former, a comparison is made between things that are incomparable.

Given these considerations, it is remarkable and somewhat perplexing that certain corporations should seek to defend practices that are in fact instances of killing innocent persons for profit. Take, for example, the corporate practice of dumping known carcinogens into rivers. On Milton Friedman's view, we should not regulate or prevent such companies from dumping their effluents into the environment. Rather we should, if we like, tax the company after the effluents are in the water and then have the tax money used to clean up the environment.[5] For Friedman, and others, the fact that so many people will die as a result of this practice seems to be just part of the cost of doing business and making a profit. If there is any moral difference between such corporate practices and murdering innocent human beings for money, it is hard to see what it is. It is even more difficult to see how anyone could justify the practice and see it as no more than a business practice not to be regulated by moral concern. And there are a host of other corporate activities that are morally equivalent to deliberate killing of innocent persons for money. Such practices number among them contributing funds to "destabilize" a foreign government, advertising cigarettes, knowingly to market children's clothing having a known cancer causing agent, and refusing to recall (for fear of financial loss) goods known to be sufficiently defective to directly maim or kill a certain percentage of their unsuspecting users because of the defect. On this latter item, we are all familiar, for example, with convincingly documented charges that certain prominent automobile and tire manufacturers will knowingly market equipment sufficiently defective to increase the likelihood of death as a direct result of the defect and yet refuse to recall the product because the cost of recalling and repairing would have a greater adverse impact on profit than if the product were not recalled and the company paid the projected number of predictably successful suits. Of course, if the projected cost of the predictably successful suits were to outweigh the cost of recall and repair, then the product would be recalled and repaired, but not otherwise. In cases of this sort, the companies involved may admit to having certain marketing problems or a design problem, and they may even admit to having made a mistake; but, interestingly enough, they do not view themselves as immoral or as murderers for keeping their product in the market place when they know people are dying from it, people who would not die if the defect were corrected.

The important point is not whether in fact these practices have occurred in the past, or occur even now; there can be no doubt that such practices have occurred and do occur. Rather the point is that when companies act in such ways as a matter of policy, they must either not know what they do is murder (i.e., unjustifiable killing of an innocent person), or knowing that it is murder, seek to justify it in terms of profit. And I have been arguing that it is difficult to see how any corporate manager could fail to see that these policies amount to murder for money, although there may be no civil statute against such corporate behavior. If so, then where such policies exist, we can only assume that they are designed and implemented by corporate managers who either see nothing wrong with murder for money (which is implausible) or recognize that what they do is wrong but simply refuse to act morally because it is more financially rewarding to act immorally.

Of course, it is possible that corporate executives would not recognize such acts as murder. They may, after all, view murder as a legal concept involving one noncorporate person or persons deliberately killing another noncorporate person or persons and prosecutable only under existing civil statute. If so, it is somewhat understandable how corporate executives might fail, at least psychologically, to see such corporate policies as murder rather than as, say, calculated risks, tradeoffs, or design errors. Still, for all that, the logic of the situation seems clear enough.

IV   Conclusion

In addition to the fact that the only two plausible arguments favoring the Friedman doctrine are unsatisfactory, a strong case can be made for the claim that corporations *do* have a clear and noncontroversial moral responsibility not to design or implement, for reasons of profit, policies that they know, or have good reason to believe, will kill or otherwise seriously injure innocent persons affected by those policies. Moreover, we have said nothing about wage discrimination, sexism, discrimination in hiring, price fixing, price gouging, questionable but not unlawful competition, or other similar practices that some will think businesses should avoid by virtue of responsibility to society. My main concern has been to show that since we all agree that murder for money is generally wrong, and since there is no discernible difference between that and certain corporate policies that are not in fact illegal, then these corporate practices are clearly immoral (that is, they ought not to be done) and incapable of being morally justified by appeal to the Friedman doctrine since that doctrine does not admit of adequate evidential support. In itself, it is sad that this argument needs to be made and, if it were not for what appears to be a fairly strong commitment within the business community to the Friedman doctrine in the name of the unquestionable success of the free enterprise system, the argument would not need to be stated.

The fact that such practices do exist—designed and implemented by corporate managers who, for all intents and purposes, appear to be upright members of the moral community—only heightens the need for effective social prevention. Presumably, of course, any company willing to put human lives into the profit and loss column is not likely to respond to moral censure. Accordingly, I submit that perhaps the most effective way to deal with the problem of preventing such corporate behavior would consist in structuring legislation such that senior corporate managers who knowingly concur in practices of the sort listed above can effectively be tried, at their own expense, for murder, rather than censured and fined a sum to be paid out of corporate profits. This may seem a somewhat extreme or unrealistic proposal. However, it seems more unrealistic to think that aggressively competitive corporations will respond to what is morally necessary if failure to do so could be very or even minimally profitable. In short, unless we take strong and appropriate steps to prevent such practices, society will be reinforcing a destructive mode of behavior that is maximally disrespectful of human life, just as society will be reinforcing a value system that so emphasizes monetary gain as a standard of human success that murder for profit could be a corporate policy if the penalty for being caught at it were not too dear.

In the long run, of course, corporate and individual willingness to do what is clearly immoral for the sake of monetary gain is a patent commitment to a certain view about the nature of human happiness and success, a view that needs to be placed in the balance with Aristotle's reasoned argument and reflections to the effect that money and all that it brings is a means to an end, and not the sort of end in itself that will justify acting immorally to attain it. What that beautiful end is and why being moral allows us to achieve it, may well be the most rewarding and profitable subject a human being can think about. Properly understood and placed in perspective, Aristotle's view on the nature and attainment of human happiness could go a long way toward alleviating the temptation to kill for money.

In the meantime, any ardent supporter of the capitalistic system will want to see the system thrive and flourish; and this it cannot do if it invites and demands government regulation in the name of the public interest. A *strong* ideological commitment to what I have described above as the Friedman doctrine is counterproductive and not in anyone's long-range interest because it is most likely to beget an ever-increasing regulatory climate. The only way to avoid such encroaching regulation is to find ways to move the business community into the long-term view of what is in its interest, and effect ways of both determining and responding to social needs before society moves to regulate business to that end. To so move the business community is to ask business to regulate its own modes of competition in ways that may seem very difficult to achieve. Indeed, if what I have been suggesting is correct, the only kind of enduring capitalism is humane capitalism, one that is at least as socially responsible as society needs. By the same token, contrary to what is sometimes felt in the business community, the Friedman doctrine, ardently adopted for the dubious reasons generally given, will most likely undermine capitalism and motivate an economic socialism by assuring an erosive regulatory climate in a society that expects the business community to be socially responsible in ways that go beyond just making legal profits.

In sum, being socially responsible in ways that go beyond legal profit-making is by no means a dubious luxury for the capitalist in today's world. It is a necessity if capitalism is to survive at all; and, presumably, we shall all profit with the survival of a vibrant capitalism. If anything, then, rigid adherence to the Friedman doctrine is not only philosophically unjustified, and unjustifiable, it is also unprofitable in the long run, and therefore, downright subversive of the long-term common good. Unfortunately, taking the long-run view is difficult for everyone. After all, for each of us, tomorrow may not come. But living for today only does not seem to make much sense either, if that deprives us of any reasonable and happy tomorrow. Living for the future may not be the healthiest thing to do; but do it we must, if we have good reason to think that we will have a future. The trick is to provide for the future without living in it, and that just requires being moral.[6]

Footnotes

1. Adam Smith, *The Wealth of Nations*, ed. Edwin Canaan (Modern Library, N.Y., 1937), p. 423.

2. See Milton Friedman, "The Social Responsibility of Business Is to Increase Its Profits" in *The New York Times Magazine* (September 13, 1970), pp. 33, 122–126 and "Milton Friedman Responds" in *Business and Society Review* (Spring, 1972, No. 1), p. 5 ff.

3. Albert Z. Carr, "Is Business Bluffing Ethical?" *Harvard Business Review* (January-February 1968).

4. Milton Friedman in "Milton Friedman Responds" in *Business and Society Review* (Spring 1972, No. 1), p. 10.

5. Milton Friedman in "Milton Friedman Responds" in *Business and Society Review* (Spring 1972, No. 1), p. 10.

6. I would like to thank C.G. Luckhardt, J. Humber, R.L. Arrington, and M. Snoeyenbos for their comments and criticisms of an earlier draft.

Shortly after this paper was initially written, an Indiana superior court judge refused to dismiss a homicide indictment against the Ford Motor Company. The company was indicted on charges of reckless homicide stemming from a 1978 accident involving a 1973 Pinto in which three girls died when the car burst into flames after being slammed in the rear. This was the first case in which Ford, or any other automobile manufacturer, had been charged with a criminal offense.

The indictment went forward because the state of Indiana adopted in 1977 a criminal code provision permitting corporations to be charged with criminal acts. At the time, twenty-two other states allowed as much.

The judge, in refusing to set aside the indictment, agreed with the prosecutor's argument that the charge was based not on the Pinto design fault, but rather on the fact that Ford had permitted the car "to remain on Indiana highways knowing full well its defects."

The case went to trial, a jury trial, and Ford Motor Company was found innocent of the charges. Of course, the increasing number of states that allow corporations to fall under the criminal code is an example of social regulation that could have been avoided had corporations and corporate managers not followed so ardently the Friedman doctrine.

Review Questions

1. Almeder gives some examples of apparently immoral corporate behavior. What are they?

2. Almeder claims that corporate executives attempt to justify their seemingly immoral actions in two ways. What are these ways?

3. How does Almeder attack these two forms of justification?

4. Why does Almeder think that killing an innocent person for money is wrong?

5. How does he reply to the utilitarian who tries to justify such killing?

6. When would it be justified to kill an innocent person in Almeder's view?

7. Almeder charges corporations with killing innocent persons for profit. What examples does he give to support this claim?

8. Explain Almeder's conclusion.

Discussion Questions

1. Do you agree that corporations have acted

immorally in the examples that Almeder gives? Are they guilty of killing innocent people for profit? Explain your position.

2. Does Almeder successfully refute the two conservative arguments or not? Do the conservatives have any reply? Explain your answer.

Problem Cases

1. Air Bags and Automobile Manufacturers Air bags are passive restraints that deploy automatically in a crash. The bags inflate within a few milliseconds of impact, and act as cushions to protect the occupants from crashing against the interior of the automobile. Of course seat belts perform the same function. But the advantage of air bags is that, unlike seat belts, they do not require any active participation by the occupants to be effective, and the percentage of those who wear seat belts in the United States is fairly low.

In the United States about 50,000 people die every year in automobile accidents. The auto industry and the National Highway Traffic Safety Administration basically agree that putting air bags in automobiles would reduce fatalities and injuries in at least some kinds of auto crashes. Yet the auto makers remain firmly opposed to putting air bags in their cars. They consistently cite cost-of-production figures. It would be expensive for auto makers to redesign and retool their cars to make automobile air bags, and auto makers insist that they cannot absorb these costs and remain profitable. If the additional costs are passed onto the consumers, then the auto makers claim that they could not remain competitive with foreign car producers. Furthermore, they assert that the air bags could be a hazard and a potential cause of accidents if they accidently inflate—although there is not enough actual experience with air bags to either confirm or disprove this supposition. The automobile insurance industry, on the other hand, supports air bag regulations because they are convinced that air bags will save lives and reduce health and insurance costs.

Should auto makers be required to put air bags in their cars? What is your position?

2. Marketing Infant Formula Since 1970 Nestle and other companies who market infant formula in third world countries have been the subject of criticism made by various health organizations (e.g., UNICEF and the World Health Organiza-

tion), the popular press, and religious groups. These critics charge that the prepared infant formula sold by these companies in poor third world countries is often improperly used and leads to malnutrition, diarrhea, and death. The women who buy the infant formula often fail to understand the instructions. Since they have inadequate water supplies, they cannot properly clean the bottles and mix them with pure water. The infant formula typically costs from twenty-five to forty-five percent of the family's income; consequently the mothers sometimes overdilute the prepartion to make it go further, and this results in malnutrition, diarrhea, increased susceptibility to disease, and death by starvation. Furthermore, and the most damaging criticism, is that the infant formula is unnecessary. It is universally agreed that from a medical, nutritional, and psychological point of view, breastfeeding by a healthy mother is the superior way to feed infants.

Do Nestle and the other companies have a moral obligation to stop marketing infant formula in third world countries? Why or why not?

3. Listerine Listerine has been marketed since 1879 and is the leading mouthwash in the United States. Listerine's marketshare is about fifty percent. It is the only brand of mouthwash that has kept its medicine-bottle shape. It was advertised as a remedy for colds and sore throats from 1938 to 1972. The label said:

LISTERINE
Antiseptic
Kills Germs
By Millions
On Contact

For Bad Breath, Colds and Resultant Sore Throats
For Colds and Resultant Sore Throats—Gargle with
    Listerine Antiseptic Full Strength at the First Sign of
    Your Cold.

In print advertisements, Listerine's effectiveness as a cold fighter was emphasized:

Colds-catching season is here again! Nothing can cold-proof you—but Listerine Antiseptic gives you a fighting chance! For fewer colds, milder colds, try this:
Get plenty of rest.
Watch your diet.
Gargle twice a day with full-strength Listerine.

The Federal Trade Commission evaluated the label and the advertisements for Listerine and concluded that they deceptively portrayed Listerine as a cure for colds and sore throats. The FTC argued that colds are caused by viruses and not bacteria or germs, that there are no treatments that can cure a cold or shorten its severity, and that catching a cold is not related to diet, rest, or exposure to the elements. The FTC did allow that gargling could relieve symptoms of a cold, but that warm water was just as effective as Listerine for this purpose.

The Warner-Lambert company, producers of Listerine, replied that their position was only that Listerine would help prevent colds and sore throats if used along with proper rest and diet. They denied that they were falsely claiming that Listerine would prevent colds or sore throats by itself.

Is Warner-Lambert guilty of deceptive advertising?

In general, what responsibility for truthfulness does a company have when it advertises? Is deceptive advertising allowable?

4. Polygraph Tests Companies faced with thefts and dishonest employees have resorted to using polygraph tests or lie detector tests to screen employees. For example, the Aldolph Coors Brewery in Golden, Colorado has used these tests to screen job applicants.

Do companies have a right to do this? Why or why not?

Suggested Readings

(1) Arrington, Robert L. "Advertising and Behavior Control." *Journal of Business Ethics* I (1982): 3–12. Arrington discusses questionable advertising techniques such as puffery, indirect information, and subliminal suggestion. He finds that advertising can control behavior, produce compulsive behavior, and create irrational desires.

(2) Beauchamp, Tom L., *Case Studies in Business, Society, and Ethics.* Englewood Cliffs, NJ: Prentice-Hall, Inc., 1983. This book is a collection of interesting case studies of business. Some examples are "The DC–10's Defective Doors," "Procter and Gamble's Rely Tampons," "Dow Chemical Company and Napalm–B," and "The Manufacture and Regulation of Laetrile."

(3) Carr, Albert. "Is Business Bluffing Ethical?" *Harvard Business Review* (Jan.-Feb., 1968): 143–153. Carr defends the use of deception in business as an essential part of the legal pursuit of profits.

(4) Donaldson, Thomas, and Patricia H. Werhane, eds. *Ethical Issues in Business.* Englewood Cliffs, NJ: Prentice-Hall, Inc., 1979. This collection of readings includes articles on profit motive, business and employee rights and obligations, business responsibility and liability with respect to the consumer, and business and environmental issues.

(5) Goldman, Alan H. "Business Ethics: Profits, Utilities, and Moral Rights." *Philospohy & Public Affairs* vol. 9, no. 3 (Spring 1980). Goldman argues that business executives ought to follow the same moral principles as everyone else, and that they cannot defend their actions by claiming that the legal pursuit of profits is a moral end in itself.

(6) Goodpaster, Kenneth E., and John B. Matthews, Jr. "Can a Corporation Have a Conscience?" *Harvard Business Review* (Jan.-Feb., 1982). Goodpaster and Matthews argue that there is an analogy between the individual and the corporation such that corporations can be just as morally responsible as individuals.

(7) Hoffman, W. Michael, and Jennifer Mills Moore, eds. *Business Ethics.* New York: McGraw-Hill Book Co., 1984. This is an excellent anthology covering many different issues in business ethics. There are articles on the nature of the corporation, employee rights and duties, hiring practices such as preferential hiring and reverse discrimination, governmental regulation, the consumer, multinational business, deception, bribery, and anticompetitive behavior.

(8) Hospers, John. *Libertarianism.* Los Angeles: Nash Publishing Co., 1971. Hospers defends the libertarian view that people should be free to pursue profits in a free market system, and that taxation is a violation of a person's rights.

(9) Michalos, Alex C. "Advertising: Its Logic, Ethics, and Economics." In *Informal Logic: The First International Symposium,* edited by J.A. Blair and R.H. Johnson. Pt. Reyes, CA: Edgepress, 1980. Michalos discusses various types of deception in advertising.

(10) Snoeyenbos, Milton, Robert Almeder, and James Humber, eds. *Business Ethics.* Buffalo, NY: Prometheus Books, 1983. This collection has readings on business and social responsibility, employee obligations and rights, trade secrets and patents, ethics and the accounting profession, business and the consumer, business and the environment, and multinational corporations.

Glossary

Eleemosynary nonprofit, and receiving all or a great part of sustaining funds from donations or gifts, charitable, philanthropic.

Effluent liquid discharged as waste.

Ethical nihilism the view that there are no values at all, nothing is really right or wrong, good or bad; or the view that it does not make sense to talk about values.

Ethical relativism the belief that values are relative to either individuals or the standard beliefs of a society. This belief is sometimes expressed by saying, "If I think x is right, then x is right for them," or "If Eskimoes believe it is right to let old people die, then this is right for them." As opposed to ethical objectivism which holds that values are independent of the beliefs of an individual or a society. For example, utilitarianism is an objective ethical theory.

Fiduciary one that holds a relation of trust with another who needs aid or protection (as the trust department of a bank).

Positivism as applied to ethics, logical positivism is a view which holds that ethical statements are meaningless because they are neither true nor false by definition nor susceptible to empirical verification (or falsification).

Rule utilitarian a person who accepts a version of utilitarianism which says that everyone should follow those rules that bring about the greatest good for the greatest number. Usually contrasted with act utilitarianism which holds that everyone ought to do those acts which produce the greatest good for the greatest number.

Chapter 6

Discrimination and Affirmative Action

Introduction

Facts about Discrimination In the last century women were denied many of the legal rights they have today. They could not vote, own property, enter into contracts, serve on juries, or enter certain male-dominated professions. There was also blatant racial discrimination. Blacks were not allowed to vote in some states, they were excluded from union membership, they were denied access to nonmenial jobs, they could not marry whites, they had to sit in certain places on buses and in restaurants, and they received an inferior eduction.

In the late 1960s and early 1970s, two laws were passed that benefited women and minorities to some extent. The Equal Pay Act of 1963 asserted that men and women have to be given equal pay for equal work. Title VII of the Civil Rights Act of 1964 prohibited any discrimination on the basis of race, color, religion, sex, or national origin.

Despite these antidiscrimination laws sexual and racial discrimination continue, although perhaps not as blatantly as before they were enacted. Consider some of the state laws that unfairly discriminate against women: there are laws which permit women to be imprisoned for three years for habitual drunkenness, while for males the penalty for the same offense is thirty days; there are laws which excuse all women from jury duty; laws which permit the withholding of credit from married women on the grounds that they are financially dependent on their husbands; laws which permit the plea of passion killing for wronged husbands but not wronged wives; laws which give the husband right of action in divorce cases of adultery but not the

209

wife; and so on. Why not eliminate these obivously sexist laws? That is one of the goals of the ERA or Equal Rights Amendment which simply states that "equality of rights under the law shall not be denied or abridged by the United States or by any state on account of sex." Yet even though this amendment was proposed by Alice Paul in 1923, and approved by Congress in 1971, it has not been ratified by three-fourths of the state legislatures, and it is now dead.

The evidence for discrimination against women and minorities in employment is enormous and hard to summarize. Nevertheless, it seems clear that women and minorities are at a distinct disadvantage. Let us review a few statistics. (1) At all occupational levels, women make less money than men, even for the same work, and despite the Equal Pay Act of 1963. According to Labor Department statistics from 1979, women's earnings in 1977 were 58.9 percent of men's. That is actually a *drop* of more than 5 percent from what it was in 1955, when women's earnings were 64 percent of men's. (2) According to the United States Census statistics from 1980, the most desirable occupations (management and administration, professions and technical jobs, sales, and crafts) were dominated by whites, while the less desirable jobs (service and farm work) were dominated by blacks, Hispanics, and other ethnic minorities. Women predominated in the poorest-paying jobs: librarians, nurses, elementary teachers, sales clerks, secretaries, bank tellers, and waitresses. At the same time men dominated the best-paying jobs: lawyers, doctors, sales representatives, insurance agents, and so on. (3) In the well-known AT & T case, this enormous company signed a settlement giving tens of millions of dollars to women and minority workers, thus admitting to massive discrimination against women and minorities. (4) Female college professors with identical credentials in terms of publications and experience are promoted at almost exactly one-half the rate of their male counterparts. (4) Eight thousand workers were employed in May, 1967 in the construction of the Bay Area Rapid Transit system, but not one electrician, ironworker, or plumber was black. There is more evidence, but why go on? It seems clear that there is racial and sexual discrimination in employment and pay.

Why is discrimination wrong? Discrimination on the basis of sex or race is not always wrong. It does not seem to matter much that restrooms are segregated by sex, and it does not seem unjust to make a movie about black people in Harlem using only black actors. On the other hand, it does seem unfair to not hire a qualified person as a lawyer just because she is a woman, or to not admit a qualified student to medical school just because he is black.

What is it about racial and sexual discrimination that makes it wrong? The standard view is that sexual and racial discrimination are wrong when race and sex are *irrelevant* to whether a person should be given a job, the vote, higher education, or some other benefit. Qualifications are relevant to getting these benefits, but not race or sex. If a woman or minority person is not allowed to vote just because of their sex or race, then this is wrong—it is wrong because sex and race are irrelevant to voting. But sex is relevant when it comes to maternity leave, and race may be relevant when one is making a movie about black people and their culture.

A theory of justice is used to support this standard view. According to Aristotle, justice requires that equals be treated equally, and that unequals be treated unequally. It must immediately be added that the equality or inequality should be relevant to the treatment in question. When we are concerned with employment, for example, the inequality of the job applications with respect to qualifications is obviously relevant and justifies unequal treatment. In other words, it is not unjust to hire the most qualified candidate. But it is unjust to not hire a qualified person because of race or sex.

However, there are problems with the standard view. One difficulty is that it forbids us to take race or sex into account in employment and admission to school, since in most cases race or sex is irrelevant. But as we shall see, defenders of affirmative action programs which involve preferential treatment or reverse discrimination do want to take race or sex into account when it comes to employment or admission to school. Furthermore, the standard view allows sexual or racial discrimination when sex or race is relevant to the treatment in question, and this seems to allow objectionable racial or sexual discrimination. For example, landlords may refuse to rent apartments to black people because the white tenants will move out. Even though this racial discrimination is in the landlord's self-interest, and thus is not arbitrary, it does not seem to be morally justified. Or consider women in combat. It may be true that, on the average, women are not as strong and aggressive as men, and thus they are not as good in combat as men. So sex does seem relevant when it comes to choosing people for combat duty. Does this mean that sexual discrimination is justified in this case? Again some people want to deny this, but the reason can't be that sex is irrelevant to the treatment in question.

Because of objections like these, Peter Singer (11) rejects the standard view that discrimination is wrong when race and sex are irrelevant. In his view it is wrong when it violates a basic moral principle—the principle of equal consideration of interests. This principle says that in our treatment of people we must give equal consideration to equal interests. Let us apply this principle

to the two problematic cases mentioned in the preceding paragraph. Suppose we have qualified women and men who have an equal interest in combat duty—they want to do this because it is easier to get a promotion in the army if one does combat duty. According to Singer's principle of equality, we must give equal consideration to the interests of both the men and the women; we are not justified in choosing the men and refusing the women. Or suppose we have both a black family and a white family who want to rent an apartment. Since their interest in renting is equal, we must give them equal consideration, and we cannot refuse the black family just because of their race.

In the first reading for this chapter, Richard Wasserstrom (14) agrees with Singer that discrimination is not wrong because it is arbitrary. In his view, racial and sexual discrimination are wrong because they create objectionable institutions, roles, beliefs, and attitudes. Human slavery, for example, is wrong not because of the way people were arbitrarily assigned to be slaves; rather slavery was and is wrong because of the practice itself—the fact that people are owned and have no freedom. Similarly, Wasserstrom says that the traditional female role of serving men is objectionable in itself, and not because women are assigned to play this role rather than men. In Wasserstrom's view, the assignment of any individual to play a role as slave or servant is objectionable because the role is unjustifiable in a decent society.

How can unjust discrimination be corrected? If it is a fact that people have been wrongfully discriminated against in the past, and continue to be discriminated against in the present, then what should we do about it? Is there a way to correct this injustice? Two sorts of solutions have been proposed. Backward-looking solutions to the problem of unjust discrimination seek to compensate groups or individuals who have been unfairly discriminated against in the past. The compensation could take the form of payment, as when, for example, the claim is made that American Indians should be paid for the land and water rights that were taken from them, or it could be in the form of jobs given to women or minorities who could not get them in the past.

Forward-looking solutions try to realize a future society free of discrimination, or at least with reduced discrimination. For example, Richard Wasserstrom advocates an assimilationist ideal where race and sex are no more significant than eye color is in our society. He thinks that this ideal is preferable to nonassimilationist ideals because it provides for more individual autonomy.

Bernard R. Boxill attacks Wasserstrom's assimilationist ideal. He argues that it has unacceptable costs, in particular it requires the elimination of sport and other activities which involve sex-activity correlations, and it removes opportunities to acquire self-esteem. Rather than trying to suppress opportunities, the ideal society, in Boxill's view, should multiply and diversify them, and this means allowing sex-activity correlations.

Affirmative Action As amended by the Equal Employment Opportunity Act of 1972, the Civil Rights Act of 1964 requires businesses that have substantial dealings with the federal government to undertake so-called affirmative-action programs which are supposed to correct imbalances in employment that exist as a result of past discrimination. The programs that have been the focus of most debate are often called "preferential treatment" programs (by those who favor them) or "reverse discrimination" (by those who oppose them). Two sorts of preferential treatment programs are at issue. The first type involves quotas or specific numerical goals; a school or employer will specify some set number or proportion of women or minority applicants who must

be accepted or hired. The second type involves no quota or numerical goal, but requires that women or minorities be given preferential treatment over white men who are equally or even better qualified.

The first type of program has resulted in some landmark lawsuits. One of these, *University of California* v. *Bakke* (1978) went to the Supreme Court, and is described in more detail in the Problem Cases for this chapter. In this case the Court ruled that the Medical School of the University of California at Davis acted illegally in using a specific quota approach, and in refusing to admit Alan Bakke while admitting less qualified minority students. Another famous case is *DeFunis* v. *Odegaard* (1973). In that case, Marco DeFunis, a nonminority applicant, was denied admission to the University of Washington Law School's class of 1971. He filed a suit claiming that he had been treated unfairly insofar as he had been denied admission on the basis of race. Preferential treatment that year was accorded to blacks, American Indians, Chicanos, and Filipinos—thirty-seven of these minority applicants were accepted, and eighteen actually enrolled. The Law School Admission Test scores and projected grade point averages of almost all these minority students were lower than those of some of the rejected nonminority students. The Supreme Court of the state of Washington ruled against DeFunis. The court argued that racial classifications are not unconstitutional, that their use is acceptable if there is a compelling state interest, and that the shortage of minority attorneys constituted a compelling state interest. The case was appealed to the United States Supreme Court, but the Court did not hand down a ruling. DeFunis had been attending law school while the case was being appealed; consequently the case was declared moot.

The unequal treatment given Bakke and DeFunis is sometimes called *reverse discrimination,* usually by those who disapprove of it. This label describes actions or practices that discriminate against an individual or a group on the basis of some characteristic that is usually considered to be irrelevant, such as race. One common objection is that it is inconsistent. If discrimination is wrong, then reverse discrimination cannot be right. As Lisa Newton puts it, "All discrimination is wrong *prima facie* because it violates justice, and that goes for reverse discrimination too." In her view, discrimination is unjust if it involves unequal treatment when citizens ought to have equal treatment under the law, and this applies to reverse discrimination as well as ordinary discrimination. Besides the charge of inconsistency, Newton raises various practical problems for reverse discrimination. For example, how much reverse discrimination will compensate those who have been discriminated against?

By contrast, Richard Wasserstrom offers a limited defense of programs which have quotas for the admission of minority students, such as those used by the University of California at Davis and the University of Washington. First, he replies to those who charge that such programs are inconsistent because they now offer preferential treatment that was considered wrong in the past. He claims that the social realities of distribution of resources and opportunities make the present preferential treatment programs very different from quota systems in the past. Second, he makes several points in reply to the charge that such programs unjustifiably ignore individual qualifications: qualifications are not connected to social effectiveness, the most qualified don't deserve benefits, and the programs require at least some minimal set of qualifications for admission.

The defense of Wasserstrom is *forward-looking* because the basic idea seems to be that preferential treatment at the present time will help reduce discrimination in the future. The other main type of defense is *backward-looking* because it rests on the claim that women or minorities deserve to be compensated for past unjust discrimination. For example, Mary Anne Warren, in our readings, gives a backward-looking defense when she argues that preferential treatment of women in the form of numerical quotas for hiring and promotion are justified to compensate women for past and ongoing discriminatory practices that have put women at a disadvantage.

Richard Wasserstrom

Racism and Sexism

Richard Wasserstrom is professor of philosophy at the University of California at Santa Cruz. He is

From Richard A. Wasserstrom, "Racism and Sexism," in R.A. Wasserstrom, *Today's Moral Problems,* 2d ed. (New York: Macmillan Publishing Co., 1979) pp. 75–105. Reprinted with permission of the author. [Some of the footnotes have been renumbered.–Ed.]

editor of Today's Moral Problems *(3d ed., 1985), and author of* Philosophy and Social Issues: Five Studies *(1980).*

Wasserstrom begins by distinguishing between four different questions, or domains of inquiry, which he thinks should be separated in order to avoid confusion about racism and sexism. These four are the question of social realities, the question of explanation, the question of ideals, and the question of instrumentalities. He is mainly concerned with answering the first and third questions in the following essay. After describing the social reality of racism and sexism, he turns to the third question, the one con-

*cerning what an ideal nonracist and nonsexist society would be like. He discusses three possible ideals. In the assimilationist ideal, the one that Wasserstrom finds to be best, race and sex would be no more important than eye color is in our present society. Both the ideal of diversity and the ideal of tolerance (the second and third possible ideals) make race and sex like religious identity. In the ideal of diversity, a plurality of races and sexes is considered to be desirable, just as religious **heterodoxy** can be viewed as desirable. By contrast, the ideal of tolerance considers a diversity of races and sexes to be an undesirable but necessary evil, just as religious heterodoxy is tolerated as a necessary evil. After examining and rejecting some objections to the assimilationist ideal, Wasserstrom concludes that it is the best because it provides for a kind of individual autonomy that cannot be found in a nonassimilationist society.*

INTRODUCTION

Racism and sexism are two central issues that engage the attention of many persons living within the United States today. But while there is relatively little disagreement about their importance as topics, there is substantial, vehement, and apparently intractable disagreement about what individuals, practices, ideas, and institutions are either racist or sexist—and for what reasons. In dispute are a number of related questions concerning how individuals ought to regard and respond to matters relating to race or sex.

There are, I think, a number of important similarities between issues of racism and issues of sexism, but there are also some significant differences. More specifically, while the same general method of analysis can usefully be employed to examine a number of the issues that arise in respect to either, the particular topics of controversy often turn out to be rather different. What I want to do in this essay is first propose a general way of looking at issues of racism and sexism, then look at several of the respects in which racism and sexism are alike and different, and then, finally, examine one somewhat neglected but fundamental issue; namely that of what a genuinely nonracist or nonsexist society might

look like.

There are, I think, at least four questions that anyone interested in issues of racism and sexism ought to see as both distinct and worth asking. The first is what I call the question of the social realities. That question is concerned with rendering a correct description of the existing social arrangements, including the existing institutional structures, practices, attitudes and **ideology.** The second is devoted to the question of explanation. Given a correct understanding of what the existing social reality is, there can be a variety of theories to explain how things got that way and by what mechanisms they tend to be perpetuated. Much of the feminist literature, for example, is concerned with the problem of explanation. Complex and sophisticated accounts have been developed which utilize the theories of Freud, Levi-Strauss, and Marx to explain the oppression of women. Other, equally complex accounts have insisted on the nonreductionist character of the nature and causes of the present sexual arrangements. Although important in their own right, as well as for the solution of other problems, I will have virtually nothing else to say about these explanatory issues in this essay.

The third question, and one that I will concentrate upon, is what I term the question of ideals. I see it as concerned with asking: If we had the good society, if we could change the social reality so that it conformed to some vision of what a nonracist or nonsexist society would be like, what would that society's institutions, practices, and ideology be in respect to matters of racial or sexual differentiation? Here, what I find especially interesting, is the question of whether anything like the ideal that is commonly accepted as a very plausible one for a nonracist society can be as plausibly proposed for a conception of a nonsexist society.

The fourth and final question is that of instrumentalities. Once one has developed the correct account of the social realities, and the most defensible conception of what the good society would look like, and the most comprehensive theory of how the social realities came about and are maintained, then the remaining question is the instrumental one of social change: How, given all of this, does one most effectively and fairly move from the social realities to a closer approximation of the ideal. This, too, is a question with which I will not be concerned in what follows, although it is, for instance, within this context and this perspective that, it seems to me, all of the significant questions concerning the justifiability of programs of preferential treatment arise. That is to say, the way to decide whether such programs are justifiable is to determine whether they are appropriate means by which to bring about a particular, independently justifiable end.

These, then, are four central questions which any inquiry into sexism, racism or any other comparable phenomenon must distinguish and examine. I turn first to an examination of this question of the social realities and then to a consideration of ideals and the nature of a nonracist or a nonsexist society.

SOCIAL REALITIES

A. The Position of Blacks and Women

Methodologically, the first thing it is important to note is that to talk about social realities is to talk about a particular social and cultural context. And in our particular social and cultural context race and sex are socially very important categories. They are so in virtue of the fact that we live in a culture which has, throughout its existence, made race and sex extremely important characteristics of and for all the people living in the culture.[1]

It is surely possible to imagine a culture in which race would be an unimportant, insignificant characteristic of individuals. In such a culture race would be largely if not exclusively a matter of superficial physiology; a matter, we might say, simply of the way one looked. And if it were, then any analysis of race and racism would necessarily assume very differ-ent dimensions from what they do in our society. In such a culture, the meaning of the term "race" would itself have to change substantially. This can be seen by the fact that in such a culture it would literally make no sense to say of a person that he or she was "passing."[2] This is something that can be said and understood in our own culture and it shows at least that to talk of race is to talk of more than the way one looks.[3]

Sometimes when people talk about what is wrong with affirmative action programs, or programs of preferential hiring, they say that what is wrong with such programs is that they take a thing as superficial as an individual's race and turn it into something important.[4] They say that a person's race doesn't matter; other things do, such as qualifications. Whatever else may be said of statements such as these, as descriptions of the social realities they seem to be simply false. One complex but true empirical fact about our society is that the race of an individual is much more than a fact of superficial physiology. It is, instead, one of the dominant characteristics that affects both the way the individual looks at the world and the way the world looks at the individual. As I have said, that need not be the case. It may in fact be very important that we work toward a society in which that would not be the case, but it is the case now and it must be understood in any adequate and complete discussion of racism. That is why, too, it does not make much sense when people sometimes say, in talking about the fact that they are not racists, that they would not care if an individual were green and came from Mars, they would treat that individual the same way they treat people exactly like themselves. For part of *our* social and cultural history is to treat people of certain races in a certain way, and we do not have a social or cultural history of treating green people from Mars in any particular way. To put it simply, it is to misunderstand the social realities of race and racism to think of them simply as questions of how some people respond to other people whose skins are of different hues, irrespective of the social context.

I can put the point another way: Race does not function in our culture as does eye color. Eye color is an irrelevant category; nobody cares what color people's eyes are; it is not an important cultural fact; nothing turns on what eye color you have. It is important to see that race is not like that at all. And this truth affects what will and will not count as cases of racism. In our culture to be non-white—especially to be black [5]—is to be treated and seen to be a member of a group that is different from and inferior to the group of standard, fully developed persons, the adult white males. To be black is to be a member of what was a despised minority and what is still a disliked and oppressed one.[6] That is simply part of the awful truth of our cultural and social history, and a significant feature of the social reality of our culture today.

We can see fairly easily that the two sexual categories, like the racial ones, are themselves in important respects products of the society. Like one's race, one's sex is not merely or even primarily a matter of physiology. To see this we need only realize that we can understand the idea of a transsexual. A transsexual is someone who would describe himself or herself as a person who is essentially a female but through some accident of nature is trapped in a male body, or a person who is essentially a male but through some accident of nature is trapped in the body of a female. His (or her) description is some kind of a shorthand way of saying that he (or she) is more comfortable with the role allocated by the culture to people who are physiologically of the opposite sex. The fact that we regard this assertion of the transsexual as intelligible seems to me to show how deep the notion of sexual identity is in our culture and how little it has to do with physiological differences between males and females. Because people do pass in the context of race and because we can understand what passing means; because people are transsexuals and because we can understand what transsexuality means, we can see that the existing social

categories of both race and sex are in this sense creations of the culture.

It is even clearer in the case of sex than in the case of race that one's sexual identity is a centrally important, crucially relevant category within our culture. I think, in fact, that it is more important and more fundamental than one's race. It is evident that there are substantially different role expectations and role assignments to persons in accordance with their sexual physiology, and that the positions of the two sexes in the culture are distinct. We do have a **patriarchal** society in which it matters enormously whether one is a male or a female.[7] By almost all important measures it is more advantageous to be a male rather than a female.

Women and men are socialized differently. We learn very early and forcefully that we are either males or females and that much turns upon which sex we are. The evidence seems to be overwhelming and well-documented that sex roles play a fundamental role in the way persons think of themselves and the world—to say nothing of the way the world thinks of them.[8] Men and women are taught to see men as independent, capable, and powerful; men and women are taught to see women as dependent, limited in abilities, and passive. A woman's success or failure in life is defined largely in terms of her activities within the family. It is important for her that she marry, and when she does she is expected to take responsibility for the wifely tasks: the housework, the child care, and the general emotional welfare of the husband and children.[9] Her status in society is determined in substantial measure by the vocation and success of her husband.[10] Economically, women are substantially worse off than men. They do not receive any pay for the work that is done in the home. As members of the labor force their wages are significantly lower than those paid to men, even when they are engaged in similar work and have similar educational backgrounds.[11] The higher the prestige or the salary of the job, the less present women are in the labor force. And, of course, women are conspicuously absent from most positions of authority and power in the major economic and political institutions of our society.

As is true for race, it is also a significant social fact that to be a female is to be an entity or creature viewed as different from the standard, fully developed person who is male as well as white. But to be female, as opposed to being black, is not to be conceived of as simply a creature of less worth. That is one important thing that differentiates sexism from racism: The ideology of sex, as opposed to the ideology of race, is a good deal more complex and confusing. Women are both put on a pedestal and deemed not fully developed persons. They are idealized; their approval and admiration is sought; and they are at the same time regarded as less competent than men and less able to live fully developed, fully human lives—for that is what men do.[12] At best, they are viewed and treated as having properties and attributes that are valuable and admirable for humans of this type. For example, they may be viewed as especially empathetic, intuitive, loving, and nurturing. At best, these qualities are viewed as good properties for women to have, and, provided they are properly muted, are sometimes valued within the more well-rounded male. Because the sexual ideology is complex, confusing, and variable, it does not unambiguously proclaim the lesser value attached to being female rather than being male, nor does it unambiguously correspond to the existing social realities. For these, among other reasons, sexism could plausibly be regarded as a deeper phenomenon than racism. It is more deeply embedded in the culture, and thus less visible. Being harder to detect, it is harder to eradicate. Moreover, it is less unequivocally regarded as unjust and unjustifiable. That is to say, there is less agreement within the dominant ideology that sexism even implies an unjustifiable practice or attitude. Hence, many persons announce, without regret or embarrassment, that they are sexists or male chauvinists; very few announce openly that they are racists.[13] For all of these reasons sexism may be a more insidious evil than racism, but there is little merit in trying to decide between two seriously objectionable practices which one is worse.

While I do not think that I have made very controversial claims about either our cultural history or our present-day culture, I am aware of the fact that they have been stated very imprecisely and that I have offered little evidence to substantiate them. In a crude way we ought to be able both to understand the claims and to see that they are correct if we reflect seriously and critically upon our own cultural institutions, attitudes, and practices. But in a more refined, theoretical way, I am imagining that a more precise and correct description of the social reality in respect to race and sex would be derivable from a composite, descriptive account of our society which utilized the relevant social sciences to examine such things as the society's institutions, practices, attitudes and ideology[14]—if the social sciences could be value-free and unaffected in outlook or approach by the fact that they, themselves, are largely composed of persons who are white and male.[15]

Viewed from the perspective of social reality it should be clear, too, that racism and sexism should not be thought of as phenomena that consist simply in taking a person's race or sex into account, or even simply in taking a person's race or sex into account in an arbitrary way. Instead, racism and sexism consist in taking race and sex into account in a certain way, in the context of a specific set of institutional arrangements and a specific ideology which together create and maintain a specific *system* of institutions, role assignments, beliefs and attitudes. That system is one, and has been one, in which political, economic, and social power and advantage is concentrated in the hands of those who are white and male.

The evils of such systems are, however, not all of a piece. For instance, sometimes people say that what was wrong with the system of racial discrimination in the South was that it took an irrelevant characteristic, namely race, and used it systematically to allocate social benefits and burdens of various sorts. The defect was the irrelevance of the characteristic used, i.e., race, for that meant that individuals ended up being treated in a manner that was arbitrary and capricious.

I do not think that was the central flaw at all—at least of much of the system. Take, for instance, the most hideous of the practices, human slavery. The primary thing that was wrong with the institution was not that the particular individuals who were assigned the place of slaves were assigned there arbitrarily because the assignment was made in virtue of an irrelevant characteristic, i.e., their race. Rather, it seems to me clear that the primary thing that was and is wrong with slavery is the practice itself—the fact of some individuals being able to own other individuals and all that goes with that practice. It would not matter by what criterion individuals were assigned; human slavery would still be wrong. And the same can be said for many of the other discrete practices and institutions that comprised the system of racial discrimination even after human slavery was abolished. The practices were unjustifiable—they were oppressive—and they would have been so no matter how the assignment of victims had been made. What made it worse, still, was that the institutions and ideology all interlocked to create a system of human oppression whose effects on those living under it were as devastating as they were unjustifiable.

Some features of the system of sexual oppression are like this and others are different. For example, if it is true that women are socialized to play the role of servers of men and if they are in general assigned that position in the society, what is objectionable about that practice is the practice itself. It is not that women are being arbitrarily or capriciously assigned the social role of server, but rather that such a role is at least *prima facie* unjustifiable as a role in a decent society. As a result, the assignment on any basis of individuals to such a role is objectionable.

The assignment of women to primary responsibility for child rearing and household maintenance may be different; it may be objectionable on grounds of unfairness of another sort. That is to say, if we assume that these are important but undesirable aspects of social existence—if we assume that they are, relatively speaking, unsatisfying and unfulfilling ways to spend one's time, then the objection is that women are unduly and unfairly allocated a disproportionate share of unpleasant, unrewarding work. Here the objection, if it is proper, is to the degree to which the necessary burden is placed to a greater degree than is fair on women, rather than shared equally by persons of both sexes.

Even here, though, it is important to see that the essential feature of both racism and sexism consists in the fact that race or sex is taken into account in the context of a specific set of arrangements and a specific ideology which is systemic and which treats and regards persons who are nonwhite or female in a comprehensive, systemic way. Whether it would be capricious to take either a person's race or a person's sex into account in the good society, because race and sex were genuinely irrelevant characteristics is a question that can only be answered after we have a clearer idea of what the good society would look like in respect either to race or sex....

IDEALS

The second perspective, described at the outset, which is also important for an understanding and analysis of racism and sexism, is the perspective of the ideal. Just as we can and must ask what is involved today in our culture in being of one race or of one sex rather than the other, and how individuals are in fact viewed and treated, we can also ask different questions: namely, what would the good or just society make of race and sex, and to what degree, if at all, would racial and sexual distinctions ever be taken into account? Indeed, it could plausibly be argued that we could not have an adequate idea of whether a society was racist or sexist unless we had some conception of what a thoroughly nonracist or nonsexist society would look like. This perspective is an extremely instructive as well as an often neglected one. Comparatively little theoretical literature that deals with either racism or sexism has concerned itself in a systematic way with this perspective.

In order to ask more precisely what some of the possible ideals are of desirable racial or sexual differentiation, it is necessary to see that we must ask: "In respect to what?" And one way to do this is to distinguish in a crude way among three levels or areas of social and political arrangements and activities. These correspond very roughly to the matters of status, role, and temperament identified earlier. First, there is the area of basic political rights and obligations, including the rights to vote and to travel, and the obligation to pay income taxes. Second, there is the area of important, nongovernmental institutional benefits and burdens. Examples are access to and employment in the significant economic markets, the opportunity to acquire and enjoy housing in the setting of one's choice, the right of persons who want to marry each other to do so, and the duties (nonlegal as well as legal) that persons acquire in getting married. And third, there is the area of individual, social interaction, including such matters as whom one will have as friends, and what aesthetic preferences one will cultivate and enjoy.

As to each of these three areas we can ask, for example, whether in a nonracist society it would be thought appropriate ever to take the race of the individuals into account. Thus, one picture of a nonracist society is that which is captured by what I call the assimilationist ideal: a nonracist society would be one in which the race of an individual would be the functional equivalent of the eye color of individuals in our society today.[16] In our society no basic political rights and obligations are determined on the basis of eye color. No important institutional benefits and burdens are connected with eye color. In-

deed, except for the mildest sort of aesthetic preferences, a person would be thought odd who even made private, social decisions by taking eye color into account. And for reasons that we could fairly readily state we could explain why it would be wrong to permit anything but the mildest, most trivial aesthetic preference to turn on eye color. The reasons would concern the irrelevance of eye color for any political or social institution, practice or arrangement. According to the assimilationist ideal, a nonracist society would be one in which an individual's race was of no more significance in any of these three areas than is eye color today.

The assimilationist ideal in respect to sex does not seem to be as readily plausible and obviously attractive here as it is in the case of race. In fact, many persons invoke the possible realization of the assimilationist ideal as a reason for rejecting the Equal Rights Amendment and indeed the idea of women's liberation itself. My own view is that the assimilationist ideal may be just as good and just as important an ideal in respect to sex as it is in respect to race. But many persons think there are good reasons why an assimilationist society in respect to sex would not be desirable.

To be sure, to make the assimilationist ideal a reality in respect to sex would involve more profound and fundamental revisions of our institutions and our attitudes than would be the case in respect to race. On the institutional level we would have to alter radically our practices concerning the family and marriage. If a nonsexist society is a society in which one's sex is no more significant than eye color in our society today, then laws that require the persons who are getting married to be of different sexes would clearly be sexist laws.

And on the attitudinal and conceptual level, the assimilationist ideal would require the eradication of all sex-role differentiation. It would never teach about the inevitable or essential attributes of masculinity or feminity; it would never encourage or discourage the ideas of sisterhood or brotherhood; and it would be unintelligible to talk about the virtues as well as disabilities of being a woman or a man. Were sex like eye color, these things would make no sense. Just as the normal, typical adult is virtually oblivious to the eye color of other persons for all major interpersonal relationships, so the normal, typical adult in this kind of nonsexist society would be indifferent to the sexual, physiological differences of other persons for all interpersonal relationships.

To acknowledge that things would be very different is, of course, hardly to concede that they would be undesirable. But still, perhaps the problem is with the assimilationist ideal. And the assimilationist ideal is certainly not the only possible, plausible ideal.

There are, for instance, two others that are closely related, but distinguishable. One I call the ideal of diversity; the other, the ideal of tolerance. Both can be understood by considering how religion, rather than eye color, tends to be thought about in our culture. According to the ideal of diversity, heterodoxy in respect to religious belief and practice is regarded as a positive good. On this view there would be a loss—it would be a worse society—were everyone to be a member of the same religion. According to the other view, the ideal of tolerance, heterodoxy in respect to religious belief and practice would be seen more as a necessary, lesser evil. On this view there is nothing intrinsically better about diversity in respect to religion, but the evils of achieving anything like homogeneity far outweigh the possible benefits.

Now, whatever differences there might be between the ideals of diversity and tolerance, the similarities are more striking. Under neither ideal would it be thought that the allocation of basic political rights and duties should take an individual's religion into account. And we would want equalitarianism even in respect to most important institutional benefits and burdens—for example, access to employment in the desirable vocations. Nonetheless, on both views it would be deemed appropriate to have some institu-

tions (typically those that are connected in an intimate way with these religions) that do in a variety of ways take the religion of members of the society into account. For example, it might be thought permissible and appropriate for members of a religious group to join together in collective associations which have religious, educational and social dimensions. And on the individual, interpersonal level, it might be thought unobjectionable, or on the diversity view, even admirable, were persons to select their associates, friends, and mates on the basis of their religious orientation. So there are two possible and plausible ideals of what the good society would look like in respect to religion in which religious differences would be to some degree maintained because the diversity of religions was seen either as an admirable, valuable feature of the society, or as one to be tolerated. The picture is a more complex, less easily describable one than that of the assimilationist ideal.

It may be that in respect to sex (and conceivably, even in respect to race) something more like either of these ideals in respect to religion is the right one. But one problem then—and it is a very substantial one—is to specify with a good deal of precision and care what that ideal really comes to. Which legal, institutional and personal differentiations are permissible and which are not? Which attitudes and beliefs concerning sexual identification and differences are properly introduced and maintained and which are not? Part, but by no means all, of the attractiveness of the assimilationist ideal is its clarity and simplicity. In the good society of the assimilationist sort we would be able to tell easily and unequivocally whether any law, practice, or attitude was in any respect either racist or sexist. Part, but by no means all, of the unattractiveness of any pluralistic ideal is that it makes the question of what is racist or sexist a much more difficult and complicated one to answer. But although simplicity and lack of ambiguity may be virtues, they are not the only virtues to be taken into account in deciding among competing ideals. We quite appropriately take other considerations to be relevant to an assessment of the value and worth of alternative nonracist and nonsexist societies.

Nor do I even mean to suggest that all persons who reject the assimilationist ideal in respect to sex would necessarily embrace either something like the ideal of tolerance or the ideal of diversity. Some persons might think the right ideal was one in which substantially greater sexual differentiation and sex-role identification was retained than would be the case under either of these conceptions. Thus, someone might believe that the good society was, perhaps, essentially like the one they think we now have in respect to sex: equality of political rights, such as the right to vote, but all of the sexual differentiation in both legal and nonlegal institutions that is characteristic of the way in which our society has been and still is ordered. And someone might also believe that the usual ideological justifications for these arrangements are the correct and appropriate ones.

This could, of course, be regarded as a version of the ideal of diversity, with the emphasis upon the extensive character of the institutional and personal difference connected with sexual identity. Whether it is a kind of ideal of diversity or a different ideal altogether turns, I think, upon two things: First, however pervasive the sexual differentiation is, second, whether the ideal contains a conception of the appropriateness of significant institutional and interpersonal inequality, e.g., that the woman's job is in large measure to serve and be dominated by the male. The more this latter feature is present, the clearer the case for regarding this as ideal, distinctively different from any of those described by me so far.

The next question, of course, is that of how a choice is rationally to be made among these different, possible ideals. One place to begin is with the empirical world. For the question of whether something is a plausible and attractive ideal does turn in part on the nature of the empirical world. If it is true, for example, that any particular characteristic, such as sex, is not only a socially significant category in our culture but that it is largely a socially created one as well, then many ostensible objections to the assimilationist ideal appear immediately to disappear.

What I mean is this: It is obvious that we could formulate and use some sort of a crude, incredibly imprecise physiological concept of race. In this sense we could even say that race is a naturally occurring rather than a socially created feature of the world. There are diverse skin colors and related physiological characteristics distributed among human beings. But the fact is that except for skin hue and the related physiological characteristics, race is a socially created category. And skin hue, as I have shown, is neither a necessary nor a sufficient condition for being classified as black in our culture. Race as a naturally occurring characteristic is also a socially irrelevant category. There do not in fact appear to be any characteristics that are part of this natural concept of race and that are in any plausible way even relevant to the appropriate distribution of any political, institutional, or interpersonal concerns in the good society. Because in this sense race is like eye color, there is no plausible case to be made on this ground against the assimilationist ideal.[17]

There is, of course, the social reality of race. In creating and tolerating a society in which race matters, we must recognize that we have created a vastly more complex concept of race which includes what might be called the idea of ethnicity as well—a set of attitudes, traditions, beliefs, etc., which the society has made part of what it means to be of a race. It may be, therefore, that one could argue that a form of the pluralist ideal ought to be preserved in respect to race, in the socially created sense, for reasons similar to those that might be offered in support of the desirability of some version of the pluralist ideal in respect to religion. As I have indicated, I am skeptical, but for the purposes of this essay it can well be left an open question.

Despite appearances, the case of sex is more like that of race than is often thought. What opponents of assimilationism seize upon is that sexual difference appears to be a naturally occurring category of obvious and inevitable social relevance in a way, or to a degree, which race is not. The problems with this way of thinking are twofold. To begin with, an analysis of the social realities reveals that it is the socially created sexual differences which tend in fact to matter the most. It is sex-role differentiation, not gender per se,[18] that makes men and women as different as they are from each other, and it is sex-role differences which are invoked to justify most sexual differentiation at any of the levels of society.[19]

More importantly, even if naturally occurring sexual differences were of such a nature that they were of obvious *prima facie* social relevance, this would by no means settle the question of whether in the good society sex should or should not be as minimally significant as eye color. Even though there are biological differences between men and women in nature, this fact does not determine the question of what the good society can and should make of these differences. I have difficulty understanding why so many persons seem to think that it does settle the question adversely to anything like the assimilationist ideal. They might think it does settle the question for two different reasons. In the first place, they might think the differences are of such a character that they substantially affect what would be possible within a good society of human persons. Just as the fact that humans are mortal necessarily limits the features of any possible good society, so, they might argue, the fact that males and females are physiologically different limits the features of any possible good society.

In the second place, they might think the differences are of such a character that they are relevant to the question of what would be desirable in the good society. That is to say, they might not think that the differences *determine* to a substantial degree what is possible,

but that the differences ought to be taken into account in any rational construction of an ideal social existence.

The second reason seems to me to be a good deal more plausible than the first. For there appear to be very few, if any, respects in which the ineradicable, naturally occurring differences between males and females *must* be taken into account. The industrial revolution has certainly made any of the general differences in strength between the sexes capable of being ignored by the good society in virtually all activities.[20] And it is sex-role acculturation, not biology, that mistakenly leads many persons to the view that women are both naturally and necessarily better suited than men to be assigned the primary responsibilities of child rearing. Indeed, the only fact that seems required to be taken into account is the fact that reproduction of the human species requires that the fetus develop *in utero* for a period of months. Sexual intercourse is not necessary, for artificial insemination is available. Neither marriage nor the family is required for conception or child rearing. Given the present state of medical knowledge and the natural realities of female pregnancy, it is difficult to see why any important institutional or interpersonal arrangements *must* take the existing gender difference of *in utero* pregnancy into account.

But, as I have said, this is still to leave it a wholly open question to what degree the good society *ought* to build upon any ineradicable gender differences to construct institutions which would maintain a substantial degree of sexual differentiation. The arguments are typically far less persuasive for doing so than appears upon the initial statement of this possibility. Someone might argue that the fact of menstruation, for instance, could be used as a premise upon which to predicate different social roles for females than for males. But this could only plausibly be proposed if two things were true: first, that menstruation would be debilitating to women and hence relevant to social role even in a culture which did not teach women to view menstruation as a sign of uncleanliness or as a curse;[21] and second, that the way in which menstruation necessarily affected some or all women was in fact related in an important way to the role in question. But even if both of these were true, it would still be an open question whether any sexual differentiation ought to be built upon these facts. The society could still elect to develop institutions that would nullify the effect of the natural differences. And suppose, for example, what seems implausible—that some or all women will not be able to perform a particular task while menstruating, *e.g.,* guard a border. It would be easy enough, if the society wanted to, to arrange for substitute guards for the women who were incapacitated. We know that persons are not good guards when they are sleepy, and we make arrangements so that persons alternate guard duty to avoid fatigue. The same could be done for menstruating women, even given these implausibly strong assumptions about menstruation. At the risk of belaboring the obvious, what I think it important to see is that the case against the assimilationist ideal—if it is to be a good one—must rest on arguments concerned to show why some other ideal would be preferable; it cannot plausibly rest on the claim that it is either necessary or inevitable.

There is, however, at least one more argument based upon nature, or at least the "natural," that is worth mentioning. Someone might argue that significant sex-role differentiation is natural not in the sense that it is biologically determined but only in the sense that it is a virtually universal phenomenon in human culture. By itself, this claim of virtual universality, even if accurate, does not directly establish anything about the desirability or undesirability of any particular ideal. But it can be made into an argument by the addition of the proposition that where there is a virtually universal social practice, there is probably some good or important purpose served by the practice. Hence, given the fact of sex-role differentiation in all, or almost all, cultures, we have some reason to think that substantial sex-role differentiation serves some important purpose for and in human society.

This is an argument, but I see no reason to be impressed by it. The premise which turns the fact of sex-role differentiation into any kind of a strong reason for sex-role differentiation is the premise of conservatism. And it is no more convincing here than elsewhere. There are any number of practices that are typical and yet upon reflection seem without significant social purpose. Slavery was once such a practice; war perhaps, still is.

More to the point, perhaps, the concept of "purpose" is ambiguous. It can mean in a descriptive sense "plays some role" or "is causally relevant." Or it can mean in a prescriptive sense "does something desirable" or "has some useful function." If "purpose" is used descriptively in the conservative premise, then the argument says nothing about the continued desirability of sex-role differentiation or the assimilationist ideal. If "purpose" is used prescriptively in the conservative premise, then there is no reason to think that premise is true.

To put it another way, the question is whether it is desirable to have a society in which sex-role differences are to be retained at all. The straight-forward way to think about that question is to ask what would be good and what would be bad about a society in which sex functioned like eye color does in our society. We can imagine what such a society would look like and how it would work. It is hard to see how our thinking is substantially advanced by reference to what has typically or always been the case. If it is true, as I think it is, that the sex-role differentiated societies we have had so far have tended to concentrate power in the hands of males, have developed institutions and ideologies that have perpetuated that concentration and have restricted and prevented women from living the kinds of lives that persons ought to be able to live for themselves, then this says far more about what may be wrong with any nonassimilationist ideal than does the conservative premise say what may be right about any nonassimilationist ideal.

Nor is this all that can be said in favor of the assimilationist ideal. For it seems to me that the strongest affirmative moral argument on its behalf is that it provides for a kind of individual autonomy that a nonassimilationist society cannot attain. Any nonassimilationist society will have sex roles. Any nonassimilationist society will have some institutions that distinguish between individuals in virtue of their gender, and any such society will necessarily teach the desirability of doing so. Any substantially nonassimilationist society will make one's sexual identity an important characteristic, so that there are substantial psychological, role, and status differences between persons who are males and those who are females. Even if these could be attained without systemic dominance of one sex over the other, they would, I think, be objectionable on the ground that they necessarily impaired an individual's ability to develop his or her own characteristics, talents and capacities to the fullest extent to which he or she might desire. Sex roles, and all that accompany them, necessarily impose limits—restrictions on what one can do, be or become. As such, they are, I think, at least *prima facie* wrong.

To some degree, all role-differentiated living is restrictive in this sense. Perhaps, therefore, all role-differentiation in society is to some degree troublesome, and perhaps all strongly role-differentiated societies are objectionable. But the case against sexual differentiation need not rest upon this more controversial point. For one thing that distinguishes sex roles from many other roles is that they are wholly involuntarily assumed. One has no choice whatsoever about whether one shall be born a male or female. And if it is a consequence of one's being born a male or a female that one's subsequent emotional, intellectual, and material development will be substantially controlled by this fact, then substantial, permanent, and involuntarily assumed restraints have been imposed on the most central factors concerning the way one

will shape and live one's life. The point to be emphasized is that this would necessarily be the case, even in the unlikely event that substantial sexual differentiation could be maintained without one sex or the other becoming dominant and developing institutions and an ideology to support that dominance.

I do not believe that all I have said in this section shows in any conclusive fashion the desirability of the assimilationist ideal in respect to sex. I have tried to show why some typical arguments against the assimilationist ideal are not persuasive,[22] and why some of the central ones in support of that ideal are persuasive. But I have not provided a complete account, or a complete analysis. At a minimum, what I have shown is how thinking about this topic ought to proceed, and what kinds of arguments need to be marshalled and considered before a serious and informed discussion of alternative conceptions of a nonsexist society can even take place. Once assembled, these arguments need to be individually and carefully assessed before any final, reflective choice among the competing ideals can be made. There does, however, seem to me to be a strong presumptive case for something very close to, if not identical with, the assimilationist ideal.

Footnotes

1. In asserting the importance of one's race and sex in our culture I do not mean to deny the importance of other characteristics—in particular, socioeconomic class. I do think that in our culture race and sex are two very important facts about a person, and I am skeptical of theories which "reduce" the importance of these features to a single, more basic one, *e.g.,* class. But apart from this one bit of skepticism I think that all of what I have to say is compatible with several different theories concerning why race and sex are so important—including, for instance, most versions of Marxism. *See, e.g.,* the account provided in J. Mitchell, *Woman's Estate* (1971). The correct causal explanation for the social realities I describe is certainly an important question, both in its own right and for some of the issues I address. It is particularly significant for the issue of how to alter the social realities to bring them closer to the ideal. Nonetheless, I have limited the scope of my inquiry to exclude a consideration of this large, difficult topic.

2. Passing is the phenomenon in which a person who in some sense knows himself or herself to be black "passes" as white because he or she looks white. A version of this is described in Sinclair Lewis' novel *Kingsblood Royal* (1947), where the protagonist discovers when he is an adult that he, his father, and his father's mother are black (or, in the idiom of the late 1940s, Negro) in virtue of the fact that his great grandfather was black. His grandmother knew this and was consciously passing. When he learns about his ancestry, one decision he has to make is whether to continue to pass, or to acknowledge to the world that he is in fact "Negro."

3. That looking black is not in our culture a necessary condition for being black can be seen from the phenomenon of passing. That it is not a sufficient condition can be seen from the book *Black Like Me* (1960), by John Howard Griffin, where "looking black" is easily understood by the reader to be different from being black. I suspect that the concept of being black is, in our culture, one which combines both physiological and ancestral criteria in some moderately complex fashion.

4. Mr. Justice Douglas suggests something like this in his dissent in *DeFunis:* "The consideration of race as a measure of an applicant's qualification normally introduces a capricious and irrelevant factor working an invidious discrimination." *DeFunis* v. *Odegaard,* 416 U.S. 312, 333 (1974).

5. There are significant respects in which the important racial distinction is between being white and being nonwhite, and there are other significant respects in which the fact of being black has its own special meaning and importance. My analysis is conducted largely in terms of what is involved in being black. To a considerable extent, however, what I say directly applies to the more inclusive category of being nonwhite. To the extent to which what I say does not apply to the other nonwhite racial distinctions, the analysis of those distinctions should, of course, be undertaken separately.

6. See, e.g., J. Baldwin, *The Fire Next Time* (1963); W.E.B. DuBois, *The Souls of Black Folks* (1903); R. Ellison, *Invisible Man* (1952); J. Franklin, *From Slavery to Freedom* (3d ed. 1968); C. Hamilton and S. Carmichael, *Black Power* (1967); Report of the U.S. Commission on Civil Disorders (1968); M. Kilson, "Whither Integration?," 45, *Am. Scholar* 360 (1976); and hundreds, if not thousands of other books and articles, both literary and empirical. These sources describe a great variety of features of the black experience in America: such things as the historical as well as the present day material realities, and the historical as well as present day ideological realities, the way black people have been and are thought about within the culture. In *Kingsblood Royal, supra* note 2, Lewis provides a powerful account of what he calls the "American Credo" about the Negro, circa 1946. *Id.* at 194–97.

7. The best general account I have read of the structure of patriarchy and of its major dimensions and attributes is that found in *Sexual Politics* in the chapter, "Theory of Sexual Politics." K. Millett, *Sexual Politics* 23–58 (1970). The essay seems to me to be truly a major contribution to an understanding of the subject. Something of the essence of the thesis is contained in the following:

"[A] disinterested examination of our system of sexual relationship must point out that the situation between the sexes now, and throughout history, is a case of that phenomenon Max Weber defined as *herrschaft,* a relationship of dominance and subordinance. What goes largely unexamined, often even unacknowledged (yet is institutionalized nonetheless) in our social order, is the birthright priority whereby males rule females. Through this system a most ingenious form of 'interior colonization' has been achieved. It is one which tends moreover to be sturdier than any form of segregation and more rigorous than class stratification, more uniform, certainly more enduring. However muted its present appearance may be, sexual dominion obtains nevertheless as perhaps the most pervasive ideology of our culture and provides its most fundamental concept of power.

"This is so because our society, like all other historical civilizations, is a patriarchy. The fact is evident at once if one recalls that the military, industry, technology, universities, science, political office, and finance—in short, every avenue of power within the society, including the coercive force of the police, is entirely in male hands...."

"Sexual politics obtains consent through the 'socialization' of both sexes to basic patriarchal politics with regard to temperament, role, and status. As to status, a pervasive assent to the prejudice of male superiority guarantees superior status in the male, inferior in the female. The first item, temperament, involves the formation of human personality along stereotyped lines of sex category ('masculine' and 'feminine'), based on the needs and values of the dominant group and dictated by what its members cherish in themselves and find convenient in subordinates: aggression, intelligence, force and efficacy in the male; passivity, ignorance, docility, 'virtue,' and ineffectuality in the female. This is complemented by a second factor, sex role, which decrees a consonant and highly elaborate code of conduct, gesture and attitude for each sex. In terms of activity, sex role assigns domestic service and attendance upon infants to the female, the rest of human achievement, interest and ambition to the male.... Were one to analyze the three categories one might designate status as the political component, role as the sociological, and temperament as the psychological—yet their interdependence is unquestionable and they form a chain."

Id. at 24–26 (footnotes omitted).

8. See, e.g., Hochschild, "A Review of Sex Role Research," 78 *Am.J.Soc.,* 1011 (1973), which reviews and very usefully categorizes the enormous volume of literature on this topic. *See also* Stewart, "Social Influences on Sex Differences in Behavior," in Sex Differences 138 (M. Teitelbaum, ed., 1976); Weitzman, "Sex Role Socialization," in *Women: A Feminist Perspective,* 105 (J. Freeman, ed., 1975). A number of the other pieces in *Women: A Feminist Perspective* also describe and analyze the role of women in the culture, including the way they are thought of by the culture.

9. "For the married woman, her husband and children must always come first; her own needs and desires, last. When the children reach school age, they no longer require constant attention. The emotional-expressive function assigned to the woman is still required of her.

Called the 'stroking function' by sociologist Jessie Bernard, it consists of showing solidarity, raising the status of others, giving help, rewarding, agreeing, concurring, complying, understanding, and passively accepting. The woman is expected to give emotional support and comfort to other family members, to make them feel like good and worthwhile human beings." B. Deckard, *The Women's Movement*, 59 (1975), *citing* J. Bernard, *Women and the Public Interest*, 88 (1971).

"Patriarchy's chief institution is the family. It is both a mirror of and a connection with the larger society: a patriarchal unit within a patriarchal whole. Mediating between the individual and the social structure, the family effects control and conformity where political and other authorities are insufficient."

K. Millett, *supra* note 7, at 33.

10. "Even if the couple consciously try to attain an egalitarian marriage, so long as the traditional division of labor is maintained, the husband will be 'more equal.' He is the provider not only of money but of status. Especially if he is successful, society values what he does; she is just a housewife. Their friends are likely to be his friends and co-workers; in their company, she is just his wife. Because his provider function is essential for the family's survival, major family decisions are made in terms of how they affect his career. He need not and usually does not act like the authoritarian paterfamilius [*sic*] of the Victorian age. His power and status are derived from his function in the family and are secure so long as the traditional division of labor is maintained."

B. Deckard, *supra* note 9, at 62.

11. In 1970, women workers were, on the average, paid only 59 percent of men's wages. And when wages of persons with similar educational levels are compared, women still were paid over 40 percent less than men. *Id.* at 79–81.

12. "It is generally accepted that Western patriarchy has been much softened by the concepts of courtly and romantic love. While this is certainly true, such influence has also been vastly overestimated. In comparison with the candor of 'machismo' or oriental behavior, one realizes how much of a concession traditional chivalrous behavior represents—a sporting kind of reparation to allow the subordinate female certain means of saving face. While a palliative to the injustice of woman's social position, chivalry is also a technique for disguising it. One must acknowledge that the chivalrous stance is a game the master group plays in elevating its subject to pedestal level. Historians of courtly love stress the fact that the raptures of the poets had no effect upon the legal or economic standing of women, and very little upon their social status. As the sociologist Hugo Biegel has observed, both the courtly and the romantic versions of love are 'grants' which the male concedes out of his total powers. Both have the effect of obscuring the patriarchal character of Western culture and in their general tendency to attribute impossible virtues to women, have ended by confining them in a narrow and often remarkably conscribing sphere of behavior. It was a Victorian habit, for example, to insist the female assume the function of serving as the male's conscience and living the life of goodness he found tedious but felt someone ought to do anyway."

K. Millett, *supra* note 7, at 36–37.

13. Thus, even after his "joke" about black persons became known to the public, the former secretary of agriculture, Earl Butz, took great pains to insist that this in no way showed that he was a racist. This is understandable, given the strongly condemnatory feature of being described as a racist.

Equally illuminating was the behavior of Butz's associates and superiors. Then-President Ford, for example, critized Butz for the joke, but did not demand Butz's removal until there was a strong public outcry. It was as though Butz's problem was that he had been indiscreet; he had done something rude like belching in public. What Ford, Butz, and others apparently failed to grasp is that it is just as wrong to tell these jokes in private because to tell a joke of this sort is to have a view about what black people are like: that they can appropriately be ridiculed as being creatures who care only about intercourse, shoes, and defecation. What these persons also failed to grasp is how implausible it is to believe that one can hold these views about black people and at the same time deal with them in a nonracist fashion.

14. At a minimum, this account would include (1) a description of the economic, political, and social positions of blacks and whites, males and females in the culture; (2) a description of the sexual and racial roles, *i.e.*, the rules, conventions and expectations concerning how males and females, blacks and whites, should behave, and the attitudes and responses produced by these roles; and (3) a description of the de facto ideology of racial and sexual differences. This would include popular beliefs about how males and females, blacks and whites, differ, as well as the beliefs as to what accounts for these differences, roles, and economic, political and social realities.

15. The problem of empirical objectivity is compounded by the fact that part of the dominant, white male ideology is that white males are the one group in society whose members are able to be genuinely detached and objective when it comes to things like an understanding of the place of race and sex in the culture. Thus, for example, when a sex-discrimination suit was brought against a law firm and the case was assigned to Judge Constance Motley, the defendant filed a motion that she be disqualified partly because, as a woman judge, she would be biased in favor of the plaintiff. Judge Motley denied the motion. *Blank v. Sullivan & Cromwell*, 418 F.Supp. 1 (S.D.N.Y.1975), *writ of mandamus denied sub nom. Sullivan & Cromwell v. Motley*, No. 75–3045 (2d Cir. Aug. 26, 1975). Explaining her decision, Judge Motley stated: "[I]f background or sex or race of each judge were, by *definition*, sufficient grounds for removal, no judge on this court could hear this case, or many others, by virtue of the fact that all of them were attorneys, of a sex, often with distinguished law firm or public service backgrounds." 418 F.Supp. at 4 (emphasis added).

16. There is a danger in calling this ideal the "assimilationist" ideal. That term suggests the idea of incorporating oneself, one's values, and the like into the dominant group and its practices and values. I want to make it clear that no part of that idea is meant to be

captured by my use of this term. Mine is a stipulative definition.

17. This is not to deny that certain people believe that race is linked with characteristics that prima facie are relevant. Such beliefs persist. They are, however, unjustified by the evidence. *See, e.g.,* Block and Dworkin, "IQ, Heritability and Inequality" (pts. 1–2), 3 *Phil. & Pub. Aff.,* 331, 4 *id.* 40 (1974). More to the point, even if it were true that such a linkage existed, none of the characteristics suggested would require that political or social institutions, or interpersonal relationships, would have to be structured in a certain way.

18. The term "gender" may be used in a number of different senses. I use it to refer to those anatomical, physiological, and other differences (if any) that are naturally occurring in the sense described above. Some persons refer to these differences as "sex differences," but that seems to me confusing. In any event, I am giving a stipulative definition to "gender."

19. *See, e.g.,* authorities cited in note 8 *supra;* M. Mead, *Sex and Temperament in Three Primitive Societies* (1935):

"These three situations [the cultures of the Anapesh, the Mundugumor, and the Tchambuli] suggest, then, a very definite conclusion. If those temperamental attitudes which we have traditionally regarded as feminine—such as passivity, responsiveness, and a willingness to cherish children—can so easily be set up as the masculine pattern in one tribe, and in another to be outlawed for the majority of women as well as for the majority of men, we no longer have any basis for regarding such aspects of behavior as sex-linked....

"... We are forced to conclude that human nature is almost unbelievably malleable, responding accurately and contrastingly to contrasting cultural conditions.... Standardized personality differences between the sexes are of this order, cultural creations to which each generation, male and female, is trained to conform."

Id. at 190–91.

A somewhat different view is expressed in J. Sherman. *On the Psychology of Women* (1971). There, the author suggests there are "natural" differences of a psychological sort between men and women, the chief ones being aggressiveness and strength of sex drive. *See id.* at 238. However, even if she is correct as to these biologically based differences, this does little to establish what the good society should look like.

Almost certainly the most complete discussion of this topic is E. Macoby and C. Jacklin, *The Psychology of Sex Differences* (1974). The authors conclude that the sex differences which are, in their words, "fairly well established," are: (1) that girls have greater verbal ability than boys; (2) that boys excel in visual-spacial ability; (3) that boys excel in mathematical ability; and (4) that males are more aggressive. *Id.* at 351–52. They conclude, in respect to the etiology of these psychological sex differences, that there appears to be a biological component to the greater visual-spacial ability of males and to their greater aggressiveness. *Id.* at 360.

20. As Sherman observes:

"Each sex has its own special physical assets and liabilities. The principal female liability of less muscular strength is not ordinarily a handicap in a civilized, mechanized, society.... There is nothing in the biological evidence to prevent women from taking a role of equality in a civilized society."

J. Sherman, *supra* note 19, at 11.

There are, of course, some activities that would be sexually differentiated in the assimilationist society; namely, those that were specifically directed toward, say, measuring unaided physical strength. Thus, I think it likely that even in this ideal society, weight lifting contests and boxing matches would in fact be dominated, perhaps exclusively so, by men. But it is hard to find any *significant* activities or institutions that are analogous. And it is not clear that such insignificant activities would be thought worth continuing, especially since sports function in existing patriarchal societies to help maintain the dominance of males. See K. Millett, *supra* note 7, at 48–49.

It is possible that there are some nontrivial activities or occupations that depend sufficiently directly upon unaided physical strength that most if not all women would be excluded. Perhaps being a lifeguard at the ocean is an example. Even here, though, it would be important to see whether the way lifeguarding had traditionally been done could be changed to render such physical strength unimportant. If it could be changed, then the question would simply be one of whether the increased cost (or loss of efficiency) was worth the gain in terms of equality and the avoidance of sex-role differentiation. In a nonpatriarchal society very different from ours, where sex was not a dominant social category, the argument from efficiency might well prevail. What is important, once again, is to see how infrequent and peripheral such occupational cases are.

21. *See, e.g.,* Paige, "Women Learn to Sing the Menstrual Blues," in *The Female Experience,* 17 (C. Tavis, ed., 1973).

"I have come to believe that the 'raging hormones' theory of menstrual distress simply isn't adequate. All women have the raging hormones, but not all women have menstrual symptoms, nor do they have the same symptoms for the same reasons. Nor do I agree with the 'raging neurosis' theory, which argues that women who have menstrual symptoms are merely whining neurotics, who need only a kind pat on the head to cure their problems.

"We must instead consider the problem from the perspective of women's subordinate social position, and of the cultural ideology that so narrowly defines the behaviors and emotions that are appropriately 'feminine.' Women have perfectly good reasons to react emotionally to reproductive events. Menstruation, pregnancy and childbirth—so sacred, yet so unclean—are the woman's primary avenues of achievement and self-expression. Her reproductive abilities define her femininity; other routes to success are only second-best in this society....

"... My current research on a sample of 114 societies around the world indicates that ritual observances and taboos about menstruation are a method of controlling women and their fertility. Men apparently use such rituals, along with those surrounding pregnancy and childbirth, to assert their claims to women and their children.

"... The hormone theory isn't giving us much mileage, and it's time to turn it in for a better model, one that looks to our beliefs about menstruation and

women. It is no mere coincidence that women get the blue meanies along with an event they consider embarrassing, unclean—and a curse."
Id. at 21.

22. Still other arguments against something like the assimilationist ideal and in favor of something like the idea of diversity are considered by Jaggar and shown by her to be unpersuasive.

Review Questions

1. Wasserstrom says that there are four questions which should be distinguished. What are these four questions and why is it important to distinguish between them?

2. How does Wasserstrom answer the question about the social reality of racism and sexism?

3. Why does he think that women are oppressed?

4. Wasserstrom distinguishes between three levels or areas of social and political arrangements and activities. What are they?

5. Explain what Wasserstrom calls the assimilationist ideal.

6. Distinguish between Wasserstrom's ideal of diversity and his ideal of tolerance.

7. What objections are made to the assimilationist ideal?

8. How does Wasserstrom reply to these objections?

9. Explain Wasserstrom's conclusion.

Discussion Questions

1. Try to describe a society which embodies Wasserstrom's assimilationist ideal.

2. Would such a society really be good and just? Explain your view.

3. Wasserstrom says that child rearing and household maintance are, "relatively speaking, unsatisfying and unfulfilling ways to spend one's time." Do you agree or disagree? Why or why not?

Bernard R. Boxill
Sexual Blindness and Sexual Equality

Dr. Bernard R. Boxill is associated with the National Humanities Center in North Carolina.

He attacks Wasserstrom's assimilationist view that a good and just society would be "sex-blind" and "color-blind." Although he focuses on problems that arise for the assimilationist ideal because of sexual differences, he claims that his arguments also apply to the assimilationist position on racial differences. His main objection is that the assimilationist ideal has unacceptable costs. Not only does it require the elimination of sport and other important activi-

From Bernard R. Boxill, "Sexual Blindness and Sexual Equality," *Social Theory and Practice*, vol. 6, no. 3 (Fall 1980), pp. 281–298. Reprinted with permission.

ties, it also removes opportunities to acquire self-esteem. In reply to the objection that these costs are justified for the sake of sexual equality, Boxill claims that sexual equality can be achieved without giving up sex-activity correlations, and that assimilationists incoherently sacrifice equality of respect for equality of opportunity. Rather than trying to suppress opportunities, true egalitarianism should multiply and diversify them, and this means allowing sex-activity correlations such as men and weightlifting.

In a recent important essay, Richard Wasserstrom describes what he thinks the "good or just society" would make of racial and sexual differences.[1] The good or just society, he argues, would exemplify the "assimilationist ideal."[2] That is, it would make of racial and sexual differences what present society makes of differences in eye color. In present society, no "basic political rights and obligations are determined on the basis of eye-color;" no "institutional benefits and burdens are connected with eye color;" and "except for the mildest sort of aesthetic preferences, a person would be thought odd who even made private, social decisions by taking eye-color into account." [3] In the good or just society, Wasserstrom contends, race and sex would be of no greater significance. [4] And, he continues, just as the typical adult in present society is "virtually oblivious to the eye color of other persons for all major interpersonal relationships," so the typical adult in the assimilationist society would be "indifferent to the sexual, physiological differences of other persons for all interpersonal relationships." [5]

The assimilationist vision of the sexually and racially ideal society springs, no doubt, from the most humane sentiments. We are seemingly so drawn to **invidious** discrimination against those of a different race or sex that it must be few who have not yearned for a society where people are blind to both their racial and sexual differences. Yet I shall argue that the assimilationist ideal is defective. The problem it attempts but fails to solve is the old one that has long troubled egalitarians: How are we to deal with the fact that, though we are undeniably equal, we are also undeniably different? In this essay I focus on the defects in the assimilationist argument that are due to the fact that though we are equal because we are human, we are also different because we are female and male. However, my arguments should apply as well to the assimilationist position on racial differences. My conclusion is that we cannot plan that the good and just society be either "sex-blind" or "color-blind."

1

As Wasserstrom allows, there can be no important sex-role differentiations in the assimilationist society. If women are better than men at certain significant activities, or if men are better than women at certain significant activities, people will not likely be oblivious to their sexual differences. The correlation of sexual differences with activities that are significant would tend to make sexual differences themselves appear significant. Accord-

ingly he proposes to break down all sex-activity correlations by designing activities so that women and men can succeed and excel equally at every activity. To use his illustration, if lifeguarding at the ocean as now practiced puts a premium on the kind of strength that gives men an advantage over women, the sexually ideal society would change the way lifeguarding is now practiced so that this advantage is nullified. [6]

Two misunderstandings of the nature and purpose of this reform must be forestalled. First, its purpose is not to make *equality of opportunity* more perfect. Its purpose is to equalize the *chances* for success of men and women at every activity. Equality of opportunity between the sexes does not demand this. Equality of opportunity demands only the removal of all social and environmental barriers to available positions and to the means to becoming qualified for such positions. Thus two people can have equal opportunities but not equal chances. They would have equal chances only if they had equal abilities and interests.

The second misunderstanding of the reform is thinking that it is incompatible with equality of opportunity. Some strategies for equalizing the chances of women and men are incompatible with equality of opportunity. Placing social or environmental barriers in the path of the able so that the less able have an equal chance to attain the goal is an example. But this is not Wasserstrom's strategy. It places no social and environmental barriers in anybody's path to available jobs and positions. It simply eliminates some jobs and positions.

Wasserstrom is aware that his reform may have costs. But he seems to think that the only such cost is a possible loss in efficiency. The question whether to institute his reforms, he says, is simply "whether the increased cost (or loss of efficiency) was worth the gain in terms of equality and the avoidance of sex-role differentiation." [7] But I argue that he is mistaken. There are two major possible costs he does not consider: the loss of a whole province of our most significant activities, and a loss of opportunities to acquire self-esteem.

Significant Activities

"It is likely," Wasserstrom writes, "that even in this ideal society, weight-lifting contests and boxing matches would in fact be dominated, perhaps exclusively so, by men. But it is hard to find any *significant* activities or institutions that are analogous. And it is not clear that such insignificant activities would be worth continuing, especially since sports function in existing patriarchal societies to help maintain the dominance of males." [8] But surely this conclusion is hasty. Even if sports function in *existing* patriarchal societies to help maintain male dominance, it certainly does not follow that they will perform the same function in an *ideal* society. Consequently, the inference that they would not be "worth continuing" is invalid. But the deeper difficulties concern the claim that sports are *insignificant*.

What Wasserstrom may mean by this is suggested in the next paragraph where he allows that lifeguarding, which also requires considerable unaided strength, is "nontrivial." [9] Since lifeguarding is distinguished from say, weight-lifting, because it performs a service, the implication is that sports are "trivial" and "insignificant" because they do not perform a service and (by extension) have no product. It is true that sports need not perform a service or have a product. Though "spectator sports" may be said to perform the service of entertaining the spectators, and sports in general may produce health, people can engage in sport without entertaining spectators or improving their health. But it is false that sports are for that reason "insignificant" and not worth continuing. There are many activities that, like sports, need have no product and need perform no service. But these activities are not "insignificant" or "not worth continuing." On the contrary some of them are among our more significant activities and are well worth continuing. They are

significant and well worth continuing because of what they are in themselves. These activities are unalienated activities. First I shall describe their nature. Then I shall show that sports are among them.

Alienated activity is not itself "the satisfaction of a need, but only a means to satisfy needs outside itself." [10] These needs are "outside" the activity in the sense that they can, at least conceivably, be satisfied "outside," that is, without the activity that usually provides for their satisfaction. As I understand it, what is really essential about labor's being alienated is that it is not in this sense itself the satisfaction of a need. Consequently, though Marx may have believed otherwise, I describe alienated activity as not essentially, though perhaps usually, involving the other man or capitalist who owns the alienated activity. [11] Now the products and services that happen to be demanded by society, as, for example, shoes, ships, and safe swimming are needs "outside" activities because they all can at least conceivably be satisfied without the usual human activities of shoemaking, shipbuilding and lifeguarding. Since alienated labor is "only a means" to satisfy such needs, the overwhelming consideration in its design is that it satisfy these needs efficiently. Hence, except inadvertently, that design will not allow the worker room to express himself or to "develop freely his mental and physical energies." [12] Further, if there is a need to engage in such activity, alienated labor cannot satisfy that need. Since such a need is for a particular kind of activity, and so can be satisfied only by engaging in that activity, it does not meet the condition of being "outside" the activity that satisfies it.

But if alienated labor is of this nature, unalienated activity must be activity that the worker has a need to engage in, and in particular, activity that is designed specifically to provide him with room to express and develop himself freely. This does not mean that it is unprincipled or undisciplined. As Marx wrote, "Really free labor, the composing of music, for example, is at the same time damned serious and requires the greatest effort." [13] That is to say, activity which is truly a form of self-expression and self-development is necessarily governed by the discipline of laws and principles. We can express ourselves in writing, music, painting and so on, and exercise our literary, musical, and in general our creative talents, only because there are laws governing literary, musical and artistic composition, and only if we submit ourselves to the discipline of these laws. As Marx put it most generally, in his free activity man "constructs in accordance with the laws of beauty." [14]

My account of unalienated labor is independent of the controversy of whether, for Marx, unalienated activity includes economically productive activity. [15] Whether it does or not is irrelevant to the point I wish to make, which is that some activity that is not economically productive is unalienated. A second possible misunderstanding of my account is that painting, composing, and so on, have "products" and are significant, not in themselves but as a means to these "products." But this is a misunderstanding. Paintings and compositions are significant because of the activities they result from, *not* vice versa as in the usual case. As Marx noted, spiders or bees can do certain things better than an architect. However, their activities are quite different because the architect, unlike the bee or spider, had the idea in his imagination. [16] Thus, part of the activity in question here is the working out of ideas. [17]

In elaborating his Aristotelian Principle, Rawls comes to relevantly similar conclusions. The Aristotelian Principle is a "principle of motivation" that "accounts for many of our major desires." [18] According to it "human beings enjoy the exercise of their realized capacities ... and this enjoyment increases the more the capacity is realized, or the greater its complexity." Thus, "of two activities they do equally well [people] prefer the one calling on a larger repertoire of intricate and subtle discriminations." [19] Presumably such activities are more enjoyable be-

cause they "satisfy the desire for variety and novelty of experience" and permit or even require "individual style and personal expression." [20] This desire is, moreover, "relatively strong" and it must be reckoned with in the design of social institutions; for "otherwise human beings will find their culture and form of life dull and empty. Their vitality and zest will fail as their life becomes a tiresome routine." [21] Thus human beings have a need to engage in activities that call on the exercise of their abilities "simply for their own sakes." [22]

In sum, then, activities can be significant in themselves both in the sense that they are forms of self-expression in which excellence can be achieved, and in the sense that human beings have a profound need to engage in them. I now show that the assimilationist proposes to eliminate a considerable class of these activities.

Consider first, sport: We have seen that Wasserstrom proposes to eliminate it for the sake of sexual blindness. Now in practically all cultures and societies people engage in sport for its own sake. Assuming that people tend to recognise their own needs, it would seem that engaging in sport is in itself the satisfaction of an important human need. [23] To forestall objections that this may be a "false need," I can show that sports can also be forms of self-expression in which excellence is achieved. Sports are not merely undisciplined, unprincipled explosions of physical energy. Though they are exercises of human energy that are freely engaged in because they are engaged in for themselves, they are governed by the most exacting rules. Moreover, since sport is not subservient to satisfying needs "outside" itself, in accordance with the Aristotelian Principle, its rules can be, and usually are, constructed to require the utmost in "intricate and subtle discriminations" that the players are capable of. Though Rawls allows that the Aristotelian Principle operates "even in games and pastimes," [24] he unfortunately, but I think inadvertently, gives the notion of intricacy and subtlety involved an excessively intellectual interpretation. But anyone who has tried to describe a Dr. J stuff shot, or the fastidious shifts in balance and speed of the best high jumpers or shot-putters, and who also understands that what he or she would put into words is not the spontaneous perfection of the animal, but a deliberately acquired art, must acknowledge that sport, too, calls for "intricate and subtle discriminations." Further, as Rawls notes, since it is the very complexity of activities which makes them important avenues of self-expression—"for how could everyone do them in the same way?" [25]—being complex, sports too are important avenues of self-expression. And again, to prove this we need only take an educated look at the best practitioners of any sport. As infallibly as any maestro, they, too, put their personal stamp on their best performances. Finally, many sports are to a considerable extent art forms governed by the "laws of beauty." Few who have seen an accomplished performance of gymnastics or diving, or a perfect pole vault, or a well-run hurdles race, would care to deny this. In ancient Greece, Myron captured the beauty of the discus thrower in his famous **discobolus.**

An assimilationist might grant my argument that sports are significant, but deny my conclusion that assimilationism requires the suppression of sport. What he or she needs to show is that Wasserstrom allowed too easily that sports necessarily involve the sex-activity correlations that subvert sexual blindness. Thus, a philosopher once argued to me that, even granting the physical differences between women and men, we could avoid sex-activity correlations in sport by classing competitors according to the physical talent that the particular sport called on, be it height, weight, oxygenation rate, or **testosterone** level. And he pointed out that we already do this in a rudimentary way, when we put competitors in age or weight classes. But this is too ingenious. It fails to see the forest for the trees. If one of the sexes has generally higher levels of the physical characteristic relevant to a particular sport, the other sex will simply not be represented, or well represented, in the classes of the sport that achieve real excellence. And this will do little for the cause of sex-blindness.

Wasserstrom is correct, then, in saying that the assimilationist must eliminate sport. But it is not only sport he must eliminate. The sexes do not differ only in strength. They differ also in physical appearance, flexibility, grace, and texture of voice, for example. Further, the exercise of these differences is central to many of our most aesthetically appealing and culturally important activities. The exercise of man's greater natural strength and woman's greater natural flexibility and grace is of course obvious in many forms of dance. Similarly, the importance of woman's naturally higher, and man's naturally deeper, voice is obvious in practically all forms of singing. Anyone who thinks of questioning the importance of the aesthetic value of the mix of soprano and bass voices should recall the lengths to which—including in particular the castration of little boys—the medievals went to secure it.

Finally, these losses of the assimilationist society cannot be "made up." Sport and the other activities the assimilationist would suppress have their own peculiar standards of excellence and beauty, and exercise different and peculiar sets of our abilities. Hence given the human need to engage in, and express the self in, all-around activity, though we could, for example, engage in the unalienated activity of philosophizing in the assimilationist society, we could not *replace* sport with philosophizing.

Self-Esteem

Turning to the second cost of the assimilationist ideal, I now argue that in cutting off opportunities to engage in unalienated activity, the assimilationist society cuts off opportunities to acquire self-esteem.

Following Rawls, I take self-esteem as including "a person's sense of his own value, his secure conviction that his conception of his good, his plan of life, is worth carrying out." [26] As Rawls further notes, one of the two main sorts of circumstances that support a person's self-esteem is finding his "person and deeds appreciated and confirmed by others who are likewise esteemed and their association enjoyed ... unless our endeavors are appreciated by our associates it is impossible for us to maintain the conviction that they are worthwhile." [27] This theory that a person's self-esteem depends on his associates' appreciation of his endeavors has long been recognized by social theorists. Without denying that appreciation of any of our endeavors is likely to support self-esteem, I argue that appreciation of our unalienated activity is especially important.

If alienated activity is activity one feels to be somehow not one's own activity, that is, not activity which expresses one's own ideas and aspirations, the fact that others appreciate it is unlikely to give much support to one's self-esteem. Support for one's self-esteem would seem to come more surely from others' appreciation of activity one feels to be an expression of one's own ideas and aspirations, that is, activity which is truly an expression of oneself. But such activity is unalienated activity. Further, since unalienated activity is done only for itself and for no ulterior motive, all other considerations can be set aside in order to achieve excellence and beauty. Consequently, there can be much for others to appreciate in one's unalienated activity. For these reasons, it would seem that an opportunity to engage in unalienated activity is also an important opportunity to acquire self-esteem. Hence in curtailing opportunities for unalienated activity, the assimilationists curtail opportunities to acquire self-esteem. And that is a serious cost.

However, it may seem that others' appreciation of one's endeavors, especially one's unalienated activity, is a chancy way to secure self-esteem. For what if one never achieves excellence or beauty? Must one lack self-esteem? This does not seem to be necessarily the case. If it is not, there must be another support for self-esteem that I have not mentioned. Further, if it flourishes in the assimilationist society, my present objection will seem less important.

What this other support for self-esteem could be may be suggested by Bernard Williams's distinction between regarding a person's life, and actions from a "technical point of view," and regarding them from "the human point of view." [28] It may be urged that what is important to persons' self-esteem is not so much that we appreciate their endeavors, which is only to see them from the technical point of view, but that we appreciate what it is for them to attempt what they attempted, which is to see them from the human point of view. I agree that because appreciation from the human point of view can be accorded irrespective of the success or importance of our endeavors—and is to that extent unconditional—it probably offers a far more secure support for self-esteem than the appreciation accorded from the technical point of view. The question is whether the human point of view is likely to flourish in the assimilationist society. Though it is possible, I think there is reason to doubt it. To regard persons from the "human point of view," we must consider their endeavors important just because they are important *to them*. Thus, as Williams notes, from the human point of view, we regard the failed inventor, "not merely as failed inventor, but as a man who wanted to be a successful inventor," that is, as one to whom inventing was important.[29] But, as we have seen, whatever its ultimate significance many people find sport important. Hence the assimilationist's proposal to eliminate it casts doubt on the assumption that he or she views the members of the ideal society from the human point of view.

Finally, the fact that the costs of the assimilationist society involve essentially unalienated activity shows how inadequate Wasserstrom's reassurance is that the "occupational cases" that would have to be phased out are "infrequent and peripheral." [30] It is inadequate because the important costs of his reforms are not the elimination of the few "occupational cases" that the industrial revolution would have eliminated anyway. They are the elimination of the unalienated activity that the industrial revolution, by increasing our leisure time, has simultaneously made more possible and more important. Thus, perhaps what is most paradoxical is the assimilationist's belief that the industrial and technological revolution will reduce the significance of the differences between the sexes. For if I am right the very *opposite* is the truth.

2

At this point, critics may grant that I have pointed to some hitherto unnoticed costs of the sexually blind society, but maintain that I have not shown that society to be unjustified because I have not shown that it is not *worth* the costs. In particular, they may argue that the assimilationist society is worth the costs I mention because it gains so much for sexual equality.

To forestall any unjustified egalitarian sympathy for the assimilationist society, I stress that the sexual equality allegedly gained by the assimilationist society is not equality of income between the sexes. That equality is not at issue. I can propose a distribution of income between the sexes which is as radically egalitarian as the assimilationists can propose.

My first objection is that it is not necessary to incur the costs of the assimilationist society in order to have equality of opportunity between the sexes. These costs are the loss of opportunities to engage in unalienated activities and to achieve self-esteem, which are incurred by the elimination of all sex-activity correlations. But it is not necessary to eliminate correlations between sex and activity in order to have equality of opportunity between the sexes. Sex roles do subvert that equality, and perhaps human beings do tend to change sex-activity correlations into sex roles. Thus, the bare existence of correlations between sex and activities may engen-

der a societal expectation that the sexes tend to excel at different activities, and this in turn can lead to societal factors that actively discourage women and men from pursuing certain activities.[31] When this occurs, sex roles exist and equality of opportunity ceases to exist. The point, however, is that sex-activity correlations need not thus develop into sex roles.[32] There is no reason that people cannot learn to successfully resist the tendency to move from a perception of sex-activity correlations to instituting sex roles.

Wasserstrom fails to see that it is not necessary to eliminate sex-activity correlations to have sexual equality because he blurs the distinction between a sex-activity correlation and a sex role. Sex roles, he says, "necessarily impose limits—restrictions on what one can do, be or become." They impose "substantial, permanent, and involuntarily assumed restraints . . . on the most central factors concerning the way one will shape and live one's life. The point to be emphasized is that this would *necessarily* be the case even in the unlikely event that the substantial sexual differentiation could be maintained without one sex or the other becoming dominant. . . ."[33] I could not agree more with all this *if* by "sexual differentiation" Wasserstrom means "sex roles." But if this is what he means, his statement is irrelevant to the question whether it is necessary to abolish sex-activity correlations to secure sexual equality.

Some may object that it is too risky to rely on people to control the tendency to change sex-activity correlations into sex roles. But I do not recommend this. We can provide those liable to be discriminated against with a "special bill of rights" and educate them to stand up for their rights. This would, of course, mean the end of "sexual blindness," but "sexual blindness" was never defended as intrinsically valuable.

It could be said that though abolishing sex-activity correlations is not necessary for sexual equality, it makes that equality more secure: If we do not notice our sexual differences we can hardly discriminate against each other on their basis. Further, it could be argued that the alternative arrangement I propose would leave society with a built-in potential for conflict between the sexes, and that the more harmonious society that sexual blindness would secure would be infinitely superior. But even this considerably weakened case for sexual blindness collapses. Though sexual blindness may give us a safer enjoyment of sexual equality as equality of opportunity between the sexes, it does so at the expense of a more fundamental precept of egalitarianism, in terms of which equality of opportunity is itself justified.

That precept, which I refer to as equality of respect, is that each person has an equal right to the maximum opportunity, compatible with a like opportunity for others, to express himself or herself and to exercise and develop his or her talents as he or she sees fit.[34] It is clearly a stronger requirement than equality of opportunity. As I defined it, and as it is commonly understood, equality of opportunity is equality of opportunity to gain available positions or careers. Hence, since we can express ourselves and exercise and develop our talents *outside* our positions and careers, equality of respect makes broader and stronger demands than equality of opportunity. More importantly—for the egalitarian at least—it is the precept in terms of which equality of opportunity is justified. Thus one reason why equality of opportunity is so important is that although careers are not the only avenues of self-expression and self-realization, they are major avenues of self-expression and self-realization.

Now the assimilationists do propose to sacrifice equality of respect for equality of opportunity. As we have seen, they propose to eliminate a substantial portion of our unalienated activities for the sake of sexual blindness. These activities are an especially rich medium of self-expression and self-realization, and probably for some people more than others. Consequently, to eliminate such activities for the sake of sexual blindness is to sacrifice equality of respect for sexual blind-

ness. But the purpose of sexual blindness is that it secures equality of opportunity between the sexes. Hence the assimilationists propose to sacrifice equality of respect for equality of opportunity. Finally, since it is equality of respect which justifies equality of opportunity, their position is incoherent.

The immediate objection may be that I have been unfair in arguing that Wasserstrom pursues equality of opportunity at the expense of equality of respect. For, in arguing against sex roles, Wasserstrom appeals explicitly to an egalitarian ideal which is practically identical with what I have called "equality of respect." Sex roles are objectionable, he argues, because "they necessarily impair an individual's ability to develop his or her own characteristics, talents and capacities to the fullest extent to which he or she might desire." [35] Thus it may seem that if Wasserstrom focuses mainly on equality of opportunity for positions and careers, this is only because this equality is very important to equality of respect; so ultimately his proposal is intended to secure equality of respect.

But if this is indeed its purpose, it is very unlikely to secure it. His proposal will probably be bad for both men and women. Consider first the case for women. There are certainly activities at which women are better than men. These activities are not necessarily among the scorned "domestic" activities. Indeed, some are among those activities that the assimilationists want to eliminate: sports. Women's relative lack of success in sports is not written in the nature of things. It is merely a sign of our **provincialism** and lack of imagination. The very anatomical and physiological differences which place women at a disadvantage in some sports give them a decided advantage in other sports. As Jane English notes, "what is a physiological disadvantage in one activity may be an advantage in others: weight is an asset to a Sumo wrestler and a drawback for marathon running; height is an aid in basketball but not on the balance beam." Consequently, as she goes on to conclude, "in some sports, women have natural advantages over men. The hip structure that slows running gives a lower center of gravity" and this gives women an advantage on the balance beam. Similarly, "fat provides insulation and an energy source for running fifty mile races," and "the hormones that hinder development of heavy muscles promote flexibility," and give women an advantage over men in ballet.[36] The point I wish to stress here is that the pursuit of sexual blindness would require the elimination of all these activities. Let us see how unfair and unequal this is. Suppose there are women whose main talents are precisely those most strongly correlated to excellence in the above-mentioned activities. The assimilationists propose to eliminate these activities and to make the talents of these women "unimportant." But why is this fair? The men disadvantaged in these activities may already be richly and variously talented. And exactly parallel arguments apply to the case for eliminating activities for which men have natural advantages.

This argument is not decisive because it depends on assumptions which, though plausible, are clearly contingent. The decisive objection is that it is mistaken in principle to eliminate activities for the reasons the assimilationist gives. This may seem a bit extreme. The assimilationist may point out that for a safe enjoyment of equality we already rule out activities that are of the very kind that I would protect. For example, we have laws against reckless driving and even some sports. These activities could conceivably be classified as unalienated activity, and quite obviously engaging in them seems to help many people's self-esteem. Yet it seems clear that we are justified in eliminating them. In a similar vein he or she may continue that on my own account economic inequalities can be eliminated or reduced if they threaten equality of respect. But if so, why can't sex-role correlations be eliminated for the same reason?

These arguments depend, however, on a very questionable assumption. That assumption is that the factors which militate against,

say, reckless driving militate also against, say, weightlifting, but this is far from clear. The factors which militate against reckless driving are that it risks harming others because it risks maiming, disfiguring and killing them. On the assimilationist's account the factors which militate against weightlifting are that the sex-activity correlations it engenders risk harming others by being the occasion by which they may come to have *false beliefs*.

For similar reasons, any parallel between the effects of allowing all activities to flourish and the effects of allowing great economic inequalities to flourish is highly questionable. For example, Norman Daniels has urged that the economic inequalities allowed by Rawls's second principle of justice militate against the equal liberties demanded by his first principle of justice.[37] Similarly, Gerald Cohen has argued against the wide economic inequalities permitted in Nozick's system.[38] Whatever the force of these arguments, they are of little help to the assimilationist. For what they maintain is that economic inequalities harm the poor because they diminish the poor's objective opportunities, *not* that they harm the poor because in contemplating them the poor may come to have false beliefs which harm them.

But if we can eliminate reckless driving because it risks harming others, why can't we eliminate sex-activity correlations on the ground that they too risk harming others? Why should it matter that the harm involved in the latter case is false belief or stems from false belief? In Chapter II of *On Liberty*, Mill argues that it is wrong for a government to restrict acts of expression, though these acts may harm certain individuals by being the occasion by which these individuals come to have "false beliefs." Following Thomas Scanlon, I defend Mill's position on the ground that the autonomous person could not allow the state to protect him against false beliefs. If a person did allow the state to do this he or she would be surrendering to it the authority to decide what he or she should believe. But in the relevant sense, an autonomous person is one who sees herself or himself as "sovereign in deciding what to believe and in weighing competing reasons for action."[39] Hence, autonomous persons could not allow the state to protect them against false beliefs by restricting activities. In particular, they could not allow the state to protect them against false beliefs about the sexes by restricting activities which generate sex-activity correlations.

Critics may feel that the sudden intrusion here of the notion of the state is unfair. But I do not see how it can really be avoided. The state seems the most likely agency to institute the reforms of the assimilationist society. But it may be argued that if that society were some sort of participatory democracy its members could freely decide to impose on themselves the restrictions in question. In this way the notion of an autocratic state, at odds with the autonomy of its members, could seem to be dispelled. That is, of course, a well-known and attractive solution to the old conflict between the individual and the state. It is, for example, Rousseau's solution. There is conceptually no difficulty in imagining people in their "cool moments" collectively deciding to outlaw actions which they know could lead them to have false beliefs. The difficulty is that this offers no help to the assimilationists. If, to break down sex-activity correlations, the autonomous members of a participatory democracy denied themselves the opportunity to engage in certain kinds of unalienated activity, then they could not be sexually blind. Remember the considerable costs of eliminating unalienated activity. Is it even intelligible to think that we could impose these costs on ourselves just to prevent correlations from arising between activities and persons different in a way we barely notice? Is it even intelligible to think that we could impose these costs on ourselves just to prevent correlations from arising between activities and persons different in ways to which we are "indifferent," or think have "no significance"? Can we imagine autonomous persons in present society

eliminating *any* activity just to prevent correlations from arising between activities and persons who are different in eye-color?

3

So the pursuit of sexual blindness is the pursuit of a **chimera.** The sexually blind or assimilationist society is either unequal in the most fundamental sense and incompatible with the autonomy of its members, or else it is impossible. The assimilationists fail to see these paradoxes because they try to describe the sexually ideal society in terms of equality of opportunity in abstraction from other values. But this is sure to lead to lop-sided results. If we give due weight to all our values—in particular, to autonomy, to the uplifting use of our leisure time, to excellence and beauty in all its forms, as well as to equality of opportunity and equality of respect—we get a society that is saner, kinder, more equal, more familiar, and also more interesting and exciting than the bizarre and bleak world of the assimilationists.

For rather than requiring us to suppress opportunities, a true egalitarianism requires us to multiply and diversify them. For example, if men excel at firefighting and other activities requiring strength, we better use our ingenuity in the service of sex-equality to create activities women can excel at rather than to **superannuate** activities men excel at. Similarly, turning to activities we find valuable in themselves, if men dominate weightlifting, the way to sex equality is not to abolish weightlifting—that is only the way to a dreary sex-blind world—but to design activities women will dominate. As Jane English saw clearly, sexual equality does not require abolishing sports—indeed she never even considers that option—but rather inventing "alternative sports using women's distinctive abilities."[40]

Given that this is the right way to proceed, though I expect that individuals in a society that enjoys a genuine sexual equality will have a far wider appreciation of talents than we do, I do not expect that we shall no longer find that certain excellences are largely peculiar to one of the sexes or that the sex-activity correlations so dreaded by the assimilationist will have disappeared. On the contrary, I expect that they will be more numerous, more varied, and more striking.

In such a society, of course, there will be a danger of sex roles emerging. Just because sex-activity correlations exist we will tend to influence others to choose activities their sex excels at, and even to assign others to activities because of their sex. Consequently, we shall have to be on guard. We shall have to watch ourselves, and watch others. Further, organizations created and designed to protect women's rights (and men's rights too) will not disappear. Perhaps the law will have to mention sex (and color) explicitly, and perhaps there may have to be special bills of rights for women or any racial or other group that is liable to need them. Perhaps these are costs. On the other hand, they are not without usefulness. Vigilance builds character and self-respect, and I do not anticipate the end of morality. Also we must not exaggerate the danger of sex roles emerging. No doubt much of the tendency of sex-activity correlations to develop into sex roles is due to inequalities in income and power which traditionally have been correlated with activities. But as egalitarians we need not tolerate such inequalities. Finally, we should not exaggerate either the value of that "harmony" which sexual blindness promises to bestow on us. The pursuit of harmony has often subverted equality.

Once we see how little can be said for sex-blindness and how much can be said against it, it should be easier to see why its associated principle of "color-blindness" should be accepted only with circumspection. Insofar as that principle means that we should be "color-blind" in the sense that we should ignore racial differences and, except in order to make compensation, set them aside as irrelevant to what positions others can fill—then, of course, it is secure. But if it means that we should institute reforms to *make* us "color-blind" in a sense analogous to "sexual blindness" in the assimilationist society, then it should be viewed with the gravest suspicion. Even in the ideal society, we must not let "color-blindness" (or "sexual blindness") distract us from equality.[41]

Footnotes

1. Richard A. Wasserstrom, "Racism, Sexism and Preferential Treatment: An Approach to the Topics," *UCLA Law Review,* 24 (February 1977), 603.

2. Ibid., p. 604.

3. Ibid.

4. Ibid., p. 605.

5. Ibid., p. 606.

6. Ibid., p. 611 n. 59.

7. Ibid.

8. Ibid., italics in the original.

9. Ibid.

10. Karl Marx, "Alienated Labour." In David McLellan ed., *Karl Marx Selected Writings,* (Oxford: Oxford University Press, 1977), p. 80.

11. For further discussion of this, see Richard Schact, *Alienation* (Garden City, N.Y.: Anchor Books, 1971), pp. 100, 101.

12. Karl Marx, "Alienated Labour" in *Karl Marx Selected Writings,* p. 80.

13. Karl Marx, "Grundrisse" in *Karl Marx Selected Writings,* p. 368.

14. Karl Marx, "Alienated Labour" in *Karl Marx Selected Writings,* p. 82.

15. Karl Marx, *Capital,* Volume I in *Karl Marx Selected Writings,* p. 456.

16. For a discussion of this see G.A. Cohen, "Marx's Dialectic of Labour," *Philosophy and Public Affairs,* 3 (1974), 235–61.

17. See further Karl Marx, "Alienated Labour," in *Karl Marx Selected Writings,* p. 80.

18. John Rawls, *A Theory of Justice* (Cambridge: Harvard University Press, 1971), p. 427.

19. Ibid., p. 426.

20. Ibid., p. 427.

21. Ibid., p. 429.

22. Ibid., p. 431.

23. Jan Boxill develops this theme in "Sport as unalienated activity," unpublished manuscript.

24. Rawls, *A Theory of Justice,* p. 429.

25. Ibid., p. 427.

26. Ibid., p. 440.

27. Ibid., p. 441.

28. Bernard Williams, "The Idea of Equality." In Joel Feinberg, ed. *Moral Concepts* (London: Oxford University Press, 1970), p. 159.

29. Ibid.

30. Wasserstrom, "Racism, Sexism, and Preferential Treatment," p. 611, n. 59.

31. On this point see Joyce Trebilcot, "Sex Roles: The Argument From Nature." In Jane English ed. *Sex Equality* (Englewood Cliffs, N.J.: Prentice-Hall, Inc., 1977), p. 125. From *Ethics,* (1975), 249–55.

32. Ibid.

33. Wasserstrom, "Racism, Sexism, and Preferential Treatment," p. 614.

34. This conception is close, though not identical with Dworkin's "equality of respect and concern." See Ronald Dworkin, *Taking Rights Seriously* (Cambridge: Harvard University Press, 1977), pp. 272, 273.

35. Wasserstrom, "Racism, Sexism, and Preferential Treatment," p. 614.

36. Jane English, "Sex Equality in Sports," *Philosophy and Public Affairs,* 7 (1978), 275.

37. Norman Daniels, "Equal Liberty and Unequal Worth of Liberty." In Norman Daniels ed. *Reading Rawls* (New York: Basic Books, 1975), pp. 253–83.

38. Gerald Cohen, "Robert Nozick and Wilt Chamberlain." In John Arthur and William Shaw eds. *Justice and Economic Distribution* (Englewood Cliffs, N.J.: Prentice-Hall, Inc., 1978), pp. 246–62.

39. Thomas Scanlon, "A Theory of Freedom of Expression," *Philosophy and Public Affairs,* 1 (1972), 215, 216.

40. English, "Sex Equality in Sports," p. 277.

41. I thank Professor Wasserstrom, Jan Boxill, and the referees of *Social Theory and Practice* for helpful comments. My criticisms of Professor Wasserstrom do not depreciate the value of his work. No one has dealt with the subjects treated here with greater sensitivity and intelligence.

Review Questions

1. What old problem does Boxill raise for Wasserstrom's assimilationist ideal?

2. Boxill forestalls two misunderstandings of Wasserstrom's position. What are they?

3. Explain Boxill's attack on Wasserstrom's assimilationist ideal.

4. How does Boxill reply to the claim that the assimilationist society is worth the cost because it provides sexual equality?

5. Explain Boxill's principle of equality of respect.

6. What is Rousseau's solution to the conflict between the individual and the state, and why isn't this solution any help to the assimilationist according to Boxill?

7. Explain Boxill's conclusion about the assimilationist ideal.

8. In Boxill's view, what would *true egalitarianism* require in sports and other activities?

Discussion Questions

1. Do you agree with Boxill's view about the importance of sports? Why or why not?

2. Boxill talks only about sexual differences, not racial differences. But at the beginning of his article he claims that his arguments also apply to the assimilationist position on race. Is this true? What do you think?

Lisa Newton

Reverse Discrimination as Unjustified

Lisa Newton is professor of philosophy at Fairfield University and adjunct professor of philosophy at

From Lisa Newton, "Reverse Discrimination as Unjustified," *Ethics,* vol. 83, 1973, pp. 308–312, © University of Chicago Press.

Sacred Heart University.

Newton distinguishes between the moral ideal of equality which says that all humans should be citizens under the law, and justice in the political sense which says that those who are citizens should receive equal treatment under the law. Discrimination is unjust if it involves unequal treatment when citizens ought to have equal treatment under the law; for example, when the southern employer refuses to hire blacks for white-collar jobs. But reverse discrimination violates this political equality just as much as ordinary discrimination, and as such, it does not advance equality, but actually undermines it. Besides this theoretical objection to reverse discrimination,

Newton also raises some practical problems. How do we determine which groups have been sufficiently discriminated against in the past to deserve preferred treatment in the present? How much reverse discrimination will compensate those who have been discriminated against? She conlcudes that reverse discrimination destroys justice, law, equality and citizenship itself.

I have heard it argued that "simple justice" requires that we favor women and blacks in employment and educational opportunities, since women and blacks were "unjustly" excluded from such opportunities for so many years in the not so distant past. It is a strange argument, an example of a possible implication of a true proposition advanced to dispute the proposition itself, like an octopus absentmindedly slicing off his head with a stray tentacle. A fatal confusion underlies this argument, a confusion fundamentally relevant to our understanding of the notion of the rule of law.

Two senses of justice and equality are involved in this confusion. The root notion of justice, progenitor of the other, is the one that Aristotle (*Nicomachean Ethics* 5.6; *Politics* 1.2; 3.1) assumes to be the foundation and proper virtue of the political association. It is the conclusion which free men establish among themselves when they "share a common life in order that their association bring them self-sufficiency"—the regulation of their relationship by law, and the establishment, by law, of equality before the law. Rule of law is the name and pattern of this justice; its equality stands against the inequalities—of wealth, talent, etc.—otherwise obtaining among its participants, who by virtue of that equality are called "citizens." It is an achievement—complete, or, more frequently, partial—of certain people in certain concrete situations. It is fragile and easily disrupted by powerful individuals who discover that the blind equality of rule of law is inconvenient for their interests. Despite its obvious instability, Aristotle assumed that the establishment of justice in this sense, the creation of

citizenship, was a permanent possibility for men and that the resultant association of citizens was the natural home of the species. At levels below the political association, this rule-governed equality is easily found; it is exemplified by any group of children agreeing together to play a game. At the level of the political association, the attainment of this justice is more difficult, simply because the stakes are so much higher for each participant. The equality of citizenship is not something that happens of its own accord, and without the expenditure of a fair amount of effort it will collapse into the rule of a powerful few over an apathetic many. But at least it has been achieved, at some times in some places; it is always worth trying to achieve, and eminently worth trying to maintain, wherever and to whatever degree it has been brought into being.

Aristotle's parochialism is notorious; he really did not imagine that persons other than Greeks could associate freely in justice, and the only form of association he had in mind was the Greek *polis.* With the decline of the *polis* and the shift in the center of political thought, his notion of justice underwent a sea change. To be exact, it ceased to represent a political type and became a moral ideal: the ideal of equality as we know it. This ideal demands that all men be included in citizenship—that one Law govern all equally, that all men regard all other men as fellow citizens, with the same guarantees, rights, and protections. Briefly, it demands that the circle of citizenship achieved by any group be extended to include the entire human race. Properly understood, its effect on our associations can be excellent: It congratulates us on our achievement of rule of law as a process of government but refuses to let us remain complacent until we have expanded the associations to include others within the **ambit** of the rules, as often and as far as possible. While one man is a slave, none of us may feel truly free. We are constantly prodded by this ideal to look for possible unjustifiable discrimination, for inequalities not absolutely required for the functioning of the society and advantageous to all. And after twenty centuries of pressure, not at all constant, from this ideal, it might be said that some progress has been made. To take the cases in point for this problem, we are now prepared to assert, as Aristotle would never have been, the equality of sexes and of persons of different colors. The ambit of American citizenship, once restricted to white males of property, has been extended to include all adult free men, then all adult males including ex-slaves, then all women. The process of acquisition of full citizenship was for these groups a sporadic trail of half-measures, even now not complete; the steps on the road to full equality are marked by legislation and judicial decisions which are only recently concluded and still often not enforced. But the fact that we can now discuss the possibility of favoring such groups in hiring shows that over the area that concerns us, at least, full equality is presupposed as a basis for discussion. To that extent, they are full citizens, fully protected by the law of the land.

It is important for my argument that the moral ideal of equality be recognized as logically distinct from the condition (or virtue) of justice in the political sense. Justice in this sense exists *among* a citizenry, irrespective of the number of the populace included in that citizenry. Further, the moral ideal is parasitic upon the political virtue, for "equality" is unspecified—it means nothing until we are told in what respect that equality is to be realized. In a political context, "equality" is specified as "equal rights"—equal access to the public realm, public goods and offices, equal treatment under the law—in brief, the equality of citizenship. If citizenship is not a possibility, political equality is unintelligible. The ideal emerges as a generalization of the real condition and refers back to that condition for its content.

Now, if justice (Aristotle's justice in the political sense) is equal treatment under law for all citizens, what is injustice? Clearly, in-

justice is the violation of that equality, discrimination for or against a group of citizens, favoring them with special immunities and privileges or depriving them of those guaranteed to the others. When the southern employer refuses to hire blacks in white-collar jobs, when Wall Street will only hire women as secretaries with new titles, when Mississippi high schools routinely flunk all the black boys above ninth grade, we have examples of injustice, and we work to restore the equality of the public realm by ensuring that equal opportunity will be provided in such cases in the future. But of course, when the employers and the schools *favor* women and blacks, the same injustice is done. Just as the previous discrimination did, this reverse discrimination violates the public equality which defines citizenship and destroys the rule of law for the areas in which these favors are granted. To the extent that we adopt a program of discrimination, reverse or otherwise, justice in the political sense is destroyed, and none of us, specifically affected or not, is a citizen, a bearer of rights—we are all petitioners for favors. And to the same extent, the ideal of equality is undermined, for it has content only where justice obtains, and by destroying justice we render the ideal meaningless. It is, then, an ironic paradox, if not a contradiction in terms, to assert that the ideal of equality justifies the violation of justice; it is as if one should argue, with William Buckley, that an ideal of humanity can justify the destruction of the human race.

Logically, the conclusion is simple enough: All discrimination is wrong *prima facie* because it violates justice, and that goes for reverse discrimination too. No violation of justice among the citizens may be justified (may overcome the *prima facie* objection) by appeal to the ideal of equality, for that ideal is logically dependent upon the notion of justice. Reverse discrimination, then, which attempts no other justification than an appeal to equality, is wrong. But let us try to make the conclusion more plausible by suggesting some of the implications of the suggested practice of reverse discrimination in employment and education. My argument will be that the problems raised there are insoluble, not only in practice but in principle.

We may argue, if we like, about what "discrimination" consists of. Do I discriminate against blacks if I admit none to my school when none of the black applicants are qualified by the tests I always give? How far must I go to root out cultural bias from my application forms and tests before I can say that I have not discriminated against those of different cultures? Can I assume that women are not strong enough to be roughnecks on my oil rigs, or must I test them individually? But this controversy, the most popular and well-argued aspect of the issue, is not as fatal as two others which cannot be avoided: If we are regarding the blacks as a "minority" victimized by discrimination, what is a "minority"? And for any group—blacks, women, whatever—that has been discriminated against, what amount of reverse discrimination wipes out the initial discrimination? Let us grant as true that women and blacks were discriminated against, even where laws forbade such discrimination, and grant for the sake of argument that a history of discrimination must be wiped out by reverse discrimination. What follows?

First, are there other groups which have been discriminated against? For they should have the same right of restitution. What about American Indians, Chicanos, Appalachian Mountain whites, Puerto Ricans, Jews, Cajuns, and Orientals? And if these are to be included, the principle according to which we specify a "minority" is simply the criterion of "ethnic (sub) group," and we're stuck with every hyphenated American in the lower middle class clamoring for special privileges for *his* group—and with equal justification. For be it noted, when we run down the Harvard roster, we find not only a scarcity of blacks (in comparison with the proportion in the population) but an even more striking scarcity of those second-, third-, and fourth-generation ethnics who make up the loudest voice of Middle America. Shouldn't they demand *their* share? And eventually, the WASPs will have to form their own lobby; for they too are a minority. The point is simply this: There is no "majority" in American who will not mind giving up just a bit of their rights to make room for a favored minority. There are only other minorities, each of which is discriminated against by the favoring. The initial injustice is then repeated dozens of times, and if each minority is granted the same right of restitution as the others, an entire area of rule governance is dissolved into a pushing and shoving match between self-interested groups. Each works to catch the public eye and political popularity by whatever means of advertising and power politics lend themselves to the effort, to capitalize as much as possible on temporary popularity until the restless mob picks another group to feel sorry for. Hardly an edifying spectacle, and in the long run no one can benefit: The pie is no larger—it's just that instead of setting up and enforcing rules for getting a piece, we've turned the contest into a free-for-all, requiring much more effort for no larger a reward. It would be in the interests of all the participants to reestablish an objective rule to govern the process, carefully enforced and the same for all.

Second, supposing that we do manage to agree in general that women and blacks (and all the others) have some right of restitution, some right to a privileged place in the structure of opportunities for a while, how will we know when that while is up? How much privilege is enough? When will the guilt be gone, the price paid, the balance restored? What recompense is right for centuries of exclusion? What criterion tells us when we are done? Our experience with the Civil Rights movement shows us that agreement on these terms cannot be presupposed: A process that appears to some to be going at a mad gallop into a black takeover appears to the rest of us to be at a standstill. Should a practice of reverse discrimination be adopted, we may safely predict that just as some of us begin to see "a satisfactory start toward righting the balance," others of us will see that we "have already gone too far in the other direction" and will suggest that the discrimination ought to be reversed again. And such disagreement is inevitable, for the point is that we could not *possibly* have any criteria for evaluating the kind of recompense we have in mind. The context presumed by any discussion of restitution is the context of the rule of law: Law sets the rights of men and simultaneously sets the method for remedying the violation of those rights. You may exact suffering from others and/or damage payments for yourself if and only if the others have violated your rights; the suffering you have endured is not sufficient reason for them to suffer. And remedial rights exist only where there is law: Primary human rights are useful guides to legislation but cannot stand as reasons for awarding remedies for injuries sustained. But then, the context presupposed by any discussion of restitution is the context of preexistent full citizenship. No remedial rights could exist for the excluded; neither in law nor in logic does there exist a right to *sue* for a standing to sue.

From these two considerations, then, the difficulties with reverse discrimination become evident. Restitution for a disadvantaged group whose rights under the law have been violated is possible by legal means, but restitution for a disadvantaged group whose grievance is that there was no law to protect them simply is not. First, outside of the area of justice defined by the law, no sense can be made of "the group's rights," for no law recognizes that group or the individuals in it, qua members, as bearers of rights (hence *any* group can constitute itself as a disadvantaged minority in some sense and demand similar restitution). Second, outside of the area of

protection of law, no sense can be made of the violation of rights (hence the amount of the recompense cannot be decided by any objective criterion). For both reasons, the practice of reverse discrimination undermines the foundation of the very ideal in whose name it is advocated; it destroys justice, law, equality, and citizenship itself, and replaces them with power struggles and popularity contests.

Review Questions

1. What is the "root notion" of justice according to Newton?

2. What is the second sense of justice explained by Newton? What is the ideal of equality?

3. Newton claims that the ideal of equality is logically distinct from justice in the political sense. What is justice in the political sense, and how is it related to the ideal of equality?

4. What is injustice in Newton's account?

5. Why does Newton find reverse discrimination to be unjust?

6. In Newton's view, what is wrong with saying that the ideal of equality justifies the violation of justice?

7. What problems does Newton raise for reverse discrimination?

8. What is her conclusion?

Discussion Questions

1. Do you agree that the problems Newton raises for reverse discrimination are really insoluble? Why or why not?

2. Newton says that when an employer refuses to hire blacks for white-collar jobs an injustice is done, and that the *same* injustice is done when employers favor blacks. Is this true? Explain your answer.

Mary Anne Warren

Secondary Sexism and Quota Hiring

Mary Anne Warren teaches at San Francisco State University. She is the author of several articles including "Do Potential People Have Moral Rights?", "On the Moral and Legal Status of Abortion," and "The Rights of the Nonhuman World."

Warren begins by distinguishing between primary and secondary sexism. Primary sexism is simply unfair discrimination on the basis of sex. Secondary sexism involves the use of sex-correlated criteria which are not valid measures of merit. One such criterion is: Does the candidate have an uninterrupted work record? This criterion discriminates against women who have interrupted their careers to have and raise children. To counteract primary and secondary sexist hiring practices which have put women at a disadvantage, Warren favors mandatory hiring quotas of a minimum sort based on the proportion of women among qualified and available candidates. Even though employers may have to use weak discrimination in favor of women to meet these quotas, Warren does not think that this is especially unfair to men. She feels that men have benefited in the past and will benefit in the future from sexist discrimination against women.

I want to call attention to a pervasive form of discrimination against women, one which helps to explain the continuing male monopoly of desirable jobs in the universities, as elsewhere. Discrimination of this sort is difficult to eliminate or even, in some cases, to recognize, because (1) it is not explicitly based on sex, and (2) it typically *appears* to be justified on the basis of plausible moral or

From Mary Anne Warren, "Secondary Sexism and Quota Hiring," *Philosophy and Public Affairs*, vol. 6, no. 3 (Spring 1977), pp. 240–261. Copyright © 1977 by Princeton University Press. Reprinted with permission of Princeton University Press. [Some of the footnotes have been renumbered.–Ed.]

practical considerations. The recognition of this form of discrimination gives rise to a new argument for the use of numerical goals or quotas in the hiring of women for college and university teaching and administrative positions.

I shall argue that because of these de facto discriminatory hiring practices, minimum numerical quotas for the hiring and promotion of women are necessary, not (just) to compensate women for past discrimination or its results, or to provide women with role models, but to counteract this *ongoing* discrimination and thus make the competition for such jobs more nearly fair. Indeed, given the problems inherent in the compensatory justice and role-model arguments for reverse discrimination, this may well be the soundest argument for the use of such quotas.

I PRIMARY AND SECONDARY SEXISM

Most of us try not to be sexists; that is, we try not to discriminate unfairly in our actions or attitudes toward either women or men. But it is not a simple matter to determine just which actions or attitudes discriminate unfairly, and a sincere effort to avoid unfair discrimination is often not enough. This is true of both of the forms of sexism that I wish to distinguish.

In its primary sense, "sexism" means *unfair discrimination on the basis of sex*. The unfairness may be unintentional; but the cause or reason for the discrimination must be the sex of the victim, not merely some factor such as size or strength that happens to be correlated with sex. Primary sexism may be due to dislike, distrust, or contempt for women, or, in less typical cases, for men or **hermaphrodites.** Or it may be due to sincerely held but objectively unjustified beliefs about women's properties or capacities. It may also be due to beliefs about the properties women *tend* to have, which are objectively justified but inappropriately applied to a particular case, in which the woman discriminated against does not have those properties.

For instance, if members of a philosophy

department vote against hiring or promoting a woman logician because they dislike women (logicians), or because they think that women cannot excel in logic, or because they know that most women do not so excel and wrongly conclude that this one does not, then they are guilty of primary sexism. This much, I think, is noncontroversial.

But what should we say if they vote to hire or promote a man rather than a woman because he has a wife and children to support, while she has a husband who is (capable of) supporting her? Or because they believe that the woman has childcare responsibilities which will limit the time she can spend on the job? What if they hire a woman at a lower rank and salary than is standard for a man with comparable qualifications, for one of the above reasons? These actions are not sexist in the primary sense because there is no discrimination on the basis of sex itself. The criteria used *can* at least be applied in a sex-neutral manner. For instance, it might be asserted that if the woman candidate had had a spouse and children who depended upon her for support, this would have counted in her favor just as much as it would in the case of a man.

Of course, appeals to such intrinsically sex-neutral criteria may, in some cases, be mere rationalizations of what is actually done from primary sexist motives. In reality, the criteria cited may not be applied in a sex-neutral manner. But let us assume for the sake of argument that the application of these criteria *is* sex-neutral, not merely a smoke screen for primary sexism. On this assumption, the use of such criteria discriminates against women only because of certain contingent features of this society, such as the persistence of the traditional division of labor in marriage and childrearing.[1]

Many people see nothing morally objectionable in the use of such intrinsically sex-neutral yet de facto discriminatory criteria. For not only may employers who use such criteria be free of primary sexism, but their actions may appear to be justified on both moral and pragmatic grounds. It might, for instance, be quite clear that a department will really do more to alleviate economic hardship by hiring or promoting a man with dependents rather than a woman with none, or that a particular woman's domestic responsibilities will indeed limit the time she can spend on the job. And it might seem perfectly appropriate for employers to take account of such factors.

Nevertheless, I shall argue that the use of such considerations is unfair. It is an example of secondary sexism, which I define as comprising all those actions, attitudes and policies which, while not using sex itself as a reason for discrimination, do involve sex-correlated factors or criteria and do result in an unfair impact upon (certain) women. In the case of university hiring policies, secondary sexism consists in the use of sex-correlated selection criteria which are not valid measures of academic merit, with the result that women tend to be passed over in favor of men who are not, in fact, better qualified. I call sexism of this sort *secondary,* not because it is any less widespread or harmful than primary sexism, but because (1) it is, in this way, indirect or covert, and (2) it is typically parasitic upon primary sexism, in that the injustices it perpetuates—for example, those apparent from the male monopoly of desirable jobs in the universities—are usually due in the first instance to primary sexism.

Two points need to be made with respect to this definition. First, it is worth noting that, although in the cases we will be considering the correlations between sex and the apparently independent but de facto discriminatory criteria are largely due to past and present injustices against women, this need not always be the case. The discriminatory impact of excluding pregnancy-related disabilities from coverage by employee health insurance policies, for example, probably makes this an instance of secondary sexism. Yet it is certainly not (human) injustice which is responsible for the fact that it is only women who become pregnant. The fact that the correlation is due to biology rather than prior injustice does not show that the exclusion is not sexist. Neither does the fact that pregnancy is often undertaken voluntarily. If such insurance programs fail to serve the needs of women employees as well as they serve those of men, then they can escape the charge of sexism only if—as seems unlikely—it can be shown that they cannot possibly be altered to include disabilities related to pregnancy without ceasing to serve their mutually agreed upon purposes, and/or producing an even greater injustice.

This brings us to the second point. It must be stressed that on the above definition the use of valid criteria of merit in hiring to university positions is not an instance of secondary sexism. Some might argue that merit criteria discriminate unfairly against women, because it is harder for women to earn the advanced degrees, to write the publications, and to obtain the professional experience that are the major traditional measures of academic merit. But it would be a mistake to suppose that merit criteria as such are therefore sexist. They are sexist only to the extent that they understate women's actual capacity to perform well in university positions; and to that extent, they are invalid as criteria of merit. To the extent that they are valid, that is, the most reliable available measurements of capacities which are indeed crucial for the performance of the job, they are not unjust, even though they may result in more men than women being hired.

If this seems less than obvious, the following analogy may help. It is surely not unjust to award first prize in a discus throwing contest to the contestant who actually makes the best throw (provided, of course, that none of the contestants have been unfairly prevented from performing up to their capacity on this particular occasion), even if some of the contestants have in the past been wrongly prevented from developing their skill to the fullest, say by sexist discrimination in school athletic programs. Such contestants may be entitled to other relevant forms of compensa-

tion, for example, special free training programs to help them make up for lost time, but they are not entitled to win this particular contest. For the very *raison d'être* of an athletic contest dictates that prizes go to the best performers, not those who perhaps *could* have been the best, had past conditions been ideally fair.

So too, a university's central reasons for being dictate that positions within it be filled by candidates who are as well qualified as can be found. Choosing less qualified candidates deprives students of the best available instruction, colleagues of a more intellectually productive environment, and—in the case of state-funded universities—the public of the most efficient use of its resources.[2] To appoint inferior candidates defeats the primary purposes of the university, and is therefore wrong-headed, however laudable its motivations. It is also, as we shall see, a weapon of social change which is apt to backfire against those in whose interest it is advocated. . . .

II SECONDARY SEXISM IN UNIVERSITY HIRING

Consider the following policies, which not infrequently influence hiring, retention, and promotion decisions in American colleges and universities:

1. Antinepotism rules, proscribing the employment of spouses of current employees.
2. Giving preference to candidates who (are thought to) have the greater financial need, where the latter is estimated by whether someone has, on the one hand, financial dependents, or, on the other hand, a spouse capable of providing financial support.
3. The "last hired-first fired" principle, used in determining who shall be fired or not rehired as a result of staffing cutbacks.
4. Refusing promotions, tenure, retention seniority, or pro-rata pay to persons employed less than full time, where some are so employed on a relatively long-term basis and where there is no evidence that

such persons are (all) less well qualified than full time employees.

5. Hiring at a rank and salary determined primarily by previous rank and salary rather than by more direct evidence of a candidate's competence, for example, degrees, publications, and student and peer evaluations.

6. Counting as a negative factor the fact that a candidate has or is thought to have, or to be more likely to have, childcare or other domestic responsibilities which may limit the time s/he can spend on the job.

7. Giving preference to candidates with more or less uninterrupted work records over those whose working careers have been interrupted (for example, by raising children) in the absence of more direct evidence of a present difference in competence.

8. Not hiring, especially to administrative or supervisory positions, persons thought apt to encounter disrespect or lack of cooperation from peers or subordinates, without regard for whether this presumed lack of respect may be itself unjustified, for example, as the result of primary sexism.

9. Discriminating against candidates on the grounds of probable mobility due to the mobility of a spouse, present or possible.

Each of these practices is an example of secondary sexism, in that while the criterion applied does not mention sex, its use nevertheless tends to result in the hiring and promotion of men in preference to women who are not otherwise demonstrably less well qualified. I suggest that in seeking to explain the continuing underrepresentation of women in desirable jobs in the universities, we need to look not only toward primary sexist attitudes within those institutions, and certainly not toward any intrinsic lack of merit on the part of women candidates,[3] but toward covertly, and often unintentionally, discriminatory practices such as these.

Of course, none of these practices operates to the detriment of women in every case; but each operates against women much more often than against men, and the cumulative effect is enormous. No doubt some of them are more widespread than others and some (for example, the use of antinepotism rules) are already declining in response to pressures to remove barriers to the employment of women. Others, such as policies 3 and 4, are still fairly standard and have barely begun to be seriously challenged in most places. Some are publicly acknowledged and may have been written into law or administrative policy, for example, policies 1, 3, 4, and 5. Others are more apt to be private policies on the part of individual employers, to which they may not readily admit or of which they may not even be fully aware, for example, policies 2, 6, 7, and 8. It is obviously much more difficult to demonstrate the prevalence of practices of the latter sort. Nevertheless, I am certain that all of these practices occur, and I strongly suspect that none is uncommon, even now.

This list almost certainly does not include all of the secondary sexist practices which influence university hiring. But these examples are typical, and an examination of certain of their features will shed light on the way in which secondary sexism operates in the academic world and on the reasons why it is morally objectionable.

In each of these examples, a principle is used in choosing between candidates that in practice acts to discriminate against women who may even be better qualified intrinsically than their successful rivals, on any reliable and acceptable measure of merit.[4] Nevertheless, the practice may *seem* to be justified. Nepotism rules, for instance, act to exclude women far more often than men, since women are more apt to seek employment in academic and/or geographical areas in which their husbands are already employed than vice versa. Yet nepotism rules may appear to be necessary to ensure fairness to those candidates and appointees, both male and female, who are *not* spouses of current employees and who, it could be argued, would otherwise be unfairly disadvantaged. Similarly, giving jobs or promotions to those judged to have the greatest financial need may seem to be simple humanitarianism, and the seniority system may seem to be the only practical way of providing job security to *any* portion of the faculty. For policies 5 through 9, it could be argued that, although the criteria used are not entirely reliable, they may still have *some* use in predicting job performance.

Thus each practice, though discriminatory in its results, may be defended by reference to principles which are not intrinsically sex-biased. In the context of an otherwise sexually egalitarian society, these practices would probably not result in de facto discrimination against either sex. In such a society, for instance, men would not hold a huge majority of desirable jobs, and women would be under no more social or financial pressure than men to live where their spouses work rather than where they themselves work; thus they would not be hurt by nepotism rules any more often, on the average, than men.[5] The average earning power of men and women would be roughly equal, and no one could assume that women, any more than men, ought to be supported by their spouses, if possible. Thus the fact that a woman has an employed spouse would not be thought to reduce her need for a job any more—or any less—than in the case of a man. We could proceed down the list; in a genuinely nonsexist society, few or none of the conditions would exist which cause these practices to have a discriminatory impact upon women.

Of course, there may be other reasons for rejecting these practices, besides their discriminatory impact upon women. Nepotism rules might be unfair to married persons of both sexes, even in a context in which they were not *especially* unfair to women. My point is simply that these practices would not be instances of sexism in a society which was otherwise free of sexism and its results. Hence, those who believe that the test of the justice of a practice is whether or not it would unfairly disadvantage any group or individual *in the context of an otherwise just society* will see no sexual injustice whatever in these practices.

But surely the moral status of a practice, as it operates in a certain context, must be determined at least in part by its actual consequences, in that context. The fact is that each of these practices acts to help preserve the male monopoly of desirable jobs, in spite of the availability of women who are just as well qualified on any defensible measure of merit. This may or may not suffice to show that these practices are morally objectionable. It certainly shows that they are inconsistent with the "straight merit" principle, that is, that jobs should go to those best qualified for them on the more reliable measures of merit. Hence, it is ironic that attempts to counteract such de facto discriminatory practices are often interpreted as attacks on the "straight merit" principle.

III WHY SECONDARY SEXISM IS UNFAIR

Two additional points need to be stressed in order to show just why these practices are unfair. In the first place, the contingent social circumstances which explain the discriminatory impact of these practices are themselves morally objectionable, and/or due to morally objectionable practices. It is largely because men *are* more able to make good salaries, and because married women are still expected to remain financially dependent upon their husbands, if possible, that the fact that a woman has an employed husband can be seen as evidence that she doesn't "need" a job. It is because a disproportionate number of women must, because of family obligations and the geographical limitations these impose, accept part-time employment even when they would prefer full time, that the denial of tenure, promotion and pro-rata pay to part-time faculty has a discriminatory impact upon women. That women accept such obligations and limitations may seem to be their own free choice; but, of course, that choice is heavily conditioned by financial pressures—for example, the fact that the husband can usually make more money—and by sexually stereotyped social expectations.

Thus, the effect of these policies is to compound and magnify prior social injustices against women. When a woman is passed over on such grounds, it is rather as if an athlete who had without her knowledge been administered a drug to hamper her performance were to be disqualified from the competition for failing the blood-sample test. In such circumstances, the very least that justice demands is that the unfairly imposed handicap not be used as a rationale for the imposition of further handicaps. If the unfair handicaps that society imposes upon women cause them to be passed over by employers because of a lack of straight merit, that is one thing, and it is unfortunate, but it is not obvious that it involves unfairness on the part of the employers. But if those handicaps are used as an excuse for excluding them from the competition regardless of their merit, as all too often happens, this is quite another thing, and it is patently unfair.

In the second place, practices such as these often tend to perpetuate the very (unjust) circumstances which underlie their discriminatory impact, thus creating a vicious circle. Consider the case of a woman who is passed over for a job or promotion because of her childcare responsibilities. Given a (better) job, she might be able to afford day care, or to hire someone to help her at home, or even to persuade her husband to assume more of the responsibilities. Denying her a job because of her domestic responsibilities may make it almost impossible for her to do anything to lessen those responsibilities. Similarly, denying her a job because she has a husband who supports her may force him to continue supporting her and her to continue to accept that support.

Both of these points may be illustrated by turning to a somewhat different sort of example. J.R. Lucas has argued that there are cases in which women may justifiably be discriminated against on grounds irrelevant to their merit. He claims, for example, that it is "not

so evidently wrong to frustrate Miss Amazon's hopes of a military career in the Grenadier Guards on the grounds not that she would make a bad soldier, but that she would be a disturbing influence in the mess room." [6]

But this is a paradigm case of secondary, and perhaps also primary, sexism; it is also quite analogous to practice 8. To exclude women from certain jobs or certain branches of the military on the grounds that certain third parties are not apt to accept them, when that nonacceptance is itself unreasonable and perhaps based on sexual bigotry, is to compound the injustice of that bigotry. If it is inappropriate for soldiers to be disturbed or to make a disturbance because there are women in the mess room, then it is wrong to appeal to those soldiers' attitudes as grounds for denying women the opportunities available to comparably qualified men. It is also to help ensure the perpetuation of those attitudes, by preventing male soldiers from having an opportunity to make the sorts of observations which might lead to their eventually accepting women as comrades.

Thus, these practices are morally objectionable because they compound and perpetuate prior injustices against women, penalizing them for socially imposed disadvantages which cannot be reliably shown to detract from their actual present capacities. We may conclude that the hiring process will never be fair to women, nor will it be based on merit alone, so long as such practices persist on a wide scale. But it remains to be seen whether numerical hiring quotas for women are a morally acceptable means of counteracting the effects of sexist hiring practices.

IV WEAK QUOTAS

I shall discuss the case for mandatory hiring quotas of a certain very minimal sort: those based on the proportion of women, not in the population as a whole, but among qualified and available candidates in each academic field. Such a "weak" quota system would require that in each institution, and ideally within each department and each faculty and administrative rank and salary, women be hired and promoted at least in accordance with this proportion. If, for instance, a tenured or tenure-track position became available in a given department on an average of every other year, and if women were twenty percent of the qualified and available candidates in that field, then such a quota system would require that the department hire a woman to such a position at least once in ten years.[7]

Needless to say, this is not a formula for rapid change in the sexual composition of the universities. Suppose that the above department has twenty members, all male and all or almost all tenured, that it does not grow, and that it perhaps shrinks somewhat. Under these not atypical circumstances, it could easily take over forty years for the number of women in the department to become proportional to the number of qualified women available, even if the quota is strictly adhered to, and the proportion of qualified women does not increase in the meantime. Consequently, some would argue that such a quota system would be inadequate.[8]

Furthermore, it *could* be argued that if the job competition were actually based on merit, women would be hired and promoted at a *higher* rate than such a weak quota system would require, since the greater obstacles still encountered by women on the way to obtaining qualifications ensure that only very able women make it.[9] Or, it might be argued that women should be hired and promoted in more than such proportional numbers, in order to compensate for past discrimination or to provide other women with role models. Indeed, some existing affirmative action plans, so I am told, already require that women be hired in more than proportional numbers. Nevertheless, I will not defend quotas higher than these minimal ones. For, as will be argued in Section VIII, higher quotas at least give the appearance of being unfair to male candidates, and it is not clear that either the compensatory justice or the role-model argument is sufficient to dispel that appearance.

V QUOTAS OR GOALS?

Before turning to the case for such minimal hiring quotas, we need to comment on the "quotas vs. goals" controversy. Those who oppose the use of numerical guidelines in the hiring of women or racial minorities usually refer to such guidelines as *quotas,* while their defenders usually insist that they are not quotas but *goals.* What is at issue here? Those who use the term "quotas" pejoratively tend to assume that the numerical standards will be set so high or enforced so rigidly that strong reverse discrimination—that is, the deliberate hiring of demonstrably less well qualified candidates—will be necessary to implement them.[10] The term "goal," on the other hand, suggests that this will not be the case, and that good faith efforts to comply with the standards by means short of strong reverse discrimination will be acceptable.[11]

But whatever one calls such minimum numerical standards, and whether or not one suspects that strong reverse discrimination has in fact occurred in the name of affirmative action, it should be clear that it is not *necessary* for the implementation of a quota system such as I have described. Neither, for that matter, is weak reverse discrimination—that is, the deliberate hiring of women in preference to equally but not better qualified men.[12] For if hiring decisions were solely based on reliable measures of merit and wholly uncorrupted by primary or secondary sexist policies, then qualified women would *automatically* be hired and promoted at least in proportion to their numbers, except, of course, in statistically abnormal cases.[13] Consequently, reverse discrimination will *appear* to be necessary to meet proportional quotas only where the hiring process continues to be influenced by sexist practices—primary or secondary, public or private.

In effect, the implementation of a minimum quota system would place a price upon the continued use of sexist practices. Employers would be forced to choose between eliminating sexist practices, thus making it possible for quotas to be met without discriminating for or against anyone on the basis of sex, and practicing reverse discrimination on an ad hoc basis in order to meet quotas without eliminating sexist practices. Ideally, perhaps, they would all choose the first course, in which case the quota system would serve only to promote an ongoing check upon, and demonstration of, the non-sexist nature of the hiring process.

In reality, however, not all secondary sexist practices can be immediately eliminated. Some forms of secondary sexism have probably not yet been recognized, and given the nature of the interests involved it is likely that new forms will tend to spring up to replace those which have been discredited. More seriously, perhaps, some secondary sexist policies, such as the seniority system, cannot be eliminated without an apparent breach of contract (or of faith) with present employees. Others—for example, hiring on the basis of need—may survive because they are judged, rightly or wrongly, to be on the whole the lesser evil. A quota system, however, would require that the impact of such secondary sexist practices be counterbalanced by preferential treatment of women in other instances. Furthermore, it would hasten the elimination of all sexist policies by making it in the interest of all employees, men as well as women, that this be done, since until it is done both will run the risk of suffering from (sexist or reverse) discrimination. Certainly their elimination would be more probable than it is at present, when it is primarily women who have a reason based on self-interest for opposing them, yet primarily men who hold the power to eliminate or preserve them.

The most crucial point, however, is that under such a quota system, even if (some) employers do use weak discrimination in favor of women to meet their quota, this will not render the job competition especially unfair to men. For, as I will argue, unfairness would result only if the average male candidate's chances of success were reduced to below what they would be in an ongoing, just society, one in which men and women had complete equality of opportunity and the competition was based on merit alone; and I will argue that the use of weak reverse discrimination to meet proportional hiring quotas will not have this effect.

VI QUOTAS AND FAIRNESS

Now one way to support this claim would be to argue that in an ongoing, just society women would constitute a far higher proportion of the qualified candidates in most academic fields and that therefore the average male candidate's chances would, other things being equal, automatically be reduced considerably from what they are now. Unfortunately, however, the premise of this argument is overly speculative. It is possible that in a fully egalitarian society women would still tend to avoid certain academic fields and to prefer others, much as they do now, or even that they would fail to (attempt to) enter the academic profession as a whole in much greater numbers than at present.

But whatever the proportion of male and female candidates may be, it must at least be the case that in a just society the chances of success enjoyed by male candidates must be no greater, on the average, and no less than those enjoyed by comparably qualified women. Individual differences in achievement, due to luck or to differences in ability, are probably inevitable; but overall differences in the opportunities accorded to comparably qualified men and women, due to discrimination, would not be tolerated.

The question, then, is: Would the use of weak discrimination in favor of women, to a degree just sufficient to offset continuing sexist discrimination against women and thus to meet minimum quotas, result in lowering the average chances of male candidates to below those of comparably qualified women? The answer, surely, is that it would not, since by hypothesis men would be passed over, in order to fill a quota, in favor of women no better qualified only as often as women continue to be passed over, because of primary or secondary sexism, in favor of men no better qualified.

In this situation, individual departures from the "straight merit" principle might be no less frequent than at present; indeed, their frequency might even be doubled. But since it would no longer be predominantly women who were repeatedly disadvantaged by those departures, the overall fairness of the competition would be improved. The average long-term chances of success of *both* men and women candidates would more closely approximate those they would enjoy in an ongoing just society. If individual men's careers are temporarily set back because of weak reverse discrimination, the odds are good that these same men will have benefited in the past and/or will benefit in the future—not necessarily in the job competition, but in *some* ways—from sexist discrimination against women. Conversely, if individual women receive apparently unearned bonuses, it is highly likely that these same women will have suffered in the past and/or will suffer in the future from primary or secondary sexist attitudes. Yet, the primary purpose of a minimum quota system would not be to compensate the victims of discrimination or to penalize its beneficiaries, but rather to increase the overall fairness of the situation—to make it possible for the first time for women to enjoy the same opportunity to obtain desirable jobs in the universities as enjoyed by men with comparable qualifications.

It is obvious that a quota system implemented by weak reverse discrimination is not the ideal long-term solution to the problem of sexist discrimination in academic hiring. But it would be a great improvement over the present situation, in which the rate of unemployment among women Ph.D.'s who are actively seeking employment is still far higher than among men with Ph.D.'s, and in which women's starting salaries and chances of promotion are still considerably lower than those

of men.[14] Strong reverse discrimination is clearly the least desirable method of implementing quotas. Not only is it unfair to the men who are passed over, and to their potential students and colleagues, to hire demonstrably less well qualified women, but it is very apt to reinforce primary sexist attitudes on the part of all concerned, since it appears to presuppose that women cannot measure up on their merits. But to presume that proportional hiring quotas could not be met without strong reverse discrimination is also to make that discredited assumption. If, as all available evidence indicates, women in the academic world are on the average just as hard-working, productive, and meritorious as their male colleagues, then there can be no objection to hiring and promoting them at least in accordance with their numbers, and doing so will increase rather than decrease the extent to which success is based upon merit.

VII   ARE QUOTAS NECESSARY?

I have argued that minimum proportional quotas such as I have described would not make the job competition (especially) unfair to men. But it might still be doubted that quotas are necessary to make the competition fair to women. Why not simply attack sexist practices wherever they exist and then let the chips fall as they may? Alan Goldman argues that quotas are not necessary, since, he says, other measures—for example, "active recruitment of minority candidates, the advertisement and application of nondiscriminatory hiring criteria ... and the enforcement of these provisions by a neutral government agency" [15] would suffice to guarantee equal treatment for women. Goldman claims that if women candidates are as well qualified as men then, given these other measures, they will automatically be hired at least in proportion to their numbers. Indeed, he suggests that the only basis for doubting this claim is "an invidious suspicion of the real inferiority of women ... even those with Ph.D.'s." [16] That discrimination against women might continue to occur in spite of such affirmative measures short of quotas, he regards as "an untested empirical hypothesis without much *prima facie* plausibility."[17]

In a similar vein, George Sher has argued that blacks, but not women, are entitled to reverse discrimination in hiring, since the former but not the latter have suffered from a poverty syndrome which has denied them the opportunity to obtain the qualifications necessary to compete on an equal basis with white men.[18] He views reverse discrimination—and presumably hiring quotas—as primarily a way of compensating those who suffer from present competitive disadvantages due to past discrimination, and claims that since women are not disadvantaged with respect to (the opportunity to obtain) qualifications, they are not entitled to reverse discrimination.

What both Goldman and Sher overlook, of course, is that women suffer from competitive disadvantages quite apart from any lack of qualifications. Even if primary sexism were to vanish utterly from the minds of all employers, secondary sexist practices such as those we have considered would in all likelihood suffice to perpetuate the male monopoly of desirable jobs well beyond our lifetimes. Such practices cannot be expected to vanish quickly or spontaneously; to insist that affirmative action measures stop short of the use of quotas is to invite their continuation and proliferation.

VIII THE COMPENSATORY JUSTICE AND ROLE–MODEL ARGUMENTS

Most of the philosophers who have recently defended the use of goals or quotas in the hiring of women and/or minority group members have assumed that this will necessarily involve at least weak and perhaps strong reverse discrimination, but have argued that it is nevertheless justified as a way of compensating individuals or groups for past injustices or for present disadvantages stemming from past injustices.[19] Others have argued that reverse discrimination is justified not (just) as a form of compensatory justice, but as a means of bringing about certain future goods—for example, raising the status of downtrodden groups,[20] or providing young women and blacks with role models and thus breaking the grip of self-fulfilling expectations which cause them to fail.[21]

If one is intent upon arguing for a policy which would give blacks or women "advantages in employment . . . greater than these same blacks or women would receive in an ongoing just society,"[22] then perhaps it is necessary to appeal to compensatory justice or to the role model or to other utilitarian arguments to justify the *prima facie* unfairness to white males which such a policy involves. But there is no need to use these arguments in justifying a weak quota system such as the one described here, and indeed, it is somewhat misleading to do so. For, as we have seen, such a system would not lower the average male candidate's overall chances of success to below what they would be if the selection were based on merit alone. It would simply raise women's chances, and lower men's, to a closer approximation of what they would be in an ongoing just society, in which the "straight merit" principle prevailed. This being the case, the fact that quotas may serve to compensate some women for past or present wrongs, or to provide others with role models, must be seen as a fortuitous side effect of their use and not their primary reasons for being. The primary reason for weak quotas is simply to increase the present fairness of the competition.

Furthermore, there are problems with the compensatory justice and role-model arguments which make their use hazardous. It is not clear that either suffices to justify any use of reverse discrimination beyond what may in practice (appear to) be necessary to implement weak quotas. For, granted that society as a whole has some obligation to provide compensation to the victims of past discrimination, and assuming that at least some women candidates for university positions are suitable beneficiaries of such compensation, it is by no means clear that male candidates should be forced to bear most of the burden for providing that compensation. It would be plausible to argue on the basis of compensatory justice for, say, tax-supported *extra* positions for women, since then the burden would be distributed relatively equitably. But compensatory justice provides no case for placing an extra, and seemingly punitive, burden on male candidates, who are no more responsible for past and present discrimination against women than the rest of us.

Similarly, however badly women may need role models, it is not clear that male candidates should be disproportionately penalized in order to provide them. It can be argued on the basis of simple fairness that male candidates' chances should not be allowed to remain *above* what they would be in a just society; but to justify reducing them to *below* that point requires a stronger argument than simply appealing to compensatory justice or the need for role models.

Nor does it help to argue that the real source of the injustice to male candidates, if and when preferential hiring of women results in lowering the former's chances to below what they would be in a just society, is not the preferential hiring policy itself, but something else. Thomas Nagel, for instance, argues that reverse discrimination is not seriously unjust, even if it means that it is harder for white men to get certain sorts of jobs than it is for women and blacks who are no better qualified, since, he suggests, the real source of the injustice is the entire system of providing differential rewards on the basis of differential abilities.[23] And Marlene Fried argues that the root of the injustice is not preferential hiring, but the failure of those with the power to do so to expand job opportunities so that blacks and women could be hired in increasing numbers without hiring fewer men.[24]

Unfortunately, we cannot, on the one hand, reject secondary sexist practices because of their contingent and perhaps unintended discriminatory effects, and, on the other hand, accept extenuations such as these for a policy which would, in practice, discriminate unfairly against (white) men. These other sources of injustice are real enough; but this does not alter the fact that if reverse discrimination were practiced to the extent that certain men's chances of success were reduced to below those enjoyed, on the average, by comparably qualified women, then it would at least give every appearance of being unfair to those men. After all, the primary insight necessary for recognizing the injustice of secondary sexist policies is that a policy must be judged, at least in part, by its consequences in practice, regardless of whether or not these consequences are a stated or intended part of the policy. If a given policy results in serious and extensive injustice, then it is no excuse that this injustice has its roots in deeper social injustices which are not themselves easily amenable to change, at least not if there is any feasible way of altering the policy so as to lessen the resulting injustice.

I think we may conclude that while proportional quotas for the hiring of women are justified both on the basis of the merit principle and as a way of improving the overall fairness of the competition, it is considerably more difficult to justify the use of higher quotas. The distinction between such weak quotas and higher quotas is crucial, since although higher quotas have in practice rarely been implemented, the apparent injustice implied by what are typically *assumed* to be higher quotas has generated a backlash which threatens to undermine affirmative action entirely. If quotas are abandoned, or if they are nominally adopted but never enforced, then employers will be free to continue using secondary and even primary sexist hiring criteria, and it is probable that none of us will see the day when women enjoy job opportunities commensurate with their abilities and qualifications.

Footnotes

1. I mean, of course, the tradition that the proper husband earns (most of) the family's income, while the proper wife does (most of) the housekeeping and child-rearing.

2. It might be argued that the hiring process ought not to be based on merit alone, because there are cases in which being a woman, or being black, might itself be a crucial job qualification. As Michael Martin points out, this might well be the case in hiring for, say, a job teaching history in a previously all white-male department which badly needs to provide its students with a more balanced perspective. See "Pedagogical Arguments for Preferential Hiring and Tenuring of Women Teachers in the University." *The Philosophical Forum* 5, no. 2: 325–333. I think it is preferable, however, to describe such cases, not as instances requiring a departure from the merit principle, but as instances in which sex or race itself, or rather certain interests and abilities that are correlated with sex or race, constitutes a legitimate qualification for a certain job, and hence a measure of merit, vis-à-vis that job.

3. With respect to one such measure, books and articles published, married women Ph.D.'s published as much or slightly more than men, and unmarried women only slightly less. See "The Woman Ph.D.: A Recent Profile," by R.J. Simon, S.M. Clark, and K. Galway, in *Social Problems* 15, no. 2 (Fall 1967): 231.

4. I am assuming that whether a candidate is married to a current employee, or has dependents, or a spouse capable of supporting her, whether she is employed on a part-time or a full-time basis, her previous rank and salary, the continuity of her work record, and so on, are not in themselves reliable and acceptable measures of merit. As noted in example 5, more direct and pertinent measures of merit can be obtained. Such measures as degrees, publications, and peer and student evaluations have the moral as well as pragmatic advantage of being based on the candidate's actual past performance, rather than on unreliable and often biased conjectures of various sorts. Furthermore, even if there is or were *some* correlation (it would surely not be a *reliable* one) between certain secondary sexist criteria and job performance, it could still be argued that employers are not morally entitled to use such criteria, because of the unfair consequences of doing so. As Mary Vetterling has observed, there might well be some correlation between having "a healthy and active sex life" and "the patience and good humor required of a good teacher"; yet employers are surely not entitled to take into account the quality of a person's sex life in making hiring and promotion decisions. "Some Common Sense Notes on Preferential Hiring," *The Philosophical Forum* 5, no. 2: 321.

5. Unless, perhaps, a significant average age difference between wives and husbands continued to exist.

6. J.R. Lucas, "Because You are a Woman," *Moral Problems*, ed. James Rachels (New York: Harper & Row, 1975), p. 139.

7. In practice problems of statistical significance will probably require that quotas be enforced on an institution-wide basis rather than an inflexible department-by-department basis. Individual departments, especially if they are small and if the proportion of qualified women in the field is low, may fail to meet hiring quotas, not because of primary or secondary sexism, but because the best qualified candidates happen in fact to be men. But if no real discrimination against women is occurring, then such statistical deviations should be canceled out on the institutional level, by deviations in the opposite direction.

8. See Virginia Held, "Reasonable Progress and Self-Respect," *The Monist* 57, no. 1: 19.

9. Gertrude Ezorsky cites in support of this point a study by L.R. Harmon of over 20,000 Ph.D.'s, which showed that "Women ... Ph.D.'s are superior to their male counterparts on all measures derived from high school records, in all ... specializations." *High School Ability Patterns: A Backward Look from the Doctorate*, Scientific Manpower [*sic*] Report No. 6, 1965, pp. 27–28; cited by Ezorsky in "The Fight Over University Women," *The New York Review of Books* 21, no. 8 (16 May 1974): 32.

10. See, for instance, Paul Seaburg, "HEW and the Universities," *Commentary* 53, no. 2 (February 1972): 38–44.

11. In practice, strong reverse discrimination is specifically prohibited by HEW affirmative action guidelines, and good faith efforts to implement affirmative action programs without resorting to strong reverse discrimination have been accepted as adequate. Nevertheless, though I would not wish to see *these* features of affirmative action policies changed, I prefer the term "quota" for what I am proposing, because this term suggests a standard which will be enforced, in one way or another, while the term "goal" suggests—and affirmative action is in great danger of becoming—a mere expression of good intentions, compliance with which is virtually unenforceable.

12. The distinction between strong and weak reverse discrimination is explored by Michael Bayles in "Compensatory Reverse Discrimination in Hiring," *Social Theory and Practice* 2, no. 3: 303–304, and by Vetterling, "Common Sense Notes," pp. 320–323.

13. This conclusion can be avoided only by assuming either that qualified women would not want better jobs if these were available, or that they are somehow less meritorious than comparably qualified men. The first assumption is absurd, since women who do not want desirable jobs are not apt to take the trouble to become qualified for them; and the second assumption is amply refuted by empirical data. See, for instance, the studies cited in fn. 9.

14. Elizabeth Scott tells me that her survey of 1974–1976 figures reveals that, in spite of affirmative action policies, unemployment among women Ph.D.'s who are actively seeking work is about twice as high as among men Ph.D.'s and that the starting salaries of women Ph.D.'s average $1,200 to $1,500 lower than those of men.

15. Alan H. Goldman, "Affirmative Action," *Philosophy & Public Affairs* 5, no. 2 (Winter 1976): 185.

16. Goldman, p. 186.

17. Goldman, p. 185.

18. Sher, p. 168.

19. See Bayles and Sher, respectively.

20. Irving Thalberg, "Reverse Discrimination and the Future," *The Philosophical Forum* 5, no. 2: 307.

21. See Marlene Gerber Fried, "In Defense of Preferential Hiring," *The Philosophical Forum* 5, no. 2: 316.

22. Charles King, "A Problem Concerning Discrimination," *Reason Papers*, no. 2 (Fall 1975), p. 92.

23. Thomas Nagel, "Equal Treatment and Compensatory Justice," *Philosophy & Public Affairs* 2, no. 4 (Summer 1973): 348–363, especially p. 353.

24. Fried, p. 318.

Review Questions

1. According to Warren, what is primary sexism?

2. What is secondary sexism, as it is explained by Warren?

3. Why does Warren think that secondary sexism is unfair?

4. What is the "weak" quota system recommended by Warren?

5. How does Warren characterize the "quota vs. goals" controversy?

6. According to Warren why isn't the use of weak reverse discrimination to meet proportional hiring quotas not unfair?

7. Why does Warren think that quotas are necessary to make competition for jobs fair for women?

8. What are the compensatory justice and role-model arguments?

9. Why doesn't Warren accept these arguments?

Discussion Questions

1. Is the sort of weak reverse discrimination advocated by Warren unfair to men? Explain your position.

2. Are the use of hiring quotas really necessary as Warren says? What do you think?

Problem Cases

1. The University of California v. *Bakke* (1978) In the years 1973 and 1974, Allan Bakke, a white male, applied for admission to the Medical School of the University of California at Davis. In both years, his application was rejected even though other applicants who had lower grade point averages and lower Medical College Admissions Test scores were admitted under a special program. After the second rejection in 1974, Bakke filed a lawsuit in the Superior Court of California. He alleged that the special program which admitted less-qualified minority students operated to exclude him from the school on the basis of race, in violation of his rights under Title VI of the Civil Rights Act of 1964 and the Equal Protection Clause of the Fourteenth Amendment. The trial court found that the special program operated as an unconstitutional racial quota because minority applicants were rated only against one another, and sixteen places in the class of 100 were reserved for them. But the court refused to order Bakke's admission. Bakke appealed and the case went to the Supreme Court of the United States. The justices of the Supreme Court were divided four-to-four on the issues in the case, with Justice Powell providing the decisive vote. Justice Powell sided with Chief Justice Warren Burger and three other justices in holding that the admissions program was unconstitutional, and that Bakke must be admitted to the school. But Justice Powell also sided with the other four justices in holding that colleges and universities can consider race as a factor in the admissions process.

Are quotas based on race or ethnic status unjust? What is your view?

Is it acceptable to consider race or sex as a factor in admissions? Why or why not?

2. A Case of Academic Hiring Suppose that the philosophy department of a state university has a tenure-track opening. The position is advertised and there are numerous applications, including one from a woman. It is not possible to determine the race of the applicants from the documents provided, and the department does not plan to interview the candidates. One of the male applicants has really outstanding credentials—a Ph.D. degree from Harvard with a dissertation on justice written under the direction of John Rawls (the dissertation is being published as a book by Harvard University Press), several articles published in leading journals, evidence of being an excellent teacher, and very flattering letters of recommendation. By comparison, the woman's credentials are good, but not really outstanding. She does not yet have a Ph.D. degree, although she says that her dissertation on feminism is almost done, and she has not published any articles. However, she does possess evidence of being a good teacher and shows positive letters of recommendation.

Should the department hire the apparently less qualified woman? Why or why not?

Suppose that it is discovered that one of the candidates is a black man; this fact is mentioned in one of the letters of recommendation. This man's credentials seem to be roughly equal to those of the woman. Should he be hired rather than the woman? What choice should be made in this case?

Suppose that the woman's credentials seem roughly equal to that of the leading man; that is, she has a Ph.D. degree from a good school, publications, good letters of recommendation, and so on. Should the department hire her rather than the man? What do you think?

3. *Women in Combat Jets* The current policy of the United States Air Force is that women are not allowed to fly combat jets. But suppose that a qualified woman pilot demands to fly one of these jets. She has logged many hours of flight time; she holds the rank of major; she is in excellent physical condition; she is unmarried and has no children; and she is a black belt in karate. Are there any good reasons for refusing to let her fly? What are they?

4. *Selling a House* Suppose that Bob and Mary Smith have been trying to sell their three-bedroom house for two years. The house is only five years old and it is located in a pleasant middle-class neighborhood of Denver. The house has been appraised at $200,000, and the Smiths started out asking that price for the house. But they have come down in price several times, and

now they are asking for only $150,000. They feel that they cannot really go any lower in price because they have a $100,000 mortgage on the house, and they have spent at least $50,000 on various improvements. One day their real estate agent calls and says he has qualified buyers who are willing to pay $150,000 for the house. The only problem is that the buyers, Ralph and Sara Jones, are black. The real estate agent advises the Smiths to turn the offer down. He points out that the house is in an all-white neighborhood, and that if they sell to blacks, the property values in the area will go down dramatically. He has seen this happen in east Denver where houses that once sold for $500,000 are now selling for $50,000. Also, the real estate agent claims that the neighbors will be very angry if the Smiths sell their house to black people. On the other hand, the Smiths have a legal right to sell their house to qualified buyers, and the Joneses are definitely qualified. Ralph Jones is a successful lawyer, and his wife Sara is a grade-school teacher. They have three children, and they would be delighted to have the house.

Should the Smiths sell their house to the Joneses? Explain your position.

5. *The Equal Rights Amendment* The proposed Equal Rights Amendment reads as follows:

"Section 1. Equality of rights under the law shall not be denied or abridged by the United States or by any state on account of sex.

"Section 2. The Congress shall have the power to enforce, by appropriate legislation, the provisions of this article.

"Section 3. This amendment shall take effect two years after the date of ratification."

This amendment was originally proposed by Alice Paul in 1923, just three years after women in the United States received the right to vote. It was approved by Congress in 1971, but it has not been ratified by the required three-fourths of the state legislatures and is now dead unless Congress revives it.

Should this amendment be ratified? Defend your position.

Suggested Readings

(1) Beauchamp, Tom. "The Justification of Reverse Discrimination." In *Social Justice and Preferential Treatment,* edited by William T. Blackstone and Robert Heslep. Athens: University of Georgia Press, 1976. Beauchamp argues that reverse discrimination in hiring is justified in order to elimi-

nate present discriminatory practices. To prove that serious discrimination exists in our society, he presents an array of statistical and linguistic evidence.

(2) Blackstone, William T. "Reverse Discrimination and Compensatory Justice." In *Social Justice and Preferential Treatment,* edited by William T. Blackstone and Robert Heslep. Athens: University of Georgia Press, 1976. Blackstone is concerned to defeat the view that reverse discrimination is justified in order to repair past wrongs done to women and minorities. His argument is utilitarian. Even though an appeal to utility is often used to justify reverse discrimination, Blackstone thinks that this appeal gives just the opposite conclusion—that more harm than good results from reverse discrimination, and consequently it is not justifiable.

(3) Boxill, Bernard R. "The Morality of Preferential Hiring." *Philosophy & Public Affairs* vol. 7, no. 3 (Spring 1978): 246–268. Boxill tries to refute two objections to preferential hiring: first, that preferential hiring benefits those who do not deserve compensation, and second, that it is unfair to young white men.

(4) Cohen, Marshall, Thomas Nagel, and Thomas Scanlon, eds. *Equality and Preferential Treatment.* Princeton, NJ: Princeton University Press, 1977. With one exception, all of the articles in this book originally appeared in the journal *Philosophy & Public Affairs.* The exception is Ronald Dworkin's article on two important legal decisions, one dealing with a 1945 admittance policy which denied a black man admittance to the University of Texas Law School, and the other on a 1971 admittance policy which denied a white male (DeFunis) admission to the University of Washington Law School.

(5) Dworkin, Ronald. "Why Bakke Has No Case," *The New York Review of Books* (Nov. 19, 1977). Dworkin argues that Bakke's rights were not violated by the University of California at Davis policy of having a quota of sixteen places out of a class of 100 reserved for minority students. Soon after this article was published, the Supreme Court ruled five-to-four that the quota system at Davis was unconstitutional. *See* the Problem Cases for this chapter.

(6) Ferguson, Ann. "Andrognyny As an Ideal for

Human Development." In *Feminism and Philosophy,* edited by Mary Vetterling-Braggin, Frederick A. Elliston, and Jane English, 45–69. Totowa, NJ: Littlefield, Adams and Co., 1977. Ferguson recommends androgyny as an ideal for human development rather than traditional sex roles. As she explains it, the ideal androgynous person would not be both masculine and feminine (the usual meaning of androgynous), but would transcend these categories.

(7) Goldberg, Steven. *The Inevitability of Patriarchy.* New York: William Morrow & Company, 1973. Goldberg defends the sexist view that the male hormone testosterone gives men an aggression advantage over women, making it impossible for women to successfully compete aginst men for high-status positions. Consequently women are better off if they accept male dominance and play traditional female roles involving helping and nurturing.

(8) Gross, Barry, ed. *Reverse Discrimination.* Buffalo, NY: Prometheus Books, 1977. This anthology includes articles by Sidney Hook, Lisa Newton, Bernard Boxill, and Alan Goldman.

(9) Sher, George. "Justifying Reverse Discrimination in Employment." *Philosophy & Public Affairs* vol. 4, no. 2 (Winter 1975). After examining and criticizing several arguments used to support reverse discrimination, Sher argues that a case can be made for reverse discrimination. It is justified when it is compensation for lost ability to compete on equal terms due to inadequate education, or factors such as an inadequate diet, or lack of early intellectual stimulation.

(10) _____. "Reverse Discrimination, the Future, and the Past." *Ethics* vol. 90 (October 1979): 81–87. Sher distinguishes between backward-looking defenses and forward-looking defenses of preferential treatment. The first makes the basic claim that in the past women and minorities were unfairly discriminated against, and so they deserve to be compensated for this past injustice. The second claim is that preferential treatment at the present time will reduce or prevent discrimination in the future. Sher raises difficulties for both of these types of defense.

(11) Singer, Peter. "Is Racial Discrimination Arbitrary?" In *Moral Issues,* edited by Jan Narveson,

308–342. New York: Oxford University Press, 1983. Instead of holding that discrimination is wrong because it is arbitrary, Singer holds that it is wrong when it violates the principle of equal consideration of interests.

(12) Thalberg, Irving. "Justification of Institutional Racism." *Philosophical Forum* vol. 3 (Winter 1972): 243–264. Thalberg attacks the arguments of opponents of changes to equalize the economic and political status of blacks.

(13) Trebilcot, Joyce. "Sex Roles: The Argument from Nature." *Ethics* vol. 85, no. 3 (April 1975): 249–255. Trebilcot critically examines three arguments used to support sexism, including Steven Goldberg's argument that alleged psychological differences between the sexes make sex roles and male dominance inevitable.

(14) Wasserstrom, Richard. "A Defense of Programs of Preferential Treatment." *National Forum, The Phi Kappa Phi Journal* vol. LVIII, no. 1 (Winter 1978): 15–18. Wasserstrom gives a limited defense of programs which have quotas for the admission of minority students.

Glossary

Ambit the sphere of action, expression, or influence.

Chimera a she-monster in Greek mythology having a lion's head, goat's body, and a dragon's or serpent's tail.

Discobolus a discus thrower.

Hermaphrodite an individual having both male and female reproductive organs.

Heterodoxy the state of being heterodox or different from an established religious point of view. As contrasted with orthodoxy, the established religious viewpoint.

Ideology abstract speculation; when used in a depreciatory sense, unpractical or visionary theorizing or speculation.

Invidious unpleasant or objectionable.

Patriarchy a social organization marked by the supremacy of the father in the family, the legal dependence of the wife and children, and the reckoning of descent and inheritance in the male line.

Polis a Greek city-state.

Provincialism an exclusive attachment to one's own region.

Superannuate to make or declare obsolete or out-of-date.

Testosterone the male sex hormone.

Chapter 7

Sexual Morality

Introduction

The Traditional Christian View The traditional Christian (and Jewish and Islamic) view of sex is that nonmarital sex is morally wrong. Nonmarital sex includes activities such as adultery, premarital sex, fornication, prostitution, masturbation, and homosexuality. An influential statement of the Christian view of sex is given in the Vatican Declaration on Sexual Ethics in our readings.

The Vatican position has been attacked by both those inside and outside the Church. One prominent critic has been Father Curren, professor of moral theology at the Catholic University of America. Another critic is Russell Vannoy, whose view is presented in our readings. Despite this criticism, the Church seems unlikely to change its position. Father Curren has been suspended from his teaching duties, and the Vatican has recently issued a statement reaffirming its condemnation of homosexuality. Furthermore, it made a declaration condemning nonstandard methods of reproduction, such as artificial insemination and surrogate parenting.

There is also controversy concerning the use of contraceptives. The official teaching of the Roman Catholic Church, stated in the 1969 papal encyclical *Humane Vitae,* is that artificial birth control is immoral. But there are plenty of Catholics and non-Catholic Christians who think that there is nothing wrong with using artificial means of birth control.

Natural Law Theory To understand the traditional Christian view of sex, it is useful to know something about the natural law theory that is often used to support this view. The term ***natural law*** is used to mean

261

a set of prescriptive rules of conduct that are binding on all human beings simply because of human nature. In the natural law theory, human action is naturally directed towards certain goals and purposes such as life and procreation. These natural goals and purposes are good, and the pursuit of them is morally right, while interfering with them is morally wrong. The natural goal or purpose of sexual activity is reproduction within the context of marriage. Interfering with this natural goal or purpose of sex is morally wrong.

This natural law theory is espoused in the Vatican Declaration. According to this declaration, masturbation is a "seriously disordered act" because it "contradicts its finality," that is, it opposes the natural end of sex, which is procreation. Homosexuality is also a serious disorder for the same reason. Premarital sexual relations are condemned because they often exclude the prospect of children, and even if children are produced, they will be deprived of a proper and stable environment.

Russell Vannoy attacks the natural law view. He finds nothing particularly wrong with so-called perversions such as masturbation and homosexuality. He makes a number of points in reply to the view that such acts are perverse and wrong because they are unnatural in the sense of being nonprocreative: sex for pleasure is just as natural as reproductive sex, perhaps even more so; we cannot assume that whatever is natural is good, for nature can inflict evil on us; sex as an expression of love is natural even if it is not procreative; and how do we know that God or nature intends sex only for procreation, given the fact that sex seems to have other purposes?

Adultery Adultery is not discussed in the Vatican declaration, but it seems clear that it would be wrong on the view the declaration endorses, since it is sex outside the context of marriage, and it usually does not include the prospect of children. But is adultery

wrong? Richard Wasserstrom discusses various reasons for saying that it is wrong, such as the claims that it involves the breaking of promises and deception. He concludes with a consideration of the importance of fidelity as a support for marriage, and suggests that adultery may be wrong because it constitutes an attack on the institution of marriage. He does not consider this reason conclusive, however, for it assumes that marriage is a morally desirable and just institution, and he does not think that this is obvious or easy to demonstrate.

Richard Taylor discusses a number of issues raised by extramarital and nonmarital love affairs: the nature of the love affair, the motives of the lovers, fidelity, and the benefits and costs of monogamy. He emphasizes the value of love affairs and defends the right to have them.

Another important problem in sexual morality that is not discussed in the Vatican declaration is rape. Presumably it would be wrong in the Vatican view when it occurs outside of marriage. (Whether rape can occur in marriage is an interesting question; certainly there have been cases where wives have charged their husbands with rape.) But why is rape wrong? It does not ordinarily involve any sexually perverse act, and it can produce children. The standard view of rape (of women) is that it is wrong because it treats women as objects, as entities inferior to men, and also because it is using a person without her consent.

Pamela Foa objects to that view of rape because it does not point out the special wrongness of rape. Rape is wrong even if it is not an act between equals; thus rape of children is just as bad as rape of adults, even though children do not have the same status as adults. Moreover, Foa does not agree with Donald Levy's view (6) that rape is wrong because it is in some sense *unnatural*. Unnatural acts are not wrong in the first place and, besides, rape can be the fulfillment of a natural sexual impulse. Nor is rape just a kind of wrongful assault on a person; being raped is not being wronged in the same way as being assaulted. What makes rape specially wrong, according to Foa, is the societal attitude that victims of rape enjoy themselves in a nonprivate and nonintimate environment. This societal attitude makes rape particularly shameful and humiliating. In fact, she says, rape in our society is only different in degree from marriage: both involve sex without real intimacy. The alternative to our society's rape model of sexuality, she suggests, is sex between friends who are willing to be intimate with each other.

AIDS and its Implications   None of the authors considered thus far have discussed AIDS (acquired immune deficiency syndrome) and its implications. But this disease is now recognized to have important implications for sexual morality and ethics in general.

Not all the facts about AIDS are known, but we do know that it is caused by a virus (called by various names: HTLV–III, LAV, ARV, and most recently, HIV). This AIDS virus infects and damages cells of the immune system; it can also infect cells of the central nervous system, causing mental and emotional disorders. AIDS is most often spread through sexual contact or sharing infected intravenous drug needles. More specifically, it is spread through sexual contact in which blood or body fluids (semen, urine, feces, vaginal secretions) are transmitted from an infected person to an uninfected person. It can also be spread by sharing drug needles contaminated with the AIDS virus, by prenatal transmission (that is, an infected woman can pass the virus to her child before, during, or shortly after birth), or by transfusion of blood or blood components contaminated with the AIDS virus.

The article by Ronald Bayer in our readings gives some facts about the spread of AIDS, and discusses some of the ethical dilemmas raised by the disease. In the United States, the disease has thus far occurred most often in the homosexual population. Of all the cases reported in the United States since 1981, seventy-three percent have been sexually active homosexual and bisexual men (this figure includes homosexual and bisexual men who are also intravenous drug abusers—eight percent, and men who have had sex with another man since 1977—sixty-five percent). Only four percent of the cases have been heterosexual men and women (this is the latest figure; the one cited by Bayer in our reading, .9 percent, is already inaccurate). But it is important to note that the heterosexual population is at risk too. In Central Africa, the disease has reached epidemic proportions in the heterosexual population; so it is clear that the disease can and is spread by heterosexual intercourse, and not just by homosexual activities.

One of the troubling features of AIDS is that people can be infected with the AIDS virus and yet remain healthy and free of symptoms for months or even years. (The latency period between the time the virus is acquired and the disease develops is unknown.) The situation is further complicated by the fact that some of those who have been exposed to the AIDS virus develop AIDS-related complex (ARC), which may include symptoms of diarrhea, fever, and swollen glands, and some people with ARC may never develop AIDS.

There is, however, a reliable test for the AIDS virus that is considered to be 100 percent certain by experts. But who should get this test for AIDS? It seems reasonable to hold that everyone in the high-risk population (sexually active homosexual and bisexual men) should be tested. But some of these people refuse to be tested; they are afraid of being quarantined, losing their jobs, losing their health insurance, and so on. Do they have a right to not be tested? Or should we have mandatory testing for AIDS? These questions are raised in the first Problem Case at the end of the chapter.

Other ethical problems arising from the AIDS epidemic are discussed by Bayer. How should we control the spread of this disease? Should people abstain from sex altogether outside of marriage or should they use safeguards (such as condoms)? Is it permissible to quarantine those exposed to the AIDS virus? Should gay baths and bars be closed? Does the fact that the disease is found mostly in gay men justify discriminating against them in various ways?

Another serious problem briefly discussed by Bayer, and explained in more detail by Oppenheimer and Padgag (7), is the challenge the AIDS crisis poses for the American health care system, which depends heavily on private insurance to pay medical bills. Private insurance carriers are turning to AIDS testing to eliminate poor risks. Some employers have attempted to fire AIDS patients or to exclude AIDS coverage from group insurance policies. As a result, many people who get AIDS will not have insurance coverage. Who will pay the enormous medical costs? Oppenheimer and Padgag discuss various solutions to this problem: Persons with AIDS could be covered under Medicare; there could be state-sponsored health insurance pools; or a national health insurance program could be developed.

The Vatican

Declaration on Sexual Ethics

The Declaration on Sexual Ethics was issued in Rome by the Sacred Congregation for the Doctrine of the Faith on December 29, 1975.

The authors defend the Christian doctrine that "every genital act must be within the framework of marriage." Premarital sex, masturbation, and homosexuality are specifically condemned, and chastity is recommended as a virtue.

1. According to contemporary scientific research, the human person is so profoundly affected by sexuality that it must be considered as one of the factors which give to each individual's life the principal traits that distinguish it. In fact it is from sex that the human person receives the characteristics which, on the biological, psychological and spiritual levels, make that person a man or a woman, and thereby largely condition his or her progress towards maturity and insertion into society. Hence sexual matters, as is obvious to everyone, today constitute a theme frequently and openly dealt with in books, reviews, magazines, and other means of social communication.

In the present period, the corruption of morals has increased, and one of the most serious indications of this corruption is the unbridled exaltation of sex. Moreover, through the means of social communication and through public entertainment this corruption has reached the point of invading the field of education and of infecting the general mentality.

In this context certain educators, teachers, and moralists have been able to contribute to a better understanding and integration into life of the values proper to each of the sexes; on the other hand there are those who have put forward concepts and modes of behavior which are contrary to the true moral exigencies of the human person. Some members of the latter group have even gone so far as to favor a licentious **hedonism.**

As a result, in the course of a few years, teachings, moral criteria, and modes of living hitherto faithfully preserved have been very much unsettled, even among Christians. There are many people today who, being confronted with so many widespread opinions opposed to the teachings which they received from the Church, have come to wonder what they must still hold as true.

2. The Church cannot remain indifferent to this confusion of minds and relaxation of morals. It is a question, in fact, of a matter which is of the utmost importance both for the personal lives of Christians and for the social life of our time.[1]

The Bishops are daily led to note the growing difficulties experienced by the faithful in obtaining knowledge of wholesome moral teaching, especially in sexual matters, and of the growing difficulties experienced by pastors in expounding this teaching effectively. The Bishops know that by their **pastoral** charge they are called upon to meet the needs of their faithful in this very serious matter, and important documents dealing with it have already been published by some of them or by Episcopal Conferences. Nevertheless, since the erroneous opinions and resulting deviations are continuing to spread everywhere, the Sacred Congregation for the Doctrine of the Faith, by virtue of its function in the universal Church [2] and by a mandate of the Supreme Pontiff, has judged it necessary to publish the present Declaration.

3. The people of our time are more and more convinced that the human person's dignity and vocation demand that they should discover, by the light of their own intelligence, the values innate in their nature, that they should ceaselessly develop these values and realize them in their lives, in order to achieve an ever greater development.

In moral matters man cannot make value judgments according to his personal whim: "In the depths of his conscience, man detects a law which he does not impose on himself, but which holds him to obedience.... For man has in his heart a law written by God. To obey it is the very dignity of man; according to it he will be judged." [3]

Moreover, through his revelation God has made known to us Christians his plan of salvation, and he has held up to us Christ, the Saviour and Sanctifier, in his teaching and example, as the supreme and immutable law of life: "I am the light of the world; anyone who follows me will not be walking in the dark, he will have the light of life." [4]

Therefore there can be no true promotion of man's dignity unless the essential order of his nature is respected. Of course, in the history of civilization many of the concrete conditions and needs of human life have changed and will continue to change. But all evolution of morals and every type of life must be kept within the limits imposed by the immutable principles based upon every human person's constitutive elements and essential relations—elements and relations which transcend historical contingency.

These fundamental principles, which can be grasped by reason, are contained in "the divine law—eternal, objective, and universal—whereby God orders, directs, and governs the entire universe and all the ways of the human community, by a plan conceived in wisdom and love. Man has been made by God to participate in this law, with the result that, under the gentle disposition of divine Providence, he can come to perceive ever increasingly the unchanging truth." [5] This divine law is accessible to our minds.

4. Hence, those many people are in error who today assert that one can find neither in human nature nor in the revealed law any absolute and immutable norm to serve for particular actions other than the one which expresses itself in the general law of charity and respect for human dignity. As a proof of their assertion they put forward the view that so-called norms of the natural law or precepts of Sacred Scripture are to be regarded only as given expressions of a form of particular culture at a certain moment of history.

But in fact, divine Revelation and, in its own proper order, philosophical wisdom, emphasize the authentic exigencies of human nature. They thereby necessarily manifest the existence of immutable laws inscribed in the constitutive elements of human nature and which are revealed to be identical in all beings endowed with reason.

Furthermore, Christ instituted his Church as "the pillar and bulwark of truth." [6] With the Holy Spirit's assistance, she ceaselessly preserves and transmits without error the truths of the moral order, and she authentically interprets not only the revealed positive law but "also . . . those principles of the moral order which have their origin in human nature itself" [7] and which concern man's full development and sanctification. Now in fact the Church throughout her history has always considered a certain number of precepts of the natural law as having an absolute and immutable value, and in their transgression she has seen a contradiction of the teaching and spirit of the Gospel.

5. Since sexual ethics concern certain fundamental values of human and Christian life, this general teaching equally applies to sexual ethics. In this domain there exist principles and norms which the Church has always unhesitatingly transmitted as part of her teaching, however much the opinions and morals of the world may have been opposed to them. These principles and norms in no way owe their origin to a certain type of culture, but rather to knowledge of the divine law and of human nature. They therefore cannot be considered as having become out of date or doubtful under the pretext that a new cultural situation has arisen.

It is these principles which inspired the exhortations and directives given by the Second Vatican Council for an education and an organization of social life taking account of the equal dignity of man and woman while respecting their difference.[8]

Speaking of "the sexual nature of man and the human faculty of procreation," the Council noted that they "wonderfully exceed the dispositions of lower forms of life." [9] It then took particular care to expound the principles and criteria which concern human sexuality in marriage, and which are based upon the finality of the specific function of sexuality.

In this regard the Council declares that the moral goodness of the acts proper to **conjungal** life, acts which are ordered according to true human dignity, "does not depend solely on sincere intentions or on an evaluation of motives. It must be determined by objective standards. These, based on the nature of the human person and his acts, preserve the full sense of mutual self-giving and human procreation in the context of true love." [10]

These final words briefly sum up the Council's teaching—more fully expounded in an earlier part of the same Constitution [11]—on the finality of the sexual act and on the principal criterion of its morality: it is respect for its finality that ensures the moral goodness of this act.

This same principle, which the Church holds from divine Revelation and from her authentic interpretation of the natural law, is also the basis of her traditional doctrine, which states that the use of the sexual function has its true meaning and moral rectitude only in true marriage.[12]

6. It is not the purpose of the present declaration to deal with all the abuses of the sexual faculty, nor with all the elements involved in the practice of chastity. Its object is rather to repeat the Church's doctrine on

certain particular points, in view of the urgent need to oppose serious errors and widespread aberrant modes of behavior.

7. Today there are many who vindicate the right to sexual union before marriage, at least in those cases where a firm intention to marry and an affection which is already in some way conjugal in the psychology of the subjects require this completion, which they judge to be **connatural**. This is especially the case when the celebration of the marriage is impeded by circumstances or when this intimate relationship seems necessary in order for love to be preserved.

This opinion is contrary to Christian doctrine, which states that every genital act must be within the framework of marriage. However firm the intention of those who practice such premature sexual relations may be, the fact remains that these relations cannot ensure, in sincerity and fidelity, the interpersonal relationship between a man and a woman, nor especially can they protect this relationship from whims and caprices. Now it is a stable union that Jesus willed, and he restored its original requirement, beginning with the sexual difference. "Have you not read that the creator from the beginning made them male and female and that he said: This is why a man must leave father and mother, and cling to his wife, and the two become one body? They are no longer two, therefore, but one body. So then, what God has united, man must not divide." [13] Saint Paul will be even more explicit when he shows that if unmarried people or widows cannot live chastely they have no other alternative than the stable union of marriage: ". . . it is better to marry than to be aflame with passion." [14] Through marriage, in fact, the love of married people is taken up into that love which Christ irrevocably has for the Church,[15] while dissolute sexual union [16] defiles the temple of the Holy Spirit which the Christian has become. Sexual union therefore is only legitimate if a definitive community of life has been established between the man and the woman.

This is what the Church has always understood and taught,[17] and she finds a profound agreement with her doctrine in men's reflection and in the lessons of history.

Experience teaches us that love must find its safeguard in the stability of marriage, if sexual intercourse is truly to respond to the requirements of its own finality and to those of human dignity. These requirements call for a conjugal contract sanctioned and guaranteed by society—a contract which establishes a state of life of capital importance both for the exclusive union of the man and the woman and for the good of their family and of the human community. Most often, in fact, premarital relations exclude the possibility of children. What is represented to be conjugal love is not able, as it absolutely should be, to develop into paternal and maternal love. Or, if it does happen to do so, this will be to the detriment of the children, who will be deprived of the stable environment in which they ought to develop in order to find in it the way and the means of their insertion into society as a whole.

The consent given by people who wish to be united in marriage must therefore be manifested externally and in a manner which makes it valid in the eyes of society. As far as the faithful are concerned, their consent to the setting up of a community of conjugal life must be expressed according to the laws of the Church. It is a consent which makes their marriage a Sacrament of Christ.

8. At the present time there are those who, basing themselves on observations in the psychological order, have begun to judge indulgently, and even to excuse completely, homosexual relations between certain people. This they do in opposition to the constant teaching of the **Magisterium** and to the moral sense of the Christian people.

A distinction is drawn, and it seems with some reason, between homosexuals whose tendency comes from a false education, from a lack of normal sexual development, from habit, from bad example, or from other similar causes, and is transitory or at least not incurable; and homosexuals who are definitively such because of some kind of innate instinct or a pathological constitution judged to be incurable.

In regard to this second category of subjects, some people conclude that their tendency is so natural that it justifies in their case homosexual relations within a sincere communion of life and love analogous to marriage insofar as such homosexuals feel incapable of enduring a solitary life.

In the pastoral field, these homosexuals must certainly be treated with understanding and sustained in the hope of overcoming their personal difficulties and their inability to fit into society. Their culpability will be judged with prudence. But no pastoral method can be employed which would give moral justification to these acts on the grounds that they would be consonant with the condition of such people. For according to the objective moral order, homosexual relations are acts which lack an essential and indispensable finality. In Sacred Scripture they are condemned as a serious depravity and even presented as the sad consequence of rejecting God.[18] This judgment of Scripture does not of course permit us to conclude that all those who suffer from this anomaly are personally responsible for it, but it does attest to the fact that homosexual acts are intrinsically disordered and can in no case be approved.

9. The traditional Catholic doctrine that masturbation constitutes a grave moral disorder is often called into doubt or expressly denied today. It is said that psychology and sociology show that it is a normal phenomenon of sexual development, especially among the young. It is stated that there is real and serious fault only in the measure that the subject deliberately indulges in solitary pleasure closed in on self ("ipsation"), because in this case the act would indeed be radically opposed to the loving communion between

persons of different sex which some hold is what is principally sought in the use of the sexual faculty.

This opinion is contradictory to the teaching and pastoral practice of the Catholic Church. Whatever the force of certain arguments of a biological and philosophical nature, which have sometimes been used by theologians, in fact both the Magisterium of the Church—in the course of a constant tradition—and the moral sense of the faithful have declared without hesitation that masturbation is an intrinsically and seriously disordered act.[19] The main reason is that, whatever the motive for acting in this way, the deliberate use of the sexual faculty outside normal conjugal relations essentially contradicts the finality of the faculty. For it lacks the sexual relationship called for by the moral order, namely the relationship which realizes "the full sense of mutual self-giving and human procreation in the context of true love."[20] All deliberate exercise of sexuality must be reserved to this regular relationship. Even if it cannot be proved that Scripture condemns this sin by name, the tradition of the Church has rightly understood it to be condemned in the New Testament when the latter speaks of "impurity," "unchasteness," and other vices contrary to chastity and continence.

Sociological surveys are able to show the frequency of this disorder according to the places, populations, or circumstances studied. In this way facts are discovered, but facts do not constitute a criterion for judging the moral value of human acts.[21] The frequency of the phenomenon in question is certainly to be linked with man's innate weakness following original sin; but it is also to be linked with the loss of a sense of God, with the corruption of morals engendered by the commercialization of vice, with the unrestrained licentiousness of so many public entertainments and publications, as well as with the neglect of modesty, which is the guardian of chastity.

On the subject of masturbation modern psychology provides much valid and useful information for formulating a more equitable judgment on moral responsibility and for orienting pastoral action. Psychology helps one to see how the immaturity of adolescence (which can sometimes persist after that age), psychological imbalance, or habit can influence behavior, diminishing the deliberate character of the act and bringing about a situation whereby subjectively there may not always be serious fault. But in general, the absence of serious responsibility must not be presumed; this would be to misunderstand people's moral capacity.

In the pastoral ministry, in order to form an adequate judgment in concrete cases, the habitual behavior of people will be considered in its totality, not only with regard to the individual's practice of charity and of justice but also with regard to the individual's care in observing the particular precepts of chastity. In particular, one will have to examine whether the individual is using the necessary means, both natural and supernatural, which Christian asceticism from its long experience recommends for overcoming the passions and progressing in virtue. . . .

Footnotes

1. See Vatican II, *Pastoral Constitution on the Church in the World of Today,* no. 47: *Acta Apostolicae Sedis* 58 (1966) 1067 [*The Pope Speaks* XI, 289–290].

2. See the Apostolic Constitution *Regimini Ecclesiae universae* (August 15, 1967), no. 29: *AAS* 59 (1967) 897 [*TPS* XII, 401–402].

3. Pastoral Constitution on the Church in the World of Today, no. 16: *AAS* 58 (1966) 1037 [*TPS* XI, 268].

4. Jn 8, 12.

5. Declaration on Religions Freedom, no. 3: *AAS* 58 (1966) 931 [*TPS* XI, 86].

6. 1 *Tm* 3, 15.

7. Declaration on Religious Freedom, no. 14: *AAS* 58 (1966) 940 [*TPS* XI, 93]. See also Pius XI, Encyclical *Casti Connubii* (December 31, 1930): *AAS* 22 (1930) 579–580; Pius XII, Address of November 2, 1954 *AAS* 46 (1954) 671–672 [*TPS* I 380–381]; John XXIII, Encyclical *Mater et Magistra* (May 25, 1961), no. 239: *AAS* 53 (1961) 457 [*TPS* VII, 388]; Paul VI, Encyclical *Humanae Vitae* (July 25, 1968), no. 4: *AAS* 60 (1968) 483 [*TPS* XIII, 331–332].

8. See Vatican II, *Declaration on Christian Education,* nos. 1 and 8: *AAS* 58 (1966) 729–730, 734–736 [*TPS* XI, 201–202, 206–207]; *Pastoral Constitution on the Church in the World of Today,* nos. 29, 60, 67: *AAS* 58 (1966) 1048–1049, 1080–1081, 1088–1089 [*TPS* XI, 276–277, 299–300, 304–305].

9. Pastoral Constitution on the Church in the World of Today, no. 51: *AAS* 58 (1966) 1072 [*TPS* XI, 293].

10. Loc. cit.; see also no. 49: *AAS* 58 (1966) 1069–1070 [*TPS* XI, 291–292].

11. See *Pastoral Constitution on the Church in the World of Today,* nos. 49–50: *AAS* 58 (1966) 1069–1072 [*TPS* XI, 291–293].

12. The present Declaration does not review all the moral norms for the use of sex, since they have already been set forth in the encyclicals *Casti Connubii* and *Humanae Vitae.*

13. Mt 19, 4–6.

14. 1 *Cor* 7, 9.

15. See *Eph* 5, 25–32.

16. Extramarital intercourse is expressly condemned in *1 Cor* 5, 1; 6, 9; 7, 2; 10, 8; *Eph* 5, 5–7; *1 Tm* 1, 10; *Heb* 13, 4; there are explicit arguments given in *1 Cor* 6, 12–20.

17. See Innocent IV, Letter *Sub Catholicae professione* (March 6, 1254) (*DS* 835); Pius II, Letter *Cum sicut accepimus* (November 14, 1459) (*DS* 1367); Decrees of the Holy Office on September 24, 1665 (*DS* 2045) and March 2, 1679 (*DS* 2148); Pius XI, Encyclical *Casti Conubii* (December 31, 1930): *AAS* 22 (1930) 538–539.

18. Rom 1:24–27: "In consequence, God delivered them up in their lusts to unclean practices; they engaged in the mutual degradation of their bodies, these men who exchanged the truth of God for a lie and worshiped and served the creature rather than the Creator—blessed be he forever, amen! God therefore delivered them to disgraceful passions. Their women exchanged natural intercourse for unnatural, and the men gave up natural intercourse with women and burned with lust for one another. Men did shameful things with men, and thus received in their own persons the penalty for their perversity." See also what St. Paul says of sodomy in *1 Cor* 6, 9; *1 Tm* 1, 10.

19. See Leo IX, Letter *Ad splendidum nitentes* (1054) (*DS* 687–688); Decree of the Holy Office on March 2, 1679 (*DS* 2149); Pius XII, Addresses of October 8, 1953: *AAS* 45 (1953) 677–678, and May 19, 1956: *AAS* 48 (1956) 472–473.

20. Pastoral Constitution on the Church in the World of Today, no. 51: *AAS* 58 (1966) 1072 [*TPS* XI, 293].

21. See Paul VI, Apostolic Exhortation *Quinque iam anni* (December 8, 1970): *AAS* 63 (1971) 102 [*TPS* XV, 329]: "If sociological surveys are useful for better discovering the thought patterns of the people of a particular place, the anxieties and needs of those to whom we proclaim the word of God, and also the oppositions made to it by modern reasoning through the widespread notion that outside science there exists no legitimate form of knowledge, still the conclusions drawn from such surveys could not of themselves constitute a determining criterion of truth."

Review Questions

1. What is the traditional Christian doctrine about sex, according to the declaration?

2. Why does the declaration find premarital sexual relations to be immoral?

3. What is the declaration's objection to homosexuality?

4. What is wrong with masturbation, according to the declaration?

Discussion Questions

1. Is celibacy a violation of natural law? Explain your view.

2. Is contraception wrong too? Defend your answer.

3. Is procreation the only natural purpose of sex? Defend your position.

Russell Vannoy

Sexual Perversion: Is There Such a Thing?

Russell Vannoy teaches philosophy at the State University College of New York at Buffalo.

Vannoy attacks the natural law view of sex. He claims that sex for pleasure is just as natural as reproductive sex, that we cannot assume that whatever is natural is good, and that sex can be a natural expression of love even if it is not procreative.

INTRODUCTORY CONSIDERATIONS

One of my students once insisted that he could conclusively prove that homosexuality was immoral. "What," he asked, "if everyone were a homosexual? The human race would perish." My own response was to ask, "Since you are a deeply religious person, what if everyone became a priest? The human race would also perish." It seems that the very sort of argument that proves that homosexuals are immoral also proves that priests are immoral as well—an odd

conclusion indeed. (Of course, not everyone is going to become a priest, but not everyone is going to become a homosexual, either.) Arguments of the purely hypothetical "what if everybody did it" sort are very common in accusations against sexual deviancy, yet in this instance it goes nowhere. Just how does one prove that perversions are immoral or "sick?" Can one even prove that there *are* such things as perversions—some of society's and some psychiatrists' convictions notwithstanding?

Another example of perversion given by a student was that of necrophilia or sex with a dead body, an example that immediately sent a shock wave of disgust through the lecture room. But if one uses the criterion that an act is immoral if it causes pain to the victim, such a criterion would hardly be applicable to a corpse! Of course such sex suffers from a distinct lack of responsiveness from the object of one's affections, but this is hardly a *moral* objection to such sex. One seems to be left only with one's shock, horror, and disgust with such a phenomenon, but this is hardly a criterion either; for conservative people are shocked by the sight of innocent lovemaking in a public park. Disgust seems to reveal more about the nature and conditioning of the one who is disgusted than it does about the object of one's disgust.

Even certain enlightened writers about sexual morality who avoid superficial moral arguments nevertheless insist on finding strained arguments to attack homosexuality. The Whiteleys, for example, do a brilliant job of exposing the manifold fallacies in condemnation of homosexuality as "unnatural," yet they persist in labeling such sex "unfruitful":

In family life, two parents are biologically necessary to produce children and, it would seem, psychologically desirable to bring them up. The homosexual is usually a person who opts out of family life and parenthood, provides no children, and deprives whoever might have been his wife (or her husband) of the opportunity for family life. A community of such people stands apart from and at odds with the rest of society. A selfish, pleasure-seeking pattern of living is common among them, not because they are constitutionally like this, but because their manner of life leaves them less incentive for the taking of responsibility. They rarely achieve the full personal relationship between partners marriage makes possible. Love affairs are common amongst them, but they are usually short-lived; they lack the support of law and custom.... They can hardly avoid some degree of estrangement from their normal associates....[1] *(Emphasis mine.)*

But the Whiteleys never stop to think where the real blame for the estrangement of homosexuals lies. For is it not the heterosexual majority who formulate the laws and customs that force homosexuals into a group alienated from the rest of society? Does this rejection not breed the self-hate that prevents long-lasting love attachments between homosexuals? (One must love oneself before one can love another.) And if the homosexual feels his creative accomplishments will be rejected by society because he is homosexual, will he not be driven to "selfish pleasure-seeking" as a form of compensation and to find some degree of happiness?

If homosexuals can be accused of being perverts because they are isolated from the rest of society, we can imagine an even more extreme case of lonely sex. Joe, for example, is a loner, who finds that reality is no match for the beautiful fantasies and orgasms he can have while his Accu-Jac machine masturbates him. What could be more in tune with this world of labor-saving devices, he asks, than to sit back and to avoid the hassle and ex-

pense of putting up with the demands and unpredictable whims of other people? Can we say that Joe is a pervert if he prefers this form of sex to the exclusion of penile-vaginal intercourse? Or must we say that if Joe is satisfied with his Accu-Jac, then that, for him, is the best sex? Nor should we call it perverted or even "bad sex" if it harms no one and brings him the gratification he seeks.

It might, however, be argued that even if we do not wish to label Joe a pervert, his is nevertheless "bad sex," for bringing relief from sexual tension is surely not the same as full sexual gratification. We can imagine someone who likes steak more than anything else but then discovers that he can eat a certain kind of pill that gives him identical nourishment and a sense of a full stomach. But although his hunger has been relieved, he has not been truly satisfied in the way he would have been had he eaten steak. Is his case like Joe's?

But this reply would not hold for someone who prefers sex of a very simple sort to one who wants a "full course" treatment. In aesthetics we sometimes contrast a "thin" sense of aesthetic perception with a "thick" sense of perception; the former perceiver prefers to focus on the pure form of the work of art itself, while the latter prefers to enrich his perception by bringing to it all the associations the work calls to his mind, such as memories of his childhood, the tragedy of the human condition, and so forth. Yet each experience can be as intense and rich in its own way as the other. The advocates of "thin" aesthetic experiences feel that the intensity of such experiences is diluted by having one's total absorption in the work for its own sake distracted by irrelevant associations. Someone who prefers masturbation to other forms of sex could then be said to prefer a "thin" sexual experience for reasons similar to those who prefer thin aesthetic experiences of works of art.[2] Nor need masturbation always be viewed as a "thin" form of sex concerned solely with an orgasmic release of sexual tension. For when it is accompanied by fantasies or by one's sensuous caresses of one's own body or by the enjoyment of sexual arousal for its own sake, it may be as rich or "thick" an experience as any other form of sex.

One's response to Joe's preference for masturbation does, I think, tend to reveal more about the lifestyle and value system of Joe's critic then it does about Joe himself. Can Joe be refuted in any objective way by saying that his sex life is lonely, nonproductive, impersonal, self-centered, or mechanistic if Joe himself has tried both types of sex and has decided on the type he thinks is best for him? Does this sort of example reveal that the concept of a nonperverted act has built into it a concept of what "good" sex is, what the good life is, what is presumably necessary to hold society together into a community of procreative, interacting individuals? If so, it is far from the clinically objective term it is often presented as being, and it is riddled with value systems that are subject to dissent and disagreement without one's necessarily being sick or perverted if he does dissent from what society considers to be healthy or normal sex.

Let us now look at some of the things that have been called sexual perversions, a phrase that has been used to cover such diverse phenomena as sadism and masochism, sex with corpses, homosexuality, voyeurism, exhibitionism, erotic attachments to certain types of clothing, or any sex that departs from the usual penile-vaginal sort, such as oral or anal sex. From time to time we receive mysterious pronouncements from psychiatrists that certain of these acts have been "declassified" as sicknesses; for example, psychiatrists (by a majority vote!) no longer classify homosexuals as sick, provided they have successfully adapted to and accepted their condition; oral and anal sex between heterosexuals has similarly been declassified, on grounds that they are commonly practiced by humans and animals. But many psychiatrists will still condemn such practices if they are allowed to take predominance over "normal" penile-vaginal intercourse, rather than being occasional supplements to the "normal" routine.

A philosopher who is looking for some clear principle to distinguish the perverted from the normal will obviously find this to be a chaotic situation, indeed. He may well wonder how many more such acts will be similarly freed from the stigma of being labeled as perverted. Is the concept of perversion, after all, perhaps an all-too-human interpretation or value judgment placed on certain sexual phenomena rather than an objective or descriptive term? Can we, for example, see the perverted quality of a sex act in the way that there can be a consensus in seeing the awkward quality of an inept dancer? Can we see the disorder in perverted sex in the same way we can see the disorder of someone undergoing an epileptic seizure? Surely there is no consensus that this could be the case, except among those who have already been conditioned to believe there must be something disordered in perverted sex.

THE "HARMONY OF OPPOSITES" PRINCIPLE

One of the most commonly offered criteria for perversion is that it is somehow a violation of the natural order of things. It has been argued, for example, that nature is governed by a "harmony of opposites" between the male and female principles. The male is active, the female passive; the active male penis is a shaft, which by nature "fits" its opposite, the passive vaginal emptiness. The male is the aggressive provider who goes forth into the world to provide for the family; the female's role is stay home, raise the children, and with her feminine tenderness help her husband relax after a long day. Each gives what the other presumably lacks, and this is supposed to be a beautiful phenomenon indeed.

It is clear, however, that the entire principle as traditionally expressed rests on sexist stereotypes of "active" males and "passive" females that have been vigorously challenged for several years now. Furthermore, the defenders of the principle overlook the obvious fact that there can be a harmony of opposites that need not involve differences of gender at all. Opposites can take many forms; between a passive and an active male, for example, an opposite exists on the psychological as well as on the physiological level. The possibility of **sodomy** between two males, with one male preferring the active or masculine role of penetrating the anus and the other preferring the passive feminine role of being penetrated, is but one illustration of how there could also be a harmony of opposites between homosexuals. The fact that traditional defenders of the principle speak of "male and female genders" rather than "masculine and feminine temperaments," two sets of concepts that need have no connection, shows clearly that the defenders of the principle have interpreted it to rationalize their heterosexual preferences that antedated the formulation of the principle itself. Indeed, if defenders of such a principle could be brought to see the validity of forms of sex other than the traditional penile-vaginal sort, they would discover many sexual practices that do not require the two partners to take "harmoniously opposite" active-passive roles at all. For example, certain forms of mutual oral stimulation of the sexual organs can be performed in the lateral position by partners of the same or opposite sex. Both are active; neither dominate the other.

Indeed, as I have noted before, my own research from student term papers reveals a decided difference in sexual philosophy between males and females, with the former preferring the more aggressive, quick sexual act and the latter preferring the more prolonged, relaxed, "loving" sensuous eroticism. If there is any "harmony" here, it is apparent that one of the two sexes is subordinating its wishes to the other, and in a sexist society it is no mystery which gender is doing the surrendering.

Furthermore, there is the curious phenomenon of males wooing females in the most devoted fashion, yet also condoning or fostering a sexist society where women are not treated as equals. It is as if men down through history said, "I love you, but stay in the kitchen where you belong and take care of the children." If true love is love between equals, each complementing the other in a harmonious attitude of mutual respect for each other's dignity, then one wonders how much true heterosexual love has existed in history.

IS PERVERSION "UNNATURAL"?

Perhaps the most familiar use of the term *natural* in a sexual context is the claim that the sexual organs have a certain natural purpose: that nature or God intended them for procreation. It is, however, apparent that nature also gives sexual desires and sexual pleasures to those who cannot procreate, either temporarily or permanently, such as those who are too young or too old, or those who are sterile or who are in a temporarily nonreproductive cycle.

The reply might be that nonreproductive intercourse could still be "natural," provided it is the sort of intercourse that could lead to procreation *were conditions normal*. But this reply would mean that a female who is in a temporarily nonreproductive cycle is somehow abnormal. Yet the period of the month when she is fertile and the years of her life when she can bear children are quite brief compared to the times she cannot reproduce. Her fertile period could then just as easily be characterized as an abnormal phenomenon. Furthermore, the number of times people have sex for pleasure so vastly outnumbers the times when sex is meant for procreation that one could argue that sex for procreation is kind of statistical abnormality. And if our sexual desires come from nature, the abnormality is not merely statistical.

Indeed, the ability to have sexual pleasure rather than the ability to or the desire to reproduce would seem to be what defines us as sexual beings. For if we could only reproduce but not have sexual feelings, we would not speak of sexual acts or sexual organs at all; rather we would speak only of reproductive acts or reproductive organs.

But the main difficulty is that there seems to be a contradiction in nature, in giving us desires for nonprocreative sex when procreation is said to be its *sole* sexual purpose. What then becomes of the claim that an act that violates nature is a sexual disorder if nature is confused about its purposes? And what becomes of the theory that nature is created by a deity or presided over by a biology that arranges all things in an orderly means-end relationship directed toward procreation if nature is contradicting herself in also allowing—indeed making us desire—nonprocreative sex?

The deeper question, however, is whether and how anything unnatural can happen in the world of nature at all. Is there some point in the universe where nature ceases and the unnatural begins? We might, for example, compare the universe to a solid bowl of pure Jello; wherever we bite into the gelatin, we will find that its creator has included in it nothing other than Jello. There would thus be no basis for saying that one should eat only the Jello and avoid anything that deviates from what its creator intended the bowl to contain. Thus, just as one would be puzzled as to how anything that is Jello could be non-gelatinous, one might equally well wonder how anything in the world of nature could be unnatural. For if something were unnatural it couldn't be part of our universe at all; the universe *is* nature, and thus everything in it is natural.

If, then, one feels an urge to commit sodomy, has one discovered some mysterious gap in the world of nature where nature does not exist? Or cannot one say that the prompting is as much a part of nature as any other? Such an urge may be unusual and widely deplored, but so is a hurricane, which is a perfectly natural phenomenon. Perhaps what we should say is that the only thing that is sexually unnatural is whatever nature does not allow us to do. A man might, for example, have the desire to ejaculate by penetrating someone's ear canal and engage in thrusting motions of the penis much as he would in a vagina. But nature clearly makes this mode of ejaculation out of the question; thus it would be unnatural. One could, of course, masturbate and shoot his semen into someone's ear (or onto any part of someone's body, for that matter). Such an act would be natural, since nature does not forbid it by making it impossible to do so.

It might, however, be argued that such an argument about the naturalness of all things that are possible destroys a perfectly familiar distinction: that between the natural and antinatural (or artificial or synthetic). Self-preservation is a natural phenomenon, yet why is it that so many people kill themselves? Isn't suicide "unnatural"? Germs are a part of nature, yet we develop man-made (that is, unnatural) drugs to destroy germs.

Indeed, if all these things were natural, wouldn't nature be contradicting herself if both disease and the drugs to conquer disease were natural, or if nature gave both the desire for self-preservation and, to some, a desire for self-destruction?

None of these considerations, however, necessarily disprove the principle that whatever exists and whatever we desire and can do is natural. Nietzsche, for example, argued that nature is a battleground of conflicting wills to power, with each one trying to expand its influence and strength and destroying whatever stands in its way. A virus or cancer, for example, is a phenomenon of nature that tries to conquer the body, and we try to conquer the virus and cancer in turn because of another phenomenon of nature—our instinct for self-preservation. The materials we use to conquer disease may be man-made, but their ingredients can be traced back to nature, as well as the natural ingenuity we use to create these materials. Furthermore, there may not be only an instinct for self-preservation; as Freud once noted, there may also exist a natural death wish, of which suicide would be the most extreme example.

It is clear, therefore, that the term *natural* can be defined to refer to many things, even if one still wanted to insist that some things are unnatural. Those who claim that only one kind of sex, procreative sex, is natural are simply selecting one aspect of our sexual nature to suit their own moral presuppositions about what the purpose of sex ought to be. Furthermore, those who attempt to give a religious or moralistic backing to such sexual doctrines make the following questionable assumptions.

— They assume that they know exactly what God's will is in sexual matters, that He intended sex only for the purpose of procreation, despite the fact that the deity has clearly created us with many other sexual needs and desires.

— They assume that whatever is natural is good, despite the fact that nature daily, through no fault of man's, inflicts on us catastrophes of all sorts. Furthermore, many would hold that aggression is a perfectly natural instinct: witness infants' screams and kicking of feet and pounding of fists when they are frustrated. Babies didn't learn to be aggressive; and if one holds that one learns aggression from society, how did society come to be aggressive in the first place and require endless laws to keep the social order? But if aggression is natural and if whatever is natural is held to be good, then under the "obey nature" philosophy, one would be driven to the highly unwelcome conclusion that rape is natural and therefore good.

— Defenders of the philosophy that nature intends sex only for procreation assume that all men have the same basic nature, even though some men (they say) willfully violate nature. This overlooks the fact that nature has clearly made us all different in some respects; could it not therefore be true that nature has created some persons with a unique sexual nature of their own that has nothing to do with procreation? But if this is true, then under the "obey nature" philosophy one should allow such persons to fulfill their own individual natures (so long as they do not harm others) rather than accuse them of having committed so-called crimes against nature.

One can therefore say that if someone who differs from what is usually considered natural and who commits acts most persons would find perverted, then the fact that such a person was endowed by nature with (1) the imagination to conceive the act, (2) the desire to perform the act, (3) the ability to carry it out, and (4) the ability to enjoy it, makes that act perfectly natural for him or her. If nature had not intended a person to perform such acts, it would have been impossible to acquire these four abilities. (If some persons claim they do not desire or cannot enjoy something that deviates from the norm, this may only mean that their unique nature has been buried under layers of repressive social conditioning.)

— It should be noted further that to reduce human sex to procreation is, in effect, to reduce sex to the purely animal level where sex is performed in only one way for one purpose—the reproduction of the species. But men and women are also beings with free will and powers of reason and imagination, and these are completely overlooked when one reduces sex to a purely animalistic function. If nature gives man freedom and imagination, doesn't nature want him to use these talents to conceive of and freely choose forms of sex other than the purely animal one? Some defenders of procreation try to meet this charge that they are reducing sex to an animal level by allowing sex to have a secondary function: sex as an expression of love. Then they condemn sex with a non-lover that is for pleasure alone, even though nature clearly gives pleasure to non-lovers, as well. Nor can one call sex for sex's sake animalistic, for it seems to be uniquely human. This is particularly true if such sex is performed with imagination, thereby utilizing a distinctively human ability.

— If sex for procreation were a law of nature implanted in all living creatures by, say, an all-powerful God, it is difficult to see why defenders of procreation have to write elaborate treatises and deliver endless sermons telling us we ought to obey the dictates of nature. For if there is a natural law regarding procreation, it would seem plausible to assume that we would all have to obey it automatically as a matter of course, just as we must all obey the natural dictates to breathe, defecate, and eventually die. But the fact that defenders of nature have to struggle to convince us to procreate (or else face eternal damnation), and the fact that so many heterosexuals do not procreate (nor do any homosexuals), indicate that there are no natural laws compelling us to procreate or even to be heterosexual.

— Defenders of procreation make the mistaken assumption that if X results from Y, X was the purpose of Y. Babies, of course, do result from sex quite frequently (although not, oddly enough, during a female's infertile period, despite the fact that nature gave her sexual desires during this period, a fact the procreation theorist cannot explain). But, once again, because X results from Y, it does not follow that X was the exclusive or main goal or purpose of Y. All sorts of things result from sex, everything from ecstatic pleasure to venereal disease. (Certainly one would not say that gonorrhea is a purpose of sex, even though it is an all too common result of sex.)

Turning from this brief critique of traditional moral and religious views on the one true purpose of sex, we also find that there are those who have questioned the idea that sex is a natural instinct at all—whatever its purpose. Ti-Grace Atkinson, for example, argues that the desire for sex is really a function of the male's desire to dominate the female in the bedroom. When this need to dominate—and the correlative culturally conditioned desire in the female to surrender—is obliterated in some future era when the sexes are equal and feel no need for the dominance-submission

syndrome, sexual desire will reveal itself for the culturally conditioned phenomenon it is and, according to Ms. Atkinson, will simply disappear.[3] The difficulty with Ms. Atkinson's theory is that she, like the conservative defenders of the natural-instinct philosophy, has assumed there is only one motive for sex: the culturally conditioned desire for dominance and submission. The fact that sex can have many purposes escapes both Ms. Atkinson and the defender of a natural instinct for procreation alone. In response to Ms. Atkinson's argument that sex will disappear when the dominance-submission syndrome is ended by overcoming sexist social conditioning, one could hold that since there are many other purposes sex might have (be they natural or socially conditioned), desires for sex will continue even after sexism is eliminated.

Finally, it might be noted that those who give up any attempt to define perversion as something that violates nature often turn to another criterion: A pervert is someone who disobeys social norms. But adultery violates a social norm, and it is not considered a perversion. Furthermore, such things as kissing in public and oral sex once violated social norms, though they are now widespread social phenomena that only a few conservatives would condemn. Basing a concept of perversion on disobedience to what is often a narrow-minded society, therefore, commits a person to basing his philosophy on the shifting sands of obedience to current fashions in sex. Anyone who prides himself on thinking for himself and on being able to transcend social conditioning would be revolted (and justifiably so) by such a socially defined concept of perversion....

Footnotes

1. C.H. and Winifred Whiteley, *Sex and Morals* (New York: Basic Books, 1967), p. 91.

2. This "thin" versus "thick" example of sexual experience is also aptly illustrated by the dark-room orgy example that we might use to prove that "an orgasm is an orgasm," that is, that one orgasm is as good as another no matter how obtained and that there is no such thing as a perversion or bad sex. Suppose, for example, that a heterosexual male were placed in a dark room which, without his knowing it, contained a man, a woman, and perhaps even a sheep. Suppose further that he had sexual intercourse with each person or animal and that he could not tell which was which. Wouldn't he be equally satisfied with each? Of course, for those who want just an orgasm, the example is perfectly apt; but for those who want to know precisely whom they are having intercourse with, with all the psychological associations that entails, the example would not work. Whether they *should* be concerned about whom they have sex with, and whether they should not rather learn that any object is a potential object of sexual enjoyment if one only tries to learn to enjoy it is another question. De Sade would regard our selectivity as merely the product of our own socially conditioned hangups.

3. Ms. Atkinson's views are summarized in Elizabeth Rapaport, "On the Future of Love: Rousseau and the Radical Feminists," *The Philosophical Forum* 5 (Fall-Winter, 1973–74): 188.

Review Questions

1. What is the most common account of sexual perversion, according to Vannoy?

2. Why doesn't Vannoy accept this account?

3. What are Vannoy's main criticisms of the view that the natural purpose of sex is procreation?

Discussion Questions

1. Does sex have other purposes besides procreation? What are they?

2. How do we tell when an activity is natural? Explain your view.

Richard Wasserstrom

Is Adultery Immoral?

Richard Wasserstrom is professor of philosophy at the University of California at Santa Cruz. He is the editor of Today's Moral Problems *(3d ed., 1985), and the author of* Philosophy and Social Issues: Five Studies *(1980).*

Wasserstrom discusses three arguments for saying that adultery is immoral. The first is that it is immoral because it involves the breaking of a promise. The second is that adultery is immoral because it involves deception. The third argument is that the prohibition against adultery is justified because it helps maintain the institution of marriage and the nuclear family. But Wasserstrom does not find these arguments to be conclusive; he raises problems for each.

From Richard A. Wasserstrom, "Is Adultery Immoral?" in R.A. Wasserstrom, *Today's Moral Problems* (New York: Macmillan Publishing Co., 1975), pp. 240–252. Reprinted with permission of author.

. . . I propose in this paper to think about the topic of sexual morality, and to do so in the following fashion. I shall consider just one kind of behavior that is often taken to be a case of sexual immorality—adultery. I am interested in pursuing at least two questions. First, I want to explore the question of in what respects adulterous behavior falls within the domain of morality at all: For this surely is one of the puzzles one encounters when considering the topic of sexual morality. It is often hard to see on what grounds much of the behavior is deemed to be either moral or immoral, for example, private homosexual behavior between consenting adults. I have purposely selected adultery because it seems a more plausible candidate for moral assessment than many other kinds of sexual behavior.

The second question I want to examine is that of what is to be said about adultery, without being especially concerned to stay within the area of morality. I shall endeavor, in other words, to identify and to assess a number of the major arguments that might be advanced against adultery. I believe that they are the chief arguments that would be given in support of the view that adultery is immoral, but I think they are worth considering even if some of them turn out to be nonmoral arguments and considerations.

A number of the issues involved seem to me to be complicated and difficult. In a number of places I have at best indicated where further philosophical exploration is required without having successfully conducted the exploration myself. The paper may very well be more useful as an illustration of how one might begin to think about the subject of sexual morality than as an elucidation of important truths about the topic.

Before I turn to the arguments themselves there are two preliminary points that require some clarification. Throughout the paper I shall refer to the immorality of such things as breaking a promise, deceiving someone, etc. In a very rough way, I mean by this that there is something morally wrong that is done in doing the action in question. I mean that the action is, in a strong sense of *"prima facie"* *prima facie* wrong or unjustified. I do not mean that it may never be right or justifiable to do the action; just that the fact that it is an action of this description always does count against the rightness of the action. I leave entirely open the question of what it is that makes actions of this kind immoral in this sense of "immoral."

The second preliminary point concerns what is meant or implied by the concept of adultery. I mean by "adultery" any case of extramarital sex, and I want to explore the arguments for and against extramarital sex, undertaken in a variety of morally relevant situations. Someone might claim that the concept of adultery is conceptually connected with the concept of immorality, and that to characterize behavior as adulterous is already to characterize it as immoral or unjustified in the sense described above. There may be something to this. Hence the importance of making it clear that I want to talk about extramarital sexual relations. If they are always immoral, this is something that must be shown by argument. If the concept of adultery does in some sense entail or imply immorality, I want to ask whether that connection is a rationally based one. If not all cases of extramarital sex are immoral (again, in the sense described above), then the concept of adultery should either be weakened accordingly or restricted to those classes of extramarital sex for which the predication of immorality is warranted.

One argument for the immorality of adultery might go something like this: what makes adultery immoral is that it involves the breaking of a promise, and what makes adultery seriously wrong is that it involves the breaking of an important promise. For, so the argument might continue, one of the things the two parties promise each other when they get married is that they will abstain from sexual relationships with third persons. Because of this promise both spouses quite reasonably entertain the expectation that the other will behave in conformity with it. Hence, when one of the parties has sexual intercourse with a third person he or she breaks that promise about sexual relationships which was made when the marriage was entered into, and defeats the reasonable expectations of exclusivity entertained by the spouse.

In many cases the immorality involved in breaching the promise relating to extramarital sex may be a good deal more serious than that involved in the breach of other promises. This is so because adherence to this promise may be of much greater importance to the parties than is adherence to many of the other promises given or received by them in their lifetime. The breaking of this promise may be much more hurtful and painful than is typically the case.

Why is this so? To begin with, it may have been difficult for the nonadulterous spouse to have kept the promise. Hence that spouse may feel the unfairness of having restrained himself or herself in the absence of reciprocal restraint having been exercised by the adulterous spouse. In addition, the spouse may perceive the breaking of the promise as an indication of a kind of indifference on the part of the adulterous spouse. If you really cared about me and my feelings—the spouse might say—you would not have done this to me. And third, and related to the above, the spouse may see the act of sexual intercourse with another as a sign of affection for the other person and as an additional rejection of the nonadulterous spouse as the one who is loved by the adulterous spouse. It is not just that the adulterous spouse does not take the feelings of the spouse sufficiently into account, the adulterous spouse also indicates through the act of adultery affection for someone other than the spouse. I will return to these points later. For the present, it is sufficient to note that a set of arguments can be developed in support of the proposition that certain kinds of adultery are wrong just because they involve the breach of a serious promise which, among other things, leads to the intentional infliction of substantial pain by one spouse upon the other.

Another argument for the immorality of adultery focuses not on the existence of a promise of sexual exclusivity but on the connection between adultery and deception. According to this argument, adultery involves deception. And because deception is wrong, so is adultery.

Although it is certainly not obviously so, I shall simply assume in this paper that deception is always immoral. Thus the crucial issue for my purposes is the asserted connection between extramarital sex and deception. Is it plausible to maintain, as this argument does, that adultery always does involve deception and is on that basis to be condemned?

The most obvious person on whom deceptions might be practiced is the nonparticipating spouse; and the most obvious thing about which the nonparticipating spouse can be deceived is the existence of the adulterous act. One clear case of deception is that of lying. Instead of saying that the afternoon was spent in bed with A, the adulterous spouse asserts that it was spent in the library with B, or on the golf course with C.

There can also be deception even when no lies are told. Suppose, for instance, that a person has sexual intercourse with someone other than his or her spouse and just does not tell the spouse about it. Is that deception? It may not be a case of lying if, for example, the spouse is never asked by the other about the situation. Still, we might say, it is surely deceptive because of the promises that were exchanged at marriage. As we saw earlier, these promises provide a foundation for the reasonable belief that neither spouse will engage in sexual relationships with any other persons. Hence the failure to bring the fact of extramarital sex to the attention of the other spouse deceives that spouse about the present state of the marital relationship.

Adultery, in other words, can involve both active and passive deception. An adulterous spouse may just keep silent or, as is often the fact, the spouse may engage in an increasingly complex way of life devoted to the concealment of the facts from the nonparticipating spouse. Lies, half-truths, clandestine meetings, and the like may become a central feature of the adulterous spouse's existence. These are things that can and do happen, and when they do they make the case against adultery an easy one. Still, neither active nor passive deception is inevitably a feature of an extramarital relationship.

It is possible, though, that a more subtle but pervasive kind of deceptiveness is a feature of adultery. It comes about because of the connection in our culture between sexual intimacy and certain feelings of love and affection. The point can be made indirectly at first by seeing that one way in which we can, in our culture, mark off our close friends from our mere acquaintances is through the kinds of intimacies that we are prepared to share with them. I may, for instance, be willing to reveal my very private thoughts and emotions to my closest friends or to my wife, but to no one else. My sharing of these intimate facts about myself is from one perspective a way of making a gift to those who mean the most to me. Revealing these things and sharing them with those who mean the most to me is one means by which I create, maintain, and confirm those interpersonal relationships that are of most importance to me.

Now in our culture, it might be claimed, sexual intimacy is one of the chief currencies through which gifts of this sort are exchanged. One way to tell someone—particularly someone of the opposite sex—that you have feelings of affection and love for them is by allowing to them or sharing with them sexual behaviors that one doesn't share with the rest of the world. This way of measuring affection was certainly very much a part of the culture in which I matured. It worked something like this. If you were a girl, you showed how much you liked someone by the degree of sexual intimacy you would allow. If you liked a boy only a little, you never did more than kiss—and even the kiss was not very passionate. If you liked the boy a lot and if your feeling was reciprocated, necking, and possibly petting, was permissible. If the attachment was still stronger and you thought it might even become a permanent relationship, the sexual activity was correspondingly more intense and more intimate, although whether it would ever lead to sexual intercourse depended on whether the parties (and particularly the girl) accepted fully the prohibition on nonmarital sex. The situation of the boy was related, but not exactly the same. The assumption was that males did not naturally link sex with affection in the way in which females did. However, since women did, males had to take this into account. That is to say, because a woman would permit sexual intimacies only if she had feelings of affection for the male and only if those feelings were reciprocated, the male had to have and express those feelings, too, before sexual intimacies of any sort would occur.

The result was that the importance of a correlation between sexual intimacy and feelings of love and affection was taught by the culture and assimilated by those growing up in the culture. The scale of possible positive feelings toward persons of the opposite sex ran from casual liking at the one end to the love that was deemed essential to and characteristic of marriage at the other. The scale of possible sexual behavior ran from brief, passionless kissing or hand-holding at the one end to sexual intercourse at the other. And the correlation between the two scales was quite precise. As a result, any act of sexual intimacy carried substantial meaning with it, and no act of sexual intimacy was simply a pleasurable set of bodily sensations. Many such acts were, of course, more pleasurable to the participants because they were a way of saying what the participants' feelings were. And sometimes they were less pleasurable for the same reason. The point is, however, that in any event sexual activity was much more than mere bodily enjoyment. It was not like eating a good meal, listening to good music, lying in the sun, or getting a pleasant back rub. It was behavior that meant a great deal concerning one's feelings for persons of the opposite sex in whom one was most interested and with whom one was most involved. It was among the most authoritative ways in which one could communicate to another the nature and degree of one's affection.

If this sketch is even roughly right, then several things become somewhat clearer. To begin with, a possible rationale for many of the rules of conventional sexual morality can be developed. If, for example, sexual intercourse is associated with the kind of affection and commitment to another that is regarded as characteristic of the marriage relationship, then it is natural that sexual intercourse should be thought properly to take place between persons who are married to each other. And if it is thought that this kind of affection and commitment is only to be found within the marriage relationship, then it is not surprising that sexual intercourse should only be thought to be proper within marriage.

Related to what has just been said is the idea that sexual intercourse ought to be restricted to those who are married to each other as a means by which to confirm the very special feelings that the spouses have for each other. Because the culture teaches that sexual intercourse means that the strongest of all feelings for each other are shared by the lovers, it is natural that persons who are married to each other should be able to say this to each other in this way. Revealing and confirming verbally that these feelings are present is one thing that helps to sustain the relationship; engaging in sexual intercourse is another.

In addition, this account would help to provide a framework within which to make sense of the notion that some sex is better than other sex. As I indicated earlier, the fact that sexual intimacy can be meaningful in the sense described tends to make it also the case that sexual intercourse can sometimes be more enjoyable than at other times. On this view, sexual intercourse will typically be more enjoyable where the strong feelings of affection are present than it will be where it is merely "mechanical." This is so in part because people enjoy being loved, especially by those whom they love. Just as we like to hear words of affection, so we like to receive affectionate behavior. And the meaning enhances the independently pleasurable behavior.

More to the point, moreover, an additional rationale for the prohibition on extramarital sex can now be developed. For given this way of viewing the sexual world, extramarital sex will almost always involve deception of a deeper sort. If the adulterous spouse does not in fact have the appropriate feelings of affection for the extramarital partner, then the adulterous spouse is deceiving that person about the presence of such feelings. If, on the other hand, the adulterous spouse does have the corresponding feelings for the extramarital partner, but not toward the nonparticipating spouse, the adulterous spouse is very probably deceiving the nonparticipating spouse about the presence of such feelings toward that spouse. Indeed, it might be argued, whenever there is no longer love between the two persons who are married to each other, there is deception just because

being married implies both to the participants and to the world that such a bond exists. Deception is inevitable, the argument might conclude, because the feelings of affection that ought to accompany any act of sexual intercourse can only be held toward one other person at any given time in one's life. And if this is so, then the adulterous spouse always deceives either the partner in adultery or the nonparticipating spouse about the existence of such feelings. Thus extramarital sex involves deception of this sort and is for this reason immoral even if no deception vis-à-vis the occurrence of the act of adultery takes place.

What might be said in response to the foregoing arguments? The first thing that might be said is that the account of the connection between sexual intimacy and feelings of affection is inaccurate. Not inaccurate in the sense that no one thinks of things that way, but in the sense that there is substantially more divergence of opinion than that account suggests. For example, the view I have delineated may describe reasonably accurately the concepts of the sexual world in which I grew up, but it does not capture the sexual *weltanshauung* of today's youth at all. Thus, whether or not adultery implies deception in respect to feelings depends very much on the persons who are involved and the way they look at the "meaning" of sexual intimacy.

Second, the argument leaves to be answered the question of whether it is desirable for sexual intimacy to carry the sorts of messages described above. For those persons for whom sex does have these implications, there are special feelings and sensibilities that must be taken into account. But it is another question entirely whether any valuable end—moral or otherwise—is served by investing sexual behavior with such significance. That is something that must be shown and not just assumed. It might, for instance, be the case that substantially more good than harm would come from a kind of demystification of sexual behavior: one that would encourage the enjoyment of sex more for its own sake and one that would reject the centrality both of the association of sex with love and of love with only one other person.

I regard these as two of the more difficult, unresolved issues that our culture faces today in respect to thinking sensibly about the attitudes toward sex and love that we should try to develop in ourselves and in our children. Much of the contemporary literature that advocates sexual liberation of one sort or another embraces one or the other of two different views about the relationship between sex and love.

One view holds that sex should be separated from love and affection. To be sure sex is probably better when the partners genuinely like and enjoy each other. But sex is basically an intensive, exciting sensuous activity that can be enjoyed in a variety of suitable settings with a variety of suitable partners. The situation in respect to sexual pleasure is no different from that of the person who knows and appreciates fine food and who can have a very satisfying meal in any number of good restaurants with any number of congenial companions. One question that must be settled here is whether sex can be so demystified; another, more important question is whether it would be desirable to do so. What would we gain and what might we lose if we all lived in a world in which an act of sexual intercourse was no more or less significant or enjoyable than having a delicious meal in a nice setting with a good friend? The answer to this question lies beyond the scope of this paper.

The second view seeks to drive the wedge in a different place. It is not the link between sex and love that needs to be broken; rather, on this view, it is the connection between love and exclusivity that ought to be severed. For a number of the reasons already given, it is desirable, so this argument goes, that sexual intimacy continue to be reserved to and shared with only those for whom one has very great affection. The mistake lies in thinking that any "normal" adult will only have those feelings toward one other adult during his or her lifetime—or even at any time in his or her life. It is the concept of adult love, not ideas about sex, that, on this view, needs demystification. What are thought to be both unrealistic and unfortunate are the notions of exclusivity and possessiveness that attach to the dominant conception of love between adults in our and other cultures. Parents of four, five, six, or even ten children can certainly claim and sometimes claim correctly that they love all of their children, that they love them all equally, and that it is simply untrue to their feelings to insist that the numbers involved diminish either the quantity or the quality of their love. If this is an idea that is readily understandable in the case of parents and children, there is no necessary reason why it is an impossible or undesirable ideal in the case of adults. To be sure, there is probably a limit to the number of intimate, "primary" relationships that any person can maintain at any given time without the quality of the relationship being affected. But one adult ought surely to able to love two, three, or even six other adults at any one time without that love being different in kind or degree from that of the traditional, monogamous, lifetime marriage. And as between the individuals in these relationships, whether within a marriage or without, sexual intimacy is fitting and good.

The issues raised by a position such as this one are also surely worth exploring in detail and with care. Is there something to be called "sexual love" which is different from parental love or the nonsexual love of close friends? Is there something about love in general that links it naturally and appropriately with feelings of exclusivity and possession? Or is there something about sexual love, whatever that may be, that makes these feelings especially fitting here? Once again the issues are conceptual, empirical, and normative all at once: What is love? How could it be different? Would it be a good thing or a bad thing if it were different?

Suppose, though, that having delineated these problems we were now to pass them by.

Suppose, moreover, we were to be persuaded of the possibility and the desirability of weakening substantially either the links between sex and love or the links between sexual love and exclusivity. Would it not then be the case that adultery could be free from all of the morally objectionable features described so far? To be more specific, let us imagine that a husband and wife have what is today sometimes characterized as an "open marriage." Suppose, that is, that they have agreed in advance that extramarital sex is—under certain circumstances—acceptable behavior for each to engage in. Suppose, that as a result there is no impulse to deceive each other about the occurrence or nature of any such relationships, and that no deception in fact occurs. Suppose, too, that there is no deception in respect to the feelings involved between the adulterous spouse and the extramarital partner. And suppose, finally, that one or the other or both of the spouses then has sexual intercourse in circumstances consistent with these understandings. Under this description, so the agreement might conclude, adultery is simply not immoral. At a minimum, adultery cannot very plausibly be condemned either on the ground that it involves deception or on the ground that it requires the breaking of a promise. . . .

The remaining argument . . . seeks to justify the prohibition by virtue of the role that it plays in the development and maintenance of nuclear families. The argument, or set of arguments, might, I believe, go something like this.

Consider first a farfetched nonsexual example. Suppose a society were organized so that after some suitable age—say, 18, 19, or 20—persons were forbidden to eat anything but bread and water with anyone but their spouse. Persons might still choose in such a society not to get married. Good food just might not be very important to them because they have underdeveloped taste buds. Or good food might be bad for them because there is something wrong with their digestive system. Or good food might be important to

them, but they might decide that the enjoyment of good food would get in the way of the attainment of other things that were more important. But most persons would, I think, be led to favor marriage in part because they preferred a richer, more varied, diet to one of bread and water. And they might remain married because the family was the only legitimate setting within which good food was obtainable. If it is important to have society organized so that persons will both get married and stay married, such an arrangement would be well suited to the preservation of the family, and the prohibitions relating to food consumption could be understood as fulfilling that function.

It is obvious that one of the more powerful human desires is the desire for sexual gratification. The desire is a natural one, like hunger and thirst, in the sense that it need not be learned in order to be present within us and operative upon us. But there is in addition much that we do learn about what the act of sexual intercourse is like. Once we experience sexual intercourse ourselves—and in particular once we experience orgasm—we discover that it is among the most intensive, short-term pleasures of the body.

Because this is so, it is easy to see how the prohibition upon extramarital sex helps to hold marriage together. At least during that period of life when the enjoyment of sexual intercourse is one of the desirable bodily pleasures, persons will wish to enjoy those pleasures. If one consequence of being married is that one is prohibited from having sexual intercourse with anyone but one's spouse, then the spouses in a marriage are in a position to provide an important source of pleasure for each other that is unavailable to them elsewhere in the society.

The point emerges still more clearly if this rule of sexual morality is seen as of a piece with the other rules of sexual morality. When this prohibition is coupled, for example, with the prohibition on nonmarital sexual intercourse, we are presented with the inducement both to get married and to stay married. For if sexual intercourse is only legitimate within marriage, then persons seeking that gratification which is a feature of sexual intercourse are furnished explicit social directions for its attainment; namely marriage.

Nor, to continue the argument, is it necessary to focus exclusively on the bodily enjoyment that is involved. Orgasm may be a significant part of what there is to sexual intercourse, but it is not the whole of it. We need only recall the earlier discussion of the meaning that sexual intimacy has in our own culture to begin to see some of the more intricate ways in which sexual exclusivity may be connected with the establishment and maintenance of marriage as the primary heterosexual, love relationship. Adultery is wrong, in other words, because a prohibition on extramarital sex is a way to help maintain the institutions of marriage and the nuclear family.

Now I am frankly not sure what we are to say about an argument such as this one. What I am convinced of is that, like the arguments discussed earlier, this one also reveals something of the difficulty and complexity of the issues that are involved. So, what I want now to do—in the brief and final portion of this paper—is to try to delineate with reasonable precision what I take several of the fundamental, unresolved issues to be.

The first is whether this last argument is an argument for the *immorality* of extramarital sexual intercourse. What does seem clear is that there are differences between this argument and the ones considered earlier. The earlier arguments condemned adulterous behavior because it was behavior that involved breaking of a promise, taking unfair advantage, or deceiving another. To the degree to which the prohibition on extramarital sex can be supported by arguments which invoke considerations such as these, there is little question but that violations of the prohibition are properly regarded as immoral. And such a claim could be defended on one or both of two distinct grounds. The first is that things

like promise-breaking and deception are just wrong. The second is that adultery involving promise-breaking or deception is wrong because it involves the straightforward infliction of harm on another human being—typically the nonadulterous spouse—who has a strong claim not to have that harm so inflicted.

The argument that connects the prohibition on extramarital sex with the maintenance and preservation of the institution of marriage is an argument for the instrumental value of the prohibition. To some degree this counts, I think, against regarding all violations of the prohibition as obvious cases of immorality. This is so partly because hypothetical imperatives are less clearly within the domain of morality than are categorical ones, and even more because instrumental prohibitions are within the domain of morality only if the end they serve or the way they serve it is itself within the domain of morality.

What this should help us see, I think, is the fact that the argument that connects the prohibition on adultery with the preservation of marriage is at best seriously incomplete. Before we ought to be convinced by it, we ought to have reasons for believing that marriage is a morally desirable and just social institution. And this is not quite as easy or obvious a task as it may seem to be. For the concept of marriage is, as we have seen, both a loosely structured and a complicated one. There may be all sorts of intimate, interpersonal relationships which will resemble but not be identical with the typical marriage relationship presupposed by the traditional sexual morality. There may be a number of distinguishable sexual and loving arrangements which can all legitimately claim to be called *marriages*. The prohibitions of the traditional sexual morality may be effective ways to maintain some marriages and ineffective ways to promote and preserve others. The prohibitions of the traditional sexual morality may make good psychological sense if certain psychological theories are true, and they may be purveyors of immense psychological mischief if other psychological theories are true.

The prohibitions of the traditional sexual morality may seem obviously correct if sexual intimacy carries the meaning that the dominant culture has often ascribed to it, and they may seem equally bizarre when sex is viewed through the perspective of the counterculture. Irrespective of whether instrumental arguments of this sort are properly deemed moral arguments, they ought not to fully convince anyone until questions like these are answered.

Review Questions

1. State and explain Wasserstrom's first argument for saying that adultery is immoral (i.e., the argument concerning promise breaking).

2. Explain the second argument given by Wasserstrom, the one about deception.

3. How does Wasserstrom respond to these two arguments?

4. Wasserstrom considers two different views about the relationship between sex and love. Describe these two views.

5. State and explain the third argument that Wasserstrom discusses, the one about preserving the marriages.

6. Wasserstrom raises some difficulties for this third argument. What are they?

Discussion Questions

1. Which view about the relation between sex and love do you find the most acceptable? Why?

2. Do you think that there is anything morally objectionable about an *open marriage* ? If so, what is it?

3. Is the institution of marriage a morally desirable and just institution? Explain your view.

Richard Taylor
Having Love Affairs

Richard Taylor is professor of philosophy at the University of Rochester and adjunct Levitt-Spencer professor of philosophy at Union College.

Taylor's book, Having Love Affairs, *from which our reading selection is taken, is based on extensive interviews with people who have had extramarital or other love affairs. According to Taylor, these love affairs have joys that go beyond the joys of sex; they also satisfy needs for affection, recognition, and friendship. He thinks that they are usually deadly serious and deeply meaningful. But he admits that they can also be dangerous and destructive, particularly for married people. As for the morality of these*

Reprinted from *Having Love Affairs,* © 1982 by Richard Taylor, with permission of Prometheus Books, Buffalo, New York.

affairs, Taylor insists that people have a right to them, as "clear a right as any right can be." Furthermore, he thinks that there is nothing wrong or immoral with extralegal marriages, that is, people living together without being legally married.

The joy of a love affair is that someone seems to love you who does not have to, or who, in fact, positively should not. Married people have many reasons—one almost wants to say ulterior motives—for caring about each other, and one can always wonder whether these might not really be the basis for affection. They are likely to have a house and other possessions, children, common endeavors which neither could pursue alone, and, above all, some sort of position in the community which is enhanced by their being married and would suffer by their separation. In other words, there are many things holding married people together besides love, and these are sometimes sufficient even when there is little or no love in the marriage. This is well and good, of course. No one can doubt that, from the standpoint of children, for example, a family is usually much better when intact than broken, even though some of the things holding it together are mundane. Nevertheless, these considerations rob marriage of the romance that everyone craves.

Partners in a love affair, on the other hand, have none of these things to hold them together, but have, on the contrary, the same kinds of forces working to drive them apart—for example, the need for secrecy and deception, which is sometimes degrading; often the existence, in the background, of a husband or wife or both; and, in such cases, the blame and condemnation the lovers risk if they are discovered. All they have, it seems to them, is passionate love—which is of course a lot, but it is still only one significant thing. This certainly does attest to the power of passionate love to hold people together, sometimes, as it must seem to them, against the whole world. That is not an illusion. It is very doubtful whether there can be found in any human experience anything as totally fulfilling as being loved in this way—intensely, intimately, and gratuitously. No one should say that it is bad, just because it is so easily condemned and so dangerous. It is still the ultimate joy that everyone wants more than anything else. The most vehement condemnations of it seem to come from those who have abandoned hope of experiencing it, and who therefore represent it to themselves as something base in order to assuage their own sense of deprivation. A person involved in such a love affair—overwhelming, forbidden, explosively dangerous—can think to himself, with some truth at least, that there is one person in the world who cares for him for no ulterior reason at all, who has nothing to gain by it and very much to lose, but who does nevertheless love. The feelings, together with this thought, are so totally intoxicating that those who have never experienced them, and especially those who have given up hope of them and perhaps taken complacent pride in this deprivation, should withhold their condemnation of others.

This does not mean that love affairs are better than marriage, for they seldom are. Love between married persons can, in the long run, be so vastly more fulfilling that none but the hopelessly romantic could suggest otherwise. The passionate love that so explosively blooms in an affair is not, moreover, as gratuitous as it may seem. While the usual ulterior reasons for it may be lacking, others are certainly present, and in particular, the ordinary and not very romantic needs of its partners. For it is certainly true that lovers are drawn to each other, not by some Platonic beauty that each finds in the other, but by some very ordinary need that each finds in himself, sometimes nothing more noble than vanity.

It is nevertheless true that the joys of illicit and passionate love, which include but go far beyond the mere joys of sex, are incomparably good. And it is undeniable that those who never experience love affairs, and who perhaps even boast of their faultless monogamy year in and year out, have really missed something. Virtuous they may be—even this can be questioned—but truly blessed they are not quite. Such a person lives in a kind of lifelong total eclipse, or a house without windows. He is like someone who has never heard a nocturne of Chopin's, tasted caviar, or beheld the Alps—except that what he has missed is something with which these tepid things do not even begin to compare. . . .

People who think of love affairs as nothing more than sexual adventures, and often casual ones at that, are . . . very much mistaken. On the contrary, these relationships are usually deadly serious and deeply meaningful. Perhaps one reason some people find this fact difficult to accept is that social convention has reserved such meaning for the presumably lifelong relationship of marriage; an affair is quite naturally thought of as a rival to this marital arrangement. Therefore, the only acceptable conception of extramarital love is a trivialized one that excludes every source of affection except sex.

In fact sexual intimacy is only one ingredient of a love affair and, to those involved, it is likely to be considered secondary. People have all kinds of needs that have little to do with sex: they need affection, recognition, a sense of self worth, simple friendship, and the banishment of loneliness. Any of these can serve as a strong basis of a love affair. Whenever I have asked those with whom I have talked whether their relationships might have been possible even without sexual contact, many have said they would have, though it must be added that this view was expressed more often by women than by men.

Still, the rare case does occur in which a love affair rests upon sexual attraction almost to the exclusion of everything else. There are, in fact, men and women who have a strong and immediate sexual attraction to each other, often inexplicable, but sometimes instantly known to both of them. From what I have seen of this it does not fit the usual stereotype of physical attractiveness. Sometimes it is referred to as a kind of "chemistry" between two people, and the metaphor is apt, suggesting a strong but irrational action and reaction. This chemistry is sometimes lamentably weak between husbands and wives, who care deeply for each other and whose marriages are genuinely happy. I have even known a man, of unusual attractiveness and sophistication, who had felt no sexual attraction whatever for his beautiful wife in nearly fifty years of marriage, even though they had always, from mutual desire, slept together. Needless to say, he was a veteran of several love affairs.

I am convinced that the presence of such feelings, or the lack of them, is totally beyond the control of people, and equally beyond their understanding—something which should, by itself, be enough to exhibit the foolishness of those who want to condemn them. With the exception of Schopenhauer, who gave a metaphysical explanation of passionate love, hardly any philosopher has attempted a serious explanation. There is no comprehending *why* a given man or woman is swept up in a tide of sexual passion for just one particular person, and quite unable to muster such feelings for another with whom he or she might be genuinely and deeply in love, who is recognized as a better person in all ways. . . .

Love affairs are dangerous and often destructive, particularly for married people. They risk not only the deep injury of eventual rejection, but the destruction of homes and damage to children. Even unmarried people, such as those in college, sometimes scrupulously avoid sexual intimacies, usually on moral or religious principles, and there is no doubt that they thereby avoid certain risks. Passionate love is strong, and sometimes explosive in its effects.

People who value safety, orderliness, and a certain predictability in their lives—especially married people of this temperament—are probably wise to avoid temptation and hold firmly to accepted values, drawing comfort from a socially approved pre-marital virginity and then monogamous marriage.

At the same time, no one should assume that everyone ought to avoid love affairs, or that even married people should necessarily abstain. Dangerous as love affairs may be, no one would suggest that they are without joy. In fact, the vehemence with which they are condemned from some quarters is indicative of how absolutely exhilarating they can be.

Nor should love affairs be thought of as casual and light-hearted, mere games that are easily entered into and just as easily abandoned. This idea, common to popular journalism, is closer to fantasy than fact. The idea that love affairs add spice to marriage, or that an affair can be a tonic to revive a faltering marriage, is simply naive. Love affairs are deadly serious, and the popular references to "playing around" are merely intended to belittle them by distortion. Perhaps life would be simpler if sex were not serious business. Certainly human relations would be easier and we would be spared a great deal of misery. But that is not how we were made. The most powerful passions in life cannot be made trivial.

In this realm we are where every person must decide for himself and accept his own responsibility. No one can tell another person what is and is not permissible with respect to whom he or she will love, and when or where, or under what conditions. No clergyman can make that decision for you, nor can any moralist, teacher, parent, or functionary. It is your decision and yours alone, to which you need answer to no one but yourself. Nor can such a decision be made by one partner in a marriage for the other; for to pass the choice to someone else—anyone else—is not to act correctly, but simply not to act at all. It is to relinquish all responsibility for one's decisions and actions with respect to the choice in question.

However inadvisable it may be to seek love outside the conventional restraints, the *right* to do so is about as clear as any right can be. For we are here dealing with what is ultimately personal and private, with that realm into which no one else can step without trespassing. Everyone has a right to be in anyone's arms he chooses. Other people can think what they like and do as they like with their own lives and loves, but they cannot decide for you. Only you can do that....

Monogamous love was never the deliverance of nature. It was the invention of frightened human beings, motivated originally by no better motive than the selfish regard for ownership; adultery was originally thought of, in our religious tradition, as a violation of a man's (not a woman's) property. "*My* wife" had exactly the connotation as "*my* chattel"; it still does, the moment the ownership expressed by "my" appears to any husband to have been violated. The "my" of "my husband," on the other hand, is less an expression of a property relation than it is an expression of subordination and deference, as in the case of "my master." It is for this reason that the idea of a cuckolded husband is easily understood, but no one ever speaks of a cuckolded wife. If a wife is discovered in an adulterous relationship, then her husband is thought to have been put upon, and made a fool of—cuckolded, in the archaic but apt vocabulary of our ancestors. The wife of a husband thus discovered is, on the other hand, merely pitied. Her security and her home have been unsettled, but not her ownership of a person, for this was never thought to exist for her in the first place....

The home, it is thought, must by all means be preserved; and having no other means of keeping it intact, societies have resorted to rules and ceremony. Needless to say, this does not work. A society can, to be sure, render the legal dissolution of a marriage impossible, as has been done in some countries; but all this has ever achieved is the preservation of the thinnest outward appearance. A church can, of course, with much solemnity, formalize the state of matrimony, even declare it incorruptible and indissoluble; but this, too, only creates the outward appearance. Marriage itself can in no way be created by any priest or servant of the state. It cannot be preserved by them nor by any other power of heaven or earth, except in appearance. Nor can it really be terminated by them; they can at best only recognize what has already ended. Marriage is entirely the work of those who enter into it. Its successes, and rewards of rejoicing, the warmth and fulfillment it gives, are theirs alone. Its failure, and the inner desolation this produces, are theirs too. The rest of the world can look on, but only they will have the blessings if they succeed, and of the anguish if they do not.

Of course this implies that marriage, being the creation of two persons, can be made ethical or moral by them alone. No priest, no political functionary, no state, no church, no rules, and no laws can confer moral rightness on this relationship, nor can any of these make that relationship morally wrong. Only lovers can do these things. It is lovers who make a marriage. No priest makes it. It is lovers, or former lovers, who destroy a marriage. No court dissolves it. Really, all a church or court can do is to confer outward legality on a state of affairs that the individuals involved have already established.

This truly goes to the heart of the matter, so far as morality is concerned. For there is a popular conception to the very contrary; that is, it is widely thought, even regarded as obvious, that *only* an authorized functionary of the church or government, a clergyman or judge, can make the relationship of lovers ethical, and indeed, that marriage between lovers is the very creation of such persons or the rituals they perform. People become married, it is thought, at a stroke, by the ceremonious pronouncement of words and the signing of documents, as though there were no more to it than this. Of course that formality is required for the *legality* of a marriage relationship. This is a truism. But to suppose it to be required for the *morality* or even the existence of that relationship is a naive, even vulgar confusion of genuine morality with law. Not all that the law requires measures up to any significant moral standard, nor does everything that is forbidden by law violate morality. If it were otherwise, then the merest infractions of parking regulations, or unintentional tax delinquencies, would be violations of morality, while, on the other hand, the total and casual disregard of human suffering, which is permitted by law, would violate no moral requirement. What is required or forbidden by law is often but not always the same as what is required or forbidden by morality. To suppose that the deepest and most precious feelings of which human beings are capable—the very feelings that are the basis not only of all social life, but life itself, the feelings of love and passion between the sexes—can be significantly influenced by any outsiders at all, or that any outsider can confer either morality or immorality upon them, is to suppose what is plainly absurd. Worse than that, it is to try to chuck onto the shoulders of some functionary a responsibility that no person can possibly relinquish, namely, the responsibility of lovers to create their own marriage. They will not accomplish this through the approval of others nor the approval of their church nor even through the approval of the whole of mankind, who are forever outside that relationship and all its implications.

There is, therefore, absolutely nothing wrong or immoral in the marriage relationships so commonly established between young people, especially those entered into at college, and society as a whole is gradually coming to realize this. Persons involved in such extralegal relationships should make no attempt to conceal them, and if this outrages their parents, then it is actually the parents who ought to be ashamed, rather than their children. The legality of a marriage relationship adds nothing whatever to its morality, and the absence of such legality takes nothing away from it. All that legality does is to suggest a greater permanence, being considered the expression of a stronger commitment on the part of the partners; but it by no means guarantees this. And it has nothing to do with the rightness or wrongness of the relationship. . . .

There is a tendency among human beings to convert things that are truly good and noble into something else, some counterfeit of the original, and then, quite forgetting the noble thing they began with, to treat the imitation as that which is good, even calling it by the same name as the original.

Patriotism is an example of this. In its original sense, patriotism is the love for one's country; and if we think of such love in its true sense, as resting upon the perception of the beauty and goodness of one's country, its institutions, and history, then it is surely in every sense a good and inspiring thing. But, over time, this originally noble idea has been doubly corrupted. The love that is embodied in it has been reduced to a kind of blind and mindless allegiance, and the object of such love has become no longer one's beautiful country, but the *symbols* of that country, such as the flag or, worse yet, the instruments and weapons of war. Thus a patriot is now thought of as someone who, without thought, displays the flag of his country here and there and who can be counted on to support war and the preparations for war. Quite obviously, this is not genuine patriotism, but a counterfeit so skillfully done that virtually everyone is gulled into accepting it as the real thing.

Another example is religion, which originally stood for the love for God. Conceived in this sense, it can hardly be doubted that it, too, is a noble and inspiring thing, assuming (as some of course would not) that it rests upon a true perception of the goodness of God. At the hands of human beings, however, religion has come to mean a devotion, often mindless and blind, to the *symbols* of religion, and to certain practices that have come to be associated with religion. Sometimes, in fact, it tends to deteriorate into a devotion to an *institution,* namely the church, and to the officials who administer the affairs of the church—a bishop or pope, for example—even when devotion of this kind is condemned as idolatrous. The corruption of religion becomes so complete that the counterfeit reduces the original almost to nothing, and millions of devotees imagine themselves actually to be religious, even deeply so, when in fact their devotion to the mere symbols of religion has made it impossible for them to be truly religious at all, in the original sense of the term. Thus they deceive themselves, their devotion to a counterfeit rendering them no longer capable of recognizing, or even of forming a very clear idea of, a genuine devotion to God. Nor, of course, do they deceive only themselves. If we see someone whose thoughts are much preoccupied with his church, who spends much of his life ritualistically observing the practices fostered by his church, and who venerates its priests or other officials, then it is difficult *not* to think of him as "religious." But this only shows how totally distorted the idea has become in the minds of most people.

The very same can be said of marital fidelity. Originally, fidelity meant faithfulness, which translates into constancy of love when we are speaking of the love between men and women. But like patriotism, religion, and oth-

er noble things, fidelity has been corrupted and replaced by a counterfeit. Fidelity in a marriage relationship has been reduced to mere sexual exclusiveness and, what is worse, this is thought of as more important than the constancy of love itself. Thus people see no contradiction in saying of some wife, for example, that even though she long since stopped loving her husband, she at least remained "faithful," in spite of the numerous infidelities on his part.

There are innumerable ways lovers can break faith with each other having nothing whatever to do with sexual inconstancy; and, equally important, from the standpoint of ethics, it is perfectly possible for lovers, and for husbands and wives, to be faithful to each other even in spite of sexual nonexclusiveness. People sometimes find this hard to understand, but that is only because they have forgotten what fidelity actually means and have, in their own minds, substituted another, less important, conception of it....

The purpose of what follows is to set forth, not a comprehensive ethic of marriage, but only the ethical principles and [definitions] that should govern a part of that relationship, namely, that pertaining to sexual fidelity....

Infidelity is everywhere treated as though it were simply synonymous with adultery, illustrating once more the vulgarization of the ethic which seems everywhere to accompany its ritualization. Some persons look upon the wedding band as a kind of "no trespassing" sign, and upon the marriage certificate as a type of permit or license to make love, a right which must then have been lacking until conferred by that document! Yet, as we have already noted, the real and literal meaning of fidelity is *faithfulness;* and what thinking person could imagine that there is only one way in which someone can fail to keep faith with another? Faithfulness is a state of one's heart and mind. It is not the mere outward conformity to rules. There are countless ways that it can fail which have nothing whatever to do with sexual intimacy nor, indeed, with outside persons. It can be fulfilled in various ways as well, even in spite of sexual nonexclusiveness, though this is sometimes more difficult to see.

To illustrate this, imagine a man who has long been married to one person, a man who has never lapsed from the rule of strict sexual constancy, nor has he ever appeared to, and who could never be suspected of this by anyone with the slightest knowledge of his character. This man, we shall imagine, assumes without doubt the rightness of his behavior, is scornful of anyone whose standards are less strict, would not permit a violation of this rule by anyone under his own roof, and would consider no circumstances to mitigate the breach of it. So far, so good; he is, it would seem to most persons, a faithful husband.

But now let us add to the picture that this same man, being of a passive nature and having somewhat of an aversion to sex, has never yielded to temptations for the simple reason that he has had no temptations placed before him. His intimacy with his own wife is perfunctory, infrequent, dutiful, and quite devoid of joy for himself or his spouse. They are, in fact, essentially strangers to each other's feelings. In this light, the nobility of his austere ethic begins to appear less impressive, does it not?

But we are not finished with our description. Let us add to the foregoing that these two persons appear to the world as hard workers, but still quite poor. He works monotonously as a sales clerk in a declining drug store, we can suppose, while she adds what she can to the family's resources by putting in long hours assisting in the local public library. Appearances are misleading, however, for behind this facade of meager resources there are, unbeknown to anyone but the husband, and scrupulously kept secret from his wife, eight savings accounts, which have been built up over the years, each in his name only, and none containing less than thirty thousand dollars. At every opportunity—sometimes by shrewd dealing, often by sheer penurious-

ness, and always by the most dedicated selfishness—the husband squirrels away more savings, so that by this time the total, augmented by interest compounded over the years, adds up to a most impressive sum.

Has the rule of good faith been breached?

But to continue the description: We now suppose that the long suffering wife of this dreary marriage is stricken, let us say, with cancer, and undergoes a radical mastectomy as the only hope of saving her life. Whereupon whatever small affection her husband ever had for her evaporates completely. He turns sullen, distant, and only dimly aware of his wife's presence, finding all the comfort for his life in those growing and secret savings accounts. He never thinks of sexual infidelity, and congratulates himself for this, as well as for other things, such as his thrift.

Finally, let us suppose that his wife has always been a poet of considerable creative power, whose creations have never received the attention they deserve, least of all her husband's, he being only dimly aware that they even exist. Yet they are finally seen and sincerely praised by another sensitive soul having the qualities of mind necessary to appreciate them, and through his encouragement, we shall imagine, she is finally able to have a sense of meaningfulness in her life, hitherto found only meagerly in the lonely creation of poetic beauty. This same new found friend is, moreover, oblivious to the scars of her illness; he cares only for her, and, unlike her husband, his love is sincere, impulsive, passionate, imaginative, and as frequent as conditions allow.

We could expand this story, but the point of it is abundantly clear by now. It is found in answering the question: *Who has been faithless to whom?* In that answer one finds not only the essential meaning of infidelity, which is a betrayal of the promise to love, but also, by contrast, the true meaning of fidelity....

Review Questions

1. How does Taylor describe love affairs? Why do people have them?

2. Explain Taylor's account of monogamous love and marriage.

3. What is Taylor's view of fidelity and infidelity?

Discussion Questions

1. Are love affairs morally wrong? What is Taylor's view? What is your view?

2. Do you agree with Taylor's account of marriage and fidelity? Why or why not?

Pamela Foa

What's Wrong with Rape

Pamela Foa teaches philosophy at the University of Pittsburgh.

Foa wants to discover what is specially wrong about rape. It is wrong even if it is not an act between equals, but it is not wrong because it is in some sense "unnatural." What makes rape specially wrong, in Foa's view, is our society's rape model of sexuality.

It is clear that rape is wrong. It is equally clear that the wrongness of rape is not completely explained by its status as a criminal assault. Dispute begins, however, when we attempt to account for the special features of rape, the ways in which its wrongness goes beyond its criminal character. I shall argue against those who maintain that the special wrongness of rape arises from and is completely explained by a societal refusal to recognize women as *people*. I shall offer a different explanation: The special wrongness of rape is due to, and is only an exaggeration of, the wrongness of our sexual interactions in general. Thus, a clear analysis of the special wrongness of rape will help indicate some of

Pamela Foa, "What's Wrong with Rape" from Mary Vetterling-Braggin, Frederick A. Elliston, and Jane English, eds., *Feminism and Philosophy*, Littlefield, Adams and Co., 1981, pp. 347–359. Reprinted with permission.

the essential features of healthy, nonrapine sexual interactions.

THE WRONGNESS OF RAPE GOES BEYOND ITS CRIMINALITY

It is to be expected during this period of resurgent feminism that rape will be seen primarily as a manifestation of how women are mistreated in our society. For example, consider these remarks of Simone de Beauvoir:

All men are drawn to B[rigitte] B[ardot]'s seductiveness, but that does not mean that they are kindly disposed towards her.... They are unwilling to give up their role of lord and master.... Freedom and full consciousness remain their [the men's] right and privilege.... In the game of love BB is as much a hunter as she is a prey. The male is an object to her, just as she is to him. And that is precisely what wounds the masculine pride. In the Latin countries where men cling to the myth of "the woman as object," BB's naturalness seems to them more perverse than any possible sophistication. It is to assert that one is man's fellow and equal, to recognize that between the woman and him there is a mutual desire and pleasure....

But the male feels uncomfortable, if, instead of a doll of flesh and blood, he holds in his arms a conscious being who is sizing him up. "You realize," an average Frenchman once said to me, "that when a man finds a woman attractive, he wants to be able to pinch her behind." A ribald gesture reduces a woman to a thing that a man can do with as he pleases without worrying about what goes on in her mind and heart and body.[1]

And rape is apparently the quintessential instance of women being viewed as objects, of women being treated as entities other than, and morally inferior to, men. It is implicit in this object-view that if men, and therefore society, viewed women as full moral equals, rape would be an assault no different in kind than any other. Thus, it is a consequence of this view that the special wrongness of rape is to be found in the nonsexual aspects of the act.

To this end, Marilyn Frye and Carolyn Shafer suggest in their paper "Rape and Respect" that the wrongness of rape is twofold: first, it is the use of a person without her consent in the performance of an act or event that is against her own best interests; and second, it is a social means of reinforcing the status of women as kinds of entities who lack and ought to lack the full privileges of personhood—importantly, the freedom to move as they will through what is rightfully their domain.[2] What is good about this account is that it provides one way of understanding the sense of essential violation of one's *person* (and not mere sexual abuse), which seems to be the natural concomitant of rape.

This account, further, gives one explanation for the continuous social denial of the common fact of criminal rape. On this view, to recognize rape as a criminal act, one must recognize the domains of women. But if domains are inextricably connected with personhood—if personhood, in fact, is to be analyzed in terms of domains—then it ought to be obvious that where there is no domain there can be no criminal trespass of domain; there can only be misperceptions or misunderstandings. To recognize domains of consent is to recognize the existence of people at their centers. Without such centers, there can be no rape.

Unfortunately, I do not believe that this kind of account can serve as an adequate explanation of what's wrong with rape. I find irrelevant its emphasis on the **ontological** status of women as persons of the first rank. It is granted that in any act of rape a person is used without proper regard to her personhood, but this is true of every kind of assault. If there is an additional wrongness to rape, it must be that more is wrong than the mere treatment of a person by another person without proper regard for her per-

sonhood. Later in this paper, I shall show that there is no need to differentiate ontologically between victim and assailant in order to explain the special wrongness of rape. However, it is important to recognize that rape is profoundly wrong even if it is not an act between ontological equals.

The special wrongness of rape cannot be traced to the fact that in this act men are not recognizing the full array of moral and legal rights and privileges that accrue to someone of equal status. Rape of children is at least as heinous as rape of adults, though few actually believe that children have or ought to have the same large domain of consent adults (male and female) ought to have. In part, this is what is so disturbing about a recent English decision I shall discuss in a moment: it seems to confuse the ontological with the moral. Men's wishes, intentions, and beliefs are given a different (and more important) weight, just because they are (wrongly in this case, perhaps rightly in the case of children) viewed as different kinds of entities than women.

But even if one thinks that women are not people, or that all people (for example, children) do not have the same rights or, *prima facie,* the same domains of consent, it seems that rape is still especially horrible, awful in a way that other assaults are not. There is for example, something deeply distressing, though not necessarily criminal, about raping one's pet dog. It is disturbing in ways no ordinary assault, even upon a person, seems to be disturbing. It may here be objected that what accounts for the moral outrage in these two cases is that the first is an instance of **pedophilia,** and the second of **bestiality.** That is, the special wrongness of these acts is due to the "unnatural" direction of the sexual impulse, rather than to the abusive circumstances of the fulfillment of a "natural" sexual impulse.

I would argue in response that outrage at "unnatural" acts is misdirected and inappropriate. The notion that acting "against" nature is immoral stems from the false belief that how things are in the majority of cases is, morally speaking, how things always ought to be. Acting unnaturally is not acting immorally unless there is a moral design to the natural order—and there is no such structure to it. This means, then, that if it is reasonable to feel that something very wrong has occurred in the above two cases, then it must be because they are rapes and not because they are "unnatural acts." However, even if this argument is not conclusive, it must be agreed that the random raping of a mentally retarded adult is clearly wrong even though such an individual does not, in our society, have all the legal and moral rights of normal people.[3]

Of course, another very reasonable point to make here may well be that it is not just people who have domains, and that what's wrong with rape is the invasion by one being into another's domain without consent or right. But if something like this is true, then rape would be wrong because it was an "incursion" into a domain. This would make it wrong in the same way that other assaults are wrong. The closer the incursion comes to the center of a person's identity, the worse the act.

The problem here is that such an argument suggests that rape is wrong the same way, and only the same way, that other assaults are wrong. And yet the evidence contradicts this. There is an emotional concomitant to this assault, one that is lacking in nonsexual criminal assaults. What must be realized is that when it comes to sexual matters, people—in full recognition of the equal ontological status of their partners—treat each other abominably. Contrary to the Frye/Shafer theory, I believe that liberated men and women—people who have no doubts about the moral or ontological equality of the sexes—can and do have essentially rape-like sexual lives.

The following case is sufficient to establish that it is not just the assault upon one's person, or the intrusion into one's domain, that makes for the special features of rape. In New York twenty or so years ago, there was a man who went around Manhattan slashing people with a very sharp knife. He did not do this as part of any robbery or other further bodily assault. His end was simply to stab people. Although he was using people against their own best interests, and without their consent—that is, although he was broadly violating domains—to be the victim of the Mad Slasher was not to have been demeaned or dirtied as a person in the way that the victim of rape was demeaned or dirtied. It was not to be wronged or devalued in the same way that to be raped is to be wronged or devalued. No one ever accused any of the victims of provoking, initiating, or enjoying the attack.

Yet the public morality about rape suggests that unless one is somehow mutilated, broken, or killed in addition to being raped, one is suspected of having provoked, initiated, complied in, consented to, or even enjoyed the act. It is this public response, the fear of such a response, and the belief (often) in the rationality of such a response (even from those who do unequivocally view you as a person) that seems to make rape especially horrible.

Thus, what is especially bad about rape is a function of its place in our society's sexual views, not in our ontological views. There is, of course, nothing necessary about these views, but until they change, no matter what progress is made in the fight for equality between the sexes, rape will remain an especially awful act.

SEX, INTIMACY, AND PLEASURE

Our response to rape brings into focus our inner feelings about the nature, purpose, and morality of all sexual encounters and of ourselves as sexual beings. Two areas that seem immediately problematic are the relation between sex and intimacy and the relation between sex and pleasure.

Our Victorian ancestors believed that sex in the absence of (at least marital) intimacy was morally wrong and that the only women who experienced sexual pleasure were **nym-**

phomaniacs.[4] Freud's work was revolutionary in part just because he challenged the view of "good" women and children as asexual creatures.[5] Only with Masters and Johnson's work, however, has there been a full scientific recognition of the capacity of ordinary women for sexual pleasure.[6] But though it is now recognized that sexual pleasure exists for all people at all stages of life and is, in its own right, a morally permissible goal, this contemporary attitude is still dominated by a Victorian atmosphere. It remains the common feeling that it is a kind of pleasure that should be experienced only in private and only between people who are and intend to be otherwise intimate. Genital pleasure is private not only in our description of its physical location, but also in our conception of its occurrence or occasion.

For the rape victim, the special problem created by the discovery of pleasure in sex is that now some people believe that *every* sex act must be pleasurable to some extent, including rape.[7] Thus, it is believed by some that the victim in a rape must at some level be enjoying herself—and that this enjoyment in a nonintimate, nonprivate environment is shameful. What is especially wrong about rape, therefore, is that it makes evident the essentially sexual nature of women, and this has been viewed, from the time of Eve through the time of Victoria, as cause for their humiliation. Note that on this view the special evil of rape is due to the feminine character and not to that of her attacker.[8]

The additional societal attitude that sex is moral only between intimates creates a further dilemma in assessing the situation of the rape victim. On the one hand, if it is believed that the sex act itself creates an intimate relationship between two people, then, by necessity, the rape victim experiences intimacy with her assailant. This may incline one to deny the fact of the rape by pointing to the fact of the intimacy. If one does not believe that sex itself creates intimacy between the actors, but nonetheless believes that sex is immoral in the absence of intimacy, then the event of sex in the absence of an intimate relationship, even though involuntary, is cause for public scorn and humiliation. For the rape victim, to acknowledge the rape is to acknowledge one's immorality. Either way, the victim has violated the social sexual taboos and she must therefore be ostracized.

What is important is no longer that one is the victim of an assault, but rather that one is the survivor of a social transgression. This is the special burden that the victim carries.

There is support for my view in Gary Wills' review of Tom Wicker's book about the Attica prisoners' revolt.[9] What needs to be explained is the apparently peculiar way in which the safety of the prisoners' hostages was ignored in the preparations for the assault on the prison and in the assault itself. What strikes me as especially important in this event is that those outside the prison walls treated the *guards* exactly like the *prisoners*. The critical similarity is the alleged participation in taboo sexual activity, where such activity is seen as the paradigm of humiliating behavior. In his review Wills says,

Sexual fantasy played around Attica's walls like invisible lightning. Guards told their families that all the inmates were animals....

When the assault finally came, and officers mowed down the hostages along with the inmates, an almost religious faith kept faked stories alive against all the evidence—that the hostages were found castrated; that those still living had been raped.... None of it was true, but the guards knew what degradation the prisoners had been submitted to, and the kind of response that might call for....

One has to go very far down into the human psyche to understand what went on in that placid town.... The bloodthirsty hate of the local community was so obvious by the time of the assault that even Rockefeller ... ordered that no correction personnel join the attack.... [Nonetheless] eleven men managed to go in.... Did they come to save the hostages, showing more care for them than outsiders could? Far from it. They fired as early and indiscriminately as the rest. Why? I am afraid Mr. Wicker is a bit too decent to understand what was happening, though his own cultural background gives us a clue. Whenever a white girl was caught with a black in the old South, myth demanded that a charge of rape be brought and the "boy" be lynched. But a shadowy ostracism was inflicted on the girl. Did she fight back? Might she undermine the myth with a blurted tale or a repeated episode? At any rate, she was tainted. She had, willed she or nilled she, touched the untouchable and acquired her own evil halo of contamination. Taboos take little account of "intention." In the same way, guards caught in that yard were tainted goods. . . . They were an embarrassment. The white girl may sincerely have struggled with her black assailant; but even to imagine that resistance was defiling—and her presence made people imagine it. She was a public pollution—to be purged. Is this [comparison] fanciful? Even Wicker . . . cannot understand the attitude of those in charge who brought no special medical units to Attica before the attack began. . . . The lynch mob may kill the girl in its urgency to get at the boy—and it will regret this less than it admits.[10]

Accounts like the one offered by Frye and Shafer might explain why the *prisoners* were treated so callously by the assaulting troops, but they cannot explain the brutal treatment of the hostages. Surely they cannot say that the guards who were hostages were not and had never been viewed as people, as ontological equals, by the general society. And yet there was the same special horror in being a hostage at Attica as there is for a woman who has been raped. In both cases the *victim* has acquired a "halo of contamination" that permanently taints. And this cannot be explained by claiming that in both cases society is denying personhood or domains of consent to the victim.

The victim in sexual assault cases is as much a victim of our confused beliefs about sex as of the assault itself. The tremendous strains we put on such victims are a cruel result of our deep confusion about the place of, and need for, sexual relationships and the role of pleasure and intimacy in those relationships.

In spite of the fact, I believe, that as a society we share the *belief* that sex is only justified in intimate relationships, we act to avoid real intimacy at almost any cost. We seem to be as baffled as our predecessors were about the place of intimacy in our sexu-

al and social lives. And this is, I think, because we are afraid that real intimacy creates or unleashes sexually wanton relationships, licentious lives—and this we view as morally repugnant. At the same time, we believe that sex in the absence of an intimate relationship is whoring and is therefore also morally repugnant. It is this impossible conflict that I think shows us that we will be able to make sense of our response to rape only if we look at rape as the model of all our sexual interactions, not as its antithesis.

THE MODEL OF SEX: RAPE

Though we may sometimes speak as though sexual activity is most pleasurable between friends, we do not teach each other to treat our sexual partners as friends. Middle-class children, whom I take to be our cultural models, are instructed from the earliest possible time to ignore their sexual feelings. Long before intercourse can be a central issue, when children are prepubescent, boys are instructed to lunge for a kiss and girls are instructed to permit nothing more than a peck on the cheek. This encouragement of miniature adult sexual behavior is instructive on several levels.

It teaches the child that courting behavior is rarely spontaneous and rarely something that gives pleasure to the people involved—that is, it is not like typical playing with friends. It gives the child a glimpse of how adults do behave, or are expected to behave, and therefore of what is expected in future life and social interactions. Importantly, boys are instructed *not* to be attentive to the claims of girls with respect to their desires and needs. And girls are instructed *not* to consult their feelings as a means of or at least a check on what behavior they should engage in.

Every American girl, be she philosopher-to-be or not, is well acquainted with the slippery-slope argument by the time she is ten. She is told that if she permits herself to become involved in anything more than a peck on the cheek, anything but the most innocent type of sexual behavior, she will inevitably become involved in behavior that will result in intercourse and pregnancy. And such behavior is wrong. That is, she is told that if she acquiesces to any degree to her feelings, then she will be doing something immoral.

Meanwhile, every American boy is instructed, whether explicitly or not, that the girls have been given this argument (as a weapon) and that therefore, since everything that a girl says will be a reflection of this argument (and not of her feelings), they are to ignore everything that she says.

Girls are told never to consult their feelings (they can only induce them to the edge of the slippery slope); they are always to say "no." Boys are told that it is a sign of their growing manhood to be able to get a girl way beyond the edge of the slope, and that it is standard procedure for girls to say "no" independently of their feelings. Thus, reasonably enough, boys act as far as one can tell independently of the explicit information they are currently receiving from the girl.

For women, it is very disconcerting to find that from the age of eight or nine or ten, one's reports of one's feelings are no longer viewed as accurate, truthful, important, or interesting. R.D. Laing, the English psychiatrist and theorist, claims that it is this type of adult behavior that creates the environment in which insanity best finds its roots.[11] It is clear, at least, that such behavior is not a model of rationality or health. In any event, rape is a case in which only the pretense of listening has been stripped away. It is the essence of what we have all been trained to expect.

In a sexually healthier society, men and women might be told to engage in that behavior that gives them pleasure as long as that pleasure is not (does not involve actions) against anyone's will (including coerced actions) and does not involve them with responsibilities they cannot or will not meet (emotional, physical, or financial).

But as things are now, boys and girls have no way to tell each other what gives them pleasure and what not, what frightens them and what not; there are only violence, threats of violence, and appeals to informing on one or the other to some dreaded peer or parental group. This is a very high-risk, high-stake game, which women and girls, at least, often feel may easily become rape (even though it is usually played for little more than a quick feel in the back seat of the car or corner of the family sofa). But the ultimate consequences of this type of instruction are not so petty. Consider, for example, the effects of a recent English high-court decision:

Now, according to the new interpretation, no matter how much a woman screams and fights, the accused rapist can be cleared by claiming he believed the victim consented, even though his belief may be considered unreasonable or irrational.

On a rainy night seven months ago, a London housewife and mother of three claims she was dragged into this dilapidated shed. Annie Baker says she screamed for help and she fought but she was raped. Mrs. Baker lost her case in court because the man claimed he thought when she said no, she meant yes.

One member of Parliament [predicts juries will] "now have the rapist saying that the woman asked for what she got and she wanted what they [sic] gave her."

However, the Head of the British Law Society maintains, "Today juries are prepared to accept that the relationship between the sexes has become much more promiscuous, and they have to look much more carefully to see whether the woman has consented under modern conditions.... One mustn't readily assume that a woman did not consent, because all indications are that there is a greater willingness to consent today than there was thirty years ago."[12]

"The question to be answered in this case," said Lord Cross of Chelsea, "as I see it, is whether, according to the ordinary use of the English language, a man can be said to have committed rape if he believed that the woman was consenting to the intercourse. I do not think he can."[13]

This is the most macabre extension imaginable of our early instruction. It is one that makes initially implausible and bizarre any suggestion that the recent philosophical analyses of sexuality as the product of a mutual desire for communication—or even for orgasm or sexual satisfaction—bear any but the most tangential relation to reality.[14]

As we are taught, sexual desires are

desires woman ought not to have and men must have. This is the model that makes necessary an eternal battle of the sexes. It is the model that explains why rape is the prevalent model of sexuality. It has the further virtue of explaining the otherwise puzzling attitude of many that women will cry "rape" falsely at the slightest provocation. It explains, too, why men believe that no woman can be raped. It is as though what was mildly unsatisfactory at first (a girl's saying "no") becomes, over time, increasingly erotic, until the ultimate turn-on becomes a woman's cry of "rape!"

AN ALTERNATIVE: SEX BETWEEN FRIENDS

Understanding what's wrong with rape is difficult just because it is a member of the most common species of social encounter. To establish how rape is wrong is to establish that we have *all* been stepping to the wrong beat. Rape is only different in degree from the quintessential sexual relationship: marriage.

As Janice Moulton has noted, recent philosophical attention to theories of sexuality seem primarily concerned with sex between strangers.[15] On my view, we can explain this primary interest by noticing that our courting procedures are structured so that the couple must remain essentially estranged from each other. They do not ever talk or listen to each other with the respect and charity of friends. Instead, what is taken as the height of the erotic is sex without intimacy.

As long as we remain uncertain of the legitimacy of sexual pleasure, it will be impossible to give up our rape model of sexuality. For it can only be given up when we are willing to talk openly to each other without shame, embarrassment, or coyness about sex. Because only then will we not be too afraid to listen to each other.

Fortunately, to give this up requires us to make friends of our lovers.[16] Once we understand that intimacy enlarges the field of friendship, we can use some of the essential features of friendship as part of the model for sexual interaction, and we can present the pleasures of friendship as a real alternative to predatory pleasures.

I am not here committing myself to the view that the correct model for lovers is that of friends. Though I believe lovers involved in a healthy relationship have a fairly complex friendship, and though I am at a loss to find any important feature of a relationship between lovers that is not also one between friends, it may well be that the two relationships are merely closely related and not, in the end, explainable with the identical model.

It remains an enormously difficult task to throw over our anachronistic beliefs, and to resolve the conflict we feel about the sexual aspects of ourselves. But once this is done, not only will there be the obvious benefits of being able to exchange ignorance and denial of ourselves and others for knowledge, and fear for friendship, but we will also be able to remove the taboo from sex—even from rape. There will be no revelation, no reminder in the act of rape that we will need so badly to repress or deny that we must transform the victim into a guilt-bearing survivor. An act of rape will no longer remind us of the "true" nature of sex or our sexual desires.

Where there is nothing essentially forbidden about the fact of our sexual desires, the victim of rape will no longer be subject to a taboo or be regarded as dirty and in need of societal estrangement. The victim can then be regarded as having been grievously insulted, without simultaneously and necessarily having been permanently injured.

Further, if the model of sexual encounters is altered, there will no longer be any motivation for blaming the victim of rape. Since sex and rape will no longer be equated, there will be no motive for covering our own guilt or shame about the rapine nature of sex in general by transferring our guilt to the victim and ostracizing her. Rape will become an unfortunate aberration, the act of a criminal individual, rather than a symbol of our systematic ill-treatment and denial of each other.

Footnotes

1. Simone de Beauvoir, *Brigitte Bardot and the Lolita Syndrome* (London: New English Library, 1962), pp. 28, 30, 32.

2. Frye and Shafer characterize a domain as "where ... a person ... lives.... Since biological life and health are prerequisites for the pursuit of any other interests and goals, ... everything necessary for their maintenance and sustenance evidently will fall very close to the center of the domain. Anything which exerts an influence on ... a person's will or dulls its intelligence or affects its own sense of its identity ... also comes very near the center of the domain. Whatever has a relatively permanent effect on the person, whatever effects its relatively constant surroundings, whatever causes it discomfort or distress—in short, whatever a person has to live with—is likely to fall squarely within its domain."

3. This societal attitude, however, that the mentally retarded are not the equals of normal people is not one with which I associate myself.

4. Francoise Basch, *Relative Creatures: Victorian Women in Society and the Novel* (New York: Schocken Books, 1974), pp. 8–9, 270–71.

5. See *The Basic Writings of Sigmund Freud,* ed. A.A. Brill (New York: Random House, 1948), pp. 553–633.

6. William H. Masters and Virginia E. Johnson, *Human Sexual Response* (Boston: Little, Brown, 1966).

7. It may well be that Freud's theory of human sexuality is mistakenly taken to support this view. See Sigmund Freud, *A General Introduction to Psychoanalysis* (New York: Washington Square Press, 1962), pp. 329–47.

8. What is a complete non sequitur, of course, is that the presence of such pleasure is sufficient to establish that no criminal assault has occurred. The two events are completely independent.

9. Tom Wicker, *A Time to Die* (New York: Quadrangle Books, 1975).

10. Gary Wills, "The Human Sewer," *New York Review of Books,* 3 April 1975, p. 4.

11. See, for example, R.D. Laing and A. Esterson, *Sanity, Madness and the Family* (Baltimore: Penguin, Pelican Books, 1970).

12. CBS Evening News with Walter Cronkite, 22 May 1975.

13. *New American Movement Newspaper,* May 1975, p. 8.

14. See R.C. Solomon, "Sex and Perversion," Tom Nagel, "Sexual Perversion," and Janice Moulton, "Sex and Reference," in *Philosophy and Sex,* ed. Robert Baker and Frederick Elliston (Buffalo, NY: Prometheus Books, 1975).

15. Janice Moulton, "Sex and Sex," unpublished manuscript.

16. See Lyla O'Driscoll, "On the Nature and Value of Marriage," in Mary Vettereing-Braggin, Frederick A. Elliston, and Jane English, eds., *Feminism and Philosophy* (Littlefield, Adams and Co., 1981). She argues that marriage and the sexual relations it entails should be based on friendship rather than romantic love.

Review Questions

1. How do Frye and Shafer explain the wrongness of rape?

2. What are Foa's criticisms of this account?

3. How is rape different from other sorts of assault according to Foa?

4. What is Foa's account of the Victorian view of sex?

5. How does she think that this view influences contemporary thinking about rape?

6. Explain Foa's notion of the "halo of contamination" that permanently taints rape victims.

7. Explain what Foa calls the rape model of sex.

8. Explain Foa's friendship model of sex.

Discussion Questions

1. Is it true that "rape is only different in degree from the quintessential sexual relationship: marriage?"

2. Is Foa's friendship model of sex acceptable? Defend your answer.

Ronald Bayer
AIDS and the Gay Community

Ronald Bayer is Associate for Policy Studies at the Hastings Center, and the author of Homosexuality and American Psychiatry *(1981).*

Bayer begins with a description of the epidemiology of AIDS; the number of cases is rapidly increasing—there may be as many as 40,000 new cases within the next two years, and it is estimated that between 500,000 to 1 million Americans may already have been exposed to the virus. The public response to the AIDS epidemic was slow in coming, Bayer claims, because at first the victims were mostly male homosexuals, and homophobia prevented the press from covering the story. Religious leaders such as Jerry Falwell saw the disease as God's punishment on an immoral society.

Bayer goes on to discuss various problems resulting from the AIDS crisis: How should we stop the spread of the disease? Should homosexuality be treated as a disease or mental disorder or should we accept homosexuality and urge homosexuals to engage in safe sexual practices and use moderation? Was the closing of gay bathhouses justified? Should there be a quarantine of those infected with AIDS?

Another issue discussed by Bayer is that of privacy. Many in the gay community are afraid of being labeled, incarcerated, or deprived of employment and insurance. Consequently, they are reluctant to be tested or to participate in AIDS research.

The Epidemiology of AIDS

... Four years ago the Centers for Disease Control (CDC) began to report the appearance, in previously healthy gay men, of diseases that had occurred only in individuals whose immune systems had been severely compromised. In June 1981, *Morbidity and Mortality Weekly Reports,* CDC's publication, described an outcropping of five cases of **pneumocystis carinii pneumonia** in Los Angeles. Terming this occurrence "unusual," the *Reports* suggested the possibility of "an association between some aspect of homosexual lifestyle or disease acquired from sexual contact and pneumocystis pneumonia in this population." [1]

The next month, CDC reported that in the prior two and a half years **Kaposi's sarcoma,** a malignancy unusual in the United States, had been diagnosed in twenty-six gay men. Eight of those patients had died within two years of diagnosis. In each of these cases, two factors were striking: the youth of the victims—in the past, Kaposi's had been reported only in elderly Americans—and its "fulminant" course. [2]

During the next year the CDC continued to record the toll of what was now called acquired immune deficiency syndrome (AIDS). By May 28, 1982, 355 cases of Kaposi sarcoma, pneumocystis pneumonia, and other opportunistic infections among those who had not been previously diagnosed with immune suppressed conditions had been reported. Of these, 79 percent were either gay or bisexual. Among the heterosexual patients, the dominant feature was illicit intravenous drug use. Though there was no definitive explanation of how AIDS spread, there was increasingly suggestive evidence that some factor transmitted through sexual contact or the sharing of needles by drug users was involved. Why recent immigrants from Haiti seemed to be overrepresented among the heterosexual AIDS cases was a mystery.

In the first year of AIDS reporting, the pattern of morbidity and mortality seemed largely limited to three distinct groups—gay and bisexual men, drug users, and Haitians. The population at large seemed unaffected. In July 1982, however, CDC reported AIDS in three heterosexuals with **hemophilia.** [3] Two had died, one was critically ill. These cases suggested the possibility that the disease could be transmitted by blood or blood

From Ronald Bayer, "AIDS and the Gay Community," *Social Research,* vol. 52, no. 3 (Autumn 1985), pp. 581–606). Reprinted by permission of the author and *Social Research.* [The footnotes have been renumbered.–Ed.]

products. These fears were confirmed when the case of a twenty-month-old infant with an unexplained cellular immune deficiency along with opportunistic infection was reported. The child had received multiple transfusions after birth. One of these had come from a donor who, though apparently in good health at the time of his donation, had subsequently developed the first symptoms of AIDS.[4]

Each year, since the first reports of AIDS were made by the CDC, the number of cases has mounted. By April 1985, 9,400 cases had come to the attention of public health authorities. There had been more than 4,500 deaths. The overall mortality of just less than 50 percent conceals the course of the disease and its toll. Of those reported in 1981 and earlier, 85 percent were dead by April 1985. This was true of 70 percent of those reported in 1982, 63 percent of those reported in 1983, and 47 percent of those reported in the first six months of 1984.[5]

It is a grim fact about the statistics on AIDS that these numbers will be painfully outdated by the time this article is read. Though just fewer than 9,000 cases had been reported as of December 1984, there is little doubt that there will be an additional 9,000 cases in 1985. With the long-hoped-for "flattening of the epidemiological curve" still elusive, some have suggested that there may be as many as 40,000 new cases within the next two years.[6] Though some small progress has been made in treatment, there is little reason to believe that the mortality figures will show much improvement.

Despite the increase in numbers, the distribution of AIDS among various subgroups in the population has remained relatively constant (Table 1). Haitians, it will be noted, have been eliminated as a designated risk group, ostensibly for statistical reasons.[7] What remains uncertain at this point is how deeply AIDS will penetrate the at-risk populations, and whether the relatively circumscribed features of the current epidemiological pattern will be maintained.

Table 1
Distribution of AIDS Cases in April, 1985

Homosexual or bisexual men	73.6%
Intravenous drug users	16.9
Transfusion-associated	1.3
Heterosexual contact	0.9
Hemophiliacs	0.7
No officially designated risk group	6.6

A recently developed antibody test for HTLV–III/LAV, the virus now believed to be causative of AIDS, makes it possible to estimate the level of viral exposure and provides some indication of the dimensions of the problem. In one study it was found that virtually all **hemophiliacs** examined were antibody-positive. In San Francisco 65 percent of homosexual patients attending a clinic for sexually transmissible diseases were antibody-positive in 1984. In the same year 87 percent of the intravenous drug users admitted to a detoxification program in New York were antibody-positive.[8] James Curran of the CDC has estimated that overall between 500,000 and 1 million Americans may already have been exposed to the virus.[9] It is unknown at present how many of those who are antibody-positive will actually develop full-blown AIDS. Epidemiologists suggest, however, that the figure may be as high as 5–20 percent. Summarizing the complex and uncertain data, one recent report concluded: "Given what is already known about the high and rising sero prevalence of HTLV–III in known risk groups and the potential for spread to other populations, the implications of the presence of this virus in a community are staggering." [10]

The Public Reaction

The reaction to AIDS, as well as the debate over how to resolve the pressing ethical issues that have emerged as a result of that reaction, have been indelibly affected by the unique social distribution of the disease. With more than 90 percent of reported cases coming from those of marginal social status (gay and bisexual men, intravenous drug users, Haitians), it is hardly surprising that the fears associated with a deadly disease of unknown **etiology** have merged with those associated with contamination from below and without.

The response of the public to AIDS was slow to take form.[11] With few exceptions, there was little media interest in the unique and troubling pattern of disease that at first seemed to affect only male homosexuals. What reporting of the nascent AIDS epidemic there was tended to focus on technical medical issues, with little concern evidenced for the impact upon the gay community. As long as AIDS was restricted to intravenous drug users, to Haitians, to homosexual and bisexual males, it seemed unworthy of broad attention. One former *New York Times* reporter, commenting on the behavior of her own newspaper in the early years of the epidemic, stated, "I think that the story was ignored in all of its aspects for a long time because of who was being affected."[12]

Silence in the press was for the gay community an indication of prevailing homophobia. It represented an unwillingness to respond to the suffering of gays, a refusal to marshal the medical and technical resources for the tasks of discovering the causes of AIDS, of developing preventive strategies, and of providing clinical interventions that could interrupt the course of the disease. But at the same time there were those in the gay community who feared the consequence of too much public discussion of a disease that was so closely identified with male homosexuals. Might not such discussion provoke fears about a "gay plague"? Might it not provoke a backlash that would threaten the very important though modest advances made in the prior decade of efforts to advance the legal and social status of homosexuals?[13]

Fears of what form a broadened public awareness might take were in fact confirmed. As one analysis of the press coverage of AIDS has noted: For one and a half years it seemed that no one was suffering at all. Suddenly, in late 1982, the press began to warn that everyone could fall victim.[14] Discussions that glided from what was suspected about sexual contact in the spread of AIDS to references about "intimate" and then "close" contact provoked fears about the risks of contagion and of the possible spread of the disease by casual public encounters with members of high-risk groups. Reports began to appear that detailed the refusal of prison guards, undertakers, garbage collectors, and even health care workers to perform their duties with those suspected of having AIDS as well as with AIDS patients themselves.[15]

These reactions were punctuated by the extreme responses from those who sought to use the occasion of public consternation over AIDS to underscore their own antipathy to homosexuality and to what they viewed as the disastrous social consequence of greater social tolerance in sexual matters. The *Moral Majority Report*[16] featured a front-cover photograph of a family wearing surgical masks to introduce a story entitled "AIDS: Homosexual Disease Threatens American Families." Jerry Falwell demanded strong action against the homosexual carriers of AIDS: "If the Reagan administration does not put its full weight against what is now a gay plague in this country, I feel a year from now [the President] personally will be blamed [when this] awful disease breaks out among the innocent American public."[17] Invoking the image of divine retribution for sexual licentiousness, the Moral Majority leader asserted that AIDS represented a "spanking": "Herpes, AIDS, veneral disease.... are a definite form of judgment of God upon society."[18] Patrick Buchanan, the conservative political columnist and now White House director of communications, [Buchanan has since resigned his White House post.–Ed.] invoked a naturalistic vision of the punishment of gays when he wrote in the *New York Post,* "The poor homosexuals—they have declared war upon Nature, and now Nature is exacting an awful retribution."[19]

In the most extreme cases, there were

calls for the incarceration of homosexuals "until and unless they can be cleansed of their medical problems." [20] Even the traditionally sacrosanct public commitment to the medical treatment of the sick was not spared the assault of those who viewed AIDS as emblematic of the moral degradation of society: "What I see is a commitment to spend our tax dollars on research to allow these diseased homosexuals to go back to their perverted practices." [21] These declamations, typically though not exclusively expressed in the idiom of religious fundamentalism, were amplified by and at times fueled the broader public consternation about the threat of AIDS.

What accounts for the shift from the relative silence of the first year or so of AIDS reporting to the dramatic attention of the subsequent period? Both the rise in the number of cases and the rising mortality certainly played a role. In all of 1981, there had been 255 reported cases. There were more than that number in the first six months of 1982. In the last six months of the year there were 625 new cases—more than had been reported in the prior year and a half. But more was clearly involved. The emergence of AIDS cases among hemophiliacs dependent upon Factor VIII—the clotting agent derived from large numbers of blood donations—and the occurrence of cases among blood-transfusion recipients, and especially among infants and children, provoked a sense of dread about the spread of a deadly disease to "vulnerable" and "innocent" bystanders. In the very act of responding to the possible spread of AIDS the community expressed not only its fears about contagion but also its moral judgment. Gay males and drug users were victims, but were implicated by their own behavior, in the onset of the disease. Those in need of transfusions and Factor VIII were "innocents" who could do little to protect themselves.

Time magazine typified the sense of alarm provoked by fears of transfusion-associated cases of AIDS when it asserted that "a majority of experts believe that what was once known as the 'gay plague' will enter the general population" and that the most likely route of entry would be through blood.[22] On one widely watched television program the newscaster, Geraldo Rivera, urged that those who might be in need of transfusions "store up" their own blood.[23] Others urged a break with the important social practice of drawing appropriately matched blood products from the general public, and argued for directed donations from family and friends believed to be safe.

The debate that swirled around the necessity of developing appropriate blood practices in the face of AIDS was emblematic of those that were to emerge in the next two years over every dimension of public health policy and the response to AIDS. On the one hand, there was a realization that the welfare of the community required the development of measures designed to inhibit spread of AIDS. On the other hand, gays and their political allies feared that incautiously crafted policies might stigmatize the homosexual community, thus adding scientific and medical fuel to the social antipathy directed at those who had so recently succeeded in making strides toward social toleration, if not integration.

In early 1983, the National Hemophilia Foundation moved to gain agreement from commercial plasma companies to ban donations from all male homosexuals. Gay leaders, aware of the symbolic significance of being excluded from the blood donor pool and fearful of the stigma that might well be associated with the charge of "bad blood," urged that efforts be made to exclude only those homosexuals who it was believed were at specially high risk—those who had engaged in sexual relations with many partners. An overriding concern was the protection of the gay community from rashly designed medical policies that would serve as a subterfuge for antihomosexual prejudice. Central to that effort was the determination that no official policy of exclusion be enunciated. Rather, gays should exercise prudence and discretion, imposing upon themselves appropriate restrictions.[24] But with increasing recognition that gays could inadvertently contaminate the blood supply, it was only a matter of time before the Public Health Service (PHS) would issue its first exclusionary recommendations. In March 1983, the PHS called upon members of all high risk groups, including "sexually active homosexual or bisexual men with multiple partners," [25] to refrain from blood donations. Those responsible for collecting blood were to inform all potential donors of those federal standards. These were the most liberal of what were to be an increasingly restrictive series of recommendations. Eventually, virtually all homosexual males were to be excluded from the donor pool. In its recommendations of December 1984, the PHS urged the exclusion of "all males who have had sex with more than one male since 1979, and males whose male sex partner has had sex with more than one male since 1979." [26]

Sexuality and the Fears of Medicalization

The debate over the nation's blood supply was set against the background of a far broader set of concerns within the gay community, responsive to the troubling recognition that homosexuality was once again becoming the focus of medical attention, debate, scrutiny, and policy. A central feature of the contemporary struggle for gay liberation had been a long and acrimonious debate centering on the demedicalization of homosexuality.[27] Against psychiatry, which had classed homosexuality as a disease, the homophile movement of the 1960s had sought to demonstrate that a pseudoscientific ideology had masked the moral strictures that had long dominated Western attitudes toward sexual activity among those of the same sex. Prodded by a well-organized challenge that was at once political, theoretical, and moral, the American Psychiatric Association was forced to confront its own diagnostic presuppositions. After a bitter intraprofessional encounter that entailed reconsideration of the scope of the concept "disease," America's psychiatrists yielded to gay pressures in 1973 by removing homosexuality from their official classification of mental disorders. Now, a decade later, faced by the threat of disease and death, the power of medicine was being brought into intimate contact with the gay community. The power of medicine was at once the sole hope for halting the spread of the disease that threatened to devastate the homosexual community and the specter threatening to subvert the achievements of the prior twenty years. Not only was there a risk that medical justifications would be used to reverse the public victories won as the result of great organizational efforts, but that every dimension of private sexual expression would become the target of medical scrutiny, diagnosis, and challenge.

As gays had forced psychiatry to confront itself, now medicine was compelling the gay community to examine its own behavior. Within the gay community, the epidemiological linkage that had been suggested by researchers between "fast lane" behavior and the enhanced risk for contracting AIDS forced a reflection upon the most intimate dimensions of sexual behavior. Some suggested that AIDS might be the consequence of repeated assaults on the immune system that resulted from certain sexual acts, including anal intercourse. Others argued that indiscriminate sexual contact with large numbers of anonymous partners simply enhanced the prospect of being exposed to the disease-bearing agent.

Joseph Sonnabend, a physician who cares for AIDS patients and former medical director of the AIDS Medical Foundation, has emerged as the leading advocate of the immunological-overload theory. "There is such a thing as sexual excess, though to say that sounds like some throwback to Victorian morality," he has asserted. "Put simply, I believe one of the biggest risks is to be exposed anally to semen from many different partners, especially in a large urban area where the risks of coming into contact with cytomegalovirus, which I think is a causative agent somehow, is very high." Sonnabend was especially critical of physicians who, because of political and social concerns, recoiled from the implications of these data: "Gay men have been poorly served by their doctors in the last decade. There was no clear and positive message about the dangers of promiscuity. We must admit that our desire to be nonjudgmental has interfered with our primary commitment to our patients." [28]

For many gay physicians, Sonnabend's unvarnished challenge passed beyond the bounds of appropriate clinical and professional discourse. Writing in the *Journal of the American Medical Association*, Neil Schram and Dennis McShane, of the American Association of Physicians for Human Rights, asserted:

It is important to note that terms such as profound promiscuity, *when used by medical personnel to describe multiple sex partners, have a strong judgmental quality, and, as such, are not suitable to the scientific and medical literature. Those physicians caring for homosexual males with or without AIDS have been encouraged to be supportive of their patients. It is terms like "promiscuity" that make many homosexuals reluctant to discuss their sexual orientation with their medical care providers, even though doing so clearly improves the quality of medical care.* [29]

But however the scientific issues were framed, a clear message was derived from the earliest scientific evidence. "Safe" sexual practices, sexual moderation, and caution were necessary. Lawrence Mass, a physician active in gay circles, writing in the *New York Native*, emphasized this point. While rejecting the moralistic undertones of the religious challenge to homosexual practice, he cautioned prudence upon his readers: "A major priority at this time is to discourage sexual lifestyles that involve many different, especially anonymous, partners." [30] Some gay men perceived this message as a challenge to their behavior, adopting an extremely harsh

perspective on their own past activities. Others, using a hydraulic image, sought to argue that an excessive preoccupation with sexuality had poorly served their community. Michael Callen, who has AIDS, and who is an ally of Dr. Sonnabend, thus asserted: "All the great sex we've been having for the past ten years has syphoned off our collective anger that might otherwise have been translated into social and political action." [31]

The calls for restraint, for the observance of "immunological Lent," and even for monogamy, were not, however, always greeted so enthusiastically. Some viewed them as representing a thinly disguised scientific call for a return to sexual conventionality. Once again, physicians were seeking to establish their dominance over homosexuality, a dominance that so recently had been discarded. Writing in the *Body Politic*, a Canadian gay journal, Michael Lynch stated: "Gays are once again allowing the medical profession to define, restrict, pathologize us." To follow the advice of physicians would involve renunciation of "the power to determine our own identity," and would represent "a communal betrayal of gargantuan proportions" of gay liberation founded upon a "sexual brotherhood of promiscuity." [32] Doubting the scientific validity of the data on the basis of which the cautionary advice was being proffered, another wrote, "I feel that what we are being advised to do involves all of the things I became gay to get away from. . . . So we have a disease for which supposedly the cure is to go back to all the styles that were preached at us in the first place. It will take a lot more evidence before I'm about to do that." [33] In a particularly vitriolic attack upon Jonathan Lieberson's essay on AIDS that appeared in the New York Review of Books, John Rechy wrote, "How eagerly do even perhaps 'good heterosexuals' impose grim sentences of abstinence on others." [34]

Bathhouses and Quarantine: The Fears of State Power

While the encounter with medicine over sexual behavior centered on how its cultural authority could affect the personal and private choices of gay men, the controversy surrounding the operation of gay bathhouses focused on medicine's interaction with government. Here the possibility that medical and epidemiological evidence might be used by the public health authorities as a justification for imposing the power of the state in the effort to interrupt the spread of AIDS was central. The gay bathhouse has emerged as a powerful symbol of the struggle for greater social toleration for homosexuality. The existence of such establishments reflects not only the willingness of certain cities to tolerate the flourishing of gay social institutions but the willingness to accept the existence of commercial establishments in which homosexual activity occurs. It is therefore not surprising that suggestions that these centers be closed would provoke an enormous political controversy.

For those who have advocated the closing of the baths the logic has been rather straightforward. Since the bathhouse exists to facilitate sexual encounters among strangers, any public health strategy committed to **prophylaxis** requires that it be eliminated. For civil libertarians, efforts to move in such a direction represented potential infringement on privacy and on the right of individuals to congregate. Some gay leaders, though by no means all, feared that the baths would be the first target of those committed to an assault on the communal institutions of the gay world. Shrouded in the mantle of medicine, protected from scrutiny by the ideology of public health, such an attack, some have believed, would ultimately extend to gay bars, businesses, and the employment possibilities of homosexual men.[35] Given this perspective, it is not surprising that at least on one occasion outrage took the form of a hyperbolic comparison between efforts to close the baths and the Nazi assault on Jewish cultural institutions.[36]

Not all public health officials have supported bathhouse closure. Their arguments have been moral and political as much as they have been medical. Dr. David Sencer, the commissioner of health in New York City, thus opposed Dr. Mervyn Silverman of San Francisco, who had sought to close his city's baths,[37] stating:

I can see no reason why we would close the bathhouses. I don't think that changing the habitat is necessarily going to change the behavior. There are other places people can go and have indiscriminate sexual relations if they want to. To try to legislate changes in lifestyle has never been effective. Public education through the routes of organized groups who are at risk is the most important thing.[38]

Others within and outside the gay community have seen the refusal or the inability of public health officials to close the baths as a capitulation in the face of irresponsible political pressure. The community's interests were thus sacrificed in an effort to appease those who did not understand the critical importance of removing the aura of public toleration from establishments that so unmistakably symbolized anonymous sexual activity. In an interview published in *San Francisco Magazine*, an AIDS' patient thus said: "I was at a friend's house, a doctor, and he was just furious that they were thinking about closing the baths—that it was taking away gay rights. Well, you know, when there are hundreds of lives involved, gay rights go right out the window, as far as I am concerned." [39]

While the debate over the baths captured public attention, a far more critical matter regarding the relationship between medical and state authority was being considered—quarantine. Once a central feature of the public health response to contagious disease, the isolation of individuals during the infectious period of illness had fallen into **desuetude.** Now with AIDS perceived as a threat to the public health, the legitimacy of quarantine received renewed attention. But unlike earlier discussions of this extreme measure that centered on matters of necessity and efficacy, the debate now took on an essentially political character. Given the vulnerable social status of the population at risk and the contemporary anxiety in liberal public health circles about the potential abuses of state authority, the debate could not have been different.

When, if ever, would it be appropriate to consider the isolation of those with AIDS to prevent the spread of the disease? Would a refusal to desist from sexual activity on the part of an individual who had AIDS warrant state intervention? Should prostitutes with AIDS be held in custody to prevent them from contaminating those with whom they might engage in sexual contact? Should women with AIDS be permitted to have children?

Like the bathhouse controversy, the quarantine debate took on its most salient form in California. In December 1983, James Chin, chief of the infectious disease section of the California Department of Health, proposed a course of action designed to provide control over the "recalcitrant" AIDS patient.[40] "Modified isolation" would be invoked if such an individual, after due warning, refused to abstain from sexual activities, which "could transmit a possible AIDS agent to sexual contacts who were unaware that he had AIDS." If such efforts failed to produce compliance with the behavior deemed medically necessary by the authorities, they would be permitted to proceed with the quarantine of the patient's residence by "posting a placard at his residence which indicates that a person with a communicable disease which can be spread by intimate contact resides in the household." Though California did not proceed with this proposal, Dr. Chin's office was informed that statutory authority already existed to charge with a misdemeanor any individual with an infectious disease who willfully exposed another person. Since special authorization was thus unnecessary to control "recalcitrant" AIDS patients, only a symbolic provocative public health gesture would have been involved in forcing the issue of quarantine.

Connecticut did adopt a quarantine statute that could include those with AIDS. That move resulted in expressions of outrage from those who viewed it as an unwarranted medicopolitical threat against both civil liberties and the rights of gay men.

The executive director of the Connecticut Civil Liberties Union asserted that the new statute would permit the state to "sweep a person off the streets on mere suspicion." [41] Dr. Alvin Novick, who has been active in gay medical circles, stated:

Quarantine is such a devastating blow to someone's life. If it were invoked for someone with AIDS, it would forever after deprive them of jobs ... social life. It would be used as a statement of official oppression that is not unknown in our society, but that today is hardly tolerable. People in public health are not precluded from being ignorant or evil, and there are people in public health who are evil and ignorant. [42]

Epidemiology and the Threat to Privacy

That the debate over bathhouse closure and quarantine would have directly engaged gay political leaders is not surprising. More unusual has been their close and watchful involvement in the conduct of public and private research into the etiology, course, and epidemiology of AIDS. Fear of being labeled, of being incarcerated, and of being deprived of access to employment and insurance has marked the ongoing conflict between the representatives of the gay community concerned with privacy and researchers who have asserted that the public health requires the conduct of epidemiological studies based upon the most intimate details about AIDS patients' lives and identities. The conflict arose early as the Centers for Disease Control sought the names of AIDS patients reported to public health authorities throughout the country. Recognizing the critical importance of longitudinal studies to a broad research program, gay leaders were nevertheless fearful that providing federal health officials with such data would create the circumstances for the deprivation of the civil rights of gay men, intravenous drug users, and undocumented aliens. For them, the technical requirements of research had to be viewed within a broad political and ethical context.

How much did federal researchers need to know? Could codes be substituted for names? Were codes inviolable? Could the CDC's professional scientists be trusted to protect the confidentiality of their data? What were the links between public health researchers and public health enforcers? These were the questions that proved so troublesome.

Doubts about the capacity or willingness of federal researchers to protect the privacy interests of AIDS patients came from many sources. The commissioner of health in the District of Columbia thus stated:

I wouldn't trust the CDC one moment not to give up information to the FBI, the CIA, or the Social Security Administration. The CDC is a federal agency. You and I both know that federal agencies do exchange information, and they will always do that on what they understand to be an appropriate need-to-know basis. And they will not consider that a breach of confidentiality.[43]

Virginia Apuzzo, executive director of the National Gay Task Force, underscored the social context of the confidentiality debate:

In this country we [gays] are illegal in half of the states. We can't serve in the armed forces, we can't raise our own kids in many states, and we sure as hell can't teach other people's kids. When you tell us you're interested in our social security numbers, when we know we are not permitted to have security clearance, we would . . . be naive, at best, not to ask "What will you do with the information? Can we trust you enough?"[44]

The dilemma posed for gay leaders was pinpointed by Jeff Levi of the National Gay Task Force: "We could not be more interested in the gathering of accurate information about AIDS, but we also firmly believe that reporting mechanisms must guarantee confidentiality."[45]

While some believed that no tension existed between the imposition of ironclad protections and the conduct of epidemiological research, others felt it imperative to note

that, while it was possible to strike a compromise position, all such efforts involved trade-offs in the speed and ease with which data could be gathered and subjected to analysis. The *New York Native*, a gay newspaper, soberly observed:

Confidentiality and epidemiology may not be as mutually compatible as some gay leaders would have us think. Confidentiality and epidemiology are matters of tense negotiation, not marriage. We are in a gray area in which abuses on both sides could occur. On the one hand, someone could illegally obtain a list of people with AIDS and try to create havoc. On the other hand, some well-intentioned gay leaders who think that AIDS is primarily a civil liberties issue may be endangering research.[46]

In a remarkable and quite unusual process, representatives of gay organizations entered into a complex set of negotiations over the nature of the confidentiality protections that were to be afforded to AIDS research subjects. Out of this process of negotiation and confrontation, compromises were fashioned for the protection of confidentiality. While some have asserted that the interests of public health have been sacrificed, others have acknowledged that the volatile setting of AIDS research required such adjustments. A refusal to yield would have produced inadequate or inaccurate reporting. James Allen of the CDC thus noted, "It clearly is a compromise position, which will make it more difficult to do our work. But if we are not getting reports, we can't do it either."[47]

The issue of confidentiality and of potential risks to the subjects of AIDS research surfaced in a particularly focused form in 1984, as efforts to create a test for the presence of the antibody to HTLV–III were moving to success. Developed primarily to screen blood donations in order to limit the still-troubling problem of the transfusion-associated cases of AIDS, the antibody test was also viewed as providing an important source of data for researchers seeking to determine the extent to which those exposed to the HTLV–III virus actually developed full-blown cases of AIDS.

Because it was feared that the results of the tests would not be protected from scrutiny of private insurers, law enforcement officials, and employers, and because it was assumed that the test would serve as a surrogate marker for homosexuality, an extraordinary effort was mounted by gay leaders to discourage individuals from being tested by private practitioners.[48] More significantly, they called upon members of the gay community to refuse participation in crucial research studies unless the guarantees of confidentiality were made more explicit.[49] Thus Nancy Langer of the Lambda Legal Defense Fund stated, "We don't want to be a roadblock to government research into AIDS; indeed, the opposite is true. But we don't want research to boomerang and become *the* major threat to the rights of gays and lesbians in this decade."[50] Once again, compromise and negotiation of an unprecedented kind resulted in additional protections for those who would be the subjects of research.

Research, Medical Care, and the Fears of Neglect

Despite the enormous consternation generated by the threat of the abuse of medical authority, those who have been most active in the medical politics surrounding AIDS have consistently and forcefully challenged the federal government, state officials, and the scientific community to increase drastically the resources available for research into the disease. A sense of despair has imbued the repeated calls for an enhanced research commitment and the critique of what has been done thus far. For gay leaders the "torpid" federal [51] response to AIDS was but another indication of a homophobia that discounted the lives and suffering of homosexuals.

Government officials, including the secretary of health and human services, have repeatedly asserted that research into AIDS has been given the highest priority. Gay leaders and their political allies within the scientific bureaucracies have viewed these assertions as cynical efforts to mask an unwillingness to treat AIDS as a true crisis. Dr. Donald Francis, CDC's AIDS coordinator for laboratory resources, thus wrote in April 1983: "The time wasted pursuing money from Washington ... has sandwiched those responsible for research and control between mass pressure to do what is right and an unmovable wall of inadequate resources ... our government's response to this disaster has been far too little."[52] This personal observation was buttressed in the same year by a report of the Committee on Government Operations of the House of Representatives. In "The Federal Response to AIDS,"[53] the Committee charged that inadequate funding had hampered Public Health Service efforts to "fight the AIDS epidemic." Two years later the Office of Technology Assessment found a similar pattern of inadequate funding, noting in addition that administration requests had been consistently below the levels deemed necessary by the Congress.[54]

The irony of being dependent upon more research into AIDS, while dreading the potential social consequences of efficiently organized and well-funded undertakings, was never really lost from view. Dennis Altman, a perceptive and trenchant analyst of gay politics, thus noted: "The very research demanded by the gay movement mean[t] greater surveillance and possible controls over us."[55]

Not only was this irony manifested in the discussions of research, however. The enormous costs generated by the medical care of AIDS patients (about $150,000 per patient from the moment of diagnosis) has provoked fears that those who were the victims of this illness would become the victims of neglect as well. For years gays had struggled to protect themselves against the ministrations of physicians who had defined their sexuality as pathological; now they feared that their pathologies would be ignored because they were homosexual.

Because health insurance in the United States is typically linked to employment, those who are chronically or even temporarily unemployed often find themselves without protection. Those who are so unprotected are sometimes treated as charity cases, more often by public hospitals. Studies of the health care system make it clear, however, that a lack of insurance coverage results in great hardships for those in need of care. Since patients with AIDS, especially in its advanced stages, cannot work, they often confront economic difficulties when seeking access to the health care system, especially when outpatient care is involved.

Concerned about the personal financial burden of needed medical attention and about the willingness of government to provide the resources for such care, gay leaders have been forced to confront the inequities of the American health system. Some have attempted to construe the problem narrowly by suggesting that federally underwritten categorical programs be expanded to protect AIDS patients. Others have argued that the problems faced by those with AIDS simply underscore the necessity of a more far-reaching reform of the American health care system: "The real point is that access to health care in the United States is not equally distributed. The poor, the nonwhite, the old, also die of neglect." [56]

AIDS thus forced a confrontation with the most basic question of justice and the health care system.

Hope and Fear

In October 1984, New York's gay newspaper, The Native, published two editorials, the juxtaposition of which exquisitely exhibits the tensions posed for those desperate to bring an end to AIDS as they confront both the promise and specter of medicine.[57] The first editorial, entitled "What Curran Should Do," was a denunciation of the inadequate funding of research into AIDS: "The time has come for [James] Curran [head of CDC's AIDS task force] to commit the bravest, most powerful act of his career: to call a press conference on the steps of Congress and announce that he is considering resignation because he will no longer be the front man for an ineffective,

often homophobic public health response to a national emergency." The second editorial, "Don't Take This Test," was a warning to gays about the risks that would attend the availability of the antibody test for HTLV–III: "Will test results be used to identify the sexual orientation of millions of Americans? Will a list of names be made? How can such information be kept truly confidential? Who will be able to keep the list out of the hands of insurance companies, employers, landlords, and the government itself?"

Spurred by the hopes evoked by medicine's power and by the fears about how that power might be used, the gay community has sparked an important debate that will test the capacity of American society to respond effectively and humanely to an unfolding tragedy. To this point the confluence of political and social forces that has emerged in the public encounter with AIDS has permitted a sympathetic hearing of the moral concerns that have been central to bioethics. Whether the social crisis that will be created if the spread of AIDS continues unabated will provide so hospitable a setting for those liberal values within which privacy and voluntarism are so important is far from certain.

Footnotes

1. U.S. Department of Health and Human Services, *Morbidity and Mortality Weekly Reports (MMWR)*, June 5, 1981.

2. *MMWR*, July 3, 1981.

3. *MMWR*, July 16, 1982.

4. *MMWR*, Dec. 10, 1982.

5. Telephone interview, Centers for Disease Control.

6. "Perspectives on the Future of AIDS," *Journal of the American Medical Association*, Jan. 11, 1985, p. 247.

7. For discussions of the debate over whether Haitians should constitute a special risk group, a debate in which Haitians had argued that such a designation represented a scientifically unwarranted stigmatization, see the *New York Times*, July 29, 1983, and the *Los Angeles Times*, Sept. 5, 1983.

8. Sheldon Landesman, Harold Ginzburg, Stanley Weiss, "The AIDS Epidemic," *New England Journal of Medicine*, Feb. 21, 1985, p. 521.

9. J. Silberner, "AIDS: Disease, Research Efforts Advance," *Science News*, Apr. 27, 1985, p. 260.

10. Landesman, Ginzburg, Weiss, "The AIDS Epidem-

ic," p. 522.

11. Harry Schwartz, Appendix to *Science in the Streets,* Report to the Twentieth Century Fund Task Force on the Communication of the Scientific Risk, 1984.

12. Julius Genachowski, "Press Covering AIDS," *Broadway,* Sept. 15, 1983, p. 11.

13. See, in general, Dennis Altman, "The Politicization of an Epidemic," *Socialist Review,* November/December 1984.

14. Genachowski, "Press Covering AIDS."

15. See, for example, "Morticians Balk at AIDS Victims," *Washington Post,* June 18, 1983.

16. Moral Majority Report, July 1983.

17. Washington Post, July 6, 1983.

18. Ibid.

19. New York Post, May 24, 1983.

20. New York Times, Aug. 7, 1983.

21. Cited in Genachowski, "Press Covering AIDS," p. 14.

22. Time, Mar. 28, 1983.

23. Newsweek, July 4, 1983, p. 21.

24. Discussed in Ronald Bayer, "Gays and the Stigma of Bad Blood," *Hastings Center Report,* April 1983, pp. 5–7.

25. U.S. Department of Health and Human Services, Memorandum from the Director, Office of Biologics, National Center for Drugs and Biologics, "Recommendations to Decrease the Risk of Transmitting Acquired Immune Deficiency Syndrome from Plasma Donors," Mar. 24, 1983.

26. U.S. Department of Health and Human Services, Memorandum from Acting Director, Office of Biologics Research and Review, "Research Recommendations to Decrease the Risk of Transmitting an Immunodeficiency Syndrome (AIDS) from Blood and Plasma Donors," Dec. 14, 1984.

27. Ronald Bayer, *Homosexuality and American Psychiatry: The Politics of Diagnosis* (New York: Basic Books, 1981).

28. American Medical News, Jan. 20, 1984, p. 3.

29. Journal of the American Medical Association, Jan. 20, 1984, p. 341.

30. Lawrence Mass, "The Case Against Medical Panic," *New York Native,* Jan. 17–30, 1983, p. 23.

31. Jonathan Lieberson, "Anatomy of an Epidemic," *New York Review of Books,* Aug. 18, 1983, p. 20.

32. Ibid, p. 19.

33. Ibid, p. 22.

34. John Rechy, Letter to the *New York Review of Books,* Oct. 13, 1983, p. 43.

35. Kenneth W. Payne and Stephen J. Risch, "The Politics of AIDS," *Science for the People,* September/October 1984, p. 23.

36. Charles Krauthammer, "The Politics of a Plague," *The New Republic,* Aug. 1, 1983, p. 19.

37. David Black, "The Plague Years," *Rolling Stone,* Apr. 25, 1985, p. 44.

38. Lieberson, "Anatomy of an Epidemic," p. 21.

39. Frank Cron, "Conversation with a Victim," *San Francisco Magazine,* April 1985, p. 66.

40. "AIDS—A New Reason to Regulate Homosexuality," *Journal of Contemporary Law,* 1984, pp. 340–341.

41. Black, "The Plague Years," p. 60.

42. Ibid.

43. Washington Post, July 18, 1983, p. 4.

44. Washington Post, July 18, 1983.

45. " 'Confidentiality' Issue May Cloud Epidemologic Studies of AIDS," *Journal of the American Medical Association,* Oct. 21, 1983, p. 1945.

46. New York Native, Nov. 7–20, 1983.

47. Washington Post, July 18, 1983.

48. New York Times, Oct. 12, 1984.

49. "Why You Should Not Be Tested for HTLV–III," *New York Native,* Oct. 8–21, 1984.

50. "Consent Form for AIDS Research Urged on Brandt," *The Advocate,* Oct. 16, 1984.

51. Lieberson, "Anatomy of an Epidemic," p. 18.

52. Judith Randal, "Too Little for AIDS," *Technology Review,* August/September 1984, p. 10.

53. U.S. House of Representatives, Committee on Government Operations, "The Federal Response to AIDS," Nov. 30, 1983.

54. U.S. Congress, Office of Technology Assessment, *Review of the Public Health Services' Response to AIDS: A Technical Memorandum* (Washington, D.C., February 1985).

55. Altman, "Politicization of an Epidemic," p. 107.

56. Ibid., p. 108.

57. New York Native, Oct. 8, 1984.

Review Questions

1. How does Bayer describe the epidemiology of AIDS?

2. According to Bayer, what was the initial public response to the AIDS epidemic?

3. How did doctors respond to the crisis, according to Bayer?

4. Describe the gay bathhouse controversy.

5. Explain the debate about the quarantine proposal.

6. Why does AIDS research pose a threat to privacy, in Bayer's view?

7. According to Bayer, why have gays been afraid to take the AIDS test?

Discussion Questions

1. Do you agree with Jerry Falwell's claim that herpes, AIDS, and veneral disease are a definite form of God's judgment? Explain your answer.

2. Do gay people have a right to have homosexual sex?

3. Should there be a quarantine of those infected with the AIDS virus?

4. Who do you think should pay the enormous costs of medical care for AIDS patients? What if the patient is unable to pay?

Problem Cases

1. *The AIDS Test* We now have tests for the presence of the AIDS virus that are as reliable as any diagnostic test in medicine. An individual who tests positive can be presumed with near certainty to carry the virus, whether he or she has symptoms of the disease or not. In fact the test correlates so consistently with the presence of the virus in bacteria cultures as to be considered 100 percent certain by experts.

Who should be tested? Some doctors recommend that everyone in the high-risk population (homosexual or bisexual men) should be tested for AIDS; otherwise the epidemic will get worse. Yet some people in the high-risk population refuse to be tested, claiming that they have a right not to be tested. They are afraid of being labeled, quarantined, losing their jobs, or losing their health insurance. Are these people justified in refusing to be tested? What is your view?

One proposal is that there be some sort of mandatory testing for AIDS. For example, people who get marriage licenses could be required to get an AIDS test or there could be mandatory testing of prison inmates. What do you think? Should we have some kind of mandatory testing for AIDS? If so, how should it be carried out? And if not, why not?

2. *The Jim Bakker Case* Jim Bakker (pronounced "baker") was the head of the Christian PTL ("Praise the Lord") organization (with 129 million in revenues in 1986), and with his wife Tammy hosted a television evangelist show, "The Jim and Tammy Show," watched by millions of people. A rival television evangelist, Louisiana-based Jimmy Swaggart, charged that Bakker had had a one-night stand with a former church secretary, twenty-seven year old Jessica Hahn, in 1981 when Jessica was only twenty-one years old. Both Hahn and Bakker admitted to the sexual encounter, but they gave rather different stories about the incident. Bakker said that he was the bewildered and inexperienced victim of an evil tempt-

ress who "knew all the tricks of the trade." Hahn said that she was drugged and then forcibly seduced by Bakker who appeared in her hotel room wearing only a white cloth swimsuit.

Assuming that it was an act between consenting adults, and not rape, was this sexual encounter morally wrong? If it was wrong, then why?

Suppose that Bakker's story is true. Would you excuse him from any wrongdoing? Why or why not?

On the other hand, suppose that Hahn's story is the accurate one. Would would excuse her from wrongdoing? What do you think?

What about Jimmy Swaggart's actions? Did he do the right thing in publically exposing this act of adultery? Explain your answer.

3. *The Gary Hart Case* In the spring of 1987, Gary Hart was the front runner for the 1988 Democratic presidential nomination. Yet just twenty-five days after formally announcing his candidacy, he suddenly withdrew from the race. His reason for this abrupt withdrawal was the scandal caused by a newspaper story in the *Miami Herald* which claimed that he had spent the night in his Washington D.C. townhouse with a twenty-nine year old model named Donna Rice. Miami Herald reporters kept Hart's townhouse under surveillance, and they asserted that they had observed Rice enter the house in the evening and leave the next morning. Although they had no proof, the reporters implied in their story that Hart and Rice had engaged in illicit sexual behavior during the night. Hart and Rice both denied that they had done anything immoral, and in his withdrawal speech, Hart accused the media of treating him unfairly. But when he was asked pointblank if he had ever committed adultery, Hart refused to answer. This was taken by the media as a tacit admission of adultery, at least at some time in the past.

This case raises some interesting questions:

a. Is the sexual behavior of a candidate for public office relevant in assessing the candidate's qualifications?

b. Should newspapers actively investigate the sexual behavior of public figures, or do these people have a right to sexual privacy?

c. Suppose, for the sake of discussion, that Hart was indeed guilty of committing adultery with his friend Rice. In your opinion, would this fact make him unqualified to hold public office? Why or why not?

4. Petit v. State Board of Education, 1973 Mrs. Petit was a teacher of retarded, elementary-school children in the public-school system. She and her husband joined a private club in Los Angeles called The Swingers. An undercover policeman attended a private party during which Mrs. Petit was observed in several acts of oral copulation. She was arrested, charged with oral copulation under the California Penal Code, and she pleaded guilty to the lesser charge of outraging public decency. After disciplinary proceedings, her teaching credentials were revoked on the grounds that her conduct involved moral turpitude. Although Mrs. Petit petitioned the courts to order the State Board of Education to restore her teaching credentials, the courts denied her request.

Was Mrs. Petit's conduct at the party morally wrong? Defend your view.

Should there be a law against private sex acts performed by consenting adults? Why, or why not?

5. Doe v. Commonwealth's Attorney for City of Richmond, 1975 In this case, two anonymous homosexuals sought to have the Virginia sodomy statute making homosexual activity a crime declared unconstitutional. In a two-to-one decision, the District Court in Richmond, Virginia, upheld the constitutionality of the statute. The case was subsequently appealed to the United States Supreme Court, but in 1976, by a vote of six to three, the Court refused to hear arguments and affirmed the lower-court ruling.

Should there be a law making sodomy a crime? Defend your position.

Suggested Readings

(1) Baker, Robert, and Frederick Elliston, eds. *Philosophy and Sex, New Revised Edition*. Buffalo, NY: Prometheus, 1984. This anthology contains a number of useful articles relevant to sexual morality.

(2) Barnhart, J.E., and Mary Ann Barnhart. "Marital Faithfulness and Unfaithfulness." *Journal of Social Philosophy* vol. 4 (April 1973). They argue that we should recognize different marriage styles as legitimate, including the marriage style that allows extramarital sex.

(3) Bertocci, Peter A. *Sex, Love, and the Person*. New York: Sheed & Ward, 1967. Bertocci defends conventional sexual morality.

(4) Cameron, Paul. "A Case Against Homosexuality." *Human Life Review* 4 (Summer 1978): 17–49. Cameron is a psychologist who provides us with facts about homosexuality. He maintains that it is an undesirable lifestyle.

(5) Leiser, Burton. *Liberty, Justice and Morals*, 2d ed. New York: Macmillan, 1979. In Chapter 2, Leiser discusses and attacks various arguments that are made for saying that homosexuality is morally wrong.

(6) Levy, Donald. "Perversion and the Unnatural as Moral Categories," In *The Philosophy of Sex* edited by Alan Soble, 169–189. Littlefield Totowa, NJ, Adams, and Co., 1980. Levy gives a survey of various definitions of "sexual perversion," and then gives his own account.

(7) Oppenheimer, Gerald M., and Robert A. Padgag. "AIDS: The Risks to Insurers, The Threat to Equity." *Hastings Center Report* (October 1986); 18–22. They discuss the problems the AIDS crisis poses for the insurance industry.

(8) Pierce, Christine, and Donald VanDeVeer, eds. *AIDS: Ethics and Public Policy*. Wadsworth, forthcoming September, 1987. This collection of readings includes David Mayo, "AIDS, Quarantines, and Non-Compliant Positives;" Donald Chambers, "AIDS testing: An Insurer's Viewpoint;" Ronald Bayer and Gerald Oppenheimer, "AIDS in the Work Place: The Ethical Ramifications;" Kenneth R. Howe, "Why Mandatory Screening for AIDS is a Very Bad Idea;" and many

other interesting articles on AIDS and its implications.

(9) Punzo, Vincent C. *Reflective Naturalism.* Macmillan, 1969. Punzo argues against premarital sexual intercourse. On his view, marriage is constituted by mutual and total commitment, and apart from this committment, sexual unions are morally deficient.

(10) Wellman, Carl. *Morals and Ethics.* Glenview, IL: Scott-Foresman, 1975. In Chapter 5, Wellman considers arguments given for and against the morality of premarital sex.

Glossary

Bestiality   sexual relations between a human being and a nonhuman animal.

Conjugal   of or relating to marriage.

Connatural   connected to nature; inborn, inherent.

Desuetude   discontinuance from use, practice, exercise, or function.

Epidemiology   the sum of factors controlling the presence or absence of a disease.

Etiology   the factors that contribute to the occurrence of a disease.

Hedonism   in ethics, the theory that only pleasure is intrinsically good, or good in itself.

Hemophilia   a sex-linked hereditary blood defect of males characterized by delayed clotting of the blood and consequent difficulty in controlling bleeding even after minor injuries.

Hemophiliacs   those affected with hemophilia.

Homophobia   fear of homosexuals or homosexuality.

Kaposi's sarcoma   an often fatal type of skin cancer that appears as purplish patches on the skin or inside the mouth, nose, or eyelids.

Magisterium of the Church   the church's teaching power.

Natural law   prescriptive rules of conduct based on human nature.

Nymphomaniac   one affected with nymphomania, an excessive desire for sexual activity (attributed to females rather than males).

Ontological   of or related to being or existence.

Pastoral   (as the word is used in the Vatican declaration) of or relating to the spiritual care of a congregation or a group of Christians.

Pedophilia   sexual interest in children.

Pneumocystis carinii pneumonia   an often fatal parasitic infection of the lungs.

Prophylaxsis   the prevention of disease.

Sodomy   the entry of the male organ into the mouth or anus of another.

Weltanshauung   world view, a philosophical view or understanding of the universe including human beings, society, and its institutions.

Chapter 8

Animals and the Environment

Introduction

Humans cause a great deal of animal suffering. Consider this example of animal experimentation taken from Peter Singer's book *Animal Liberation*. At the Lovelace Foundation in New Mexico experimenters forced sixty-four beagles to inhale radioactive strontium 90. Twenty-five of the dogs died; initially most of them were feverish and anemic, and had hemorrhages and bloody diarrhea. One of the deaths occurred during an epileptic seizure, and another resulted from a brain hemorrhage. In a similar experiment, beagles were injected with enough strontium 90 to produce early death in fifty percent of the group. Are experiments such as these really necessary? It was already known that strontium 90 was unhealthy, and that the dogs would suffer and die. Furthermore, these experiments did not save any human lives or have any important benefits for humans. So why were they done?

Another common human practice that produces considerable animal suffering is factory farming. Take the treatment of veal calves for example. In order to make their flesh pale and tender, these calves are given special treatment. They are put in narrow stalls and tethered with a chain so that they cannot turn around, lie down comfortably, or groom themselves. They are fed a totally liquid diet to promote rapid weight gain. This diet is deficient in iron and, as a result, the calves lick the sides of the stall, which are impregnated with urine containing iron. They are given no water because thirsty animals eat more than those who drink water. Is this cruel treatment morally justified? Should we do this to animals just because we enjoy eating their flesh?

Speciesism   In his book *Animal Liberation,* Singer introduces the term **"speciesism."** As he defines it, speciesism is "a prejudice or attitude of bias toward the interests of members of one's own species and against those of members of other species." Singer goes on to argue that speciesism is analogous to racism and sexism. It is unjust to discriminate against blacks because of their color, or against women because of their sex. Their interests—e.g., their interest in voting—have to be considered equally to those of whites and men. Similarly, it is unjust to discriminate against nonhuman animals because of their species. Their interests, and particularly their interest in not suffering, have to be considered too.

But how do we go about reducing animal suffering? Does this mean that we should become vegetarians and eat no meat? Singer thinks so, but of course this is a very controversial proposal in our meat-eating society. In Singer's view we should stop eating meat in order to eliminate factory farming or at least to protest against it, and also because we should not treat animals as "means to our end."

These arguments for vegetarianism are attacked by Leslie Pickering Francis and Richard Norman (3). Even though they agree that it is wrong to cause animal suffering, other things being equal, Francis and Norman do not agree that this principle requires us to embrace vegetarianism or abandon animal experimentation that serves human needs. They maintain that human beings can justifiably give more weight to their own interests than to animal interests because human beings have important relations to other human beings that they do not have to animals. Thus speciesism is justified to some extent, and it is not analogous to racism or sexism.

Tom Regan has a different view of the matter. He contends that the duty to become a vegetarian cannot be based on utilitarianism as Singer thinks. Utilitarianism is not an acceptable moral theory because it

incorrectly makes the morality of individual acts depend on how others behave. Nevertheless, Regan does think that we ought to be vegetarians and oppose commercial animal agriculture. The reason for doing this is not that there will be good consequences, but because some animals are persons who have moral rights, and commercial animal agriculture violates these rights.

R.G. Frey has a different line of attack on Singer's view. Unlike Francis and Norman, he does not agree that animals have interests in the first place. He rejects Singer's claim that the capacity for pain is a necessary and/or sufficient condition for having interests, and he denies that pain is intrinsically evil. Consequently, he finds that animals have neither interests nor moral rights.

Rights Theory   In his defense of vegetarianism, Regan relies heavily on the concept of a moral right, but there is controversy about the meaning of the concept of a right and how it should be applied.

According to Joel Feinberg (2), to have a right is to have a claim *to* something and *against* someone." In Feinberg's view, only beings who are capable of having interests are capable of claiming these rights. But animals do have interests, so they can have rights.

H.J. McCloskey (7) has a different theory of rights. In McCloskey's analysis, a right is an entitlement to something and not a claim against someone. A person could have a right and not have a claim against someone else, for example, if he or she were the last person on earth. Nevertheless, McCloskey holds that being able to make a claim, either directly or through a representative, is essential to the possession of rights. Since animals cannot do this, they cannot be possessors of rights.

Regan agrees with Feinberg that in order for an individual to have a right, there must be other people; it would not make sense to say that the last person on earth has any rights. In Regan's account, if an individual has a moral right, then there must be other moral agents who have a duty to respect it. But who possesses rights? Regan's answer is different from that of Feinberg or McCloskey. Regan's position is that only individuals who have *inherent value* have rights, where inherent value is a value that does not depend on utility. Those who have this inherent value are persons, and according to Regan, some animals are persons who have rights.

Sentientism   Singer assumes that only beings with mental states are a subject of moral concern. But isn't this sentientism (to put a label on it) just another kind of prejudice? He has escaped one prejudice, speciesism, only to embrace another, namely sentientism. Why not say that nonsentient things such as forests are of moral concern too? After all, human beings are rapidly destroying and polluting the natural environment. Isn't this morally wrong?

Holism   One way of defending environmental conservation and preservation is to argue that the environment has instrumental value for humans and animals. But William Godfrey-Smith argues that instrumental justifications for environmental conservation— saving the wilderness because it is a cathedral, a laboratory, a silo, or a gymnasium— all fail to provide a satisfactory rationale. Not only are there conflicts between the activities justified, there is also the feeling that the wilderness has more than instrumental value, that it has an **intrinsic value.** Instead of sentientism or an anthropocentric view, Godfrey-Smith suggests that we adopt a "holistic conception" of nature where we think of humans and nature together forming a moral community, and where we must engage in cooperative behavior (not exploitive behavior) to preserve the health of the whole community. This means that we should have empathy for nature, and not think of ourselves as separate from it or superior to it.

Animal Liberation v. *Environmental Holism*   We have two different views before us, the animal liberation view that nonhuman animals have rights, and the environmental holism view that the nonhuman environment has intrinsic value. Are these two views compatible?

Some writers believe that they are not compatible; if you accept one, then you must reject the other. For example, Tom Regan, the animal liberationist, thinks that environmental holism amounts to "environmental fascism" because it implies that we are morally obligated to save wild grasses at the expense of the life and welfare of people. It is morally obvious, at least to Regan, that the interests of people are more important than the health and existence of wild grasses.

Some defenders of environmental holism, on the other hand, think that animal liberation is at odds with the goal of preserving the environment. As an example of the conflict between the environmental ethic and the ascription of rights to animals, Alastair Gunn (5) describes a situation on certain islands off the coast of New Zealand, where feral goats, pigs, and cats have had to be exterminated in order to protect indigenous species and habitats. This extermination cannot be justified with the animal rights view because it involves a violation of the rights of individual animals. However, this situation reveals the flaw in the animal rights view. Not only does it show no concern for the protection of the environment, it doesn't even recognize the importance of saving endangered species of plants and animals. Furthermore, animal liberationists are opposed to hunting, fishing, and rearing animals for food, but environmentalists such as Aldo Leopold (6) have no objection to these practices provided they do not harm the environment. Indeed they believe hunting and fishing can help preserve natural habitats by preventing overpopulation.

Mary Anne Warren attempts to resolve the differences between these two rival positions. She argues that a "harmonious marriage" between the two is possible provided that each side makes some compromises. The animal liberationist must recognize that animal rights are not the same as human rights, and that animal rights can be overriden by environmental or utilitarian concerns more easily than human rights. The environmentalist must realize that nonsentient natural entities do not have moral rights in the same way that sentient creatures with interests have rights, even though they do have an intrinsic value that makes them worth preserving. If it is stated in this way, the environmental view is fully compatible with animal liberation, and indeed supplements it. For it shows us why we should protect *species* of animals and plants, and not just individual animals.

Peter Singer

All Animals Are Equal

Peter Singer is Professor of Philosophy at Monash University in Australia. His publications include Animal Liberation *(1975) and* Practical Ethics *(1979).*

Singer defines speciesism as a prejudice towards the interests of members of one's own species and against those of members of other species. He argues that speciesism is analogous to racism and sexism. If it is unjust to discriminate against women and blacks by not considering their interests, it is also unfair to ignore the interests of animals, particularly their interest in not suffering.

"Animal Liberation" may sound more like a parody of other liberation movements than a serious objective. The idea of "The Rights of Animals" actually was once used to parody the case for women's rights. When Mary Wollstonecraft, a forerunner of today's femi-

From Peter Singer, *Animal Liberation* (The New York Review, 1975). Reprinted by permission of the author. Copyright © Peter Singer 1975. [One footnote has been deleted and the remaining ones renumbered.– Ed.]

nists, published her *Vindication of the Rights of Women* in 1792, her views were widely regarded as absurd, and before long an anonymous publication appeared entitled *A Vindication of the Rights of Brutes.* The author of this satirical work (now known to have been Thomas Taylor, a distinguished Cambridge philosopher) tried to refute Mary Wollstonecraft's arguments by showing that they could be carried one stage further. If the argument for equality was sound when applied to women, why should it not be applied to dogs, cats, and horses? The reasoning seemed to hold for these "brutes" too, yet to hold that brutes had rights was manifestly absurd; therefore the reasoning by which this conclusion had been reached must be unsound, and if unsound when applied to brutes, it must also be unsound when applied to women, since the very same arguments had been used in each case.

In order to explain the basis of the case for the equality of animals, it will be helpful to start with an examination of the case for the equality of women. Let us assume that we wish to defend the case for women's rights against the attack by Thomas Taylor. How should we reply?

One way in which we might reply is by saying that the case for equality between men and women cannot validly be extended to nonhuman animals. Women have a right to vote, for instance, because they are just as capable of making rational decisions about the future as men are; dogs, on the other hand, are incapable of understanding the significance of voting, so they cannot have the right to vote. There are many other obvious ways in which men and women resemble each other closely, while humans and animals differ greatly. So, it might be said, men and women are similar beings and should have similar rights, while humans and nonhumans are different and should not have equal rights.

The reasoning behind this reply to Taylor's analogy is correct up to a point, but it does not go far enough. There *are* important differences between humans and other animals, and these differences must give rise to *some* differences in the rights that each have. Recognizing this obvious fact, however, is no barrier to the case for extending the basic principle of equality to nonhuman animals. The differences that exist between men and women are equally undeniable, and the supporters of Women's Liberation are aware that these differences may give rise to different rights. Many feminists hold that women have the right to an abortion on request. It does not follow that since these same feminists are campaigning for equality between men and women they must support the right of men to have abortions too. Since a man cannot have an abortion, it is meaningless to talk of his right to have one. Since a dog can't vote, it is meaningless to talk of its right to vote. There is no reason why either Women's Liberation or Animal Liberation should get involved in such nonsense. The extension of the basic principle of equality from one group to another does not imply that we must treat both groups in exactly the same way, or grant exactly the same rights to both groups. Whether we should do so will depend on the nature of the members of the two groups. The basic principle of equality does not require equal or identical *treatment;* it requires equal *consideration.* Equal consideration for different beings may lead to different treatment and different rights.

So there is a different way of replying to Taylor's attempt to parody the case for women's rights, a way that does not deny the obvious differences between humans and nonhumans but goes more deeply into the question of equality and concludes by finding nothing absurd in the idea that the basic principle of equality applies to so-called brutes. At this point such a conclusion may appear odd; but if we examine more deeply the basis on which our opposition to discrimination on grounds of race or sex ultimately rests, we will see that we would be on shaky ground if we were to demand equality for blacks, women, and other groups of oppressed humans while denying equal consideration to nonhumans. To make this clear we need to see first, exactly why racism and sexism are wrong.

When we say that all human beings, whatever their race, creed, or sex, are equal, what is it that we are asserting? Those who wish to defend hierarchical, inegalitarian societies have often pointed out that by whatever test we choose it simply is not true that all humans are equal. Like it or not we must face the fact that humans come in different shapes and sizes; they come with different moral capacities, different intellectual abilities, different amounts of benevolent feeling and sensitivity to the needs of others, different abilities to communicate effectively, and different capacities to experience pleasure and pain. In short, if the demand for equality were based on the actual equality of all human beings, we would have to stop demanding equality.

Still, one might cling to the view that the demand for equality among human beings is based on the actual equality of the different races and sexes. Although, it may be said, humans differ as individuals there are no differences between the races and sexes *as such.* From the mere fact that a person is black or a woman we cannot infer anything about that person's intellectual or moral capacities. This, it may be said, is why racism and sexism are wrong. The white racist claims that whites are superior to blacks, but this is false—although there are differences among individuals, some blacks are superior to some whites in all of the capacities and abilities that could conceivably be relevant. The opponent of sexism would say the same: a person's sex is no guide to his or her abilities, and this is why it is unjustifiable to discriminate on the basis of sex.

The existence of individual variations that cut across the lines of race or sex, however, provides us with no defense at all against a more sophisticated opponent of equality, one who proposes that, say, the interests of all those with IQ scores below 100 be given less consideration than the interests of those with ratings over 100. Perhaps those scoring below the mark, would, in this society, be made the slaves of those scoring higher. Would a hierarchical society of this sort really be so much better than one based on race or sex? I think not. But if we tie the moral principle of equality to the factual equality of the different races or sexes, taken as a whole, our opposition to racism and sexism does not provide us with any basis for objecting to this kind of inegalitarianism.

There is a second important reason why we ought not to base our opposition to racism and sexism on any kind of actual equality, even the limited kind that asserts that variations in capacities and abilities are spread evenly between the different races and sexes: we can have no absolute guarantee that these capacities and abilities really are distributed evenly, without regard to race or sex, among human beings. So far as actual abilities are concerned there do seem to be certain measurable differences between both races and sexes. These differences do not, of course, appear in each case, but only when averages are taken. More important still, we do not yet know how much of these differences is really due to the different genetic endowments of the different races and sexes, and how much is due to poor schools, poor housing, and other factors that are the result of past and continuing discrimination. Perhaps all the important differences will eventually prove to be environmental rather than genetic. Anyone opposed to racism and sexism will certainly hope that this will be so, for it will make the task of ending discrimination a lot easier; nevertheless it would be dangerous to rest the case against racism and sexism on the belief that all significant differences are environmental in origin. The opponent of, say, racism who takes this line will be unable to avoid conceding that *if* differences in ability do after all prove to have some genetic connection with race, racism would in some way be defensible.

Fortunately there is no need to pin the case for equality to one particular outcome of a scientific investigation. The appropriate response to those who claim to have found evidence of genetically based differences in ability between the races or sexes is not to stick to the belief that the genetic explanation must be wrong, whatever evidence to the contrary may turn up: instead we should make it quite clear that the claim to equality does not depend on intelligence, moral capacity, physical strength, or similar matters of fact. Equality is a moral idea, not an assertion of fact. There is no logically compelling reason for assuming that a factual difference in ability between two people justifies any difference in the amount of consideration we give to their needs and interests. *The principle of the equality of human beings is not a description of an alleged actual equality among humans; it is a prescription of how we should treat humans.*

Jeremy Bentham, the founder of the reforming utilitarian school of moral philosophy, incorporated the essential basis of moral equality into his system of ethics by means of the formula: "Each to count for one and none for more than one." In other words, the interests of every being affected by an action are to be taken into account and given the same weight as the like interests of any other being. A later utilitarian, Henry Sidgwick, put the point in this way: "The good of any one individual is of no more importance, from the point of view (if I may say so) of the Universe, than the good of any other." More recently the leading figures in contemporary moral philosophy have shown a great deal of agreement in specifying as a fundamental presupposition of their moral theories some similar requirement that operates so as to give everyone's interests equal consideration—although these writers generally cannot agree on how this requirement is best formulated.[1]

It is an implication of this principle of equality that our concern for others and our readiness to consider their interests ought not to depend on what they are like or on what abilities they may possess. Precisely what this concern or consideration requires us to do may vary according to the characteristics of those affected by what we do: concern for the well-being of a child growing up in America would require that we teach him to read; concern for the well-being of a pig may require no more than that we leave him alone with other pigs in a place where there is adequate food and room to run freely. But the basic element—the taking into account of the interests of the being, whatever those interests may be—must, according to the principle of equality, be extended to all beings, black or white, masculine or feminine, human or nonhuman.

Thomas Jefferson, who was responsible for writing the principle of the equality of men into the American Declaration of Independence, saw this point. It led him to oppose slavery even though he was unable to free himself fully from his slaveholding background. He wrote in a letter to the author of a book that emphasized the notable intellectual achievements of Negroes in order to refute the then common view that they had limited intellectual capacities:

Be assured that no person living wishes more sincerely than I do, to see a complete refutation of the doubts I have myself entertained and expressed on the grade of understanding allotted to them by nature, and to find that they are on a par with ourselves ... but whatever be their degree of talent it is no measure of their rights. Because Sir Isaac Newton was superior to others in understanding, he was not therefore lord of the property or person of others.[2]

Similarly when in the 1850s the call for women's rights was raised in the United States a remarkable black feminist named Sojourner Truth made the same point in more robust terms at a feminist convention:

... they talk about this thing in the head; what do they call it? ["Intellect," whispered someone near by.] That's it. What's that got to do with women's rights or Negroes' rights? If my cup won't hold but a pint and yours holds a quart, wouldn't you be mean not to let me have my little half-measure full?[3]

It is on this basis that the case against racism and the case against sexism must both ultimately rest; and it is in accordance with this principle that the attitude that we may call "speciesism," by analogy with racism, must also be condemned. Speciesism—the word is not an attractive one, but I can think of no better term—is a prejudice or attitude of bias toward the interests of members of one's own species and against those of members of other species. It should be obvious that the fundamental objections to racism and sexism made by Thomas Jefferson and Sojourner Truth apply equally to speciesism. If possessing a higher degree of intelligence does not entitle one human to use another for his own ends, how can it entitle humans to exploit nonhumans for the same purpose?[4]

Many philosophers and other writers have proposed the principle of equal consideration of interests, in some form or other, as a basic moral principle, but not many of them have recognized that this principle applies to members of other species as well as to our own. Jeremy Bentham was one of the few who did realize this. In a forward-looking passage written at a time when black slaves had been freed by the French but the British dominions were still being treated in the way we now treat animals, Bentham wrote:

The day may come when the rest of the animal creation

*may acquire those rights which never could have been withholden from them but by the hand of tyranny. The French have already discovered that the blackness of the skin is no reason why a human being should be abandoned without redress to the caprice of a tormentor. It may one day come to be recognized that the number of the legs, the **villosity of the skin,** or the termination of the os sacrum are reasons equally insufficient for abandoning a sensitive being to the same fate. What else is it that should trace the insuperable line? Is it the faculty of reason, or perhaps the faculty of discourse? But a full-grown horse or dog is beyond comparison a more rational, as well as a more conversable animal, than an infant of a day or a week or even a month old. But suppose they were otherwise, what would it avail? The question is not, Can they reason? nor Can they talk? but, Can they suffer?* [5]

In this passage Bentham points to the capacity for suffering as the vital characteristic that gives a being the right to equal consideration. The capacity for suffering—or more strictly, for suffering and/or enjoyment or happiness—is not just another characteristic like the capacity for language or higher mathematics. Bentham is not saying that those who try to mark "the insuperable line" that determines whether the interests of a being should be considered happen to have chosen the wrong characteristic. By saying that we must consider the interests of all beings with the capacity for suffering or enjoyment Bentham does not arbitrarily exclude from consideration any interests at all—as those who draw the line with reference to the possession of reason or language do. The capacity for suffering and enjoyment is *a prerequisite for having interests at all,* a condition that must be satisfied before we can speak of interests in a meaningful way. It would be nonsense to say that it was not in the interests of a stone to be kicked along the road by a schoolboy. A stone does not have interests because it cannot suffer. Nothing that we can do to it could possibly make any difference to its welfare. A mouse, on the other hand, does have an interest in not being kicked along the road, because it will suffer if it is.

If a being suffers there can be no moral justification for refusing to take that suffering into consideration. No matter what the nature of the being, the principle of equality requires that its suffering be counted equally with the like suffering—insofar as rough comparisons can be made—of any other being. If a being is not capable of suffering, or of experiencing enjoyment or happiness, there is nothing to be taken into account. So the limit of **sentience** (using the term as a convenient if not strictly accurate shorthand for the capacity to suffer and/or experience enjoyment) is the only defensible boundary of concern for the interests of others. To mark this boundary by some other characteristic like intelligence or rationality would be to mark it in an arbitrary manner. Why not choose some other characteristic, like skin color?

The racist violates the principle of equality by giving greater weight to the interests of members of his own race when there is a clash between their interests and the interests of those of another race. The sexist violates the principle of equality by favoring the interests of his own sex. Similarly the speciesist allows the interests of his own species to override the greater interests of members of other species. The pattern is identical in each case.

Most human beings are speciesists. Ordinary human beings—not a few exceptionally cruel or heartless humans, but the overwhelming majority of humans—take an active part in, acquiesce in, and allow their taxes to pay for practices that require the sacrifice of the most important interests of members of other species in order to promote the most trivial interests of our own species. . . .

Animals can feel pain. As we saw earlier, there can be no moral justification for regarding the pain (or pleasure) that animals feel as less important than the same amount of pain (or pleasure) felt by humans. But what exactly does this mean, in practical terms? To prevent misunderstanding I shall spell out what I mean a little more fully.

If I give a horse a hard slap across its rump with my open hand, the horse may start, but it presumably feels little pain. Its skin is thick enough to protect it against a mere slap. If I slap a baby in the same way, however, the baby will cry and presumably does feel pain, for its skin is more sensitive. So it is worse to slap a baby than a horse, if both slaps are administered with equal force. But there must be some kind of blow—I don't know exactly what it would be, but perhaps a blow with a heavy stick—that would cause the horse as much pain as we cause a baby by slapping it with our hand. That is what I mean by "the same amount of pain" and if we consider it wrong to inflict that much pain on a baby for no good reason then we must, unless we are speciesists, consider it equally wrong to inflict the same amount of pain on a horse for no good reason.

There are other differences between humans and animals that cause other complications. Normal adult human beings have mental capacities that will, in certain circumstances, lead them to suffer more than animals would in the same circumstances. If, for instance, we decided to perform extremely painful or lethal scientific experiments on normal adult humans, kidnapped at random from public parks for this purpose, every adult who entered a park would become fearful that he would be kidnapped. The resultant terror would be a form of suffering additional to the pain of the experiment. The same experiments performed on nonhuman animals would cause less suffering since the animals would not have the anticipatory dread of being kidnapped and experimented upon. This does not mean, of course, that it would be right to perform the experiment on animals, but only that there is a reason, which is *not* speciesist, for preferring to use animals rather than normal adult humans, if the experiment is to be done at all. It should be noted, however, that this same argument gives us a reason for preferring to use human infants—orphans perhaps—or retarded humans for experiments, rather than adults, since infants and retarded humans would also have no idea of what was going to happen to them. So far as this argument is concerned

nonhuman animals and infants and retarded humans are in the same category; and if we use this argument to justify experiments on nonhuman animals we have to ask ourselves whether we are also prepared to allow experiments on human infants and retarded adults; and if we make a distinction between animals and these humans, on what basis can we do it, other than a barefaced—and morally indefensible—preference for members of our own species?

There are many areas in which the superior mental powers of normal adult humans make a difference: anticipation, more detailed memory, greater knowledge of what is happening, and so on. Yet these differences do not all point to greater suffering on the part of the normal human being. Sometimes an animal may suffer more because of his more limited understanding. If, for instance, we are taking prisoners in wartime we can explain to them that while they must submit to capture, search, and confinement they will not otherwise be harmed and will be set free at the conclusion of hostilities. If we capture a wild animal, however, we cannot explain that we are not threatening its life. A wild animal cannot distinguish an attempt to overpower and confine from an attempt to kill; the one causes as much terror as the other.

It may be objected that comparisons of the sufferings of different species are impossible to make, and that for this reason when the interests of animals and humans clash the principle of equality gives no guidance. It is probably true that comparisons of suffering between members of different species cannot be made precisely, but precision is not essential. Even if we were to prevent the infliction of suffering on animals only when it is quite certain that the interests of humans will not be affected to anything like the extent that animals are affected, we would be forced to make radical changes in our treatment of animals that would involve our diet, the farming methods we use, experimental procedures in many fields of science, our approach to wildlife and to hunting, trapping and the wearing of furs, and areas of entertainment like circuses, rodeos, and zoos. As a result, a vast amount of suffering would be avoided.

So far I have said a lot about the infliction of suffering on animals, but nothing about killing them. This omission has been deliberate. The application of the principle of equality to the infliction of suffering is, in theory at least, fairly straightforward. Pain and suffering are bad and should be prevented or minimized, irrespective of the race, sex, or species of the being that suffers. How bad a pain is depends on how intense it is and how long it lasts, but pains of the same intensity and duration are equally bad, whether felt by humans or animals.

The wrongness of killing a being is more complicated. I have kept, and shall continue to keep, the question of killing in the background because in the present state of human tyranny over other species the more simple, straightforward principle of equal consideration of pain or pleasure is a sufficient basis for identifying and protesting against all the major abuses of animals that humans practice. Nevertheless, it is necessary to say something about killing.

Just as most humans are speciesists in their readiness to cause pain to animals when they would not cause a similar pain to humans for the same reason, so most humans are speciesists in their readiness to kill other animals when they would not kill humans. We need to proceed more cautiously here, however, because people hold widely differing views about when it is legitimate to kill humans, as the continuing debates over abortion and euthanasia attest. Nor have moral philosophers been able to agree on exactly what it is that makes it wrong to kill humans, and under what circumstances killing a human being may be justifiable.

Let us consider first the view that it is always wrong to take an innocent human life. We may call this the "sanctity of life" view. People who take this view oppose abortion and euthanasia. They do not usually, however, oppose the killing of nonhumans—so perhaps it would be more accurate to describe this view as the "sanctity of *human* life" view.

The belief that human life, and only human life, is sacrosanct is a form of speciesism. To see this, consider the following example.

Assume that, as sometimes happens, an infant has been born with massive and irreparable brain damage. The damage is so severe that the infant can never be any more than a "human vegetable," unable to talk, recognize other people, act independently of others, or develop a sense of self-awareness. The parents of the infant, realizing that they cannot hope for any improvement in their child's condition and being in any case unwilling to spend, or ask the state to spend, the thousands of dollars that would be needed annually for proper care of the infant, ask the doctor to kill the infant painlessly.

Should the doctor do what the parents ask? Legally, he should not, and in this respect the law reflects the sanctity of life view. The life of every human being is sacred. Yet people who would say this about the infant do not object to the killing of nonhuman animals. How can they justify their different judgments? Adult chimpanzees, dogs, pigs, and may other species far surpass the brain-damaged infant in their ability to relate to others, act independently, be self-aware, and any other capacity that could reasonably be said to give value to life. With the most intensive care possible, there are retarded infants who can never achieve the intelligence level of a dog. Nor can we appeal to the concern of the infant's parents, since they themselves, in this imaginary example (and in some actual cases), do not want the infant kept alive.

The only thing that distinguishes the infant from the animal, in the eyes of those who claim it has a "right to life," is that it is, biologically, a member of the species Homo sapiens, whereas chimpanzees, dogs, and pigs are not. But to use *this* difference as the basis for granting a right to life to the infant and not to the other animals is, of course, pure speciesism.[6] It is exactly the kind of arbitrary difference that the most crude and overt kind of racist uses in attempting to justify racial discrimination.

This does not mean that to avoid speciesism we must hold that it is as wrong to kill a dog as it is to kill a normal human being. The only position that is irredeemably speciesist is the one that tries to make the boundary of the right to life run exactly parallel to the boundary of our own species. Those who hold the sanctity of life view do this because while distinguishing sharply between humans and other animals they allow no distinctions to be made within our own species, objecting to the killing of the severely retarded and the hopelessly senile as strongly as they object to the killing of normal adults.

To avoid speciesism we must allow that beings that are similar in all relevant respects have a similar right to life—and mere membership in our own biological species cannot be a morally relevant criterion for this right. Within these limits we could still hold that, for instance, it is worse to kill a normal adult human, with a capacity for self-awareness, and the ability to plan for the future and have meaningful relations with others, than it is to kill a mouse, which presumably does not share all of these characteristics; or we might appeal to the close family and other personal ties that humans have but mice do not have to the same degree; or we might think that it is the consequences for other humans, who will be put in fear of their own lives, that makes the crucial difference; or we might think it is some combination of these factors, or other factors altogether.

Whatever criteria we choose, however, we will have to admit that they do not follow precisely the boundary of our own species. We may legitimately hold that there are some features of certain beings which make their lives more valuable than those of other beings; but there will surely be some nonhuman animals whose lives, by any standards, are more valuable than the lives of some humans. A chimpanzee, dog, or pig, for instance, will have a higher degree of self-awareness and a greater capacity for meaningful relations with others than a severely retarded infant or someone in a state of advanced senility. So if we base the right to life on these characteristics we must grant these animals a right to life as good as, or better than, such retarded or senile humans.

Now this argument cuts both ways. It could be taken as showing that chimpanzees, dogs, and pigs, along with some other species, have a right to life and we commit a grave moral offense whenever we kill them, even when they are old and suffering and our intention is to put them out of their misery. Alternatively one could take the argument as showing that the severely retarded and hopelessly senile have no right to life and may be killed for quite trivial reasons, as we now kill animals.

Since the focus here is on ethical questions concerning animals and not on the morality of euthanasia I shall not attempt to settle this issue finally. I think it is reasonably clear, though, that while both of the positions just described avoid speciesism, neither is entirely satisfactory. What we need is some middle position that would avoid speciesism but would not make the lives of the retarded and senile as cheap as the lives of pigs and dogs now are, nor make the lives of pigs and dogs so sacrosanct that we think it wrong to put them out of hopeless misery. What we must do is bring nonhuman animals within our sphere of moral concern and cease to treat their lives as expendable for whatever trivial purposes we may have. At the same time, once we realize that the fact that a being is a member of our own species is not in itself enough to make it always wrong to kill that being, we may come to reconsider our policy of preserving human lives at all costs, even when there is no prospect of a meaningful life or of existence without terrible pain.

I conclude, then, that a rejection of speciesism does not imply that all lives are of equal worth. While self-awareness, intelligence, the capacity for meaningful relations with others, and so on are not relevant to the question of inflicting pain—since pain is pain, whatever other capacities, beyond the capacity to feel pain, the being may have—these capacities may be relevant to the question of taking life. It is not arbitrary to hold that the life of a self-aware being, capable of abstract thought, of planning for the future, of complex acts of communication, and so on, is more valuable than the life of a being without these capacities. To see the difference between the issues of inflicting pain and taking life, consider how we would choose within our own species. If we had to choose to save the life of a normal human or a mentally defective human, we would probably choose to save the life of the normal human; but if we had to choose between preventing pain in the normal human or the mental defective—imagine that both have received painful but superficial injuries, and we only have enough painkiller for one of them—it is not nearly so clear how we ought to choose. The same is true when we consider other species. The evil of pain is, in itself, unaffected by the other characteristics of the being that feels the pain; the value of life is affected by these other characteristics.

Normally this will mean that if we have to choose between the life of a human being and the life of another animal we should choose to save the life of the human, but there may be special cases in which the reverse holds true, because the human being in question does not have the capacities of a normal human being. So this view is not speciesist, although it may appear to be at first glance. The preference, in normal cases, for saving a human life over the life of an animal when a choice *has* to be made is a preference based on the characteristics that normal humans have, and not on the mere fact that they are members of our own species. This is why when we consider members of our own species who lack the characteristics of normal humans we can no longer say that their lives are always to be preferred to those of other animals. In general, the ques-

tion of when it is wrong to kill (painlessly) an animal is one to which we need give no precise answer. As long as we remember that we should give the same respect to the lives of animals as we give to the lives of those humans at a similar mental level, we shall not go far wrong.

In any case, the conclusions that are argued for here flow from the principle of minimizing suffering alone. The idea that it is also wrong to kill animals painlessly gives some of these conclusions additional support that is welcome, but strictly unnecessary. Interestingly enough, this is true even of the conclusion that we ought to become vegetarians, a conclusion that in the popular mind is generally based on some kind of absolute prohibition on killing.

Footnotes

1. For Bentham's moral philosophy, see his *Introduction to the Principles of Morals and Legislation,* and for Sidgwick's see *The Methods of Ethics* (the passage quoted is from the seventh edition, p. 382). As examples of leading contemporary moral philosophers who incorporate a requirement of equal consideration of interests, see R.M. Hare, *Freedom and Reason* (New York, Oxford University Press, 1963) and John Rawls, *A Theory of Justice* (Cambridge: Harvard University Press, Belknap Press, 1972). For a brief account of the essential agreement on this issue between these and other positions, see R.M. Hare, "Rules of War and Moral Reasoning," *Philosophy and Public Affairs* 1 (1972).

2. Letter to Henri Gregoire, February 25, 1809.

3. Reminiscences by Francis D. Gage, from Susan B. Anthony, *The History of Woman Suffrage,* vol. 1; the passage is to be found in the extract in Leslie Tanner, ed., *Voices from Women's Liberation* (New York: Signet, 1970).

4. I owe the term "speciesism" to Richard Ryder.

5. Introduction to the Principles of Morals and Legislation, chapter 17.

6. I am here putting aside religious views, for example the doctrine that all and only humans have immortal souls, or are made in the image of God. Historically these views have been very important, and no doubt are partly responsible for the idea that human life has a special sanctity. Logically, however, these religious views are unsatisfactory, since a reasoned explanation of why it should be that all humans and no nonhumans have immortal souls is not offered. This belief too, therefore, comes under suspicion as a form of speciesism. In any case, defenders of the "sanctity of life" view are generally reluctant to base their position on purely religious doctrines, since these doctrines are no longer as widely accepted as they once were.

1. Explain the principle of equality that Singer adopts.

2. How does Singer define speciesism?

3. What is the "sanctity of life" view? Why does Singer reject this view?

1. Is speciesism analogous to racism and sexism? Why, or why not?

2. Is there anything wrong with killing animals painlessly? Defend your view.

3. Do human interests outweigh animal interests? Explain your position.

Tom Regan

Ethical Vegetarianism and Commercial Animal Farming

Tom Regan teaches philosophy at North Carolina State University. He has written numerous books and articles, and he has edited many textbooks. His most recent books on the subject of animal rights are All That Dwell Therein: Essays on Animal Rights and Environmental Ethics *(1982) and* The Case for Animal Rights *(1983).*

Regan begins with a discussion of moral **anthropocentrism***, the view of Kant and others that only human interest should be morally considered. This view is rejected by utilitarianism and by some proponents of moral rights including Regan. Regan does not find the utilitarianism of Bentham and Singer to be morally acceptable. Instead he defends a rights theory. On this theory, moral rights imply a duty to respect the rights. Persons with "inherent value" possess rights, and some animals are persons. So we have a duty to respect animal rights by abolishing commercial animal farming and becoming vegetarians.*

INTRODUCTION

Time was when a few words in passing usually were enough to exhaust the philosophical interest in the moral status of animals other than human beings. "Lawless beasts," writes Plato. "Of the order of sticks and stones," opines the nineteenth-century Jesuit W.D. Ritchie. True, there are notable exceptions, at least as far back as Pythagoras, who advocated vegetarianism on ethical grounds—Cicero, Epicurus, Herodotus, Horace, Ovid, Plutarch, Seneca, Virgil: hardly a group of "animal crazies"! By and large, however, a few words would do nicely, thank you, or, when one's corpus took on grave proportions, a few paragraphs or pages. Thus we find Kant, for example, by all accounts one of the most influential philosophers in the history of ideas, devoting almost two full pages to the question of our duties to animals, while St. Thomas Aquinas, easily the most important philosopher-theologian in the Catholic tradition, bequeaths perhaps ten pages to the topic at hand.

Times change. Today an even modest bibliography listing titles of the past decade's work on the moral status of animals would easily equal the length of Kant's and Aquinas' treatments combined, a quantitative symbol of the changes that have taken place, and continue to take place, in philosophy's attempts to rouse slumbering prejudices lodged in the anthropocentrism of western thought.

With relatively few speaking to the contrary (St. Francis always comes to mind in this context), theists and humanists, rowdy bedfellows in most quarters, have gotten along amicably when questions were raised about the moral center of the terrestrial universe: *Human* interests form the center of that universe. Let the theist look hopefully beyond the harsh edge of bodily death, let the humanist denounce, in Freud's terms, this "infantile view of the world," at least the two could agree that the moral universe revolves around us humans—our desires, our needs, our goals, our preferences, our love for one another. The intense dialectic now characterizing philosophy's assaults on the traditions of humanism and theism, assaults aimed not only at the traditional account of the moral status of animals but at the foundation of our moral dealings with the natural environment, with Nature generally—these assaults should not be viewed as local skirmishes between obscure academicians each bent on occupying a deserted fortress. At issue are the validity of alternative visions of the scheme of things and our place in it. The growing philosophical debate over our treatment of animals and the environment is both a symptom and a cause of a culture's attempt to come to critical terms with its past as it attempts to shape its future.

At present there are three major challenges being raised against moral anthropocentrism. The first is the one issued by *utilitarians;* the second, by proponents of *moral rights;* and the third emanates from the camp of those who advocate what we shall term a *holistic ethic.* This essay offers brief summaries of each position with special reference to how their advocates answer two questions: (a) Is vegetarianism required on ethical grounds? and (b) Judged ethically, what should we say, and what should we do, about commercial animal agriculture? To ask whether vegetarianism is required on ethical grounds is to ask whether there are reasons other than those that relate to one's own welfare (for example, other than those that relate to one's own health or financial well-being) that call for leading a vegetarian way of life.

As for the expression "commercial animal agriculture," that should be taken to apply to the practice of raising animals to be sold for food. The ethics of other practices that involve killing animals (for example, hunting, the use of animals in science, "the family farm" where the animals raised are killed and eaten by the people who raise them, etc.) will not be considered, except in passing, not because the ethics of these practices should not demand our close attention but because space and time preclude our giving them this attention here. Time and space also preclude anything approaching "complete" assessments of the three views to be discussed. None can be proven right or wrong in a few swift strokes. Even so, it will be clear where my own sympathies lie.

TRADITIONAL MORAL ANTHROPOCENTRISM

Aquinas and Kant speak for the anthropocentric tradition. That tradition does not issue a blank check when it comes to the treatment of animals. Morally, we are enjoined to be kind to animals and, on the other side of the coin, not to be cruel to them. But we are not enjoined to be the one and prohibited from being the other because we owe such treatment to *animals themselves*—not, that is, because we have any duties *directly* to nonhumans; rather, it is because of *human* interests that we have these duties regarding animals. "So far as animals are concerned," writes Kant, "we have no direct duties.... Our duties to animals are merely indirect duties to mankind." In the case of cruelty, we are not to be cruel to animals because treating them cruelly will develop a habit of cruelty, and a habit of cruelty, once it has taken up lodging in our breast, will in time include human beings among its victims. "(H)e who is cruel to animals becomes hard also in his dealings with men." And *that* is why cruelty to animals is wrong. As for kindness, "(t)ender feelings towards dumb animals develop humane feelings toward mankind." [1] And *that* is why we have a duty to be kind to animals.

So reasons Kant. Aquinas, predictably, adds theistic considerations, but the main storyline is the same, as witness the following passage from his *Summa Contra Gentiles*.

Hereby is refuted the error of those who said it is sinful for a man to kill dumb animals: for by divine providence they are intended for man's use in the natural order. Hence it is no wrong for man to make use of them, either by killing, or in any other way whatever.... And if any passages of Holy Writ seem to forbid us to be cruel to dumb animals, for instance to kill a bird with its young: this is either to remove men's thoughts from being cruel to other men, and lest through being cruel to animals one becomes cruel to human beings: or because injury to an animal leads to the temporal hurt of man, either of the doer of the deed, or of another: or on account of some (religious) signification: thus the Apostle expounds the prohibition against muzzling the ox that treadeth the corn.[2]

To borrow a phrase from the twentieth-century English philosopher Sir W.D. Ross, our treatment of animals, both for Kant and Aquinas, is "a practice ground for moral virtue." The *moral game* is played between human players or, on the theistic view, human players plus God. The way we treat animals is a sort of moral warmup, character calisthenics, as it were, for the moral game in which animals themselves play no part.

THE UTILITARIAN CHALLENGE

The first fairly recent spark of revolt against moral anthropocentrism comes, as do other recent protests against institutionalized prejudice, from the pens of the nineteenth-century utilitarians, most notably Jeremy Bentham and John Stuart Mill. These utilitarians—who count the balance of pleasure over pain for all sentient creatures as the yardstick of moral right and wrong, and who reject out of hand Descartes' famous teaching that animals are "nature's machines," lacking any trace of conscious awareness—recognize the direct moral significance of the pleasures and pains of animals. In an oft-quoted passage, Bentham enfranchises animals within the utilitarian moral community by declaring that

"(t)he question is not, Can they talk?, or Can they reason?, but, Can they suffer?"[3] And Mill stakes the credibility of utilitarianism itself on its implications for the moral status and treatment of animals, writing that "(w)e (that is, those who subscribe to utilitarianism) are perfectly willing to stake the whole question on this one issue. Granted that any practice causes more pain to animals than it gives pleasure to man: is that practice moral or immoral? And if, exactly in proportion as human beings raise their heads out of the slough of selfishness, they do not with one voice answer 'immoral' let the morality of the principle of utility be forever condemned."[4] The duties we have regarding animals, then, are duties we have *directly to them*, not indirect duties to humanity. For utilitarians, animals are themselves involved in the moral game.

Viewed against this historical backdrop, the position of the contemporary Australian moral philosopher Peter Singer can be seen to be an extension of the attack on the tradition of moral anthropocentrism initiated by his utilitarian forebears. For though this sometimes goes unnoticed by friend and foe alike, Singer, whose book *Animal Liberation* is unquestionably the most influential work published in the 1970s on the topic of the ethics of our treatment of animals, is a utilitarian.[5] That view requires, he believes, observance of the equality of interests principle. This principle requires that, before we decide what to do, we consider the interests (that is, the preferences) of all those who are likely to be affected by what we do *and* weigh equal interests equally. We must not, that is, refuse to consider the interests of some of those who will be affected by what we do because, say, they are Catholic, or female, or black. *Everyone's* interests must be considered. And we must not discount the importance of comparable interests because they are the interests of, say, a Catholic, woman, or black. Everyone's interests must be weighed *equitably*. Of course, to ignore or discount the importance of a woman's interests *because she is a woman* is the very **paradigm** of the moral prejudice we call sexism, just as to ignore or discount the importance of the interests of blacks (or Native Americans, Chicanos, etc.) are paradigmatic forms of racism. It remained for Singer to argue, which he does with great vigor, passion, and skill, that a similar moral prejudice lies at the heart of moral anthropocentrism, a prejudice that Singer, borrowing a term first coined by the English author and animal activist Richard Ryder, denominates *speciesism.* [6] *Like Bentham and Mill before him, Singer, the utilitarian, denies that we are to treat animals well in the name of the betterment of humanity, denies that we are to do this because this will help us discharge our duties to our fellow humans, denies that acting dutifully toward animals is a moral warmup for the real moral game played between humans, or, as theists would add, between humans-and-humans-and-God. We owe it to those animals who have interests to take their interests into account, just as we also owe it to them to count their interests equitably.* Our duties regarding animals are, in these respects, *direct* duties we have to them, not indirect duties to humanity. To think otherwise is to give sorry testimony to the prejudice of speciesism Singer is intent upon unmasking.

FARMING TODAY

Singer believes that the utilitarian case for ethical vegetarianism is strengthened when we inform ourselves of the changes taking place in commercial animal farming today. In increasing numbers, animals are being brought in off the land and raised indoors, in unnatural, crowded conditions—raised "intensively," to use the jargon of the animal industry, in structures that look for all the world like factories. Indeed, it is now common practice to refer to such commercial ventures as *factory farms.* The inhabitants of these "farms" are kept in cages, or stalls, or pens, or closely-confined in other ways, living out their abbreviated lives in a technologically created and sustained environment: automated feeding, automated watering, automated light cycles, automated waste removal, auto-

automated what-not. And the crowding: as many as nine hens in cages that measure eighteen by twenty-four inches; veal calves confined to twenty-two inch wide stalls; hogs similarly confined, sometimes in tiers of cages—two, three, four rows high. Could any impartial, morally sensitive person view what goes on in a factory farm with benign approval? Certainly many of the basic interests of the animals are simply ignored or undervalued, Singer claims, because they do not compute economically. Their interest in physical freedom or in associating with members of their own species, these interests routinely go by the board. And for what? So that we humans can dine on steaks and chops, drumsticks and roasts, food that is simply inessential for our own physical well-being. Add to this sorry tale of speciesism on today's farm the enormous waste that characterizes animal industry, waste to the tune of six or seven pounds of vegetable protein to produce a pound of animal protein in the case of beef cattle, for example, and add to the accumulated waste of nutritious food the chronic need for just such food throughout the countries of the Third World, whose populations characteristically are malnourished at best and literally starving to death at worst—add all these factors together and we have, Singer believes, the basis for the utilitarian's answers to our two questions. In response to the question, "Is vegetarianism required on ethical grounds?" the Singer-type utilitarian replies affirmatively. For it is not for self-interested reasons that Singer calls us to vegetarianism (though such reasons, including a concern for one's health, are not irrelevant). It is for ethical reasons that we are to take up a vegetarian way of life. And as for our second question, the one that asks what we should think and do about commercial animal farming, Singer's utilitarian argument prescribes, he thinks, that we should think ill of today's factory farms and act to bring about significant humane improvements by refusing to purchase their products. Ethically considered, we ought to become vegetarians.

THE CHALLENGE
TO UTILITARIANISM

Singer, then, is the leading contemporary representative of the utilitarian critique of the anthropocentric heritage bequeathed to us by humanism and theism. How should we assess his critique? Our answer requires answering two related questions. First, How adequate is the general utilitarian position Singer advocates? Second, How adequate is Singer's application of this general position to the particular case of commercial animal agriculture and, allied with this, the case for ethical vegetarianism? A brief response to each question, beginning with the second, will have to suffice. Consider Singer's claim that each of us has a duty to become a vegetarian. How can this alleged duty be defended on *utilitarian* grounds? Well, on this view, we know, the act I *ought* to perform, the act I have a *duty* to do, is the one that will bring about the best consequences for all those affected by the outcome, which, for Singer, means the act that will bring about the optimal balance of preference satisfaction over preference frustration. But it is naive in the extreme to suppose that, were I individually henceforth to abstain from eating meat and assiduously lead a vegetarian existence, this will improve the lot of a single animal. Commercial animal farming simply does not work in this way. It does not, that is, fine-tune its production to such a high degree that it responds to the decisions of each individual consumer. So, no, the individual's abstention from meat will not make the slightest dent, will not effect the smallest change, in commercial animal agriculture. No one, therefore, Singer included, can ground *the individual's* ethical obligation to be vegetarian on the effects *the individual's* acts will have on the welfare of animals.

Similar remarks apply to the other presumed beneficiaries of the individual's conversion to vegetarianism. The starving, malnourished masses of the Third World will not receive the food they need if I would but stop eating animals. For it is, again, naive in the extreme to suppose that the dietary decisions and acts of any given *individual* will make the slightest difference to the quality of life for any inhabitant in the Third World. Even were it true, which it is not (and it is not true because commercial animal agriculture is not so fine-tuned in this respect either), that a given amount of protein-rich grain *would not be fed to animals* if I abstained from eating meat, it simply would not follow that this grain *would find its way to any needy human being.* To suppose otherwise is to credit one's individual acts and decisions with a kind of godlike omnipotence a robust sense of reality cannot tolerate. Thus, since the type of utilitarianism Singer advocates prescribes that we decide what our ethical duties are by asking what will be the consequences of our acts, and since there is no realistic reason to believe that the consequences of my abstaining from meat will make any difference whatever to the quality of life of commercially raised farm animals or the needy people of the Third World, the alleged duties to become a vegetarian and to oppose commercial animal agriculture lack the kind of backing a utilitarian like Singer requires.

Here one might attempt to defend Singer by arguing that it is the total or sum of the consequences of *many* people becoming vegetarians, not just the results of each individual's decisions, that will spare some animals the rigors of factory farms and save some humans from malnutrition or starvation. Two replies to this attempted defense may be briefly noted. First, this defense at most gives *a sketch of a possible* reply; it does not give a finished one. As a utilitarian, Singer must show that the consequences for everyone involved would be better if a number of people became vegetarians than if they did not. But to show this, Singer must provide a thorough rundown of what the consequences would be, or would be in all probability, if we abstained from eating meat, *or* ate less of it, *or* ate none at all. And this is no easy task. Would the grains not fed to animals even be grown if the animal industry's requirements for them were reduced or eliminated? Would there be an economically viable market for corn, oats, and other grains if we became vegetarians? Would farmers have the necessary economic incentive to produce enough grain to feed the world's hungry human beings? Who knows? In particular, does Singer know? One looks in vain to find the necessary empirical backing for an answer here. Or consider: Suppose the grain is available. From a utilitarian point of view, would it be best (that is, would we be acting to produce the best consequences) if we made this grain available to the present generation of the world's malnourished? Or would it be better in the long run to refuse to aid these people at this point in time? After all, if we assist them now, will they not simply reproduce? And won't their additional numbers make the problem of famine for the next generation even more tragic? Who knows what the correct answers to these questions are? Who knows what is even "most likely" to be true? It is not unfair to a utilitarian such as Singer to mark the depths of our ignorance in these matters. And neither is it unfair to emphasize how our ignorance stands in the way of his attempt to ground the obligatoriness of vegetarianism on utilitarian considerations. If we simply do not know what the consequences of our becoming vegetarians would be, or are most likely to be, and if we simply do not know whether the consequences that would result would be, or are most likely to be, better than those that would obtain if we did not become vegetarians, then we simply lack any semblance of a utilitarian justification for the obligation to become vegetarians or for amounting a frontal assault on commercial animal agriculture. The decision to lead a vegetarian way of life and, by doing so, to lodge a moral complaint against commercial animal agriculture, viewed from the perspective of Singer's utilitarianism, must be diagnosed as at best symbolic gestures.

Aside from these matters, what can be said about the adequacy of utilitarianism in general? That is a question raised earlier to which we must now direct our attention.

There is a vast literature critical of utilitarian theory, and it will obviously not be possible to survey it here. Here let us note just one difficulty. Utilitarianism, at least as understood by Singer, implies that whether *I* am doing what I ought to do is crucially dependent on what *other* people do. For example, although the consequences of *my* abstaining from eating meat are too modest to make any difference to how animals are raised or whether grains are made available to needy people, if enough *other* people join me in a vegetarian way of life we could collectively bring about changes in the number of animals raised, how they are raised, what use is made of grain, etc. The situation, in other words, is as follows: If enough people join me so that the consequences of what we do *collectively* makes some impact, then what I do might be right, whereas if too few people join me, with the result that the consequences of what we do fails to make any difference to how animals are raised, etc., then I am *not* doing what is right.

To make the morality of an individual's acts depend on how others behave is a highly unsatisfactory consequence for any moral theory. When people refuse to support racist or sexist practices (for example, in employment or education), they do what is right, but their doing what is right does not depend on how many *other* people join them. The number of people who join them determines how many people do or support what is right, *not* what is right in the first place. Utilitarianism, because it makes *what is right* dependent in many cases on how many people act in a certain way, puts the moral cart before the horse. What we want is a theory that illuminates moral right and wrong independently of how many people act in this or that way. And that is precisely what utilitarianism, at least in the form advocated by Singer, fails to give us. For all its promise as an attack on the anthropocentric traditions of humanism and theism, for all its insistence on the direct relevance of the interests of animals, and despite the radical sounding claims made by utilitarians in criticism of current practices on the farm and in the laboratory, utilitarianism proves to be more ethical shadow than substance. If we look beyond the rhetoric and examine the arguments, utilitarianism might not change these practices as much as it would fortify them.[7]

THE RIGHTS VIEW

An alternative to the utilitarian attack on anthropocentrism is what we shall call "the rights view."[8] Those who accept this view hold that (1) certain individuals have certain moral rights, (2) these individuals have these rights independently of considerations about the value of the consequences of treating them in one way or another, and (3) the duty the individual has to respect the rights of others does not depend on how many other people act in ways that respect these rights. The first point distinguishes proponents of the rights view from, among others, those utilitarians like Bentham and Singer who deny that individuals have moral rights; the second distinguishes advocates of the rights view from, among others, those utilitarians such as Mill who hold that individuals have moral rights if, and only if, the general welfare would be promoted by saying and acting as if they do; and the third point distinguishes those who champion the rights view from, among others, any advocate of utilitarianism who holds that my duty to act in certain ways depends on how many other people act in these ways. According to the rights view, certain individuals have moral rights, and my duty to act in ways that respect such an individual's (A's) rights is a duty I have directly to A, a duty I have to A that is not grounded in considerations about the value of consequences for all those affected by the outcome, and a duty I have to A whatever else others might do to A. *Those who advocate animal rights, understanding this idea after the fashion of the rights view, believe that some of those individuals who have moral rights, and thus some of those to whom we have duties of the type just described, are animals.*

GROUNDS FOR THE RIGHTS VIEW

To proclaim "the moral rights of Man" sounds good but is notoriously difficult to defend. Bentham, who writes more forcefully to support what he rejects than to establish what he accepts, dismisses rights other than legal rights as "nonsense upon stilts." So we will not settle the thorny question about human rights of an essay's reading or writing. And, it goes without saying, the moral rights of animals must remain even less established. Were Bentham in his grave (in fact he remains above ground, encased in glass in an anteroom in University College, London, where he is dutifully brought to dinner each year on the occasion of his birthday) he would most certainly roll over at the mere mention of *animal* rights! Still, something needs to be said about the rational grounds for the rights view.

An important (but not the only possible) argument in this regard takes the following form: Unless we recognize that certain individuals have moral rights, we will be left holding moral principles that sanction morally reprehensible conduct. Thus, in order to avoid holding principles that allow such conduct, we must recognize that certain individuals have moral rights. The following discussion of utilitarianism is an example of this general line of argument.

Utilitarians cut from the same cloth as Bentham would have us judge moral right and wrong by appeal to the consequences of what we do. Well, suppose aged Aunt Bertha's heirs could have a lot more pleasure than she is likely to have in her declining years if she were to die. But suppose that neither nature nor Aunt Bertha will cooperate: She simply refuses to die as expeditiously as, gauged by the interest of her heirs, is desirable. Why not speed up the tempo of her demise? The reply given by Bentham-type utilitarians shows how far they are willing to twist our moral intuitions to save their theory. If we were to kill Aunt Bertha, especially if we took care to do so painlessly, then, these utilitarians submit, we would do no wrong to

Aunt Bertha. However, if *other* people found out about what we did, they would quite naturally grow more anxious, more insecure about their own safety and mortality, and these mental states (anxiety, insecurity, and the like) are painful. Thus, so we are told, killing Aunt Bertha is wrong (if it is) because of the painful consequences for others!

Except for those already committed to a Bentham-style utilitarianism, few are likely to find this account satisfactory. Its shortcomings are all the more evident when we note that *if* others did not find out about our dastardly deed (and so were not made more anxious and insecure by their knowledge of what we did), and *if* we have a sufficiently undeveloped conscience not to be terribly troubled by what we did, and *if* we do not get caught, and *if* we have a jolly good time with Aunt Bertha's inheritance, a much better time, in fact, than we would have had if we had waited for nature to run its course, then Bentham-style utilitarianism implies that we did nothing wrong in killing Aunt Bertha and, indeed, acted as we morally ought to have acted. People who, in the face of this kind of objection, remain Bentham-type utilitarians, may hold a consistent position. But one pays a price for a "foolish consistency." The spectacle of people "defending their theory to the last" in spite of its grave implications must, to put it mildly, take one's moral breath away.

There are, of course, many ethical theories in addition to utilitarianism, and many versions of utilitarianism in addition to the one associated with Bentham. So even if the sketch of an argument against Bentham's utilitarianism proves successful, the rights view would not thereby "win" in its competition with other theories. But the foregoing does succeed in giving a representative sample of one argument deployed by those who accept the rights view: If you deny moral rights, as Bentham does, then the principles you put in their place, which, in Bentham's case, is the principle of utility, will sanction morally reprehensible conduct (for example, the murder of Aunt Bertha). If those who affirm and defend the rights view could show this given *any* initially plausible theory that denies moral rights, and if they could crystalize and defend the methodology on which this argument depends, then they would have a powerful reason for their position.

THE VALUE OF THE INDIVIDUAL

The rights view aspires to satisfy our intellect, not merely our appetite for rhetoric, and so it is obliged to provide a theoretical home for moral rights. Part, but by no means not the whole, of this home is furnished by the rights views' theory of value. Unlike utilitarian theories (for example, value hedonism), the rights view recognizes *the value of individuals,* not just the value of their mental states (for example, their pleasures). Following custom, let us call these latter sorts of value "intrinsic values" and let us introduce the term "inherent value" for the type of value attributed to individuals. Then the notion of inherent value can be explained as follows. First, the inherent value of an individual who has such value is not the same as, is not reducible to, and is incommensurate with the intrinsic value of that individual's, or of any combination of individuals', mental states. The inherent value of an individual, in other words, is not equal to any sum of intrinsic values (for example, any sum of pleasures). Second, all individuals who have inherent value have it equally. Inherent value, that is, does not come in degrees; some who have it do not have it more or less than others. One either has it or one does not, and all who have it have it to the same extent. It is, one might say, a categorical concept. Third, the possession of inherent value by individuals does not depend on their utility relative to the interests of others, which, if it were true, would imply that some individuals have such value to a greater degree than do others, because some (for example, surgeons) have greater utility than do others (for example, bank thieves). Fourth, and relatedly, individuals cannot acquire or lose such value by anything they do. And fifth, and finally, the inherent value of individuals does not depend on what or how others think or feel about them. The loved and admired are neither more nor less inherently valuable than the despised and forsaken.

Now, the rights view claims that any individual who has inherent value is due treatment that respects this value (has, that is, a *moral right* to such treatment), and though not everything can be said here about what such respect comes to, at least this much should be clear: We fail to treat individuals with the respect they are due whenever we assume that how we treat them can be defended *merely* by asking about the value of the mental states such treatment produces for those affected by the outcome. This must fail to show appropriate respect since it is tantamount to treating these individuals as if they lacked inherent value—as if, that is, we treat them as we ought whenever we can justify our treatment of them *merely* on the grounds that it promotes the interests other individuals have in obtaining preferred mental states (for example, pleasure). Since individuals who have inherent value have a kind of value that is not reducible to their utility relative to the interests of others, we are not to treat them merely as a means to bringing about the best consequences. We ought not, then, kill Aunt Bertha, given the rights view, even if doing so brought about "the best" consequences. That would be to treat her with a lack of appropriate respect, something she has a moral right to. To kill her for these reasons would be to violate her rights.

WHICH INDIVIDUALS HAVE INHERENT VALUE?

Even assuming the rights view could succeed in providing a coherent, rationally persuasive theoretical framework for "the rights of Man," further argument would be necessary to illuminate and justify the rights of animals. That argument, not surprisingly, will be long and torturous. At least we can be certain of two things, however. First, it must include considerations about the criteria of right pos-

session; and, second, it will have to include an explanation and defense of how animals meet these criteria. A few remarks about each of these two points will have to suffice.

Persons [9] are the possessors of moral rights, and though most human beings are persons, not all are. And some persons are not human beings. Persons are individuals who have a cluster of actual (not merely potential or former) abilities. These include awareness of their environment, desires and preferences, goals and purposes, feelings and emotions, beliefs and memories, a sense of the future and of their own identity. Most adult humans have these abilities and so are persons. But some (the irreversibly comatose, for example) lack them and so are not persons. Human fetuses and infants also are not persons, given this analysis, and so have no moral rights (which is not to say that we may therefore do anything to them that we have a mind to; there are moral constraints on what we may do in addition to those constraints that involve respect for the moral rights of others—but this is a long story . . . !).

As for nonhumans who are persons, the most famous candidate is God as conceived, for example, by Christians. When believers speak of "the blessed Trinity, three persons in one," they don't mean "three human beings in one." Extraterrestrials are another obvious candidate, at least as they crop up in standard science fiction. The extraterrestrials in Ray Bradbury's *Martian Chronicals,* for example, are persons, in the sense explained, but they assuredly are not human beings. But, of course, the most important candidates for our purposes are animals. And they are successful candidates if they perceive and remember, believe and desire, have feelings and emotions, and, in general, actually possess the other abilities mentioned earlier.

Those who affirm and defend the rights of animals believe that some animals actually possess these abilities. Of course, there are some who will deny this. All animals, they will say, lack all, or most, or at least some of the abilities that make an individual a person. In a fuller discussion of the rights view, these worries would receive the respectful airing they deserve. It must suffice here to say that the case for animal rights involves the two matters mentioned and explained—first, considerations about the criteria of right possession (or, alternatively, personhood), and, second, considerations that show that some animals satisfy these criteria. Those who would squelch the undertaking before it gets started by claiming that "it's *obvious* that animals cannot be persons!" offer no serious objection; instead, they give sorry expression to the very speciesist prejudice those who affirm and defend the rights of animals seek to overcome.

LINE DRAWING

To concede that some animals are persons and so have moral rights is not to settle the question, *Which* animals are persons? "Where do we draw the line?" it will be asked; indeed, it must be asked. The correct answer seems to be: We do not know with certainty. Perhaps there is no exact line to be drawn in this case, any more than there is an exact line to be drawn in other cases (for example, "Exactly how tall do you have to be to be tall?" "Exactly how old must you be before you are old?"). What we must ask is where in the animal kingdom we find individuals who are *most like* paradigmatic persons—that is, most like us, both behaviorally and physiologically. The greater the similarity in these respects, the stronger the case for believing that these animals have *a mental life similar to our own* (including memory and emotion, for example), a case that is strengthened given the major thrust of evolutionary theory. So, while it remains a matter of uncertainty *exactly* where we are to draw this line, it is implausible to deny that adult mammalian animals have the abilities in question (just as, analogously, it would be implausible to deny that eighty-eight-year-old Aunt Bertha is old because we don't know exactly how old someone must be before they are old). To get this far in the argument for animal rights is not to finish the story, but it is to give a rough outline of a major chapter in it.

THE INHERENT VALUE OF ANIMALS

Moral rights, as explained earlier, need a theoretical home, and the rights view provides this by its use of the notion of inherent value. Not surprisingly, therefore, the rights view affirms this value in the case of those animals who are persons; not to do so would be to slide back into the prejudice of speciesism. Moreover, because all who possess this value possess it equally, the rights view makes no distinction between the inherent value human persons possess as distinct from that possessed by those persons who are animals. And just as *our* inherent value, as persons, does not depend on our utility relative to the interests of others, or on how much we are liked or admired, or on anything we do or fail to do, the same must be true in the case of animals who, as persons, have the same inherent value we do.

To regard animals in the way advocated by the rights view makes a truly profound difference to our understanding of what, morally speaking, we may do to them, as well as how, morally speaking, we can defend what we do. Those animals who have inherent value have a moral right to respectful treatment, a right we fail to respect whenever we attempt to justify what we do to them by appeal to "the best consequences." What these animals are due, in other words, is the same respectful treatment we are. We must never treat them in this or that way merely because, we claim, doing so is necessary to bring about "the best consequences" for all affected by the outcome.

The rights view therefore calls for the total dissolution of commercial animal agriculture as we know it. Not merely "modern" intensive rearing methods must cease. For though the harm visited upon animals raised in these circumstances is real enough and is morally to be condemned, its removal would not eliminate the basic wrong its presence compounds. The *basic* wrong is that animals raised for commercial profit are viewed and treated in ways that fail to show respect for their moral right to respectful treatment. *They are not* (though of course they may be treated as if they are) "commodities," "economic units," "investments," "a renewable resource," etc. They are, like us, persons and so, like us, are owed treatment that accords with their right to be treated with respect, a respect we fail to show when we end their life before doing so can be defended on the grounds of mercy. Since animals are routinely killed on grounds other than mercy in the course of commercial animal agriculture, that human enterprise violates the rights of animals.

Unlike the utilitarian approach to ethical vegetarianism, the rights view basis does not require that we know what the consequences of our individual or collective abstention from meat will be. The moral imperatives to treat farm animals with respect and to refuse to support those who fail to do so do not rest on calculations about consequences. And unlike a Singer-type utilitarianism, the rights view does not imply that the individual's duty to become a vegetarian depends on how many other people join the ranks. *Each individual* has the duty to treat others with the respect they are due independently of how many others do so, and each has a similar duty to refrain in principle from supporting practices that fail to show proper respect. Of course, anyone who accepts the rights view must profoundly wish that others *will* act similarly, with the result that commercial animal agriculture, from vast agribusiness operations to the traditional family farm, will go the way of the slave trade—will, that is, cease to exist. But the *individual's* duty to cease to support those who violate the rights of animals does not depend on humanity in general doing so as well.

The rights view is, one might say, a "radical" position, calling, as it does, for the total abolition of a culturally accepted institution to wit, commercial animal farming. The way to "clean up" this institution is not by giving animals bigger cages, cleaner stalls, a place to roost, thus and so much hay, etc. When an institution is grounded in injustice, because it fails to respect the rights of those involved, there is no room for internal house cleaning. Morality will not be satisfied with anything less than its total abolition. And that, for the reasons given, is the rights view's verdict regarding commercial animal agriculture.

HOLISM

The "radical" implications of the rights view suggest how far some philosophers have moved from the anthropocentric traditions of theism and humanism. But, like the utilitarian attacks on this tradition, one should note that the rights view seeks to make its case by working within the major ethical categories of this tradition. For example, hedonistic utilitarians do not deny the moral relevance of human pleasures and pain, so important to our humanist forebears; rather, they accept this and seek to extend our moral horizons to include the moral relevance of the pleasures and pains of animals. And the rights view does not deny the distinctive moral importance of the individual, a central article of belief in theistic thought; rather, it accepts this moral datum and seeks to widen the class of individuals who are to be thought of in this way to include many animals.

Because both the positions discussed in the preceding work with major ethical categories handed down to us by our predecessors, some influential thinkers argue that these positions are, despite all appearances, in the hip pocket, so to speak, of the *Weltanschauung* they aspire to overturn. What is needed, these thinkers contend or imply, is not a broader interpretation of traditional categories (for example, the category of "the rights of the individual"); rather, what is required is the overthrow of these categories. Only then will we have a new vision, one that liberates us from the last vestiges of anthropocentrism.

"THE LAND ETHIC"

Among those whose thought moves in this direction, none is more influential than Aldo Leopold.[10] *Very* roughly, Leopold can be seen as rejecting the "atomism" dear to the hearts of those who build their moral thinking on "the value (or rights) of the individual." What has ultimate value is not the individual but the collective, not the "part" but the "whole," whereby "the whole" is meant the entire biosphere: the *totality* of the things and systems in the natural order. Acts are right, Leopold claims, if they tend to promote the integrity, beauty, diversity, and harmony of the biosphere; they are wrong if they tend contrariwise. As for individuals, be they humans or animals, they are merely "members of the **biotic** team," having neither more nor less value in themselves than any other member—having, that is, *no* value "in themselves." What good individuals have, so far as this is computable at all, is instrumental only: They are good to the extent that they promote the "welfare," so to speak, of the biosphere. For a Leopoldian, the rights view rests on the fictional view that individuals have a kind of value they in fact lack.

Traditional utilitarianism, not just the rights view, goes by the board, given Leopold's vision. To extend our moral concern to the experiences of animals (for example, their pleasures and pains) is not to overcome the prejudices indigenous to anthropocentrism. One who does this is still in the grip of these prejudices, supposing that mental states that matter to humans must be the yardstick of what matters morally. Utilitarians are people who escape from one prejudice (speciesism) only to embrace another (what we might call "sentientism," the view that mental states allied with or reducible to pleasure and pain are what matter morally). "Animal liberation" is not "nature liberation." In order to forge an ethic that liberates us from our anthropocentric tradition, we must develop a holistic understanding of things, a molecular, rather than an atomistic, vision of the scheme of things and our place

in it. "The land" must be viewed as meriting or moral concern. Water, soil, plants, rocks—inanimate, not just animate, existence must be seen to be morally considerable. All are "members" of the same team—the "biotic team."

HOLISM AND ETHICAL VEGETARIANISM

The holism Leopold advocates has interesting implications regarding how we should approach the issue of ethical vegetarianism. Appeals to the rights of animals, of course, are ruled out from the start. Based, as they are, on ideas about the independent value of the individual, such appeals are the voice of anthropocentrism past. That ghost can be exorcised once and for all only if we see the illusoriness of the atomistic view of the individual, *any* individual, as having an independent value, dignity, sanctity, etc. Standard versions of utilitarianism, restricted, as they are, to sentient creation, are similarly out of place. The "moral community" is comprised of all that inhabits the biosphere, not just some select portion of it, and there is no guarantee that what optimizes the balance of, say, pleasure over pain for sentient creation would be the right thing to do, when gauged by what promotes the "welfare" of the biosphere as a whole. If we are to approach the question of ethical vegetarianism with a clear head, therefore, we should refuse the guidance of both the rights view and utilitarianism.

Holism implies that the case for or against ethical vegetarianism must be decided by asking how certain practices involving animals promote or diminish the integrity, diversity, beauty, and harmony of the biosphere. This will be no easy task. Utilitarianism, as was noted earlier, encounters a very serious problem, when it faces the difficulty of saying what the consequences will be, or are most likely to be, if we do one thing rather than another. And this problem arises for utilitarians despite the fact that they restrict their calculations just to the effects on sentient creation. How much more difficult it must be, then, to calculate the consequences for *the biosphere!* There is some danger that "the Land Ethic" will not be able to get off the ground.

Let us assume, however, that this challenge could be met. Then it seems quite likely that the land ethic might judge some practices involving animals morally right, others wrong. For example, raising cattle on nonarable pastures might promote the biosphere's "welfare," whereas destroying a delicately balanced **ecosystem** in order to construct a factory farm, or allowing chemicals used in animal agriculture to pollute a stream or pond, might be roundly condemned as "unhealthy" for the biosphere. Holism, in short, presumably would decide the ethics of animal agriculture on a case by case basis. When a given commercial undertaking meets the principles of the land ethic, it is right, and we are free to support it by purchasing its wares. When a given commercial undertaking fails to meet the appropriate principles, it is wrong, and we ought not to help it along by buying its products. So far as the matter of the pain, stress, and deprivations that might be caused farm animals in a commercial endeavor that promotes the "welfare" of the biosphere, these "mental states" simply do not compute, and to be morally troubled by such concerns is unwittingly to slip back into the misplaced atomistic concern for the individual holism aspires to redirect.

HOLISM AS ENVIRONMENTAL FASCISM

Few will be easily won over to this "new vision" of things. Like political fascism, where "the good of the State" supercedes "the good of the individual," what holism gives us is a fascist understanding of the environment. Rare species of wild grasses doubtless contribute more to the diversity of the biosphere than do the citizens of Cleveland. But are we therefore morally obliged to "save the wild grasses" at the expense of the life or welfare of these people? If holism is to hold its ground, it must acknowledge that it has this implication, and, in acknowledging this it

must acknowledge further that its theoretical boat will come to grief on the shoals of our considered moral beliefs. Of course, those who are determined to awaken us to holism's virtues may be expected to reply that they are out to *reform* our moral vision, to *change* it, and so should not be expected to provide us with a theory that conforms with our "moral intuitions"—intuitions that, they are likely to add, are but another layer of our uncritical acceptance of our anthropocentric traditions and the ethnocentrism with which they are so intimately allied.

Well, perhaps this is so. Everything depends on the arguments given to support these bold pronouncements. What those arguments come to, or even if they come, must be considered elsewhere.[11] Here it must suffice to note that people who remain sympathetic to notions like "the rights of Man" and "the value of the individual" will not find environmental fascism congenial. And that is a crucial point, given the debate over ethical vegetarianism and commercial animal agriculture. For one cannot consistently defend meat-eating or commercial animal agriculture by appeal to the principles of "the Land Ethic," on the one hand, and, on the other, appeal to principles involving human rights and the value of the individual to defend one's convictions about how human beings should be treated. Environmental fascism and *any* form of a rights theory are like oil and water; they don't mix.

SUMMARY

Two related questions have occupied our attention throughout: (1) Is vegetarianism required on moral grounds? and (2) Judged ethically, what should we say, and what should we do, about commercial animal agriculture? Three different ways to approach these questions have been characterized: utilitarianism, the rights view, and holism. Of the three, the rights view is the most "radical"; it calls for the total abolition of commercial animal agriculture and argues that, as individuals, we have an obligation to cease eating meat, including the meat produced by the animal industry, independently of how many other people do so and independently of the actual consequences our individual abstention have on this industry. Since this industry routinely violates the rights of farm animals, those who support it, not just those who run and profit from it, have "dirty hands."

Some utilitarians evidently seek the same answers offered by the rights view, but their arguments are radically different. Since what we ought to do depends on the consequences, and since our individual abstention from meat eating would not make a whit of difference to any individual animal, it seems we cannot have an obligation to be vegetarians, judged on utilitarian grounds. If, in reply, we are told that it is the consequences of *many* people becoming vegetarians, not just those that flow from the individual's abstention, that grounds the obligation to be vegetarian, utilitarians are, so to speak, out of the frying pan but into the fire. First, we do not know what the consequences will be (for example, for the economy, the starving masses of the Third World, or even farm animals) if many people became vegetarians, and, second, it distorts our very notion of the duties of the individual to suppose that these duties depend on how many other people act in similar ways. So, no, these utilitarians do not succeed in showing *either* that we have an obligation to be vegetarians *or* that commercial animal agriculture is morally to be condemned. These utilitarians may want the conclusions the rights view reaches, but, paradoxically, their utilitarianism stands in the way of getting them.

Holism (the kind of theory we find in Aldo Leopold's work, for example) was the third view considered. So long as we have reason to believe that this or that commercial endeavor in farm animals is not contrary to the beauty, harmony, diversity, and integrity of the biosphere, we have no reason to condemn its operation nor any reason to refuse to consume its products. If, however, particular commercial ventures are destructive of these qualities of the biosphere, we ought to bring them to a halt, and one way of helping to do this is to cease to buy their products. Holism, in short, answers our two questions, one might say, with an unequivocal "Yes and no." Very serious questions remain, however, concerning how we can know what, according to holism, we must know, before we can say that a given act or practice is right or wrong. Can we really presume to know the consequences of our acts "for the biosphere?" Moreover, holism implies that individuals are of no consequence apart from their role as "members of the biotic team," a fascist view of the individual that would in principle allow mass destruction of the members of a plentiful species (for example, Homo sapiens) in order to preserve the last remaining members of another (for example, a rare wild flower), all in the name of preserving "the diversity" of the biosphere. Few will find holism intuitively congenial, and none can rely on it to answer our two questions and, in mid-stride, invoke "the rights of man" to defend a privileged moral status for human beings. At least none can consistently do this.

Despite their noteworthy differences, the three views we have examined speak with one voice on the matter of the tradition of anthropocentrism bequeathed to us by humanism and theism. That tradition is morally bankrupt. On that the three are agreed. And on this, it seems, we may all agree as well. That being so, and while conceding that the foregoing does not "prove" its merits, it can be no objection to the rights view's answers to our two questions to protest that they are at odds with our moral traditions. To be at odds with these traditions is devoutly to be wished.

Nor is it an objection to the rights view to claim that because it proclaims the rights of animals, it must be unmindful of "the rights of Man" or insensitive to the beauty or integrity of the environment. The rights view does not deny "the rights of Man"; it only refuses to be species-bound in its vision of inherent value and moral rights. No principle it upholds opposes making grains not fed to animals available to needy humans, as commercial animal agriculture winds down. It simply insists that *these* (real or imaginary) consequences of the dissolution of commercial animal agriculture are not the reason why we ought to seek to dissolve it. As for the natural environment, one can only wonder what more one could do to ensure that its integrity and beauty are promoted or retained, than to act in ways that show respect to animals, including wild animals. In respecting the rights of this "part" of the biosphere, will not the "welfare of the whole" be promoted?

CONCLUSION

Theories are one thing; our practice quite another. And so it may seem that all this talk about rights and duties, utility and preferences, the biosphere and anthropocentrism comes to naught. People are people, and they will do what they are used to doing, what they like to do. History gives the lie to this lazy acquiescence in the face of custom and convenience. Were it true, whites would still own blacks, women would still lack the vote, and people could still be put to death for sodomy. Times and customs change, and one (but by no means not the only) force for change are the ideas that trickle down over time into the language and thought of a culture. The language of "animal rights" is in the air, and the thought behind those words is taking root. What not too long ago could be laughed out of court now elicits serious concern. Mill says it well: "All great movements go through three stages: ridicule, discussion, adoption." The movement for animal rights is beyond the stage of ridicule. For those persuaded of its truth, it is an irresistible force. Commercial animal agriculture is the movable object.

Footnotes

1. Immanuel Kant, "Duties to Animals and Spirits," *Lectures on Ethics*, trans. Louis Infield (New York: Harper and Row, 1963), pp. 239–41. Collected in *Animal Rights and Human Obligations*, Tom Regan and Peter Singer, eds. (Englewood Cliffs, NJ: Prentice-Hall Inc., 1976), pp. 122–23.

2. St. Thomas Aquinas, *Summa Contra Gentiles*, literally translated by the English Dominican Fathers (Benzinger Books, 1928), Third Book, Part II, Chap. C XII. Collected in *Animal Rights and Human Obligations*, op. cit., pp. 58–59.

3. Jeremy Bentham, *The Principles of Morals and Legislation* (1789: many editions), Chapter XVII, Section 1. Collected in *Animal Rights and Human Obligations*, op. cit., pp. 129–30.

4. John Stuart Mill, "Whewell on Moral Philosophy," *Collected Works*, Vol. X, pp. 185–87. Collected in *Animal Rights and Human Obligations*, op. cit., pp. 131–32.

5. Peter Singer, *Animal Liberation* (New York: Avon Books, 1975). By far the best factual account of factory farming is J. Mason and Peter Singer, *Animal Factories* (New York: Collier Books, 1982).

6. Richard Ryder, "Experiments on Animals," in *Animals, Men and Morals*, ed. S. and R. Godlovitch and J. Harris (New York: Taplinger, 1972). Collected in *Animal Rights and Human Obligations*, op. cit., pp. 33–47.

7. These criticisms of utilitarianism are developed at greater length in my *The Case For Animal Rights* (Berkeley: University of California Press. London: Routledge and Kegan Paul, 1983).

8. The rights view is developed at length in *The Case For Animal Rights*, ibid.

9. I use the familiar idea of "person" here because it is helpful. I do not use it in *The Case For Animal Rights*. I do not believe anything of substance turns on its use or nonuse.

10. Aldo Leopold, *A Sand County Almanac* (New York: Oxford University Press, 1949). For additional criticism and suggested readings, see William Aiken, "Ethical Issues in Agriculture," in Tom Regan, ed., *Earthbound: New Introductory Essays in Environmental Ethics* (New York: Random House (paper); Philadelphia: Temple University Press (cloth), 1983), pp. 268–70.

11. See *The Case For Animal Rights*, op. cit., ch. 5.

Review Questions

1. Explain Regan's account of traditional moral anthropocentrism.

2. What is the utilitarian objection to this view according to Regan?

3. What objections does Regan make to Singer's position?

4. What is the rights view as Regan expounds it?

5. What is inherent value in Regan's view?

6. Who has rights according to Regan?

7. Why does Regan think that commercial animal agriculture violates the rights of animals?

8. What is the holistic view advocated by Leopold (according to Regan)?

9. Why doesn't Regan accept this view?

Discussion Questions

1. Does Regan refute utilitarianism or not? Explain your answer.
2. Is Regan's notion of inherent value coherent?
3. Do you agree that some animals are persons?

Defend your answer.

4. Do you eat meat? If so, do you think that there is anything morally wrong with this practice? Defend your position.

R.G. Frey

The Case Against Animal Liberation

R.G. Frey is senior lecturer in philosophy at the University of Liverpool.

Frey attacks Singer's view that we should morally consider the interests of animals, particularly their interest in not feeling pain. As Frey interprets him, Singer merely assumes without proof that the capacity to feel pain is a necessary condition for having interests at all. But according to Frey, this assumption is false. Humans who are injured or comatose or fetuses may not be able to feel pain, but they have interests nonetheless. The capacity to feel pain is not a sufficient condition for having interests either, or at least it is not the sole sufficient condition. What is sufficient, namely being a human being, is not likely to be accepted by animal liberationists such as Singer. Finally, Frey raises doubts about the utilitarian claim that pain is intrinsically evil; in the Christian tradition, it is sin and not pain that is intrinsically evil. The conclusion that Frey reaches is that animals have neither interests nor moral rights.

An enormous volume of material has already appeared on the conditions under which animals live and die on factory farms,[1] and more is almost certainly on the way. Much of this material is upsetting in the extreme, and it is

difficult to imagine any normal person reading or hearing of it without being revolted. Indeed, our feeling of revulsion may be so intense that we simply can no longer bring ourselves to eat meat. In other words, we become vegetarians, not through any decision of principle, but through being unable to bring ourselves to continue to dine upon the flesh of animals. We become vegetarians in this way, however, only if we are revolted to a degree sufficient to overcome our fondness or liking for meat; and whether we are *going to be* sufficiently revolted by what we read and hear cannot be known in advance by the advocate of vegetarianism. If our liking for meat is in fact more intense than our revulsion at the suffering endured on factory farms, then we are going to remain meateaters, with the result that, if the vegetarian has grounded his case in an appeal to our feelings, then that case is in jeopardy. In order to protect himself, therefore, he is not likely to rest his case upon (an appeal to) the state and intensities of our feelings.

What the vegetarian wants, surely, is that we should stop eating meat even if our liking for it *exceeds* our revulsion at the suffering endured on factory farms. And this would seem to be possible only if vegetarianism is based upon principle and not upon feeling. That is, if what the vegetarian wants is that we should stop eating meat even if we like eating it and even if our liking for it greatly exceeds our revulsion at the suffering of animals in being raised and slaughtered for food, then a decision to stop eating meat would seem to amount to a decision of principle. It does not *follow* that this principle, which becomes the ground or basis of our vegetarianism, will be a *moral* one; but the overwhelming likelihood is that it will be, in view of the fact that it must convince and compel us to give up eating meat even when our inclinations, habits, and feelings run strongly in the opposite direction. If vegetarianism *has* a moral basis, a ground rooted in moral principle, then all of us, if we take morality seriously, must earnestly examine our present eating practices, however intense our liking for meat.

In his book *Animal Liberation,* Peter Singer argues that vegetarianism has just such a basis in moral principle; and the whole point to his book is that, if we care about morality at all, this principle compels us to become vegetarians. In what follows, I deny that vegetarianism has the moral basis Singer alleges it has, and I deny this in a way which does not raise quibbles about whether I am taking morality seriously.

According to Singer, the principle of the equal consideration of interests "requires us to be vegetarians". This is a moral principle, and states that "the interests of every being affected by an action are to be taken into account and given the same weight as the like interests of any other being". Interests arise, Singer contends, from the capacity to feel pain, which he labels a "prerequisite" for having interests at all, and animals can and do suffer, can and do feel pain. The principle of the equal consideration of interests, therefore, applies to them, which in turn means that we are not morally justified in ignoring, disregarding, or otherwise neglecting their interests. ...

PAIN AS A NECESSARY CONDITION

Animals have interests, according to Singer, in virtue of the fact that they can suffer; and he emphasizes a number of times that the capacity for suffering is a "prerequisite" for having interests at all. By "prerequisite", I understand "something required", in this case that the condition of being able to suffer

be satisifed, if a creature is to have interests. That is, a prerequisite is *at least a necessary* condition, whereby I mean to allow that satisfaction of the condition may also suffice to establish the point at issue. In the United States, Philosophy 101 is a prerequisite for admission into Philosophy 201, in the sense that the successful completion of course 101 is at least a necessary condition for admission into course 201, while, in Britain, successful completion of Part I of the BA degree is a prerequisite or at least a necessary condition for admission into Part II of the degree. Singer is claiming, then, I take it, that the capacity for suffering is a necessary condition for the possession of interests, which condition, if satisfied, may also suffice for the possession of interests. ...

My argument is simply this: Singer's prerequisite for having interests is dubious, if not false, since we can and do speak of interests in cases where the capacity for feeling pain is muted in non-trivial ways and where this capacity is entirely absent.[2]

While serving in Vietnam, a soldier friend of mine received such severe and extensive head, spinal, and nervous injuries that, amongst other things, though he was conscious, he was no longer able to feel pain. Did he, therefore, cease to have interests? On Singer's prerequisite, it would seem that he did; but surely his interest in being cared for while ill was *more,* not less, pronounced because of his wounds? And what about his interest in having his wife and children looked after, and his interest in retaining his good name? Certainly, it would be very peculiar to maintain that one has an interest in a good name, only so long as one can feel pain; for one's good name can be sullied and one's interests thereby damaged whether or not one feels any pain in the process and, indeed, even if one remains forever in the dark about the allegations which do the harm. Certainly, too, this is an interest of my friend and others which the courts acknowledge and protect, even if the individual whose interests are in question cannot feel pain. Of course, an action brought in a case such as my friend's is brought by someone else on his behalf; but it does not follow that it is not *his interests* which are in jeopardy of being harmed and which the courts will and do protect.[3]

Another type of case which is relevant to the evaluation of Singer's prerequisite is that exemplified by Karen Quinlan, in which an individual does not and cannot feel pain as the result of being in a comatose state, which state can last from a few hours to decades.[4] Does Karen Quinlan have interests? Once again, since she cannot feel pain, on Singer's prerequisite it appears that she does not; but here, too, I would urge on her behalf those considerations presented on behalf of my friend. And other considerations spring to mind at once. For example, if a photographer slips into her room and photographs Karen Quinlan, her interest in having her privacy respected is presumably not violated, since she has no interests. Importantly, the argument that her privacy cannot be invaded because she cannot *know* her privacy is invaded—a highly questionable argument, in any event—is not Singer's; for according to his prerequisite, it is not because a Karen Quinlan cannot *know* anything, but because she cannot *feel pain* that she has no interests. In other words, the state of her knowledge is immaterial to the question of whether she has interests, a view which an animal liberationist such as Singer seems bound to be attracted by, since people in general are much more ready to accept that animals feel pain than they are to accept that they can have knowledge. Thus, for Singer, because she can feel no pain, Karen Quinlan can have no interests, not even an interest in having her privacy respected, which, even in non-comatose individuals like ourselves, seems to be an interest that has nothing whatever to do with being able to feel pain. Again, if we are trying to discover whether it would be right to switch off Karen Quinlan's life-sustaining machines, we can consult the interests of her parents, her doctors, the hospital staff, the taxpayers, and so on; but if Singer is right, we

cannot include among the interests to be consulted her own, since she does not have any. Hence the individual who, in an ordinary, straightforward sense of the term, may well die if the life-sustaining machines are switched off is deemed to have no interest whatever to be weighed in deciding whether to switch them off, and not because she cannot know of, consent to, or appreciate this decision, but merely because she cannot feel pain.[5] The point has moral implications: her doctors and others have argued that Karen Quinlan's interests will best be served if her life-sustaining machines are left on, whereas her parents and others have argued that her interests will best be served if she is allowed "to die with dignity". On Singer's prerequisite, however, both doctors and parents are wrong in thinking Karen Quinlan has any interests at all, so the questions of how to weigh her interests morally, of how much weight to give them, and of how best to serve them cannot even arise in the first place. It is impossible, therefore, to ignore, undervalue, or damage Karen Quinlan's interests, which leaves us with the bizarre conclusion that any decision about the machines, any decision whatever, including the decision to turn off the machines for the fun of it, cannot fail to do justice to her interests.

Now one of the things which underlies our talk of interests in cases like these is this: we regard my friend and Karen Quinlan as human beings or persons, and, in virtue of that fact, deem them to have a genuine stake in certain things, quite independently of whether they can feel pain; and what we deem them to have a genuine stake in, we deem them to have an interest in.[6] In this way, human beings or persons are deemed to have a genuine stake and, therefore, an interest in receiving medical attention while ill, in having their families cared for, in retaining their good name, in having their privacy respected, and in life itself. Whether they are able to feel pain is neither here nor there to their being deemed to have these interests, and the law reflects this fact. For one can invade the privacy of or libel, for example, comatose as well as non-comatose individuals; and it is *neither a legal nor a moral* defence to libel that the individual libelled cannot feel pain. Thus, the interests of human beings or persons can be harmed, even though, as in the cases of my friend and Karen Quinlan, those whose interests they are cannot thereby be physically hurt; and this fact too the law recognizes, in distinguishing between harming interests and hurting individuals and in allowing the interests of individuals to be harmed even though these same individuals are not thereby hurt, as when my privacy is invaded unknown to me.[7]

If, then, one is going to call into question whether my friend and Karen Quinlan have interests, it would seem that one must show not that they cannot feel pain but that—what is by no means the same thing—they are not human beings or persons. This is brought out very clearly, I think, in the controversy surrounding another type of case which deserves mention in respect of evaluating Singer's prerequisite, namely that of abortion. For many have wanted to argue that, in addition to the interests of the mother, the father, the other members of the family, society, etc., there are the interests of the foetus to consider, both in deciding in individual cases whether to abort and in deciding on the moral rightness of abortion *per se*. Yet, though the foetus may react to stimuli, there is no ready consensus that it feels pain. Those who argue that the foetus *does have interests* typically advance as the ground for their view that the foetus is a human being or person; but there is no attempt whatever on their part to identify being a human being or person with being able to feel pain, since we do not allow that everything which might be able to feel pain is a human being or person, and animals are precisely the exception we have in mind. Of course, accepting this point, one may nevertheless go on to insist that, because it remains unborn, the foetus *is not* a human being or person and, therefore, has no interests; [8] and this challenge—that the foetus is not a human

being or person—highlights the claim I think we shall want established, both in this case and in those of my friend and Karen Quinlan, if we are to take the ascription of interests in these cases to be misplaced. It is precisely because some people *are* doubtful that the foetus is a human being or person, a doubt which is far less likely to arise or to be widespread in the cases of my friend and Karen Quinlan, that talk of weighing the interests of the foetus is sometimes objected to.

Once the decision to consider foetuses human beings or persons has been taken, however, it seems clear that we then (i) deem foetuses to have interests, (ii) extend moral and perhaps legal protection to these interests, and (iii) commit ourselves to weighing those interests in reaching decisions affecting foetuses. In the cases of my friend and Karen Quinlan, on the other hand, a decision of this sort is unnecessary, since they have been and are human beings or persons and so are already deemed to have interests, which can be legally and morally protected and which can be considered and weighed in reaching decisions affecting them. Of course in the last of these two cases it is sometimes doubted that the being in question still is a human being or person, though almost always a distinction is drawn; that is, it is sometimes argued that a human "vegetable", though a human being, has ceased to be a person.[9] In this regard, it is significant that human "vegetables", even if we concede for the sake of argument that they are not persons but merely human beings, can, for example, be libelled and have their privacy invaded and can have their interests in these regards protected by the courts, as well as by the rest of us adopting moral sanctions against the offending parties.

None of the above cases hold any comfort for Singer. This is not only because we do not regard being able to feel pain as having anything essentially to do with them, so far as the ascription of interests goes, and because we do not identify or otherwise equate being a human being or person with being able to feel pain, but also because Singer thinks animals have interests and so is most unlikely to accept being a human being or person as a prerequisite for having interests. I do not, however, wish to be misunderstood: I am not defending anything about these cases. I am not suggesting that we should continue to talk of interests in them, that we should not reform the law in order to avoid having to concede interests to my friend and Karen Quinlan, that we should not be at liberty to photograph and say what we like about them, that we should not be at liberty to switch off their life-sustaining machines, that we should not be able to regard and to dispose of foetuses in any way we like, and that we should not drop altogether the elusive talk of being a human being or person. Some of these things I think, others I do not. All I am maintaining is that, *contra* Singer, we can and do speak of the interests of my friend and Karen Quinlan, can and do acknowledge moral and legal protection of these interests, can and do concede that their interests are able to be harmed and benefited by us, can and do assign moral blame and legal responsibility in respect of such harm, in spite of the fact that these individuals are not able to feel pain. Unless, therefore, Singer turns his prerequisite for having interests into a stipulative one, so that it now becomes true by stipulation that only beings which are able to feel pain have interests, we have grounds for rejecting that prerequisite as false. . . .

PAIN AS A SUFFICIENT CONDITION

It is possible, appearances notwithstanding, that Singer's case for vegetarianism will be taken to revolve around the claim that being able to feel pain is a sufficient condition for the possession of interests. In other words, by "prerequisite", it is possible, in spite of the passages I have quoted to the contrary, that we are to understand a sufficient condition. A word on this possibility, therefore, is required.

The major difficulty with the claim that being able to feel pain is a sufficient condi-

tion for the possession of interests is that it is an unargued claim. Certainly Singer nowhere argues for it in *Animal Liberation,* nor do I know of an argument in the literature on animal rights and vegetarianism or on moral rights in general specifically devoted to establishing it. Of course, assuming the claim to be true and then taking its truth for granted has the convenient consequence of eliminating counter-examples in respect of animals; for to point to animals as creatures which feel pain but do not have interests only invites the retort that, if they feel pain, then that suffices to endow them with interests. In this way, the burden of proof is quietly shifted from the back of the proponent of the claim on to the back of the individual who queries whether animals do have interests.

Merely saying that X is a necessary or a sufficient or a necessary and sufficient condition for Y does not make it so. Argument is needed, and argument is precisely what is lacking. Singer's whole case for a moral basis to vegetarianism rests upon the claim that being able to feel pain is a "prerequisite" for having interests; yet, to establish this crucial claim, he simply quotes favourably a passage from Bentham, which itself only states the claim, and passes on.[10] Nor is Singer alone in shunning argument: recent discussions of animal rights and of moral rights in general commonly betray this sort of thing. For example, in his book *Animal Rights,* Andrew Linzey suggests that, if we take sentiency (understood as being able to experience pain) as a "criterion" for the possession of moral rights, then animals can have such rights;[11] but why should we take sentiency as a "criterion" for the possession of rights in the first place? Linzey has no answer to this question, except to observe that, if we were to adopt such a "criterion", we might obtain a view of the issues which is more favourable to animals than some other views.[12] Even if true, and even if we want a view of the issues which is favourable (or more favourable than some other view) to animals, this would not show that sentiency actually *is* a criterion for the possession of moral rights. Again, in her noteworthy paper "Do Potential People Have Moral Rights?", Mary Anne Warren claims that "sentience is a necessary and sufficient condition for the possession of moral rights".[13] And what is her argument to support this claim? It is this:

. . . morality is or ought to be a system designed to promote the interests of sentient beings. Which sentient beings? Ideally, all there are and all there ever will be. Sentience is the ultimate source of all moral rights; a being that has experiences and that prefers experiences of some sorts to those of other sorts, has on that basis alone a prima facie *right that those preferences be respected by beings that have the intelligence to comprehend this fact.*[14]

Even if one happens to agree with all these assertions, as I know a good many people do, we have not really been given any reason to think that what Warren says is the case.

Perhaps understandably enough, what has gone wrong in these cases, I think, is that a value judgment about the intrinsic evilness of pain has come to take the place of argument. That is, a moral conviction that pain is an intrinsic evil is in fact the ultimate ground for the claim that being able to feel pain is a necessary or sufficient or necessary and sufficient condition for possessing interests and/or rights. In his widely influential paper "The Moral Basis of Vegetarianism", Regan has this to say:

. . . if it is true that animals can and do experience pain; and if, furthermore, it is true, as I think it is, that pain is an intrinsic evil; then it must be true that the painful experience of an animal is, considered intrinsically, just as much of an evil as a comparable experience of a human being.[15]

And Regan's support for the claim that pain is an intrinsic evil? This claim, he says, is a "value judgment".[16] This represents at bottom, I believe, the central core of what is common not only to the work of Singer, Linzey, Warren, and Regan himself but also to the work of all those who want to make sentiency out to be either the prerequisite for having interests or the prerequisite for having rights (or both).

This value judgment, however, compounds our problem. As we have seen, Singer's claim that being able to feel pain is a "prerequisite" for having interests is unargued for; but it seems reasonable to suppose, given his fondness for Bentham, that the alleged intrinsic evilness of pain is intimately connected with this pre-eminent role pain is assigned in determining the possession of interests. If, however, we seek for the argument by which he shows that pain *is* an intrinsic evil, we shall seek in vain; there is not one to be found. Nor do Linzey, Warren, or Regan assist us in this regard either. . . . I want here to draw attention to one obvious aspect of our moral autonomy and its effect upon the issue of what possesses intrinsic value.

I am aware, as many vegetarians at a conference on animal rights at Trinity College, Cambridge in August 1977 were quick to point out to me, that one very prominent view of intrinsic value is that it is not something one argues for and establishes but something much more primitive than this; it is something which, so to speak, one finds or "sees" in things. For example, some people claim that human life is intrinsically valuable. Generally speaking, what I think they mean when they say this is that they do not justify, for instance, acts of respecting human life in terms of some other value, such as the production of greater amounts of pleasure, but in terms of itself. If one cannot accept that human life is intrinsically valuable, if one cannot regard or "see" human life in this way, then there is a clear sense in which one's justification of acts of respecting human life—if, indeed, one can justify them—is going to be at odds with the justification of one who does accept or "see" this. The difference in justification reflects the difference in values. . . .

Why *should* unpleasant sensations be regarded as intrinsically evil? The reply that a good many utilitarian theories demand that they be cuts no ice whatever with someone who is not a utilitarian. The point is worth pausing over. In Roman Catholic and Anglican orthodoxy, for example, though cardinal sins are regarded as intrinsically evil, the mere having of unpleasant sensations is not. Sin and unpleasant sensations are not the same thing, as Peter Geach has recently stressed in his discussion of animal pain in *Providence and Evil.*[17] One can sin without inflicting unpleasant sensations, and one can inflict unpleasant sensations without sinning. It is sin, not pain, which exercises the orthodox Christian, sin and not pain which he is anxious to guard against. If the alternative to blaspheming is suffering unpleasantness, this is literally not a choice situation to the orthodox; for sin is not to be committed merely in order to avoid inflicting pain, either upon oneself or others. It is certainly not clear that the orthodox are *obviously* wrong in regarding sin but not pain as an intrinsic evil.

In short, we plumb the true depths of the reader's predicament *vis-à-vis* Singer's book only when we realize that he provides neither an argument to show that being able to feel pain *is* a "prerequisite" for having interests nor, if we assume that his claim is supposed to be intimately connected with and perhaps even to reflect the alleged intrinsic evilness of pain, an argument to show that pain *is* intrinsically evil. Yet his case for animal interests, and through interests a moral basis to vegetarianism, turns upon the first of these, which in turn connects with the second.

What we have so far, however, is a purely negative attack upon Singer and the contention that his "prerequisite", since it cannot be a necessary condition for the possession of interests, must, therefore, be a sufficient condition.

A more positive line is possible. Either there is more than one sufficient condition for the possession of interests or there is only this one, viz., being able to feel pain. If there is only this one, and it is, after all, all that Singer endorses or thinks required to make his case, as we have seen; and if a creature must be able to feel pain in order to have interests, as Singer alleges; then it would appear that being able to feel pain becomes a necessary and sufficient condition for the possession of interests. But I have earlier in this chapter already shown that pain is not a necessary condition for having interests. If, however, there is more than one sufficient condition for the possession of interests, then what are these others? More especially, how are they related to the condition of being able to feel pain? On these questions, Singer is silent; it is being able to feel pain alone which is, he says, *the* "prerequisite" for animal interests. (Nor is he alone in this: as the literature attests, pain is by far the principal hope of the animal rights/vegetarian camp.) The effect, I believe, is to turn pain into a necessary and sufficient condition for the possession of interests, and I can show this view mistaken by showing that pain is not a necessary condition for having interests.

Let me develop this positive line a bit further. What underlay the earlier examples of this chapter was the view that my friend, Karen Quinlan, foetuses, and future beings either are or will be human beings and that they have a stake and, therefore, an interest in those things which creatures of their kind typically desire. Now one might try to gloss my discussion of these examples by suggesting that being human is a sufficient condition for possessing interests. If so, then what is the relationship between *this* sufficient condition and the sufficient condition of being able to feel pain? Plainly, no one such as Singer, who wants animals to have interests, can regard being human and being able to feel pain as *a set* of sufficient conditions, with the occurrence or presence of *the set* as what is required in order to establish the presence of interests; for this set excludes animals from the class of interest-holders.

No, it is not accidental that Singer appeals to pain and to nothing else whatever in order to make a case for animal interests, or that, for example, Linzey in *Animal Rights* appeals only to pain in order to make a case for animal rights; for anything else, if it is to form part of *a set* of sufficient conditions, runs the risk of jeopardizing the inclusion of animals within the class of interest-holders and/or right-holders. The reason for this is obvious from past chapters: to everyone except rabid Cartesians (who, I expect, are an extinct species anyway), animals feel pain, or, as I would prefer to say, since I think they lack this concept, have unpleasant sensations; on nothing else on which one is likely to base the possession of interests and/or rights is there anything like this degree of agreement over the case of animals. For example, I have already argued that animals do not have desires, beliefs, language, emotions, reasons, etc.; so to rely upon one of these, together with being able to feel pain, in order to form a set of sufficient conditions for interests and or rights results in the exclusion of animals from the relevant class. The same is true for the other possible grounds we have touched upon; thus, if being able to feel pain and rationality are cited as the set of sufficient conditions for the possession of interests and/or rights, then there is going to be widespread disagreement on whether animals are rational and very widespread disagreement if one looks at all but a few (types of) animals or if one uses any but very minimal tests of rationality. No, appealing to pain and only to pain is important to Singer and the others here, since it is, today, noncontroversial that animals have or can have unpleasant sensations; to base one's argument for animal interests and/or rights on anything else in addition to this places in jeopardy the reasonably secure ground of that argument.

The position, then, is this: being able to feel pain is, according to Singer, the one and only "prerequisite" for the possession of interests, and beings which cannot feel pain cannot, he stresses, have interests. In this way, being able to feel pain is, I think, turned into a necessary and sufficient condition for having interests, and this view succumbs to the earlier argument of this chapter. . . .

What I hope to have conveyed to the reader in the present chapter is that Singer's philosophical case for animal interests collapses, with the result that he has failed to establish his absolutely critical, his absolutely fundamental claim that animals do have interests, upon which his entire case for a moral basis to vegetarianism rests. . . . In short, though it should be borne in mind that we have not examined all possible analyses of the concept of an interest or all possible arguments for the claim that animals can be the logical subject of rights, nevertheless, in respect of the widely held, centrally important, and significantly influential analysis and argument we have examined, we can conclude that animals have neither interests nor moral rights, with consequent effect upon some alleged moral bases to vegetarianism.

Footnotes

1. For the uninitiated, a good introduction to this material is to be found in Singer's *Animal Liberation*, pp. 96–166. The notes to these pages, pp. 167–70, give the many sources of his material. Another well-known work in this regard is Ruth Harrison's *Animal Machines* (Vincent Stuart, London, 1964). A good, representative sample of the kinds of scientific experiments presently being conducted on animals can be found in Richard Ryder's *Victims of Science* (Davis-Poynter, London, 1975), in Dallas Pratt's *Painful Experiments on Animals* (Argus Archives, New York, 1977), and in *Alternatives to Laboratory Animals*, a journal of abstracts published in London by the Fund for the Replacement of Animals in Medical Experiments (FRAME).

2. I do not make only a verbal point here, about what we can and do say. As will be seen, the cases which follow can be and are hotly contested, in ways which they could not be if Singer's prerequisite were correct.

3. I am trying to show that interests are conceded in such cases as this one by appealing, first, to the way in which the cases are contested precisely because interests are attributed in them and, second, to the fact that the courts acknowledge and protect the interests at risk in them. I came to the first part of this argument by reflecting on cases such as my friend's and reaching the position (i) that the individuals in such cases have vital concerns in respect of what happens to them and theirs, (ii) that these vital concerns represent interests they have, (iii) that these concerns are things in which they have an interest in spite of the fact that there are things in which they cannot take an interest, and (iv) that these interests do not simply vanish the moment an individual such as my friend steps upon an anti-personnel mine or lapses into a coma. Having this part of the argument in mind, which I will shortly develop further, I then saw how to wed it to the second part and to anchor my criticism of Singer's prerequisite in the

whole, as the result of reading and reflecting upon the following passage in Joel Feinberg's *Social Philosophy* (Prentice-Hall, Englewood Cliffs, N.J., 1973, p. 26): "Legal writers classify interests in various ways. One of the more common lists 'Interests of Personality,' 'Interests of Property,' 'Interests in Reputation,' 'Interest in Domestic Relations,' and 'Interest in Privacy,' among others. A humanly inflicted harm is conceived as the violation of one of a person's interests, an injury to something in which he has a genuine stake. In the lawyer's usage, an interest is something a person always possesses in some condition, something that can grow and flourish or diminish and decay, but which can rarely be totally lost." In my view, this is not mere "lawyer's usage"; on the contrary, it is an important fact in our thinking about people that the stake they have in the concerns of life is not lost through, for instance, having suffered damage to their nervous system. (The first part of this chapter, then, owes a debt to pp. 26–7 of Feinberg's book, not least because I am going to exploit the notion of having a stake in it, in order to underpin the first part of my argument here.)

4. The case of Karen Ann Quinlan has become familiar, as the result of the publicity surrounding her parents' petition to allow her to die and her doctors' refusal to go along with this. (Both parties, of course, clearly believed that she was not already dead; see Ch. III, n. 11). Among the books on the case, see M.D. Heifetz *et al.*, *The Right to Die* (Berkley Publishing Corporation, New York, 1975); and B.D. Colen, *Karen Ann Quinlan: Dying in the Age of Eternal Life* (Nash Publishing Co., New York, 1976). Of related interest is *Ethical Issues in Death and Dying*, eds. T.L. Beauchamp, S. Perlin (Prentice-Hall, Englewood Cliffs, N.J., 1978), Part IV.

5. On the question of whether the comatose are already dead, see Ch. III, n. 11. In the Quinlan case, the New Jersey Superior Court decided in 1976 that the respirator could be switched off, and this was subsequently done, without, much to the surprise of the doctors, death ensuing. This fact does not affect my point here, which is that, on Singer's prerequisite, Karen Quinlan has no interests to be weighed in reaching the decision to turn off the respirator, though it is she who is affected by that decision. (For a discussion of whether turning off the respirator amounts to injuring Karen Quinlan, see Marvin Kohl, "Euthanasia and the Right to Life", in *Philosophical Medical Ethics: Its Nature and Significance*, eds. S.F. Spicker, H.T. Engelhardt, Jr. (D. Reidel, Dordrecht, 1977), pp. 79 ff. Of related interest are H.K. Beecher's "Ethical Problems Created by the Hopelessly Unconscious Patient", *New England Journal of Medicine*, 278 (1968), 1425–30; and G. Fletcher's "Prolonging Life", 42 *Washington Law Review* [1967] 999.) The complete record of the Quinlan case in the New Jersey Superior Court, Morristown, New Jersey, including medical testimony, can be found in *In the Matter of Karen Quinlan* (University Publications of America, Inc., Arlington, Virginia, 1975, 1976).

Singer has indicated to me that, though the implications I spell out here will appear to many as unfortunate ones, just as the labelling of such people as "vegetables" is to me regrettable, he still prefers the view that Karen Quinlan has no interests. If I read Feinberg correctly, he is of the same opinion; see "The Rights

of Animals and Unborn Generations", pp. 60 f.

6. See n. 3 above; see also Feinberg, *Social Philosophy*, p. 26. This sense of "interest" is probably the most common in ordinary parlance; after all, a person who has an interest in something often has a stake, a financial stake at that, in that thing. But it would be wrong to treat the financial overtones of this sense as basic to it; for a husband and father has a stake in the vital concerns of life, both for himself and his family, and it would be wholly erroneous to think that the stake he has in what happens to his wife and children is tied to his financial support of them. Rather, as I shall argue, they are a part of his extended well-being, in respect of which human beings typically have certain desires.

7. See Feinberg, *Social Philosophy*, p. 27; see also his "The Rights of Animals and Unborn Generations", pp. 59 f.

8. This is the typical utilitarian position (minus my comments about our deeming a creature to be a human being or person). Singer has indicated to me that he accepts it entirely and so regards foetuses as lacking all interests. Feinberg accepts it as well; see "The Rights of Animals and Unborn Generations", pp. 62 f.

9. Michael Tooley's paper "Abortion and Infanticide" is sometimes cited in this connection. See Ch. VIII.

10. *Animal Liberation*, p. 9.

11. *Animal Rights*, p. 26.

12. Ibid. 26 ff.

13. pp. 186–7.

14. p. 284.

15. p. 283.

16. p. 187.

17. Cambridge University Press, Cambridge, 1977, pp. 67–83. Geach's main point in these pages is that the pains of animals cannot morally be attributed to God, since sympathy with these pains cannot be a virtue to a nature, the Divine Nature, which is in no wise animal.

Review Questions

1. According to Frey, why is it unwise for the vegetarian to ground his case on the appeal to feelings?

2. How does Frey interpret Singer's claim that the capacity for suffering is a prerequisite for having interests, and why does he reject this claim?

3. What is Frey's view of Karen Quinlin's moral status?

4. What is his view of the moral status of the fetus?

5. What does Frey think is the major difficulty with the claim that being able to feel pain is a sufficient condition for possession of interests?

6. According to Frey, what is intrinsically evil?

7. Summarize Frey's negative attack on Singer's view.

8. What is his positive attack?

9. Explain Frey's conclusions.

Discussion Questions

1. Mary Anne Warren says that sentience (the capacity to be conscious) is the necessary and sufficient condition for having interests, and hence moral rights. Does her view escape Frey's attack? Why or why not?

2. Frey thinks that Karen Quinlan has interests, e.g., an interest in privacy. Do you agree? Why or why not?

3. Frey does not discuss abortion or euthanasia per se, but how would his view apply to those problems?

4. How would Singer's view apply to those problems?

5. Is pain intrinsically evil? What is your view?

6. Has Frey refuted Singer's position? What do you think?

William Godfrey-Smith

The Value of Wilderness

William Godfrey-Smith teaches philosophy at Australian National University (Canberra, Australia).

Godfrey-Smith explores two kinds of justification for wilderness preservation, an instrumental justification and a holistic one based on the intrinsic value of the wilderness. He finds that the instrumental justifications for conservation—saving the wilderness because it is a cathedral, a laboratory, a silo, or a gymnasium—all fail to provide a satisfactory rationale. Instead he suggests a holistic conception of nature where we think of humans and nature together forming a moral community, and where we must engage in cooperative behavior for the sake of the whole community.

Wilderness is the raw material out of which man has hammered the artifact called civilization.[1]

Aldo Leopold

From William Godfrey-Smith, "The Value of Wilderness," *Environmental Ethics* (1979), pp. 309–310. Reprinted with permission of *Environmental Ethics* and the author.

The framework that I examine is the framework of *Western* attitudes toward our natural environment, and wilderness in particular. The philosophical task to which I shall address myself is an exploration of attitudes toward wilderness, especially the sorts of justification to which we might legitimately appeal for the preservation of wilderness: what grounds can we advance in support of the claim that wilderness is something that we should *value?*

There are two different ways of appraising something as valuable. It may be that the thing in question is good or valuable *for the sake* of something that we hold to be valuable. In this case the thing is not considered to be good in itself; value in this sense is ascribed in virtue of the thing's being a *means* to some valued end, and not as an *end in itself.* Such values are standardly designated *instrumental* values. Not everything that we hold to be good or valuable can be good for the sake of something else; our values must ultimately be *grounded* in something that is held to be good or valuable in itself. Such things are said to be *intrinsically* valuable. As a matter of historical fact, those things that have been held to be intrinsically valuable, within our Western traditions of thought, have nearly always been taken to be states or conditions of *persons*, e.g., happiness, pleasure, knowledge, or self-realization, to name but a few.

It follows from this that a very central assumption of Western moral thought is that value can be ascribed to the nonhuman world only insofar as it is good for the sake of the well-being of human beings.[2] Our entire attitude toward the natural environment, therefore, has a decidedly anthropocentric bias, and this fact is reflected in the sorts of justification that are standardly provided for the preservation of the natural environment.

A number of thinkers, however, are becoming increasingly persuaded that our anthropocentric morality is in fact inadequate to provide a satisfactory basis for a moral philosophy of ecological obligation. It is for this reason that we hear not infrequently the claim that we need a "new morality." A new moral framework—that is, a network of recognized obligations and duties—is not, however, something that can be casually conjured up in order to satisfy some vaguely felt need. The task of developing a sound biologically based moral philosophy, a philosophy that is not anthropocentrically based, and that provides a satisfactory justification for ecological obligation and concern, is, I think, one of the most urgent tasks confronting moral philosophers at the present. It will entail a radical reworking of accepted attitudes—attitudes that we currently accept as "self-evident"—and this is not something that can emerge suddenly. Indeed, I think the seminal work remains largely to be done, though I suggest below the broad outline that an environmentally sound moral philosophy is likely to take.

In the absence of a comprehensive and convincing ecologically based morality we naturally fall back on *instrumental* justifications for concern for our natural surroundings, and for preserving wilderness areas and animal species. We can, I think, detect at least four main lines of instrumental justification for the preservation of wilderness. By *wilderness* I understand any reasonably large tract of the earth, together with its plant and animal communities, which is substantially unmodified by humans and in particular by human technology. The natural contrast to *wilderness*

and *nature* is an *artificial* or *domesticated* environment. The fact that there are borderline cases that are difficult to classify does not, of course, vitiate this distinction.

The first attitude toward wilderness espoused by conservationists to which I wish to draw attention is what I shall call the "cathedral" view. This is the view that wilderness areas provide a vital opportunity for spiritual revival, moral regeneration, and aesthetic delight. The enjoyment of wilderness is often compared in this respect with religious or mystical experience. Preservation of magnificent wilderness areas for those who subscribe to this view is essential for human well-being, and its destruction is conceived as something akin to an act of vandalism, perhaps comparable to—some may regard it as more serious than [3]—the destruction of a magnificent and moving human edifice, such as the Parthenon, the Taj Mahal, or the Palace of Versailles.

Insofar as the "cathedral" view holds that value derives solely from human satisfactions gained from its contemplation it is clearly an instrumentalist attitude. It does, however, frequently approach an *intrinsic value* attitude, insofar as the feeling arises that there is importance in the fact that it is there to be contemplated, whether or not anyone actually takes advantage of this fact. Suppose for example, that some wilderness was so precariously balanced that *any* human intervention or contact would inevitably bring about its destruction. Those who maintained that the area should, nevertheless, be preserved, unexperienced and unenjoyed, would certainly be ascribing to it an intrinsic value.

The "cathedral" view with respect to wilderness in fact is a fairly recent innovation in Western thought. The predominant Greco-Christian attitude, which generally speaking was the predominant Western attitude prior to eighteenth- and nineteenth-century romanticism, had been to view wilderness as threatening or alarming, an attitude still reflected in the figurative uses of the expression *wilderness,* clearly connoting a degenerate state to be avoided. Christianity, in general, has enjoined "the transformation of wilderness, those dreaded haunts of demons, the ancient nature-gods, into farm and pasture,"[4] that is, to a domesticated environment.

The second instrumental justification of the value of wilderness is what we might call the "laboratory" argument. This is the argument that wilderness areas provide vital subject matter for scientific inquiry that provides us with an understanding of the intricate interdependencies of biological systems, their modes of change and development, their energy cycles, and the source of their stabilities. If we are to understand our own biological dependencies, we require natural systems as a norm, to inform us of the biological laws that we transgress at our peril.

The third instrumentalist justification is the "silo" argument, which points out that one excellent reason for preserving reasonable areas of the natural environment intact is that we thereby preserve a stockpile of genetic diversity, which it is certainly prudent to maintain as a backup in case something should suddenly go wrong with the simplified biological systems that, in general, constitute agriculture. Further, there is the related point that there is no way of anticipating our future needs, or the undiscovered applications of apparently useless plants, which might turn out to be, for example, the source of some pharmacologically valuable drug—a cure, say, for leukemia. This might be called, perhaps, the "rare herb" argument, and it provides another persuasive instrumental justification for the preservation of wilderness.

The final instrumental justification that I think should be mentioned is the "gymnasium" argument, which regards the preservation of wilderness as important for athletic or recreational activities.

An obvious problem that arises from these instrumental arguments is that the various activities that they seek to justify are not always possible to reconcile with one another. The interests of the wilderness lover who subscribes to the "cathedral" view are not always reconcilable with those of the ordinary vacationist. Still more obvious is the conflict between the recreational use of wilderness and the interests of the miner, the farmer, and the timber merchant.

The conflict of interest that we encounter here is one that it is natural to try and settle through the economic calculus of cost-benefit considerations. So long as the worth of natural systems is believed to depend entirely on instrumental values, it is natural to suppose that we can sort out the conflict of interests within an objective frame of reference, by estimating the human satisfactions to be gained from the preservation of wilderness, and by weighing these against the satisfactions that are to be gained from those activities that may lead to its substantial modification, domestication, and possibly even destruction.

Many thinkers are liable to encounter here a feeling of resistance to the suggestion that we can apply purely economic considerations to settle such conflicts of interest. The assumption behind economic patterns of thought, which underline policy formulation and planning, is that the values that we attach to natural systems and to productive activities are commensurable; this is an assumption that may be called into question. It is not simply a question of the difficulty of quantifying what value should be attached to the preservation of the natural environment. The feeling is more that economic considerations are simply out of place. This feeling is one that is often too lightly dismissed by tough-minded economists as being obscurely mystical or superstitious; but it is a view worth examining. What it amounts to, I suggest, is the belief that there is something *morally* objectionable in the destruction of natural systems, or at least in their wholesale elimination, and this is precisely the belief that natural systems, or economically "useless" species do possess an *intrinsic* value. That is, it is an attempt to articulate the rejection of the anthropocentric view that all value, ultimately, resides in *human* interests and concerns.

But it is a difficult matter to try to provide justification for such attitudes, and this is, for reasons that are deeply bound up with the problems of resolving basic value conflict, a problem that I have discussed elsewhere.[5]

The belief that all values are commensurable, so that there is no problem *in principle* in providing a satisfactory resolution of value conflict, involves the assumption that the quantitative social sciences, in particular economics, can provide an *objective* frame of reference within which all conflicts of interest can be satisfactorily resolved. We should, however, note that in the application of cost-benefit analyses there is an inevitable bias in the sorts of values that figure in the calculation, to wit, a bias toward those considerations that are readily quantifiable, and toward those interests that will be staunchly defended. This is a fairly trivial point, but it is one that has substantial consequences, for there are at least three categories of values and interests that are liable to be inadequately considered, or discounted altogether.[6] First, there are the interests of those who are too widely distributed spatially, or too incrementally affected over time, to be strongly supported by any single advocate. Second, there are the interests of persons not yet existing, to wit, future generations, who are clearly liable to be affected by present policy, but who are clearly not in a position to press any claims. Third, there are interests not associated with humans at all, such as the "rights" of wild animals.[7]

This last consideration, in particular, is apt to impress many as ludicrous, as quite simply "unthinkable." It is an unquestioned axiom of our present code of ethics that the class of individuals to which we have obligations is the class of humans. The whole apparatus of rights and duties is in fact based on an ideal of reciprocal contractual obligations, and in terms of this model the class of individuals to whom we may stand in moral relations—i.e., those with whom we recognize a network of rights, duties, and obligations—is the class of humans. A major aspect of a satis-factory ethic of ecological obligation and concern will be to challenge this central anthropocentric assumption. I return to this point below.

Even restricting our attention to the class of human preference havers, however, we should be wary of dismissing as simply inadmissible the interests of future generations. The claims of posterity tend to be excluded from our policy deliberations not, I suspect, because we believe that future generations will be unaffected by our policies, but because we lack any clear idea as to how to set about attaching weight to their interests. This is an instance of the familiar problem of "the dwarfing of soft variables." In settling conflicts of interest, any consideration that cannot be precisely quantified tends to be given little weight or, more likely, left out of the equation altogether: "If you can't measure it, it doesn't exist."[8] The result of ignoring soft variables is a spurious appearance of completeness and precision, but in eliminating all soft variables from our cost-benefit calculations, the conclusion is decidedly biased. If, as seems plausible, it is *in principle* impossible to do justice to soft variables, such as the interests of posterity, it may be that we have to abandon the idea that the economic models employed in cost-benefit calculations are universally applicable for sorting out all conflicts of interest. It may be necessary to abandon the economic calculus as the universal model for rational deliberation.[9]

Another category of soft variable that tends to be discounted from policy deliberations is that which concerns economically unimportant species of animals or plants. A familiar subterfuge that we frequently encounter is the attempt to invest such species with spurious economic value, as illustrated in the rare herb argument. A typical example of this, cited by Leopold, is the reaction of ornithologists to the threatened disappearance of certain species of songbirds: they at once came forward with some distinctly shaky evidence that they played an essential role in the control of insects.[10] The dominance of economic modes of thinking is again obvious: the evidence has to be economic in order to be acceptable. This exemplifies the way in which we turn to instrumentalist justifications for the maintenance of biotic diversity.

The alternative to such instrumentalist justifications, the alternative that Leopold advocated with great insight and eloquence, is to widen the boundary of the moral community to include animals, plants, the soil, or collectively *the land*.[11] This involves a radical shift in our conception of nature, so that land is recognized not simply as property, to be dealt with or disposed of as a matter of expediency; land in Leopold's view is not a commodity that belongs to us, but a community to which we belong. This change in conception is far-reaching and profound. It involves a shift in our metaphysical conception of nature—that is, a change in what sort of thing we take our natural surroundings to *be*. This is a point that I would like to elaborate, albeit sketchily.

The predominant Western conception of nature is exemplified in—and to no small extent is a consequence of—the philosophy of Descartes, in which nature is viewed as something separate and apart, to be transformed and controlled at will. Descartes divided the world into conscious thinking substances—minds—and extended, mechanically arranged substances—the rest of nature. It is true that we find in Western thought alternatives to the Cartesian metaphysical conception of nature—the views of Spinoza and Hegel might be mentioned in particular [12]—but the predominant spirit, especially among scientists, has been Cartesian. These metaphysical views have become deeply embedded in Western thought, which has induced us to view the world through Cartesian spectacles. One of the triumphs of Descartes' mechanistic view of nature has been the elimination of occult qualities and forces from the explanation of natural events. The natural world is to be understood, in the Cartesian model, in purely mechanistic terms. An unfortunate consequence of the triumph, nevertheless, has been a persistent fear among some thinkers that the rejection of Cartesian metaphysics may lead to the reinstatement of occult and mystical views of nature.

An important result of Descartes' sharp ontological division of the world into active mental substances and inert material substances, has been the alienation of man from the natural world. Although protests have been raised against Cartesian metaphysics ever since its inception, it has exercised a deep influence on our attitudes toward nature. Descartes' mechanistic conception of nature naturally leads to the view that it is possible in principle to obtain complete mastery and technical control over the natural world. It is significant to recall that for Descartes the paradigm instance of a natural object was a lump of wax, the perfect exemplification of malleability. This conception of natural objects as wholly pliable and passive is clearly one that leaves no room for anything like a network of obligations.

A natural corollary of the mechanistic conception of nature, and integral to the Cartesian method of inquiry, is the role played by reductive thinking. In order to understand a complex system one should, on this view, break it into its component parts and examine them. The Cartesian method of inquiry is a natural correlate of Cartesian metaphysics, and is a **leitmotif** of our science-based technology.

It should be stressed that a rejection of the Cartesian attitude and its method of inquiry need *not* involve a regression to occult and mystical views about the "sacredness" of the natural world, and the abandoning of systematic rational inquiry. It must be conceded, however, that the rejection of the view that nature is an exploitable commodity has, unfortunately, frequently taken this form. This sort of romantic nature mysticism *does* provide a powerful exhortation for exercising restraint in our behavior to the natural world, but it carries with it a very clear danger. This is that while prohibiting destructive acts toward the natural world, it equally prohibits constructive acts; we surely cannot rationally adopt a complete "hands off" policy with respect to nature, on the basis of what looks like the extremely implausible—and highly cynical—a priori assumption that *any* attempt to modify our surroundings is bound to be for the worse.

It may, however, be that advocates of the "sacredness" of nature are attempting to do no more than articulate the idea that natural systems have their own intrinsic value, and adopt this manner of speaking as a convenient way of rejecting the dominant anthropocentric morality. If *this* is all that is being claimed, then I have no quarrel with it. And it may be inevitable that this mode of expression is adopted in the absence of a developed ecologically sound alternative morality. But I think we should be wary of this style of justification; what is needed, as Passmore has nicely expressed it, is not the spiritualizing of nature, but the naturalizing of man.[13] This involves a shift from the piecemeal reductive conception of natural items to a *holistic* or systemic view in which we come to appreciate the **symbiotic** interdependencies of the natural world. On the holistic or total-field view, organisms—including man—are conceived as **nodes** in a biotic web of intrinsically related parts.[14] That is, our understanding of biological organisms requires more than just an understanding of their structure and properties; we also have to attend seriously to their interrelations. Holistic or systemic thinking does not deny that organisms are complex physicochemical systems, but it affirms that the methods employed in establishing the high-level functional relationships expressed by physical laws are often of very limited importance in understanding the nature of biological systems. We may now be facing, in the terminology of Thomas Kuhn,[15] a shift from a physical to a biological paradigm in our understanding of nature. This seems to me to be an important aspect of the rejection of Cartesian metaphysics.

The limitations of the physical paradigm have long been accepted in the study of human society, but the tendency has been to treat social behavior and human action as quite distinct from the operations of our natural surroundings. The inappropriateness of the physical paradigm for understanding *human* society seems to me to be quite correct; what is comparatively new is the post-Cartesian realization that the physical paradigm is of more limited application for our understanding of *nature* than was previously supposed.

The holistic conception of the natural world contains, in my view, the possibility of extending the idea of community beyond human society. And in this way biological wisdom does, I think, carry implications for ethics. Just as Copernicus showed us that man does not occupy the physical center of the universe, Darwin and his successors have shown us that man occupies no *biologically* privileged position. We still have to assimilate the implications that this biological knowledge has for morality.

Can we regard man and the natural environment as constituting a community in any morally significant sense? Passmore, in particular, has claimed that this extended sense of community is entirely spurious.[16] Leopold, on the other hand, found the biological extension of community entirely natural.[17] If we regard a community as a collection of individuals who engage in cooperative behavior, Leopold's extension seems to me entirely legitimate. An ethic is no more than a code of conduct designed to ensure cooperative behavior among the members of a community. Such cooperative behavior is required to underpin the health of the community, in this biologically extended sense, *health* being understood as the biological capacity for self-renewal,[18] and *ill-health* as the degeneration or loss of this capacity.

Man, of course, cannot be placed on "all fours" with his biologically fellow creatures in all respects. In particular, man is the only creature who can act as a full-fledged moral agent, i.e., an individual capable of exercising reflective rational choice on the basis of principles. What distinguishes man from his fellow creatures is not the capacity to *act,* but the fact that his actions are, to a great extent, free from programming. This capacity to modify our own behavior is closely bound up with the capacity to acquire knowledge of the natural world, a capacity that has enabled us, to an unprecedented extent, to manipulate the environment, and—especially in the recent past—to alter it rapidly, violently, and globally. Our hope must be that the capacity for knowledge, which has made ecologically hazardous activities possible, will lead to a more profound understanding of the delicate biological interdependencies that some of these actions now threaten, and thereby generate the wisdom for restraint.

To those who are skeptical of the possibility of extending moral principles in the manner of Leopold, to include items treated heretofore as matters of expediency, it can be pointed out that extensions have, to a limited extent, already taken place. One clear—if partial—instance, is in the treatment of animals. It is now generally accepted, and this is a comparatively recent innovation,[19] that we have at least a *prima facie* obligation not to treat animals cruelly or sadistically. And this certainly constitutes a shift in moral attitudes. If—as seems to be the case—cruelty to animals is accepted as intrinsically wrong, then there *is* at least one instance in which it is *not* a matter of moral indifference how we behave toward the nonhuman world.

More familiar perhaps are the moral revolutions that have occurred within the specific domain of human society—witness the progressive elimination of the "right" to racial, class, and sex exploitation. Each of these shifts involves the acceptance, on the part of some individuals, of new obligations, rights, and values that, to a previous generation, would have been considered unthinkable.[20] The essential step in recognizing an enlarged community involves coming to see, feel, and understand what was previously perceived as alien and apart: it is the evolution of the capacity of *empathy.*

I have digressed a little into the history of ideas, stressing in particular the importance of the influence of Descartes.[21] My justification for this excursion is that our present attitudes toward nature, and toward wilderness, are very largely the result of Descartes' metaphysical conception of what nature is, and the concomitant conception that man has of himself. Our metaphysical assumptions are frequently extremely influential invisible persuaders; they determine the boundaries of what is thinkable. In rejecting the Cartesian conception the following related shifts in attitudes can, I think, be discerned.

1. A change from reductive convergent patterns of thought to divergent holistic patterns.
2. A shift from man's conception of himself as the center of the biological world, to one in which he is conceived of as a component in a network of biological relations, a shift comparable to the Copernican discovery that man does not occupy the *physical* center of the universe.
3. An appreciation of the fact that in modifying biological systems we do not simply modify the properties of a substance, but alter a network of relations. This rejection of the Cartesian conception of nature as a collection of independent physical parts is summed up in the popular ecological maxim "it is impossible to do only one thing."
4. A recognition that the processes of nature are independent and indifferent to human interests and concerns.
5. A recognition that biological systems are items that possess intrinsic value, in Kant's terminology, that they are "ends in themselves."

We can, however, provide—and it is important that we can provide—an answer to the question: "What is the *use* of wilderness?" We certainly ought to preserve and protect wilderness areas as gymnasiums, as laboratories, as stockpiles of genetic diversity, and as cathedrals. Each of these reasons provides a powerful and sufficient instrumental justification for their preservation. But note how the very posing of this question about the *utility* of wilderness reflects an anthropocentric system of values. From a genuinely ecocentric point of view the question "What is the *use* of wilderness?" would be as absurd as the question "What is the *use* of happiness?"

The philosophical task is to try to provide adequate justification, or at least clear the way for a scheme of values according to which concern and sympathy for our environment is immediate and natural, and the desirability of protecting and preserving wilderness self-evident. When once controversial propositions become platitudes, the philosophical task will have been successful.

I will conclude, nevertheless, on a deflationary note. It seems to me (at least much of the time) that the shift in attitudes that I think is required for promoting genuinely harmonious relations with nature is too drastic, too "unthinkable," to be very persuasive for most people. If this is so, then it will be more expedient to justify the preservation of wilderness in terms of instrumentalist considerations, and I have argued that there *are* powerful arguments for preservation that can be derived from the purely anthropocentric considerations of human self-interest. I hope, however, that there will be some who feel that such anthropocentric considerations are not wholly satisfying, i.e., that they do not really do justice to our intuitions. But at a time when *human* rights are being treated in some quarters with a great deal of skepticism it is perhaps unrealistic to expect the rights of nonhumans to receive sympathetic attention. Perhaps, though, we should not be too abashed by this; extensions in ethics have seldom followed the path of political expediency.

Footnotes

1. Aldo Leopold, *A Sand County Almanac* (New York: Oxford University Press, 1949), p. 188.

2. Other cultures have certainly included the idea that nature should be valued for its own sake in their moral codes, e.g., the American Indians (cf. Chief Seattle's letter to President Franklin Pierce of 1854, reprinted in *The Canberra Times*, 5 July 1966, p. 9), the Chinese (cf. Joseph Needham, "History and Human Values," in H. and S. Rose, eds. *The Radicalisation of Science* [London: Macmillan, 1976], pp. 90–117), and the Australian Aborigines (cf. W.E.H. Stanner, *Aboriginal Man in Australia* [Sydney: Angus and Robertson, 1965], pp. 207–237).

3. We can after all *replace* human artifacts such as buildings with something closely similar, but the destruction of a wilderness or a biological species is irreversible.

4. John Passmore, *Man's Responsibility for Nature* (London: Duckworth, 1974; New York: Charles Scribner's Sons, 1974), p. 17; cf. ch. 5.

5. In "The Rights of Non-humans and Intrinsic Values," in M.A. McRobbie, D. Mannison, and R. Routley, eds. *Environmental Philosophy* (Canberra: Australian National University Research School of Social Sciences, forthcoming).

6. Cf. Laurence H. Tribe, "Policy Science: Analysis or Ideology?" *Philosophy and Public Affairs* 2 (1972–3): 66–110.

7. I should mention that I am a skeptic about "rights"; it seems to me that talk about rights is always eliminable in favor of talk about legitimate claims for considerations, and obligations to respect those claims. Rights-talk does, however, have useful rhetorical effect in exhorting people to recognize claims. The reason for this is that claims pressed in these terms perform the crucial trick of shifting the onus of proof. This is accomplished by the fact that a *denial* of a right appears to be a more positive and deliberate act than merely refusing to acknowledge an obligation.

8. Laurence H. Tribe, "Trial by Mathematics: Precision and Ritual in Legal Process," *Harvard Law Review* 84 (1971): 1361.

9. Of course, in practice cost-benefit considerations *do* operate within deontic constraints, and we do *not* accept economics unrestrictedly as providing the model for rational deliberation. We would not accept exploitative child labor, for example, as a legitimate mode of production, no matter how favorable the economics. This is not just because we attach too high a cost to this form of labor; it is just unthinkable.

10. Aldo Leopold, "The Land Ethic," in *A Sand County Almanac*, p. 210.

11. Cf. Aldo Leopold, "The Conservation Ethic," *Journal of Forestry* 31 (1933): 634–43, and "The Land Ethic," *Sand County Almanac*.

12. Cf. John Passmore, "Attitudes to Nature," in R.S. Peters, ed., *Nature and Conduct* (London: Macmillan, 1975), pp. 251–64.

13. Ibid., p. 260.

14. Cf. Arne Naess, "The Shallow and the Deep, Long-Range Ecology Movement," *Inquiry* 16 (1973): 95–100.

15. T.S. Kuhn, *The Structure of Scientific Revolutions* (Chicago: University of Chicago Press, 1962).

16. Passmore, *Man's Responsibility for Nature*, ch. 6; "Attitudes to Nature," p. 262.

17. Leopold, "The Land Ethic."

18. Ibid., p. 221.

19. Cf. Passmore, "The Treatment of Animals," *Journal of the History of Ideas* 36 (1975): 195–218.

20. Cf. Christopher D. Stone, "Should Trees Have Standing? Toward Legal Rights for Natural Objects," *Southern California Law Review* 45 (1972): 450–501.

21. Here I differ from the well-known claim of Lynn White ("The Historical Roots of Our Ecological Crisis," *Science* 155 [1967]: 1203–7) that the Judeo-Christian tradition is predominantly responsible for the development of Western attitudes toward nature.

Review Questions

1. Distinguish between instrumental value and intrinsic value.

2. How does Godfrey-Smith define "wilderness?"

3. What is the "cathedral view?"

4. Explain the "laboratory argument."

5. What is the "silo" argument?

6. What is the "gymnasium argument?"

7. What problems arise for these instrumental justifications for preserving wilderness areas?

8. What is the dominant Western conception of nature?

9. Explain the "holistic conception" of the natural world.

Discussion Questions

1. Is the "holistic conception" of the natural world acceptable? Defend your position.

2. Should human beings frustrate important interests in order to preserve the natural environment? Defend your answer.

Mary Anne Warren

The Rights of the Nonhuman World

Mary Anne Warren teaches philosophy at San Francisco State University.

Warren wants to propose a "harmonious marriage" between the animal liberation view and Leopold's land ethic. Despite apparent conflicts between the two views, she thinks that a compromise can be reached provided certain concessions are made by each side. Briefly, the animal liberationist must allow that animal rights are different from human rights in both strength and content, and that animal rights can be easily overridden by environmental and

From Mary Anne Warren, "The Rights of the Nonhuman World," Robert Elliot and Arran Gare, eds., *Environmental Philosophy* (London and University Park: The Penn State University Press, 1983), pp. 109–134, Reprinted by permission of Dr. Mary Anne Warren, San Francisco State University.

utilitarian reasons, reasons that would not suffice to override stronger human rights. The environmentalists, for their part, should grant that mountains, oceans, and other natural objects do not have moral rights. But we should still preserve them because they have not only instrumental value to us and future generations, but also instrinsic value. The result of this compromise, Warren contends, is a more complete nonhomocentric moral theory. It explains why we ought to protect not only individual animals, but also species of plants and animals, and the natural environment.

Western philosophers have typically held that human beings are the only proper objects of human moral concern. Those who speak of *duties* generally hold that we have duties only to human beings (or perhaps to God), and that our apparent duties towards animals, plants and other nonhuman entities in nature are in fact indirect duties to human beings.[1] Those who speak of moral *rights* generally ascribe such rights only to human beings.

This strictly **homocentric** (human-centered) view of morality is currently challenged from two seemingly disparate directions. On the one hand, environmentalists argue that because humanity is only one part of the natural world, an organic species in the total, interdependent, planetary biosystem, it is necessary for consistency to view all of the elements of that system, and not just its human elements, as worthy of moral concern in themselves, and not only because of their usefulness to us. The ecologist Aldo Leopold was one of the first and most influential exponents of the view that not only human beings, but plants, animals and natural habitats, have moral rights. We need, Leopold argued, a new ethical system that will deal with our relationships not only with other human individuals and with human society, but also with the land, and its nonhuman inhabitants. Such a "land ethic" would seek to change "the role of *Homo sapiens* from conqueror of the land community to plain member and citizen of it".[2] It would judge our interaction with the nonhuman world as "right when it tends to preserve the integrity, stability, and beauty of the biotic community", and "wrong when it tends otherwise".[3]

On the other hand, homocentric morality is attacked by the so-called animal liberationists, who have argued, at least as early as the eighteenth century (in the Western tradition), that insofar as (some) nonhuman animals are sentient beings, capable of experiencing pleasure and pain,[4] they are worthy in their own right of our moral concern.[5] On the surface at least, the animal liberationist ethic appears to be quite different from that of ecologists such as Leopold. The land ethic is *wholistic* in its emphasis: it treats the good of the biotic *community* as the ultimate measure of the value of individual organisms or species, and of the rightness or wrongness of human actions. In contrast, the animal-liberationist ethic is largely inspired by the utilitarianism of Jeremy Bentham and John Stuart Mill.[6] The latter tradition is individualist in its moral focus, in that it treats the needs and interests of individual sentient beings as the

ultimate basis for conclusions about right and wrong.

These differences in moral perspective predictably result in differences in the emphasis given to specific moral issues. Thus, environmentalists treat the protection of endangered species and habitats as matters for utmost concern, while, unlike many of the animal liberationists,[7] they generally do not object to hunting, fishing or rearing animals for food, so long as these practices do not endanger the survival of certain species or otherwise damage the natural environment. Animal liberationists, on the other hand, regard the inhumane treatment or killing of animals which are raised for meat, used in scientific experimentation and the like, as just as objectionable as the killing or mistreatment of "wild" animals.[8] They oppose such practices not only because they may sometimes lead to environmental damage, but because they cause suffering or death to sentient beings.

Contrasts such as these have led some philosophers to conclude that the theoretical foundations of the Leopoldian land ethic and those of the animal-liberationist movement are fundamentally incompatible,[9] or that there are "intractable practical differences" between them.[10] I shall argue on the contrary, that a harmonious marriage between these two approaches is possible, provided that each side is prepared to make certain compromises. In brief, the animal liberationists must recognize that although animals do have significant moral rights, these rights are not precisely the same as those of human beings; and that part of the difference is that the rights of animals may sometimes be overriden, for example, for environmental or utilitarian reasons, in situations where it would not be morally acceptable to override human rights for similar reasons. For their part, the environmentalists must recognize that while it may be acceptable, as a legal or rhetorical tactic, to speak of the rights of trees or mountains,[11] the logical foundations of such rights are quite different from those of the rights of human and other sentient beings. The issue is of enormous importance for moral philosophy, for it centres upon the theoretical basis for the the ascription of moral rights, and hence bears directly upon such disputed cases as the rights of (human) foetuses, children, the comatose, the insane, etc. Another interesting feature is the way in which utilitarians and **deontologists** often seem to exchange sides in the battle—the former insist upon the universal application of the principle that to cause unnecessary pain is wrong, while the latter refuse to apply that principle to other than human beings, unless there are utilitarian reasons for doing so.

In section I, I will examine the primary line of argument presented by the contemporary animal-rights advocates, and suggest that their conclusions must be amended in the way mentioned above. In section II, I will present two arguments for distinguishing between the rights of human beings and those of (most) nonhuman animals. In section III, I will consider the animal liberationists' objection that any such distinction will endanger the rights of certain "nonparadigm" human beings, for example, infants and the mentally incapacitated. In section IV, I will reply to several current objections to the attempt to found basic moral rights upon the sentience, or other psychological capacities, of the entity involved. Finally, in section V, I will examine the moral theory implicit in the land ethic, and argue that it may be formulated and put into practice in a manner which is consistent with the concerns of the animal liberationists.

I WHY (SOME) ANIMALS HAVE (SOME) MORAL RIGHTS

Peter Singer is the best known contemporary proponent of animal liberation. Singer maintains that all sentient animals, human or otherwise, should be regarded as morally equal; that is, that their interests should be given equal consideration. He argues that sentience, the capacity to have conscious experiences such as pain or pleasure, is "the only

defensible boundary of concern for the interests of others".[12] In Bentham's often-quoted words, "the question is not, Can they reason? nor, Can they talk? but Can they suffer?"[13] To suppose that the interests of animals are outside the scope of moral concern is to commit a moral fallacy analogous to sexism or racism, a fallacy which Singer calls *speciesism.* True, women and members of "minority" races are more *intelligent* than (most) animals—and almost certainly no less so than white males—but that is not the point. The point does not concern these complex capabilities at all. For, Singer says, "The claim to equality does not depend on intelligence, moral capacity, physical strength, or similar matters of fact."[14]

As a utilitarian, Singer prefers to avoid speaking of moral *rights,* at least insofar as these are construed as claims which may sometimes override purely utilitarian considerations.[15] There are, however, many other advocates of animal liberation who do maintain that animals have moral rights, rights which place limitations upon the use of utilitarian justifications for killing animals or causing them to suffer.[16] Tom Regan, for example, argues that if all or most human beings have a right to life, then so do at least some animals.[17] Regan points out that unless we hold that animals have a right to life, we may not be able to adequately support many of the conclusions that most animal liberationists think are important, for example, that it is wrong to kill animals painlessly to provide human beings with relatively trivial forms of pleasure.[18]

This disagreement between Singer and Regan demonstrates that there is no single well-defined theory of the moral status of animals which can be identified as *the* animal liberationist position. It is clear, however, that neither philosopher is committed to the claim that the moral status of animals is completely identical to that of humans. Singer points out that his basic principle of equal *consideration* does not imply identical *treatment.*[19] Regan holds only that animals have *some* of the same moral rights as do human beings, not that *all* of their rights are necessarily the same.[20]

Nevertheless, none of the animal liberationists have thus far provided a clear explanation of how and why the moral status of (most) animals differs from that of (most) human beings; and this is a point which must be clarified if their position is to be made fully persuasive. That there is such a difference seems to follow from some very strong moral intuitions which most of us share. A man who shoots squirrels for sport may or may not be acting reprehensibly; but it is difficult to believe that his actions should be placed in *exactly* the same moral category as those of a man who shoots women, or black children, for sport. So too it is doubtful that the Japanese fishermen who slaughtered dolphins because the latter were thought to be depleting the local fish populations were acting quite *as* wrongly as if they had slaughtered an equal number of their human neighbours for the same reason.

Can anything persuasive be said in support of these intuitive judgments? Or are they merely evidence of unreconstructed speciesism? To answer these questions we must consider both certain similarities and certain differences between ourselves and other animals, and then decide which of these are relevant to the assignment of moral rights. To do this we must first ask just what it means to say than an entity possesses a certain moral right.

There are two elements of the concept of a moral right which are crucial for our present purposes. To say that an entity, X, has a moral right to Y (some activity, benefit or satisfaction) is to imply at least the following:

1. that it would be morally wrong for any moral agent to intentionally deprive X or Y without some sufficient justification;
2. that this would be wrong, at least in part, *because of the (actual or potential) harm which it would do to the interests of X.*

On this (partial) definition of a moral right, to ask whether animals have such rights is to ask whether there are some ways of treating them which are morally objectionable because of the harm done to the animals themselves, and not merely because of some *other* undesirable results, such as damaging the environment or undermining the moral character of human beings. As Regan and other animal liberationists have pointed out, the arguments for ascribing at least some moral rights to sentient nonhuman animals are very similar to the arguments for ascribing those same rights to sentient human beings.[21] If we argue that human beings have rights not to be tortured, starved or confined under inhumane conditions, it is usually by appealing to our knowledge that they will suffer in much the same ways that we would under like circumstances. A child must learn that other persons (and animals) can experience, for example, pain, fear or anger, on the one hand; pleasure or satisfaction, on the other, in order to even begin to comprehend why some ways of behaving towards them are morally preferable to others.

If these facts are morally significant in the case of human beings, it is attractive to suppose that they should have similar significance in the case of animals. Everything that we know about the behaviour, biology and neurophysiology of, for instance, nonhuman mammals, indicates that they are capable of experiencing the same basic types of physical suffering and discomfort as we are, and it is reasonable to suppose that their pleasures are equally real and approximately as various. Doubts about the sentience of other animals are no more plausible than doubts about that of other human beings. True, most animals cannot use human language to *report* that they are in pain, but the vocalizatons and "body language" through which they *express* pain, and many other psychological states, are similar enough to our own that their significance is generally clear.

But to say this is not yet to establish that animals have moral rights. We need a connecting link between the premise that certain ways of treating animals cause them to suffer, and the conclusion that such actions are *prima facie* morally wrong, that is, wrong unless proven otherwise. One way to make this connection is to hold that it is a *self-evident truth* that the unnecessary infliction of suffering upon any sentient being is wrong. Those who doubt this claim may be accused (perhaps with some justice) of lacking empathy, the ability to "feel with" other sentient beings, to comprehend the reality of their experience. It may be held that it is possible to regard the suffering of animals as morally insignificant only to the extent that one suffers from blindness to "the **ontology** of animal reality",[22] that is, from a failure to grasp the fact that they are centres of conscious experience, as we are.

This argument is inadequate, however, since there may be those who fully comprehend the fact that animals are sentient beings, but who still deny that their pains and pleasures have any direct moral significance. For them, a more persuasive consideration may be that our moral reasoning will gain in clarity and coherence if we recognize that the suffering of a nonhuman being is an evil of the same general sort as that of a human being. For if we do not recognize that suffering is an intrinsic evil, something which ought not to be inflicted deliberately without just cause, then we will not be able to fully understand why treating *human beings* in certain ways is immoral.

Torturing human beings, for example, is not wrong merely because it is illegal (where it is illegal), or merely because it violates some implicit agreement amongst human beings (though it may). Such legalistic or contractualistic reasons leave us in the dark as to why we *ought* to have, and enforce, laws and agreements against torture. The essential reason for regarding torture as wrong is that it *hurts,* and that people greatly prefer to avoid such pain—as do animals. I am not arguing, as does Kant, that cruelty to animals is wrong because it causes cruelty to human be-

ings, a position which consequentialists often endorse. The point, rather, is that unless we view the deliberate infliction of needless pain as inherently wrong we will not be able to understand the moral objection to cruelty of *either* kind.

It seems we must conclude, therefore, that sentient nonhuman animals have certain basic moral rights, rights which they share with all beings that are psychologically organized around the pleasure/pain axis. Their capacity for pain gives them the right that pain not be intentionally and needlessly inflicted upon them. Their capacity for pleasure gives them the right not to be prevented from pursuing whatever pleasures and fulfillments are natural to creatures of their kind. Like human rights, the rights of animals may be overriden if there is a morally sufficient reason for doing so. What *counts* as a morally significant reason, however, may be different in the two cases.

II HUMAN AND ANIMAL RIGHTS COMPARED

There are two dimensions in which we may find differences between the rights of human beings and those of animals. The first involves the *content* of those rights, while the second involves their strength; that is, the strength of the reasons which are required to override them.

Consider, for instance, the right to liberty. The *human* right to liberty precludes imprisonment without due process of law, even if the prison is spacious and the conditions of confinement cause no obvious physical suffering. But it is not so obviously wrong to imprison animals, especially when the area to which they are confined provides a fair approximation of the conditions of their natural habitat, and a reasonable opportunity to pursue the satisfactions natural to their kind. Such conditions, which often result in an increased lifespan, and which may exist in wildlife sanctuaries or even well-designed zoos, need not frustrate the needs or interests of animals in any significant way, and thus do not clearly violate their rights. Similarly treated human beings, on the other hand (e.g., native peoples confined to prison-like reservations), do tend to suffer from their loss of freedom. Human dignity and the fulfillment of the sorts of plans, hopes and desires which appear (thus far) to be uniquely human, require a more extensive freedom of movement than is the case with at least many nonhuman animals. Furthermore, there are aspects of human freedom, such as freedom of thought, freedom of speech and freedom of political association, which simply do not apply in the case of animals.

Thus, it seems that the human right to freedom is more extensive; that is, it precludes a wider range of specific ways of treating human beings than does the corresponding right on the part of animals. The argument cuts both ways, of course. *Some* animals, for example, great whales and migratory birds, may require at least as much physical freedom as do human beings if they are to pursue the satisfactions natural to their kind, and this fact provides a moral argument against keeping such creatures imprisoned.[23] And even chickens may suffer from the extreme and unnatural confinement to which they are subjected on modern "factory farms". Yet it seems unnecessary to claim for *most* animals a right to a freedom quite as broad as that which we claim for ourselves.

Similar points may be made with respect to the right to life. Animals, it may be argued, lack the cognitive equipment to value their lives in the way that human beings do. Ruth Cigman argues that animals have *no* right to life because death is no misfortune for them.[24] In her view, the death of an animal is not a misfortune, because animals have no desires which are *categorical;* that is which do not "merely presuppose being alive (like the desire to eat when one is hungry), but rather answer the question whether one wants to remain alive".[25] In other words, animals appear to lack the sorts of long-range hopes, plans, ambitions and the like, which give human beings such a powerful interest in

continued life. Animals, it seems, take life as it comes and do not specifically desire that it go on. True, squirrels store nuts for the winter and deer run from wolves; but these may be seen as instinctive or conditioned responses to present circumstances, rather than evidence that they value life as such.

These reflections probably help to explain why the death of a sparrow seems less tragic than that of a human being. Human lives, one might say, have greater intrinsic value, because they are worth more *to their possessors.* But this does not demonstrate that no nonhuman animal has *any* right to life. Premature death may be a less *severe* misfortune for sentient nonhuman animals than for human beings, but it is a misfortune nevertheless. In the first place, it is a misfortune in that it deprives them of whatever pleasures the future might have held for them, regardless of whether or not they ever *consciously anticipated* those pleasures. The fact that they are not here afterwards, to *experience* their loss, no more shows that they have not lost anything than it does in the case of humans. In the second place, it is (possibly) a misfortune in that it frustrates whatever future-oriented desires animals *may* have, unbeknownst to us. Even now, in an age in which apes have been taught to use simplified human languages and attempts have been made to communicate with dolphins and whales, we still know very little about the operation of nonhuman minds. We know much too little to assume that nonhuman animals never consciously pursue relatively distant future goals. To the extent that they do, the question of whether such desires provide them with *reasons for living* or merely *presuppose* continued life, has no satisfactory answer, since they cannot contemplate these alternatives—or, if they can, we have no way of knowing what their conclusions are. All we know is that the more intelligent and psychologically complex an animal is, the more *likely* it is that it possesses specifically future-oriented desires, which would be frustrated even by *painless* death.

For these reasons, it is premature to conclude from the apparent intellectual inferiority of nonhuman animals that they have no right to life. A more plausible conclusion is that animals do have a right to life but that it is generally somewhat weaker than that of human beings. It is, perhaps, weak enough to enable us to justify killing animals when we have no other ways of achieving such vital goals as feeding or clothing ourselves, or obtaining knowledge which is necessary to save human lives. Weakening their right to life in this way does not render meaningless the assertion that they have such a right. For the point remains that *some* serious justification for the killing of sentient nonhuman animals is always necessary; they may not be killed merely to provide amusement or minor gains in convenience.

If animals' rights to liberty and life are somewhat weaker than those of human beings, may we say the same about their right to *happiness;* that is, their right not to be made to suffer needlessly or to be deprived of the pleasures natural to their kind? If so, it is not immediately clear why. There is little reason to suppose that pain or suffering are any less unpleasant for the higher animals (at least) than they are for us. Our large brains *may* cause us to experience pain more intensely than do most animals, and *probably* cause us to suffer more from the anticipation or remembrance of pain. These facts might tend to suggest that pain is, on the whole, a worse experience for us than for them. But it may also be argued that pain may be *worse* in some respects for nonhuman animals, who are presumably less able to distract themselves from it by thinking of something else, or to comfort themselves with the knowledge that it is temporary. Brigid Brophy points out that "pain is likely to fill the sheep's whole capacity for experience in a way it seldom does in us, whose intellect and imagination can create breaks for us in the immediacy of our sensations".[26]

The net result of such contrasting considerations is that we cannot possibly claim to know whether pain is, on the whole, worse

for us than for animals, or whether their pleasures are any more or any less intense than ours. Thus, while we may justify assigning them a somewhat weaker right to life or liberty, on the grounds that they desire these goods less intensely than we do, we cannot discount their rights to freedom from needlessly inflicted pain or unnatural frustration on the same basis. There may, however, be *other* reasons for regarding all of the moral rights of animals as somewhat less stringent than the corresponding human rights.

A number of philosophers who deny that animals have moral rights point to the fact that nonhuman animals evidently lack the capacity for moral autonomy. Moral autonomy is the ability to act as a moral agent; that is, to act on the basis of an understanding of, and adherence to, moral rules or principles. H.J. McCloskey, for example, holds that "it is the capacity for moral autonomy . . . that is basic to the possibility of possessing a right".[27] McCloskey argues that it is inappropriate to ascribe moral rights to any entity which is not a moral agent, or *potentially* a moral agent, because a right is essentially an entitlement granted to a moral agent, licensing him or her to *act* in certain ways and to *demand* that other moral agents refrain from interference. For this reason, he says, "Where there is no possibility of [morally autonomous] action, potentially or actually . . . and where the being is not a member of a kind which is normally capable of [such] action, we withhold talk of rights." [28]

If moral autonomy—or being *potentially* autonomous, or a member of a kind which is *normally* capable of autonomy—is a necessary condition for having moral rights, then probably no nonhuman animal can qualify. For moral autonomy requires such probably uniquely human traits as "the capacity to be critically self-aware, manipulate concepts, use a sophisticated language, reflect, plan, deliberate, choose, and accept responsibility for acting".[29]

But why, we must ask, should the capacity for autonomy be regarded as a precondition for possessing moral rights? Autonomy is clearly crucial for the *exercise* of many human moral or legal rights, such as the right to vote or to run for public office. It is less clearly relevant, however, to the more basic human rights, such as the right to life or to freedom from unnecessary suffering. The fact that animals, like many human beings, cannot *demand* their moral rights (at least not in the words of any conventional human language) seems irrelevant. For, as Joel Feinberg points out, the interests of non-morally autonomous human beings may be defended by others, for example, in legal proceedings; and it is not clear why the interests of animals might not be represented in a similar fashion.[30]

It is implausible, therefore, to conclude that because animals lack moral autonomy they should be accorded *no moral rights whatsoever.* Nevertheless, it may be argued that the moral autonomy of (most) human beings provides a second reason, in addition to their more extensive interests and desires, for according somewhat *stronger* moral rights to human beings. The fundamental insight behind contractualist theories of morality[31] is that, for morally autonomous beings such as ourselves, there is enormous mutual advantage in the adoption of a moral system designed to protect each of us from the harms that might otherwise be visited upon us by others. Each of us ought to accept and promote such a system because, to the extent that others also accept it, we will all be safer from attack by our fellows, more likely to receive assistance when we need it, and freer to engage in individual as well as cooperative endeavours of all kinds.

Thus, it is the possibility of *reciprocity* which motivates moral agents to extend *full and equal* moral rights, in the first instance, only to other moral agents. I respect your rights to life, liberty and the pursuit of happiness in part because you are a sentient being, whose interests have intrinsic moral significance. But I respect them as *fully equal to my own* because I hope and expect that you will do the same for me. Animals, insofar as they lack the degree of rationality necessary for moral autonomy, cannot agree to respect our interests as equal in moral importance to their own, and neither do they expect or demand such respect from us. Of course, domestic animals may expect to be fed, etc. But they do not, and cannot, expect to be treated as moral equals, for they do not understand that moral concept or what it implies. Consequently, it is neither pragmatically feasible nor morally obligatory to extend to them the same *full and equal* rights which we extend to human beings.

Is this a speciesist conclusion? Defenders of a more extreme animal-rights position may point out that this argument, from the lack of moral autonomy, has exactly the same form as that which has been used for thousands of years to rationalize denying equal moral rights to women and members of "inferior" races. Aristotle, for example, argued that women and slaves are naturally subordinate beings, because they lack the capacity for moral autonomy and self-direction;[32] and contemporary versions of this argument, used to support racist or sexist conclusions, are easy to find. Are we simply repeating Aristotle's mistake, in a different context?

The reply to this objection is very simple: animals, unlike women and slaves, really *are* incapable of moral autonomy, at least to the best of our knowledge. Aristotle certainly *ought* to have known that women and slaves are capable of morally autonomous action; their capacity to use moral language alone ought to have alerted him to this likelihood. If comparable evidence exists that (some) nonhuman animals are moral agents we have not yet found it. The fact that some apes (and, possibly, some **cetaceans**) are capable of learning radically simplified human languages, the terms of which refer primarily to objects and events in their immediate environment, in no way demonstrates that they can understand abstract moral concepts, rules or principles, or use this understanding to regulate their own behaviour.

On the other hand, this argument implies

that if we *do* discover that certain nonhuman animals are capable of moral autonomy (which is certainly not impossible), then we ought to extend full and equal moral rights to those animals. Furthermore, if we someday encounter extraterrestrial beings, or build robots, **androids** or supercomputers which function as self-aware moral agents, then we must extend full and equal moral rights to these as well. Being a member of the human species is not a necessary condition for the possession of full "human" rights. Whether it is nevertheless a *sufficient* condition is the question to which we now turn.

III THE MORAL RIGHTS OF NONPARADIGM HUMANS

If we are justified in ascribing somewhat different, and also somewhat stronger, moral rights to human beings than to sentient but non-morally autonomous animals, then what are we to say of the rights of human beings who happen not to be capable of moral autonomy, perhaps not even potentially? Both Singer and Regan have argued that if any of the superior intellectual capacities of normal and mature human beings are used to support a distinction between the moral status of *typical,* or paradigm, human beings, and that of animals, then consistency will require us to place certain "nonparadigm" humans, such as infants, small children and the severely retarded or incurably brain damaged, in the same inferior moral category.[33] Such a result is, of course, highly counterintuitive.

Fortunately, no such conclusion follows from the autonomy argument. There are many reasons for extending strong moral rights to nonparadigm humans; reasons which do not apply to most nonhuman animals. Infants and small children are granted strong moral rights in part because of their *potential* autonomy. But *potential* autonomy, as I have argued elsewhere,[34] is not in itself a sufficient reason for the ascription of full moral rights; if it were, then not only human foetuses (from conception onwards) but even ununited human sperm-egg pairs would have

to be regarded as entities with a right to life the equivalent of our own—thus making not only abortion, but any intentional failure to procreate, the moral equivalent of murder. Those who do not find this extreme conclusion acceptable must appeal to reasons other than the *potential* moral autonomy of infants and small children to explain the strength of the latter's moral rights.

One reason for assigning strong moral rights to infants and children is that they possess not just *potential* but *partial* autonomy, and it is not clear how much of it they have at any given moment. The fact that, unlike baby chimpanzees, they are already learning the things which will enable them to *become* morally autonomous, makes it likely that their minds have more subtleties than their speech (or the lack of it) proclaims. Another reason is simply that most of us tend to place a very high value on the lives and well-being of infants. Perhaps we are to some degree "programmed" by nature to love and protect them; perhaps our reasons are somewhat egocentric; or perhaps we value them for their potential. Whatever the explanation, the fact that we do feel this way about them is in itself a valid reason for extending to them stronger moral and legal protections than we extend to nonhuman animals, even those which may have just as well or better-developed psychological capacities.[35] A third, and perhaps the most important, reason is that if we did *not* extend strong moral rights to infants, far too few of them would ever *become* responsible, morally autonomous adults; too many would be treated "like animals" (i.e., in ways that it is generally wrong to treat even animals), and would consequently become socially crippled, antisocial or just very unhappy people. If any part of our moral code is to remain intact, it seems that infants and small children *must* be protected and cared for.[36]

Analogous arguments explain why strong moral rights should also be accorded to other nonparadigm humans. The severely retarded or incurably senile, for instance, may have no potential for moral autonomy, but there are apt to be friends, relatives or other people who care what happens to them. Like children, such individuals may have more mental capacities than are readily apparent. Like children, they are more apt to achieve, or return to moral autonomy if they are valued and well cared for. Furthermore, any one of us may someday become mentally incapacitated to one degree or another, and we would all have reason to be anxious about our own futures if such incapacitation were made the basis for denying strong moral rights.[37]

There are, then, sound reasons for assigning strong moral rights even to human beings who lack the mental capacities which justify the general distinction between human and animal rights. Their rights are based not only on the value which they themselves place upon their lives and well-being, but also on the value which other human beings place upon them.

But is this a valid basis for the assignment of moral rights? Is it consistent with the definition presented earlier, according to which X may be said to have a moral right to Y only if depriving X of Y is *prima facie* wrong *because of the harm done to the interests of X,* and not merely because of any further consequences? Regan argues that we cannot justify the ascription of stronger rights to nonparadigm humans than to nonhuman animals in the way suggested, because "what underlies the ascription of rights to any given X is that X has value independently of anyone's valuing X".[38] After all, we do not speak of expensive paintings or gemstones as having rights, although many people value them and have good reasons for wanting them protected.

There is, however, a crucial difference between a rare painting and a severely retarded or senile human being; the latter not only has (or may have) value for other human beings but *also* has his or her own needs and interests. It may be this which leads us to say that such individuals have intrinsic value. The sentience of nonparadigm humans, like that of sentient nonhuman animals, gives them a place in the sphere of rights holders. So long as the moral rights of all sentient beings are given due recognition, there should be no objection to providing some of them with *additional* protections, on the basis of our interests as well as their own. Some philosophers speak of such additional protections, which are accorded to X on the basis of interests other than X's own, as *conferred* rights, in contrast to *natural* rights, which are entirely based upon the properties of X itself.[39] But such "conferred" rights are not necessarily any weaker or less binding upon moral agents than are "natural" rights. Infants, and most other nonparadigm humans have the *same* basic moral rights that the rest of us do, even though the reasons for ascribing those rights are somewhat different in the two cases.

IV OTHER OBJECTIONS TO ANIMAL RIGHTS

We have already dealt with the primary objection to assigning *any* moral rights to nonhuman animals; that is, that they lack moral autonomy, and various other psychological capacities which paradigm humans possess. We have also answered the animal liberationists' primary objection to assigning somewhat *weaker,* or less-extensive rights to animals; that is, that this will force us to assign similarly inferior rights to nonparadigm humans. There are two other objections to animal rights which need to be considered. The first is that the claim that animals have a right to life, or other moral rights, has absurd consequences with respect to the natural relationships *among* animals. The second is that to accord rights to animals on the basis of their (differing degrees of) sentience will introduce intolerable difficulties and complexities into our moral reasoning.

Opponents of animal rights often accuse the animal liberationists of ignoring the realities of nature, in which many animals survive only by killing others. Callicott, for example, maintains that, whereas environmentally aware persons realize that natural predators are a vital part of the biotic community, those who believe that animals have a right to life are forced to regard all predators as "merciless, wanton, and incorrigible murderers of their fellow creatures".[40] Similarly, Ritchie asks whether, if animals have rights, we are not morally obligated to "protect the weak among them against the strong? Must we not put to death blackbirds and thrushes because they feed on worms, or (if capital punishment offends our humanitarianism) starve them slowly by permanent captivity and vegetarian diet?"[41]

Such a conclusion would of course be ridiculous, as well as wholly inconsistent with the environmental ethic. However, nothing of the sort follows from the claim that animals have moral rights. There are two independently sufficient reasons why it does not. In the first place, nonhuman predators are not moral agents, so it is absurd to think of them as wicked, or as *murdering* their prey. But this is not the most important point. Even if wolves and the like *were* moral agents, their predation would still be morally acceptable, given that they generally kill only to feed themselves, and generally do so without inflicting prolonged or unnecessary suffering. If we have the right to eat animals, in order to avoid starvation, then why shouldn't animals have the right to eat one another, for the same reason?

This conclusion is fully consistent with the lesson taught by the ecologists, that natural predation is essential to the stability of biological communities. Deer need wolves, or other predators, as much as the latter need them; without predation they become too numerous and fall victim to hunger and disease, while their overgrazing damages the entire ecosystem.[42] Too often we have learned (or failed to learn) this lesson the hard way, as when the killing of hawks and other predators produces exploding rodent populations—which must be controlled, often in ways which cause further ecological damage. The control of natural predators may *sometimes* be necessary, for example, when human pressures upon the populations of certain species become so intense that the latter cannot endure continued *natural* predation. (The controversial case of the wolves and caribou in Alaska and Canada may or may not be one of this sort.) But even in such cases it is preferable, from an environmentalist perspective, to reduce human predation enough to leave room for natural predators as well.

Another objection to assigning moral rights to sentient nonhuman animals is that it will not only complicate our own moral system, but introduce seemingly insoluble dilemmas. As Ritchie points out, "Very difficult questions of casuistry will ... arise because of the difference in grades of sentience."[43] For instance, is it morally worse to kill and eat a dozen oysters (which are at most minimally sentient) or one (much more highly sentient) rabbit? Questions of this kind, considered in isolation from any of the practical circumstances in which they might arise, are virtually unanswerable. But this ought not to surprise us, since similarly abstract questions about the treatment of human beings are often equally unanswerable. (For instance, would it be worse to kill one child or to cause a hundred to suffer from severe malnutrition?)

The reason such questions are so difficult to answer is not just that we lack the skill and knowledge to make such precise comparisons of interpersonal or interspecies utility, but also that these questions are posed in entirely unrealistic terms. Real moral choices rarely depend entirely upon the comparison of two abstract quantities of pain or pleasure deprivation. In deciding whether to eat **molluscs** or mammals (or neither or both) a human society must consider *all* of the predictable consequences of each option, for example, their respective impacts on the **ecology** or the economy, and not merely the individual interests of the animals involved.

Of course, other things being equal, it would be morally preferable to refrain from killing *any* sentient animal. But other things are never equal. Questions about human diet involve not only the rights of individual animals, but also vital environmental and human concerns. On the one hand, as Singer points out, more people could be better fed if food suitable for human consumption were not fed to meat-producing animals.[44] On the other hand, a mass conversion of humanity to vegetarianism would represent "an increase in the efficiency of the conversion of solar energy from plant to human biomass",[45] with the likely result that the human population would continue to expand and, in the process, to cause greater environmental destruction than might occur otherwise. The issue is an enormously complex one, and cannot be solved by any simple appeal to the claim that animals have (or lack) certain moral rights.

In short, the ascription of moral rights to animals does not have the absurd or environmentally damaging consequences that some philosophers have feared. It does not require us to exterminate predatory species, or to lose ourselves in abstruse speculations about the relative degrees of sentience of different sorts of animals. It merely requires us to recognize the interests of animals as having intrinsic moral significance; as demanding some consideration, regardless of whether or not human or environmental concerns are also involved. We must now consider the question of how well the animal rights theory meshes with the environmental ethic, which treats not only animals but plants, rivers and other nonsentient elements of nature as entities which may demand moral consideration.

V ANIMAL LIBERATION AND THE LAND ETHIC

The fundamental message of Leopold's land ethic, and of the environmentalist movement in general, is that the terrestrial biosphere is an integrated whole, and that humanity is a part of that natural order, wholly dependent upon it and morally responsible for maintaining its integrity.[46] Because of the wholistic nature of biotic systems, it is impossible to determine the value of an organism simply by considering its individual moral rights: we

must also consider its relationship to other parts of the system. For this reason, some philosophers have concluded that the theoretical foundations of the environmentalist and animal liberation movements are mutually contradictory.[47] Alastair Gunn states: "Environmentalism seems incompatible with the Western obsession with individualism, which leads us to resolve questions about our treatment of animals by appealing to the essentially atomistic, competitive notion of rights." [48]

As an example of the apparent clash between the land ethic and the ascription of rights to animals, Gunn points to the situation on certain islands off the coast of New Zealand, where feral goats, pigs and cats have had to be exterminated in order to protect indigenous species and habitats, which were threatened by the introduced species. "Considered purely in terms of rights," he says, "it is hard to see how this could be justified. [For,] if the goats, etc. are held to have rights, then we are violating these rights in order perhaps to save or increase a rare species." [49]

I maintain, on the contrary, that the appearance of fundamental contradiction between the land ethic and the claim that sentient nonhuman animals have moral rights is illusory. If we were to hold that the rights of animals are *identical to those of human beings,* then we would indeed be forced to conclude that it is wrong to eliminate harmful introduced species for the good of the indigenous ones or of the ecosystem as a whole—just as wrong as it would be to exterminate all of the human inhabitants of North America who are immigrants, however greatly this might benefit the native Americans and the natural ecology. There is no inconsistency, however, in the view that animals have a significant right to life, but one which is somewhat more easily overridden by certain kinds of utilitarian or environmental considerations than is the human right to life. On this view, it is wrong to kill animals for trivial reasons, but not wrong to do so when there is no other way of achieving a vital goal, such as the preservation of threatened species.

Another apparent point of inconsistency between the land ethic and the animal liberation movement involves the issue of whether sentience is a *necessary,* as well as *sufficient,* condition for the possession of moral rights. Animal liberationists sometimes maintain that it is, and that consequently plants, rivers, mountains and other elements of nature which are not themselves sentient (though they may *contain* sentient life forms) cannot have moral rights.[50] Environmentalists, on the other hand, sometimes argue for the ascription of moral rights to even the nonsentient elements of the biosphere.[51] Does this difference represent a genuine contradiction between the two approaches?

One argument that it does not is that the fact that a particular entity is not accorded moral rights does not imply that there are no sound reasons for protecting it from harm. Human health and survival alone requires that we place a high value on clean air, unpolluted land, water and crops, and on the maintenance of stable and diverse natural ecosystems. Furthermore, there are vital scientific, spiritual, aesthetic and recreational values associated with the conservation of the natural world, values which cannot be dismissed as luxuries which benefit only the affluent portion of humanity.[52] Once we realize how *valuable* nature is, it may seem immaterial whether or not we also wish to speak of its nonsentient elements as possessing moral *rights.*

But there is a deeper issue here than the precise definition of the term "moral rights". The issue is whether trees, rivers and the like ought to be protected *only* because of their value to us (and to other sentient animals), or whether they also have *intrinsic* value. That is, are they to be valued and protected because of what they are, or only because of what they are good for? Most environmentalists think that the natural world is intrinsically valuable, and that it is therefore wrong to wantonly destroy forests, streams, marshes and so on, even where doing so is not *obviously* inconsistent with the welfare of human beings. It is

this conviction which finds expression in the claim that even nonsentient elements of nature have moral rights. Critics of the environmental movement, on the other hand, often insist that the value of the nonhuman world is purely instrumental, and that it is only sentimentalists who hold otherwise.

John Passmore, for instance, deplores "the cry ... for a new morality, a new religion, which would transform man's attitude to nature, which would lead us to believe that it is *intrinsically* wrong to destroy a species, cut down a tree, clear a wilderness."[53] Passmore refers to such a call for a nonhomocentric morality as "mystical rubbish".[54] In his view, nothing in the nonhuman world has *either* intrinsic value or moral rights. He would evidently agree with William F. Baxter, who says that "damage to penguins, or to sugar pines, or geological marvels is, without more, simply irrelevant.... Penguins are important [only] because people enjoy seeing them walk about the rocks."[55]

This strictly instrumentalist view of the value of the nonhuman world is rejected by animal liberationists and environmentalists alike. The animal liberationists maintain that the sentience of many nonhuman animals constitutes a sufficient reason for regarding their needs and interests as worthy of our moral concern, and for assigning them certain moral rights. Sentience is, in this sense, a sufficient condition for the possession of intrinsic value. It does not follow from this that it is also a *necessary* condition for having intrinsic value. It may be a necessary condition for having individual moral *rights;* certainly it is necessary for *some* rights, such as the right not to be subjected to unnecessary pain. But there is room to argue that even though mountains and trees are not subject to pleasure or pain, and hence do not have rights of the sort we ascribe to sentient beings, nevertheless they have intrinsic value of another sort, or for another reason.

What sort of intrinsic value might they have? The environmentalists' answer is that they are valuable as organic parts of the natural whole. But this answer is incomplete, in that it does not explain why we ought to value the natural world *as a whole,* except insofar as it serves our own interests to do so. No clear and persuasive answer to this more basic question has yet been given. Perhaps, as Thomas Auxter has suggested, the answer is to be found in a teleological ethic of the same general sort of that of Plato or Aristotle, an ethic which urges us "to seek the highest good, which is generally understood as the most perfect or complete state of affairs possible".[56] This most perfect or complete state of affairs would include "a natural order which encompasses the most developed and diverse types of beings",[57] one in which "every species finds a place ... and ... the existence and functioning of any one species is not a threat to the existence and functioning of any other species".[58]

It is not my purpose to endorse this or any other philosophical explanation of why even the nonsentient elements of nature should be regarded as having intrinsic value. I want only to suggest that better answers to this question can and should be developed, and that there is no reason to presume that these answers will consist entirely of "mystical rubbish". Furthermore, I would suggest that the claim that mountains and forests have intrinsic value of *some* sort is intuitively much more plausible than its denial.

One way to test your own intuitions, or unformulated convictions, about this claim is to consider a hypothetical case of the following sort. Suppose that a virulent virus, developed by some unwise researcher, has escaped into the environment and will inevitably extinguish all animal life (ourselves included) within a few weeks. Suppose further that this or some other scientist has developed another virus which, if released, would destroy all plant life as well, but more slowly, such that the effects of the second virus would not be felt until after the last animal was gone. If the second virus were released *secretly,* its release would do no further damage to the well-being of any sentient creature; no one would

suffer, even from the knowledge that the plant kingdom is as doomed as we are. Finally, suppose that it is known with certainty that sentient life forms would never re-evolve on the earth (this time from plants), and that no sentient aliens will ever visit the planet. The question is would it be morally preferable, in such a case, *not* to release the second virus, even secretly? If we tend to think that it would be, that it would certainly be better to allow the plants to survive us than to render the earth utterly lifeless (except perhaps for the viruses), then we do not really believe that it is only sentient—let alone only human—beings which have intrinsic value.

This being the case, it is relatively unimportant whether we say that even nonsentient natural entities may have moral *rights,* or whether we say only that, because of their intrinsic value, they ought to be protected, even at some cost to certain human interests. Nevertheless, there is an argument for preferring the latter way of speaking. It is that nonsentient entities, not being subject to pleasure or pain, and lacking any preferences with respect to what happens to them, cannot sensibly be said to have *interests.* The Gulf Stream or the south wind may have value because of their role in the natural order, but if they were to be somehow altered or destroyed, *they* would not experience suffering, or lose anything which it is in *their* interest to have. Thus, "harming" them would not be wrong *in and of itself,* but rather because of the kinds of environmental efforts which the land ethic stresses. In contrast, harm done to a sentient being has moral significance even if it has no further consequences whatsoever.

The position at which we have arrived represents a compromise between those animal liberationists who hold that only sentient beings have *either* intrinsic value or moral rights, and those environmentalists who ascribe *both* intrinsic value and moral rights to even the nonsentient elements of nature. Mountains and trees should be protected not because they have moral rights, but because they are intrinsically—as well as instrumentally—valuable.

So stated, the land ethic is fully compatible with the claim that individual sentient animals have moral rights. Indeed, the two positions are complementary; each helps to remedy some of the apparent defects of the other. The animal liberation theory, for instance, does not in itself explain why we ought to protect not only *individual* animals, but also threatened *species* of plants as well as animals. The land ethic, on the other hand, fails to explain why it is wrong to inflict needless suffering or death even upon domestic animals, which may play little or no role in the maintenance of natural ecosystems, or only a negative role. Practices such as rearing animals in conditions of severe confinement and discomfort, or subjecting them to painful experiments which have no *significant* scientific purpose, are wrong primarily because of the suffering inflicted upon individual sentient beings, and only secondarily because of any social or environmental damage they may incidentally cause.

Thus, it is clear that as we learn to extend our moral concern beyond the boundaries of our own species we shall have to take account of both the rights of individual animals *and* the value of those elements of the natural world which are not themselves sentient. Respecting the interests of creatures who, like ourselves, are subject to pleasure and pain is in no way inconsistent with valuing and protecting the richness, diversity and stability of natural ecosystems. In many cases, such as the commercial slaughter of whales, there are both environmental and humane reasons for altering current practices. In other cases, in which humane and environmental considerations appear to point in opposite directions e.g., the case of the feral goats on the New Zealand islands) these factors must be weighed against each other, much as the rights of individual human beings must often be weighed against larger social needs. In no case does a concern for the environment preclude *also* considering the rights of individual animals; it may, for instance, be possible to trap and deport the goats alive, rather than killing them.

VI SUMMARY AND CONCLUSION

I have argued that the environmentalist and animal liberationist perspectives are complementary, rather than essentially competitive or mutually inconsistent approaches towards a nonhomocentric moral theory. The claim that animals have certain moral rights, by virtue of their sentience, does not negate the fact that ecosystems are complexly unified wholes, in which one element generally cannot be damaged without causing repercussions elsewhere in the system. If sentience is a necessary, as well as sufficient, condition for having moral rights, then we cannot ascribe such rights to oceans, mountains and the like; yet we have a moral obligation to protect such natural resources from excessive damage at human hands, both because of their value to us and to future generations, and because they are intrinsically valuable, as elements of the planetary biosystem. It is not necessary to choose between regarding biological communities as unified systems, analogous to organisms, and regarding them as containing many individual sentient creatures, each with its own separate needs and interests; for it is clearly both of these things at once. Only by *combining* the environmentalist and animal rights perspectives can we take account of the full range of moral considerations which ought to guide our interactions with the nonhuman world.

Footnotes

1. See, for instance, Immanuel Kant, "Duties to Animals and Spirits", in *Lectures on Ethics,* trans. Louis Infield (New York: Harper and Row, 1964), excerpted in *Animal Rights and Human Obligations* ed. Tom Regan and Peter Singer (Englewood Cliffs, N.J.: Prentice-Hall, 1976), pp. 122–23.

2. Aldo Leopold, *A Sand County Almanac* (New York: Oxford University Press, 1949), p. 204.

3. Ibid., p. 225.

4. Here, as elsewhere in this paper, the terms "pleasure" and "pain" should not be understood in the narrow sense in which they refer only to particular sorts of *sensation,* but rather as an abbreviated way of referring to the fulfillment or frustration, respectively, of the needs, interests and desires of sentient beings.

5. See, for example, the selections by Jeremy Bentham, "A Utilitarian View"; John Stuart Mill, "A Defence of Bentham"; and Henry S. Salt, "The Humanities of Diet", "Animal Rights", and "The Logic of the Larder", in *Animal Rights,* ed. Regan and Singer.

6. Ibid.

7. See, Maureen Duffy, "Beasts for Pleasure", in *Animals, Men and Morals,* ed. Stanley and Rosalind Godlovitch (New York: Taplinger Publishing Co. 1972), pp. 111–24.

8. See, Stephen R.L. Clark, *The Moral Status of Animals* (Oxford: Clarendon Press, 1977); Tom Regan, "Animal Rights, Human Wrongs", *Environmental Ethics* 2, no. 2 (Summer 1980): 99–120; Richard Ryder, "Experiments on Animals", in *Animal Rights,* ed. Regan and Singer, pp. 33–47; and Peter Singer, *Animal Liberation: A New Ethics for Our Treatment of Animals* (New York: Avon, 1975), especially chaps. 2 and 3.

9. J. Baird Callicott, "Animal Liberation: A Triangular Affair", *Environmental Ethics* 2, no. 4 (Winter 1980): 315.

10. Ibid., p. 337.

11. See Christopher D. Stone, *Should Trees Have Standing? Toward Legal Rights for Natural Objects* (Los Altos, Calif.: William Kaufman, 1974).

12. Singer, *Animal Liberation,* p. 9.

13. Jeremy Bentham, *The Principles of Morals and Legislation* (1789), chap. 18, sec. 1; cited by Singer, *Animal Liberation,* p. 8.

14. Singer, *Animal Liberation,* p. 5.

15. Peter Singer, "The Fable of the Fox", *Ethics* 88, no. 2 (January 1978): 122.

16. See, for instance, Brigid Brophy, "In Pursuit of a Fantasy", in *Animals, Men and Morals,* pp. 125–45; Joel Feinberg, "The Rights of Animals and Unborn Generations", in *Philosophy and Environmental Crisis,* ed. William T. Blackstone (Athens, Ga. University of Georgia Press, 1974), pp. 43–68; Rosalind Godlovitch, "Animals and Morals", in *Animals, Men and Morals,* pp. 156–71; Lawrence Haworth, "Rights, Wrongs and Animals", *Ethics* 88, no. 2 (January 1978): 95–105; Anthony J. Povilitis, "On Assigning Rights to Animals and Nature", *Environmental Ethics* 2 (Spring 1980): 67–71; and Tom Regan, "Do Animals Have a Right to Life?", in *Animal Rights,* ed. Regan and Singer, pp. 197–204.

17. Regan, "Right to Life?"

18. Ibid., p. 203.

19. Singer, *Animal Liberation,* p. 3.

20. Regan, "Right to Life?"; see also, idem, "An Examination and Defence of One Argument Concerning Animal Rights", *Inquiry* 22, nos. 1–2 (1979): 189–217.

21. Regan, "Right to Life?", p. 197.

22. T.L.S. Sprigge, "Metaphysics, Physicalism, and Animal Rights", *Inquiry* 22, nos. 1–2 (1979): 101.

23. See John C. Lilly, *Lilly on Dolphins* (New York: Anchor Books, Garden City, 1975), p. 210. Lilly, after years of experimenting with dolphins and attempting to communicate with them, concluded that keeping them captive was wrong because they, like us, suffer from such confinement.

24. Ruth Cigman, "Death, Misfortune, and Species Inequality", *Philosophy and Public Affairs* 10, no. 1 (Winter 1981): p. 48.

25. Ibid., pp. 57–58. The concept of a categorical desire is introduced by Bernard Williams, "The Makropoulous Case", in his *Problems of the Self* (Cambridge: Cambridge University Press), 1973.

26. Brophy, "Pursuit of Fantasy", p. 129.

27. H.J. McCloskey, "Moral Rights and Animals", *Inquiry* 22, nos. 1–2 (1979): 31.

28. Ibid., p. 29.

29. Michael Fox, "Animal Liberation: A Critique", *Ethics* 88, no. 2 (January 1978): 111.

30. Feinberg, "Rights", pp. 46–47.

31. Such as that presented by John Rawls, *A Theory of Justice* (Oxford: Oxford University Press, 1972).

32. Aristotle *Politics* 1. 1254, 1260, and 1264.

33. Singer, *Animal Liberation,* pp. 75–76; Regan, "One Argument Concerning Animal Rights".

34. Mary Anne Warren, "Do Potential People Have Moral Rights?", *Canadian Journal of Philosophy* 7, no. 2 (June 1977): 275–89.

35. This argument does not, as one might suppose, justify placing restrictions upon (early) abortions which are as severe as the restrictions upon infanticide or murder, although there are certainly many people who place a high value upon the lives of foetuses. The reason it does not is that such restrictions, unlike restrictions upon infanticide (given the possibility of adoption), violate all of the most basic moral rights of women, who are not morally obligated to waive their own rights to life, liberty and happiness, in order to protect the sensibilities of human observers who are not directly affected.

36. Anthropological evidence for this claim may be found in Margaret Mead's study of the Mundugumor, a Papuan tribe in New Guinea which placed little value on infants and abused them casually; adult Mundugumors, men and women alike, appear to be hostile, aggressive and generally amoral, to a degree barely compatible with social existence (Margaret Mead, *Sex and Temperament in Three Primitive Societies* [New York: William Morrow, 1963]).

37. One exception to the rule that mental incapacitation does not justify the denial of basic human rights is *total and permanent* incapacitation, such that there is no possibility of any future return to sentience. Once a person has entered a state of terminal coma, he or she has nothing to gain from continued biological life, and nothing to lose by dying. Where there is any doubt about the possibility of full or partial recovery, every benefit of the doubt should be given; but where there is clearly no such possibility, the best course is usually to allow death to occur naturally, provided that this is consistent with the wishes of the individual's family or friends. (To sanction *active* euthanasia, i.e., the deliberate *killing* of such terminally comatose persons might be unwise, in that it might lead all of us to fear [somewhat more] for our lives when we are forced to place them in the hands of medical personnel; but that is an issue which we need not settle here.)

38. Regan, "One Argument Concerning Animal Rights", p. 189.

39. See, for example, Edward A. Langerak, "Abortion, Potentiality, and Conferred Claims", (Paper delivered at the Eastern Division of the American Philosophical Association, December 1979).

40. Callicott, "Animal Liberation", p. 320.

41. D.G. Ritchie, "Why Animals Do Not Have Rights", in *Animal Rights,* ed. Regan and Singer, p. 183.

42. See Aldo Leopold, *Sand County Almanac,* pp. 129–33.

43. Ritchie, "Why Animals Do Not Have Rights".

44. Singer, *Animal Liberation* pp. 169–74.

45. Callicott, "Animal Liberation", p. 335.

46. For exposition of this holistic message, see, William T. Blackstone, "Ethics and Ecology", in *Philosophy and Environmental Crisis,* pp. 16–42; Thomas Auxter, "The Right Not To Be Eaten", *Inquiry* 22, nos. 1–2 (Spring 1979): 221–30; Robert Cahn, *Footprints on the Planet: The Search for an Environmental Ethic* (New York: Universe Books, 1978); Albert A. Fritsch, *Environmental Ethics* (New York: Anchor Press, Doubleday, 1980), p. 3; Alastair S. Gunn, "Why Should We Care About Rare Species?", *Environmental Ethics* 2, no. 1 (Spring 1980): 17–37, Eugene P. Odum, "Environmental Ethics and the Attitude Revolution", in *Philosophy and Environmental Crisis,* pp. 10–15; and, of course, Leopold, *Sand County Almanac.*

47. See Callicott, "Animal Liberation", p. 315.

48. Gunn, "Rare Species", p. 36.

49. Ibid., p. 37.

50. See Feinberg, "Rights", pp. 52–53.

51. See Stone, *Should Trees Have Standing?*

52. For example, Baxter maintains that "environmental amenities ... fall in the category of a luxury good" (William F. Baxter, *People or Penguins: The Case for Optimal Pollution* [New York and London: Columbia University Press, 1974], p. 105).

53. John Passmore, *Man's Responsibility for Nature* (London: Duckworth, 1974), p. 111.

54. Ibid., p. 173.

55. Baxter, *People or Penguins,* p. 5.

56. Thomas Auxter, "The Right Not To Be Eaten", *Inquiry* 22, nos. 1–2 (1979): 222.

57. Ibid., p. 225.

58. Ibid., p. 226.

Review Questions

1. Distinguish between the land ethic and the animal liberation view, as Warren explains them.

2. How does Warren think that the two views can be made compatible?

3. What problem does Warren find in the animal rights view?

4. How does Warren analyze the concept of a moral right?

5. According to Warren, why do animals have some rights? What are these rights?

6. In Warren's view, what are the differences in content and strength between animal and human rights?

7. According to Warren, what is the fundamental message of Leopold's land ethic?

8. Why does there appear to be a fundamental contradiction between the land ethic and the animal rights view, and how does Warren propose to resolve it?

Discussion Questions

1. Warren says, "If we someday encounter extraterrestrial beings, or build robots, androids or supercomputers which function as self-aware moral agents, then we must extend full and equal moral rights to these as well." Do you agree? Why or why not?

2. Reread the example about the virulent virus. Do you agree that it would be morally preferable not to release the second virus? Explain your view.

Problem Cases

1. Killing Chickens Suppose a farmer raises chickens on his farm. They are well fed, they have plenty of room, they have a comfortable place to sleep, in short, they are well cared for. Each year the farmer kills some of the chickens quickly and with little pain. Then he eats them with great relish. He replaces the chickens he kills with other chickens so that the chicken population remains stable. Does this farmer do anything that is morally wrong? Explain your position.

2. The Draize Test The Draize eye test is used by cosmetic companies such as Revlon and Procter and Gamble to test the eye irritancy of their products—cosmetics, hair shampoos, and so on. The substance to be tested is injected into the eyes of rabbits; more specifically, 0.1 milligrams (a large volume dose) is injected into the conjuctival sac of one eye of each of six rabbits with the other eye serving as a control. The lids are held together for one second and then the animal is released. The eyes are examined at twenty-four, forty-eight, and seventy-two hours to see if there is corneal damage. Although the test is very painful, as you can imagine, anesthetics are not used. The eyes are not washed. Very large doses are used (often resulting in permanent eye damage) to provide a large margin of safety in extrapolating the human response. No nonanimal test for eye irritancy has been developed. Should companies continue to test their new products in this way? What is your view?

3. *The Proposed Dickey-Lincoln Dam* The proposed Dickey-Lincoln Dam on the St. John River in Maine will produce hydroeclectric power, provide recreational opportunities (boating and fishing), and will increase real estate values. Environmentalists who are opposed to the project point out that it would drown more than half of the population of furbish louseworts, a rare relative of the snapdraggon. This type of plant is in danger of becoming extinct. But it seems to have little or no commercial value; it is not pretty or beautiful. Should this dam be built? Defend your position.

4. *Guerrilla Warfare in Cathedral Forest* (Reported in *Esquire*, Feb., 1987). Cathedral Forest in Oregon is one of the last large stands of virgin forest remaining on the North American continent. The forest is called old growth because the trees (Douglas firs) are among the oldest and biggest on the planet. Old growth constitutes an almost infinitesimal percentage of forested lands in the United States. Even though there is no commercial demand for the timber, the United States Forest Service has made the harvesting of the last of the old trees a priority. The Forest Service has sold Cathedral Forest to Willamette Industries, a large wood-products company.

To prevent the forest from being cut down, radical environmentalist Mike Roselle has resorted to an illegal guerrilla action called tree spiking. He has driven long nails into trees in a spiral pattern. Chain saws and saw blades will shatter when they hit the buried nails. Mike hopes that the spiked trees will prevent Willamette from cutting down the forest. Is this tree spiking morally justified? What is your view?

Suggested Readings

(1) *Environmental Ethics.* This journal is edited by Eugene C. Hargrove and is dedicated to the philosophical aspects of environmental problems.

(2) Feinberg, Joel. "The Rights of Animals and Unborn Generations." In *Philosophy and Environmental Crisis,* edited by W. Blackstone, 48–68. Athens: University of Georgia Press, 1974. On Feinberg's analysis of the concept of a right, only beings who are capable of having interests can meaningfully be said to have rights. In view of this principle, Feinberg holds that individual animals may be said to have rights, but species of animals or plants, trees, rocks, and other inanimate things cannot be said to have rights.

(3) Francis, Leslie Pickering, and Richard Norman. "Some Animals Are More Equal Than Others." *Philosophy* 53 (October 1978): 507–527. Francis and Norman agree with Singer and others that it is wrong to cause animal suffering, other things being equal, but unlike Singer they do not think that this requires us to adopt vegetarianism or abandon animal experimentation.

(4) Frankena, William K., "Ethics and the Environment." In *Ethics and Problems of the 21st Century,* edited by Kenneth Goodpaster and K.M. Sayre. Notre Dame, Indiana: University of Notre Dame Press, 1979. Frankena distinguishes between eight types of ethics: (1) ethical egoism, (2) humanism, (3) sentientism or the view that the class of moral patients includes only sentient beings, (4) the ethics of "reverence for life," (5) the view that everything should be morally considered, (6) theistic ethics, (7) combination ethics where different types of ethics are combined, and (8) naturalistic ethics. He finds ethical egoism and humanism to be morally inadequate, and he has doubts about theistic ethics and combination ethics. He concludes that sentientism provides an adequate basis for environmental ethics. His view is rejected both by Frey and by those who adopt a holistic environmental ethic.

(5) Gunn, Alastair S. "Why Should We Care about Rare Species?" *Environmental Ethics* vol. 2, no. 1 (Spring 1989): 17–37. Gunn analyzes the concept of rarity and its relation to value. He argues that the extermination of a rare species is wrong because each species, as well as ecological wholes, have intrinsic value.

(6) Leopold, Aldo. "The Land Ethic." In *A Sand County Almanac*, 217–241. New York: Oxford University Press, 1966. This is the classic presentation of Leopold's "Land Ethic." As he puts it, "The land ethic simply enlarges the boundaries of the community to include soils, waters, plants, and animals, or collectively, the land."

(7) McCloskey, H.J. "Moral Rights and Animals." *Inquiry* 22 (Spring-Summer 1979): 25–54. McCloskey attacks Feinberg's analysis of the concept of a right and presents his own account. According to McCloskey, a right is an entitlement to something and not a claim against someone. Beings who are able to make a claim, either directly or through a representative, can possess rights. But since animals cannot do this, they cannot be said to possess rights.

(8) Regan, Tom. ed. *Earthbound: New Introductory Essays in Environmental Ethics.* New York: Random House, 1984. This is a collection of original essays on a variety of topics related to the enviornment, including Alastair S. Gunn, "Preserving Rare Species;" Annette Baier, "For the Sake of Future Generations;" and Mark Sagoff, "Ethics and Economics in Environmental Law."

(9) _____. *The Case for Animal Rights* Berkeley: University of California Press, 1983. Regan argues that animals are not "thoughtless brutes," but persons who have beliefs and desires, memories and expectations, and who feel pleasure and pain. As such they have a basic moral right to be treated with respect. To do this we must eliminate commercial animal agriculture, hunting and trapping, and animal experimentation.

(10) Sagoff, Mark. "On Preserving the Natural Environment." *Yale Law Journal* 84 (December 1974): 205–167. Sagoff proposes a nonutilitarian rationale for preserving the natural environment.

(11) Stone, Christopher. *Should Trees Have Standing?* Los Altos, California: Kaufman, 1974. In this short book, Stone argues that trees and other objects in the environment should be granted legal standing so that it is possible for them to sue for their own protection.

Glossary

Android   an artifically created being with human form.

Anthropocentrism   the belief that human beings are central or most important in the universe, rather than animals or the nonhuman world. Contrasted with ecocentrism, the view that the environment is what is central or important, not human beings. See homocentrism.

Biotic   relating to life.

Cetaceans   aquatic mammals such as whales, dolphins, and porpoises.

Deontologists   those who hold a deontological ethical theory. Such a theory holds that the rightness or wrongness of an act is determined by something other than its consequences, for example, by God's commands. Contrasted with teleological ethical theories, including utilitarianism, which hold that the rightness or wrongness of an act is determined by its consequences.

Ecology   the science which deals with the interrelationships of organisms and their environments.

Ecosystem   a community of living things considered together with the nonliving factors of its environment as a unit.

Homocentrism (Homocentric)   the view that only humans have moral standing and that nonhuman animals and the environment have no moral standing.

Leitmotif a marked melodic phrase or figure in Wagnerian music expressive of a certain idea, person, or situation.

Intrinsic value something has intrinsic value or goodness if it is good in itself apart from its use or consequences. By contrast, something has instrumental value if it is good as a means of getting something else. The theory that only pleasure is intrinsically good, and only pain intrinsically bad, is called hedonism. Bentham and his follower Singer are thus hedonists, as well as being utilitarians.

Molluscs invertebrate animals including snails, mussels, octopuses, and related life forms.

Nodes knobs, protuberances.

Ontology the study of being or existence.

Os sacrum the last bone of the spine.

Paradigm an ideal or standard example.

Sentience the capacity to be conscious.

Speciesism a bias or prejudice against members of other species.

Symbiotic relating to symbiosis, the intimate living together of dissimilar organisms.

Villosity of the skin the amount of hair on the skin.

Chapter 9

Nuclear War and Deterrence

Introduction

WAR SCENARIOS

Discussions of nuclear war often include scenarios, possible ways in which nuclear weapons might be used. Of course these are hypothetical, but they could become actual very quickly with present-day missiles.

There are two main scenarios: **MAD** (mutual assured destruction) and limited or tactical war. The MAD scenario dates back to the Eisenhower-Dulles era, and it remains dominant in nonmilitary thought. This plan calls for massive first strikes (called preemptive first strikes) and massive retaliations against civilian populations. There might be more flexible responses against lesser strikes, but these are very likely to escalate into massive strikes; there would be no way to limit the exchange. Such an exchange, in which both sides use thousands of nuclear warheads (the United States and Soviet Union together have about 50,000 nuclear warheads with more being built every day) would involve enormous losses on both sides. Neither side could really be said to "win" such a war. Although it is believed that no rational leader or group would intentionally start such a war, there is still the possibility of threatening such an attack for political or military gain. For example, when President Kennedy ordered a naval blockade of Cuba in 1962 in order to halt the Soviet deployment of intermediate range missiles, he was tacitly threatening to use nuclear weapons if the Soviets did not withdraw.

Current military thinking places more emphasis on the limited use of nuclear weapons to counter setbacks in conventional military battles, and thereby

379

win the conflict. A possible conflict that is often discussed, and is being carefully planned for on both sides, is a Soviet invasion of West Germany. The Soviets have forty-seven divisions at full strength stationed within quick striking distance of the West German frontier. These troops might be committed to a sneak attack, a blitzkrieg, on West Germany. Led by tanks, the troops could quickly cross the border and overrun the surprised NATO forces. With their conventional forces overrun, the NATO leaders would be left with only one option besides surrender, and that is to use nuclear weapons. Even if the U.S. missiles are eliminated from Europe, the NATO forces still have some 4,000 nuclear weapons that could be used to respond to a Soviet attack, ranging from battlefield missiles to gravity bombs.

THE FIRST–USE POLICY

The current policy of the NATO Alliance is to initiate the use of nuclear weapons, if necessary, to turn back a conventional Soviet attack against Western Europe. Nuclear weapons are viewed as a way of balancing numerically superior Warsaw Pact ground forces.

But this policy has dangers. What would the Soviets do if the NATO forces began the use of nuclear weapons? Even if they eliminate their intermediate-range missiles, the Soviets still have various nuclear weapons including about 1,000 battlefield ballistic missiles, and they could be used to respond to NATO's first use of nuclear weapons. If the Soviets did respond with nuclear weapons, they could easily devastate Europe even if they hit only military targets.

To prevent the Soviets from using their missiles, or to retaliate against them for their attack on West Germany, the United States might launch a preemptive strike using their accurate land-based missiles. The United States has about 1,000 ICBMs (inter-continental ballistic missiles) carrying about 2,000 warheads, and 100 more MX

missiles (which are first-strike weapons) are in the planning stages. A first strike against the Soviets would be risky, of course, for as soon as they had a warning of a United States missile launch, the Soviets would be tempted to launch their own ICBMs (they have about 1,400 ICBMs with around 6,000 warheads). As the military strategists say, the Soviets would have to "use 'em or lose 'em." No doubt they would choose to use their weapons in a first-strike situation, and the result would be a nuclear holocaust.

THE EFFECTS OF NUCLEAR WAR

In his book, *The Fate of the Earth,* Jonathan Schell vividly describes the effects of an air burst of a one-megaton bomb—a bomb equal in explosive yield to a million tons of TNT. There is initial radiation, an electromagnetic pulse, a thermal pulse, a blast wave, initial radioactive fallout, and mass fires. The electromagnetic pulse would produce widespread damage to solid-state electrical circuits; this means, for one thing, that unshielded defense communications would be disrupted and electronic guidance systems on missiles would not work properly. Schell also describes some little-known global effects of nuclear bombs: delayed or worldwide radioactive fallout lasting millions of years, dust in the stratosphere cooling the earth's surface producing a nuclear winter, and destruction of the layer of ozone that shields the earth from ultraviolet radiation. He emphasizes that a nuclear holocaust in which ten thousand megatons are detonated would probably make life on earth impossible except in the ocean. The United States would become a "republic of insects and grass."

Moral Issues   Is nuclear war ever morally justified? In their pastoral letter, "The Challenge of Peace," the United States Catholic Bishops condemn any use of nuclear weapons, even in retaliation against attack. Their main reason for this condemnation is that nuclear war, whether offensive or defensive, limited or all-out, inevitably results in the massive killing of innocent noncombatants and "no Christian can rightfully carry out orders or policies deliberately aimed at killing noncombatants."

The Harvard Nuclear Study Group does not agree. They think that in some circumstances a nuclear war could be morally justified. If the war were limited, and the alternative was to submit to a "Hitler-type domination of the world in which tens of millions of innocent people would be exterminated without war," then in that case a nuclear war would be worth fighting.

But even if actual nuclear war is not morally justified, at least in most imaginable cases, there remains the difficult question about the morality of nuclear deterrence: Is it morally justifiable to threaten to use nuclear weapons? The bishops raise serious objections to the strategy of nuclear deterrence. It involves the morally objectionable intention to kill innocent people, and it continues the expensive arms race. Given these objections, one might think that the bishops would condemn a nuclear deterrence strategy as well as nuclear war. But various considerations lead them to a "strictly conditioned moral acceptance of nuclear deterrence." First, they agree with Pope John Paul II that deterrence is morally acceptable "as a step on the way toward progressive disarmament." Second, nuclear deterrence is morally acceptable if it does not violate two principles of the traditional Christian just-war theory, the **principle of discrimination** and the **principle of proportionality**. The principle of discrimination prohibits direct intentional attacks on noncombatants; attacks must discriminate between combatants and noncombatants. But note that the doctrine of double effect (which is assumed by the bishops) does allow innocent noncombatants to be killed as the

unintended and foreseen side effect of justified attacks. However, the good achieved by the attack must be proportionate to the evil resulting from the attack—this is the principle of proportionality. Some attacks that do not violate the principle of discrimination could violate the principle of proportionality: for example, a nuclear attack on a military target in a heavily populated area which causes massive civilan casualities would be morally disproportionate.

Like the bishops, George F. Kennan views nuclear war and deterrence from a Christian point of view, and he agrees with the bishops that any use of nuclear weapons is morally unacceptable because it would involve the killing of noncombatants. But unlike the Bishops, Kennan strongly condemns policies of nuclear deterrence that amount to holding innocent people hostage, and that threaten to end civilization. These considerations make him condemn the readiness to use nuclear weapons as nothing less than a blasphemy, "an indignity of monstrous dimensions."

Charles Krauthammer rejects the antinuclear view including the bishops' position of conditionally accepting nuclear deterrence while condemning the use of nuclear weapons. Keeping the weapons but vowing not to use them is "a sorry compromise, neither coherent nor convincing." It is not coherent because their entire argument undermines deterrence, rather than supports it. It is not convincing because their position turns nuclear deterrence into nuclear bluffing, and this is no deterrence at all. In order to work, Krauthammer insists, nuclear deterrence must involve the will and the intent to actually use the weapons, not an empty bluff.

The Harvard Nuclear Study Group also defends nuclear deterrence strategy. They argue that in deterrence the basic intention is not to do something evil. The threat to use nuclear weapons is intended to avoid both the horrible outcome of nuclear war and an aggressive first attack by the other side. Furthermore, not threatening to attack in retaliation would have the disastrous moral consequence of inciting the enemy to make a first strike, and thus it would make war more likely, rather than less likely.

Finally, the bishops make a number of specific proposals which are subject to debate: They recommend "progressive disarmament," a nuclear freeze agreement, bilateral cuts in weapons arsenals, a **comprehensive test ban treaty,** and a **"no first use"** policy. Charles Krauthammer rejects a nuclear freeze on the ground that a survivable nuclear force requires

continuing modernization. He is opposed to the "no first use" policy because it makes conventional war more thinkable and this in turn makes nuclear war more likely.

The Harvard Nuclear Study Group claims that disarmament is "inherently unstable," and not in the nation's best interests. Nevertheless they allow that some kind of arms control might contribute to three dimensions of stability: deterrence, arms-race stability, and crisis stability. Using these criteria, as well as negotiability and possible verification, they critically discuss a number of proposals including arms reductions, freezes, force restructuring, and stabilizing measures.

~~~

Jonathan Schell

The Effects of Nuclear Bombs

Jonathan Schell is a writer. His book The Fate of the Earth *originally appeared in* The New Yorker.

Schell describes the effects of an air burst of a one-megaton bomb (initial radiation, electromagnetic pulse, thermal pulse, blast wave, radioactive fallout, and destruction of the ozone layer), and he speculates about the effects of a nuclear holocaust on individual life, human society, and the earth as a whole.

Whereas most conventional bombs produce only one destructive effect—the shock wave—nuclear weapons produce many destructive effects. At the moment of the explosion, when the temperature of the weapon

material instantly gasified, is at the superstellar level, the pressure is millions of times the normal atmospheric pressure. Immediately, radiation, consisting mainly of gamma rays, which are a very high-energy form of electromagnetic radiation, begins to stream outward into the environment. This is called the "initial nuclear radiation," and is the first of the destructive effects of a nuclear explosion. In an air burst of a one-megaton bomb—a bomb with the explosive yield of a million tons of TNT, which is a medium-sized weapon in present-day nuclear arsenals—the initial nuclear radiation can kill unprotected human beings in an area of some six square miles. Virtually simultaneously with the initial nuclear radiation, in a second destructive effect of the explosion, an electromagnetic pulse is generated by the intense gamma radiation acting on the air. In a high-altitude detonation, the pulse can knock out electrical equipment over a wide area by inducing a powerful surge of voltage through various conductors, such as antennas, overhead power lines, pipes, and railroad tracks. The Defense Department's Civil Preparedness Agency reported in 1977 that a single multi-kiloton nu-

From *The Fate of the Earth,* by Jonathan Schell. Copyright © 1982 by Jonathan Schell. Reprinted by permission of Alfred A. Knopf, Inc. Originally appeared in *The New Yorker.*

clear weapon detonated one hundred and twenty-five miles over Omaha, Nebraska, could generate an electromagnetic pulse strong enough to damage solid-state electrical circuits throughout the entire continental United States and in parts of Canada and Mexico, and thus threaten to bring the economies of these countries to a halt. When the fusion and fission reactions have blown themselves out, a fireball takes shape. As it expands, energy is absorbed in the form of X-rays by the surrounding air, and then the air re-radiates a portion of that energy into the environment in the form of the thermal pulse—a wave of blinding light and intense heat—which is the third of the destructive effects of a nuclear explosion. (If the burst is low enough, the fireball touches the ground, vaporizing or incinerating almost everything within it.) The thermal pulse of a one-megaton bomb lasts for about ten seconds and can cause second-degree burns in exposed human beings at a distance of nine and a half miles, or in an area of more than two hundred and eighty square miles, and that of a twenty-megaton bomb (a large weapon by modern standards) lasts for about twenty seconds and can produce the same consequences at a distance of twenty-eight miles, or in an area of 2,460 square miles. As the fireball expands, it also sends out a blast wave in all directions, and this is the fourth destructive effect of the explosion. The blast wave of an air-burst one-megaton bomb can flatten or severely damage all but the strongest buildings within a radius of four and a half miles, and that of a twenty-megaton bomb can do the same within a radius of twelve miles. As the fireball burns, it rises, condensing water from the surrounding atmosphere to form the characteristic mushroom cloud. If the bomb has been set off on the ground or close enough to it so that the fireball touches the surface, in a so-called ground burst, a crater will be formed, and tons of dust and debris will be fused with the intensely radioactive fission products and sucked up into the mushroom cloud. This mixture will return to earth as radioactive fallout, most of it in the form of fine ash, in the fifth destructive effect of the explosion. Depending upon the composition of the surface, from forty to seventy percent of this fallout—often called the "early" or "local" fallout—descends to earth within about a day of the explosion, in the vicinity of the blast and downwind from it, exposing human beings to radiation disease, an illness that is fatal when exposure is intense. Air bursts may also produce local fallout, but in much smaller quantities. The lethal range of the local fallout depends on a number of circumstances, including the weather, but under average conditions a one-megaton ground burst would, according to the report by the Office of Technology Assessment, lethally contaminate over a thousand square miles. (A lethal dose, by convention, is considered to be the amount of radiation that, if delivered over a short period of time, would kill half the able-bodied young adult population.)

The initial nuclear radiation, the electromagnetic pulse, the thermal pulse, the blast wave, and the local fallout may be described as the local primary effects of nuclear weapons. Naturally, when many bombs are exploded the scope of these effects is increased accordingly. But in addition these primary effects produce innumerable secondary effects on societies and natural environments, some of which may be even more harmful than the primary ones. To give just one example, nuclear weapons, by flattening and setting fire to huge, heavily built-up areas, generate mass fires, and in some cases these may kill more people than the original thermal pulses and blast waves. Moreover, there are—quite distinct from both the local primary effects of individual bombs and their secondary effects—global primary effects, which do not become significant unless thousands of bombs are detonated all around the earth. And these global primary effects produce innumerable secondary effects of their own throughout the ecosystem of the earth as a whole. For a full-scale holocaust is more than the sum of its local parts; it is also a powerful direct blow to the **ecosphere.** In that sense, a holocaust is to the earth what a single bomb is to a city. Three grave direct global effects have been discovered so far. The first is the "delayed," or "worldwide," fallout. In detonations greater than one hundred kilotons, part of the fallout does not fall to the ground in the vicinity of the explosion, but rises high into the troposphere and into the stratosphere, circulates around the earth, and then, over months or years, descends, contaminating the whole surface of the globe—although with doses of radiation far weaker than those delivered by the local fallout. Nuclear-fission products comprise some three hundred radioactive isotopes, and though some of them decay to relatively harmless levels of radioactivity within a few hours, minutes, or even seconds, others persist to emit radiation for up to millions of years. The short-lived isotopes are the ones most responsible for the lethal effects of the local fallout, and the long-lived ones are responsible for the contamination of the earth by stratospheric fallout. The energy released by all fallout from a thermonuclear explosion is about five percent of the total. By convention, this energy is not calculated in the stated yield of a weapon, yet in a ten-thousand-megaton attack the equivalent of five hundred megatons of explosive energy, or forty thousand times the yield of the Hiroshima bomb, would be released in the form of radioactivity. This release may be considered a protracted afterburst, which is dispersed into the land, air, and sea, and into the tissues, bones, roots, stems, and leaves of living things, and goes on detonating there almost indefinitely after the explosion. The second of the global effects that have been discovered so far is the lofting, from ground bursts, of millions of tons of dust into the stratosphere; this is likely to produce general cooling of the earth's surface. The third of the global effects is a predicted partial destruction of the layer of ozone that surrounds the entire earth in the stratosphere. A nuclear fireball, by burning

nitrogen in the air, produces large quantities of oxides of nitrogen. These are carried by the heat of the blast into the stratosphere, where, through a series of chemical reactions, they bring about a depletion of the ozone layer. Such a depletion may persist for years. The 1975 N.A.S. report has estimated that in a holocaust in which ten thousand megatons were detonated in the Northern Hemisphere the reduction of ozone in this hemisphere could be as high as seventy percent and in the Southern Hemisphere as high as forty percent, and that it could take as long as thirty years for the ozone level to return to normal. The ozone layer is crucial to life on earth, because it shields the surface of the earth from lethal levels of ultraviolet radiation, which is present in sunlight. Glasstone remarks simply, "If it were not for the absorption of much of the solar ultraviolet radiation by the ozone, life as currently known could not exist except possibly in the ocean." Without the ozone shield, sunlight, the life-giver, would become a life-extinguisher. In judging the global effects of a holocaust, therefore, the primary question is not how many people would be irradiated, burned or crushed to death by the immediate effects of the bombs but how well the ecosphere, regarded as a single living entity, on which all forms of life depend for their continued existence, would hold up. The issue is the habitability of the earth, and it is in this context, not in the context of the direct slaughter of hundreds of millions of people by the local effects, that the question of human survival arises.

Usually, people wait for things to occur before trying to describe them. (Futurology has never been a very respectable field of inquiry.) But since we cannot afford under any circumstances to let a holocaust occur, we are forced in this one case to become the historians of the future—to chronicle and commit to memory an event that we have never experienced and must never experience. This unique endeavor, in which foresight is asked to perform a task usually reserved for hindsight, raises a host of special difficulties. There is a categorical difference, often overlooked, between trying to describe an event that has already happened (whether it is Napoleon's invasion of Russia or the pollution of the environment by acid rain) and trying to describe one that has yet to happen—and one, in addition, for which there is no precedent, or even near-precedent, in history. Lacking experience to guide our thoughts and impress itself on our feelings, we resort to speculation. But speculation, however brilliantly it may be carried out, is at best only a poor substitute for experience. Experience gives us facts, whereas in pure speculation we are thrown back on theory, which has never been a very reliable guide to future events. Moreover, experience engraves its lessons in our hearts through suffering and the other consequences that it has for our lives; but speculation leaves our lives untouched, and so gives us leeway to reject its conclusions, no matter how well argued they may be. (In the world of strategic theory, in particular, where strategists labor to simulate actual situations on the far side of the nuclear abyss, so that generals and statemen can prepare to make their decisions in case the worst happens, there is sometimes an unfortunate tendency to mistake pure ratiocination for reality, and to pretend to a knowledge of the future that it is not given to human beings to have.) Our knowledge of the local primary effects of the bombs, which is based both on the physical principles that made their construction possible and on experience gathered from the bombings of Hiroshima and Nagasaki and from testing, is quite solid. And our knowledge of the extent of the local primary effects of many weapons used together, which is obtained simply by using the multiplication table, is also solid: knowing that the thermal pulse of a twenty-megaton bomb can give people at least second-degree burns in an area of 2,460 square miles, we can easily figure out that the pulses of a hundred twenty-megaton bombs can give people at least second-degree burns in an area of 246,000 square miles. Nevertheless, it may be that our knowledge even of the primary effects is still incomplete, for during our test program new ones kept being discovered. One example is the electromagnetic pulse, whose importance was not recognized until around 1960, when, after more than a decade of tests, scientists realized that this effect accounted for unexpected electrical failures that had been occurring all along in equipment around the test sites. And it is only in recent years that the Defense Department has been trying to take account strategically of this startling capacity of just one bomb to put the technical equipment of a whole continent out of action.

When we proceed from the local effects of single explosions to the effects of thousands of them on societies and environments, the picture clouds considerably, because then we go beyond both the certainties of physics and our slender base of experience, and speculatively encounter the full complexity of human affairs and of the biosphere. Looked at in its entirety, a nuclear holocaust can be said to assail human life at three levels: the level of individual life, the level of human society, and the level of the natural environment—including the environment of the earth as a whole. At none of these levels can the destructiveness of nuclear weapons be measured in terms of firepower alone. At each level, life has both considerable recuperative powers, which might restore it even after devastating injury, and points of exceptional vulnerability, which leave it open to sudden, wholesale, and permanent collapse, even when comparatively little violence has been applied. Just as a machine may break down if one small part is removed, and a person may die if a single artery or vein is blocked, a modern technological society may come to a standstill if its fuel supply is cut off, and an ecosystem may collapse if its ozone shield is depleted. Nuclear weapons thus do not only kill directly, with their tremendous violence, but also kill indirectly, by breaking down the man-made and the natural systems on which individual lives collectively depend. Human beings require constant provision and care, supplied both by their societies and by the natural environment, and if these are suddenly removed people will die just as surely as if they had been struck by a bullet. Nuclear weapons are unique in that they attack the support systems of life at every level. And these systems, of course, are not isolated from each other but are parts of a single whole: ecological collapse, if it goes far enough, will bring about social collapse, and social collapse will bring about individual deaths. Furthermore, the destructive consequences of a nuclear attack are immeasurably compounded by the likelihood that all or most of the bombs will be detonated within the space of a few hours, in a single huge concussion. Normally, a locality devastated by a catastrophe, whether natural or man-made, will sooner or later receive help from untouched outside areas, as Hiroshima and Nagasaki did after they were bombed; but a nuclear holocaust would devastate the "outside" areas as well, leaving the victims to fend for themselves in a shattered society and natural environment. And what is true for each city is also true for the earth as a whole: a devastated earth can hardly expect "outside" help. The earth is the largest of the support systems for life, and the impairment of the earth is the largest of the perils posed by nuclear weapons.

The incredible complexity of all these effects, acting, interacting, and interacting again, precludes confident detailed representation of the events in a holocaust. We deal inevitably with approximations, probabilities, even guesses. However, it is important to point out that our uncertainty pertains not to *whether* the effects will interact, multiplying their destructive power as they do so, but only to *how*. It follows that our almost built-in bias, determined by the limitations of the human mind in judging future events, is to underestimate the harm. To fear interactive consequences that we cannot predict, or even imagine, may not be impossible, but it is very difficult. Let us consider, for example, some

of the possible ways in which a person in a targeted country might die. He might be incinerated by the fireball or the thermal pulse. He might be lethally irradiated by the initial nuclear radiation. He might be crushed to death or hurled to his death by the blast wave or its debris. He might be lethally irradiated by the local fallout. He might be burned to death in a firestorm. He might be injured by one or another of these effects and then die of his wounds before he was able to make his way out of the devastated zone in which he found himself. He might die of starvation, because the economy had collapsed and no food was being grown or delivered, or because existing local crops had been killed by radiation, or because the local ecosystem had been ruined, or because the ecosphere of the earth as a whole was collapsing. He might die of cold, for lack of heat and clothing, or of exposure, for lack of shelter. He might be killed by people seeking food or shelter that he had obtained. He might die of an illness spread in an epidemic. He might be killed by exposure to the sun if he stayed outside too long following serious ozone depletion. Or he might be killed by any combination of these perils. But while there is almost no end to the ways to die in and after a holocaust, each person has only one life to lose; someone who has been killed by the thermal pulse can't be killed again in an epidemic. Therefore, anyone who wishes to describe a holocaust is always at risk of depicting scenes of devastation that in reality would never take place, because the people in them would already have been killed off in some earlier scene of devastation. The task is made all the more confusing by the fact that causes of death and destruction do not exist side by side in the world but often encompass one another, in widening rings. Thus, if it turned out that a holocaust rendered the earth uninhabitable by human beings, then all the more immediate forms of death would be nothing more than redundant preliminaries, leading up to the extinction of the whole species by a hostile environment. Or if a continental ecosystem was so thoroughly destroyed by a direct attack that it could no longer sustain a significant human population, the more immediate causes of death would again decline in importance. In much the same way, if an airplane is hit by gunfire, and thereby caused to crash, dooming all the passengers, it makes little difference whether the shots also killed a few of the passengers in advance of the crash. On the other hand, if the larger consequences, which are less predictable than the local ones, failed to occur, then the local ones would have their full importance again.

Faced with uncertainties of this kind, some analysts of nuclear destruction have resorted to fiction, assigning to the imagination the work that investigation is unable to do. But then the results are just what one would expect: fiction. An approach more appropriate to our intellectual circumstances would be to acknowledge a high degree of uncertainty as an intrinsic and extremely important part of dealing with a possible holocaust. A nuclear holocaust is an event that is obscure because it is future, and uncertainty, while it has to be recognized in all calculations of future events, has a special place in calculations of a nuclear holocaust, because a holocaust is something that we aspire to keep in the future forever, and never to permit into the present. You might say that uncertainty, like the thermal pulses or the blast waves, is one of the features of a holocaust. Our procedure, then, should be not to insist on a precision that is beyond our grasp, but to inquire into the rough probabilities of various results insofar as we can judge them, and then to ask ourselves what our political responsibilities are in the light of these probabilities. This embrace of investigative modesty—this acceptance of our limited ability to predict the consequences of a holocaust—would itself be a token of our reluctance to extinguish ourselves.

There are two further aspects of a holocaust that, though they do not further obscure the factual picture, nevertheless vex our understanding of this event. The first is that although in imagination we can try to survey the whole prospective scene of destruction, inquiring into how many would live and how many would die and how far the collapse of the environment would go under attacks of different sizes, and piling up statistics on how many square miles would be lethally contaminated, or what percentage of the population would receive first-, second-, or third-degree burns, or be trapped in the rubble of its burning houses, or be irradiated to death, no one actually experiencing a holocaust would have any such overview. The news of other parts necessary to put together that picture would be one of the things that were immediately lost, and each surviving person, his vision drastically foreshortened by the collapse of his world, and his impressions clouded by his pain, shock, bewilderment, and grief, would see only as far as whatever scene of chaos and agony happened to lie at hand. For it would not be only such abstractions as "industry" and "society" and "the environment" that would be destroyed in a nuclear holocaust; it would also be, over and over again, the small collections of cherished things, known landscapes, and beloved people that made up the immediate contents of individual lives.

The other obstacle to our understanding is that when we strain to picture what the scene would be like after a holocaust we tend to forget that for most people, and perhaps for all, it wouldn't be *like* anything, because they would be dead. To depict the scene as it would appear to the living is to that extent a falsification, and the greater the number killed, the greater the falsification. The right vantage point from which to view a holocaust is that of a corpse, but from that vantage point, of course, there is nothing to report.

Review Questions

1. Describe the effects of an air burst of a one-megaton bomb.

2. What would happen in a nuclear holocaust?

1. Can you think of any circumstances in which a nuclear holocaust would be morally justified?

2. The United States presently has about 9,000 H-bombs with more being made every day, and about 20,000 smaller A-bombs like the one dropped on Hiroshima. The Soviet Union has about 240 medium-sized cities and perhaps a few hundred military targets such as air bases and missile sites. Why do we need so many bombs? Why are we building more and more?

The National Conference of Catholic Bishops

The Challenge of Peace

Following a general meeting of the United States Bishops in November, 1980, a committee of bishops was appointed to draft a pastoral letter on war and peace. The third draft of the pastoral letter was approved by the body of bishops during the plenary assembly in Chicago on May 3, 1983.

The bishops condemn any use of nuclear weapons, even in retaliation. Their reason for this condemnation is that nuclear war in any form kills innocent noncombatants and this is always morally wrong. The bishops also evaluate current strategies of deterrence, and make specific recommendations for arms control.

THE USE OF NUCLEAR WEAPONS

Establishing moral guidelines in the nuclear debate means addressing first the question of the use of nuclear weapons. That question has several dimensions.

It is clear that those in the Church who interpret the gospel teaching as forbidding all use of violence would oppose any use of nuclear weapons under any conditions. In a sense the existence of these weapons simply confirms and reinforces one of the initial insights of the nonviolent position, namely, that Christians should not use lethal force since the hope of using it selectively and restrictively is so often an illusion. Nuclear weapons seem to prove this point in a way heretofore unknown.

For the tradition which acknowledges some legitimate use of force, some important elements of contemporary nuclear strategies move beyond the limits of moral justification. A justifiable use of force must be both discriminatory and proportionate. Certain aspects of both U.S. and Soviet strategies fail both tests as we shall discuss below. The technical literature and the personal testimony of public officials who have been closely associated with U.S. nuclear strategy have both convinced us of the overwhelming probability that major nuclear exchange would have no limits.[1]

On the more complicated issue of "limited" nuclear war, we are aware of the extensive literature and discussion which this topic has generated.[2] As a general statement, it seems to us that public officials would be unable to refute the following conclusion of the study made by the Pontifical Academy of Sciences:

Even a nuclear attack directed only at military facilities would be devastating to the country as a whole. This is because military facilities are widespread rather than concentrated at only a few points. Thus, many nuclear weapons would be exploded.

Furthermore, the spread of radiation due to the natural winds and atmospheric mixing would kill vast numbers of people and contaminate large areas. The *medical facilities of any nation would be inadequate to care for the survivors. An objective examination of the medical situation that would follow a nuclear war leads to but one conclusion: prevention is our only recourse.*[3]

Moral Principles and Policy Choices

In light of these perspectives we address three questions more explicitly: (1) counter population warfare; (2) initiation of nuclear war; and (3) limited nuclear war.

Counter Population Warfare Under no circumstances may nuclear weapons or other instruments of mass slaughter be used for the purpose of destroying population centers or other predominantly civilian targets. Popes have repeatedly condemned "total war" which implies such use. For example, as early as 1954 Pope Pius XII condemned nuclear warfare "when it entirely escapes the control of man," and results in "the pure and simple annihilation of all human life within the radius of action."[4] The condemnation was repeated by the Second Vatican Council:

Any act of war aimed indiscriminately at the destruction of entire cities or of extensive areas along with their population is a crime against God and man itself. It merits unequivocal and unhesitating condemnation.[5]

Retaliatory action whether nuclear or conventional which would indiscriminately take many wholly innocent lives, lives of people who are in no way responsible for reckless actions of their government, must also be condemned. This condemnation, in our judgment, applies even to the retaliatory use of weapons striking enemy cities after our own have already been struck. No Christian can rightfully carry out orders or policies deliberately aimed at killing noncombatants.[6]

We make this judgment at the beginning of our treatment of nuclear strategy precisely because the defense of the principle of noncombatant immunity is so important for an ethic of war and because the nuclear age has posed such extreme problems for the princi-

ple. Later in this letter we shall discuss specific aspects of U.S. policy in light of this principle and in light of recent U.S. policy statements stressing the determination not to target directly or strike directly against civilian populations. Our concern about protecting the moral value of noncombatant immunity, however, requires that we make a clear reassertion of the principle our first word on this matter.

The Initiation of Nuclear War We do not perceive any situation in which the deliberate initiation of nuclear warfare, on however restricted a scale, can be morally justified. Non-nuclear attacks by another state must be resisted by other than nuclear means. Therefore, a serious moral obligation exists to develop non-nuclear defensive strategies as rapidly as possible.

A serious debate is under way on this issue.[7] It is cast in political terms, but it has a significant moral dimension. Some have argued that at the very beginning of a war nuclear weapons might be used, only against military targets, perhaps in limited numbers. Indeed it has long been American and NATO policy that nuclear weapons, especially so-called tactical nuclear weapons, would likely be used if NATO forces in Europe seemed in danger of losing a conflict that until then had been restricted to conventional weapons. Large numbers of tactical nuclear weapons are now deployed in Europe by the NATO forces and about as many by the Soviet Union. Some are substantially smaller than the bomb used on Hiroshima, some are larger. Such weapons, if employed in great numbers, would totally devastate the densely populated countries of Western and Central Europe.

Whether under conditions of war in Europe, parts of Asia or the Middle East, or the exchange of strategic weapons directly between the United States and the Soviet Union, the difficulties of limiting the use of nuclear weapons are immense. A number of expert witnesses advise us that commanders

operating under conditions of battle probably would not be able to exercise strict control; the number of weapons used would rapidly increase, the targets would be expanded
beyond the military, and the level of civilian
casualties would rise enormously.[8] No one
can be certain that this escalation would not
occur, even in the face of political efforts to
keep such an exchange "limited." The
chances of keeping use limited seem remote,
and the consequences of escalation to mass
destruction would be appalling. Former public officials have testified that it is improbable
that any nuclear war could actually be kept
limited. Their testimony and the consequences involved in this problem lead us to
conclude that the danger of escalation is so
great that it would be morally unjustifiable to
initiate nuclear war in any form. The danger
is rooted not only in the technology of our
weapons systems but in the weakness and sin-
fulness of human communities. We find the
moral responsibility of beginning nuclear war
not justified by rational political objectives.

This judgment affirms that the willingness
to initiate nuclear war entails a distinct,
weighty moral responsibility; it involves
transgressing a fragile barrier—political, psychological, and moral—which has been constructed since 1945. We express repeatedly
in this letter our extreme skepticism about
the prospects for controlling a nuclear exchange, however limited the first use might
be. Precisely because of this skepticism, we
judge resort to nuclear weapons to counter a
conventional attack to be morally unjustifiable.[9] Consequently we seek to reinforce the
barrier against any use of nuclear weapons.
Our support of a "no first use" policy must
be seen in this light.

At the same time we recognize the responsibility the United States has had and
continues to have in assisting allied nations in
their defense against either a conventional or
a nuclear attack. Especially in the European
theater, the deterrence of a *nuclear* attack may
require nuclear weapons for a time, even
though their possession and deployment

must be subject to rigid restrictions.

The need to defend against a conventional attack in Europe imposes the political and
moral burden of developing adequate, alternative modes of defense to present reliance
on nuclear weapons. Even with the best coor-
dinated effort—hardly likely in view of contemporary political division on this question—development of an alternative defense
position will still take time.

In the interim, deterrence against a conventional attack relies upon two factors: the
not inconsiderable conventional forces at the
disposal of NATO and the recognition by a
potential attacker that the outbreak of large-
scale conventional war could escalate to the
nuclear level through accident or miscalculation by either side. We are aware that
NATO's refusal to adopt a "no first use"
pledge is to some extent linked to the deterrent effect of this inherent ambiguity. Nonetheless, in light of the probable effects of initiating nuclear war, we urge NATO to move
rapidly toward the adoption of a "no first
use" policy, but doing so in tandem with development of an adequate alternative defense
posture.

Limited Nuclear War It would be possible
to agree with our first two conclusions and
still not be sure about retaliatory use of nuclear weapons in what is called a "limited
exchange." The issue at stake is the *real* as
opposed to the *theoretical* possibility of a
"limited nuclear exchange."

We recognize that the policy debate on
this question is inconclusive and that all participants are left with hypothetical projections
about probable reactions in a nuclear exchange. While not trying to adjudicate the
technical debate, we are aware of it and wish
to raise a series of questions which challenge
the actual meaning of "limited" in this discussion.

— Would leaders have sufficient
information to know what is happening in a
nuclear exchange?

— Would they be able under the conditions of stress, time pressures, and fragmentary information to make the extraordinarily precise decision needed to keep the exchange limited if this were technically possible?

— Would military commanders be able, in the midst of the destruction and confusion of a nuclear exchange, to maintain a policy of "discriminate targeting"? Can this be done in modern warfare, waged across great distances by aircraft and missiles?

— Given the accidents we know about in peacetime conditions, what assurances are there that computer errors could be avoided in the midst of a nuclear exchange?

— Would not the casualties, even in a war defined as limited by strategists, still run in the millions?

— How "limited" would be the long-term effects of radiation, famine, social fragmentation, and economic dislocation?

Unless these questions can be answered satisfactorily, we will continue to be highly skeptical about the real meaning of "limited." One of the criteria of the just-war tradition is a reasonable hope of success in bringing about justice and peace. We must ask whether such a reasonable hope can exist once nuclear weapons have been exchanged. The burden of proof remains on those who assert that meaningful limitation is possible.

A nuclear response to either conventional or nuclear attack can cause destruction which goes far beyond "legitimate defense." Such use of nuclear weapons would not be justified.

In the face of this frightening and highly speculative debate on a matter involving millions of human lives, we believe the most effective contribution or moral judgment is to introduce perspectives by which we can assess the empirical debate. Moral perspective should be sensitive not only to the quantitative dimensions of a question but to its psychological, human, and religious characteristics as well. The issue of limited war is not simply the size of weapons contemplated or the strategies projected. The debate should include the psychological and political significance of crossing the boundary from the conventional to the nuclear arena in any form. To cross this divide is to enter a world where we have no experience of control, much testimony against its possibility, and therefore no moral justification for submitting the human community to this risk.[10] We therefore express our view that the first imperative is to prevent any use of nuclear weapons and our hope that leaders will resist the notion that nuclear conflict can be limited, contained, or won in any traditional sense.

Deterrence In Principle and Practice

The moral challenge posed by nuclear weapons is not exhausted by an analysis of their possible uses. Much of the political and moral debate of the nuclear age has concerned the strategy of deterrence. Deterrence is at the heart of the U.S.–Soviet relationship, currently the most dangerous dimension of the nuclear arms race.

The Concept and Development of Deterrence Policy The concept of deterrence existed in military strategy long before the nuclear age, but it has taken on a new meaning and significance since 1945. Essentially, deterrence means "dissuasion of a potential adversary from initiating an attack or conflict, often by the threat of unacceptable retaliatory damage." [11] In the nuclear age, deterrence has become the centerpiece of both U.S. and Soviet policy. Both superpowers have for many years now been able to promise a retaliatory response which can inflict "unacceptable damage." A situation of stable deterrence depends on the ability of each side to deploy its retaliatory forces in ways that are not vulnerable to an attack (i.e., protected against a "first strike"); preserving stability requires a willingness by both sides to refrain from deploying weapons which appear to have a first-strike capability.

This general definition of deterrence does not explain either the elements of a deterrence strategy or the evolution of deterrence policy since 1945. A detailed description of either of these subjects would require an extensive essay, using materials which can be found in abundance in the technical literature on the subject of deterrence.[12] Particularly significant is the relationship between "declaratory policy" (the public explanation of our strategic intentions and capabilities) and "action policy" (the actual planning and targeting policies to be followed in a nuclear attack).

The evolution of deterrence strategy has passed through several stages of declaratory policy. Using the U.S. case as an example, there is a significant difference between "massive retaliation" and "**flexible response,**" and between "mutual assured destruction" and "countervailing strategy." It is also possible to distinguish between "**counterforce**" and "**countervalue**" targeting policies; and to contrast a posture of "minimum deterrence" with "**extended deterrence.**" These terms are well known in the technical debate on nuclear policy; they are less well known and sometimes loosely used in the wider public debate. It is important to recognize that there has been substantial continuity in U.S. action policy in spite of real changes in declaratory policy.[13]

The recognition of these different elements in the deterrent and the evolution of policy means that moral assessment of deterrence requires a series of distinct judgments. They include: an analysis of the *factual character* of the deterrent (e.g., what is involved in targeting doctrine); analysis of the *historical development* of the policy (e.g., whether changes have occurred which are significant for moral analysis of the policy); the relationship of deterrence policy and other aspects of *U.S.–Soviet affairs;* and determination of the key *moral questions* involved in deterrence policy.

The Moral Assessment of Deterrence The

distinctively new dimensions of nuclear deterrence were recognized by policymakers and strategists only after much reflection. Similarly, the moral challenge posed by nuclear deterrence was grasped only after careful deliberation. The moral and political paradox posed by deterrence was concisely stated by Vatican II:

Undoubtedly, armaments are not amassed merely for use in wartime. Since the defensive strength of any nation is thought to depend on its capacity for immediate retaliation, the stockpiling of arms which grows from year to year serves, in a way hitherto unthought of, as a deterrent to potential attackers. Many people look upon this as the most effective way known at the present time for maintaining some sort of peace among nations. Whatever one may think of this form of deterrent, people are convinced that the arms race, which quite a few countries have entered, is no infallible way of maintaining real peace and that the resulting so-called balance of power is no sure genuine path to achieving it. Rather than eliminate the causes of war, the arms race serves only to aggravate the position. As long as extravagant sums of money are poured into the development of new weapons, it is impossible to devote adequate aid in tackling the misery which prevails at the present day in the world. Instead of eradicating international conflict once and for all, the contagion is spreading to other parts of the world. New approaches, based on reformed attitudes, will have to be chosen in order to remove this stumbling block, to free the earth from its pressing anxieties, and give back to the world a genuine peace.[14]

Without making a specific moral judgment on deterrence, the council clearly designated the elements of the arms race: the tension between "peace of a sort" preserved by deterrence and "genuine peace" required for a stable international life; the contradiction between what is spent for destructive capacity and what is needed for constructive development.

In the post-conciliar assessment of war and peace, and specifically of deterrence, different parties to the political-moral debate within the Church and in civil society have focused on one aspect or another of the problem. For some, the fact that nuclear weapons have not been used since 1945 means that deterrence has worked, and this fact satisfies the demands of both the political and the moral order. Others contest this assessment by highlighting the risk of failure involved in continued reliance on deterrence and pointing out how politically and morally catastrophic even a single failure would be. Still others note that the absence of nuclear war is not necessarily proof that the policy of deterrence has prevented it. Indeed, some would find in the policy of deterrence the driving force in the superpower arms race. Still other observers, many of them Catholic moralists, have stressed that deterrence may not morally include the intention of deliberately attacking civilian populations or noncombatants.

The statements of the NCCB/USCC over the past several years have both reflected and contributed to the wider moral debate on deterrence. In the NCCB pastoral letter, *To Live In Christ Jesus* (1976), we focused on the moral limits of declaratory policy while calling for stronger measures of arms control.[15] In 1979 John Cardinal Krol, speaking for the USCC in support of **SALT II** ratification, brought into focus the other element of the deterrence problem: the actual use of nuclear weapons may have been prevented (a moral good), but the risk of failure and the physical harm and moral evil resulting from possible nuclear war remained. "This explains," Cardinal Krol stated, "the Catholic dissatisfaction with nuclear deterrence and the urgency of the Catholic demand that the nuclear arms race be reversed. It is of the utmost importance that negotiations proceed to meaningful and continuing reductions in nuclear stockpiles, and eventually to the phasing out altogether of nuclear deterrence and the threat of mutual-assured destruction."[16]

These two texts, along with the conciliar statement, have influenced much of Catholic opinion expressed recently on the nuclear question.

In June 1982, Pope John Paul II provided new impetus and insight to the moral analysis with his statement to the United Nations Second Special Session on Disarmament. The pope first situated the problem of deterrence within the context of world politics. No power, he observes, will admit to wishing to start a war, but each distrusts others and considers it necessary to mount a strong defense against attack. He then discusses the notion of deterrence:

*Many even think that such preparations constitute the way—even the only way—to safeguard peace in some fashion or at least to impede to the utmost in an efficacious way the outbreak of wars, especially major conflicts which might lead to the ultimate holocaust of humanity and the destruction of the civilization that man has constructed so laboriously over the centuries. In this approach one can see the "philosophy of peace" which was proclaimed in the ancient Roman principle: **Si vis pacem, para bellum.** Put in modern terms; this "philosophy" has the label of "deterrence" and one can find it in various guises of the search for a "balance of forces" which sometimes has been called, and not without reason, the "balance of terror."* [17]

Having offered this analysis of the general concept of deterrence, the Holy Father introduces his considerations on disarmament, especially, but not only, nuclear disarmament. Pope John Paul II makes this statement about the morality of deterrence:

In current conditions "deterrence" based on balance, certainly not as an end in itself but as a step on the way toward a progressive disarmament, may still be judged morally acceptable. Nonetheless in order to ensure peace, it is indispensable not to be satisfied with this minimum which is always susceptible to the real danger of explosion. [18]

In Pope John Paul II's assessment we perceive two dimensions of the contemporary dilemma of deterrence. One dimension is the danger of nuclear war, with its human and moral costs. The possession of nuclear weapons, the continuing quantitative growth of the arms race, and the danger of nuclear proliferation all point to the grave danger of basing "peace of a sort" on deterrence. The other dimension is the independence and freedom of nations and entire peoples, including the need to protect smaller nations from threats to their independence and integrity. Deterrence reflects the radical distrust which marks international politics, a condition identified as a major problem by Pope John XXIII in *Peace on Earth* and reaffirmed by Pope Paul VI and Pope John Paul II. Thus a balance of forces, preventing either side from achieving superiority, can be seen as a means of safeguarding both dimensions.

The moral duty today is to prevent nuclear war from ever occurring *and* to protect and preserve those key values of justice, freedom, and independence which are necessary for personal dignity and national integrity. In reference to these issues, Pope John Paul II judges that deterrence may still be judged morally acceptable, "certainly not as an end in itself but as a step on the way toward a progressive disarmament."

On more than one occasion the Holy Father has demonstrated his awareness of the fragility and complexity of the deterrence relationship among nations. Speaking to UNESCO in June 1980, he said:

Up to the present, we are told that nuclear arms are a force of dissuasion which have prevented the eruption of a major war. And that is probably true. Still, we must ask if it will always be this way.[19]

In a more recent and more specific assessment Pope John Paul II told an international meeting of scientists on August 23, 1982:

You can more easily ascertain that the logic of nuclear deterrence cannot be considered a final goal or an appropriate and secure means for safeguarding international peace.[20]

Relating Pope John Paul's general statements to the specific policies of the U.S. deterrent requires both judgments of fact and an application of moral principles. In preparing this letter we have tried, through a number of sources, to determine as precisely as possible the factual character of U.S. deter-

rence strategy. Two questions have particularly concerned us: (1) the targeting doctrine and strategic plans for the use of the deterrent, particularly their impact on civilian casualties; and (2) the relationship of deterrence strategy and nuclear war-fighting capability to the likelihood that war will in fact be prevented.

Moral Principles and Policy Choices

Targeting doctrine raises significant moral questions because it is a significant determinant of what would occur if nuclear weapons were ever to be used. Although we acknowledge the need for deterrent, not all forms of deterrence are morally acceptable. There are moral limits to deterrence policy as well as to policy regarding use. Specifically, it is not morally acceptable to intend to kill the innocent as part of a strategy of deterring nuclear war. The question of whether U.S. policy involves an intention to strike civilian centers (directly targeting civilian populations) has been one of our factual concerns.

This complex question has always produced a variety of responses, official and unofficial in character. The NCCB Committee has received a series of statements of clarification of policy from U.S. government officials.[21] Essentially these statements declare that it is not U.S. strategic policy to target the Soviet civilian population as such or to use nuclear weapons deliberately for the purpose of destroying population centers. These statements respond, in principle at least, to one moral criterion for assessing deterrence policy: the immunity of noncombatants from direct attack either by conventional or nuclear weapons.

These statements do not address or resolve another very troublesome moral problem, namely, that an attack on military targets or militarily significant industrial targets could involve "indirect" (i.e., unintended) but massive civilian casualties. We are advised, for example, that the United States strategic nuclear targeting plan (SIOP—Single Integrated Operational Plan) has identified 60 "military" targets within the city of Moscow alone, and that 40,000 "military" targets for nuclear weapons have been identified in the whole of the Soviet Union.[22] It is important to recognize that Soviet policy is subject to the same moral judgment; attacks on several "industrial targets" or politically significant targets in the United States could produce massive civilian casualties. The number of civilians who would necessarily be killed by such strikes is horrendous.[23] This problem is unavoidable because of the way modern military facilities and production centers are so thoroughly interspersed with civilian living and working areas. It is aggravated if one side deliberately positions military targets in the midst of a civilian population. In our consultations, administration officials readily admitted that, while they hoped any nuclear exchange could be kept limited, they were prepared to retaliate in a massive way if necessary. They also agreed that once any substantial numbers of weapons were used, the civilian casualty levels would quickly become truly catastrophic, and that even with attacks limited to "military" targets, the number of deaths in a substantial exchange would be almost indistinguishable from what might occur if civilian centers had been deliberately and directly struck. These possibilities pose a different moral question and are to be judged by a different moral criterion: the **principle of proportionality.**

While any judgment of proportionality is always open to differing evaluations, there are actions which can be decisively judged to be disproportionate. A narrow adherence exclusively to the principle of noncombatant immunity as a criterion for policy is an inadequate moral posture for it ignores some evil and unacceptable consequences. Hence, we cannot be satisfied that the assertion of an intention not to strike civilians directly, or even the most honest effort to implement that intention, by itself constitutes a "moral policy" for the use of nuclear weapons.

The location of industrial or militarily significant economic targets within heavily populated areas or in those areas affected by radioactive fallout could well involve such massive civilian casualties that, in our judgment, such a strike would be deemed morally disproportionate, even though not intentionally indiscriminate.

The problem is not simply one of producing highly accurate weapons that might minimize civilian casualties in any single explosion, but one of increasing the likelihood of escalation at a level where many, even "discriminating," weapons would cumulatively kill very large numbers of civilians. Those civilian deaths would occur both immediately and from the long-term effects of social and economic devastation.

A second issue of concern to us is the relationship of deterrence doctrine to war-fighting strategies. We are aware of the argument that war-fighting capabilities enhance the credibility of the deterrent, particularly the strategy of extended deterrence. But the development of such capabilities raises other strategic and moral questions. The relationship of war-fighting capabilities and targeting doctrine exemplifies the difficult choices in this area of policy. Targeting civilian populations would violate the **principle of discrimination**—one of the central moral principles of a Christian ethic of war. But "counterforce targeting," while preferable from the perspective of protecting civilians, is often joined with a declaratory policy which conveys the notion that nuclear war is subject to precise rational and moral limits. We have already expressed our severe doubts about such a concept. Furthermore, a purely counterfource strategy may seem to threaten the viability of other nations' retaliatory forces, making deterrence unstable in a crisis and war more likely.

While we welcome any effort to protect civilian populations, we do not want to legitimize or encourage moves which extend deterrence beyond the specific objective of preventing the use of nuclear weapons or other actions which could lead directly to a nuclear exchange.

These considerations of concrete elements of nuclear deterrence policy, made in light of John Paul II's evaluation, but applying it through our own prudential judgments, lead us to a strictly conditioned moral acceptance of nuclear deterrence. We cannot consider it adequate as a long-term basis for peace.

This strictly conditioned judgment yields *criteria* for morally assessing the elements of deterrence strategy. Clearly, these criteria demonstrate that we cannot approve of every weapons system, strategic doctrine, or policy initiative advanced in the name of strengthening deterrence. On the contrary, these criteria require continual public scrutiny of what our government proposes to do with the deterrent.

On the basis of these criteria we wish now to make some specific evaluations:

1. If nuclear deterrence exists only to prevent the *use* of nuclear weapons by others, then proposals to go beyond this to planning for prolonged periods of repeated nuclear strikes and counterstrikes, or "prevailing" in nuclear war, are not acceptable. They encourage notions that nuclear war can be engaged in with tolerable human and moral consequences. Rather, we must continually say "no" to the idea of nuclear war.

2. If nuclear deterrence is our goal, "sufficiency" to deter is an adequate strategy; the quest for nuclear superiority must be rejected.

3. Nuclear deterrence should be used as a step on the way toward progressive disarmament. Each proposed addition to our strategic system or change in strategic doctrine must be assessed precisely in light of whether it will render steps toward "progressive disarmament" more or less likely.

Moreover, these criteria provide us with the means to make some judgments and recommendations about the present direction of U.S. strategic policy. Progress toward a world freed of dependence on nuclear deterrence must be carefully carried out. But it must not be delayed. There is an urgent moral and political responsibility to use the "peace of a sort" we have as a framework to move toward authentic peace through nuclear arms control, reductions, and disarmament. Of primary importance in this process is the need to prevent the development and deployment of destabilizing weapons systems on either side; a second requirement is to insure that the more sophisticated command and control systems do not become mere hair triggers for automatic launch on warning; a third is the need to prevent the proliferation of nuclear weapons in the international system.

In light of these general judgments *we oppose* some specific proposals in respect to our present deterrence posture:

1. The addition of weapons which are likely to be vulnerable to attack, yet also possess a "prompt hard-target kill" capability that threatens to make the other side's retaliatory forces vulnerable. Such weapons may seem to be useful primarily in a first strike;[24] we resist such weapons for this reason and we oppose Soviet deployment of such weapons which generate fear of a first strike against U.S. forces.
2. The willingness to foster strategic planning which seeks a nuclear war-fighting capability that goes beyond the limited function of deterrence outlined in this letter.
3. Proposals which have the effect of lowering the nuclear threshold and blurring the difference between nuclear and conventional weapons.

In support of the concept of "sufficiency" as an adequate deterrent, and in light of the present size and composition of both the U.S. and Soviet strategic arsenals, *we recommend:*

1. Support for immediate, bilateral, verifiable agreements to halt the testing, production, and development of new nuclear weapons systems.[25]

2. Support for negotiated bilateral deep cuts in the arsenals of both superpowers, particularly those weapons systems which have destabilizing characteristics; U.S. proposals like those for START (Strategic Arms Reduction Talks) and INF (Intermediate-range Nuclear Forces) negotiations in Geneva are said to be designed to achieve deep cuts,[26] our hope is that they will be pursued in a manner which will realize these goals.

3. Support for early and successful conclusion of negotiations of a **comprehensive test ban treaty.**

4. Removal by all parties of short-range nuclear weapons which multiply dangers disproportionate to their deterrent value.

5. Removal by all parties of nuclear weapons from areas where they are likely to be overrun in the early stages of war, thus forcing rapid and uncontrollable decisions on their use.

6. Strengthening of command and control over nuclear weapons to prevent inadvertent and unauthorized use.

These judgments are meant to exemplify how a lack of unequivocal condemnation of deterrence is meant only to be an attempt to acknowledge the role attributed to deterrence, but not to support its extension beyond the limited purpose discussed above. Some have urged us to condemn all aspects of nuclear deterrence. This urging has been based on a variety of reasons, but has emphasized particularly the high and terrible risks that either deliberate use or accidental detonation of nuclear weapons could quickly escalate to something utterly disproportionate to any acceptable moral purpose. That determination requires highly technical judgments about hypothetical events. Although reasons exist which move some to condemn reliance on nuclear weapons for deterrence, we have not reached this conclusion for the reasons outlined in this letter.

Nevertheless, there must be no misunderstanding of our profound skepticism about the moral acceptability of any use of nuclear weapons. It is obvious that the use of any weapons which violate the principle of discrimination merits unequivocal condemnation. We are told that some weapons are designed for purely "counterforce" use against military forces and targets. The moral issue, however, is not resolved by the design of weapons or the planned intention for use; there are also consequences which must be assessed. It would be a perverted political policy or moral casuistry which tried to justify using a weapon which "indirectly" or "unintentionally" killed a million innocent people because they happened to live near a "militarily significant target."

Even the "indirect effects" of initiating nuclear war are sufficient to make it an unjustifiable moral risk in any form. It is not sufficient, for example, to contend that "our" side has plans for "limited" or "discriminate" use. Modern warfare is not readily contained by good intentions or technological designs. The psychological climate of the world is such that mention of the term "nuclear" generates uneasiness. Many contend that the use of one tactical nuclear weapon could produce panic, with completely unpredictable consequences. It is precisely this mix of political, psychological, and technological uncertainty which has moved us in this letter to reinforce with moral prohibitions and prescriptions the prevailing political barrier against resort to nuclear weapons. Our support for enhanced command and control facilities, for major reductions in strategic and tactical nuclear forces, and for a "no first use" policy (as set forth in this letter) is meant to be seen as a complement to our desire to draw a moral line against nuclear war.

Any claim by any government that it is pursuing a morally acceptable policy of deterrence must be scrutinized with the greatest care. We are prepared and eager to participate in our country in the ongoing public debate on moral grounds.

The need to rethink the deterrence policy of our nation, to make the revisions necessary to reduce the possibility of nuclear war, and to move toward a more stable system of national and international security will demand a substantial intellectual, political, and moral effort. It also will require, we believe, the willingness to open ourselves to the providential care, power, and word of God, which call us to recognize our common humanity and the bonds of mutual responsibility which exist in the international community in spite of political differences and nuclear arsenals.

Footnotes

1. The following quotations are from public officials who have served at the highest policy levels in recent administrations of our government: "It is time to recognize that no one has ever succeeded in advancing any persuasive reason to believe that any use of nuclear weapons, even on the smallest scale, could reliably be expected to remain limited." M. Bundy, G.F. Kennan, R.S. McNamara, and G. Smith, "Nuclear Weapons and the Atlantic Alliance," *Foreign Affairs* 60 (1982):757.

"From my experience in combat there is no way that [nuclear escalation] . . . can be controlled because of the lack of information, the pressure of time and the deadly results that are taking place on both sides of the battle line." Gen. A.S. Collins, Jr. (former deputy commander in chief of U.S. Army in Europe), "Theatre Nuclear Warfare: The Battlefield," in J.F. Reichart and S.R. Sturn, eds. *American Defense Policy*, 5th ed., (Baltimore: 1982), pp. 359–60.

"None of this potential flexibility changes my view that a full-scale thermonuclear exchange would be an unprecedented disaster for the Soviet Union as well as for the United States. Nor is it at all clear that an initial use of nuclear weapons—however selectively they might be targeted—could be kept from escalating to a full-scale thermonuclear exchange, especially if command-and-control centers were brought under attack. The odds are high, whether weapons were used against tactical or strategic targets, that control would be lost on both sides and the exchange would become unconstrained." Harold Brown, *Department of Defense Annual Report FY 1979* (Washington, D.C.: 1978).

Cf. also: *The Effects of Nuclear War* (Washington, DC: 1979, U.S. Government Printing Office).

2. For example, cf.: H.A. Kissinger, *Nuclear Weapons and Foreign Policy* (New York: 1957), *The Necessity for Choice* (New York: 1960); R. Osgood and R. Tucker, *Force, Order and Justice* (Baltimore: 1967); R. Aron, *The Great Debate: Theories of Nuclear Strategy* (New York: 1965); D. Ball, *Can Nuclear War Be Controlled?* Adelphi Paper # 161 (London: 1981); M. Howard, "On Fighting a Nuclear War," *International Security* 5 (1981):3–17.

3. "Statement on the Consequences of the Use of Nuclear Weapons."

4. Pius XII, "Address to the VIII Congress of the World Medical Association," in *Documents*, p. 131.

5. *Pastoral Constitution*, # 80.

6. Ibid.

7. M. Bundy, et al., "Nuclear Weapons," cited; K. Kaiser, G. Leber, A. Mertes, F.J. Schulze, "Nuclear Weapons and the Preservation of Peace," *Foreign Affairs* 60 (1982):1157–70; cf. other responses to Bundy article in the same issue of *Foreign Affairs*.

8. Testimony given to the National Conference of Catholic Bishops Committee during preparation of this pastoral letter. The testimony is reflected in the quotes found in note 61.

9. Our conclusions and judgments in this area although based on careful study and reflection of the application of moral principles do not have, of course, the same force as the principles themselves and therefore allow for different opinions.

10. Undoubtedly aware of the long and detailed technical debate on limited war, Pope John Paul II highlighted the unacceptable moral risk of crossing the threshold to nuclear war in his "Angelus Message" of December 13, 1981: "I have, in fact, the deep conviction that, in the light of a nuclear war's effects, which can be scientifically foreseen as certain, the only choice that is morally and humanly valid is represented by the reduction of nuclear armaments, while waiting for their future complete elimination, carried out simultaneously by all the parties, by means of explicit agreements and with the commitment of accepting effective controls." In *Documents*, p. 240.

11. W.H. Kincade and J.D. Porro, *Negotiating Security: An Arms Control Reader* (Washington, DC: 1979).

12. Several surveys are available, for example cf.: J.H. Kahin, *Security in the Nuclear Age: Developing U.S. Strategic Policy* (Washington, DC: 1975); M. Mandelbaum, *The Nuclear Question: The United States and Nuclear Weapons 1946–1976* (Cambridge, England: 1979); B. Brodie, "Development of Nuclear Strategy," *International Security* 2 (1978):65–83.

13. The relationship of these two levels of policy is the burden of an article by D. Ball, "U.S. Strategic Forces: How Would They Be Used?" *International Security* 7 (1982/83):31–60.

14. *Pastoral Constitution*, # 81.

15. United States Catholic Conference, *To Live in Christ Jesus* (Washington, DC: 1976), p. 34.

16. John Cardinal Krol, "Testimony on Salt II," *Origins* (1979):197.

17. John Paul II, "Message U.N. Special Session 1982," # 3.

18. Ibid., # 8.

19. John Paul II, "Address to UNESCO, 1980," # 21.

20. John Paul II, "Letter to International Seminar on the World Implications of a Nuclear Conflict," August 23, 1982, text in *NC News Documentary*, August 24, 1982.

21. Particularly helpful was the letter of January 15, 1983, of Mr. William Clark, national security adviser, to Cardinal Bernardin. Mr. Clark stated: "For moral, political and military reasons, the United States does

not target the Soviet civilian population as such. There is no deliberately opaque meaning conveyed in the last two words. We do not threaten the existence of Soviet civilization by threatening Soviet cities. Rather, we hold at risk the war-making capability of the Soviet Union— its armed forces, and the industrial capacity to sustain war. It would be irresponsible for us to issue policy statements which might suggest to the Soviets that it would be to their advantage to establish privileged sanctuaries within heavily populated areas, thus inducing them to locate much of their war-fighting capability within those urban sanctuaries." A reaffirmation of the administration's policy is also found in Secretary Weinberger's *Annual Report to the Congress* (Casper Weinberger, *Annual Report to the Congress*, February 1, 1983, p. 55): "The Reagan Administration's policy is that under no circumstances may such weapons be used deliberately for the purpose of destroying populations." Also the letter of Mr. Weinberger to Bishop O'Connor of February 9, 1983, has a similar statement.

22. S. Zuckerman, *Nuclear Illusion and Reality* (New York: 1982); D. Ball, cited, p. 36; T. Powers, "Choosing a Strategy for World War III," *The Atlantic Monthly*, November 1982, pp. 82–110.

23. Cf. the comments in Pontifical Academy of Sciences "Statement on the Consequences of the Use of Nuclear Weapons," cited.

24. Several experts in strategic theory would place both the MX missile and Pershing II missiles in this category.

25. In each of the successive drafts of this letter we have tried to state a central moral imperative: that the arms race should be stopped and disarmament begun. The implementation of this imperative is open to a wide variety of approaches. Hence we have chosen our own language in this paragraph, not wanting either to be identified with one specific political initiative or to have our words used against specific political measures.

26. Cf. President Reagan's "Speech to the National Press Club" (November 18, 1981) and "Address at Eu-

reka College" (May 9, 1982), Department of State, *Current Policy* # 346 and # 387.

Review Questions

1. What is the nonviolent position?

2. What two limits are placed on the justifiable use of force in the Christian tradition that allows this?

3. According to the bishops, why can't any Christian rightfully carry out orders or policies deliberately aimed at killing noncombatants?

4. Why don't the bishops think that the deliberate initiation of nuclear warfare can ever be justified?

5. Why don't they think that a limited nuclear exchange can be justified?

6. What two dimensions of deterrence do they discuss?

7. Explain the bishops' "strictly conditioned moral acceptance of nuclear deterrence."

Discussion Questions

1. Can you think of any exceptions to the principle "It is not morally acceptable to intend to kill the innocent?" What are they?

2. Is nuclear deterrence as a policy or strategy morally acceptable? Explain your view.

3. Do you agree with the specific recommendations made by the bishops? Why or why not?

George F. Kennan

A Christian's View of the Arms Race

George F. Kennan, former ambassador to the Soviet

From George F. Kennan, "A Christian's View of the Arms Race," *Theology Today* (1982), pp. 162–170. Reprinted with permission.

Union, is currently professor emeritus at the Institute for Advanced Study in Princeton, NJ.

Kennan argues that if nuclear arms are viewed as just another weapon, then they must be subject to the same restraints that apply to other weapons, and these restraints would be violated by any use of nuclear weapons. Specifically, they would bring death and injury to noncombatants in a massive and unavoidable way. Furthermore, these restraints are violated even by threatening to use such weapons because the threat amounts to holding innocent people hostage. Another violation is that the use of nuclear weapons could put an end to human existence. In view of these considerations, Kennan regards the readiness to use such weapons as an "indignity of monstrous dimensions."

The public discussion of the problems presented by nuclear weaponry which is now taking place in this country is going to go down in history, I suspect (assuming, of course, that history is to continue at all and does not itself fall victim to the sort of weaponry we are discussing), as the most significant that any democratic society has ever engaged in.

I myself have participated from time to time in this discussion, whenever I thought I might usefully do so; but in doing so, I have normally been speaking only in my capacity as a citizen talking to other citizens; and since not all of those other citizens were Christians, I did not feel that I could appeal directly to Christian values. Instead, I have tried only to invoke those values which, as it seemed to me, had attained the quality of accepted ideals of our society as a whole.

In this article, I would like to address myself to some of these same problems more strictly from the Christian standpoint. I do this with some hesitation, because while I hold myself to be a Christian, in the imperfect way that so many others do, I am certainly no better a one than millions of others; and I can claim no erudition whatsoever in the field of Christian theology. If, therefore, I undertake to look at the problems of nuclear weaponry from a Christian standpoint, I am aware that the standpoint, in this instance, is a primitive one, theologically speaking, and that this places limitations on its value. This is, however, the way that a great many of us have to look at the subject; and if primitive paintings are conceded to have some aesthetic value, perhaps the same sort of indulgence can be granted to a layperson's view of the relationship of nuclear weaponry to his own faith.

There are, I believe, two ways in which one may view the nuclear weapon, so-called. One way is to view it just as one more weapon, like any other weapon, only more de-structive. This is the way it is generally viewed, I am afraid, by our military authorities and by many others. I personally do not see it this way. A weapon is something that is supposed to serve some rational end—a hideous end, as a rule, but one related to some serious objective of governmental policy, one supposed to promote the interests of the society which employs it. The nuclear device seems to me not to respond to that description.

But for those who do see it this way I would like to point out that if it is to be considered a weapon like other weapons, then it must be subjected to the same restraints, to the same rules of warfare, which were supposed, by international law and treaty, to apply to other forms of weaponry. One of these was the prescription that weapons should be employed in a manner calculated to bring an absolute minimum of hardship to noncombatants and to the entire infrastructure of civilian life. This principle was of course offended against in the most serious way in World War II; and our nuclear strategists seem to assume that, this being the case, it has now been sanctioned and legitimized by precedent.

But the fact is that it remains on the books as a prescription both of the laws of war and of international treaties to which we are parties; and none of this is changed by the fact that we ourselves liberally violated it thirty or forty years ago. And even if it were not thus prescribed by law and treaty, it should, as I see it, be prescribed by Christian conscience. For the resort to war is questionable enough from the Christian standpoint even in the best of circumstances; and those who, as believing Christians, take it upon their conscience to give the order for such slaughter (and I am not saying that there are never situations where this seems to be the lesser of the two evils)—those who do this owe it to their religious commitment to assume that the sufferings brought to innocent and helpless people by the military operations are held to the absolute minimum—and this, if necessary, even at the cost of military victory. For victory itself, even at its apparent best, is a questionable concept. I can think of no judgments of statesmanship in modern times where we have made greater mistakes, where the relationship between calculations and results have been more ironic, than those which related to the supposed glories of victory and the supposed horrors of defeat. Victory, as the consequences of recent wars have taught us, is ephemeral; but the killing of even one innocent child is an irremedial fact, the reality of which can never be eradicated.

Now the nuclear weapon offends against this principle as no other weapon has ever done. Other weapons can bring injury to noncombatants by accident or inadvertence or callous indifference; but they don't always have to do it. The nuclear weapon cannot help doing it, and doing it massively, even where the injury is unintended by those who unleash it.

Worse still, of course, and utterly unacceptable from the Christian standpoint as I see it, is the holding of innocent people hostage to the policies of their government, and the readiness, or the threat, to punish them as a means of punishing their government. Yet how many times—how many times just in these recent years—have we seen that possibility reflected in the deliberations of those who speculate and calculate about the possible uses of nuclear weapons? How many times have we had to listen to these terrible euphemisms about how many cities or industrial objects we would "take out" if a government did not do what we wanted it to do, as though what were involved here were only some sort of neat obliteration of an inanimate object, the removal of somebody else's pawn on the chessboard, and not, in all probability, the killing and mutilation of innocent people on a scale previously unknown in modern times (unless it be, if you will, in the Holocaust of recent accursed memory)?

These things that I have been talking about are only those qualities of the nuclear weapon which violate the traditional limita-

tions that were supposed to rest even upon the conduct of conventional warfare. But there is another dimension to this question that carries beyond anything even conceived of in the past, and that is, of course, the possible, if not probable, effect of nuclear warfare on the entire future of civilization—and, in a sense, on its past as well. It has recently been forcefully argued (and not least in Jonathan Schell's powerful book, *The Fate of the Earth,* 1982) that not only would any extensive employment of nuclear weapons put an end to the lives of many millions of people now alive, but it would in all probability inflict such terrible damage to the ecology of the Northern Hemisphere and possibly of the entire globe as simply to destroy the very capacity of our natural environment for sustaining civilized life, and thus to put an end to humanity's past as well as its future.

Only scientists are qualified, of course, to make final judgments on such matters. But we nonscientists are morally bound, surely, to take into account not only the certain and predictable effects of our actions but also the possible and probable ones. Looking at it from this standpoint, I find it impossible not to accept Schell's thesis that in even trifling with the nuclear weapon, as we are now doing, we are placing at risk the entire civilization of which we are a part.

Just think for a moment what this means. If we were to use these devices in warfare, or if they were to be detonated on any considerable scale by accident or misunderstanding, we might be not only putting an end to civilization as we now know it but also destroying the entire product of humanity's past efforts in the development of civilized life, that product of which we are the beneficiaries and without which our own lives would have no meaning: the cities, the art, the learning, the mastery of nature, the philosophy—what you will. And it would be not just the past of civilization that we were destroying; we would, by the same token, be denying to countless generations as yet unborn, denying to them in our unlimited pride and selfishness, the very privilege of leading a life on this earth, the privilege of which we ourselves have taken unquestioning and greedy advantage, as though it were something owed to us, something to be taken for granted, and something to be conceded or denied by us to those who might come after us—conceded or denied, as we, in our sovereign pleasure, might see fit.

How can anyone who recognizes the authority of Christ's teaching and example accept, even as a humble citizen, the slightest share of responsibility for doing this—and not just for doing it, but for even incurring the risk of doing it? This civilization we are talking about is not the property of our generation alone. We are not the proprietors of it; we are only the custodians. It is something infinitely greater and more important than we are. It is the whole; we are only a part. It is not our achievement, it is the achievement of others. We did not create it. We inherited it. It was bestowed upon us; and it was bestowed upon us with the implicit obligation to cherish it, to preserve it, to develop it, to pass it on—let us hope improved, but in any case intact—to the others who were supposed to come after us.

And this obligation, as I see it, is something more than just a secular one. The great spiritual and intellectual achievements of Western civilization: the art (including the immense Christian art), the architecture, the cathedrals, the poetry, the prose literature—these things were largely unthinkable without the faith and the vision that inspired them and the spiritual and intellectual discipline that made possible their completion. Even where they were not the products of a consciously experienced faith, how can they be regarded otherwise than as the workings of the divine spirit—the spirit of beauty and elevation and charity and harmony—the spirit of everything that is the opposite of meanness, ugliness, cynicism, and cruelty?

Must we not assume that the entire human condition out of which all this has risen—our own nature, the character of the natural world that surrounds us, the mystery of the generational continuity that has shaped us, the entire environmental framework, in other words, in which the human experiment has proceeded—must we not assume that this was the framework in which God meant it to proceed—that this was the house in which it was meant that we should live—that this was the stage on which the human drama, our struggle out of beastliness and savagery into something higher, was meant to be enacted? Who are we, then, the actors, to take upon ourselves the responsibility of destroying this framework, or even risking its destruction?

Included in this civilization we are so ready to place at risk are the contributions of our own parents and grandparents—of people we remember. These were, in many instances, humble contributions, but ones wrung by those people from trouble and sacrifice, and all of them equal, the humble ones and the momentous ones, in the sight of God. These contributions were the products not just of our parents' efforts but of their hopes and their faith. Where is the place for these efforts, these hopes, that faith, in the morbid science of mutual destruction that has so many devotees, official and private, in our country? What becomes, in that mad welter of calculations about who could take out whom, and how many millions might survive, and how we might hope to save our own poor skins by digging holes in the ground, and thus perhaps surviving into a world not worth surviving into—what becomes in all this of the hopes and the works of our own parents? Where is the place, here, for the biblical injunction to "honor thy father and mother"—that father and mother who stand for us not only as living memories but as symbols of all the past out of which they, too, arose, and without which their own lives, too, had no meaning?

I cannot help it. I hope I am not being unjust or uncharitable. But to me, in the light of these considerations, the readiness to use nuclear weapons against other human beings—against people whom we do not know, whom we have never seen, and whose guilt or innocence it is not for us to establish—and, in doing so, to place in jeopardy the natural structure upon which all civilization rests, as though the safety and the perceived interests of our own generation were more important than everything that has ever taken place or could take place in civilization: this is nothing less than a presumption, a blasphemy, an indignity—an indignity of monstrous dimensions—offered to God!

Review Questions

1. Why does Kennan think that the use of nuclear weapons is unacceptable?
2. Why does he hold that it is also utterly unacceptable from the Christian standpoint to threaten to use them?

Discussion Questions

1. Do you think that there is any use of nuclear weapons that is morally acceptable? What is it?
2. Do you agree that the readiness to use nuclear weapons is an indignity of monstrous dimensions?

Charles Krauthammer

On Nuclear Morality

Charles Krauthammer writes a syndicated column for The New Republic.

Krauthammer discusses and rejects two antinuclear arguments, the prudential argument that the balance of terror is inherently unstable, and the moral argument of Kennan and others that deterrence is morally impermissible. The first argument is quickly dismissed as ineffective; the second argument gets more attention, but is eventually rejected as unsound. In Krauthammer's view, genuine deterrence which involves the will and intent to use nuclear weapons, and not mere bluffing, is a necessary evil for preventing the worse evil of nuclear war. Thus the bishops' position of merely conditionally accepting nuclear deterrence is unacceptable. He also rejects Schell's view (9) that survival requires us to abandon nuclear deterrence; in fact, he argues, history teaches us just the opposite, that survival is made possible by the pursuit of nuclear deterrence. Further-

more, **unilateral disarmament,** *far from producing survival, is actually a threat to it. Finally Krauthammer rejects the nuclear freeze, on the ground that a survivable nuclear force requires modernization; he rejects the "no first use policy" because it makes conventional war more thinkable, and this in turn makes nuclear war more likely.*

The contemporary anti-nuclear case takes two forms. There is, first, the prudential argument that the nuclear balance is inherently unstable and unsustainable over time, doomed to breakdown and to taking us with it. The animating sentiment here is fear, a fear that the anti-nuclear campaign of the 1980's has fanned with great skill. One of its major innovations has been its insistence on a technique of graphic depiction, a kind of nuclear neorealism, as a way of mobilizing mass support for its aims. Thus the Hiroshima slide show and the concentrically circular maps showing where and precisely when one will die in every home town. But there are limitations to this approach. The law of diminishing returns applies even to repeated presentations of the apocalypse. Ground Zero Day can be celebrated, as it were, once or perhaps twice, but it soon begins to lose its effectiveness. The numbing effect of detail, as well as the simple inability of any movement to sustain indefinitely a sense of crisis and imminent calamity, has led to the current decline in popularity of the pragmatic anti-nuclear case.

Consequently there has been a subtle shift in emphasis to a second line of attack, from a concern about what nuclear weapons might do to our bodies to a concern about what they are doing to our souls. Medical lectures on "the last epidemic" have been replaced by a sharper, and more elevated, debate about the ethics of possessing, building, and threatening to use nuclear weapons. (The most recent and highly publicized document on the subject is the pastoral letter of the U.S. bishops on war and peace.)

The moral anti-nuclear argument is based on the view that deterrence, the central strategic doctrine of the nuclear age, is ethically impermissible. Yet two auxiliary issues, one a requirement of deterrence, the other an extension of it, have received the most public attention and become the focus for much of the fervor of the anti-nuclear crusade. The requirement is nuclear modernization, which is opposed under the banner of "the freeze"; the extension is the American nuclear umbrella (the threat of nuclear retaliation against an attack, conventional or nuclear, on America's NATO allies), which is opposed under the slogan of "no-first-use." In examining the different strands of the anti-nuclear argument, it is useful to start with the more fundamental challenge to deterrence itself.

The doctrine of deterrence holds that a nuclear aggressor will not act if faced with a threat of retaliation in kind. It rests, therefore, on the willingness to use these weapons in response to attack. The moral critique of deterrence holds that the actual use of nuclear weapons, even in retaliation, is never justified. As the bishops put it, simply, one is morally obliged to "say no to nuclear war."

But things are not so simple. There are different kinds of retaliation, and different arguments (often advanced by different proponents) for the inadmissibility of each.

The popularly accepted notion of deterrence (often mistakenly assumed to be the only kind) is **"countervalue" retaliation,** an attack on industrial and population centers aimed at destroying the society of the aggressor. The threat to launch such retaliation is the basis of the doctrine of Mutual Assured Destruction, also known as MAD, massive retaliation, or the balance of terror. It is a balance constructed of paradox: weapons built never to be used, purely defensive weapons, like the **ABM,** more threatening to peace than offensive weapons; weapons aimed at people lessening the risk of war, weapons aimed at weapons increasing it. In Churchill's summary, "Safety will be the sturdy child of terror, and survival the twin brother of annihilation."

The bishops—and others, including non-pacifists like Albert Wohlstetter, who advocate deterrence based on a "counterforce" strategy of striking military targets—are neither assured nor amused by such paradoxes: they are appalled by them. For them MAD is unequivocally bad. Deliberate attacks on "soft targets" grossly violate the just-war doctrine of discrimination. They are inadmissible under any circumstance, because they make no distinction between combatants and noncombatants. Indeed, they are primarily aimed at innocent bystanders.

The bishops, however, reject not just a countervalue strategy, but also a counterforce strategy. Since military targets are often interspersed with civilian population centers, such an attack would kill millions of innocents, and thus violate the principle of proportionality, by which the suffering inflicted in a war must not outweigh the possible gains of conducting such a war. "It would be a perverted political policy or moral casuistry," write the bishops, "which tried to justify using a weapon which 'indirectly' or 'unintentionally' killed a million innocent people because they happened to live near a 'militarily significant target.'" The bishops also reject, in a second sense, the idea that a counterforce war would be limited. They share the widespread conviction that limited nuclear war is a fiction, that counterforce attacks must inevitably degenerate into countervalue warfare, and thus bring us full circle back to the moral objections to MAD and all-out nuclear war.

That does not leave very much. If a countervalue strategy is rejected for violating the principle of discrimination, and a counterforce strategy is rejected for violating the principle of proportionality (and also for leading back to total war), one runs out of ways of targeting nuclear weapons. That suits the bishops: they make a point of insisting that their doctrine is "no-use-ever." The logic, and quite transparent objective, of such a position is to reject deterrence in toto. However, the bishops suffer from one constraint. Vatican policy seems to contradict this position. Pope John Paul II has declared that "in current conditions 'deterrence' based on balance, certainly not as an end in itself but as a step on the way toward a progressive disarmament, may still be judged morally acceptable." What to do? The bishops settle for the unhappy compromise of not opposing deterrence itself, but simply what it takes to make deterrence work. Accordingly, they do not in principle oppose the possession of nuclear weapons when its sole intention is to deter an adversary from using his; they only oppose any plan, intent, or strategy to use these weapons in the act of retaliation. You may keep the weapons, but you may not use them. In sum, the only moral nuclear policy is nuclear bluff.

It is a sorry compromise, neither coherent nor convincing. It is not coherent, because it requires the bishops to support a policy—deterrence—which their entire argument is designed to undermine. And it is not convincing because the kind of deterrence they approve is no deterrence at all. Deterrence is not inherent in the weapons. It results from a combination of possession and the will to use them. If one side renounces, for moral or other reasons, the intent of ever actually using nuclear weapons, deterrence ceases to exist.

Pacifists unencumbered by papal pronouncements are able more openly to oppose deterrence. To take only the most celebrated recent example, in *The Fate of the Earth* Jonathan Schell makes the case the bishops would like to make, and stripped of any theological trappings. In its secular version it goes like this: biological existence is the ultimate value; all other values are conditional upon it; there can be neither liberty nor democracy nor any other value in defense of which Western nuclear weapons are deployed, if mankind itself is destroyed; and after nuclear war the earth will be "a republic of insects and grass." Therefore nothing can justify using nuclear weapons. Deterrence is more than a hoax, it is a crime.

Schell's argument enjoys a coherence that the bishops' case lacks, but it is still unsatisfying. Judged on its own terms—of finding a policy that best serves the ultimate and overriding value of biological survival—it fails.

For one thing, it willfully ignores history. Deterrence has a track record. For the entire postwar period it has maintained the peace between the two superpowers, preventing not only nuclear war, but conventional war as well. Under the logic of deterrence, proxy and brushfire wars are permitted, but not wars between the major powers. As a result, Europe, the central confrontation line between the two superpowers, has enjoyed its longest period of uninterrupted peace in a century. And the United States and the Soviet Union, the two most powerful nations in history, locked in an ideological antagonism and a global struggle as profound as any in history, have not exchanged so much as small-arms fire for a generation.

This is not to say that deterrence cannot in principle break down. It is to say that when a system that has kept the peace for a generation is to be rejected, one is morally obliged to come up with a better alternative. It makes no sense to reject deterrence simply because it may not be infallible; it only makes sense to reject it if it proves more dangerous than the alternatives. And a more plausible alternative has yet to be offered. Schell's recommended substitute is a call for a new world order in which all violence, nuclear and conventional, is renounced. Yet his 231–page brief against deterrence neglects to go into the details of exactly how this proposal is to be implemented. Of the job of remaking politics and man, he says, "I have left to others those awesome, urgent tasks."

There is one logical alternative to deterrence, and it does not require remaking man or politics, though neither Schell nor the bishops are quite willing to embrace it: unilateral disarmament. (The bishops' position that one may possess but never use nuclear weapons, however, is unilateralist in all but name.) It has a track record, too. The only nuclear war ever fought was as one-sided as it was short. It ended when the non-nuclear power suffered the destruction of two cities (and then surrendered unconditionally). Unilateralism has similar consequences in other contexts, like bacteriological warfare. In Southeast Asia today yellow rain falls on helpless tribesmen. The same Vietnamese forces in the same place a decade before never used these weapons against a far more formidable American enemy. The reason is obvious. The primitive Hmong, technologically disarmed, cannot retaliate; the Americans could. Similarly for our experience with chemical weapons in World War II, which were not used by either side even after the breakdown of peace, because both sides were capable of retaliation.

Far from being a guarantor of survival, unilateralism is a threat to it. Thus, whether one's ethical system calls its overriding value the sanctity of life or mere biological survival, unilateralism fails within its own terms, and with it the moral critique of deterrence. The breakdown of deterrence would lead to a catastrophic increase in the probability of precisely the inadmissible outcome its critics seek to avoid. The bishops unwittingly concede that point in a subsidiary argument against counterforce when they speak of such a strategy "making deterrence unstable in a crisis and war more likely."

The critics argue that no ends can justify such disproportionate and nondiscriminatory means as the use of nuclear weapons. That would be true if the ends of such a war were territory, or domination, or victory. But they are not. The sole end is to prevent a war from coming into existence in the first place. That the threat of retaliation is the best available this-world guarantee against such a war is a paradox the bishops and other pacifists are unwilling to face. As Michael Novak writes: "The appropriate moral principle is not the relation of means to ends but the choice of a moral act which prevents greater evil. Clearly, it is a more moral choice and occasions lesser evil to hold a deterrent intention than it is to allow nuclear attack."[1] Or recklessly to increase the danger of such an attack.

Nevertheless, debate does not end with the acceptance of the necessity, and thus the morality, of deterrence. Not everything is then permitted. There is a major argument between proponents of countervalue and counterforce deterrence. The former claim that counterforce threats lower the nuclear threshold and make nuclear war more likely because it becomes "more thinkable." The latter argue that to retaliate against defenseless populations is not only disproportionate and nondiscriminatory, but dangerous as well, since the threat is not credible and thus actually lowers the nuclear threshold. (Note that the countervalue vs. counterforce debate is over the relative merits of different kinds of retaliation, and not, as is sometimes pretended, between a "party of deterrence" and a "war-fighting party." The latter distinction is empty: all deterrence rests on the threat of nuclear retaliation, i.e., "war-fighting"; and all retaliatory [i.e., nonlunatic] war-fighting strategies from McNamara to today are designed to prevent attack in the first place i.e., for deterrence. The distinction between these two "parties" has to do with candor, not strategy: the "war-fighters" are willing to spell out the retaliatory steps that the "deterrers" rely on to prevent war, but which they prefer not to discuss in public.)

Nevertheless, whichever side of the intra-mural debate among deterrence advocates one takes, it seems to me that deterrence wins the debate with its opponents simply because it is a better means of achieving the ultimate moral aim of both sides—survival.

There is another argument in favor of de-terrence, though in my view it carries less weight. It appeals not to survival but to other values. It holds that (1) there are values more important than survival, and (2) nuclear weapons are necessary to protect them. The second proposition is, of course, true. The West is the guarantor of such fragile histori-cal achievements as democracy and political liberty; a whole constellation of ideals and values ultimately rests on its ability to deter those who reject these values and have a his-tory of destroying them wherever they domi-nate. Unilaterally to reject deterrence is to surrender these values in the name of surviv-al.

The rub comes with the first proposition. Are there values more important than surviv-al? Sidney Hook was surely right when he once said that when a person makes survival the highest value, he has declared that there is nothing he will not betray. But for a civili-zation self-sacrifice makes no sense since there are not survivors to give meaning to the sacrificial act. In that case, survival may be worth betrayal. If this highly abstract choice were indeed the only one, it would be hard to meet Schell's point that since all values hinge on biological survival, to forfeit that is to for-feit everything. It is thus simply not enough to say (rightly) that nuclear weapons, given the world as it is today, keep us free; one must couple that statement with another, equally true: they keep us safe. A nuclear pol-icy—like **unilateralism**—that forces us to choose between being dead or red (while in-creasing the chances of both) is a moral ca-lamity. A nuclear policy—like deterrence—that protects us from both perils is the only morally compelling alternative.

Although the attack on deterrence itself is the most fundamental assault on American nuclear doctrine, the case is difficult and complicated. It has, therefore, not seized the public imagination the way two auxiliary is-sues have. These other issues deal not with the basic assumptions of deterrence but with the weapons and some of the tactics that un-derpin it. These two campaigns have been conducted under the slogan of the "freeze" and "no-first-use."

The moral attack on the weapons them-selves takes two curiously contradictory ap-proaches. The first, a mainstay of freeze pro-ponents, is that beyond existing levels new weapons are simply redundant, that we are wasting billions of dollars on useless weapons that will do no more than make the rubble bounce, to borrow another memorable Churchillian formulation. The moral crime, it is alleged, is that these monies are being tak-en away from human needs, like housing and health care and aid to poorer countries. This theme runs through much of the moral litera-ture on armaments. It is featured, for exam-ple, in the Brandt North-South report which calculates that for every bomber one could instead build so many pharmacies in the Third World. The bishops also protest "the economic distortion of priorities—billions readily spent for destructive instruments while pitched battles are waged daily in our legislatures over much smaller amounts for the homeless, the hungry, and the helpless here and abroad."

It is extraordinary that an argument so weak can enjoy such widespread currency. Compared to other types of weapons, strate-gic nuclear weapons are remarkably cheap. In the U.S. they account for less than 10 percent of the military budget, and about one-half of 1 percent of the gross national product. The reasons are clear. Strategic nuclear weapons are not labor-intensive. Once in place, they need a minimal amount of maintenance, and fulfill their function simply by existing. In-deed, the argument turns against the anti-nuclearists. A shift away from strategic to conventional weapons would be extremely expensive. That is precisely why the West decided in the 1950's and 1960's to rely so heavily on nuclear weapons and to permit the current conventional imbalance in Europe. Rather than match the Soviet bloc tank for tank, plane for plane, the West decided to go nuclear, because this offered, in John Foster Dulles's immortal phrase, "more bang for the buck." The decision to buy cheap nuclear defense permitted the West vastly to expand social spending. A decision to move away from nuclear to conventional defense would require a willingness to divert enormous resources away from social to defense spending. Thus, if social priorities are to enter the moral calculus, as the nuclear critics demand, it is the anti-nuclear case that is undercut.

On the other hand, freeze advocates often argue that these weapons are not useless but dangerous, destabilizing, and likely to precipitate a nuclear war. The more weapons we build, the closer we come to nuclear war. The assumption is that high weapons levels *in themselves* increase the likelihood of war. That reverses cause and effect. Weapons are a result of tensions between nations, not their primary cause. It is true that distrust can be a dangerous by-product of an uncontrolled arms race. And yet arms-control agreements like SALT can reduce the risk of war by building mutual confidence and trust, while at the same time permitting *higher* weapons levels. Historically, nuclear tension simply does not correlate well with weapons levels. The worst nuclear crisis took place in October 1962, when the level of nuclear arms was much lower than it is today. And nuclear tensions were probably at their lowest during the heyday of détente in the mid–70's; at that time U.S.-Soviet relations were at their peak, while each side had by then vastly increased its capacity for multiple overkill.

There is an understandable built-in prejudice against new weapons. Even those willing grudgingly to grant the need for minimal deterrence recoil from building and deploying new weapons of mass destruction. "Enough is enough," they say. What is ig-

nored in this critique is that deterrence has requirements, and one is survivability (the ability of one's weapons to sustain a first strike and still deliver a second strike). And survivability, in an era of technological innovation, requires modernization, often to counteract non-nuclear advances like those in anti-submarine or anti-aircraft warfare (advances, incidentally, which a freeze would do nothing to curb). Thus, the proposed new American bomber, whether it be the B–1 or the Stealth, will be better able to elude destruction on the ground and Soviet defenses in the air. It will not be any more destructive—or immoral—than the B–52. Similarly for the Trident subs, which are quieter and (because they have longer-range missiles) can hide in larger areas of the ocean than Poseidons. In short, mainstream non-unilateralist freeze proponents are caught in the position of accepting the fundamental morality of deterrence but rejecting the addition of any new weapon for preserving it.

The penchant for providing ends without means also characterizes the final flank attack on deterrence: the rejection of the doctrine of "extended deterrence," the threat to use nuclear weapons, if necessary, in response to an attack (even a conventional attack) by the Soviet Union on NATO. That policy, which derives ultimately from Western unwillingness to match Soviet conventional strength in Europe, has long troubled many Americans. But since the alternatives are massive conventional rearmament or abandonment of our European allies, it has had to serve through half-a-dozen administrations as the guarantor of the Western alliance.

The campaign waged against this policy has been spearheaded by four former high administration officials, all with interesting histories. Robert McNamara and McGeorge Bundy are the authors of "flexible response" (a euphemism for limited nuclear war); George Kennan, of "containment"; and Gerard Smith, of SALT I. In an influential 1982 article in *Foreign Affairs,* they joined forces to call for adoption of a "no-first-use" policy on nuclear weapons.

This position has found an echo in many quarters, including, not surprisingly, the bishops' pastoral letter. It, too, doubts the possibility of a limited nuclear war remaining limited, and resolutely opposes ever crossing the line separating conventional from nuclear war. Therefore any nuclear retaliation against any conventional attack is rejected in principle.

Leave aside the consideration that the impossibility of limited nuclear war is both historically unproven and by no means logically necessary. Assume that limited nuclear war is indeed a fiction. We are still faced with the central problem of the no-first-use approach: its intent is to prevent any war from becoming nuclear, but its unintended consequence is to make that eventuality more likely. For thirty years war between the superpowers has been deterred at its origin. The prospect that even the slightest conventional conflict might escalate into a nuclear war has been so daunting that neither has been permitted to happen. Current policy sets the "firebreak" at the line dividing war from peace; a no-first-use policy moves it to the line dividing conventional war from nuclear war. No-first-use advocates are prepared to risk an increased chance of conventional war (now less dangerous and more "thinkable") in return for a decreased chance of any such war going nuclear. But a no-first-use pledge is unenforceable. Who will guarantee that the loser in any war will stick to such a pledge? A conventional European war would create the greatest risk ever of nuclear war. Any policy, however pious its intent, that makes conventional war more thinkable makes nuclear war more likely.

And that is the fundamental flaw in both this argument and the general attack on deterrence. It examines current policy in the light of some ideal, and finds it wanting. It ignores the fact that rejecting these policies forces the adoption of more dangerous alternatives, and makes more likely the calamities we are trying to avoid. In the end these argu-

ments defeat themselves.

Nuclear weapons are useful only to the extent that they are never used. But they are more likely to fulfill their purpose, and never be used, if one's adversary believes that one indeed has the will to use them in retaliation for attack. That will to use them is what the moralists find unacceptable. But it is precisely on that will that the structure of deterrence rests. And it is on the structure of deterrence that rest not only "secondary" values of Western civilization but also the primary value of survival in the nuclear age.

Footnotes

1. "Moral Clarity in the Nuclear Age," *National Review*, April 1, 1983.

Review Questions

1. Krauthammer says that the contemporary antinuclear case takes two forms. What are they?

2. Why does Krauthammer find the prudential argument to be ineffective?

3. How does Krauthammer characterize the doctrine of deterrence?

4. What is MAD? Why is it paradoxical according to Krauthammer? Why do the bishops think it is bad?

5. Why does Krauthammer find the bishops' position to be a "sorry compromise?"

6. Why does Krauthammer find Schell's argument unsatisfying?

7. What reason does Krauthammer give for keeping nuclear weapons and threatening to use them? Why is this reason paradoxical?

8. According to Krauthammer, why shouldn't a whole civilization sacrifice its survival for some other value?

9. Why does Krauthammer find the first argument of the freeze proponents weak? How can it be turned against them?

10. How does Krauthammer reply to their second argument, that nuclear weapons are dangerous and destabilizing?

11. According to Krauthammer, why do we need new nuclear weapons?

12. What is wrong with the "no first use" approach, according to Krauthammer?

Discussion Questions

1. Is it paradoxical to threaten war to prevent war? What do you think about this?

2. Is it ever morally right to threaten to kill innocent people? Explain your answer.

3. Are there values more important than survival? What are they? For example, would you rather be dead than red? Or would you rather be red than dead?

The Harvard Nuclear Study Group

Disarmament and Arms Control

The Harvard University Nuclear Study Group includes: Albert Carnesale, Professor of Public Policy and Academic Dean of Harvard's John F. Kennedy School of Government; Paul Doty, Director of the Center for Science and International Affairs and Mallinckrodt Professor of Biochemistry, Harvard University; Stanley Hoffmann, Chairman of the Center for European Studies and Douglas Dillon Professor of the Civilization of France, Harvard University; Samuel P. Huntington, Director of the Center for International Affairs and Clarence Dillon Professor of International Affairs, Harvard University; Joseph S. Nye, Jr., Professor of Government, Harvard University; and Scott D. Sagan, Staff Director of the project, and Ph.D. candidate in the Department of Government, Harvard University.

The group claims that disarmament is "inherently unstable" and not in the nation's best interests. They accept the common view that arms are necessary to deter aggression and to project political influence. Still they grant that some kind of arms control might contribute to deterrence, arms-race stability, and crisis stability. Using these criteria, as well as negotiability and possible verification, they critically

examine a number of proposals for arms reductions, freezes, force restructuring, and stabilizing measures.

DISARMAMENT AND DISTRUST

Successful efforts at disarmament are extremely rare, but there have been some. An outstanding example was the reduction of naval forces on the Great Lakes during the nineteenth century. Naval battles in the War of 1812 against Great Britain proved the importance of naval control of the Lakes. Both sides threatened to build more ships in the period following the war. A treaty concluded in 1817, still in force today, limits navy ships to sizes smaller than the existing fleets. As a result the U.S. and British fleets were dismantled, the threat of a future war was removed, and a major step was taken on the road that has produced the longest, enduring demilitarized border in modern history.

One reason that successful disarmament efforts are rare is that they require a degree of political accommodation that is difficult to achieve. Unless some political trust exists, efforts to disarm prove fruitless. Such trust is difficult to build, but not impossible—witness the peaceful relations between France and Germany today in contrast with the past. But political accommodation and trust are built slowly and this makes complete disarmament—as contrasted with more limited arms control—a long-term rather than an immediate prospect.

Complete disarmament would require some form of world government to deter actions of one nation against another. In a disarmed world, without such a government armed with sufficient force to prevent conflict between or among nations, differences in beliefs and interests might easily lead to a renewal of war. But any world government capable of preventing world conflict could also become a world dictatorship. And given the differences in ideology, wealth, and nationalism that now exist in the world, most states are not likely to accept a centralized government unless they feel sure of controlling it or minimizing its intrusiveness. A weak central machinery would be ineffective. And even a strong one—assuming governments would agree to set it up—could still be faced with breakdown. It is worth remembering that the central government of the United States fell apart in the mid–19th century, leading to a horrible civil war. Such a breakdown of authority in a world government would not only lead to bitter power struggles for domination of the world government in order to advance one or another national group, but could also lead to massive warfare. Individual nations would rearm. And those who could, would race to make nuclear weapons.

Disarmament would leap into the unknown; each state would accept it only if the dangers it feared could be ended or if it thought that the danger of nuclear holocaust outweighed the risks involved in nuclear disarmament. Despite the present costs of national military forces and arms competition, despite the limited gains which the threat to use force now brings, and despite the enormous risks such uses may entail, most nations still see a clear national advantage in having such forces. They provide the possibilities of deterring aggression and of projecting political influence. Disarmament would not necessarily ensure a state's position in the international contest between states. It would not necessarily ensure a state's security. Nor would disarmament guarantee that the funds saved from weapons would necessarily be devoted to raising the living standards of poor peoples. As a result, governments, even in this dangerous nuclear world, have preferred a combination of arms, self-restraint, and arms control to complete disarmament.

Ironically, while complete disarmament may be a worthy long-term goal, trying to achieve it before the requisite political conditions exist could actually increase the prospects of war. If the political pre-conditions of trust and consensus are missing, complete disarmament is inherently unstable. In a disarmed world, the first nation to acquire a few arms would be able to influence events to a much greater extent than it could in a heavily armed world. Nuclear weapons greatly magnify this effect.

On a cold January day in 1977, a little boy listened to President Carter aspire in his inaugural speech to remove nuclear weapons from the face of the earth. "Daddy, do you think he really means it?" the boy asked. "Yes," his father replied. After a moment's thought the boy responded. "Daddy, don't you think we should hide at least one?" The boy had a point. While mistrust exists, there will be strong temptation to hedge one's bets. Moreover, nuclear weapons can be easily hidden or quickly reinvented. At high numbers, even hidden bombs do not matter. But if the numbers are few and political mistrust persists, rumors of hidden bombs or fears of their reinvention by any number of nations could lead to the worst kind of nuclear arms race—a crash program of rearmament with few of the safety features that are built into existing weapons.

ARMS CONTROL

Therefore, when the consequences and risks of complete world disarmament are examined it appears that it does not guarantee peace and security if attempted before the political conditions are right. But nuclear arms races do not guarantee peace and security either. Instead they can guarantee enormous destruction if war occurs either by design, or more likely through accident, miscalculation, or misunderstanding. With no safe port in complete nuclear disarmament or in unrestricted competition, mankind has been compelled to seek safety by using arms control to lower the risks that nuclear weapons impose on peace and security.

"Arms control" has to a large extent replaced "disarmament" in the specialist's vocabulary since about 1960, but as long as disarmament is not taken to mean complete disarmament, the terms overlap. Arms control includes a wider range of actions than the removal of arms. For example, it includes steps that improve stability and help avoid accidents. Some "arms control" agreements reduce armaments; but not all do.

A common criticism of arms control and disarmament is that they mistake the symptoms for the disease. Since the origins of conflict do not reside in the weapons, its cure should not be sought in their restraint. But this is only a partial truth. The easy recourse to weapons in times of stress or panic does increase the likelihood of their use. This problem is ever so much larger in the Nuclear Age.

The parallel can be seen with handguns. Clearly they are not the sole or even the primary cause of murders, but where they are not generally available to the adult population, there are fewer murders, as in Britain, Japan, and the Soviet Union. Where guns are widely available, as in the United States, and much more so in Lebanon, murder is considerably more common. In daily life or international politics the proper control of arms, whether they are symptoms or not, can lower the risk of their being used.

Arms control alone is not enough. It is also important to attack the sources of conflicts. The ultimate hope for peace clearly lies with improving international relations to the point where conflict does not threaten to erupt into war and reconciliation replaces aggression. Whether the world eventually reaches this goal or not may depend on the combination of arms control with effective deterrence over the next decades.

DIFFICULTIES CONFRONTING ARMS CONTROL

During the past three decades the military establishments of the United States and the Soviet Union have become, by most counts, the most powerful and most expensive institutions ever created. It is no wonder that they are difficult to change. Such enormous bureaucracies often resist the changes that arms control initiatives attempt to introduce. The Arms Control and Disarmament Agency of the U.S. government is funded at an annual cost of less than the cost of the least expensive fighter aircraft! Ideally, arms control and security policy should go hand in hand. But in reality many arms control initiatives do not survive the raised eyebrows of the defense community and defense decisions may therefore ignore their arms control implications.

This uneven situation would ordinarily suppress most arms control initiatives were it not for heads of governments. It is chiefly by this route that arms control has had a role. Even so, its role is precarious and vulnerable to the changing views of successive administrations. Nevertheless, at least in democracies, polls show recurrent public support for efforts at arms control. When presidents ignore these opinions, they do so to their own political peril.

Another difficulty encountered by arms control is the unusual U.S. constitutional clause on the ratification of treaties. The United States alone among industrialized Western countries requires a two-thirds majority in the Senate to ratify treaties. This means that a minority, one that often represents much less than one-third of U.S. voters and one motivated by diverse interests, can block ratification. The role of arms control would have been much greater in the last decade if ratification required only a majority vote.

These examples, which do not exhaust the list, illustrate why arms control is often harder to accomplish than it would first appear. Two more problems deserve special attention: conflicting views about Soviet conceptions of arms control and the special limits that may be set by verification.

SOVIET ARMS CONTROL POLICY

Arms control negotiations have been a constant ingredient of Soviet-American relations for a quarter of a century. There is ample evidence that the Soviet Union, like the United States, has been motivated by an interest in preserving and managing the strategic relationship. Not only does this make for diminished risks and greater effectiveness in both sides' military planning, but it has also helped establish the Soviet Union's claim to co-equal status with the United States. As might be expected in a country that has steadily increased its military spending for two decades and where the defense programs are insulated from fluctuating public attitudes, Soviet arms control policy has been tightly integrated with Soviet military policy.

The substance of the Soviet Union's arms control positions can be summarized as follows. Until about 1960 the Soviet Union was in such an inferior position strategically that it resisted Western arms control initiatives for the understandable reason that agreements would freeze them in perpetual inferiority. However, they camouflaged this negative position by campaigns for general and complete disarmament and offers to ban weapons first and work out verification later. Nevertheless, from 1959 through the 1960s a number of agreements were negotiated that prohibited nuclear deployments in Antarctica, space, and the seabed, banned nuclear tests in the atmosphere, and created a Non-Proliferation Treaty. With the approach to parity in the 1970s it became possible to open up negotiations in the domain of central strategic forces.

The Soviet approach was limited by their concept of deterrence, which emphasizes that whichever side can deliver the greatest blow first is likely to remain in a dominant position thereafter. This explains the Soviet preoccupation with land-based, highly controlled, large ICBMs rather than bombers. Hence a main Soviet arms control objective has been to retain these forces and to ensure their modernization. They have resisted American efforts to use arms control to encourage greater Soviet reliance on their submarines (which they have regarded as an area of American advantage). At the same time, they have stressed a number of measures that do not reduce their central forces, such as a series of bans and limitations on new weapons or weapons in the planning stage. The successful treaty limiting antiballistic missile defenses was of this sort.

Another Soviet preoccupation has been with the concept of equality. Not only has the symbol of equality with the U.S. been important to them, but they have argued that "equal security" requires more than an equal number of weapons. They use the term to justify claims of compensation for geographical handicaps, for nuclear weapons in Europe, and for British, French, and Chinese nuclear forces. They are less open to U.S. claims that they have a geographical advantage because of their proximity to Europe. This complicates efforts to negotiate reductions that maintain rough "parity."

The Soviets, like the U.S., often use arms control proposals as propaganda weapons; with no effective public opinion at home, this is far easier for them to manage than for democracies. The extent to which the Soviet Union publicizes its role in negotiations seems to tell something about the seriousness with which it wants a compromise agreement. The negotiations of SALT I and SALT II were generally carried out with considerable privacy until the late stages. This seems to apply to the START negotiations as well. However, the INF negotiations have been carried out in public view almost from the beginning. One of the Soviet objectives in these negotiations is to split Western Europe from the United States and thereby halt or limit the deployment of intermediate-range forces. But if this tactic fails, an agreement may be possible.

What does the Soviet record tell us about the outlook for future arms control agreements? The picture is mixed. On the one hand, the proposals of the Reagan administration would cut deeply into the Soviet land-based missiles. These forces have been sacrosanct in the past. The "deep cuts" approach runs counter to the Soviet penchant and tradition for slow increments of change. In a period of political transition, Soviet leaders often find it especially hard to move in radical directions. Yuri Andropov was a product of this system and was beholden to military support in attaining his position of leadership. Not surprisingly, the Soviets had only offered proposals for more modest reductions and restrictions on new systems of interest to the U.S.

On the other hand, changes do occur in international politics. There are several possible catalysts for change in the Soviet situation. Andropov came into office in 1982 at the age of 68. With only a few years to leave his mark, he may have wished to move faster in arms control negotiations. More important, he faced serious political and economic problems: a decreasing Soviet work force; minority pressures for larger roles; a chronically incompetent agricultural system; inadequate consumer goods production; unrest in Eastern Europe; and most of all, a shrinking growth rate that does not provide the base it once did for the Soviet military machine. Together, these pressures may induce a more active search for maintaining the military competition with the West at lower levels of risk and expenditure.

VERIFYING ARMS CONTROL AGREEMENTS

Given the distrust between East and West, only arms control agreements that are verifiable are likely to be negotiated and ratified. How severe will this limitation be?

In the 1950s, the West routinely proposed, and the Soviet Union routinely rejected, measures to monitor arms control and disarmament agreements that involved on-site inspection, that is, provision for the physical inspection of a country's weapons and facilities by foreign experts. Until technology developed that permitted states to monitor one another at a distance, nuclear arms control was not possible. The absence of acceptable verification measures prevented the negotiation of limits on strategic weapons systems. When President Eisenhower proposed, in 1955, his Open Skies arrangement whereby the United States and the Soviet Union would exchange military blueprints and open one another's airspace to airborne reconnaissance the Russians rejected it, but in 1956 the U.S. began carrying out aerial reconnaissance photography anyway, using the U–2 aircraft. By January 1961, the first successful photo-reconnaissance satellite was launched. Such satellites have continually improved, and the level of detail gleaned by modern satellite scanners is, by all accounts, quite remarkable. In addition to photography, satellites have infra-red sensors (which work at night and through clouds) and listening devices for monitoring radio transmissions from Soviet missile tests.

The U.S. employs a variety of means, besides satellites, to determine the size of Soviet forces as well as verify Soviet compliance with arms control treaties, including large radars in the Aleutians, a space-tracking ship, line-of-sight radar stations around the Soviet periphery, and over-the-horizon radars. In combination, these systems provide detailed information on Soviet missile tests and weapons deployments. The Soviet Union has similar ships and satellites, which are collectively referred to as "national technical means" of verification.

But even such sophisticated measures as these cannot be all-seeing. There are aspects of the weapon systems production cycle that remain difficult to monitor by national technical means. The production of individual bombs, warheads, and missiles takes place in secrecy and production rates can only be inferred from scrutiny of what comes to the factories. If small changes in numbers of weapons are important, this process may be far too crude to be adequate.

It was the revolution in verification technology in the 1960s that made the more ambitious efforts of the Strategic Arms Limitation Talks possible. Of necessity the SALT process reflected the limitations of verification technology. Only delivery vehicles that were large enough to spot from space (for example, ICBM silos) or that, if mobile, could only operate from relatively few, known bases (heavy bombers and strategic submarines) could be verified. It was possible, however, to set limits on warheads and bombs, which were too small to be verified directly, by agreeing to somewhat arbitrary counting rules. A missile was counted as having the maximum number of warheads ever tested on that missile, rather than the actual number deployed (which might be much less). In this way verification was extended to what could not be seen.

While the Soviets have elaborate surveillance equipment, their interests in verification are less than those of the United States because of the very different nature of the two societies. The high level of reporting from American congressional hearings, media coverage, leaks to newspapers, and the likelihood that any violation of an agreement will find its way into newspapers make verification much easier for the Soviet Union. Hence exacting verification procedures are seen by the Soviets as something they "give" to the United States. At the same time, the Soviet Union is extremely secretive about military matters, a tradition with deep roots in the history of a frequently invaded Russian state. Many of the verification measures proposed by the U.S. look like espionage measures to the Soviets. Over the years, negotiations helped convince the Soviets that such procedures are not a cover for espionage but are an essential requirement for ratifiable arms control measures. Yet in each instance procedures must be justified in minute detail and negotiated in ways that minimize intrusiveness.

It should be remembered that the vast system of monitoring and intelligence collection that the United States must use for verification is needed whether arms control agreements exist or not. Indeed, arms control agreements, especially SALT II, have greatly increased our knowledge of the Soviet nuclear arsenal; both sides have promised not to interfere with each other's surveillance devices, and both have agreed that certain activities will not be concealed but will remain open to monitoring. Hence the verification of future agreements will have a broader foundation on which to build. Moreover, improvements in verification technology continue and it is reasonable to expect that capabilities that were not possible in the past will exist in the future.

When matters of national security are at stake, both the government and the public wish to know for certain whether agreements are being kept. But in daily life we know that we must live with some uncertainty. Verification of arms control agreements is no different; some risks are inevitable. But an untrammeled arms race also creates risks. Risks must be balanced and judgments made about adequacy. Verification must be adequate enough so that a Soviet violation of an agreement large enough to threaten our security could be detected in time for us to be able to make a sufficient response. Ironically, some of these judgments are easier to make at current high levels of weaponry than would be the case if there were deep reductions in numbers.

Much of the U.S. internal debate during the SALT II negotiations and ratification hearings focused on such judgments. Although the verification of some treaty provisions was seen to be less adequate than others, the trade-offs made between uncertainty and the importance of the item to be limited was generally agreed to be prudent.

Nevertheless, the new weaponry scheduled for deployment in this decade raises new problems. Cruise missiles will present a special challenge to verification. They are small and can be easily changed from conventional to nuclear warheads. The focus may have to be on restricting the ships and planes and geographical regions of their deployment.

Close monitoring of both sides' production plants may also help. Mobile ICBMs will require special measures as well. As greater emphasis shifts to the number of warheads and the ability to reload missile launchers, further measures will be required. In each case difficult judgments of two sorts will have to be made: what kinds of violations have significant adverse consequences on American security, and what is the probability that such violations could be detected. If one insists on absolute certainty in verification, then very little can be verified and arms cannot be controlled. On the other hand, if verification procedures are absent or lax, cheating may occur and confidence will be lost in the other side's compliance. The task is to find the right middle ground.

Verification procedures in future agreements will be subject to even greater scrutiny for two reasons. First, the Soviet Union refused to cooperate with American efforts to discover if an outbreak of anthrax in a Soviet city was a violation of the Biological Weapons Convention of 1972. Second, there is increasing evidence of the use of poison gas by the Soviet forces in Afghanistan and by the military forces they support in Cambodia. In the latter case there is a technical loophole in that the countries allegedly under attack were not themselves parties to the Geneva Protocol that prohibits such use. Those conventions did not have the elaborate verification provisions and procedures that the SALT treaties have. Soviet actions have therefore reinforced the importance of having such provisions in any future arms control agreements.

Despite all these difficulties, however, over the past twenty-five years there has been a gradual improvement in Soviet willingness to provide information, even to negotiate details of on-site inspections in the 1976 Threshold Test-Ban Treaty, and to permit the discussion of such requirements. It has been a slow process but it should not go unnoticed.

THE ROLE OF PUBLIC OPINION

Arms control has tended to succeed in the United States in periods of significant public involvement and concern. The 1963 Test-Ban Treaty and the 1972 ABM Treaty both were achieved during such periods. One of the most interesting developments of the early 1980s was the remarkable rise of public interest and public protest in the area of nuclear policy. Failure of the U.S. to ratify SALT II, after a similar failure to ratify two treaties negotiated in 1976 to further limit nuclear tests, suggested to the public that arms control was not working, and that the principal diplomatic lever for controlling the arms competition was stuck. The 1980 election was filled with rhetoric about rearmament. Concern in Europe about these events and the plans to deploy new nuclear weapons helped to stimulate mass movements. A year-long series of pronouncements by the U.S. president and his secretaries of state and defense that reflected a preoccupation with improving U.S. nuclear **war-fighting capability** and a new level of hostility toward the Soviet Union followed. This was accompanied by rapidly increasing military budgets.

As budgets and rhetoric escalated, so did the memberships and the influence of public and professional groups opposed to nuclear war. Physicians' groups, some dating from the campaign against nuclear testing two decades earlier, were particularly effective in reminding Americans of the horrible human suffering and death that would accompany nuclear war. Because of this revival of public interest in arms control, the current nuclear freeze movement, the careful examination of the moral basis of nuclear policy by the U.S. Catholic bishops, and intensified support for arms control in the scientific and professional community came into being.

The **nuclear freeze movement** began in the spring of 1980 with a call for bilateral, verifiable freeze on the production, testing, and deployment of all nuclear weapons systems in the U.S. and the USSR. Its aim is to prevent further development or deployment of counterforce and other destabilizing weapons, and to stabilize the current balance so that reductions can go forward. Various freeze resolutions were supported by the electorates in eight (of nine) states where it appeared on the ballot in November 1982. Public opinion polls at the end of 1982 showed the freeze idea appealed to some three-quarters of the public if it is verifiable and would grant no significant advantage to the Soviet Union. The same polls showed overwhelming opposition to unilateral disarmament and considerable mistrust of the Soviet Union.[1]

Earlier freezes suggested by Presidents Johnson and Carter did not have any obvious drawing power, nor have the various moratoria proposed by the Soviet Union. But with the combination of the seemingly bellicose pronouncements of the early Reagan administration and the belief that arms control was not being seriously pursued, the freeze movement took hold with the public. Considering the difficulty of any treaty of substance gaining the two-thirds Senate vote needed for ratification, this degree of public arousal may turn out to be an essential requirement for any future arms control agreement.

In Europe, the anti-nuclear opposition has focused on deployment of new NATO missiles and is strongest in northern Europe and among the Protestant churches. By contrast, in the U.S. the initiative from the religious sector has come from the Catholic bishops. This has taken the form of a well-planned, deliberate debate.

A further indication of the spread of concern is seen in the mobilization of support for arms control in the scientific community. Not only are activist scientists busy refining freeze proposals, but the establishment itself is involved. For the first time the National Academy of Sciences passed virtually unanimously a resolution urging intensified efforts at the negotiating table and adherence to the still unratified treaties. A carefully crafted statement by the presidents of scientific academies and other leading scientists on these matters was presented to Pope John Paul II in September 1982. It urged curbing "the development, production, testing and deployment of nuclear weapons systems and their reduction to substantially lower levels," claiming that "the sole purpose of nuclear weapons, as long as they exist, must be to deter nuclear war," and calling upon all nations "never to be the first to use nuclear weapons."

This brief overview cannot convey the full extent of the diversity and vigor of the new public engagement in nuclear policy. Like public involvements in the past, this one may be changed or move in new directions. But it seems likely that this new force will prove durable enough to affect government policies. . . .

THREE MORAL DILEMMAS

As long as nations have fought wars efforts have been made to place moral restraints on the violence unleashed. Medieval writers on the subject sought to encourage what they called a just-war theory. Justice in warfare required several conditions: a good cause (for example, self-defense rather than aggression); some proportion between the ends sought and the means used; and keeping the distinction between civilians and combatants, between innocent bystanders and soldiers fighting a war. Nations at war have never been able to follow this moral distinction with complete success, but many have tried. The history of warfare contains many stories of statesmen, generals, even common foot soldiers attempting to spare civilian lives even in the midst of fighting. Such actions are efforts to maintain a sense of the moral world even in the hell of war.

Have nuclear weapons made such efforts futile and destroyed the just-war tradition?

Not completely, although they have shaken some of its assumptions. Aggression can still be condemned, and in principle one can conceive of small-scale use of very low-yield nuclear weapons that would do less destruction than conventional bombs (thus meeting the criterion of proportion), and allow discrimination between enemy soldiers and civilians. The key question, however, is whether the violence would remain at that level. Once the nuclear threshold has been crossed, will conflict escalate to large-scale nuclear war where the distinction between civilians and soldiers is lost in blind ferocity, and all sense of proportion is obliterated? No one knows. And therefore, however just the cause involved, unintended consequences could transform a limited nuclear use into a highly immoral action. Certainly it is hard to envisage any circumstances in which a nuclear war that would destroy the societies in conflict would be morally justifiable.

The Catholic bishops of the United States are addressing these issues. One of the dilemmas they have discussed is whether it can ever be moral to initiate the use of nuclear weapons, even if a conventional war is being lost. If one believes that escalation is unlikely to be controlled and that a full-scale nuclear exchange would be immoral, can initiating the use of nuclear weapons ever be morally justified?

The dilemma arises because it is not known whether, in a conventional war, the use of nuclear weapons in an extremely limited fashion, to destroy a Soviet radar site for example, would be more likely to lead to nuclear escalation or to stop the conventional war. If initiating the use of nuclear weapons led to escalation, the action would have been immoral. But if it led to a quick end of the conventional war in Europe, might not the action be seen as moral? Perhaps. But every effort would have to be made to keep close control of the risks (i.e., small weapons; no delegation of authority to dispersed military units; continual communications with the Soviet Union; a clear idea of how to terminate the conflict, etc.). Even then, given the enormous cost of the unintended consequences, and the uncertainty about reaching the intended ones (a quick de-escalation or end of violence), such an action could only be a last resort. What morality and prudence dictate is

"no early use" of nuclear weapons as policy and strategy, and a highly selective and limited use if it should come to that; indeed, morality and prudence suggest that were deterrence to fail, one should have the means to carry out an alternative, non-nuclear strategy.

This brings us to the second dilemma that the bishops have raised: Can it be right to have nuclear forces and a targeting doctrine that deliberately aim at civilians? The bishops believe not. Many others differ over this issue. Some have argued that assured destruction is an immoral doctrine because it rests on the deterrent threat of disproportionate damage to civilians and industry. The American government does not aim its weapons at the Soviet population per se, and ever since the 1950s our doctrine has in practice involved military targets. But many people also powerfully argue that counterforce targeting is immoral because it makes nuclear weapons seem more usable and requires ever more war-fighting capabilities; there is no limit on the number of targets and weapons, thus the insatiable needs of the nuclear arsenal will compete with other moral claims on the resources of our society. Moreover, destruction of large parts of civilian society is an unavoidable part of any large-scale strategic nuclear war.

Targeting certainly raises an important moral issue. But it is not the theology of "counterforce versus countercity." The issue is whether our strategy and arsenal can reduce the prospect of war in a time of crisis. Since the moral claims for deterrence rest on averting large-scale nuclear war, the truly immoral behavior is to have nuclear force and doctrines that invite preemptive attack by one's opponent or by oneself. For example, a force that is highly lethal and highly vulnerable at the same time will tempt a political leader to "use it or lose it" at a time of crisis. Even an invulnerable but complete counter-silo capability may incite one's opponent to use his vulnerable missiles against some enemy targets before the missiles are lost. Morality is not just about choices at a time of crisis;

it can also be about averting terrible choices at a time of crisis. The crucial moral question about force posture and targeting doctrine therefore is: How can our current actions ensure that even in a deep crisis no general on either side can persuasively argue that it is imperative to launch his nation's strategic forces because they might otherwise be lost?

A third dilemma raised by the bishops' letter concerns neither the use nor the specific targets of nuclear weapons, but the morality of deterrence itself. It can be called the "intentions versus consequences" dilemma: Is it justifiable to threaten a nuclear attack that might destroy innocent civilians if the intention is to deter nuclear war altogether? Even if the consequences of the threat are moral—if deterrence works, in other words— is making the threat itself morally acceptable? Some theologians who stress the importance of intent believe it is not, and that therefore the whole notion of nuclear deterrence is morally unsound. They argue that it is wrong to threaten what it is wrong to do. Others would place more stress on consequences. For example, we may believe it is wrong to kill another person, but believe it moral to threaten to kill someone who is about to attack our children if such a threat would deter the act.

Most people judge the morality of actions on their intentions and their consequences. Moreover, in deterrence our intentions are not to do evil. Our threat is intended to avoid both the horrible outcome of nuclear war and aggressive behavior by the other side. Our intent in making the threat is not immoral, and the consequences depend in part upon the intentions of the other side. On the contrary, to remove the threat altogether—because it is evil to threaten to kill entire populations, or to threaten to attack military targets with weapons that are likely to be neither discriminating nor controllable— might indeed have disastrous moral effects, if it incites one's adversary to take greater risks, and thereby made war more likely.

While we differ with some details raised by the bishops' arguments about nuclear weapons, we are sympathetic to their overall conclusion that nuclear deterrence is morally tolerable as long as there is no acceptable alternative means to prevent a feared action and the intent is to avert the greater evil of nuclear war. We agree with the bishops that nuclear deterrence is only conditionally moral; the condition being that we make genuine efforts to reduce dependence on nuclear deterrence over the long run. To resort to nuclear deterrence in order to protect low stakes is a morally and politically nasty bluff. To resort to nuclear deterrence to protect *high* stakes makes political and moral sense only if the credibility of the threat is enhanced by the availability of non-nuclear weapons, which may make the actual execution of the threat unnecessary.

Those who disagree with this position would argue that deterrence implies some risk of nuclear war, and that nothing is worth nuclear war, particularly if it would end life on earth. This might be obvious if a breakdown of deterrence would really end life on earth. Trust in the existence of future generations pervades our daily life. We seek to preserve the environment, to save money, to raise children properly, all the time assuming that life will continue to exist. But a nuclear war between the superpowers today would most likely not end all human life on earth. A critical moral goal should be to avoid passing that awful threshold.

Of course that is not enough. The current inventors of 50,000 weapons could wreak indescribable devastation. Even if its use would not end human life, it would destroy the human society we now know and cherish. But that does not mean one could not imagine a moral use of nuclear weapons. Suppose a nuclear war were limited, and the alternative was to succumb to a Hitler-type domination of the world in which tens of millions of innocent people would be exterminated without war. Many people would think such a war worth fighting. Fortunately, that is not our current situation.

Even if one believes that nothing is worth fighting nuclear war, it does not follow that nothing is worth the risk of nuclear war. Imagine, for the purposes of argument, a tiny risk of a nuclear war occurring in the first place, and only a small risk of it escalating to a large scale if it did break out. But imagine that the threat of that risk helped to prevent large-scale conventional war that would cost tens of millions of innocent lives as occurred in the Second World War. Would it be immoral to rely on a small risk of nuclear war to avoid the higher probability of large-scale conventional war? We think not—so long as efforts are made to keep the risks as low as possible, and so long as one realizes that this is only an interim solution. A complacency that led one to relax about the dangers of relying on nuclear deterrence could become the source of great immorality. But so also would a utopianism that could raise both nuclear and conventional risks.

In short, nuclear deterrence can be tolerated, but never liked. Deterrence can be seen as a necessary evil. Because it is necessary, one cannot abandon it carelessly; because it is evil, one must strive to rely on it less. . . .

Footnote

1. Lou Harris Associates Polls.

Review Questions

1. According to the group, why is successful disarmament so rare?

2. What problems does the group find with complete disarmament?

3. According to the group, what are the advantages of arms control?

4. What is the Soviet position on arms control?

5. How does the group think that an arms control agreement could be verified?

6. Explain the just-war theory.

7. What are the three moral dilemmas raised by the United States Catholic Bishops?

8. How does the group agree with the bishops' position? How do they disagree?

Discussion Questions

1. Does the just-war theory apply to nuclear war? Defend your answer.

2. Can a limited nuclear war be justified? How?

3. Is the risk of nuclear war justified? Explain your view.

4. Is nuclear deterrence really a "necessary evil" as the group says? What is your view?

Problem Cases

1. A Soviet Invasion of West Germany The current policy calls for the NATO Alliance to initiate the use of nuclear weapons if there is a conventional Soviet attack against Western Europe. Suppose that the Soviets invade West Germany, and suppose that it looks as if their numerically superior ground forces will prevail over the NATO forces. Should the NATO Alliance be the first to use nuclear weapons in this case? Explain and defend your answer.

2. The Freeze Resolution The Nuclear Freeze Resolution (Senate Joint Resolution 163 and House Joint Resolution 434, 1982) introduced by Senators Edward M. Kennedy and Mark O. Hatfield: Resolved by the Senate and the House of Representatives of the United States of America in Congress assembled,

i. As an immediate strategic arms control objective, the United States and the Soviet Union should:

a. pursue a complete halt to the nuclear arms race;

b. decide when and how to achieve a mutual and verifiable freeze on the testing, production, and future deployment of nuclear warheads, missiles, and other delivery systems; and

c. give special attention to destabilizing weapons whose deployment would make such a freeze more difficult to achieve.

ii. Proceeding from this freeze, the United States and the Soviet Union should pursue major, mutual, and verifiable reductions in nuclear warheads, missiles, and other delivery systems, through annual percentages or equally effective means, in a manner that enhances stability.

Referendums in support of the freeze resolution have won in several states, and opinion polls show that the majority of people in the United States support it. Should the freeze resolution be passed by Congress? Explain your position.

3. *The Strategic Defense Initiative (SDI) or the "Star Wars" Initiative* President Reagan has proposed that the United States develop a space-based missile defense system popularly called a "Star Wars" system because it calls for the development and deployment of the sorts of high-tech weapons seen in the science-fiction movie *Star Wars*. Just exactly what weapons or systems would or could be deployed in space is a matter of speculation, but there has been much talk about the possibility of orbiting directed energy weapons in space. This speculation has usually involved three different classes of weapons: (1) conventional optical lasers, (2) particle-beam devices, and (3) a new category of systems that is supposed to include X-ray lasers powered by nuclear explosions. The technology for the first type of weapon is well known, but the second and third types of weapons are still in the research and development stage. Most scientists agree that much work needs to be done, and that it will be very expensive. The best estimates available indicate that the development of a laser battle station in space (as in the *Star Wars* movie) would be about ten times as much as that of other roughly similar modern high-technology systems, that is, it would be tens of billions of dollars as opposed to billions of dollars. Furthermore, no such system would be leak proof; at best it could only stop some attacking missiles, not all of them. Nevertheless, such a system would give the United States an advantage over the Soviet Union. Not only would it increase our chances of surviving a nuclear attack, also it would help give the United States *first-strike capability*, the ability to attack the Soviet Union in such a way that they could not effectively strike back.

Assuming that the Star Wars defense system is technically feasible, should the United States go ahead with its development? Explain your position.

4. *An Extended Nuclear War* The Reagan administration has developed plans for prevailing or winning an extended global nuclear war. These plans including building long tunnels deep underground that will be stocked with food, weapons, and supplies. The plan calls for military personnel to inhabit these tunnels for years while fighting continues on the surface of the Earth. No doubt the surface of the Earth would become uninhabitable, except perhaps by ants.

Are these plans a good idea? What do you think?

Civilians could build their own underground shelters and stock them. Should we be doing this?

5. *The Decapitation Scenario* Suppose that we have evidence of a Soviet nuclear attack on Washington D.C. at one A.M. Easter Sunday. The evidence is a radar warning coming from a station on the coast of the Atlantic Ocean. We know that there is a Soviet submarine off the coast of Washington because we have been tracking it. The radar seems to indicate that this submarine has launched two missiles, and since subs of that type are known to be carrying nuclear warheads, it is possible that these are short-range missiles armed with nuclear bombs. Or perhaps it is some kind of Soviet test or trick, to see how we will respond. Maybe it is just a false radar warning; false radar warnings have happened more than once. One time it turned out to be an unusual flock of birds; another time the computer mistook a war game for the real thing. Given the cloud cover, it is impossible to get a visual confirmation. But fighter jets have been scrambled, and are in the air with orders to hit the sub with air to surface missiles. We can justify the attack by saying that the sub was spying, and that it violated our territorial waters (although actually it is international waters). The main worry is whether it is really a nuclear attack or not, and given the speed of the missiles or apparent missiles, we have only ten minutes to decide. If it is a real attack, then there will be damage to the unprotected command and control systems of the United States; and we will lose a lot of our capacity to carry out a retaliatory response. (In strategy books, an attack on Washington or Moscow is called the *decapitation scenario.*) Also, there will be massive loss of life, including the president who is asleep at the White House. Should we launch our missiles in retaliation now, before we are hit and lose much of our command and control ability, or should we wait for ten minutes and make sure that the attack is genuine? What should we do in this crisis situation?

Suppose we wait and Washington is hit with two hydrogen bombs, resulting in a communications blackout except for the shielded connection to the hollow mountain communications center near Colorado Springs—now what? Should a response be ordered? Given the communications difficulties, it will be hard if not impossible to control a limited response. It looks like it is either an all-out, massive response, or nothing at all. Which should it be in your opinion, and given this possibility what should our policy be? Think about it.

Suggested Readings

(1) Blake, Nigel, and Kay Pole, eds. *Objections to Nuclear Defense: Philosophers on Deterrence* London: Routledge & Kegan Paul, 1984. This is a collection of articles on the morality of nuclear deterrence including an interesting article by Anthony Kenny on the slogan "Better dead than red."

(2) *Ethics* vol. 95 (April 1985). This issue has papers given at a conference on ethics and nuclear deterrence in Aspen in 1984. The authors include philosophers and strategists; they are seen to have different approaches to the problems.

(3) Hardin, Russell. "Unilateral Versus Mutual Disarmament." *Philosophy & Public Affairs* vol. 12 (Summer 1983): 236–254. Hardin rejects Lackey's argument (in "Missiles and Morals"—*See* Lackey citation) that utilitarianism recommends unilateral nuclear disarmament by the United States, and gives arguments for mutual disarmament.

(4) Kavka, Gregory S. "Doubts About Unilateral Nuclear Disarmament." *Philosophy & Public Affairs* Vol. 12 (Summer 1983); 255–260. Kavka also replies to Lackey's article; Kavka is opposed to unilateral nuclear disarmament by the United States.

(5) _____. "Some Paradoxes of Deterrence." *The Journal of Philosophy* vol. LXXV, no. 6 (June 1978): 285–302. In this classic article, Kavka argues that the standard view of deterrence results in serious moral paradoxes that challenge three widely accepted moral principles: the wrongful intention principle, the right-good principle, and the virtue preservation principle.

(6) Lackey, Douglas P. "Missiles and Morals: A Utilitarian Look at Nuclear Deterrence," *Philosophy & Public Affairs* Vol. 11 (Summer 1982): Lackey gives utilitarian arguments in favor of unilateral nuclear disarmament by the United States.

(7) _____. "Moral Principles and Strategic Defense." *The Philosophical Forum* vol. XVIII, no. 1, (Fall 1986): 1–7. Lackey attacks President Reagan's Star Wars proposal. He argues that a system of deterrence with defenses is not, as Reagan and his supporters claim, morally superior to the current system of deterrence without defenses.

(8) Maclean, Douglas, ed. *The Security Gamble: Deterrence Dilemmas in the Nuclear Age.* Totowa, NJ: Rowman & Allanheld, 1984. This is a collection of papers and responses written for a conference held at the University of Maryland in 1983. Two respond to the United States Catholic Bishops' position.

(9) Schell, Jonathan. *The Abolition.* New York: Alfred A. Knopf, Inc., 1984. In this book, Schell continues his attack on nuclear weapons and deterrence. He contends that there is no defense against nuclear weapons. Deterrence strategy recognizes this superiority of the offense and seeks to prevent a first strike, which can't be defended against, by threatening a retaliatory second strike, which also can't be defended against. To restore the superiority of defense, Schell recommends that we abolish nuclear weapons, hence the title *The Abolition.*

(10) Sterba, James P. ed. *The Ethics of War and Nuclear Deterrence.* Belmont, CA: Wadsworth, 1985. This excellent anthology includes articles about the morality of war in general, articles about nuclear war in particular, and discussions of deterrence strategies and arms negotiations. Different points of view are represented.

(11) _____. "How to Achieve Nuclear Deter-

rence without Threatening Nuclear Destruction." In *The Ethics of War and Nuclear Deterrence,* edited by James P. Sterba, 155–174. Sterba grants that nuclear deterrence is morally justified, and he also accepts the view that it is immoral to threaten nuclear destruction. As a result, he tries to combine both views by contending that we can achieve nuclear deterrence without threatening nuclear destruction.

Glossary

ABM Anti-Ballistic Missile.

Counterforce targeting or retaliation an attack on military targets, as distinguished from nonmilitary targets such as industries and cities.

Comprehensive Test Ban Treaty a proposed treaty prohibiting any testing of nuclear weapons, including underground testing. At present the United States and the Soviet Union have a Limited Test Ban Treaty (negotiated and signed in 1963) which prohibits tests in the atmosphere, outer space, and underwater, but allows them to continue underground.

Countervalue targeting or retaliation an attack on industrial and population centers, as distinguished from military targets.

Ecosphere the ecological system of the whole Earth.

Extended deterrence the threat to use nuclear weapons in response to a conventional attack by the Soviet Union on NATO territory, as distinguished from minimum deterrence where the threat is only to use nuclear weapons in response to nuclear weapons.

Flexible response a limited response to a nuclear attack using nuclear weapons, as distinguished from an all-out response using nuclear weapons or massive retaliation.

ICBM Intercontinental ballistic missile.

MAD a scenario for nuclear war that is part of the deterrence strategy; each side threatens the other with mutual assured destruction ("MAD") or an all-out global nuclear war in which both sides sustain massive damage.

No first use policy the declared intention to not be the first to use nuclear weapons in a war.

Nuclear freeze proposal (movement) this proposal has different versions; the United States Catholic Bishops put it this way: "A bilateral, verifiable agreement to halt the testing, production, and deployment of new nuclear weapons systems." See the Nuclear Freeze Resolution proposed by Senators Kennedy and Hatfield in the Problem Cases.

Principle of discrimination a principle in the Christian just-war theory which prohibits direct and intentional attacks on noncombatants and nonmilitary targets; attacks must distinguish between combatants and noncombatants.

Priniciple of proportionality a principle in the Christian just-war theory which says that the good achieved by the war must be proportionate to the evil resulting from the war. If the evil resulting outweighs the good achieved, then the war is unjust.

SALT II the second phase of the strategic-arms limitation talks which resulted in the SALT II Treaty. This treaty set various limits on strategic nuclear delivery vehicles (missiles, bombers, etc). This treaty was signed by President Carter and Soviet leader Leonid Brezhnev in 1979, but it was not ratified by the United States Congress, and President Reagan has withdrawn it from any further consideration by the Senate. Instead, President Reagan initiated a new round of negotiations, called START (Strategic Arms Reduction Talks) which thus far have produced an agreement in principle to eliminate U.S. and Soviet shorter and medium range missiles in Europe, but leaving all of the other missiles in place. Also, the United States and the U.S.S.R. do have a 1972 ABM Treaty which severely limits the deployment of ABM (anti-ballistic missile) systems.

SDI Strategic Defense Initiative; President Reagan's proposed plan for developing a space-based missile defense system; for more details see the

Problem Cases.

Si vis pacem, para bellum if you wish peace, prepare for war.

Unilateralism where one side has a weapon that the other side does not have. For example, at the end of World War II, the United States had (and used on two cities in Japan) nuclear bombs that Japan did not have.

Unilateral disarmament where one side disarms and the other doesn't, as distinguished from bilateral disarmament, where both sides disarm.

Warfighting capability the ability to fight an extended global nuclear war.

Index

Dischargeability, 136, 138–39. *See also* Hunger; Welfare

Discobolus, defined, 259

Discrimination. *See* Affirmative action; Race discrimination; Sex discrimination

Discrimination, principle of, defined, 381, 423. *See also* Nuclear war: civilians in

Distributive justice, defined, 177

Doctors. *See* Physicians

Doe v. *Commonwealth's Attorney for City of Richmond,* 313

Donne, John, 147

"Do Potential People Have Moral Rights?" (Warren), 347

Double effect, doctrine of, 50, 51–52, 83, 381. *See also* Nuclear war

Douglas, William O., 225n.4

Down's syndrome, 64, 65, 70–71, 83. *See also* Euthanasia; Mentally handicapped persons; Mongoloids, defined

Draize eye tests, 376

Duffy, Clinton, 107

Dulles, John Foster, 408

Durocher, Leo, 146

Ecocentrism, defined, 377

Ecology, defined, 377. *See also* Environmental protection

Ecosphere, defined, 423

Ecosystems, defined, 377

Ectopic pregnancies, defined, 2, 45

Effluents, defined, 207

Eichmann, Adolf, 99, 124

Eisenhower, Dwight D., 414

Eleemosynary, defined, 207

Eliot, George, 143

Embryos, defined, 1, 45

Employment discrimination. *See* Affirmative action; Race discrimination; Sex

discrimination: in employment

Ensoulment, 3, 10, 11, 45. *See also* Abortion

Environmental protection. *See also* Pollution

animal rights compared to, 370–73

anthropocentric views of, 352–53, 357–58

holistic views of, 317, 351, 356–58, 360

moral considerations regarding, 352, 354, 358n.2, 359, 360–61, 371, 372, 373

poverty's influence on, 146, 150–51, 154

utilitarian views of, 352–53, 357–58, 371

Environmental Protection Agency (EPA), 182–83, 184–85, 186

Epicurus, 327

Epidemiology, defined, 314

Equal Employment Opportunity Act of 1972, 212

Equality, elements of, 240–41

Equality of opportunity and respect, defined, 235

Equal Pay Act of 1963, 209, 210

Equal Rights Amendment (ERA), 210, 219, 257

Equivalence thesis, 134, 137, 139, 140, 141. *See also* Hunger; Welfare

Equivocation, defined, 45

ERA. *See* Equal Rights Amendment (ERA)

Ethical nihilism, objectivism, and relativism, defined, 207

Ethnocentrism, defined, 177

Etiology, defined, 314

Euthanasia. *See also* Active euthanasia; Passive euthanasia

American Medical Association's views of, 50, 51, 58–59, 62, 64, 67–68, 70, 71, 72

of babies, 64, 65, 66n.14, 70–71, 73, 74, 79

charity compared to, 63, 66n.11

consent to, 68–69, 73, 75–78, 79, 80n.5

conservative views of, 51, 53–55, 59, 60, 63, 74

defined, 49, 53

liberal views of, 51, 56–58, 59–64, 68–69, 70–71, 73, 74–79

moderate views of, 51, 64

moral considerations regarding, 25, 50, 51–52, 53, 69, 132

physicians' views of, 52, 55, 58, 59, 60–61, 62–63, 64, 65, 66n.14, 69–70, 71–72

and prolonging life, means of, 52, 59, 67, 68–70, 71–72, 73, 74, 75

quality of life's influence on, 52, 78–79, 80n.5

religious views of, 54, 74

theories regarding, 54–55

Evans, Timothy, 105, 120

Ex hypothesi, defined, 177

Extended deterrence, defined, 423. *See also* Deterrence (nuclear)

Extramarital sex. *See* Adultery

Factory farms, 340 *See also* Animals

moral considerations regarding, 330–31, 336–37, 342

weaknesses of, 315, 316, 330, 364

Fallacy of affirming the consequence, defined, 45–46

Fallout, radioactive, 383, 384 *See also* Nuclear war

Falwell, Jerry, 300, 302

Famine. *See* Hunger

Fate of the Earth, The (Schell), 380, 401, 402, 405–6, 407

Federalism, defined, 129

Fetuses, 1, 73. *See also* Abortion

Pollution. *See also* Environmental protection
corporate responsibility regarding, 198, 201–2
by Hooker Chemical Company, 179, 180, 182, 183–84, 185, 186
of Love Canal, 182, 183, 184, 185
Polygraph tests, 206
Poor persons, 131, 175. *See also* Homeless persons
capital punishment of, 102, 107
immigration's influence on, 151–53
influence on environmental protection of, 146, 150–51, 154
reproduction's influence on, 145–46, 148–50, 154–55
Positive duties, 132, 134, 177
Positivism, defined, 207
Potassium chloride, defined, 83
Poverty, Special Senate Committee Report on, 161–62
Powell, Lewis F., Jr., 86, 87, 96–97, 256
Preemptive first strikes, 380. *See also* Nuclear war
defined, 379, 421
religious views of, 389–90, 396, 398
weaknesses of, 404, 409
Preferential treatment. *See* Affirmative action
Pregnancy. *See also* Reproduction
as insurance exclusion, 245–46
responsibility for, 20–21, 25–26, 27, 39
Premarital sex, 262, 267, 269n.16. *See also* Sex
Premeditation, 105–6. *See also* Murder
Prima facie, defined, 46
Privacy rights
to abortion, 5, 7, 8
regarding AIDS, 307–8, 309, 312
background of, 6–7

to homosexuality, 305–6, 307–8
Procreation. *See* Reproduction
Products liability, 198, 202. *See also* Corporate responsibility
Property, libertarian views of, 168–71, 172
Prophylaxis, defined, 314
Proportionality, principle of, 395, 417–18. *See also* Nuclear war
defined, 381, 404, 423
Providence and Evil (Geach), 348, 350n.17
Provincialism, defined, 259
Psychology of Sex Differences, The (Macoby and Jacklin), 227n.19
Psychoses. *See* Mentally handicapped persons
Pythagoras, 327

Quality of life, 52, 78–79, 80n.5. *See also* Euthanasia
Quarantines, of AIDS patients, 305–7
Quickening, 3, 5, 37, 46. *See also* Abortion; Pregnancy
Quinlan, Karen Ann, 49, 53
background of, 80–81
rights of, 344, 345, 346, 348, 350nn.4, 5

Race discrimination, 179. *See also* Affirmative action
assimilationist views of, 219–21, 222, 223, 224, 227n.20, 228–29
background of, 209, 210
in capital punishment, 102, 105, 106, 107
sex discrimination compared to, 216, 217, 218, 222, 319–20
speciesism compared to, 316, 318, 319, 322, 361, 366
Radiotherapy, defined, 83
Rand, Ayn, 156, 159

Rape
capital punishment for, 105, 106
influence on abortion of, 2, 4, 20, 31
moral considerations regarding, 262–63, 275
sex as, 296–99
women's status in, 293, 294, 295, 296, 297–99
"Rape and Respect" (Frye and Shafer), 293
Rationalizations, defined, 176
Rawls's theory, 40, 46
Ray, James Earl, 100
Reagan, Ronald, 421, 423
Real Poverty Report, 160
Reductio arguments, defined, 177–78
Refuse Act, 184
Repatriated, defined, 178
Report of the Royal Commission on Capital Punishment (Royal Commission on Capital Punishment), 120, 121
Reprobation, defined, 129
Reproduction, 7
influence on poverty of, 145–46, 148–50, 153–54
sex as, 261, 266, 267, 268, 271, 273, 274, 275–76
sexual pleasure compared to, 273–74, 275–76
Resource Conservation and Recovery Act, 184
Respect, equality of, defined, 235
Respirators, defined, 83
Retarded persons. *See* Mentally handicapped persons
Retribution
capital punishment as, 86–87, 88, 91, 95–97, 98–99, 102, 107–8, 115–16, 117–18, 124
defined, 112, 114
revenge compared to, 112, 113
Revenge, 112, 113–14
Reverse discrimination, defined, 212–13, 250. *See also* Affirmative action
Rice, Donna, 312–13